Everybody Was So Young

It wasn't the parties that made it such a gay time.
There was such affection between everybody. You loved
your friends and wanted to see them every day, and usually
you did see them every day. It was like a great fair,
and everybody was so young.

— Sara Murphy to Calvin Tomkins
in *Living Well Is the Best Revenge*

EVERYBODY WAS SO YOUNG

Gerald and Sara Murphy

A LOST GENERATION

LOVE STORY

Amanda Vaill

Houghton Mifflin Company

Boston   New York

Library of Congress Cataloging-in-Publication Data

Vaill, Amanda.
Everybody was so young : Gerald and Sara Murphy —
a lost generation love story / Amanda Vaill.
p. cm.
Includes bibliographical references and index.
ISBN 0-395-65241-3
1. Murphy, Gerald, 1888–1964.   2. Painters—United States—Biography.
3. Murphy, Sara.   4. Painters' spouses—United States—Biography.
5. Expatriate painters—France—Biography.   I. Title.
ND237.M895V35   1998   759.13—dc21   97-49149 [B]   CIP

Book design by Anne Chalmers
Typeface: Electra

Printed in the United States of America

QUM 10 9 8 7 6 5 4 3 2

TEXT AND ILLUSTRATION CREDITS BEGIN ON PAGE 469.

In memory of my mother

PATRICIA VAILL

Contents

Everybody Was So Young

Antibes, May 28, 1926

IT WAS THEIR FRIEND Scott Fitzgerald who described the Murphys best, on the beach at Antibes in the south of France, in the summer sun of the 1920s. There is Sara, her face "hard and lovely and pitiful," her bathing suit "pulled off her shoulders" and her brown back gleaming under her rope of pearls, "making out a list of things from a book open in the sand." And there is Gerald, her husband, tall and lean in his striped maillot and a knitted cap, gravely raking the seaweed from the beach as if performing "some esoteric burlesque," to the delight of the little audience of friends they have gathered around them. On the "bright tan prayer rug of the beach," they and their friends swim, sunbathe, drink sherry and nibble crackers, trade jokes about the people with strange names listed in the "News of Americans" in the *Paris Herald*: "Mrs. Evelyn Oyster" and "Mr. S. Flesh." Their very presence is "an act of creation"; to be included in their world is, Fitzgerald says, "a remarkable experience."

Fitzgerald wasn't literally portraying the Murphys, of course; he was writing a novel, called *Tender Is the Night*, about a psychiatrist named Dick Diver and his wife, Nicole. In the novel, the woman with the pearls is recovering from a psychotic break brought on by incest, and the man with the rake ends up losing his wife, his position, everything he most cares about. These things are not known to have happened to Gerald and Sara Murphy. So when Fitzgerald insisted to Sara, after the publication of *Tender Is the Night* in 1934, that "I used you again and again in *Tender*," Sara's reaction was denial and distaste. "I hated the book when I first read it," she told her neighbor, the writer Calvin Tomkins. "I *reject categorically any* resemblance to ourselves or anyone we know — at *any* time." But Gerald made the connection at once. "I know . . . that what you said in 'Tender is the Night' is true," he wrote Fitzgerald in 1935. "Only the invented part of our life — the unreal part — has had any scheme any beauty."

By that time the life the Murphys had invented at their Villa America in Antibes, and in Paris during the 1920s, may indeed have seemed unreal. In the intervening years tragedy had tarnished the Murphys' lives: the death of one child, the mortal illness of another, Gerald's forfeiture of his career as a painter; a whole litany of loss. But on May 28, 1926, those events are in the future, and the invented part of the Murphys' lives is as real, as palpable, as the hot sand under their feet or the throbbing of cicadas or the color of the sea — an improbable turquoise in the shallows, and a deep, purplish blue, the color of blueberries, farther out.

The beach, La Garoupe, is literally Gerald's invention: Until a year or so ago, it was covered in seaweed and stones, and deserted except for the fishermen who pull up their little boats there. But Gerald saw its possibilities when the Murphys first stayed in Antibes in the summer of 1922 with Cole Porter and his wife, Linda. Gerald and Cole raked the debris from a corner of the sand, and in the years since Gerald has cleared the entire *plage* almost single-handed. Now what began as a private Murphy passion has caught on — not, it should be noted, with the local inhabitants, who cannot understand why anyone would want to go out in the midday heat and actually lie in the sun — but with fashionable Parisians and increasing numbers of visiting Americans and English from the huge *fin de siècle* hotel at the end of the Antibes peninsula, which has only recently extended its season into the summer months.

In fact, the beach has been rather crowded today: Anita Loos, the smart young American screenwriter and author of *Gentlemen Prefer Blondes*, is there; the playwright Charles MacArthur; Ada MacLeish, the soprano, with her two children, Mimi and Ken (Ada's husband, the poet Archibald MacLeish, is still in Persia with the League of Nations' Opium Commission); and Scott and Zelda Fitzgerald, who have made a rare sortie from their villa at Juan-les-Pins on the other side of the peninsula, Scott nursing a hangover and Zelda not speaking to him. Absent today, although they are often here, are Comte Étienne de Beaumont, the long-faced French aristocrat who was the model for the eponymous hero of Raymond Radiguet's scandalous roman à clef, *Le bal du Comte d'Orgel*, and his wife, Édith (who, it's whispered, has an opium habit). As is their custom, the Murphys arrived with their three children and their nanny late in the morning, after Gerald has completed the day's work on one of the precise and unsettling paintings for which he has become famous, and they have been holding a kind of impromptu party ever since, with cold sherry and little biscuits called *sablés* at noon. Now they are leaving — it is lunchtime. And they have arranged to take Hadley Hemingway, wife of the young American writer Ernest Hemingway, to pick up her husband at the Antibes railway station after lunch.

By rights, Hadley should be in Madrid with Ernest, who went there to work on a new novel, and the Hemingways' one-year-old son, John, nicknamed Bumby, should have been staying with the Murphys. But before Hadley could get away, Bumby was diagnosed with whooping cough, and Sara, who swathes the railway compartments that she and her family travel in with sheets washed in Lysol to protect her children from germs, thought it best that the little boy and his mother be quarantined until the disease has run its course. Luckily, the Fitzgeralds were able to lend Hadley their rented house in Juan-les-Pins, the Villa Paquita, which they have vacated in favor of a much grander property nearby. And Gerald and Sara, insisting that Hadley and Bumby are their guests, have been paying Bumby's doctor bills and Hadley's other expenses.

When Ernest steps off the train at the Antibes station this afternoon he is met by four people: Hadley's friend Pauline Pfeiffer, as small and dark and slender as Hadley is fair and large-boned, is also standing on the platform. Pauline is an editor at *Vogue* in Paris, and because she has already had whooping cough it holds no terrors for her. She has been staying with Hadley during this quarantine and has become a great favorite with the Murphys, who admire her stylishness and quick wit. She is a great favorite with Ernest, too — in fact, the two of them have been having a secret affair that began last winter. But the Murphys don't know this and Hadley only suspects it; and if the greeting Ernest gives his wife seems a little awkward, everyone puts it down to his exhaustion (he has had to change trains three times on the journey from Madrid), Hadley's own weariness after weeks of tending a sick child, and the lack of privacy.

In the evening Gerald and Sara stage a more formal welcome for Ernest: a caviar-and-champagne party at the little casino in Juan-les-Pins which the owner, Edouard Baudoin, has recently renovated in the hopes of turning Juan into a French Miami. Fresh caviar has never been a summer dish — it spoils too readily on the long train journey from the Caspian Sea — but some enterprising importer has recently begun flying it in, and Gerald wants to be the first to take advantage of this development. As with so many things, the Murphys are setting a fashion.

Sara is wearing a long, floating dress with vaguely semiclassical lines, nothing like the beaded chemises beloved by flapper fashion victims; her dark gold hair, recently bobbed into soft waves, frames what Scott Fitzgerald will describe as her "Viking madonna" face; her rope of pearls is wound once around her neck. Gerald, in an impeccable dinner jacket, is circulating among his guests, introducing this one to that one, starting a conversation here, changing a subject there — a friend later describes him as "stage manag[ing] his parties down to the last detail, right down to what stories people should tell."

When Scott and Zelda Fitzgerald arrive, Zelda in fuchsia with a peony pinned in her fair hair, Scott is already drunk — "you drank all the time," Zelda later tells him, speaking of that summer — and Zelda is smoldering. At first he contents himself with throwing ashtrays off the casino terrace and staring at one of the women guests until she becomes discomfited and asks him to stop. But when the Hemingways come in, with Pauline in tow, Fitzgerald starts to get dangerous.

Because he himself is already an enormously successful novelist with an established reputation, he has always thought of Hemingway as a kind of protégé: he has recognized the younger writer's talent and praised his work, and he has fixed him up with his publisher, Scribner's, which is going to publish Hemingway's first novel, *The Sun Also Rises*, this fall. Tonight, though, Fitzgerald feels their roles reversing, and watches with increasing frustration as Ernest, tanned from the Spanish sun, his white teeth flashing, becomes the center of attention.

Gerald keeps urging Ernest to talk about Spain, particularly about the fiesta of San Fermín in Pamplona, where the Murphys plan to accompany the Hemingways later this summer. And as if it were not enough for Ernest to have Hadley on one arm and Pauline on the other, soon Sara, too, is hovering over him. This is too much for Fitzgerald, who is more than half in love with her, and jealous of her attention. He finds a small throw rug in one of the anterooms, drapes it over his head and shoulders like a cloak, and crawls from room to room on his hands and knees moaning, "Sara's being mean to me." Gerald is furious, and accuses Fitzgerald of sabotaging the party — at which Fitzgerald, by now hot and disheveled, straightens up and says he doesn't care. He has never heard of anything so silly and affected as a champagne-and-caviar party. Only Gerald would think something so dated would be fun.

Although the next day everyone is civil to everyone else, the aftershocks of that evening, of things said and left unsaid, done and left undone, will be felt in the lives of almost everyone there for years to come. Something else will persist, too, something almost as durable as the reputations of Fitzgerald and Hemingway: the legend of Gerald and Sara Murphy, the "prince and princess" (as one of their friends described them) who were the evening's presiding geniuses.

Elegant, attractive, wealthy, cultured, affectionate, the Murphys had gathered around themselves at their home in France a brilliant group of American writers and artists, among them Fitzgerald, Hemingway, Cole Porter, Dorothy Parker, John Dos Passos, Archibald MacLeish, Robert Benchley, Alexander Woollcott, and Philip Barry; in addition, they numbered among their friends some of the most prominent figures of the European modernist movement, such as Pablo Picasso, Jean Cocteau, Fernand Léger, and Igor Stravinsky. Of this first manifestation of what we today might call the glitterati, Gertrude Stein is supposed to have remarked: "You are all a lost generation." But they were not lost. As Fitzgerald himself sensed, they had been found, and embraced, by two remarkable people who would enable many of them to unleash their creative powers in ways that transformed the twentieth century artistic landscape.

Early in the novel he was writing that summer — and would work on intermittently for nearly eight more years — Fitzgerald describes an alfresco dinner at his protagonists' villa:

Rosemary . . . had a conviction of homecoming, of a return from the derisive and salacious improvisations of the frontier. There were fireflies riding in the dark air and a dog baying on some low and far-away ledge of the cliff. The table seemed to have risen a little toward the sky like a mechanical dancing platform, giving the people around it a sense of being alone with each other in the dark universe, nourished by its only food, warmed by its only lights. . . . [T]he two Divers began suddenly to warm and glow and expand. . . . Just for a moment, they seemed to speak to everyone at the table, singly and together, assuring them of their friendliness, their affection. And for a moment the faces turned up toward them were like the faces of poor children at a Christmas tree.

His model for that magical moment was a dinner party at the Murphys', one of many that seem to run together in the memories of those who were lucky enough to be there. What was the special quality about Gerald and Sara Murphy — "the golden couple," the actress Marian Seldes called them — that made this alchemy possible? It wasn't just nurturing, although their generosity and supportiveness were famous. It wasn't only inspiration, although they left their imprint, or their images, in works as diverse as Hemingway's "The Snows of Kilimanjaro," Dos Passos's *The Big Money*, MacLeish's *J.B.*, or *Tender Is the Night*. It wasn't simply example — the example of lives lived with grace and, ultimately, courage in the face of personal disaster. It wasn't, even, the transformations they effected on the character and work of those close to them.

Late in his life their friend Archibald MacLeish tried to put it into words for an interviewer who had asked him what "the special pull of the Murphys" was. "No one has ever been able quite to define it," MacLeish said — but he came as close as anyone: "Scott tried in *Tender is the Night*. Dos tried in more direct terms. Ernest tried by not trying. I wrote a *Sketch for a Portrait of Madame G. M.*, a longish poem. They escaped us all. There was a shine to life wherever they were: not a decorative *added* value but a kind of revelation of inherent loveliness as though custom and habit had been wiped away and the thing itself was, for an instant, *seen*. Don't ask me how."

"A revelation of inherent loveliness" — it was a strong charm, indeed, against the confusion and ugliness of so much of their century. It enabled them to survive. More potently, it enabled those to whom they gave it to make art out of life.

1

❧

"My father, of course, had wanted *boys*"

SARA SHERMAN WIBORG MURPHY was a figure of myth long before the Fitzgeralds and the Hemingways and MacLeishes met her in France. Her father, Frank Bestow Wiborg, had been born in Cleveland, Ohio, in 1855, the son of Henry Paulinus Wiborg, a Norwegian immigrant who was either a deckhand on a lake steamer (as family legend has it) or "one of the pioneer businessmen of Cleveland" (as the *Centennial History of Cincinnati* describes him). When Frank was about twelve, his father died; according to the deckhand legend, he contracted pneumonia while saving the victims of a boat accident, and his widow, Susan, remarried a man with whom young Frank could not get along. In the best Horatio Alger tradition, Frank Wiborg then reportedly left home to seek his fortune and found his way to Cincinnati, where he managed to gain admittance to the Chickering Institute, a select college preparatory academy emphasizing the classics and sciences.

He graduated in 1874 — in his family's account, he paid his way by peddling newspapers — and got work as a salesman for a producer of printer's ink, Levi Addison Ault, and so dazzled his employer that a mere four years later Ault offered him a partnership in the company. This was the great period of printmaking, when newspaper lithographs, sheet music, poetry broadsheets, glossy magazines, and posters were the predominant mode of graphic expression, and the new company of Ault and Wiborg, which manufactured and mixed its own dry color to produce high-quality lithographer's ink, found its product in great demand, not only in the United States but worldwide. Toulouse-Lautrec was just one of the artists who used Ault and Wiborg inks for his prints; and the company commissioned him to create an advertising poster, using as a model the beautiful Misia Natanson, patron and muse of Vuillard, Proust, Bonnard, Fauré, and Ravel.

The engineer of this dynamic expansion, Frank Wiborg was the very model of the spirit of American enterprise. Young, handsome in a foursquare, musta-chioed, Teddy Roosevelt kind of way, restless, dynamic, and smart, he was clearly a man on the way up. And he gave himself an immeasurable boost by marrying, in 1882, the daughter of one of Ohio's most illustrious families.

Adeline Moulton Sherman was willowy, dark-haired, and pretty, the daugh-ter of Major Hoyt Sherman, a lawyer and banker who had served as United States paymaster during the Civil War and accumulated an enormous for-tune in Iowa, his adopted state, which he represented as a state legislator for many years. One of his brothers was Senator John Sherman of Ohio, who gave the Sherman Anti-Trust Act its name; another was the Union general William Tecumseh Sherman, who memorably marched through Georgia from Atlanta to the sea, burning and pillaging as he went, and remarked (from personal experience, no doubt) that "War is hell." Marrying Adeline transformed Frank Wiborg from up-and-coming to already-there; all that was needed was a son to set the seal on his happiness.

He was destined to be disappointed. The year after their marriage, Addie Wiborg gave birth to a daughter. "After an awful struggle," noted the new father in his diary for November 7, 1883, "at 7:15 [P.M.] a little girl baby arrives. I never experienced such great relief and we are all very happy over it." At the top of the page he wrote, in large round letters: "Sara Sherman Wiborg born." Sara was followed, four years later, by a second daughter, Mary Hoyt, and two years after *that* by a third, Olga Marie. "My father, of course, had wanted *boys*," said Sara many years afterward, "but he became resigned to girls later on and was *always wonderful* to his three daughters."

Certainly, in a material sense, he was. At the time of Sara's birth, Wiborg had already established his household outside of Cincinnati proper, in the country suburb of Clifton; soon he built a mansion for his growing family, complete with stables and a sunken garden, at the intersection of Clifton Avenue and Senator Place — the latter, almost inevitably, was named after *another* uncle of his wife's, Senator George H. Pendleton. The new house, which one reached by driving over a wooden bridge from Clifton Avenue, was a showplace, positively bristling with imported *boiserie* and fancy furniture. The lofty ceilings, towering mantels, and winding staircases were embellished with carved birds and garlands; the walls were hung with splendid tapestries; the floors were inlaid with rare woods; and in the large parlor, the drawing room, and the spacious hall, Venetian and French mirrors reflected back the glow of chandeliers. There was a library and music room, and just off the library — as one Cincinnati society reporter breathlessly noted — a little Turkish smoking room, "all the appointments of which were brought from Cairo by the Wiborgs, even to the carved jalousies through which the veiled daughters of the Turkish Beys see and remain unseen."

The Wiborg daughters, veiled or not, were emphatically not unseen. They attended Miss Ely's private school for girls in Cincinnati, to which they were driven each morning in a two-horse barouche. In winter, to protect them from the chill, the carriage was closed, causing what Sara referred to as "squeamish feelings," so that the girls arrived at school "sometimes pale and shaken." At Miss Ely's the girls worked hard: they learned French from a Madame Frédin as well as geography, arithmetic, composition, grammar, history, music, and drawing; but in the afternoons and on holidays they ran decorously wild through the woods and fields of Clifton, riding, "coasting" (sledding), and playing outdoors with the dogs — the Wiborgs kept dachshunds and wolfhounds — or picking wildflowers in the pasture.

Birthdays were celebrated with enthusiasm and much suspense over who would draw what favor out of the traditional cake: would it be the thimble (which foretold spinsterhood), the sixpence (riches), or the ring (marriage)? At other times the children played at dressing up, or bundled into bed with their friends to watch a magic lantern show. But often their amusements had a more worldly cast — a performance of the opera *Hansel and Gretel* at Christmastime, a Paderewski concert ("beautiful," pronounced twelve-year-old Sara), or an excursion to see Ellen Terry and Henry Irving in *King Arthur*.

Sara exhibited an early interest in music, but her two favorite pastimes were drawing ("I think drawing is lovely," she confided to her diary at age twelve) and dancing. "I went to dancing school and had a good time," she wrote. "Always do on Thursdays!!!" Blond and fresh-faced, with slanting eyes and delicate features, she had an elfin quality that set her apart from her equally beautiful but strikingly different sisters: the dark, intense Mary Hoyt (who was called Hoytie) and the classically serene Olga. Hoytie, an imperious, self-involved child who once protested, in a sudden summer rainstorm, "It's raining on *me!*" was her father's favorite, and she and Sara had an uneasy relationship. Sara was far closer to Olga, despite the difference in their ages.

Their father, who was known as an exacting but fair employer, ran his family the way he ran his company. He expected from his womenfolk the same enterprise and industry that had made him a millionaire by the time he was forty; and for the most part he got it. The strain of living up to Frank's expectations took its toll, however: as time passed, Adeline suffered increasingly from headaches and digestive twinges and other manifestations of late-Victorian malaise, although she soldiered on valiantly. She was a world-class party giver who could turn a drawing room into a bower of enchantment (as the society columnists were fond of saying) with the best of them. And as she progressed from entertaining *le tout Cincinnati* to consorting with the presidents and princes who were Frank's clients and associates at home and abroad, she realized that her three charming daughters were potent weapons in her social arsenal.

In 1898 the Wiborgs went to live in Germany so Frank could expand Ault and Wiborg's European presence, and the young Misses Wiborg proved themselves as adept at charming royalty as they did the citizens of Cincinnati. They had met Kaiser Wilhelm II in Norway the previous summer, when they were invited on board the imperial yacht, the *Hohenzollern,* and His Imperial Majesty had given the girls ribbons emblazoned with the ship's name for their broad-brimmed hats and had "kissed us all around," as Sara reported to an aunt. Now they renewed the acquaintance at an afternoon audience at the kaiser's Charlottenburg Palace, which fourteen-year-old Sara, aware of the event's importance, chronicled in a leather-bound journal. At the palace a footman in silver livery led the Wiborgs up a marble staircase to a waiting room where, after a few moments, "the door flew open and two large Russian hounds came bounding in and close after them the princes and the little princess. Last of all came the Kaiser and the Kaiserin."

The Wiborg girls politely kissed the empress's hand and tried to do the same to the kaiser, but — possibly sensitive about his withered left arm — he demurred. They exchanged handshakes with the princes and princess, but soon all the children were romping with the dogs on the rug. The oldest princes provided a diversion by trooping off upstairs to do their lessons and making such a clatter that, wrote Sara with typical candor, "it sounded as if the ceiling were falling down." But the kaiser and kaiserin only laughed, and offered their guests hot chocolate "with whip cream" and cakes. There was one tricky moment during this momentous occasion when eight-year-old Olga lost her gloves and thought she must have dropped them under the table — to grope, or not to grope? — but the youngest prince simply dived beneath the cloth to retrieve them, shooing away the footmen who tried to help him.

All this familial gemütlichkeit gave Frank Wiborg, and his company, a kind of most favored nation status in Germany, and enhanced Frank's standing among American industrialists as well. Four years later, when the kaiser's brother, Prince Henry of Prussia, made a trip to the United States, the Wiborgs were among his official hosts, and "lavishly entertained" him (as the *Cincinnati Enquirer*'s reporter put it) at Clifton. But by then Frank and Adeline Wiborg had extended their social horizons far beyond the banks of the Ohio.

In the last decade of the nineteenth century, New York City was the mercantile, artistic, and social capital of America. It was the fulcrum on which J. P. Morgan rested the lever of his millions; it was home to Mrs. Astor's ballroom and the four hundred blue bloods who could dance in it; it boasted the Metropolitan Opera, Andrew Carnegie's palatial Florentine-inspired Music Hall, the Metropolitan Museum of Art, the Ladies' Mile, and Madison Square Garden. If you were going to be a leader of industry or society — and the Wiborgs aspired to be both — you had to conquer New York. Cincinnati might be the Queen City of the West, but compared to New York it was sleepy and provincial.

Adeline Wiborg already had New York connections through her sister, Helen Sherman Griffith, who was married to Lieutenant General Nelson Miles, and through a cousin, Colgate Hoyt. And with Frank on the move so much of the time, shuttling between Ault and Wiborg offices and factories in Europe and Asia and South America, it made sense for her to establish some kind of *pied-à-terre* in New York. She settled on the Gotham Hotel, which had recently been built on the corner of Fifth Avenue and 55th Street, a fashionable address, with smart, up-to-date accommodations, and no servants to hire or worry about.

Many women of Adeline's class and economic bracket would have made a move to New York in order to launch their daughters on a course toward a brilliant marriage, but this thought seems to have been far from Adeline's mind. Although by now Sara was in her teens, an age when most young girls of her class were being prepared for presentation to society and then for marriage, Adeline tried to postpone this inevitable progression. Perhaps, as her granddaughter later theorized, she simply enjoyed Sara's company and wished to keep her to herself; or perhaps she and Frank were simply too busy to attend to the business of marrying Sara off. Possibly she needed Sara as a buffer against her energetic and demanding husband. Whatever the reason, their eldest daughter, like a princess in a fairy tale, grew ever taller and fairer — and still she stayed in the schoolroom with Hoytie and Olga. It was as if the three sisters were a matched set, "the Wiborg girls," traveling companions and social ornaments, to be shown off in public but enjoyed only in private.

In the late autumn of 1902, Frank Wiborg was asked to accompany his brother-in-law General Miles, who was commander in chief of the army, on a round-the-world fact-finding trip. Their party planned a stopover in Peking, where only two years previously rebellious anti-Western Chinese soldiers had held the entire foreign colony hostage, killing 234 of the 480 defenders, for fifty-five days during the Boxer Rebellion — but no such incidents marred *this* trip. After an audience with the dowager empress, Hu-Tsi, Frank and the general boarded the Trans-Siberian Railroad for St. Petersburg in January 1903, and didn't return to the U.S. until the spring. Adeline and the girls, however, missed the opportunity to kiss the hands of the empress, or the czar and czarina. They were left at home, and Sara, who at nineteen might have expected her leash to be let out a little, was instead enrolled at Miss Spence's School, an elite academy for young ladies on West 48th Street, where the rather advanced curriculum included French and Latin, literature, history, chemistry, art history, psychology, and — Frank Wiborg was doubtless delighted to discover — practical mathematics and household accounting.

She wasn't entirely happy there: she thought many of her schoolmates snobbish, and was appalled by their gossipy, boy-crazy conversation — "*so* harmful at that impressionable age," she said later. Although lively and clever, Sara wasn't as serious a student as some in her class. She didn't elect to pursue the preparatory course that Clara Spence offered to a few college-bound girls, and at her graduation in 1904 she was awarded a certificate rather than the diploma given for meeting Miss Spence's stringent academic standards. But she was now, at last, officially out of the schoolroom; she could wear her long blond hair up and her skirts down to the ground. Although her parents might not have felt ready to let her go, she was ripe for adventure.

She soon got it, in a limited form. That June, Adeline Wiborg took her two elder daughters and their cousin Sara Sherman on a trip to Europe. And in France, accompanied by a Cleveland friend of the girls, Mary Groesbeck, as well as one of Adeline's own cronies, a poker-faced Edwardian dowager named Dickson and her son, Roland, they toured the château country by automobile, a dashing, very *modern* thing to do.

The trip started out badly: in Paris it took them four tries before they could find rooms in the Continental, which (wrote Sara in her travel journal) was "a horrid place." Not that they stayed there long. By the next day Adeline had moved them to the Hôtel Campbell, on the avenue de Friedland near the Arc de Triomphe, and shortly afterward they moved yet again to a furnished apartment just up the street from the Opéra. Considering the number of trunks and valises involved in each relocation, the family's first few days in Paris must have been a nightmare of logistics and tipping.

Then there were the cars. Automobiles in the first decade of this century were still little more than horseless carriages — they had open passenger compartments with convertible accordion tops, far from watertight, and shock absorbers were still just a gleam in some automotive engineer's eye. The Wiborg party engaged two automobiles, with two chauffeurs, Georges and Eugène, as well as two "mécaniciens"; thus accompanied, and swathed in long dusters and motoring veils, they set off for Chartres, only to be soaked by rain. In the downpour the chauffeurs lost their way; next, the car containing Sara, Mary Groesbeck, Mrs. Dickson, and her son developed motor trouble;

then it got stuck in the mud. Sara, showing the sense of the absurd with which she frequently undercut her surroundings, dissolved into helpless giggles. Mrs. Dickson was not amused: *"Don't* laugh, girls!" she kept saying. "It isn't at *all* a laughing matter!" Finally Sara and Mary got out — it had stopped raining by this time — and helped the chauffeur and mécanicien push the car out of its rut. What with more tire trouble, a fresh downpour, and bad roads, the little party didn't reach Tours until 3:30 A.M., soaked to the skin after seventeen hours on the road.

Sara was undaunted by this unpromising start, and by the time the weather cleared and "Grouchy George" and Eugène had been replaced, she was pronouncing the tour "perfect." She was an enthusiastic traveler, shuddering deliciously over the chamber at Blois where the Duc de Guise was murdered by his perfidious cousin, and musing about why Queen Catherine de Medici would have forced her rival, the king's mistress, Diane de Poitiers, to swap châteaux. "Catherine certainly was a cat," pronounced Sara, "& I can't help being on Diane's side, though I suppose C. was in the right on this one occasion." (What Adeline Wiborg thought of her daughter's sympathy for the Other Woman isn't recorded.) Not that Sara saw everything uncritically: she thought the château at Blois garishly restored — "too fresh and burnished-looking . . . the general effect is horrid. . . . As Henry James says in A *Little Tour in France,* it looks like 'an expensive set in the opera.'" But she was continually delighted by unexpected details: the squalor of a "dirty picturesque village"; the "old wrinkled bent women of 80, carrying huge bundles on their backs that no Frenchman, however young or strong, would *think* of lifting"; "the beaming face of an American youth who . . . helped us find other automobiles at Tours, [who] had such a remarkable way of whistling out of one side of his mouth that Mary and I had to Kodak him on the top of the tower at Loches, unbeknownst to him, however."

Adeline Wiborg could successfully keep the young man off-limits — "We didn't meet him, or know his name, or anything," lamented Sara — but she couldn't repress her eldest daughter's evident and growing individuality. And it was this quality, more than her blond beauty or her melodious singing voice or her skill with a sailboat, that entranced a sixteen-year-old schoolboy she *did* meet at the end of the summer, at a party in East Hampton, Long Island.

In 1895 the village of East Hampton, on Long Island's eastern tip, was a peaceful backwater full of clapboard or shingle houses strung out along a grassy, elm-shaded main street that sported a seventeenth-century windmill, formerly used for grinding grain, at each end. After the Civil War the village had become a summer haven for numerous New York and Brooklyn ministers; a number of New York–based artists, among them Winslow Homer and Childe Hassam, had begun spending the summer months there as well, attracted by the flat expanses of the surrounding farmland, with their great vault of sky, the pristine beaches, and the opalescent light.

The artists had to hire carriages, or trudge on foot, from neighboring Bridgehampton, for the railroad from New York, which bore Gilded Age vacationers to the new resorts of Long Island's South Shore, didn't extend as far as East Hampton — it came to Bridgehampton, a few miles to the west, and then swerved north to the old whaling village of Sag Harbor. Progress and fashion seemed to have passed East Hampton by, literally as well as figuratively. Certainly it was an unlikely magnet for a worldly man of affairs like Frank Wiborg.

Although Frank's involvement with Ault and Wiborg meant that a permanent move from Cincinnati was out of the question, the increasing amounts of time that his wife and daughters and even he himself were spending in New York made their Gotham Hotel *pied-à-terre* seem inadequate. In fact, a summer retreat near the city — away from the sometimes oppressive heat and humidity of the Ohio valley — looked like a good idea. And Frank was nothing if not a savvy entrepreneur with an eye for emerging markets.

In 1895 Frank Wiborg began buying a substantial amount of property in East Hampton, including the first parcels of what would eventually become a six-hundred-acre tract of land that lay between the ocean and a large saltwater inlet called Hook Pond. There was a gambrel-roofed farmhouse on the property that belonged to the previous owners, a family named Pell, but it was insufficiently grand for the future that Frank Wiborg had in mind for himself and his family, and he commissioned Grosvenor Atterbury — one of the architects of New York's City Hall and of the Metropolitan Museum's American Wing — to add onto it. The result was a thirty-room mansion called the Dunes, which grew out of and ultimately subsumed the original house. When it was finished, it boasted eleven "master's bedrooms" with five baths, nine servants' rooms with three baths, a ground-floor shower and changing room for swimmers, and a huge living room that was forty-two feet wide and seventy feet long. Its walls were covered in Currier and Ives prints, marine paintings, and seventeenth-century Beauvais tapestries, its floors by enormous bear rugs with open mouths, sharp teeth, and lolling red felt tongues, its rooms filled with enormous dark mahogany furniture. It had stables and pastures and a dairy, Italian gardens and flagged terraces and shady porches. It was one of the first great summer houses in East Hampton, and it was prophetic: in 1896, the year after Frank acquired the Dunes property, the railroad was extended to East Hampton, and the town emerged as a fashionable summer resort. (Not so coincidentally, Frank Wiborg's real estate investments had an exponential increase in value.)

The Wiborgs began spending their summers — and increasingly their autumns, winters, and springs — in East Hampton, in the sprawling stucco house overlooking the ocean, where the sound of the surf resonated in every room. They swam in the ocean regularly — "in bathing" is a frequent comment in both Frank's and his daughter's diaries; they rode on the beaches; they played golf on seaside links; they learned to sail. Adeline and her daughters worked in the garden — she was an enthusiastic horticulturalist — and served tea on the porch with its view of the flower beds and the sea.

Although East Hampton was becoming a watering place for the wealthy, with vast shingled "cottages" arising along its windblown dunes and tranquil saltwater ponds, the vacationing artists had given it a distinctive flavor. An anonymous chronicler of the 1920s described East Hampton society as "based on a community of intellectual tastes rather than a feverish craving for display and excitement," unlike neighboring Southampton, which this authority depicted as "ruled by the fading remnant of the once all-powerful New York society."

Intellectual it may or may not have been, but East Hampton was relaxed, entertaining, and gay. The daughter of one of Sara's closest friends remembers it as bathed in a kind of perpetual summer light, like a William Merritt Chase painting: "the women all had tiny waists and beautiful shoes, and they wore long fluttering eyelet dresses, and veils on their hats — chiffon veils that tied under the chin — and there was always a breeze." There were golf games and amateur theatricals at the Maidstone Club, horse shows and dog shows in neighbors' paddocks, parties on friends' porches and sloping lawns — and it was at one of these that Sara Wiborg met a boy named Gerald Murphy. He was nearly five years younger than she, Olga's contemporary more than hers, a brown-haired lower middle former from the Hotchkiss School with a square jaw and diffident manner. Although, or because, he was so clearly *not* beau material, she was nice to him, drawing him out about school (he was a rather indifferent student), travel (he had been to Europe once as a small boy and longed to go again), his interests (plays, pictures, golf, music), dogs (he loved them but didn't own any).

Somehow they hit it off. For Sara, the intense, curious, and admiring boy made an audience at once stimulating and uncritical; for Gerald, the wealthy, well-traveled, beautiful Sara was like a glamorous older sister with whom he could share both his thoughts and his dreams. Soon he was a regular visitor to the Dunes, and even Adeline Wiborg saw nothing to object to about him. He was just a schoolboy, after all, and he had impeccable manners. The girls called him Cousin, and when Sara lectured him about his studies she told him to think of her as "a wise old Aunt." If she found herself daydreaming about anyone, it was about Gerald's older brother, Fred, a tall, red-haired, amusing young man who had just graduated from Hotchkiss and would start Yale in the fall. For his part, Gerald spent at least as much time with Hoytie as with Sara — she was, after all, closer in age, and much more possessive.

Things would change, but so slowly neither of them would know the precise moment when the wind shifted. He knew it first, though. And he set his course, very firmly, on this new tack.

2

"Gerald's besetting sin is inattention"

GERALD MURPHY'S PARENTS, like Frank Wiborg, came of immigrant stock — but there the resemblance ended. His father, Patrick Francis Murphy, was born in Boston in 1858, the eldest of thirteen children. He attended Boston Latin School, the city's toughest and most prestigious public school; and when he graduated in 1875, at the age of seventeen, he talked himself into a job with an up-market saddler and harness maker, Mark W. Cross, whose shop on Summer Street was the only one boasting a brick facade. His stated position was salesman, but soon he was forming, and expressing, opinions about the stock: why, he asked Cross, didn't they try to adapt fine-quality saddle leather, as well as the hand-stitching methods used for harnesses, to smaller personal items like wallets, cases, and belts? Cross took a gamble on his young salesman's idea, and the result was a trendsetting success.

When Cross died without heirs, Patrick Murphy bought the company for $6,000, which he borrowed from his father (at 6 percent interest), and relocated it to Tremont Street, then Boston's most fashionable shopping venue. At about the same time, he met and married a strong-willed, devoutly Catholic young woman named Anna Ryan and was soon the father of a son, Frederic, born in 1885. When Frederic was joined by another son, Gerald Cleary, on March 26, 1888, Anna Murphy, elevating piety over accuracy, changed the little boy's birth date in her family Bible to March 25, the Feast of the Annunciation, and always celebrated his birthday on that date.

The Murphys didn't stay in Boston for long. By the last decade of the nineteenth century the self-styled Hub of the Universe had become "a stagnant community" (as Gerald Murphy would later describe it) — a place

where "even the [trolley] conductors speak with an educated mispronunciation." It was also a city deeply divided between the Yankee descendants of the
English Puritan settlers and the more recently immigrant Irish, many of
whom were peasants fleeing the harsh economic and political conditions of
their native land. The Yankees looked down at the Irish: the "Help Wanted"
notices in windows and newspapers often bore the line "No Irish Need Apply." Irish boys didn't go to Harvard; Irish girls didn't leave their calling cards
in Back Bay drawing rooms. For Patrick Murphy, Boston was not only a
small and stagnant pond, it was a restrictive one, and he determined to move
to New York.

He rented premises for the Mark Cross Company (as he had renamed it)
on Broadway's Golden Mile, at Number 253, from Clarence Mackay, the
mining millionaire who would later become Irving Berlin's father-in-law. And
he found a modest brownstone on lower Fifth Avenue, in a genteel part of
town, to house his family. But Anna Murphy refused to go. Boston was where
she lived, and Boston was where she, and her boys, would stay. Patrick Murphy called her bluff: he went anyway. Three weeks later Anna packed and
followed.

Patrick Murphy was a distant, even chilly, father — in fact, recalled Gerald,
he avoided all "close relationships, even family ones. He was solitary and
managed, though he had a wife and children, to lead a detached life. I was
never sure what his philosophy was, except that I recall it to have been
disillusioned, if not cynical." He seemed to think of himself more as a man of
letters than a merchant, and he spent his evenings reading the classics — his
special favorites were Macaulay and Pascal — alone in his paneled library,
with its green-baize-topped table, its globe and bust of Emerson standing
guard. Balding and thin-lipped, dressed in sober suits, he looked more like a
conservative banker than a fashionable retailer. But he was known to cut loose
on occasion. On weekends he was often to be found on the golf course, his
pipe clutched between his teeth, a floppy hat protecting his bald pate from the
sun; and afterward he liked to celebrate with a libation or two. Edmund
Wilson recalled finding him and "some other gray-haired old gentleman,"
both of them clearly feeling the effects of several cocktails, "bounding about

on the lawn" at a Southampton country club, singing interminable choruses of "Sweet Adeline." He also possessed an unsuspected talent for clog dancing and for standing on his hands on the arms of a chair.

During the week, however, he was all business. At Mark Cross, he supplied to America's rich and *nouveaux riches* the luxury products enjoyed by the European upper classes: English capeskin driving gloves, Scottish golf clubs, Minton china, pigskin luggage, even the first demitasse and the first thermos bottle ever seen in the United States. He wrote all his own advertising copy: "A woman with a Cross bag wishes to be seen by two people," went one advertisement, "the man she likes best and the woman she likes least." A canny phrasemaker, he became a renowned after-dinner speaker at the numerous banquets, often seating up to two thousand captains of industry and commerce, which were a feature of New York's business and social scene. His speaking style was aphoristic, even epigrammatic, like his ad copy: "Give a woman the luxuries of life, she will dispense with the necessities," he would say; or "Choosing a husband is like choosing a mushroom. If it is a mushroom, you live, and if it is a toadstool, you die"; or "Youth has a faculty of laying up a luxuriant harvest of regrets."

He worked at his speeches with at least the same devotion that he gave to Mark Cross. He filled hundreds of small leather-bound notebooks with his own *pensées* — stream-of-consciousness sequences of ideas and phrases that he would fish in, again and again, for his seemingly spontaneous remarks. "Impromptu speeches are, of course, the best," he once said; "the great difficulty about them is the committing of them to memory." He evolved a careful formula: he always insisted on being the final speaker on the roster; he never smiled, and always kept his hands clasped behind his back; he spoke as if to an imaginary (and rather deaf) elderly lady seated in one of the upper ballroom boxes at the old Waldorf-Astoria; and his speeches lasted for no more than seven minutes, with eight more minutes allotted for laughter and applause.

Clearly this was a man who liked to control his environment, if not dominate it. He "didn't believe in being sick," according to his granddaughter, Honoria Donnelly; what he did believe in was physical toughness. He disdained overcoats and the long underwear that made cold winters (and unheated houses) bearable, and he wore summer-weight suits the year round. He thought if you ran into adverse circumstances you should grit your teeth and keep going: one winter afternoon, he and Gerald, aged about ten, were walking by the lake in Central Park when Gerald fell through the ice. Patrick pulled the boy out and insisted that he soldier on, wet clothes and all, until the two of them had finished their walk.

Anna Murphy was hardly more nurturing. In later life Gerald recalled her as "devoted, possessive, ambitious, Calvinistic, superstitious, with a faulty sense of truth. She was hypercritical and . . . ultimately resigned from most of her friendships." She was also, at this time, taken up with the care of a new baby, having given birth to a daughter, Esther, in 1898; and she had begun showing evidence of the deep depressions and anxiety attacks that increasingly gripped her as she grew older. Patrick Murphy was finding consolation elsewhere, and not always discreetly. When he took Fred to Atlantic City for some recuperative sea air after a spell of illness, the boy entered his father's room in the morning only to be greeted by the senior Murphy and a "lady" in a state of some undress. "Oh, this is Miss So-and-So," explained the patriarch. "We were just looking for her glove."

With his parents otherwise occupied, Gerald, a solemn, rather wistful-looking child, was left to the company of his siblings and the ministrations of an elderly nurse who disliked him. His one comfort was a wirehaired fox terrier named Pitz who was his special friend. He used to smuggle Pitz into his bedroom and fall asleep with the little dog clasped in his arms; but Nurse hated dogs, and if, on her nightly inspections, she discovered Pitz in Gerald's bed, she would snatch him away and lock him in the cellar.

One winter Pitz was exiled to the yard. Gerald made him a house out of a soapbox and surreptitiously threw towels and blankets out the window so the terrier could drag them into his lair to keep warm; but without human contact the little dog grew wild. In the spring Gerald was allowed to go out and play with him, and picked up a bone for him to chase, but Pitz, thinking the boy was taking it away, snapped at him. The next day Pitz was sent away forever.

Gerald had been attending Blessed Sacrament Academy, uptown on West 79th Street, where one of his younger schoolmates was Dorothy Rothschild (one day to be Dorothy Parker); but apparently his rebellious behavior over

Pitz's exile had been noticed, and his parents felt he needed a stricter environment. So Anna Murphy found him a Catholic boarding school near Dobbs Ferry, in the Hudson valley just north of New York City. Instead of a haven from the frosty atmosphere of home, however, it was more like a dress rehearsal for purgatory: the nuns, Gerald recalled, took him to the woodshed and flogged him with wooden laths for wetting his bed.

In the fall of 1903 Gerald followed Fred to Hotchkiss, a preparatory school in Lakeville, Connecticut, which was a kind of nursery for upper-class WASPs on their way to Yale or Harvard or Princeton. By this time the Murphys had moved uptown to 110 West 57th Street, just a few blocks away from the Wiborgs' *pied-à-terre* at the Gotham Hotel, and Mark Cross itself had relocated to Fifth Avenue and 34th Street. They had come a long way from Irish Catholic Boston, far enough that Gerald now began to spell his middle name "Clery" instead of the more Irish "Cleary" — and there was more of an Edith Wharton gloss on their daily life. In the evenings, when Gerald was on vacation from school, he would be permitted to join the adults in the library, where his father's drinks tray fascinated him, not because of the intoxicants it contained, but because of the alluring shapes of the bottles, glasses, and bar tools. And on Sundays his parents would take him to the Metropolitan Museum to admire their favorite paintings; years later he would recall with distaste "standing interminably in front of the enormous canvas of *Washington Crossing the Delaware* which finally destroyed for me for years all interest in painting."

At Hotchkiss, Gerald tried to put some distance between himself and his parents' expectations. He "rebelled and chose 'Chapel' rather than go to the village Roman Catholic Church," and he failed to distinguish himself academically — mathematics was a particular bête noire — so that by his second year he was put on probation, with the possibility of being left behind a year if his work didn't improve. Anna Murphy's reaction to the news was denial. "I will not put up with Gerald being dropped a class," she wrote to the headmaster, Huber Buehler. "I know he can get his lessons if he wants to apply himself." She hinted that any demotion of her son would result in his withdrawal from the school, and felt that a combination of heavy tutoring and "sharp talking to's" would do the trick.

Poor Gerald got both: summer sessions with a tutor while his parents took Esther to Lake George or Europe, and a series of jeremiads from Anna, who was anxious that he not replicate the "fiasco" of Fred's last year at Hotchkiss. Patrick Murphy seems to have had little interest in his son's progress, or lack of it. Letters sent by the school to his office went unanswered, and it was Anna who barraged the hapless Mr. Buehler with correspondence. The headmaster appeared to feel that stuffing remedial work into Gerald as if he were a Strasbourg goose was not the wisest course, but Anna was implacable. "Gerald's besetting sin is inattention," she maintained, and she grumbled that perhaps "some method other than the method at the Hotchkiss School must be brought to bear upon" him.

In February 1906 Gerald contracted what looked to the school doctor to be scarlet fever — in those pre-antibiotic days an often serious, sometimes fatal streptococcal infection — and was confined to the infirmary. His parents, however, refused to be alarmed. Patrick was famously scornful of doctors and all the hocus-pocus of illness; and Anna (as so often) knew better. "You know I have insisted that Gerald did not have scarlet fever," she wrote Mr. Buehler. Little Esther, she reported, had come down with what the family's physician described as "a peculiar form of 'Hives' brought about by intellectual indigestion . . . perfectly harmless — and occurring in children of bilious temperament." In her diagnosis, Gerald must be suffering from the same thing, and the remedy was to get him up and about as soon as possible. The school's doctor was unconvinced, however, and sent the boy home for five weeks' convalescence.

This interruption put Gerald behind again; and when, that spring, he took the preliminary entrance examinations for Yale (where Fred already was a student, and where Anna was determined to place Gerald in the fall of 1907), he failed to pass. Furthermore, there was some question of whether his academic standing would permit him to go on to his senior year with his Hotchkiss class. There followed more letters from Anna, more threats to remove him from the school entirely, more tutors. No wonder that in the few photographs that survive of Gerald during this period, he has such an uncomfortable expression on his handsome, square-jawed face.

He had, perhaps, an additional reason for unhappiness, one that he was reticent about to the end of his life, although he tried to explain it, obliquely, in a letter to a friend some twenty-five years later. It was at Hotchkiss that he first became aware of what he later called "a defect over which I have only had enough control to scotch it from time to time," something which made his "subsequent life . . . a process of concealment of the personal realities." What was this "defect" — and what was its manifestation, which so clearly impressed itself on Gerald that he dated his "subsequent life" from his sixteenth year? What could have made him "learn . . . to dread (and avoid) the responsibilities of friendship . . . believing, as I do, that I was incapable of a full one"? In the first three-quarters of this century, the term "defect" (or "defect of character") was frequently applied to an attraction for the same sex; and although this might not be such an uncommon thing for an adolescent boy in an all-male environment like Hotchkiss, one can imagine how it would have horrified the senior Murphys if they had learned of it, and how it would have frightened their son if he had felt it.

Lonely, confused, unself-confident, Gerald needed desperately to find a confidant. And that summer of 1906 he found one when Anna Murphy arranged for her family to spend much of the summer by the sea, at the Maidstone Inn in East Hampton. For there, when he was able to take a break from his studies, Gerald could renew, and deepen, his friendship with the fascinating Wiborg girls.

On Friday evening, August 24, 1906, the Maidstone Club of East Hampton presented a burlesque with libretto by "Bernard Pshaw" and music by "Victor Sherbert" entitled *Mrs. Clymer's Regrets: The Twice Suppressed but ever Popular Production.* Mr. Pshaw, the lyricist, was actually Fred Murphy, then about to start his senior year at Yale. Gerald, despite his fine voice and interest in theatricals, was evidently shackled to his desk and took no part in the production. A glance at the dramatis personae — Mrs. Clymer and her daughter; Lord Help-Us (played by Fred); the Earl of Finanhaddie; and assorted "Maidens and Rakes" — gives an idea of the plot. A "lady with money" (as she describes herself in one of the songs) tries to get her daughter married off to an English nobleman of straitened means who is visiting East Hampton in the company of his complaisant father, the earl. There are inevitable complications, but all comes right in time for the finale, which included "Imitations of Miss Ethel Barrymore" by Miss Helen Hotchkiss and something described as a "Donkey Ballet," which possibly had to be seen to be believed.

Perhaps the only girls in East Hampton that summer who might have made a transatlantic match like Miss Veroness Clymer's were Frank Wiborg's beautiful daughters, and all three of them appeared in *Mrs. Clymer's Regrets*, though not in starring roles. "Miss Sarah Wiborg" was cast in the supporting part of Dottie Dimples (one of the maidens); "Miss Hottie Wiborg" played Rosy Blush, a member of Mrs. Clymer's household; and Olga portrayed another maiden, Birdie Seed. Mrs. Clymer and her daughter — "Just the Girl I Am Looking For," as Fred dubbed her in song — were played by two other East Hampton ladies, so if Mrs. Clymer's "Grecian Garden" in East Hampton, the setting of the play, reminded anyone in the audience of the Wiborgs' Italian garden, the similarity would have been put down to coincidence.

Fred's star turn gave him an opportunity to shine for the Misses Wiborg — and, in particular, for Sara, whom he was seen to squire about with some frequency that summer. Fred lunched at the Dunes, and he danced with Sara at the well-chaperoned parties they both attended. Sara told him how much she had enjoyed the Yale Glee Club's concert in Cincinnati over the Christmas holidays, and he told her how much he and his mother hoped that Gerald would pass his Yale entrance exams in the fall. But nothing more happened between them because Adeline Wiborg was determined that it should not. If Fred Murphy, with his red hair and his height and his tenor voice, wanted to pay attention to her daughter, she would just ignore it. In her mind, and therefore in indisputable fact, Fred was not a suitor; he was a friend, just like his younger brother, the one who tagged along whenever his tutor let him off the hook.

What Adeline didn't notice was that Gerald — who was now eighteen years old, though still a schoolboy — had fallen under the Wiborgs' collective spell. How could he not? Outgoing, physically demonstrative, fun-loving, carelessly wealthy, they were everything his own family wasn't. No one nagged Hoytie and Olga and Sara to apply themselves to their studies; no one exiled their puppies to the yard.

September came all too quickly. Gerald had to travel to New Haven to take the Yale entrance examinations again — and again, despite his summer's tutoring, he failed. He went back to Hotchkiss for his final year, although even his acceptance there was in doubt until the last minute. But in the months that followed he stayed in touch with the Wiborgs. February found them traveling to London, to the girls' dismay (they wanted to stay in East Hampton); but Gerald telegraphed them a comic farewell that "helped a lot," as Olga wrote in a postcard that bore messages from all three Wiborg daughters. "Wish you were here to cheer us up," said "Sara W." in pencil; and, in ink, "Hello Jerry! Sara W." Hoytie corrected her: "That should be spelled with a 'G,' oughtn't it?" and added, in ink: "Here I am!!! — H."

Despite such distractions Gerald managed to complete his course work and graduate. In a conscious effort to compensate for the doubts he felt about who and what he was, he created for himself what he later called "the likeness of popularity and success" — his classmates remembered him as the wittiest boy in his class, and its leading "social light." According to the class yearbook, he somehow planned to enter Yale in the fall of 1907, but that spring, so far as his classmates knew, his thoughts weren't of New Haven. Under his solemn yearbook photograph appears the information that "Murph's" favorite song — his signature tune, in fact — was something called "In Cincinnati."

3

"New clothes, new friends,
and lots of parties"

GERALD MAY HAVE BEEN DREAMING of Cincinnati, but Sara Wiborg wasn't dreaming of him. She had other things on her mind. She was, by now, officially "out" — "*what* a job!" she commented later. "New clothes, new friends, and lots of parties." On December 30, 1905, she was presented to society at a "*bal masqué*" at the Cincinnati Country Club, a spectacular event that had taken every kilowatt of Adeline Wiborg's party-giving energy. The club had been swagged in smilax and forested with Christmas trees adorned with comedy masks in different colors ("my mother was so good at that," said Sara), and there were daisies — Sara's favorite flower — everywhere. The masked guests, who included the congressman and future presidential son-in-law Nicholas Longworth, were decked out as samurai, hussars, wizards, shepherdesses, and other exotic figures. Sara's friend Mary Groesbeck "personated crème de menthe or absinthe or something else green and very intoxicating" in a short green dress accessorized with a little tray and a glass of some green liquid.

Sara herself was, as she put it, "dressed to the teeth" in silver shoes, an eighteenth-century court dress of white brocade whose train could be kilted into panniers for dancing, and a powdered wig crowned with a wreath of daisies. After a ritual unmasking at the midnight supper interval, the lights were lowered and two lackeys in red, white, and gold livery bore a closed sedan chair into the ballroom. Then the lights came up, and Sara stepped out of the sedan chair to wild applause and distributed "lavish and handsome" favors — feather boas, royal insignia, tinsel flowers, cupid's quivers and bows and arrows, and dog collars and leashes — to her guests.

A few weeks after this triumphant fantasia, reality blundered in: Sara experienced what she called "the 1st real grief and shock of my life." She was out with a party of friends in a horse-drawn sleigh, all of them singing and laughing, and her little bulldog puppy was running behind them when a car ("so rare in those parts then") struck him at an intersection. Sara sprang from the sleigh to cradle the dying dog in her arms; after her companions got them both home to Clifton Avenue she "stayed in [my mother's] bed weeping for 2 days."

That Adeline Wiborg saw nothing odd in taking twenty-two-year-old Sara into her own bed for comfort shows how strong the bond was between mother and daughters. It was a strength as confining as it was comforting. After Sara's debut it would have been natural for Adeline to relax her hold a little, to encourage this young man or discourage that one, to probe her daughter's preferences gently in order to gauge the depth of her interest. But Adeline seems to have been blind to the possibility that her daughter could arouse sexual interest in a man, or feel it herself.

Yet in the two years since she had graduated from Miss Spence's, Sara had blossomed into a beauty. Her delicate features had lost the blur of late adolescence and acquired a pixieish quality, and her heavy dark gold hair, creamy skin, and mischievous, slanting eyes gave her an air of *volupté* accentuated by a deliciously ripe figure. Her friend Ellen Barry described her as "very feminine, with a big bust. And she had very pretty legs. She was rather vain about them."

She also had a daredevil streak that, according to family legend, compelled her to accompany one of the Wright brothers on a brief exhibition flight ("they told her not to wear a long scarf because it would get tangled in the propellers," recalled her daughter, Honoria). She loved sailing, and while at East Hampton often went out in Gardiners Bay in the roughest weather. A remarkable photograph of her at this age shows her at the helm of a boat, steering her own course, her eyes narrowed, her lips parted in exhilaration, and her long hair unbound and wild, like a Lorelei.

She kept her wild side hidden, however, when Adeline swept her off to

London in the spring of 1907. "Palatial domicile on opp side is where we expect to be for 2 months," wrote Sara to Gerald on May 18, in a postcard showing the Hyde Park Hotel. "Hoytie is in her element. . . . Greetings from Little H. & Sara W." The Wiborgs' extended stay in this palatial domicile had a specific purpose: Adeline had achieved the considerable coup of arranging to have her two elder girls presented to King Edward VII and Queen Alexandra at Buckingham Palace. For an American girl, being presented at court, a rite of passage for the cream of English society, ranked just short of marriage to a peer as a measure of transatlantic social success. In American society columns it became a sort of Homeric epithet, always mentioned after the subject's name ("Miss So-and-so, who was presented at court. . . .").

So it was a momentous occasion when, on June 6, Sara and Hoytie put on their specially ordered elaborate white evening dresses, fastened the requisite three white ostrich plumes in their swept-up hair, took up their ornate bouquets, and maneuvered their long court trains into the carriage that bore them to Buckingham Palace. There — once the prince and princess of Wales had arrived with their mounted escort of Life Guards from Marlborough House — they made their deep court curtsies, one by one, to the royal couple, and then mingled with the decidedly imperial throng crowding the reception rooms, which included the Princess Victoria; the maharajahs of Bikaner, Alwar, and Pudukota; the duke and duchess of Connaught (brother and sister-in-law of the king); and Lord Grey, the foreign secretary. It was a long way from the Cincinnati Country Club, where the only maharajahs were likely to be in costume; and it signaled the beginning of a new phase in the Wiborgs' life.

For Frank Wiborg — having made a fortune in the neighborhood of $2,000,000, with considerable investments in real estate and commerce which would continue to throw off substantial income — was moving toward retirement as an active partner of the Ault and Wiborg Company. The year after Sara and Hoytie made their curtsies to the king and queen, President Taft appointed Frank to a dollar-a-year post as an assistant secretary of commerce and labor, and the family moved temporarily to Washington, where they rented a house at 1626 Rhode Island Avenue. Frank even thought of running for Congress from his Ohio district if Nicholas Longworth declined to renew his bid for reelection in 1910. As it turned out, he got only lukewarm support from the Ohio Republican organization, and his candidacy came to nothing; but he was now a figure of national, even international, standing, and his wife, and particularly his daughters, had become stars whose comings and goings made copy for gossip columnists and their readers.

In New York or in London, where Olga in her turn was presented at court in 1909, Adeline marched onward as inexorably as her uncle the general, trailing her glorious daughters behind her from ball to tea party to charity benefit. Lovely in strikingly individual ways — from "Miss Sara's chic" to "Miss Hoytie's dark beauty" to "Miss Olga's delicate fairness," as one commentator put it — they were even more striking as a trio. All three girls had had years of music lessons; now they were expected to perform at society soirées, as every accomplished young lady did, at the drop of an ivory fan. Sara sang contralto, Hoytie tenor, and Olga soprano, and they would do everything from American folk songs to Wagner in three-part harmony, often accompanying themselves on the guitar or the piano. A favorite show stopper was their rendition of the Rhine Maidens' theme from *Das Rheingold*, which the girls sang bare-shouldered behind a semitransparent curtain, waving their arms about suggestively. Their act was so polished that one perplexed London hostess, thinking them to be professional performers, mistakenly offered them money to play at one of her parties, a gaffe which merited a story in the *New York Tribune*.

What Frank Wiborg made of all this is puzzling. He was proud, certainly, of the figure cut by his womenfolk: he retained a clipping service to keep track of their appearances in newspapers and fashionable magazines, and he kept the cuttings stuffed into the pockets of his diaries. But he seems to have felt that their celebrity — for it was that — was the purely natural consequence of their position as *his* wife and *his* daughters. And he complained to his diary frequently about their everyday behavior, of what he saw as their lassitude and fecklessness. "Our girls are so thoughtless and lack foresight utterly," went one entry.

If he had paid closer attention, he would have seen that Sara's behavior, at least, was a rebuke to his criticism. She put in long hours in the garden at East Hampton, trimming and weeding and spraying under the hot sun; she made curtains for the house and tended to ill or injured animals and ran errands for her mother — for between parties and shopping excursions Adeline was increasingly subject to sick headaches and digestive upsets.

Sara herself wasn't immune to feelings of frustration and depression, a word that began to creep into her own journal at about this time. But she hid them, as she hid her daredevilry and her disconcerting perceptiveness, beneath a veneer of serenity and compliance. As the eldest Wiborg daughter she was, in a sense, the captain of a team; she had a role to play, and a responsibility to see that the other team members did their part. And although it wasn't always easy for her to do so, she tried to measure up.

"This is a word of exhortation from a kind old aunt," Sara wrote from East Hampton in September 1908 to Gerald, then briefly incarcerated at a cram school called Hargrove in Fairfield, Connecticut, to prepare again for the Yale entrance exams. Her tone was jocular as well as avuncular ("We miss you greatly here, Fat Face"), and why not, as twenty-year-old Gerald was her younger sister's beau, if he was anyone's. "Your mother and Fred have *absolute* faith that you will pass your exams, and if by chance you didn't, the disappointment would be too cruel. . . . So work all night and every Sunday, for heaven's sake, rather than miss out again."

The Murphys had by now purchased a house called the Orchard in Southampton, East Hampton's stuffier, grander neighbor, where Patrick could be closer to the Shinnecock National golf links. Fred had graduated from Yale and gone to work with his father at Mark Cross, and the family lunched or dined or played golf with the Wiborgs frequently enough that Sara was well informed about her young friend's vicissitudes. After graduating from Hotchkiss in June 1907 Gerald still hadn't been able to meet Yale's entrance requirements, and had had to take another year of prep school, this time at Phillips Academy in Andover, Massachusetts. In later life he claimed that the year at Andover was a notion of his father's by which Patrick hoped to persuade his son to enter Harvard instead of Yale; but it was really an academic necessity. And even this didn't quite bring him up to Yale's standard — which is why he had gone to Hargrove for a last-minute grooming.

When he finally did manage to scrape through, just weeks before the beginning of the fall term, he arrived at a Yale that wasn't vastly different from the world he already knew. The 407 members of the class of 1912 were predominantly easterners, the bulk of them from New York or Connecticut. Many of them were familiar faces; most of the others would seem that way. Even New Haven's Romanesque vaults, Gothic towers, and white clapboard houses would have had a certain academic familiarity; and the campus rituals into which he was soon initiated differed only in degree from those at Hotchkiss and Andover.

On his first evening in New Haven he unpacked his trunk at 266 York Street and went out into a city that had seemingly been taken over by their contemporaries: the restaurants were filled with undergraduates, the streets were crowded with students and hung with banners celebrating the class of 1912. At eight o'clock a parade of Yale men, kept in line by marshals wearing white letter sweaters, marched from Chapel Street to the campus as the band played "March on Down the Field" and the townspeople gawked (and occasionally jeered); when the parade reached its destination, the seniors formed a ring of torches for wrestling matches between the sophomores and the freshmen. Afterward the freshman class gathered shoulder to shoulder on Elm Street and charged toward the sophomores, who were similarly massed at the library, in something like a medieval joust. The city trolleys had been pulled off their wires to prevent any traffic interfering with this curious rite, and if any bystanders were caught between the hurtling mobs, *noblesse oblige* yielded to *sauve qui peut.*

Gerald soon came to find such mindless, Dink Stoverish high jinks both thuggish and jejune. In later life he complained that Yale celebrated "a general tacit Philistinism. One's studies were seldom discussed. An interest in the arts was suspect. The men in your class with the most interesting minds were submerged and you never got to know them." Although riding, golf, and swimming were particular passions of his, he wasn't a jock in the usual sense. One day, crossing the campus in riding clothes, he was stung to find himself the object of sneering comments from classmates who found his getup more effete than athletic. It was also increasingly obvious that Gerald wasn't an academic star, either. He finished up his freshman year with the equivalent of gentleman's C's in all his subjects except for history, in which his marks hovered near failure. Although Anna offered him a rare pat on the back for being able to "go free of care into your sophomore year," the Murphys didn't feel his performance merited including him in the European trip upon which they and Esther embarked that summer. Gerald stayed on in New York at the Osborne, a residential hotel at 205 West 57th Street, and in a peculiar turn-about was charged with "mak[ing] Fred look after his health."

Gerald and Fred had a formal rather than fraternal relationship. According to the actor Monty Woolley, who was a class ahead of Gerald at Yale, "They always appeared to act as members of a royal family. Their politeness to one another was formidable. They never relaxed in one another's presence." But by this time Fred had already started to suffer from the recurrent infections and stomach problems that would plague his later life; and Gerald, who was trying hard to live up to everyone's expectations, took Anna's exhortation seriously.

So Gerald sweltered in hot, empty New York City, while Patrick and Anna took Esther to Paris, Switzerland, and England, and wrote him about the fine time they were having, and what a sensation little Esther — or Tess, as they called her — was making. Esther was by then eleven, a prodigious and preco-cious reader with a conversational sangfroid that disarmed (and sometimes demolished) adults. She also had a noticeable case of strabismus, or a "lazy eye," which Anna hoped could be helped by a visit to a European specialist. But despite her odd appearance and scholarly demeanor, Esther was "the belle of the ship" on the Murphys' transatlantic crossing, and "the pet of the prominent men on board." The *Amerika*'s captain had opened the ship's ball with her, reported Anna. But Esther's real triumph was the mock trial she got up to decide a "case" brought by one of the passengers, a man named McDonald, who complained that his wife smoked in bed. Appointing herself counsel for the defense, Esther won her case by, among other things, calling the prosecutor "a persecutor."

"Tess is a wonder," wrote Patrick, in a letter in which he also congratulated Gerald perfunctorily for working hard during his first year at Yale. "Never have I seen such a mind; everybody who meets her stamps her as a 'ge-nius.'" The contrast between Patrick's effusions about Esther and his luke-warm praise of Gerald must have hurt. Gerald knew he would never be a scholar, nor a star athlete. And he was still nagged by the feelings of *difference* that had surfaced for him at Hotchkiss. When he'd complained about the college atmosphere to his father the previous spring, Patrick had adjured him that "your environment is *inevitable*; you can't change that — so it is philosophy to accept it." But acceptance wasn't Gerald's style; transformation was. And when he returned to Yale in the fall he proceeded to make himself into a big man on campus by transforming his environment, devoting himself to what his class historian referred to as "the aesthetic side" of undergraduate life. He was one of the five members of the Sophomore German Committee, the organizers of the sophomore prom; he was chosen as manager of the Apollo Glee Club, an underclassmen's chorus; he was elected to DKE (or Deke), the most exclusive junior fraternity on campus; and in the spring he became assistant manager of the Musical Club.

He was becoming known as someone with a talent for arranging things — people, events, objects. He was far from the wealthiest, or most patrician, of his contemporaries. His college mates included members of the horse-racing and polo-playing Tower and Clark families, and Leonard Hanna, nephew of the Midwest millionaire and presidential kingmaker Mark Hanna, who was one of the richest men in the United States. But he was tall, well groomed, and well dressed — as a scion of the house of Mark Cross he could hardly be anything else — and he had a reputation for wit and the kind of social gallantry that made any occasion, from a dance to a picnic, go more smoothly. And so he was popular as well as successful. Robert Gardner, who chaired the Junior Prom Committee, deferred to Gerald on all questions of protocol — "my social secretary," he called him — and claimed that the New Yorker was "so metropolitan I naturally am rather afraid of him." He was such a stickler for good manners and proper form that when a group of undergraduates summoned up the nerve to invite the alluring actress Elsie Janis to tea at the college, Gerald made Gardner rewrite the invitation to make it correct.

Inevitably, however, Gerald's expanding social life took a toll on his studies: in late November the dean sent a form report to Patrick Murphy saying that Gerald's work was unsatisfactory in philosophy, economics, geology, English, and rhetoric. (In fact, he was failing three courses and barely passing the other two.) At the bottom of the form, the dean had typed a personal note: "Please urge him to devote more time and greater effort to his studies."

Patrick did so. "Come, brace up," he wrote Gerald. "You can't afford to let this thing go *now*. It means *failure*." He signed his letter "Affectionately, Papa." Gerald did manage to pull his marks up to passing that year, and he never received another probation notice, but it was clear that his real attention was elsewhere, with the "aesthetic side" of his campus existence. He left the envelope containing Patrick's exhortation lying on his desk, where a friend used it as a message pad. "Dear Gerald," ran the penciled note, "I very much want to see 'Herod.' Will you leave a ticket for a seat at the [box] office for me?"

Gerald's circle of acquaintance at Yale was wide — his roommates Harold Carhart and Esmond O'Brien were varsity stars in hockey and (in Carhart's case) in baseball — but two of his closest Yale friends were cut from somewhat different cloth than most boola-boola Old Blues: Edwin Montillion Woolley, called Monty, a stoutish homosexual actor and director of the Yale Dramatic Association who later earned fame portraying Sheridan Whiteside in *The Man Who Came to Dinner*; and a young man from Indiana named Cole Porter. Gerald met Porter in the fall of 1910 while vetting sophomore candidates for DKE. "I can still see [Porter's] room," Gerald recalled later: "there was a single electric light bulb in the ceiling, and a piano with a box of caramels on it, and wicker furniture, which was considered a bad sign at Yale. . . . And sitting at the piano was a little boy from Peru, Indiana, in a checked suit and a salmon tie, with his hair parted in the middle and slicked down, looking just like a Westerner all dressed up for the East."

Gerald, who was already something of a dandy — a photograph taken at the time shows him in a batik jacket, ascot, silk sash, and solar topee, the very image of the pukka sahib — decided to overlook the checked suit and loud tie. He discovered that Porter shared his passion for Gilbert and Sullivan, and they had a long chat about music that somehow segued into a recitation of Porter's life story. By the time Gerald had heard all the details of Porter's childhood on an apple farm, not to mention the lyrics of "Bulldog," the ditty Porter had just submitted for the football song competition, this rather unlikely pair had cemented a lifetime friendship. Perhaps each saw in the other what he kept so carefully hidden from others: the soul of an outsider concealed behind a facade of urbanity.

Gerald got Porter elected to DKE, and to the Apollo Glee Club (in which both boys sang second tenor). That winter he also managed to persuade the officers of the combined Glee, Banjo, and Mandolin clubs to allow Porter, a lowly sophomore, a solo spot in their winter tour so he could sing a song he'd written in praise of motorcars: the sight of the diminutive Porter backed by the rest of the glee club humming "Zoom, zoom, zoom," brought down the house.

Although the Glee Club appeared at the Waldorf-Astoria in New York during its tour, the Wiborg girls didn't come to the concert; they were preparing to leave for an extended European trip that would keep them abroad for nearly six months. But Gerald hadn't lost touch with them. On the contrary, he had become an even closer family initiate, although his friendship with Hoytie had cooled somewhat. It was with Sara that he had developed a new closeness: during the summer, he had spent days at a time at the Dunes, and the two of them had gardened and done chores (Gerald painted and varnished the porch chairs), or gone walking or driving together, or read Emerson aloud to each other in the evenings. And when it came time for the Yale junior prom (for which Gerald was one of the eight organizers), Sara was the girl he asked to accompany him.

At twenty-seven, Sara Wiborg was emphatically not one of the dewy debutantes his classmates swooned over. In a way that was the point. She was an unconventional choice: not a beautiful girl, but a beautiful woman. Up to now, with the exception of Hoytie, Gerald had had no real flirtations. With girls he was charming but not threatening — his friend Gardner called him "Galahad the Pure" — the boy all the mothers loved because he was at ease with *them* while he was impartially, and politely, attentive to their daughters. Whether this impartiality meant he was indifferent to them is debatable. Whatever the nature of the "defect" he had discerned in himself at Hotchkiss — and despite the fact that many of his Yale friends, such as Woolley, Hanna, and Porter, were homosexual — Gerald's sexual preferences were far from clear, even to himself. What *was* clear was that he had spent twenty-two years in a cold, withholding family, trying, not always successfully, to live up to someone else's expectations. By taking twenty-seven-year-old Sara Wiborg — who had been presented at court, who was a society sensation on two continents — to the Yale junior prom, he not only trumped everyone else's aces, he changed the game entirely.

But there was something else going on. With Sara, increasingly, Gerald felt he could let down his guard. Well traveled, well read, she was someone with whom he could discuss Emerson or music. She shared his sense of the absurd, collecting peculiar or pompous phrases she had overheard and sending them to him for his amusement. Most interesting to someone as wary and contained as Gerald had become, and most unsettling, was that edge about her, that repressed wildness, that sense that (as he later described it), "I have no idea what she will do, or say, or propose."

What Sara saw in him — whether she saw anything — he still didn't know.

4

"Thinking how nice you are"

"THE SADDEST PEOPLE," Sara said years later, "are the ones with no love in their life — I realized that, — & feared it — for a long time." It was that fear, a cold, clammy fog of doubt, that sent her into a neurasthenic gloom one August morning in 1911. Her cousin, Hoyt Sherman, and Gerald and Esther Murphy had all been staying at the Dunes for some days, but today they had left, and Sara was despondent. "Spent day in bed," Sara wrote in her diary, rather forlornly. "Got up for dinner — Horribly depressed."

Depression was a recurring theme in her journal. She was by now twenty-seven years old, an age when most of her contemporaries were married and starting up their own households. In fact, her two closest friends in New York were married — one, Rue Carpenter, to the composer John Alden Carpenter, and the other, Rachel (nicknamed Ray) Lambert, to the pharmaceutical heir Gerard Lambert. But she herself was still one of the three beautiful Wiborg girls, supporting, like a caryatid, the familial facade. She longed desperately for something more.

Since her schooldays she had had an interest in art and now she began to pursue it seriously, taking classes and drawing from the model every morning, and doing charcoal or oil studies of friends like Ray Lambert in the afternoons and evenings. Like other fashionably *au courant* New Yorkers, she also visited various artists' ateliers on "open days" in order to see their work in progress. "Went to H. Mann's studio," she wrote in February 1910, *"wonderful portraits."* Another such visit was less pleasant. She and Rue Carpenter went to look at pictures in the studio of Ben Ali Haggin, a socially prominent New York painter, but all that Sara recorded about the afternoon was a description of

"B.A.H." as "a dreadful thing," her frequent code for someone who made unwelcome advances or behaved in a louche manner.

Possibly Haggin misread her signals. She was, after all, a very pretty young woman, and a single one, whose tentative forays into the artist's *vie de bohème* might be open to misinterpretation. But Sara was no free love advocate. She was a well-brought-up millionaire's daughter who had been carefully taught, as Ray Lambert's daughter recalled, "never even to glance into the *windows* of a men's club." She had a rigorous sense of personal correctness — she was aghast to discover, for example, that little Esther Murphy, a schoolgirl in her teens, not only read but *talked about* racy French novels at the luncheon table. Whether by her own choice or her mother's, Sara led a somewhat cloistered existence; and her social life, in New York at least, had lost the giddy frenzy of her debutante days. She went to the de rigueur events, of course, like Theodore Roosevelt, Jr.'s, wedding in June, and she kept up her volunteer commitments with the Junior League, of which she was a member. But more and more it was Olga and Hoytie who went to dances at the Whitneys' or tableaux at the Clarence Mackays' — where Olga dressed as a Greek libation bearer in a Fortuny-inspired chiton — and it was Sara who stayed at home drawing, or accompanied Frank on his icy dips in the autumn Atlantic, or went to the opera or ballet with the Lamberts or the Murphys or other married friends of the family. (Her taste in music was more adventurous than that of many of her peers — she found Strauss's *Elektra* "stirring" and when she felt bemused by Debussy's *Pelléas et Mélisande* she went to a repeat performance and "liked it *much* better" the second time.)

Despite the pleasure she took in these diversions, there were many days when she felt very low. She was headachy, and she suffered from painful menstrual periods ("*awful* pains," notes one diary entry). February found her "much depressed," "frightfully depressed," and "fearfully depressed"; a family trip to Cincinnati in May, preceded by several days of "packing *hard*," left her cross and mopey; and even in her beloved East Hampton, where she busied herself with staking the driveway, sewing curtains, weeding, raking the terrace, gathering leaves, and swimming, she still felt empty and sad. Matters weren't helped when her cousin, Sara Sherman, who had lived with the Wiborgs since the death of her own parents, married Ledyard Mitchell in

July. Despite Adeline's skittishness about suitors, and despite the fact that Mitchell had been raised a Roman Catholic, Frank and Adeline Wiborg had given their blessing to their niece's marriage and held the ceremony at the Dunes in grand style. Sara Sherman (she was always referred to in the family by both names, to distinguish her from her cousin) lent Sara Wiborg her wedding veil to try on, and when the cake was cut Sara got the ring in her slice — but although the ring was supposed to signify marriage, there was no groom in sight for her.

For unlike Hoytie, who increasingly preferred women to men, or Olga, who was speculatively and publicly linked to various eligible bachelors, Sara seemed not to have any serious suitors. Her friendships with Gerald and Fred Murphy, and with Chesley Richardson, one of the usefully neutral gentlemen who would nowadays be described as a "walker," were just that — friendships. But there was another man in her life who was potentially more dangerous than they, Gerard Barnes Lambert, the husband of her friend Ray.

Lambert's father was a St. Louis man who made a fortune by inventing the household antiseptic Listerine. The son had come east to attend Princeton University, graduating with the class of 1908 and marrying Rachel Lowe the same year. At the time Sara first knew him, he was studying architecture at Columbia University; but he later went to work in his father's company, where he would distinguish himself by repositioning Listerine as a mouthwash designed to ward off bad breath, or, as Lambert put it with faux-clinical flair, "halitosis." The advertising campaign he devised — featuring a despondent debutante wondering why she has so few admirers — was one of the first to be built entirely on sex appeal, a quality Lambert himself possessed in abundance. He was so tall, long-legged, and handsome that "people just fell in love with him," recalls his daughter, Mrs. Paul Mellon. An avid sportsman, he played golf and raced oceangoing yachts.

He had a car, too, a sleek affair called a Simplex, and he used to take Sara motoring. Ray was at this time expecting a baby, her first, and might not have felt well enough to gad about with her husband and friend, which may explain why she didn't accompany them to see the Whistlers at the Metropolitan, or to the show of "The Ten's" paintings, or to the various lunches that Sara recorded in her diary. Perhaps Sara was doing her friend a favor, keeping her husband amused while she was confined. Why else would she spend so much time with a man who was so clearly off-limits? Whatever Lambert's attraction for Sara (and he was certainly attractive), it would have been counterbalanced by Sara's strict sense of propriety and loyalty. "She had a sense of austerity about these things," recalled Ellen Barry many years later, speaking of another married man and another relationship. The situation was complicated, and potentially uncomfortable.

Gerald Murphy, on the other hand, was a kind of tonic, both flattering and amusing: he was someone to whom she could describe her sighting of Halley's comet ("like a searchlight") or the "terrific" pink lightning that raged over the Dunes during a summer thunderstorm. She began calling him "Jerry," and their summer friendship only deepened when he returned to Yale for his junior year. Just after her birthday, which left her "depressed" and "feeling rottenly," she went to New Haven for the Harvard-Yale football game, although she returned to New York and dinner with Ray and Gerard Lambert directly afterward. More significantly (it was, after all, a real date), she accepted Gerald's invitation for the junior prom in January.

It was quite an event. "Will you ever forget with what trepidation you donned the newest and the best," reminisced the *History of the Class of 1912*, "and took your stand fearfully among the other social lions at the station? And then the giggling girls gushing from every car in great profusion." A slightly exotic bloom in this garden of giggling debutantes, Sara had a wonderful time, despite the watchful presence of Anna Murphy, who had come along to act as chaperon. There was lunch at the Lawn Club, and a tea and a Glee Club concert, followed by a small dance at the college's Woolsey Hall — and although she had risen early that morning to catch the train Sara danced until 3:30.

The next day, after staying in bed until nearly noon, she spent the afternoon in Gerald's rooms listening to music on the gramophone (presumably with Anna along to keep things on the level); then in the evening they went to the prom in the New Haven Armory, which had been draped in shirred bunting and spangled with Christmas lights for the occasion. Sara's dance card was filled with names like J. Biddle and R. Auchincloss and A. Harriman — in addition, naturally, to G. Murphy — and all the bright young things danced the waltz and that new dance sensation, the turkey trot. "Wonderful time," wrote Sara afterward. "To bed about 5:30. *Dead* — rheumatism in knees."

Her fling as sweetheart of DKE was short-lived. Returning to New York, she found Adeline "in bed — on strict diet — Trained nurse — Return of old trouble." Now all the dancing she did was in attendance on her mother. (Possibly this was Adeline's plan.) Inevitably Sara began "feeling like the devil" herself, and "commenced taking 2 raw eggs daily" from the supply she purchased fresh each day for Adeline. Everyone was on edge, suffering from cabin fever in their Gotham Hotel digs: Sara later described the atmosphere to Gerald as "unspeakable." February passed gloomily; at its end the whole family were delighted to flee to London on the *Mauritania*, where a fellow passenger was the actress Mrs. Patrick Campbell, then returning to England from an American tour.

Stella Campbell had first achieved fame — even notoriety — in 1893 in Arthur Pinero's *The Second Mrs. Tanqueray*, her first but by no means her last portrayal of a woman with a past. Dark-haired, white-skinned, both exotic and interestingly fragile, she had played Hedda Gabler and Elektra, as well as Mélisande to Sarah Bernhardt's Pelléas, and she was the inspiration for Shaw's Cleopatra and his Eliza Doolittle. Her marriage to Patrick Campbell, a soldier who was killed in the Boer War, had coexisted with her long romance with the actor-manager Johnston Forbes-Robertson. She had also been entangled with the young actor Gerald du Maurier (later the father of the novelist Daphne du Maurier), and at the time of her *Mauritania* crossing she was having an affair with George Cornwallis-West, then ten years younger than she and married to Winston Churchill's mother, the former Jennie Jerome. Despite her public carryings-on and her vampish onstage persona, "Mrs. Pat" counted numerous titled ladies as her friends, and her daughter had been presented by one of them at court; but such connections weren't universally impressive. In New York, Mrs. Cornelius Vanderbilt had asked the actress to attend a soirée as an entertainer for her guests, but she refused to invite Mrs. Campbell "in society as a lady."

Frank Wiborg might have shared Mrs. Vanderbilt's dubiety about this cigarette-smoking, tragic-eyed siren (he never got beyond the "Mrs. Campbell" stage with her), but Stella Campbell became a close friend of Adeline's and a mentor to the Wiborg girls. Her own daughter had embarked on a stage career and was about to announce her engagement; and Stella adopted Sara, Hoytie, and Olga as surrogates. Sara became her favorite; she would take her shopping and demand, in her famous husky voice, "Sara, darling, does the dress walk? Or does it make me look just like a cigar?"

Once settled at their usual London address, the Hyde Park Hotel, the Wiborgs plunged into a round of activity: Harrods, the theater, lunch with the countess of Wemyss and Edith Lyttelton, dashing aristocrats and friends of Stella Campbell's. "We sang afterwards," notes Sara's diary. They sang, also, at a weekend house party at Belvoir (pronounced Beaver) Castle, home of the duke and duchess of Rutland. The duchess was a notable beauty, famous for her elegant and unconventional style of dress. She wore her family tiara back to front, the better to confine her Grecian knot of hair, and looped her fabulous pearl necklace, which Charles II's mistress Nell Gwyn had worn in her portrait by Lely, around her shoulders between two diamond drop earrings — a style Sara herself later adapted. In her youth she had been one of the Souls, "a rather self-conscious group of clever young men and pretty young women" (as one historian described them) that had lionized Oscar Wilde, and her daughters — Lady Marjorie, Lady Violet, and Lady Diana Manners — were just as spirited. They took to Sara at once: "I love Sara," said Lady Diana, recognizing a kindred spirit. "She's a cat who goes her own way."

Sara felt instinctively at home in this new world. "I think I shall move here to live!" she confided to Gerald in a letter later that summer. At Belvoir, mealtimes were announced by bells and gongs, the tables were set with historic china and Cellini silver, and the guests wore buttonholes or "sprays" chosen from a silver tray carried to all the guest rooms before dinner. The ladies (recalled Lady Diana) "dressed for tea in trailing chiffon and lace and changed again for dinner into something less limp, and all the men wore white ties and drank sherry, then champagne . . . and then port and then brandy." On Sunday afternoons guests would take long walks *à deux* in order to indulge in interesting conversation. At bedtime the ladies would withdraw to one of the girls' rooms for hair brushing, where they might be joined by a number of favored gentlemen. This mixture of grandeur and wit, formality and informality, was just the sort of social cocktail Sara craved.

But she was permitted to have only a small taste of it. The stated purpose of the Wiborgs' European visit was to attend the events surrounding the coronation, in June, of the new king, George V, and new clothes were needed. This meant Paris, and the couture houses of Worth and Poiret. On April 5 the family crossed the channel in a snowstorm — "most *hideous* crossing," noted Sara; "all frightened as well as ill." So ill, in fact, that a doctor was sent for on their arrival in Paris, and despite the allure of couture fittings, nights at the Opéra, and drives in the Bois, Sara continued to feel sick and depressed for some weeks. There doesn't seem to have been anything constitutionally wrong with her, despite the heavy and painful menstrual periods she still occasionally suffered, one of which had kept her confined to bed and unable to make a return visit to Belvoir in March. It sounds as if she had had enough of living life as one of the matched pieces of her mother's luggage, but couldn't bear to admit it, much less express it.

In Paris she tried to carve out some space for herself. She had secured a letter of introduction to Rodin and used it to gain admission to his two studios — one wonders what she thought of such frankly erotic sculptures as *The Kiss* — and she enrolled in sculpture classes at the Académie Julian, where her fellow Americans Maurice Prendergast and Edward Steichen had also studied. Each student at Julian was required to draw from a live nude model, which must have raised eyebrows Chez Wiborg, and which may have led to the row that Sara described as "one of the most fearful days ever spent." But the issue was moot; by early June the Wiborgs swept her off to London and the coronation.

June was a blur of dinner parties and luncheons (for which, Sara's diary usually notes, "We sang"), of visits to the Horse Show and Royal Ascot ("nice day but bored"), and rehearsals and costume fittings for a grand coronation-eve quadrille in which the performers — all names familiar from the "Court Circular" — would represent characters from Shakespeare. (The Wiborg girls had been asked to join their well-connected countrywoman, Mrs. Waldorf Astor, in the *Merchant of Venice* figure.) This grand event — for which the Albert Hall was transformed into an enchanted Italian garden, complete with forty-foot cypress trees, yew hedges that had been clipped to resemble peacocks, vine-covered pergolas, stone statuary, and grassy banks, all under a pavilion roof of blue silk — was attended by nearly four thousand guests, including the new king and queen, who put in an appearance, along with all the "royal and distinguished guests" staying at Buckingham Palace for the coronation, after midnight. Adeline Wiborg must have been in her element, and even Sara permitted herself to enjoy it.

The coronation itself was almost an anticlimax. As commoners, and foreigners at that, the Wiborgs didn't merit a seat in Westminster Abbey, but after the customary twenty-one-gun salute woke Sara at 4:00 A.M. the family proceeded to the house of friends in Mayfair (the American newspaperman Richard Harding Davis was also a guest) for lunch and rubbernecking. "Procession passed about 2," wrote Sara in her diary, "*gorgeous* sight." Then they went on to tea with their friends the marquess and marchioness of Headfort, who — still sporting the coronets and ermine-trimmed robes they had worn to the ceremony — were able to give an authentically regal account of the morning's proceedings. The marchioness was a former showgirl, Rosie Boote, who before her marriage had been a "favorite" of the new king's womanizing father, and her spontaneity and lack of stuffiness made her a favorite of Sara's as well. "We have been having *such* a good time," she wrote to Gerald, back in East Hampton, after the coronation. "I can't remember when in years I've enjoyed myself more."

The purpose of Sara's letter to Gerald wasn't to gloat about her London season, but (as she put it) to "send you a handshake" on his election to the elite — and very secret — Yale senior society Skull and Bones, a development so momentous that his friend Keith Merrill had cabled her the news. "Would you mind," she now asked Gerald, mock-seriously, "if it is allowable thanking him about it? I am afraid to myself — I feel I could face death if needs be, but not a breach of etiquette in these matters."

The near apotheosis that election to Bones represented had been denied to Fred. "Poor old Fred," Sara wrote, "I do feel so sorry that he missed it — How much more pleased he will be about you on that account — being a most unselfish person — There is *nothing* [underlined twice] so ghastly in this world as to feel 'out of it.'" If Fred was out, Gerald was, by the standards that

Yale measured, in: That June he was also elected to a quasi-literary club called the Pundits, for which only five other incoming seniors were chosen; three of them, including his former roommate Larry Cornwall, were new Bonesmen as well. In January of his senior year, despite his rather unspectacular academic record, he was made one of eighteen undergraduate charter members of a new organization, the Elizabethan Club, which had been founded just that autumn to provide "a center for the literary life of the university" (as the *Yale Daily News* described it). Among the other "men of discriminating tastes and appreciations" on the initial membership list were the university president, Anson Phelps Stokes, and the legendary professor George Pierce Baker, soon to leave for Harvard, where one of his students would be Eugene O'Neill. The Elizabethans' white frame headquarters on College Street contained First and Second Folio editions of Shakespeare, a copy of the First Quarto edition, and first editions of numerous other Tudor and Stuart writers — certainly a contrast to the macho austerity of the Bones crypt or the big table at Mory's, where the undergraduates sat around "cussing and drinking lemonade."

Gerald was also elected manager of the Glee Club, and made a member of the Prom Committee. In the midst of all this extracurricular activity he managed to stage his best academic performance yet, earning a respectable C average (though he came close to failing geology). In February, when his classmates ranked their peers for the class history, Gerald was voted Best Dressed (he got 92 votes, nearly three times more than his nearest rival), Greatest Social Light (he was first of nine, with 58 votes), and Thorough Gent (first of 15, with 55 votes), and he was ranked fourth of ten in the category of Wittiest (Larry Cornwall was the winner). He even got seven votes for Most Brilliant, which would have startled Headmaster Buehler if he learned of it.

But these coups appear to have made little impression on the senior Murphys. Patrick intended that Gerald follow Fred to Mark Cross, and he hoped his younger son would feel more enthusiasm for this task than the elder had. "I am not disappointed in my work for Cross," he wrote Gerald. "What hurts is that Fred seems to value it so lightly." Yet he himself put so little value on his younger son's achievements that he didn't even feign regret at missing a Glee Club concert Gerald had asked him to attend: "I cannot accept your invitation for March 17th," wrote Patrick curtly, in a typed letter, presumably dictated to his secretary, from the Mark Cross factory at Walsall, in England, where he was on a business trip. "We cannot arrive until the 17th at the dock." He gave Gerald an epistolary pat on the back for his solid academic performance in his junior year — "I'm proud of you and your record," he wrote — but he seemed to take his son's extracurricular accomplishments for granted.

Inevitably, with so little encouragement from those whose approval he craved, Gerald began to find his Yale successes hollow. "Only in my senior year," he complained years later, "did I realize how dissatisfied I had been, and how little I had benefitted from my courses." It cannot have helped that he considered his achievements a kind of camouflage for his true self, a "distortion of myself into a likeness of popularity and success," as he later put it.

The person who seems to have cheered Gerald's successes most enthusiastically was Sara Wiborg, but she did so in a sisterly way, playing Jo March to Gerald's Laurie. Gerald, for his part, spent most of his last year at Yale acting as a kind of courtier to the Wiborg women. He dropped in on them at New Year's when he returned from his winter Glee Club tour; he took Sara to a Glee Club concert, a John Barrymore play, the DKE dance, and — along with Cole Porter — to see Eddie Foy in *Over the River*; he accompanied Adeline when, terrified by the sinking of the *Titanic* on April 12, she went to the Cunard offices to cancel the family's steamship tickets for a planned European trip. But Sara responded to this singular devotion with disarming casualness.

For during the spring and summer of 1912 she was again seeing a good deal of Gerard Lambert. He took her to lunch, went driving with her, took her sailing. Perhaps his attentiveness had something to do with the fact that Ray was again expecting a baby — and then again, perhaps not. The Wiborgs (and the Murphys, who were also friends of the Lamberts) were invited *en famille* to Gerard's birthday dinner on May 13; two days later Sara noted the actual anniversary in her diary, "*Gerard's birthday*," underlining it as if it had special significance.

All through the East Hampton summer she played golf or drove or went walking or met visitors' trains with Gerard. A typical entry in her diary reads:

"Golf with G. [Gerard] and Chesley 10 — In bathing — . . . L's [Lamberts] to lunch — Mother, H. and O. and Hoyt out. To Devon with G, back 4. . . . To Sagaponack with G. to see . . . about cruise — Home 7:30." As the summer progressed a note of strain crept into her relationship with the Lamberts, and the atmosphere at home worsened as well. Suddenly there were more "very depressed" notations in her diary, and a number of family quarrels broke out.

There was a brief respite in June, in the form of a trip to the Republican Convention in Chicago, where Frank Wiborg was a delegate. Sara was awed by the "terrific crowds — 11,000 people in the building"; and she returned to the convention each day, arriving at 10:30 in the morning and staying well into the night. On June 22, despite the forty-five-minute demonstration that had taken place for Roosevelt two days previously, Taft finally prevailed at 9:00 P.M. Olga, Hoytie, and Adeline had all returned to their rooms at the Blackstone Hotel by then, but Sara stayed to the end. She always did love a Scene.

When she returned to East Hampton she fell again into her easy companionship with Fred and Gerald Murphy, who were both frequent summer visitors; and Adeline, possibly relieved to have Sara going about with two blamelessly unattached young men, made no objection. It seems not to have occurred to Sara to play favorites with either, but as the summer went on Gerald contrived, subtly, to tilt things in his favor. Fred was working at Mark Cross — not entirely happily, for his father was an exacting superior — but he escaped to East Hampton on weekends and played golf with Sara, and the ubiquitous Gerald. Gerald, however, had been allowed a summer of leisure before going to work at Mark Cross, and he came to the Dunes almost daily to garden and read aloud with her, accompany her sailing on Gerard Lambert's boat, the *Wild Olive*, and act as her partner in winning a "very important [golf] match" on September 17.

One evening, Sara decided it would be fun to camp out overnight on the beach below the Dunes and she persuaded Gerald to join her. Frank Wiborg came along as a reluctant chaperon, and (Sara recalled later) the three of them bundled up in blankets on the sand and "watched very damp clouds go by — for the longest time, across the stars — at an immense distance up —

and dew fell on my face and wool cap." In the morning, when Sara awoke to crystalline sunlight and the cries of the gulls, she found that Frank had decamped to the house and Gerald was still asleep. For a long time — like Psyche and Cupid — she stared at the sleeping youth, thinking how "nice" he was. And then, feeling "awfully embarrassed" and afraid he would wake up and find her watching him, she fled in silence from the beach.

5

"I must ask you endless questions"

So CUPID SLEPT ON, and Sara tried to fill the void in her life with work. During the previous winter she had begun painting with the American impressionist William Merritt Chase in his studio on Fourth Avenue and 25th Street. Now, in the autumn of 1912, she started taking illustration classes with Thomas Fogarty at the Art Students' League. Her pictures, despite their clear palette and quick gestural shorthand reminiscent of her impressionist models, seem more those of a gifted amateur than the confident handiwork of a finished artist. But she spent long hours painting in the studio and, on weekends, in East Hampton. Certainly this work was more nourishing than another "artistic" venture she was involved in that January: an evening of *tableaux vivants* in Mrs. Orme Wilson's ballroom, in which she posed as a portrait by Romney, wearing dull blue with a rose at her bosom, for a charity audience that included such social lights as Mr. and Mrs. Reginald Vanderbilt, Theodore Roosevelt, Jr., and Mrs. J. Pierpont Morgan.

Her whole life was beginning to feel like an interminable *tableau vivant*. She was clearly under stress, suffering from a recurrent eye infection and quarreling with her family ("lunch in family and all fought" was only one such entry in her diary), even lashing out at nice Fred Murphy on at least one occasion (although she made it up with him later).

Whatever her feelings for Gerard Lambert, he was a less frequent presence in her life that winter, and it was Fred who was her nearly constant companion. But when the Wiborgs sailed at midnight on March 4 for their annual trip to Europe, Gerald was the one who saw them off. He was working, without much enthusiasm, at Mark Cross, and participating — without much more enthusiasm — in the social round expected of an eligible young bachelor. He too was increasingly beleaguered by the emptiness of his own family life. Anna was subject to deeper and deeper depressions; Esther worried so about her that she offered to come home from boarding school and take care of her. Fred's health was frail. And Patrick was frequently absent either physically or emotionally. Sara's departure clearly shook Gerald, and he looked so bereft at the prospect of parting that Sara remarked on it: "I shall see your saddened face to my dying day," she wrote him from shipboard. "Such an *unwholesome* feeling the whole thing had — sickly lights and anoemic confusion and cold relentless machinery. Wasn't it awful?" She signed the letter "Sal," which (quoting, perhaps, from a popular song?) had become "pretty Sal" by her next note to him.

After their usual London diet of theater, couture fittings, and parties, the Wiborgs moved on to Paris and then to Italy. Having dispatched Frank to New York to look after business, Adeline swept the girls off to the baths at Terme to recruit their strength for the rigors of the season to come, and then returned to Paris to outfit them at Poiret.

Sara tried briefly to assert her independence by going to study with the fashionable painter Walter Sickert when the Wiborgs returned to London, but it wasn't a good experience. For Sickert was a notorious ladies' man as well as a successful artist, and although Sara took the precaution of having her friend Ruby Peto accompany her to Sickert's Hampstead studio, her second session with the master was a "*Dreadful* day." As she recorded in her diary: "Hate man not going back." Perhaps, as he was known to do with other alluring young women, he chased her around an easel. To judge from her outraged syntax, not to mention her appearance and direct, vivacious manner, the possibility isn't unlikely.

For the remainder of the summer Sara resigned herself to being one of Mrs. Wiborg's Three Beautiful Daughters, and playing a supporting role in Adeline's triumphant season's finale, a "Vegetable Ball" held at the Ritz Hotel in London on July 24. This party was a kind of high-water mark for American social aspirations in London: among the chic and the aristocratic who joined "the preliminary scrimmage for invitations" (as one newspaper described it) were the duchess of Rutland, Mrs. Patrick Campbell, Princess Jane de San

Faustino, Lady Cunard (mother of the soon-to-be-infamous Nancy), the Russian basso and society sensation Fyodor Chaliapin, and the duchess of Westminster. Everyone came encrusted with diamonds and draped in pearls, but when it was time for the cotillion, a pseudo rusticity prevailed: Olga and Prince Colonna took the floor, followed by a servant in blackface pushing a wheelbarrow heaped with vegetables which were then handed out as favors. Apparently these Ole Plantation shenanigans sent the glittering company into gales of laughter, which can only have increased during the "ragtime potato-race," won by Lady Diana Manners, who was dressed for speed in a white ball gown trimmed with panels of red, green, and yellow brocade.

Although this event made headlines on two continents, it barely rated a mention in Sara's journal: she was much more impressed by two evenings she spent earlier in the week. On July 22, she was introduced to members of Serge Diaghilev's Ballets Russes at a party given for them at the Carlton Hotel, at which the young virtuoso Arthur Rubinstein played the piano. And the next night she went to the last London performance of the company's new ballet, *Le Sacre du printemps*. The ballet had created a sensation at its Paris premiere in May. Smartly dressed audience members had slapped their hissing neighbors, and a composer screamed for the "sluts" of the sixteenth *arrondissement* (where many of the wealthy box holders lived) to "shut up." The cause of this brouhaha was not only Nijinsky's angular choreography and Stravinsky's fierce, rhythmic score (which one contemporary observer compared to "the continuous thudding of a savage's tom-tom"); there was also the ballet's scenario, in which a young maiden is ritually sacrificed to ensure the coming of spring, a rather unsettling parallel to the female commodity-trading that made dollar princesses out of young women like the Wiborgs. Although the London audience was somewhat less vociferous than the Parisian one, the ballet was performed only three times during the Diaghilev company's London visit, and it is a mark of Sara's artistic adventurousness that she saw it at all. As one critic has noted, "musically and choreographically, *Sacre* bid adieu to the Belle Epoque." Sara Wiborg, it seems, was ready to do the same.

"It must be wonderful," Gerald wrote Sara that July, "to be doing so many things that are *new* to you." He himself had been having new experiences, but of a grim and anxious sort: shortly after his parents left for a summer in Europe, Fred had come down with mastoiditis, a life-threatening infection of the mastoid bone behind the ear. He was rushed to the hospital for two emergency operations, and there ensued what Gerald described as "a month's phantasmagoria of hospitals, operations, deliberate doctors, nurses, ether, etc. . . . he came within an hour and a half of losing his mind — or his life, — and his suffering was inhumane." Gerald, as usual, had been the one to cope with this crisis, moving into the hospital himself to keep watch over his brother. Patrick, on business in England, was "kept informed in detail," but Anna and Esther, vacationing in Switzerland, were left in ignorance, if not bliss. "I only wish I were 10 years younger and felt well," Anna sighed in one letter to Gerald.

Once Fred was on the mend, Gerald went back to work at Mark Cross; almost no one he knew was in the city, so he amused himself with reading, golf, and a new role as impresario. Esther, who was now an academically precocious schoolgirl, had written a poem, and Gerald sent it out to several magazines "for criticism only." The editors (he informed Sara with pride) had "pronounced it 'mature genius,'" and he himself felt "surer each day that she will do something with her mind." He had also been working on Sara's behalf. He had shown some of her illustrations to the editor of *Munsey's Magazine*, who "considers it all as indicative of a 'highly developed imagination,' . . . as good as anything he's *ever* seen." So, Gerald exhorted her, "I do hope you are going to work hard with your sketching when you return."

And when would that be? he asked with mock plaintiveness. In the meantime, he and Frank Wiborg had developed a rather formal friendship in the absence of Frank's womenfolk. They had had dinner together and had even gone several times to sample that curious new entertainment, the moving picture show. Gerald had spent several weekends at the Dunes, but, he confessed, he had been constantly unsettled by Sara's ghostly traces. "It was too uncanny to go through the house . . . Every now and then I would be startled by hearing you call the dogs . . . I'd wonder if you were really on the same planet with me — it made you seem much more remote."

He missed her, although he seemed afraid to tell her so. "Pretty Sal," he wrote, in the orotund style with which he often camouflaged his feelings, "I have much that I would talk to you of. Do you know I find myself wondering exactly what your opinion of certain things might be? This has made me believe that I must ask you endless questions when we are together, is it so?" It was.

Sara, Hoytie, Olga, and Adeline arrived in New York on the *Mauritania* on Friday morning, September 5, and were met by Frank and a welcoming party consisting of Gerald, his father, Chesley Richardson, and the Lamberts. Frank was in a foul temper. He had arisen at 6:30 to be at the dock by 10:00, and now here were his women surrounded by twenty trunks and innumerable valises. "Too much baggage and . . . no end of bustle," he grumbled to his diary that evening. To make matters worse, Adeline hadn't filled out her customs documents properly: she seemed to feel it was the customs inspectors' job to go through her baggage and establish what she owed in duty. When it was suggested to her that she simply put a value of $4,000 on what she had bought abroad and have done with the matter, she was mortally offended. On the contrary, she said, $500 was more like it. She wouldn't pay duty on a penny more.

After much huffing and puffing Frank got everyone waved through (although the trunks had to be taken to the general inspection area and would be sent on later), and they made the 3:30 train to East Hampton with minutes to spare. But on Monday disaster struck. In going through the Wiborgs' twenty trunks, the customs inspectors had found $5,000 worth of furs and dresses and jewelry bought on the journey, and they were determined to indict Adeline for smuggling.

Curiously, in this crisis Frank didn't turn to one of his racquet club cronies, or one of his Taft administration cohorts. It was Patrick Murphy who put the Wiborgs together with a lawyer named John B. Stanchfield, and on September 27 Stanchfield, Adeline, and Frank went to federal court, where Adeline pled not guilty to a crime that could subject her to a fine of $5,000, up to two years in prison, or both.

The newspapers had a field day: "MRS. F. WIBORG INDICTED; HELD FOR SMUGGLING," screamed the tabloids; "MILLIONAIRE'S WIFE FINED AS SMUGGLER." Adeline must have cringed; but worse must have been her very real fear of imprisonment, and of Frank's wrath if the maximum fine were imposed. The strain took its toll on her family, and tempers were frayed. "Most horrible day," wrote Sara in her diary on September 29. "S[ara] S[herman] and I dined [with] Lamberts[;] family disagreement between G[er-ard] and us." Whether Adeline's lapse had caused the quarrel, or whether Sara had flown off the handle on another account, is not clear; what *is* clear is that the authorities were determined to throw the book at the millionaire's wife, and Adeline was finally persuaded to change her plea.

On October 23 she went to court accompanied by Sara and John Stanchfield. Frank seems not to have been present. Like French aristocrats on their way to the guillotine, both women wore heavy veils, but the judge made Adeline remove hers while Stanchfield read character references from sup-porters like Henry Taft (brother of the ex-president), and argued that a prison sentence for what was really a case of ignorance or carelessness would endan-ger his client's life.

The judge relented, fining her $1,750 and letting her go. But the experi-ence had left the whole family shaken. And in some subtle way the balance of power between Gerald and Sara had been altered, too.

With Adeline's court case settled, the Wiborgs fled the country. This time, after a Christmas holiday in England, they planned an extended trip to India and Ceylon. It was proposed that Gerald take a furlough from Mark Cross and accompany them; but he was not permitted to, even though Sara argued eloquently that he "would learn more than in *years* of business." He gave Sara a rather significant going-away gift, a leather case for her drawing materials, and, she reported to him, it never left her side. "I sleep in trains with my head on it."

It was a relief to get "home" to London. Adeline was still prostrated from her ordeal and pretty much kept to her bed at the Hyde Park Hotel, but the girls went to spend Christmas at Belvoir Castle, where, Sara wrote to Gerald with characteristic irony, they had "burning plum-pudding for *every* meal except breakfast," and Hoytie and Olga rode to hounds, "*exactly* like an old English print." Other guests went shooting, pausing from the slaughter for lunch, which consisted of "a big table on the grass, many courses & heaps of port & mulled claret — all the men rather cold & cross. Everything as it should be & *rows* of dead birds going by on wagons." Concluded Sara, her tongue firmly in her cheek: "Is *anything* [underlined four times] so satisfying as to be picturesque? I am nearly dead with it."

The voyage to India was more than picturesque. It was her first encounter with a world totally outside her ken, and it awakened all her senses. "Arriving at Port Said was queer," she said of the squalid little town at the entrance to the Suez Canal which marked the beginning of Asia for P. & O. passengers. "We saw a row of lights in the distance . . . it might have been Coney Island or *anything*, — then, as we got closer — a queer smell mixed with the sea air — like something unfamiliar burning, — and *then* we were in the East — without warning — *everything* different." Port Said was "an evil little town," but it was full of "*such* [underlined three times] extraordinary people — *great* dignity & straight backs — & *such* color!! Not only lurid, but *very* subtle mixed in."

The Wiborg party landed in Bombay on March 18 and went on to Delhi, where they arrived just in time for Indian Cavalry Polo Week. This display of pukka-sahib festivity included a ball at the Viceregal Lodge, from which Sara retired early — possibly fatigued by the prospect of so many waltzes to *Der Rosenkavalier*, or two-steps to "How Do You Do, Miss Ragtime?" — and, the following evening, a presentation at the Gymkhana Club of J. M. Barrie's play, *The Twelve-Pound Look*. The program also included a "variety entertainment" in which Sara, Hoytie, and Olga stopped the show with a medley of ragtime and cakewalk tunes that the local newspaper called "coon song snatches." Although their father proudly noted that "they looked beautifully and sang well," and acknowledged that "they got much applause," he complained that the songs were a "poor selection."

He had been grumbling ever since they entered the Red Sea, calling Port Said "hot unkempt and tawdry, [full of] cheap things and cheap [music?] and not attractive." Even the Taj Mahal and the mountains of the Hindu Kush were unlikely to awaken in him the kind of sensual appreciation they did in his eldest daughter. But Gerald, who had taken Sara to an exhibition of Bakst prints and drawings in New York that autumn, could be counted on to understand her feeling that Asia was "the most marvelous place! Kipling and *all* of Bakst and Dulac come true." Her accounts of her journey, he wrote to her, "'transported me beyond delight,' — like pages torn at random from the Cripsy Dream Book."

Those letters, and his response to them, had transformed their relationship from an easy brother-and-sister camaraderie to something else. "Lately I have been made to realize," he wrote to her in April,

> how few men there are with whom I am able to carry on more than a five minute conversation, — without effort. . . . [N]ight after night, — these diners out, during coffee, — get so far with the Panama situation, or Wilson, — or the 1914 Cadillac vs. the 1914 Ford, — and then sit back. Why is it? Any mention of some important exhibition, concert, book, — editorial, — philosophy, — is at once allied with effeminacy . . . and discounted. . . . I long for someone with whom, as I walk the links, I can discuss, without conscious effort, — and with unembarrassed security, — the things that do not smack of the pavement.

He couldn't quite say it to her yet, but it was clearer and clearer that he had found that someone in Sara. With men — certain kinds of men — he couldn't be himself; with her he could. But in the nearly ten years that they had known each other they had never had the opportunity for the kind of extended and intimate conversation their correspondence now provided. Suddenly, separated by thousands of miles of ocean and a world of experience, they were alone together. And Gerald found his voice at last.

Frank Wiborg preceded his family to America, arriving in New York on March 27, somewhat exasperated to find Gerald waiting for him at the dock. "Gerald Murphy showed up," his diary notes, rather testily. But Gerald, instead of feeling cowed by Frank's bluster, found it amusing because he could joke about it with Sara. "[H]e was playing a part, you see," he confided to her (she was still in Rome): "he unearthed from inner pockets quartos of signed papers with which he fairly rustled. Assuming an air of high-bred preoccupation, he stood defiantly before his strangely-shaped 16 pieces [of luggage] with a 'bring on your U.S. Customs Officials!' air." Alas, poor Frank! As Gerald rather gleefully reported it to Sara, "No one noticed him, — no one at all."

Frank soon mellowed sufficiently to invite Gerald for a weekend at the Dunes, and the two of them went on an all-day horseback expedition to Montauk Light, some twenty-three miles away, which took them "over rolling downs, thro' pigmy forests, — with the sea sixty feet below booming and growling on an infinity of beach!" Perhaps afraid that he had portrayed himself as too much of an aesthete in previous letters, Gerald was eager to show off this active side of himself to Sara: "I felt emancipated, and wondered if I'd ever been in stuffy theatres and ball-rooms," he told her. It was all "such fun," he said. "[S]urely I am meant for that instead of padded chairs."

There was only one thing missing: "Your absence," he told her, "has embittered me." Abruptly the letter changed from gossipy recitation to breathless prose poem, in which he tried to tell her what was on his mind:

> In the garden the pansies come first to surely greet her, — but faded one by one whimpering: "she will not come." . . . Thro'out the house the clocks await in idle silence the better hour of her arrival; — on the hearth her dog sleeps and dreams of her return, — awakes, and hears no sound, — sighs: "she will not come." . . . The waves of the sea rush gleaming up the beach at her imagined approach, — but return hourly to their waters, hissing: "she will not come." The balcony stands lonely . . . with boards upon whose dust the fitful wind has traced the words: "she will not come."

He signed it, simply, "G."

6

"A relationship that
so lets loose the imagination!"

WITH GERALD'S LETTERS in her leather traveling case, Sara was on her
way back to America on the SS *Lusitania* when war was declared between
Britain, France, Germany, and the Austro-Hungarian Empire. The diplo-
matic atmosphere had been tense for days before her departure, and many on
board the ship were anxious for their safety on a British vessel if hostilities
should begin. "Damp day — many rumors," wrote Sara in her diary. "No
lights on decks, masts or bridge, and ports blanketed. About 11 — flashlight of
cruiser guns. Changed course, went like the *wind* — 30 knots through fog . . .
about 1 [o'clock] fired on — 2 shots. *Essex* convoyed us to Halifax."

In this state of heightened excitement and expectation she was reunited
with Gerald for the first time in nine months. When she had left the previous
December he was barely out of college. Now, although he claimed to disdain
the part, he was the very model of a polished young man about town, in
demand as a companion of other young dandies at the theater or for dinner at
Delmonico's or Rector's, on every society matron's guest list for tableaux and
balls and soirées. And he had changed in other ways. During their separation
her letters to him had maintained the bantering tone that had always marked
their friendship, but there can have been no mistaking the deepening seriousness of his to her. Face to face with him at last, she felt as she might have done
if he had awakened to find her staring at him on that long-ago morning at the
beach. She discovered, almost to her surprise, that she was deeply in love.

For his part, Gerald proceeded cautiously, spiriting her off to the garden or the beach at East Hampton or to plays and exhibitions in New York, and talking over *everything* — from books and pictures to food and decor and behavior — as if to work out the cosmology for a little world of two. They discussed their shared tastes in things material and spiritual, from "cold-cuts and mustard" and "creamy Italian pottery" to the music of Wagner or the sonnets of Keats. "How differently I feel about things seen and done, *with* you," Sara exclaimed to Gerald after they had been to see Euripides' *Trojan Women.* "Without you only one half of me enjoys them." They decided to shun all things effete and bourgeois, like chicken salads and "mid-summer club-porch chatter," in favor of the honest, the hand-hewn, and the candid. "Don't you love plank floors worn so that the knot holes stick up?" asked Gerald, in all seriousness. And on a reservation card he sent Sara to a "New Year's Eve Souper Dansant" at Delmonico's, New York's most fashionable restaurant, he scribbled the words: *"Aristocrats!! bah!!"*

Their talks went deeper than the surface, though. To Sara, and only to her, Gerald confided the feelings of emptiness and imposture that had haunted him ever since leaving Yale. He told her how little he enjoyed his work, and how little pleasure he derived from the superficial social contacts that charm and position afforded him. And he gave *her* an audience. He encouraged her artistic aspirations: "My heart is full of pride at your etching!" he told her, in a note urging her to continue her work at the Art Students' League. "You bless for me everything you think of and do with your hands . . . I know how gifted you are and how you have always longed to express the beauty you feel." He understood her ambivalence about her loving but restrictive family — "we've both lived too padded and policed an existence," he agreed — and he allowed her free rein to indulge in her wickedly accurate perceptiveness about her peers. "*What* a gloomy thing a funeral is," she could comment to him: "All those Jet Hats on the train — in silence — with faces lugubriously pulled — on the way up — (not quite too sad to stare awfully though — & peer to see *who* was there) — & On the way back — with lunch — they let themselves go quite a little — however — They were even quite merry — dozens of voices raised — sounded so like an afternoon tea. There *is* very little *real* feeling, don't you think?"

There was real feeling between the two of them, however; and, although it was some time before they could speak of it, a very real physical attraction as well. "You asked the other day if I thought you feminine!" wrote Gerald to Sara later that winter. "My own dear girl, if you knew how I thought of you!"

Somehow Frank and Adeline never noticed what was happening to their daughter beneath their very noses. The easy friendship that had always existed between Gerald and the Wiborgs provided camouflage and, terrified of what her possessive family would say, Sara kept her feelings secret. She couldn't hide the bloom in her face, however. As Gerald wrote her in one of the nearly daily letters that began to pass between them, "It is generally remarked this year that you are looking your best."

By the new year he was asking her, "Can you see me anywhere, everywhere and with everyone you'd ever care to see again? This is important." He had never felt this way before; he had been afraid, as she had, that he never would. "Who is there, after all, with whom you would throw in your lot in life?" he wrote her. "Am I clear?" His mind was reeling with questions: "Are we peculiar; — are we alike; do we want the same thing; will we get it together or alone?"

At last he felt sure of the answer. On February 4 he slipped away from a tea dance at the Vanderbilt Hotel and, sitting at a desk in the hotel lobby, wrote the following.

> Sal mine . . . in the past I must have pretended to much affection for people . . . In my heart I have cared for but few people. My regard for you is so different, it is so much more *real* than anything I've known. . . . I only know that I am willing for the first time to give it all to one person.
>
> Not so hysterically as you'd think,
> Gerald

Her response, when next they met, filled his cup to overflowing:

> My Sal: [he wrote her afterward]
> Those four words are ringing in my head. Could you have known what it would mean to me to say them? Take my heart in thanks.
>
> You are everything to me, — I cannot imagine life without you — and every bit of me is yours — *I am yours.*

Sara, for her part, must have felt like Sleeping Beauty, imprisoned for years behind the brambles of her well-ordered, well-protected existence, and only now awakened to a realization of what life could hold for her. "I never dreamed I'd find someone whom the same things and words delight," she told Gerald, wonderingly. "You are in my inmost heart & mind & soul, — where I never thought I'd let anyone go. You don't quite know it yet, but you are. And to say I love you seems a small, ridiculously faint idea to give of the truth. We *are* each other."

On February 8, sitting in front of the fire at her parents' residential club in New York, they were formally, but secretly, engaged — and almost immediately had to part. Sara was traveling to Montreal with her mother and sisters and would be unreachable for several days, but before she left for the station (Gerald could not bear to come and see her off) they were able to steal two hours alone together. Sara gave him a parting present of an amethyst and gold seal embossed with the figure of a turtle — a comment on the pace with which their courtship had proceeded? — accompanied by a heartbreakingly modest little note. "I am beginning to believe you love me, too," it said. Gerald's response must have seemed satisfyingly ardent: "I put [the seal] to my lips, as I would have put my lips to yours," he wrote, and placed it on a chain around his neck, where "your hands alone shall remove it."

Bereft without her, and afraid to submit himself to the scrutiny of his family, he went to stay for several days at St. Andrew's, his golf club in rural Westchester County. In a welter of emotion he wrote nearly hourly letters to Sara, bundling them up for later delivery as a proof of how desperately he had longed for her. And beside a stone wall where he and Sara had recently picnicked, he buried a little silver-stoppered glass bottle in which he had placed a Byronic *cri de coeur*, rolled and tied with green grosgrain ribbon, to "commemorate the pain and tears of this night." This wasn't hysteria, or romantic posturing: it was the release of two decades of loneliness and self-doubt. And he was both comforted and tormented by the fact that during these few days she wrote him nearly as often as he did her. One note asked if he missed her "½ as much" as she did him, and Gerald responded, "Were you here this minute I should take you in my arms in a way that would show you what you mean to me and how I *need* you." And, later that day, a postscript: "These meager words!"

❧

Almost as soon as they were betrothed Gerald and Sara began to make plans for the new life they would live together, a life "'loaded and fragrant' with everything that is beautiful." Touchingly, despite (or because of) the coldness of his own childhood, Gerald persistently peopled that future with children. "Can't you see them?" he wrote Sara: "Eager-minded, imaginative, humorous, lithe and clean — you finish it." Before they could do so, however, they had to confront their own respective families. At first they were prevented by absences from town — hers in Canada; his in the Adirondacks, where he spent a few days as the guest of J. P. Morgan's daughter Anne at the Morgans' magnificent Camp Uncas; and Frank Wiborg's in the west, where he had gone on business. Gerald was anxious to make the engagement public. "I am disappointed that it is not known today," he wrote on February 24. "What difference is it going to make — after all — *when* we tell them, as long as we don't take advantage of our knowledge and their ignorance?" But Sara was apprehensive, and made him put off speaking to her father at least once.

Finally the pressure of their feelings for each other became too much: on March 1 there was an encounter that seems to have moved their relationship to a different plane. Wrote Gerald:

> last night left me impressed, uplifted, awed (no word!) as I have never been. It may be strange for a *man* to admit of this: — but I could never take what occurred to us last night casually. I feel as if some supernatural power had whispered to me the secret of life, — as I held you last night it seemed as if somewhere within me a spirit were weeping for joy. There is so much that is pristine and *virginal* in our relation, — which makes everything so different, — we who have never been given to either man or woman are now given to each other. . . . I have been under the spell of it all day.

Whatever happened between them was clearly physical as well as emotional; and the force of it had brought Gerald to the end of his resources. "I tell you frankly that it must be told them all soon," he continued. "I cannot live alone with this feeling much longer."

Three days later Gerald presented himself to "'ply my suit with your respected male parent' (isn't it put thus in Jane Austen?)" He was apprehensive about the opposition he would face, and about his own response to it ("I have always lost my temper when anything is at stake," he confessed). Sara herself was so afraid of what her mother would say that she waited to tell her the news until Adeline was in the bathtub; then, positioning herself outside the bathroom door, she blurted out, "I'm marrying Gerald" — and fled.

Both families reacted in predictable ways. Adeline wept as if she had suffered an inestimable loss. Anna, who always took "life and the living of it so tragically," was convinced that Gerald was involving Sara in the equivalent of a suicide pact, and at first refused to receive her prospective daughter-in-law. And both fathers, who lunched together to discuss how best to deal with this crisis, conducted "an autopsy, post-mortem, coroner's inquest in one" on the folly of their children's presumption.

At the heart of the paternal objections was the disparity between the style in which Sara had been raised and Gerald's ability to support her in it. He was making $3,000 a year (roughly $50,000 in 1990s terms) and had no source of income beyond the Mark Cross Company. Sara could easily go through half that amount on clothes alone. Of course Frank Wiborg was a millionaire and could easily have settled a handsome dowry on his eldest daughter; but he seemed to regard her as an improvident and indolent child, unfit for an independent existence. "Sara Wiborg," he had grumbled in a November diary entry, "lie[s] about until 10–11 o'clock and has breakfast in bed and no attention whatever about the household management . . . I don't like it." If he was at all reluctant to subsidize Sara's marriage, Patrick Murphy was even more adamant that he should not.

Although he claimed to be "very fond of . . . both" Gerald and Sara, Patrick viewed their attachment with pessimism, and his ultimate response was to express what a "great disappointment" Gerald had been to him, "in a worldly way." His son's "vision of life [was] unsound and warped"; as Gerald reported to Sara: "I have failed to grasp the fundamental duty in life, i.e.: self-support, — and financial independence. He fears for my future and for that of anyone I'm responsible for, — because he feels that were I sent out to-morrow to earn my own living I could do little. He blames himself somewhat for having supplied me with 'the crutches on which I walk' — namely money which I do not earn. . . . He said I did not deserve to be married."

It's hard to guess how Patrick expected his son to respond to such a thorough denunciation of his character and prospects. Perhaps he felt defensive: despite his connections, despite the golf games and after-dinner speeches for which he was so sought after, Patrick Murphy was still a successful tradesman, not a millionaire industrialist, and Gerald's pursuit of F. B. Wiborg's daughter underscored the fact. But there is a coldness and a vindictiveness in his response to Gerald's declaration which seems of a piece with the banished dog, the frozen walk in wet clothes, the whole sad litany of Gerald's childhood.

Gerald refused to be deterred; he and Sara insisted that they could and would manage. Other concerns than money did occur to them, but they were reassured by a breathless note from Sara Sherman Mitchell, to whom Sara had immediately confided her news:

> I can't see that age makes any difference at all and Sara the Catholic part is hard at first terribly hard but one's point of view changes a lot after you are married and it all seems to smooth out.
>
> I could tell you a lot of things that I can't write and I *hope* I'll see you some time soon.
>
> Worlds of love Sara and it *is* so wonderful
>
> > Affectionately,
> > Sara

Despite her niece's enthusiasm, Adeline Wiborg hoped the whole thing would blow over, and refused to allow Sara and Gerald to announce their engagement officially. They told Fred, of course. He was vacationing in California for his health, and heroically wrote Sara to reassure her of his delight in their happiness: "You have no adequate idea of how overjoyed I am. My dear Sara: in all my vagaries and difficulties you have been a constant friend. I cannot express my admiration for you . . . read between the lines and understand that I am genuine and sincere in my affirmation that nothing ever made me happier."

Other friends of the couple suspected something was up: Gerald's Yale contemporary Arthur Gammell buttonholed him at the theater one evening, and said, "I've never seen you like this, you act as if you'd been refused in love!" When Gerald retorted, "Well, I haven't!" Gammell raised his eyebrows and said, "Oh! *That's* what's the matter!" causing Theodore Roosevelt, Jr., another member of the party, to quiz Gerald mercilessly. Another friend commented meaningfully to Gerald that "*Everyone* is agog about how well Sara looks, — why, she's lost all that anxiety of expression, — and now she gets herself *up* so well. I shall never forget the force in her handshake the other night. I've never seen such a changed person, it's wonderful!" But however much Gerald and Sara might have wanted to shout the explanation, they still had to keep it secret.

Limiting themselves to private lunches at a favorite restaurant and stolen kisses in "nooks in the library, stairway seats in the rear galleries of the Museum," or, on at least one occasion, "on public fire-escapes, etc." began to take a toll. "I think the tension of late may have made me a bit nutty," Gerald confessed. He began to be prey to depressions he referred to as the Black Service, in the grip of which (he told Sara), "I get quite petulant and pouty . . . which is worse [than anything] because it's small and I hate the small. I should so like to be bigger than anything that happens to me." The experience left him, he said, "a little frightened, — frightened at the way you conducted yourself in the face of my ravings. Sometimes you set me such a good example that I wonder what I can be doing for you in return." Nonsense, replied Sara: "I come wailing to you — like a child with a bruised finger — *far* [underlined three times] oftener than you do to me." Fortunately Gerald often managed to preserve a sense of self-mockery about these tempests, sending Sara a photograph of himself, scowling darkly, which he had captioned, "The Stormy Petrel in its native haunt."

By the beginning of June, although Gerald had been permitted to give her a little diamond solitaire to wear on her ring finger (she blushed uncontrollably when the clerk at Black Starr and Frost asked her which finger he should measure), the familial atmosphere was still frigid. Gerald was able to get a few private moments with her at the house of her cousin Elizabeth Hoyt ("Thank Eliz. for last night," he wrote, and for "leaving the room, too!") before he departed on a visit to Boston and New Haven, where Cole Porter was in the throes of preparing his first musical comedy and needed cheering up. But Sara was disconsolate: he was taking the Fall River Night Boat (notorious for romantic rendezvous) to Boston, and she wrote to tell him, "I *miss* you so — (I *wish* I were going on the F.R. Boat with you —)."

Instead, she had to go to East Hampton, where yet another family crisis was brewing: after well-publicized (but effectively quashed) flirtations with Jay Gould, grandson of the robber baron, and an English aristocrat, Lord Camoys, Olga had fallen in love with Sidney Fish, scion of an impeccably aristocratic, moneyed, and politically powerful New York family, and he had arrived at the Dunes to ask permission to marry her. Sara, of course, knew what game her favorite sister had afoot; so did Elizabeth Hoyt, who had also come for the weekend; but both were sworn to silence. Adeline had taken to her bed with a recurrence of her seemingly chronic digestive trouble, and Sidney broke the news to Frank Wiborg while they were both (in Sara's words) "stalking up and down the terrace." Hoytie, who had not been in on the secret, confessed to feeling "sort of *left*" when she heard of her second sister's engagement. And when Adeline was told the next morning, she broke down, wailing, "*What* do I know of this boy?" ("She didn't say *that* of you," wrote Sara to Gerald.) When Olga said she hoped her mother was pleased, Adeline moaned, "Nobody could *expect* me to be pleased with these changes" (one imagines the accusing glance at Sara). When her daughters tried to soothe her with thoughts of how long they'd all been together, "*much* longer than most families," she could only sniff, "It hasn't seemed long to *me*."

Sidney and Olga, however, were allowed to announce their engagement publicly, and the attention paid to them (while Gerald and Sara were forced to maintain silence) brought on another of Gerald's dark moods. "What an agonizing weekend!" exclaimed Sara. "You are such a pathetic figure to me — when in the grip of the Black Service — that it breaks me up. . . . I don't enjoy people not paying the slightest attention to *us* any more than you do, you know. And unreasonably — the fact that . . . they don't know anything — doesn't mitigate the resentment . . . in the least."

The only outsiders let in on Gerald's and Sara's secret were a dozen of Gerald's Skull and Bones mates, with whom he spent a bracing few days at the end of June on an island in the St. Lawrence where the society maintained a rustic, half-Gothic, half-Viking compound. Gerald went there with some feelings of trepidation. "I wonder if I shall ever recover from the feeling of being 'inspected' when with a group of men?" he confided to Sara. "I suppose the fact that I'm not the most comprehensible type to the average male mind accounts for a lot." But once among them again he was caught up in the rituals of friendship, diving from his tower balcony into the icy, seventy-five-foot-deep St. Lawrence and swapping secrets with the other Bonesmen in the campfire circle at "Stone Henge." And sharing with "the men I admire most" his feelings about "the woman . . . of my life" gave him more than a trophy pride. "You have kept alive the man in me," he wrote her. "Frankly, the game in N.Y. . . . has been played at too great a cost, I see it all now. At least I have learned it is not for me, — is not *real*. You've always known that . . . Anything that's easy for me, — such as this 'social game' — demoralizes me . . . I haven't played the game hard, — but somehow it's scattered my force, — and that's bad." With no clear compass point, he felt, he had drifted off course; but envisioning a future with Sara had given him a purpose and a direction. He returned to New York determined to "erase these smudged years of mine" and build, with her, a new life.

By July, Adeline Wiborg had thawed enough to allow the couple to set a wedding date for late in September and announce their plans, and Frank agreed to settle $15,000 a year on Sara. Patrick Murphy, who seems to have been dabbling in the New York real estate market, offered them a lease on a small house at 50 West 11th Street in Greenwich Village, a neighborhood much admired by the sprightly, artistic younger set that Gerald and Sara moved in, and one where they felt they could live "in a different place and manner from our respective and respectable families." Imagine their surprise when Adeline and Frank Wiborg, who were also in the market for a new winter residence in the city, found a mansion right around the corner at 40 Fifth Avenue!

Gerald and Sara simply ignored this development, and instead set about quite literally playing house: imagining the life they would lead together, and then trying to make it real by purchasing the objects that would exemplify it. Venetian glass, antique hatboxes, old pictures, painted Sheraton chairs and American country furniture (not the dark mahogany that filled the rooms they had grown up in), pink lusterware. "Such wantable things," said Sara, who loved prowling antique shops and "finding good things among trash."

Gerald tried to apply himself with renewed energy to his work at Mark Cross. As he'd said to Sara, "Better men than I am have made humbler beginnings. It's all very well for me to see beyond it; — but I should have done my work well in the meantime." But somehow Patrick managed to frustrate his attempts to show initiative. "I hope your father will realize . . . that once given *responsibility*, (*not* just given a vague chance to 'find something' but real responsibility) . . . there is *no one* more worthy of filling and distinguishing a position of trust — than you," wrote Sara, when it appeared that just such a possibility would be extended — but the position was given to someone else, and Patrick instead returned to all his old criticisms of his son's fecklessness and impracticality.

This "court martial" (as Gerald referred to it) may have been merely "one of those 'tests of equilibrium' . . . parents seem to find necessary to put their children . . . to, just to see if they can *confuse* them." But that, and Adeline's inability to cope with her daughter's marriage, forced a postponement of the wedding date. "I think I am right about putting things off," wrote Sara regretfully. "I am *not* considering your father, — or my own family — in this. . . . It is because I honestly think it is best for *you*. I want you to feel *at peace* (for lack of a better phrase) with your work."

Patrick's "court martial" must have seemed particularly unjust to Gerald coming at this time, for he had just acquitted himself nobly in handling a family emergency for which his father, as so frequently happened, was unavailable. In late July, Fred suddenly developed a bleeding ulcer and had to be hospitalized for tests and possible surgery at the Mayo Clinic in Rochester, Minnesota; Patrick was in Europe, so it fell to Gerald to play paterfamilias and accompany his mother and brother to Minnesota to arrange the details of Fred's treatment. Fred was in great pain and considerable danger, and Anna suffered nearly as much: "Her tenderness and devotion to him . . . is touching to see," reported Gerald to Sara. "The mother cherishing her weaker offspring. At times as I watch I wonder that women are made to bring children into the world to see them suffer."

The whole atmosphere in Rochester was one of suffering, however. Gerald's description is practically Dantesque:

A half-grown Western city, with cheap but pretentious civic buildings, — and the entire interest revolving about the clinical buildings and hospital. The place is crawling with cripples and sick. I waited to-day with 200 people in the rotunda of the examination hall while farmers and their flat-chested,

scrawny wives in hats and dressing-gowns came in awed silence, broken
senators, the Prince Troubetskoy, — young husbands with pale brides, then
whole families surrounding their cherished invalid member. The tenderness
in public is heart-rending, weak women helping and wheedling strong but
maimed men thro' the streets — all humanity seems afflicted! . . . The very
air is disinfected, — a sign outside the hotel dining-room reads, "Guests are
requested not to discuss operations during meals" — a crude assault upon
the feelings?! Illness and death and their avoidance — !!

Ultimately the Mayo doctors concluded that Fred did not require surgery, and
he gradually recovered. And as the days went on, Gerald found some amusement in the peculiarities of Rochester — the "mange-cures for 'dandruff'"
advertised in barbershops, the toothpicks used by all and sundry unconcealed,
and the townsfolk who presented themselves for restaurant dinners at 2 P.M.,
rigged out in full evening dress. But the visions of suffering he saw at the clinic
haunted him, and were to be horrifyingly revisited in his later life.

Only Sara seemed to know what effect this trip had on Gerald: when he set
out she wrote him of how much she pitied him his "long, hard journey . . .
with hospital atmosphere & doctors again — at the end of it." She saw something else, too: "You don't know *what* it does to me — though — the unhesi-
tating way in which you set out to do things. It really is times like these that
show me your character — a situation arises and though there may be 1000s
of other people in it with you — it is *always you* who takes charge of it — you
step into command & everyone does as you say — I've *never* seen it fail."

If only Patrick Murphy had shared his prospective daughter-in-law's opinion of his son! Instead, however, he seemed intent on infantilizing him.
Possibly trying to give Gerald a good scare, he now reneged on his promise of
50 West 11th Street to the engaged couple, and put the property on the market
in early October at a price of $25,000. As it turned out, either Messrs. Pease
and Elliman (the brokers) found no takers, or Patrick changed his mind yet
again. In the end, Gerald and Sara got the house and were able to paper the
front hall gray, paint the exterior white, and order all the majolica and Sheraton chairs they could afford. Still, this latest paternal blow must have hurt.

It was only partially offset by the fact that a new date, December 30, had been set for the wedding, and that the engagement could now be publicly and officially announced, with Sara's dreamy profile emblazoned on the cover of *Town and Country* magazine. This exposure, of a kind to which Adeline Wiborg's daughters had been accustomed almost from childhood, mortified Sara horribly, as she explained to Gerald in a note scribbled on the East Hampton train: "The youngest newsboy (with the bad complexion) has just come to a full — & rather dramatic — stop in the aisle — and held open the 'Town and Country' that has my fat photo — for frontispiece — before my shocked eyes for inspection — you will never ask me to do a thing like that again — will you? It reminds me of Tecla pearls [cheap imitation jewelry]. I know you won't — it isn't the *least* like us — in *any* way."

Although Gerald longed to travel to Europe with Sara, the war made a transatlantic honeymoon out of the question. In the spirit of adventure which they hoped characterized their relationship, they made plans instead for a wedding trip to Panama, with stopovers in Havana, Jamaica, and Costa Rica. A friend living in Panama, Gladys Rousseau, offered to organize a trip into the rain forest for them, and they started buying khakis and puttees for the jungle, as well as (for Sara) a new bathing suit and umbrella silk for new parasols. "*Won't* it seem funny — our starting forth to strange lands, together — we who have always had the heavy hand of chaperonage weighing us down?!" wrote Sara with palpable anticipation. (She was dating all her letters with notations like "Eight weeks until we sail!") "I looked up the moon — It will be, I am afraid, just over when we are starting out — but we *should* have one — on the way home — Home to 11th Street!"

They went to have their passport photos taken — Gerald sober in a homburg and starched collar, Sara rather drawn and anxious in a smart veiled hat topped by what looks like velvet confetti — and made final arrangements for the wedding ceremony itself. It was to be a very small gathering, in the drawing room at 40 Fifth Avenue, with only family and intimate friends. Adeline had already expended her energies on Olga's wedding to Sidney Fish, and Gerald and Sara were so eager to tie the knot at last that they hardly cared. They did manage a few festive touches: "I am *delighted* that we can have the 3 little boys with candles," wrote Sara to Gerald. "We'll pulverize them yet!"

On Wednesday morning, December 30, a florist delivered Sara's bouquet of orange blossoms to Number 40. With them was a note in Gerald's exquisite draftsman's hand: "Here are some blossoms for you, my own Sal, — no amount of pen, ink and paper could do as well toward this morning's message."

That afternoon, preceded by Hoytie and Olga, each in blue-green brocade with coronets of silver leaves, Sara stepped into her parents' drawing room wearing a white satin gown trimmed with lace and embroidered with pearls. Her only ornament was a simple strand of pearls at her throat. Her white tulle veil trailed behind her as she walked between the rows of guests to the music of Wagner's *Lohengrin* wedding march, played by a trio of organ, cello, and harp. Gerald, with Fred at his side, was waiting for her in the bay window at the room's east end, where an altar and prie-dieu had been placed in front of blue and gold ecclesiastical tapestries. And there, eleven years after they had first met, Father William Martin of St. Patrick's Cathedral made them man and wife.

"Think of a relationship that not only does not bind, but actually *so lets loose* the imagination!" Gerald had written her at their engagement. "Think of it, Sal, — and thank heaven!" Now, finally, they would give each other that freedom.

7

"Don't let's *ever* separate again"

AT MIDNIGHT ON NEW YEAR'S EVE, 1916, Mr. and Mrs. Gerald C. Murphy, liberated at last from the heavy hand of chaperonage, stood on the deck of the United Fruit Company's ship *Pastores* as she sailed down the Hudson. To all intents and purposes they were bound for Havana and Panama, but they were traveling as well into a new world of sexual experience for which neither was very well prepared.

Although Sara was thirty-two, she had been raised in the strictest propriety, and the word *sex* was not in her vocabulary (nor would it ever be). Yet she had a passionate, sensual nature — thirty years later Gerald could still marvel at her need for "communicated affection" — that was long overdue for fulfillment, and a candor and directness that was the polar opposite of Gerald's extreme diffidence. Such a disparity in natures between two partners might be considered fatal to a marriage, but in this case Sara's eagerness and honesty seem to have thrilled Gerald; whatever his doubts and fears about himself, she erased them, or overrode them. And, at least at first, his reserve gave her the opportunity to bloom. They were making things up rather as they went along, but the improvisation seemed to work.

At the end of January they came "home to 11th Street," where the view, literally and metaphorically, was somewhat different from what they had been used to. The street itself looked away from Fifth Avenue, and toward Sixth, where quaint brick storefronts faced one another under the tracks of the rather noisy and dirty elevated train. At the end of the block, near Sixth, was the tiny triangular cemetery of the Spanish and Portuguese Synagogue, whose congregation had moved on but had left its stone memorial tablets and a tree-shaded brick walk behind. Around the corner, at 51-55 West 10th Street, was the Studio Building, a six-story edifice designed by the architect Richard Morris Hunt specifically to house the studios of such artists as J. F. Kensett, Albert Bierstadt, and Frederick Church, all of whom had leased space there in their heyday. Although that day was long past, the Studio Building was still home to less-renowned artists and illustrators.

Number 50 West 11th — one of a group of identical brick row houses on the south side of the street with pilastered front doors and scrolled wrought-iron stoops — had been built in the mid-nineteenth century for residents who were middle-class rather than wealthy; there were grander residences up the street, not to mention the mansions of Fifth Avenue or Washington Square, just blocks away. Although the house was four stories high, the ground floor, given over to kitchen and utility rooms, was several steps below street level, and the top story — with rooms for Rose, the cook, and Mollie, the maid — had squat little half-height windows, with ceilings to match. As a result Number 50, and the houses adjacent to it, had a cottagey look.

The interiors were cottage-scale as well. In the Murphys' house the single sitting room faced the street, and behind that was a dining room with a little breakfast room opening off it that overlooked the tiny rear garden. On the floor above were just two bedrooms, only one of which had a bathroom; and instead of the steam heat boasted by any self-respecting modern residence, all the rooms had fireplaces. But despite its modest proportions and lack of modern conveniences, Number 50 became the first of a series of legendary Murphy houses, an artful composition that expressed not just its owners' taste, but also their attitudes about life.

Gerald had had the house's brick facade freshly whitewashed in the autumn, and the gray patterned wallpaper that he and Sara had chosen was hung in the hall; the wide-plank floors were covered with hooked rugs that Sara had pilfered from the Dunes. If some of these details could have been lifted from the pages of Elsie De Wolfe's recent best seller, *The House in Good Taste*, the rest were highly individual. Instead of the highly carved Herter or Belter settees their parents might have craved, or the pastel French bergères Miss De Wolfe recommended, Gerald and Sara filled their rooms with carefully placed early nineteenth-century American and English pieces — squat, stubby chairs and sofas, Empire chests, and Sheraton benches — and brightened them with fresh flowers in Empire vases and old opalescent glass jugs. On the walls they hung tinsel pictures on glass, old gilt mirrors, and folk art paintings. A particular favorite of Gerald's depicted "a black and white guinea pig making every effort to appear indifferent to . . . an idealized bunch of grapes." Most of these finds had come from secondhand shops and more than a few were refinished or retouched by Gerald and Sara themselves. The result was a house that updated "Old Worldy" virtues with fresh paint, and combined traditional elements in new and surprising ways. The look they were after — eccentric, elegant, original — was emphatically not a fashion statement: it was the outward and visible sign of the inward and spiritual neoclassicism they both yearned for. Gerald had once tried to articulate it in a letter to Sara describing a friend's house in Roslyn, New York:

> It's very old — wide corridors, bedrooms with ball-room dimensions, aged furniture, the grains and knots of the wood of which are outlined with deep cracks, the brocades on the chairs are worn nearly thro'; but have not been replaced. On my writing-desk is an elaborate silver stand containing ink and a shaker full of powdered sand! . . . To the modern it would all appear as "shabby genteel" — but these people love their worn rugs and cracked teacups. You and I prefer "shabby genteel" to its inverse i.e. "smart chintzed apartments" with their skillful imitation hyacinths in painted pots, — and general air of having been inspired by Vogue's latest hints to the housekeeper.

"Smart apt," in fact, became a private term of opprobrium, used to dismiss anything that smelled of the chichi. "A bit too smart apt," they would say to each other, with a barely perceptible arch of the eyebrows.

Gerald went back to work at Mark Cross, leaving his cozy nineteenth-century nest every morning to mope in the sterile modern surroundings of his Fifth Avenue office, where Sara would send him little notes during the course of the day which said no more than "how much and how dearly I love you." At this point, when they were at last together, separation of any kind was wrenching. A short summer visit by Gerald to his Yale friend Arthur Howe was so unnerving that Gerald had to comfort himself by going to an antique store and purchasing "2 blue vases for your room, a glass bottle of an indescribable colour, a lamp with a lyre base and two painted globes you'll love, 3 white glass goblets, 2 monstrous bird pictures done in feathers, etc." As he wrote Sara then, "You were beside me at every step, and I felt so near you that I dreaded going out into the street."

She was spending the summer with her family at the Dunes (the shackles of daughterhood proving rather hard to shake off), and Gerald was commuting to East Hampton on weekends, as he had during their courtship; the only difference was that now they were permitted to share a bed. Even that comfort was denied Sara come Tuesdays, though; "this A.M. — I was *just* going to say something to you," she wrote him plaintively, "when I remembered — with a pang, that you weren't there — There was *such* a strange unwelcome *flatness* in the bottom of your mattress."

They both hoped desperately for a child — "the real rock of our future happiness," as Gerald described it — and thought Sara might be pregnant in the autumn. She was doing hospital volunteer work at the time and had caught a persistent cold, which brought on a torrent of maternal concern. "The work you are doing is *very dangerous* when you have any kind of a cold," wrote Adeline warningly from East Hampton, "and really you should *not go* about in hospitals while you are so susceptible to all infection." She barraged her daughter with cold prescriptions that, she said, should be filled *immediately* (she enclosed $1 to pay for them). In the end she persuaded Sara to come back to the Dunes to be coddled.

The pregnancy proved to be a false alarm, however; and in November, Adeline's own health took a turn for the worse. Although she had dwindled of late into a kind of professional state of delicacy, this new development seemed potentially critical: returning to New York alone, having left Sara in East Hampton, Gerald felt a preliminary pang of regret. "I'm so glad to have seen your mother," he told Sara in a note written from the train. "I wish I'd kissed her hand. Do it for me." His sense of farewell was prophetic: just after the New Year, Adeline Wiborg died at home at 40 Fifth Avenue.

In five scrapbooks, bound in black leather and individually wrapped in the gaily printed cotton called *tissu de Provence*, Sara Wiborg Murphy chronicled the first dozen years of her new life with Gerald. Photographs, lovingly cap-tioned, alternate with clippings and bits of memorabilia: cards, snippets of fabric, locks of hair. In the first scrapbook, the first entry is a clipping taken from the *New York Herald* on the Friday after Olga's wedding to Sidney Fish: "MISS WIBORG TO BE BRIDE OF GERALD MURPHY," it says. There is no trace of Adeline Wiborg's tersely correct obituary, which appeared in the *New York Times* on January 4, 1917, and mentioned neither the date nor the cause of its subject's demise. Instead, the next item in Sara's scrapbook is a rather saccharine poem, cut from a newspaper, entitled "First Born." It begins, "Your little hands clutch at the world / As something new and strange." Under it Sara has written a date, December 19, 1917. On that day, as Gerald noted in Sara's diary (Sara being too weak to do so), "Honoria Adeline [was] born at 8 P.M. Showed much spirit and alertness even when held up by the heels."

Gerald always claimed, in later life, that his daughter was not named for anyone in either family; but in fact she carried the name not only of his late mother-in-law, but also of Honoria Roberts Murphy, his great-grandmother, who had emigrated from Ireland in 1832. You could put this lapse down to forgetfulness, or you could suspect that Gerald was covering his tracks. Among the papers he left behind after his death is a loose sheet bearing a litany of names redolent of Celtic twilight — Cormac, Aongus, Baoth, Niall, Brighid, and "Honor or Onora." Elsewhere, in a little pigskin notebook, is a similar list containing the name Honoria Adeline Murphy. It seems as if, in naming her, Gerald was covertly reaffirming the Irishness that Patrick Murphy had come to New York to escape. And in adding Adeline's name to Honoria's, just as he and Sara had furnished their house with the quaint cast-offs of their parents' generation, he made another nod in the direction of the past.

Certainly the past must have seemed safer that December than the bright future they had imagined for themselves. In April the United States had entered the Great War, and all through the summer and fall Gerald's class-mates and contemporaries had been enlisting in the fight. Fred, at first re-jected because of his physical frailty, fought his way into the army as a private in the Sixth Field Artillery Division and by the end of the year was waiting to be shipped out to France. Hoytie, distressed, as they all were, by stories of the casualties in the trenches, had decided to volunteer as a nurse in the ambulance corps. Gerald tried for months to arrange an officer's commission — one intercessor on behalf of "my friend, Gerald Murphy" was the muckraker Ida Tarbell — and in November, the week after Sara's birthday, he went to Washington in person to try to move things along. But he was discouraged to learn that it would probably take at least two months more before he could be commissioned. He and Sara were anxiously awaiting Honoria's birth, which perhaps made him feel all the more strongly the need to commit himself. On November 22 he, like Fred, enlisted in the army as a private. To commemorate the occasion he had a photographic portrait taken: in it he stands, braced and solemn, in his private's khakis, his breeches neatly creased, his puttees wrapped as tightly as mummy bandages. His face, under his broad-brimmed doughboy's hat, appears apprehensive and uncomfortable. It is perhaps the only photograph of Gerald in costume in which he does not seem completely at ease, as if this were one part for which he was miscast.

That Christmas was a bittersweet one for the Murphys. They were still in mourning for Adeline, and Sara was confined to bed, recovering from a painful and difficult delivery. They made a brave effort at gaiety: they put a small Christmas tree in Sara's room and trimmed it with miniature ornaments; they pinned a sprig of mistletoe to Honoria's crib, and placed her Christmas and birthday gifts — a silver mug from Anna Murphy, silk dresses, jewelry, money, and a bank passbook from Frank Wiborg — under the little tree. But over their celebration hung the pall of Gerald's imminent departure.

On December 30, her parents' second wedding anniversary, Honoria was baptized at home, wearing a christening dress of cherry-colored silk overlaid with embroidered lace — "royal and overpowering — but quaint in effect," commented her mother, who was still forbidden to get up and had to watch the proceedings, which took place in the adjoining bedroom, in a "courting mirror" held by Helen Stewart, the baby nurse. As an anniversary present (or a christening gift?) Frank Wiborg bought 50 West 11th Street from Patrick Murphy and presented the deed to his daughter and soldier son-in-law. Now, whatever happened, they had a home that was truly their own. Two days later, on New Year's Day, came "the greatest anguish of our lives": kissing his wife and infant daughter good-bye, Gerald went to Pennsylvania Station for the train that would carry him to Ground Officers' Training School in Texas, and thence, he hoped, to war.

The train journey was miserable: it was bitterly cold, and the men were crowded into narrow berths in a mostly unheated sleeping car. Gerald had a sore throat and runny nose, and dosed himself from the traveling medicine chest Sara had given him. For comfort he had packed one of Honoria's little baby shirts, and through the night he held it next to his cheek. The warmth of it, and its sweet baby scent, contrasted with the "ugliness" and the "permeating smell of cold steel" that enveloped him, and, he wrote Sara, "brought me back with a pang to you both in that lovely white room with its suffused candle-light and flowers."

Fort Kelly, a mile and a half outside of San Antonio, was a long way away from that lovely white room. Rows of dark khaki tents flanked a central drill ground, with the whole surrounded by "miles of flat dust-lands, not white with a good clear glare, — but black & cruel yellow-black, stale and unprofitable." Gerald had at first been attracted by the endless space and "featureless horizon" of the level Texas landscape, but soon the rigors of the recruit's life made him see it differently. The men slept nearly thirty to a tent on canvas cots with straw mattresses; the showers (cold) were situated at the end of the barracks, and the only working latrine was outside. The climate was fierce: a week after Gerald's arrival the camp was devastated by a sandstorm that filled the air with black dust, blotted out the sun, blew down tents, sent pack mules on a rampage, and caused truck drivers to crash blindly into barracks. In two hours, the thermometer plunged sixty-one degrees as rain, sleet, and finally snow mixed with the flying dust. During the night four enlisted men froze to death and four more killed themselves out of desperation and terror. Those less afflicted still suffered from the dust, which brought with it pinkeye and all kinds of bronchial ailments. At night the tents were so filled with the barking sound of coughing that they sounded like a kennel. And it was so cold and damp that Gerald slept in a woolen union suit, sweater, muffler, bathrobe, and bed boots under four layers of blankets.

Sara, distressed at his situation, kept sending him packets of clothing — puttees, pajamas, shirts from Brooks Brothers, caps lovingly knitted by her mother's sister, Aunt Mame — as well as homemade bran muffins and squares of washed cheesecloth for him to use as disposable handkerchiefs. Anna Murphy was less sympathetic, writing him "that I must get a lot out of this experience, that it was good for me and that the War was 'a great developer.'" Anna had written him the same sort of letters at school "and I thought her heartless," Gerald said, but now he could bear such exhortations with equanimity. For he had Sara and "our fragrant garden baby," whose tiny shirt he kept under his pillow. "It gives me such courage now to think of us established as a little family," he wrote Sara. "I believe so in us — it is my creed — we can do anything with ourselves."

At the end of January, to his relief, he was accepted for the School of Aeronautics and was shipped out to Ohio. The train trip to Columbus took three days and nights, all spent sitting up in three overcrowded day coaches. Gerald discovered two Yale friends, the Kentuckian Menefee Clancy and Dan Nugent of St. Louis, among his comrades-in arms, and after the three sons of Eli had sat up all night in their uniforms Nugent suggested they disembark during a stopover in St. Louis and accompany him to the Racquet Club for a shower. Although Gerald was suffering from a cold, he thought the whole experience was a fine adventure. But when he telephoned Sara to regale her (the first time they had spoken since he left), the sound of his hoarse voice undid her.

"It has made me too homesick for you — to hear your voice," she wrote him in a tearstained note immediately afterward; "some things seem too much for one — to be borne — I try not to cry — on account of Honoria, but today I can't succeed." Then, scrawling, "I'll go on with this tomorrow," she enclosed a rose petal that she and Honoria had kissed.

This breakdown was uncharacteristic, for in general Sara had kept busy and cheerful learning to look after Honoria and getting her own strength back. Her letters were full of the baby's looks and doings — her weight (satisfactorily gaining), her "*brilliant* dark gray blue" eyes, her "pale *bronze* lashes," her way of stretching her toes to the fire or staring intently into her mother's face. But although Sara clearly reveled in every aspect of her new life as a mother, it was far from the only thing on her mind. She was keeping up with the war news, sending Gerald clippings from the New York papers about the likelihood of a German counteroffensive along the Marne, and speculating about the divisive effects of the Bolshevik revolution on the internal affairs of Austria and

Germany. "What a triumph for Socialism," she wrote, "the war won by Psychology, — instead of Steel — what a slap in the eye for Force of Arms. . . . (How we should love it, shouldn't we?)"

She had drawn together a kind of nursery salon on 11th Street: her old friend Rue Carpenter came with her husband, John, whose new symphony was about to have its premiere in New York; and Monty Woolley dropped by to update her on his vicissitudes with the draft board (he was trying to get exempted from military service). He was charmed by Honoria, to Sara's surprise — but not everyone was so comfortable with the novel and unembarrassed way Sara blended her roles as mother and hostess. Two gentleman friends were present one afternoon when (as Sara wrote Gerald afterward, with endearing candor) the baby had "the *most fearful* movement . . . a real cannonnade (too many n's — never mind) . . . But instead of laughing, — as I hoped they would — as honest men, — they became most offhand — & talked loudly of other matters — their faces growing more & more refined — How *false* to try to 'carry off' anything of the kind. And it put me in the position of 'Mortified Young Mother' whereas I felt nothing of the kind."

Her serenity and composure stood in some contrast to the emotional storms raging around the corner at 40 Fifth Avenue, where her family were all "miserable." Hoytie was preparing to leave for France and the ambulance corps; Frank, doubtless anxious about the menace of German submarines and concerned about the dangers his daughter would face behind the lines, went into scolding paterfamilias mode, warning her to get her affairs in order before she sailed because *she might not come back* — but no one paid him any attention. Olga, grass-widowed when Sidney Fish joined the army, had come to stay at Number 40, and she and Hoytie and Frank had been quarreling fearfully over trifles like the amount of time each family member spent on the telephone; after one particularly stinking row Olga moved to the Brevoort Hotel in a huff. Everyone had colds, and Frank had come down with what was at first thought to be mumps (it was only a bad sore throat). But Sara reported to Gerald that she felt "exactly as though I were in a calm backwater, — watching logs and débris piling and plunging along in the flood. I don't even enter the fights as umpire now, — as I always used to be tempted to do, — (thereby invariably being drawn in, sooner or later)."

It helped that she had a place of her own, "surrounded by the beautiful things" he had picked out for them. In the days of their courtship she and Gerald had often dreamed of some pastoral place to which they could escape. In their recent, wartime letters "our little farm" had been a recurring theme, and 11th Street represented an urban version. Like the Australian bower-bird that attracts its mate by furnishing its nest with bright found objects, feathers, and flowers, the Murphys took turns embellishing "our beautiful house." Even on his way to San Antonio Gerald had found time, during a brief stopover in New Orleans, to acquire an Empire chest of drawers, six oyster plates ("only .75 each") with an antique M in the middle, a pair of Empire candelabra, assorted old vases and lamps, curtain tiebacks, a hot toddy set, a "strange large lavender pitcher for Honoria's bath," and a set of antique children's plates, each decorated with a French puzzle sentence — a marvelously eccentric list. Now Sara was busying herself making new mulberry red curtains for the sitting room — to drape over the pale blue chiffon under-curtains already in the window ("the blue makes quite a lovely light," she commented) — and looking for an old pier glass to hang between the windows.

But as much comfort as she took in it, "our house — where I have never been without you" — made her wistful, too. "I still find my ears straining for your key in the lock — and that bang of the knocker when the door is opened — and then I have a sinking recollection, when it turns out to be Miss Stewart, coming in. Jerry dearest, — don't let's *ever* separate again. . . . Because without you I am only existing — I am *less* than half of myself." She missed him so much, it was a tangible, physical hunger. "I was thinking today," Sara wrote, as Gerald was on his way to Columbus, "of how much I'd like to kiss that little hole in the front of your neck — or either side of your mouth — Perhaps I will — very soon."

With Gerald's transfer to flight training school a reunion now became possible: Sara could come out to Columbus and he could join her and the baby at a hotel in town when he had liberty. The very thought threw Sara into a spasm of anxiety: Would Gerald be embarrassed by her appearance, dressed as she still was "in rusty black" in mourning for her mother? Would the lunch and supper hours Gerald was allowed conflict with Honoria's nursing schedule? Gerald's own temper was short: there was a mix-up about her hotel reservation which delayed her arrival by a day, and he grouchily accused her of staying in New York to see Hoytie off for France (she hadn't), wasting a whole twenty-four hours of the leave he had arranged for himself. But finally Sara, Honoria, and Miss Stewart, accompanied by enough equipment and clothing to outfit a small army, arrived at the Hotel Deshler in Columbus for a ten-day stay.

The reunion was sweet, even if it was only for ten days in less than ideal circumstances: they could share meals in tearooms and laugh at the surly waitress, play with their adored baby daughter, hold hands and whisper in darkened taxis, even (when Gerald had no guard duty) spend the night together. It had been a long time since they had been able to be with each other in this way, and Sara was desolate when Frank Wiborg came out to Columbus to accompany his daughter and her entourage home. "You see," she wrote Gerald afterward, "I can *only* be happy where you are."

For the next few months Gerald buckled down to his preflight studies as he never had to his undergraduate work at Yale. To prepare for the dreaded elimination exams he woke at 3:30 A.M. to pore over his books in the latrines, the only place with enough light to read by, until 6:00. Sara hoped the result would be a staff posting in Washington or, even better, at Mineola on Long Island, where she could set up housekeeping with Olga, and she offered to have Frank Wiborg pull some strings to make this happen. But Gerald wanted the real thing: flight training and transfer to the front lines in France, where Fred, who had transferred to the Tank Corps and been promoted to the rank of second lieutenant, had already seen action.

By the end of March, Gerald had passed his exams and was commissioned as a second lieutenant, assigned to the 838th Aero Squadron in Garden City, New York. In June he was made intelligence officer of the post, but by the end of the summer he was no closer to France; and on August 22 he was transferred again, to the Aviation Recruit Receiving Depot at Fort Wayne, outside of Detroit, where he was pigeonholed as a "casual," to serve as and when needed, a real blow to his pride. Although he formed warm friendships with his brother officers, he disliked his superiors, who, "while the British in Palestine destroy two whole Turkish Armies," spent their time bickering over "whether the girls in the Motor Corps and Canteens are of sufficiently good social standing to be given a dance." Impatient to get overseas, he pulled every string he could: he approached a former Yale and Hotchkiss colleague who was an officer in the Aviation Section in Washington; Frank Wiborg wrote a general he knew; Fred and Hoytie were delegated to try to wangle him a staff job with General Henry T. Allen in France; Patrick Murphy's friend J. M. Tumulty, President Wilson's secretary, did "everything I properly can to be of service."

Uncertain about his situation, he wanted desperately to see Sara but couldn't quite commit to the idea of having her move to Michigan to be with him. He was able to get them married officers' quarters on the base, and she began shuttling back and forth from New York to Detroit by train, spending weekends with Gerald and speeding back to Honoria afterward. Their visits were sweet. "What fun we had — all week! in that fusty old place! And *how much* [underlined with two squiggly lines] I love you," Sara wrote. But the partings were painful. They clung to each other so passionately at the railway station on one occasion that a fellow passenger remarked on it sympathetically in the train afterward. They comforted themselves with talismans: when Gerald found her unfinished cigarette in their quarters he lit it and smoked it down to the end, just to feel closer to her — then he saved the holder.

A greater comfort than talismans was the possibility that Sara might be pregnant again. By the end of September they were certain of it, and Gerald was cautioning her not to take any risks that might endanger her health or the baby's. Soon there was more encouraging news: a wire and then a letter from Tumulty, followed by orders from the War Department, announced Gerald's transfer to the Air Service Training Brigade in Mineola, Long Island. "You ought to be proud of this boy," wrote Tumulty to Patrick Murphy — the sort of praise Gerald had so rarely heard from his father's lips. It appeared as if he might finally be on the verge of going overseas. But then, on November 11, the guns along the western front fell silent for the first time in four years. The German army had surrendered, and the Great War was over.

"Jerry my Berry dearest," wrote Sara, using a nickname she had invented early in their courtship:

Just a line before I go to bed to say how much I love you and *how* [underlined twice] I look forward . . . to the time when our little family (of 3 ½) will be all together under one roof. . . . And the little one half will arrive to a happy, united family and not one separated, or about to separate. . . . I wonder if you have regrets — about not going to France — even though I cannot (personally) help thinking . . . that it *might* not have done you good but harm. . . . For us — (so it seems to me) separation does *not* bring a spiritual development, rather it delays it. . . . But I could not bear it if you felt you had missed a chance — that it was something you would half regret and have to *explain* — always. . . .

God bless you and keep you safe — I love you.

Your wife,

Sal

He did have regrets. Not just about missing action, but about what he felt his war service had shown him about his character. On December 11, as the men who had served under him filed past and shook his hand in farewell, he was surprised to find himself "completely knocked out."

I must have cared for them more than I knew — and more than they knew. It is this that pains. All that I have made them feel is a cold kindness and a decent interest in their welfare, — while *all* the time I have loved them! . . . It enrages me to think that this *consciousness* of relationship that I feel toward those whom I want to have like me — should blur my true feelings. I longed so to have them know — and they are gone. . . . It is my fault. How meagerly equipped I am for human expression. . . . I have felt — at all times — complex and forced in my efforts to show these men how I felt. . . . I must resign from the world of human relationship — I'm no good at it, if I have failed to show these simple souls my real feelings. . . . Thank God for you — to whom I — alone — feel that I have shown in full the love I bear.

It was the old story for Gerald — this feeling that he existed as if behind a glass wall that kept him from honestly connecting with the people he truly cared for. And it would become a familiar one in the years to come, as he and Sara began in earnest to make the life they had been dreaming of since their marriage.

8

"The idea is thrilling to me"

TO CELEBRATE HONORIA ADELINE MURPHY'S second Christmas her parents gave gifts in her name to the Red Cross and the Belgian Babies' Fund. Remembering those whom fate had treated less kindly than their own "little family of 3 ½," they also sent checks to Fatherless Children of France in lieu of lavish presents to each other or to others in their families. But even as they enjoyed the blessings of peace, they found themselves wondering what the next step was.

They loved their pretty house on 11th Street (Sara was already planning additions for when the new baby arrived), and they played the part of young parents with enthusiasm, dressing Honoria in a dazzling array of Kate Greenaway–inspired outfits and chronicling her every weight gain or new tooth in Sara's scrapbook. When Honoria was separated for a few days from her favorite playmate, a neighbor's boy of her own age, Gerald concocted an excruciatingly polite miniature letter from the little boy, saying he had been ill but would be able to play with her soon. The letter was enclosed in a tiny envelope no bigger than a postage stamp with a tiny dot of "sealing wax" and a tiny pretend stamp with a tiny cancelation mark on it.

Entertaining though such nursery games were, they were only games. Gerald was going to have to do something to "get a grip on our future," as he put it. Mark Cross, it was clear, was worse than a dead end for him. He had always felt ill at ease, like an impostor, in the boardrooms and at the dinner tables that were his father's natural habitat, and he had failed in his one attempt to leave his imprint on the company. In 1915, before the war, Patrick had asked him to try his hand at designing an inexpensive safety razor, and

Gerald was on the verge of patenting the result when King Gillette beat him to market with his own version. Now, he felt, his father would always second-guess him, as he did Fred (who was demobilized and working for Cross in England). When the elder Murphy asked Gerald what he planned to do when his demobilization papers came through, he made a life-changing decision. He wanted to go to Harvard, he said, and study landscape architecture.

"I had to say something," he explained later, "and that's what came out." But it wasn't quite so haphazard a response as he maintained. He had always had an eye for space and color: even his bleakest wartime letters were lit up by images — of the Mexican market in San Antonio with its jumble of colors, of the "spangled tights" of a Seuratesque tightrope walker at a street fair, or the "enormously fat Percherons" he saw pulling a sledge in Columbus, "dappled grey (handpainted!) with heavy manes and fetlocks, soft grey noses, and the beloved crease down the back." That winter, after his demobilization, he had been studying drawing in New York with a Miss Weir at the School of Design and Liberal Arts, a pursuit Sara applauded: "I do think it so remarkable, — not that you could do it, — but that, as you *could* do it as well as that, you had never found it out before now. It's *amazing*."

"My parents had a plan," Honoria said many years afterward, a plan that sounds like something one of Tolstoy's utopian-minded characters might have sketched out at the dinner table. Part of the plan was a bucolic setting ("our little farm"), but a more important part of it was a life centered around some kind of artistic endeavor, where work and life were one, and where man and wife could — would — be able to work shoulder to shoulder. As Gerald envisioned it: "When we wake up in the morning *the* question and work of the day will *belong* to *both* of us. *Think* what this means!! To be able to work *together* over the *same* thing. What husbands and wives can do this?! Think of our being able to add to all that we already share — the very work of our hands and brains. The idea is thrilling to me." Whether they were making gardens, like Candide and Cunégonde, or painting or potting seemed almost beside the point.

As bitter a pill as Gerald's repudiation of Mark Cross may have seemed to Patrick Murphy, he swallowed it with good grace, possibly because his wife uncharacteristically supported her son's decision. And whatever his feelings, he was jubilant when he, Fred, Frank Wiborg, and Hoytie (all of whom were in London at the time) received a cablegram announcing the birth, in New York, of a "male Murphy" on May 13, 1919. "There was wild yelling," reported Sara, "and they all opened champagne and caroused over the heir — & the grandpapas did a lot of handshaking & yelling — Hoytie says Father takes on as though he had given birth to a son himself."

The new baby was named Baoth Wiborg Murphy (Baoth was one of those old Irish names on Gerald's original list), but for the first few months of his life his parents called him either "the boy" or (Sara's preference) "Dubbedy," which may have been Honoria's version of "the baby." Sara was enchanted with his gold hair and merry face — "How alike we are!" she wrote on the back of one photograph of him. Soon her scrapbook was full of exquisite watercolor sketches of Baoth, in celadon greens, pinks and peaches and golds, like the ones she had done of Honoria.

Gerald did not have long to enjoy his little son, however, for by the beginning of June he was in Cambridge, Massachusetts, living at the Brattle Inn and enrolled in Harvard's School of Landscape Architecture. He was immediately enthralled by the work: surveying a lily pond at the botanical gardens, covered with white, yellow, pink, and lavender blooms; bisecting tree trunks "at 300 ft. distance with a telescope which has a double lens with cobwebs [crosshairs?] transversely across it"; or cramming Latin for botanical classifications. He had got Sara a catalogue for the Women's School — which offered identical graduate classes with the same professors, but under a different roof — so she could enroll in the same courses he had. And he was scouting out houses for them in the fall. They had decided, reluctantly, to give up 50 West 11th. They still loved the house but "look[ed] upon it as an invaded retreat," subject to sudden incursions from 40 Fifth Avenue and surrounded by the alien forces of New York society. So Gerald got Alice James (the wife of William James, Jr., and one of Cambridge's social and intellectual arbiters) to go with him while he looked at square Georgian clapboards and modern stucco villas and even "one *manor* with immemorial elms on the lawn, barricades of lilac, a cupola, etc."

Rue and John Carpenter had also turned up in Cambridge (John was a

Harvard graduate, class of 1897), and through them Gerald was introduced to Amy Lowell, the cigar-smoking scholar, poet, and scion of a definitively Brahmin Boston family. Lowell had taken over leadership of the imagist school of poetry from Ezra Pound in 1914, and she had recently published a pioneering study of new verse, *Tendencies in Modern American Poetry*. She was "an amazing creature — rather like a large, formidable frog, with a brain like a dynamo" — and she startled Gerald by demanding that he and the Carpenters come to dinner with her that very evening.

Lowell lived in grand style in Brookline, across the river from Cambridge, in a beautiful Georgian house built by her ancestors and surrounded by pre-Revolutionary gardens that fascinated the neophyte landscape architect. She and Gerald had much to talk about, for in addition to her passion for gardening — she had become a keen student of the work of the English landscape designer Gertrude Jekyll — she was deeply versed in an astonishing array of other subjects. Her interests ranged from fairy tales and Orientalia to carriage-driving and English literature (her collection of Keats editions and incunabula was remarkable) and coaching, and at the time she was immersed in translating a collection of Chinese poetry, written in 700 B.C., from the Mandarin. As Gerald discovered, she had a rather mandarin quality herself.

After dinner, while her companion, the actress Ada Russell, entertained the ladies, Lowell offered her favorite cigars to the gentlemen and then spirited Gerald off for a discussion of Russian novels. He wasn't the least bit nonplussed by the postprandial arrangements, being a habitué of Elizabeth Marbury's, Anne Morgan's, and Elsie De Wolfe's dinner parties. But his tête-à-tête with Lowell took an alarming turn when he observed that he found many of the characters in Russian fiction to be "such weak animals that the hopelessness of it all becomes unreal." Whirling on him, Lowell demanded, "Repeat that!" And when he did, rather haltingly, she whipped out a pencil, wrote down his words, and then muttered, "Weak animals, weak animals is right, weak animals is good!" To the consternation of the other awestruck guests, Gerald roared with laughter. "She knows everything *about* everything," he told Sara, "yet she's so cordial and human."

What Lowell represented for Gerald was something he had been hungering for, a combination of unconventional aristocracy and intellectualism, of social and cultural engagement. *This* was a world where he and Sara could flourish, and he could hardly wait until they could be transplanted to it. The only element of uncertainty was financial: somehow, with the return to civilian life, Baoth's birth, the removal to Cambridge, and other expenses, Gerald was overextended, and it took an infusion of cash from Fred to pay off his outstanding bills. Gerald was grateful, but inclined to be a little defiant. Although he lamented his inability "to anticipate the need, use, and value of money," he felt that his own family, and his in-laws, paid entirely too much attention to the subject. "I'm so glad," he told Sara huffily, "that there's no evidence of it up here."

Perhaps he felt he could afford to be grand, for Frank Wiborg had decided, like King Lear, to divide his assets among his three daughters before his death, and Sara would soon be mistress of a substantial amount of capital. In preparation, Frank had taken to thrusting pamphlets about "The Safe Keeping of Securities" into her hands at opportune moments. Sara tried to be appreciative but admitted to feeling mystified. "Who can we get to teach us about amortization, & assessments & depletion?" she asked. "It all sounds like diseases to me. . . . Can't we just go on trusting in God & the Columbia Trust Co.?" Of course she knew they couldn't: although she told Gerald she agreed with him in principle that money wasn't a fit object for obsession, "Nothing, I think, chains one so much to it, as entirely disregarding it does. Mismanagement brings it *always* before the eye."

With 11th Street rented out, Sara had packed up all their belongings and, with the children and Miss Stewart, moved to East Hampton for the summer. Although the sea and the sand held a perpetual allure for her, she felt "exasperated" by this return to her old life. "I've never been *away* from it enough as yet, — and I feel its claws still in me," she told Gerald. Frank, as usual, was "running the legs off his guests" with mornings of nonstop golf, lawn bowling, and croquet, punctuated by walks about the estate to view the livestock and drives to Montauk or other points of interest, and Hoytie and Olga (Gerald referred to them as Scylla and Charybdis) were at each other's throats again. Hoytie had given Olga a surprise party for her birthday, hanging lanterns in the trees and smuggling a dance band and caterers and all of Olga's best friends into the house while Sidney and Olga were out to dinner. But instead of being pleased, Olga was furious, complaining that the house had been overrun by "hoodlums" who misplaced the bric-a-brac. She went off to bed in the middle of the party and spent all the next day complaining about the noise and the damage, to which Hoytie responded histrionically, "Things, things: Olga's life is made up of nothing but *things*."

Caught in the middle yet again, Sara blamed herself for not being able to keep the peace, and raged inwardly that her own plans and hopes seemed to be so easily blown off course by these familial storms. Gerald comforted her long distance as best he could: "I believe in you so," he wrote. "Our new life is but one thing: *your* ideals and principles and character organized and put into actuality by me. You were a woman and couldn't do it — on account of your family — I am a man and can, in spite of everything. Don't you see, my dear girl, how you taught me to do the things that life and society forbade you to?!" In fact she was beginning to see it, and was beginning to put her ideals and principles into practice by herself.

At the end of July the country had been shocked by an outbreak of racial violence in Washington, D. C., that began when a white mob spearheaded by two hundred sailors and marines swept through black neighborhoods searching for two youths who had been apprehended and released after reportedly insulting the wife of a naval officer. A policeman was shot in the process, setting off a rampage in which black men and women were beaten and their homes burned, and blacks in their turn invaded white neighborhoods; there were many injuries and at least ten deaths, and more than two thousand troops and police officers were required to restore order. Against this background of racial unrest, Mary McLeod Bethune, one of the leaders of the National Association of Colored Women, arrived in Long Island on a fundraising tour for the Daytona Normal and Industrial Institute for Negro Girls, a school she had founded in Florida. And when her train pulled into the East Hampton station, Sara Wiborg Murphy was there to meet it.

Despite her father's political connections and aspirations, Sara was something less than activist: she didn't march for women's suffrage or sign petitions. But Bethune, the seventeenth child of former slaves, stirred her: her "dignity of labor" philosophy, her kindness, directness, and grace, spoke to Sara, and she felt impelled to help Bethune's cause. Hoytie was less enthusiastic (Frank was away in Washington consulting to the Tariff Commission), and she drew the line at inviting Bethune to spend the night at the Dunes. What, she asked her sister, would the servants think? Reluctantly Sara compromised on allowing Bethune to stay with a local black family, but she insisted on inviting her to spend the day at the Dunes, and held a fund-raising meeting to which the eleemosynarily inclined of East Hampton's elite were invited. They had lunch in the enormous baronial dining room — the Irish maids frostily handing around the peas — and discussed the Washington riots. Bethune's comments were "frightfully interesting," thought Sara. Earlier she had proudly showed off Honoria and Baoth to her visitor. "Has she ever seen a Negro before?" Bethune inquired about Honoria and, when Sara admitted that she hadn't, remarked, "Oh, then she will be afraid of me." Said Sara to Gerald later, "I was *so* glad that she wasn't."

At the end of September the Murphys moved to 149 Brattle Street in Cambridge, a pleasant, square frame house with a wide porch, shaded by old trees. Sara was delighted with the change. "We *need* a new place," she had sighed in her last weeks at East Hampton. "Isn't it amazing what a refreshed outlook it gives one?"

Gerald certainly showed its effects: he had done unusually well in his summer courses and now took on a substantial load of new ones, freehand drawing and architecture, as well as courses in landscaping. Unfortunately, burdened with setting up a new household and satisfying the demands of two very small children, Sara couldn't join him. Her scrapbooks tell the story: whereas she had chronicled the great events of Honoria's infancy — first step, first tooth, first haircut — with pasted photos and carefully inked captions, Baoth's milestones were recorded on slips of white paper tucked into the book, as if awaiting some leisurely afternoon (which never materialized) when she would have time to do it all *properly*.

She did find the time to begin cultivating a widening circle of friends, among them her girlhood friend Hester Chanler, who was studying seriously to be a painter and had married a proper Bostonian (and rising young historian) named Edward Pickman; William and Alice James; the portraitist John

Singer Sargent, whose lectures Gerald attended at the Boston Museum of Fine Arts; and the collector Isabella Stewart Gardner, patron of Bernard Berenson. One acquaintance they did *not* make was that of a Harvard Law School student who had been at Yale, and in Bones, just three years behind Gerald: Archibald MacLeish was beginning to be known as a poet; his wife, Ada, was a promising singer of opera and art songs; both were friends of Amy Lowell's; and they would have seemed a perfect fit for the socially connected but artistically aspiring Murphys. But MacLeish, who knew that Gerald was a fellow Bonesman, felt skittish about them, a residue, perhaps, of the Yale wariness with which the gridiron star MacLeish viewed the social butterfly Murphy. When he saw Gerald on the street in Cambridge he said to himself, "He isn't the real thing — he just doesn't look right to me!" Later MacLeish amended this story, claiming to have admired Sara and Gerald from a distance. "I would like to know those people," he said he thought. "They look so well-laundered."

Certainly the Murphys were moving in exalted circles. The formidable Mrs. Gardner invited them to dinner (with the Jameses and Sargent) at Fenway Court, the neo-Venetian palazzo she had filled with Bellinis, Giottos, Vermeers, and what the transplanted Boston exquisite Harry Crosby would later refer to as "the next-best Raphael I ever saw." Afterward she begged them to sing some of the duets for which their own parties were famous. Instead of Wagnerian numbers like those Sara had once performed with her sisters, the Murphys' entertainments had a distinctively American stamp: Gerald had been collecting old sheet music for some time and had built up a considerable library of forgotten American songs of the late nineteenth century. He had also become interested in African American spirituals, which were virtually unknown at the time except as arcane folkloric artifacts. Somehow he had stumbled across some examples in the Boston Public Library and laboriously copied out the scores and the words. So for Mrs. Gardner he mingled his tenor with Sara's contralto in "Oh, Graveyard" and "Sometimes I Feel Like a Motherless Child." The next day, in a typical gesture, the Murphys sent their hostess a copy of Henry Krehbiel's *Afro-American Folk-Songs*, the academic classic on the subject, as a bread-and-butter present.

Their gift was an expression of their interest and respect for African American culture and their wish to share what they felt about it — an attitude light-years away from the condescending burlesques of Edwardian "coon song" performances. Although Eugene O'Neill's African drama *The Emperor Jones*, starring the Negro actor Charles Gilpin, was raising eyebrows on the New York stage in 1920, and although Countee Cullen's poetry — which urged God to "Make a poet black, and bid him sing!" — was beginning to be published in literary magazines, people of the Murphy's class rarely took black people, or black culture, seriously. While the Murphys' peers were clapping their hands for the finale of the 1919 *Ziegfeld Follies*, Irving Berlin's "I'd Rather See a Minstrel Show," which featured "The Follies Pickaninnies" and blacked-up white men like Eddie Cantor, Sara and Gerald had left the "coon song snatches" of their youth behind. Now, on trips to New York, they found excitement in the emerging Harlem club scene and the music of artists like Fats Waller (Sara's self-proclaimed favorite). As in other things, Sara and Gerald had begun to go their own way.

Despite their passion for American art forms, they were also beginning to be aware of artistic developments in Europe. In the autumn of 1920 they traveled to New York with Sargent to see the first American exhibition of the work of Nicholas Roerich, the exiled Russian cubist who had designed the décors for the Ballets Russes' *Sacre du printemps*. Both Gerald and Sara had been to the legendary Armory Show of 1913, which had awakened America to the possibilities of modern art, but only Sara had been particularly stimulated by it. She had, in fact, wanted to buy some of the exhibited works, but was "dissuaded by reactionaries." Now Roerich's pictures stirred them both equally. Later Gerald told of how two of Sargent's Boston Museum auditors — one of whom was William James, Jr. — disparaged Roerich to the master, and Sargent replied, "A little of Roerich's virus would do you good!" Gerald never identified the other speaker; perhaps it was himself. If so, the virus was already in his system, and the symptoms were about to appear.

The Murphys spent the summer of 1920 in a spacious Greek Revival house in Litchfield, Connecticut, called the Glebe; another season in East Hampton, with the merry-go-round of guests and the constant family sniping, was simply impossible to contemplate. Sara was pregnant again, and the cool rooms and luxuriant gardens of the Glebe were a tranquil refuge: it was the closest she and Gerald had yet come to that idyllic country existence they had once imagined for themselves. In Connecticut, Baoth's hair was trimmed for the first time, and Sara saved the gold wisps in her scrapbook. He and Honoria romped under the shade of the great trees in dresses and playsuits of gossamer linen, all lovingly captured by Gerald's Kodak. In September they returned to Cambridge, this time to a larger house at 4 Willard Street; and there, on October 18, Patrick Francis Murphy II was born.

By this time Gerald had begun to feel again a nagging dissatisfaction with the direction their life was taking. The landscape architecture program at Harvard was, he felt, increasingly "veering away from designing estates," his passion, "to town planning and engineering. Unsatisfactory." Certainly for someone with his lack of interest or aptitude in mathematics, it was. Nor had Sara been able, as they had envisioned, to take her place by his side at the school; for the past year and a half she had been either pregnant or nursing a baby. Gerald's work began to suffer from his disaffection: he found himself unable, or unwilling, to complete some of his course assignments. The old cycle of inattention and loss of direction, which had plagued him at Yale, at Mark Cross, and in the army, seemed to be repeating itself.

Perhaps the "new place" just wasn't new enough. Malcolm Cowley later described "Cambridge in the early 1900s" as "good manners, tea parties, Browning, young women with their minds adequately dressed in English tweeds. I think it was T. S. Eliot who said that life there was so intensely cultured it had ceased to be civilized." Things hadn't changed much by 1920, and although Sara and Gerald had formed some happy friendships there, Cambridge itself had come to seem confining. And the increasingly philistine and isolationist feeling of American society in general made them uncomfortable.

During the time the Murphys were in Cambridge, *The Dial*, a literary magazine with which Amy Lowell was closely associated, had been publishing a series of essays by Harold Stearns which inveighed against the conformity and mediocrity of the American cultural scene; these essays must have been an item of table talk at Brattle Street dinner parties, and they would have found a sympathetic partisan in Gerald. Certainly he was familiar with the work of Waldo Frank, who in 1919 was writing about the repressive force of Puritanism in American society: "Whole departments of [the American's] psychic life must be repressed. Categories of desire must be inhibited. Reaches of consciousness must be lopped off." Gerald himself described it somewhat flippantly when he claimed that "a government that could pass the Eighteenth Amendment [prohibiting the sale or consumption of alcohol], could, and probably would, do a lot of other things to make life in the States as stuffy and bigoted as possible." He and Sara resented the fact that if they wanted a glass of wine with dinner or a cocktail — that daring new invention — beforehand, they had to seek refuge in "the basements of old sandstone houses." He had put up with so much bluenosed disapproval from his own family during his lifetime that he was disinclined to put up with more from his country.

And that, finally, was the problem. All the disapproval, the materialism, the stifling restrictiveness that he and Sara had experienced within their re-spective families now seemed to be manifested by society at large. How could they reinvent themselves in such an atmosphere? It was a question asked by others than themselves. During the years since the war increasing numbers of Americans had left the United States for Europe: in 1921 there were six thousand Americans in Paris; by 1924, thirty thousand. Although some were war veterans returning to taste the fruits of peace in the lands they had fought over, still others were artists, writers, musicians, intellectuals, who, "feeling like aliens in the commercial world" of the 1920s, as Malcolm Cowley put it, "sailed for Europe as soon as they had money enough to pay for the steamer tickets." Suddenly Europe seemed like the answer, at least for the short term. Gerald and Sara were, for the first time in their lives, financially independent, thanks to Frank Wiborg's property settlement. In Europe, where in 1920 the dollar was strong, Sara's income, which now came to about $7,000 a year, would go that much further. They could put the Atlantic Ocean between themselves and what Gerald thought of as their "two powerful families," and make a new start in an old place.

They didn't plan very far ahead. Gerald asked for a leave of absence from Harvard; he hadn't completed his course work for the 1920–21 academic year, and he was a number of credits short of qualifying for his degree. Although he told Harvard that he would return in February 1922, he took the somewhat ambiguous step of having the family's passports stamped "Foreign Residents." He and Sara intended to spend at least the summer in England. Perhaps, if things worked out, he could find work as a landscape designer there, and they could settle abroad. They gave up the lease on Willard Street, put their furniture into storage, and on June 11, 1921 — accompanied by Honoria, now three and a half; Baoth, two; Patrick, eight months; and their nurse, Lillie Nyberg — sailed for Southampton on the SS *Cedric*.

9

"An entirely new orbit"

THE SUMMER OF 1921 was hot and dry, and although Sara dutifully escorted Gerald on a tour of the houses she had been welcomed in as one of the beautiful Wiborg sisters, the gardens of England's stately homes were parched and brown and most unrewarding to study. London, although they could renew friendships with Stella Campbell, the Headforts, and others, "didn't seem to fill the bill," as Sara put it, so the Murphys repaired to Croyde Bay, a seaside village in Devon, for the remainder of the summer. Then, following Wiborg tradition, they proceeded to Paris, where on September 3 they installed themselves and the children at the Hôtel Beau-Site in the rue de Presbourg near the Étoile.

It was meant to be a short stay; frustrated by their English sojourn, Gerald and Sara had decided to return to the United States sooner rather than later. But then they discovered that their Boston friends, the Pickmans, had settled in Paris temporarily (Edward Pickman was gathering material for a book). And Cole Porter had set up residence near the Eiffel Tower with his new wife, Linda Lee Thomas, an American "alimony millionairess" some eight years older than himself who was reputed to be the most beautiful woman in the world. Although the Pickmans and the Porters didn't find one another entirely congenial (Hester Pickman, with old money's queasiness at ostentation, thought Linda Porter "overdressed"), they were both agreed on one thing: the Murphys *must* stay in Paris, if only for the winter.

So Gerald and Sara found a furnished apartment on the rue Greuze, a curved bow of a street that arced away from the place du Trocadéro in Passy, a chic, modern district of leafy streets and substantial limestone apartment houses bordered by the Seine on one side, the Bois de Boulogne on another, and the green belt of the avenue Foch on another. The area might reek of "smart apt," but the children could play in the Trocadéro gardens nearby, or in the Bois, and with the franc at less than twenty cents on the dollar the rent seemed like nothing. And, as the Murphys soon discovered, something was going on in Paris that made it unlike any other place in the world.

In the autumn of 1921 Paris was a city transformed by the twentieth century. Although pounded by zeppelins and cannonades during the war, most of the buildings had survived. The wide boulevards were still shaded by plane trees, and the cafés, which had been forced to close during the worst of the bombardments, had put out their awnings again. But in the streets the war's effects were readily apparent. "The thing I used to notice in Paris," said Archibald MacLeish, who would arrive in the city in 1923, "was the total absence of the young. . . . The youth of [France] had been slaughtered." In their place had come other young people — and some not so young — from Russia or Spain or Ireland or America, all of them drawn by a feeling that here they could (as one of their number, Ezra Pound, famously put it) "make it new."

James Joyce had already published *Portrait of the Artist as a Young Man* and was living on the boulevard Raspail in Montparnasse, working on the manuscript that would become *Ulysses*. The Catalan painter Joan Miró had joined his compatriot Pablo Picasso, already famous as the pioneer of cubism, on the roster of the dealer Jean Rosenberg. The American painter and photographer Man Ray had been persuaded by Marcel Duchamp to come to Paris, where he was experimenting with a new kind of photography he called "the rayograph." Igor Stravinsky and Sergei Prokofiev were composing in Paris rather than in newly Bolshevik Russia. They were all there, or on their way there: George Antheil, Virgil Thomson, Harry and Caresse Crosby, Samuel Beckett, Berenice Abbott, John Dos Passos, Léonide Massine, Josephine Baker, Ernest Hemingway, Sylvia Beach, Bricktop, Ford Madox Ford, e. e. cummings, Aaron Copland, Scott Fitzgerald, Isadora Duncan, Constantin Brancusi, George Balanchine — an infinite roll call of modernism.

And, *pace* MacLeish, there were any number of survivors of the prewar avant-garde, all of whom found themselves stimulated by this infusion of fresh talent, with noisy and dramatic results. The year immediately preceding the Murphys' arrival in Paris had opened with the first dada *manifestation* at the Palais des Fêtes on January 23, 1920. Dada — the name is a nursery term for "hobbyhorse" — was an anarchic artistic movement that grew out of, and made serious fun of, the nihilistic despair caused by the war; and this first *manifestation* was a kind of multimedia performance-art happening that included a reading and literary discussion by André Breton, Louis Aragon, and Philippe Soupault; a recitation by Tristan Tzara of the entire text of a newspaper article he had chosen at random, accompanied by clanging cowbells, clattering castanets, and rattles; and the ritual erasing, by Breton, of a chalk painting by Francis Picabia that hung amid an installation of work by Fernand Léger, Juan Gris, and Giorgio de Chirico. The audience, whose initial befuddlement at the proceedings had given way to frustration and rage, went wild, whistling, hissing, and hurling insults at the delighted dadaists.

But it wasn't long before dadaism was everywhere. In February the wiry-haired, sad-eyed poet Jean Cocteau joined forces with the composer Darius Milhaud to present a dadaist opéra bouffe entitled *Le Boeuf sur le toit* (*The Ox on the Roof*; the English equivalent would be "shaggy-dog story"), which featured the Fratellinis — clowns from the Cirque Médrano — and a jazzy, Latin-inspired score. It drew its audience equally from the aristocratic salons of the Right Bank and the artists' ateliers of the Left Bank. And when the show closed Milhaud had the bright idea of reincarnating it as a nightclub, also called Le Boeuf sur le toit, where the walls were covered in artists' sketches, and Les Six — Milhaud, Poulenc, and fellow composers Georges Auric, Louis Durey, Germaine Taillefer, and Arthur Honneger — would jam into the wee hours.

The same mix of society and avant-garde that had made a sensation of *Le Boeuf sur le toit* filled the Opéra on May 15, when Serge Diaghilev — the astute, dandyish impresario who had dazzled Sara Wiborg with *Le Sacre du printemps* in 1913 — opened his first Ballets Russes season after the war. Always at the cutting edge, Diaghilev had produced the first cubist-inspired ballet, *Parade*, in 1917, with music by Erik Satie, décors and costumes by Picasso, and a program note by Guillaume Apollinaire which introduced the word *surrealism* into the popular lexicon. Now he celebrated the arrival of the postwar era with a quadruple bill that exemplified the eclecticism and excitement of the moment: *La Boutique fantasque* (music by Gioacchino Rossini, orchestration by Ottorino Respighi, sets and costumes by André Derain); *Le Chant du Rossignol* (music by Igor Stravinsky, sets and costumes by Henri Matisse); *Le Tricorne*, also known as *The Three-Cornered Hat* (music by Manuel de Falla, sets and costumes by Picasso); and *Pulcinella* (music by Stravinsky after Giambattista Pergolesi, sets, costumes, and drop curtain by Picasso).

The premiere was followed by a legendary party given by Prince Firouz of Persia at a château just outside Paris owned by an ex-convict named René de Amouretti. As one guest, the artist and set designer Jean Hugo, recalled it: "The ground floor was taken up by an enormous room with a balcony running around it onto which opened the doors to the bedrooms. . . . We drank a lot of champagne. Stravinsky got drunk and went up to the bedrooms, grabbed all the pillows, bolsters, and feather beds, and hurled them from the balcony down into the great hall. We all had a pillow fight and the party ended at three in the morning."

Prominent among the revelers at this not-to-be-missed event were Auric, Poulenc, Picasso, the choreographer and leading *danseur* Léonide Massine, Diaghilev, the Count and Countess Étienne de Beaumont, Cocteau, and Cocteau's object of affection, a beautiful seventeen-year-old youth named Raymond Radiguet. Radiguet must have stayed fairly sober because he noticed everything and then committed it to fiction in the form of a roman à clef entitled *Le Bal du comte d'Orgel*. And one of Radiguet's characters in that novel, the tall, rather comically drunk American heiress Hester Wayne, was a barely disguised portrait of none other than Hoytie Wiborg.

Hoytie was now living in Paris in an elegant apartment on the quai de Conti which had been conferred on her for her lifetime in gratitude for her services to France during the war. As beautiful as always but haughtier and more peremptory than ever, she had conceived a hopeless crush on Diaghilev's patroness, the fascinating Marie Godebska Natanson Edwards Sert. Misia, as everyone called her, had been an inspiration and support to painters, poets, and musicians since Hoytie was just a little girl and *she* was Madame Natanson, Toulouse-Lautrec's model for Ault and Wiborg's signature poster; now, married to the Spanish painter José María Sert, she exercised her charm upon and dispensed favors to a circle that included Stravinsky, Picasso, Gabrielle (Coco) Chanel, Poulenc, Cocteau, and a host of others.

Misia didn't return Hoytie's passionate attention (reportedly she called her *l'emmerdeuse,* an extremely vulgar term meaning "the Nuisance"), but she put up with her. Everyone did, in fact, and Hoytie had a wide and influential group of friends to whom it became her pleasure to introduce her newly arrived sister and her husband. Although Gerald and Sara were both leery of what Gerald referred to as Hoytie's tactics of "subjugation and domination," they had to admit that "she knew everybody." And pretty soon, so did they.

One of the people she introduced them to was the original of Count Orgel himself. A tall, long-faced, blue-blooded aesthete with a squeaky voice and prominent blue eyes, Étienne de Beaumont "opened the ball after the war" (as Radiguet said of Orgel), meaning he originated the spectacular costume parties that characterized Parisian social life in the twenties and thirties. These glittering entertainments, which the French call *travestis,* each had a theme — the age of Louis Quatorze, Perrault's fairy tales, card games, legendary heroes, sea creatures — and each was organized with the precision of a military campaign. Once the date was chosen, de Beaumont would drop hints of the planned treat to a chosen few, partly to get a buzz of gossip going and partly to give everybody time to worry whether this year he (or she) would be In or Out. By the time the little pasteboard invitation cards went out, delivered in person by a de Beaumont footman, some people would be ill from anxiety. But the parties themselves were never anticlimactic.

The Murphys might not have been at the Bal de Mer, where Jean Hugo, impersonating one of four waiters from Prunier's, carried in a tray on which reclined the maharanee of Kapurthala, disguised as caviar; Hugo had had a little too much champagne and let his corner of the tray drop, unseating the maharanee and causing the maharajah to mutter, "In India he would have been put to death at once." But they were almost certainly invited to the New Year's party with which the de Beaumonts welcomed 1922 — and at which, the count announced, Marcel Proust was expected. During the course of the evening Celeste, Proust's housekeeper, telephoned several times to make sure there were no drafts and to ask if the hypersensitive author's herbal tea had been prepared. Finally, about midnight, recalled Hugo, "there was a stir in the crowd, and we knew that Proust was there. He had come in with the new year, that of his death. . . . His sallow face had become puffy; he had acquired a paunch. He only spoke to dukes. 'Oh, look,' Picasso said to me. 'He's sticking to his theme.'"

The milieu in which the Murphys now found themselves was, as another contemporary chronicler put it, "a world somewhere between *Guermantes' Way* and *Sodom*," where "a well-set-up young man would attract the glances of as many men as women." It was alluring, polymorphous, perverse: utterly unlike anything Gerald and Sara had ever experienced. Hoytie, seemingly, had taken to it as a duck to water — survivors of the circle, and their descendants, still speak of her with affection — and Sara and Gerald were diverted by it. But they had come to Paris looking for more than diversion. Almost by accident, they found it.

It is October 1921. The last of the summer heat has left the pavements, and the sky is that peculiar pearlescent blue of the Île-de-France. Gerald Murphy is walking under the yellowing chestnut trees on the avenue des Champs-Élysées. He is wearing an exquisitely tailored suit, gloves, a felt hat; his malacca cane is jauntily deployed. His long-legged stride carries him past the Hôtel de Langeac, a beautiful eighteenth-century mansion that was Thomas Jefferson's home in Paris, and Fouquet's, the smart café-restaurant where the Irish writer James Joyce is somewhat improbably to be found in the evenings. At the corner of the rue la Boétie, the street where the city's fashionable art dealers have their galleries, he turns.

Perhaps he has been reading about the forthcoming sale — the second in a series liquidating the holdings of the German dealer Kahnweiler — of work by cubist painters, among them Derain, Braque, Vlaminck, Gris, Léger, and Picasso; perhaps he is mildly curious about the pictures of artists whose scenery for Diaghilev's Ballets Russes is all the rage. Perhaps he is just on his way to lunch. But through the glass of a gallery window he sees a series of paintings that, literally, stop him in his tracks.

"There was," Gerald wrote later, "a shock of recognition which put me into an entirely new orbit." He couldn't remember the pictures themselves, or even — accurately — where he had seen them, whether they were all at one gallery or in a series of windows he peered through that autumn day. Picasso, Derain, Gris, Braque, a kaleidoscope of color and form. "I was astounded that there were paintings of that kind," Gerald later recalled, perhaps forgetting his brief glimpse of the Armory Show. But in New York in 1913 he had been too busy trying to fit the mold of the up-and-coming young businessman to pay sympathetic attention to avant-garde art. Now, in the adventurous light of Paris in 1921, he could *see*. He returned from his walk transfigured. "If that's painting," he told Sara, "that's the kind of painting that *I* would like to do."

It was a life-changing decision, and characteristically Sara was galvanized by it. They had money to support themselves; they had leisure; they had a nanny to look after the children; why not study painting? As it turned out, Hester Pickman was eager to explore a new direction in her own work, so the three of them found a teacher, a Russian émigré named Natalia Goncharova — a descendant and namesake of the wife of Aleksandr Pushkin — who had designed a number of productions for the Ballets Russes. She was an inspired choice. Although barely forty, Goncharova had made a considerable reputation for herself in Russia before the revolution, when she was one of the founders of rayonism. She worked in two genres: a blend of cubism and futurism which used strong shapes and colors in energetic semiabstract compositions, and a neoprimitive pictorial style that had its source in Russian folk and religious art. It was in this latter mode that she had designed the scenery and costumes for Diaghilev's production of *Le Coq d'Or*, which Sara had seen in New York during the war and adored: "a crazy Russian fairy tale," she had called it, "done. . . with *color*, — and irresponsible childishness." There was no irresponsible childishness, however, in the way Goncharova proceeded with her new American pupils.

Every morning the three of them would travel to Goncharova's Left Bank studio in the rue de Seine and set to work. A "charming, extraordinarily attractive" woman, according to Hester Pickman, Goncharova was a rigorous teacher. "She started us with *absolutely* abstract painting," Gerald recalled, still sounding bemused nearly forty years later. "Absolutely nonrepresentational." They would subdivide their canvases into nonfigurative shapes, and then — depending on whether the shapes were stronger or

weaker — they would color the shapes, making the weaker ones more striking, the stronger ones less so. Goncharova's one rule was that her students
could commit nothing to canvas that resembled in any way anything they had
ever seen. "No apple on a dish," commented Sara dryly.

For Gerald this discipline was a liberation. All his life he had responded to
the beauty of objects, not for what they connoted but for their shapes and
surfaces: the worn plank floors, luster pitchers, and squatty Empire chests he
and Sara had rhapsodized about, or a doe in the Adirondack snow, a red
locomotive, the draft horses and tightrope walkers he had written about in his
letters to Sara. The kind of art he despised, such as his childhood pet hate,
Leutze's *Washington Crossing the Delaware,* commanded him to "feel" something. Goncharova's triangles and rays simply pleased him.

He and Sara and Hester worked with Goncharova for six months, painting
nearly all day and then, in the evenings, taking criticism from her and from
her companion, another Russian futurist named Michel Larionov. (Although
they had lived together for some twenty years, Goncharova "was still Mademoiselle because she didn't approve of religious marriage.") Larionov was also
in the Ballets Russes loop, and had designed settings and costumes for *Contes
russes* and *Chout.* Stravinsky described him as "a huge, blond mujik [peasant]
of a man . . . who had an uncontrollable temper [and] once knocked Diaghilev down." He was also, according to the composer of *Le Sacre du printemps* and *Firebird,* chronically lazy. Stravinsky believed that Goncharova did
all his work for him. But Gerald and Sara found him enchanting, and they
were particularly amused by "how he rushed up at the sight of you and kissed
you *'plein sur la bouche'* (full on the mouth)."

Soon the American novices had distinguished themselves enough for their
teacher to speak of them to Diaghilev, who saw in them, as he saw in so many
others, a means to an end. A number of sets for his ballets had fallen victim to
wear and tear and careless handling — Goncharova used to mourn that working in the theater was "a sad business, because the costumes and décors are
only beautiful when they're new." They needed to be refurbished quickly for
the company's spring season at the Opéra. But, alas (and as usual), Diaghilev
had no money. Would Mademoiselle Goncharova's pupils like to paint sets
for him, *gratis,* in the Ballets Russes scenery shop? They would.

It was, Gerald remembered, "serious and trying work." Diaghilev's atelier was located in the run-down district of Belleville on the outskirts of Paris. There were six other workers, all young Russian émigrés, and the new apprentices coped with their paints and glue pots and huge muslin flats and drop curtains in a language that was probably French, or French mixed with Russian. Certainly it wasn't English. The canvases were fastened to the floor, and the scene painters used soft brushes with long handles, like janitors' brooms, to spread the paint on them. Then they had to climb thirty-foot ladders and look down at their work to get the proper perspective. Diaghilev, a sleek, portly man with a streak of white in his glossy black hair, "hovered, — but pleasantly," peering through his monocle at the finished flats, and the artists whose designs they were executing, Braque and Derain and Picasso, came in to supervise and offer corrections.

Pablo Picasso was already a familiar figure to the Murphys, at least from a distance, but up close he made an indelible impression. "A dark, powerful, physical presence [who] always reminded me of the bulls of Goya," was how Gerald recalled him. He was nothing like the other artists they had known, the Sargents, Chases, and Sickerts who handled a teacup with the same facility as a paintbrush. Although Hester Pickman might pronounce him "very attractive," Picasso was emphatically not the kind of person who would have been welcome in the drawing rooms she and Sara had grown up in. First there were his pictures themselves, unsettling deconstructions that didn't look anything like the objects they were supposed to represent. And then there was Picasso's reputation. Although he had recently married one of Diaghilev's ballerinas, Olga Kokhlova (reportedly it was the only way he could get her to go to bed with him), Picasso had a famously roving eye and a long string of mistresses with whom he had lived openly. But the Murphys were irresistibly drawn to him, and soon they were all on friendly enough terms to arouse the suspicious ire of Hoytie Wiborg, who swept into the atelier one day and reprimanded them, "What are you all doing down here wasting your time?"

In fact, they had been caught up in what Gerald later called "a sort of movement," the group of artists and musicians and amateurs and hangers-on that clustered around the Ballets Russes. "You knew everyone in it," said Gerald, "and you were expected to go to the rehearsals, and they wanted your opinion and they discussed it with you." Sometimes the new recruits gave even more material aid: Gerald and Sara were watching one rehearsal for Stravinsky's new ballet *Le Renard*, a Russian fable with snow-encrusted scenery by Larionov, when Stravinsky lost his temper with Bronislava Nijinska, who was playing the fox, because she seemed not to be paying attention to his directions. She protested that she couldn't hear what he was saying because the scarf she was wearing around her head muffled the sound of his voice.

"Then we must cut it in two," thundered Stravinsky. He was legendarily short-tempered, and Gerald had once seen him leap out of the orchestra pit to the stage, using the laps of two violinists as stepping-stones, in order to berate a dancer. Now he grabbed the scarf from Nijinska — "a *beautiful* scarf," remembered Sara wistfully; "I'd give my eyes to have it" — and snapped, "Who has a scissors?"

Almost against her will, Sara piped up. "I always have my scissors," she said, digging in her bag and handing them over.

Stravinsky beamed at her. "Only Americans have scissors," he said.

"He was a wonderful man," Sara said fondly afterward.

His work with the Ballets Russes had given Gerald the confidence that he was a painter, not just a dilettante, and he now felt ready to start working on his own. He enlisted a cousin of Diaghilev's whom he'd met at the atelier, a former naval cadet named Vladimir Orloff, to act as a technical assistant, and began looking for studio space. Obviously the Murphys' rented quarters in the rue Greuze were unsuitable. Unlike Picasso, who had an atelier upstairs from his apartment in the rue la Boétie, Gerald could not find an appropriate space nearby. But he discovered a sculptor's studio in a shabby block of what looked like old stables on the rue Froidevaux, a street that ran along the southern perimeter of the Cimetière du Montparnasse. This leafy necropolis, crisscrossed with access roads that have the character of country lanes, was full of mausolea inscribed with the name of this or that upper bourgeois Parisian family; the lack of any other buildings in the vicinity meant that the studio got wonderful light. For obvious reasons, it was also very quiet.

Gerald's quarters consisted of one spacious room with a cement floor and skylight. There was a gas stove in one corner, and in the other a stairway went up to a kind of loft that could be used for sleeping or for storage. He whitewashed the walls and hung a curtain to separate the loft from the rest of the studio; he bought oil and tempera paint, brushes, canvas, and other supplies. He even began sporting a broad-brimmed black hat and red sideburns in the style of a Toulouse-Lautrec poster. He was ready to begin.

Because the space at his disposal was huge — the studio ceiling was approximately thirty feet high — and because he had been working on a large scale in his theatrical painting, Gerald seemed from the first to have conceived his pictures in monumental terms. "I seemed to see in miniature detail," he said many years afterward, "but in giant scale." The influence of his theatrical mentors, the futurists Goncharova and Larionov, also made itself felt in his initial choice of subject matter. Futurism and its near descendant, constructivism, exalted the powers and materials of technology — the "iron, glass, concrete, circle, cube, cylinder, synthetically combined with mathematical precision and structural logic," as the painter Louis Lozowick described it in a 1922 article in the little magazine *Broom*. So Gerald began painting machines. The shapes themselves, their order and their raw power, fascinated him.

It's not clear which picture he started first — those first paintings are lost now, and he never could remember correctly the order in which he'd done them. He called one of them *Turbines*, the other *Pressure* (or *Pression*). The former was a closely cropped, nearly abstract close-up view of the parts of a nameless machine, the latter a perspectival rendering of the working heart of an ocean liner, an enormous engine with the name of the manufacturer emblazoned (including a Dadaist typo) on the side of the engine block. He worked on each painting the same way, as if he were preparing and executing a scenic design: he made a maquette, or sketch, in tempera on paper; then, painstakingly, using a pencil and a grid, he transferred the outlines of the picture onto airplane linen that had been mounted on three-ply veneer panels; finally he painted in the design in oils on the canvas. It was a deliberate process, and it showed: the surface of the paintings had the sharp, even clarity of something, well, machine-made. Cogs, wheels, pistons, crankshafts, all of them gleaming and impermeable.

He worked all morning or all afternoon, for the first time in his life completely absorbed in what he was doing. He had never, he told an acquaintance later, been truly happy until that moment.

On June 12 Gerald put aside his brushes and paints to accompany Sara, the children, and the children's nanny, Mademoiselle Henriette Géron, to Houlgate, a seaside resort on the English Channel in Normandy. The Channel beaches were the summertime refuge of fashionable Parisians, and the Murphys must have thought of Houlgate as the French equivalent of East Hampton. They would be looking forward to the sort of summer they remembered from their youth — minus, of course, the familial strains that had made the Dunes so difficult in recent years.

They settled in for the summer at the Hôtel des Clématites, and Honoria, Baoth, and even little Patrick enjoyed riding donkeys along the beach and digging in the sand. The children acquired a dog, a liver-and-white English spaniel named Asparagus, and they didn't lack for company because the Pickmans and their five children were nearby in the Villa Germaine. But the weather was all wrong, chilly and gray, perfect for a polite stroll along the promenade in layers of fashionable clothes, but not good for the basking or sea-bathing the Murphys craved. So when Cole and Linda Porter asked them to come down to stay for a week or so in a château they'd rented in Antibes, on the Mediterranean coast, Gerald and Sara accepted.

The Côte d'Azur was not yet a byword in chic circles. Largely the haunt of English and German vacationers who didn't swim or sunbathe and came only for a short January-to-May season, it was deserted in summertime. But Cole Porter "always had a great flair, a sense of the avant garde, about places," recalled Gerald. "So we went down there in that hot, hot summer . . . and on the Cap d'Antibes was this little tiny beach — I think only about 3 or 4 hundred yards long — covered with a bed of seaweed that must have been there for ages. It was three or four feet thick. We dug a little corner of it out and bathed and sat in the most wonderful sun — absolutely dry weather, cool evenings, constant breeze in the evenings and clear, sunny days one after the other, and this perfectly beautiful, crystalline water." It seemed like paradise. And at the end of their stay, they knew they would come back.

10

"A prince and a princess"

THERE WERE MANY SIGNS of spring in Paris, from the setting out of the café tables at the Closerie des Lilas to the budding of chestnut trees in the Bois; but for the people who cared about art, the opening of the Salon des Indépendents was the first sign that winter was over.

The Société des Artistes Indépendents was an organization of antiestablishment artists united under the slogan *"Ni jury ni récompenses"* ("Neither jury nor rewards"); its thirty-fourth exposition opened on February 10, 1923, in the Grand Palais, a monumental art nouveau fantasy of stone, glass, and steel built for the Universal Exhibition of 1900, the first world's fair in Paris. Since the Indépendents required of their exhibitors only the desire to be seen and the payment of a small entrance fee, the number of works on view was enormous, as the glossy arts journal, *Shadowland,* made clear: "Think for a moment of a place as large as Madison Square Garden, with two floors divided into about seventy rooms. Think then of all the paintings of every known and unknown school, of all the pieces of sculpture, illustrations and designs for carpets and tapestries; and imagine them to the tune of six thousand sent in by almost two thousand artists and you begin to have a vague idea of what this Salon means."

Visitors milling under the Grand Palais's domed and vaulted glass roof could look at paintings by Pierre Bonnard, Max Ernst, Fernand Léger, Tsuguharu-Léonard Foujita, Francis Picabia, Michel Larionov, and Natalia Goncharova — but the point of the Indépendents was to discover new talent, and this season there were four pictures by an unfamiliar name: Gerald Murphy.

In the course of little more than six months of painting Gerald had produced four pictures for the Salon: two oils, *Turbines* and *Pression*; one watercolor, *Taxi*; and one drawing, *Crystaux*. This was their first public viewing; in fact, because Gerald preferred to avoid criticism of his work in progress, it was the first time he had had any real reaction to it. The results had to please him: his "cubistic studies of machinery" were singled out for special mention in *Shadowland*, and the *Paris Herald's* reviewer gave his "very personal point of view in the study of machinery" a new label: "centrifugalist." Mr. Murphy, the *Herald* declared, revealed "a feeling for mass and a sense of decorative effect."

It was the beginning of a kind of *annus mirabilis* for Gerald Murphy. Having his pictures hung in the Salon des Indépendents was one thing, but even more cachet attached to his invitation to design the "American" booth at a spectacular charity benefit given to raise money for impoverished Russian émigrés. This four-day bazaar, featuring art, crafts, and entertainment, opened on February 23 with a fantasy Bal des Artistes Russes at which four orchestras, including a jazz band, played the latest dance music. The guests showed up in Russian folk dress or in costumes derived from current avant-garde paintings (there were a lot of harlequins and cubist-inspired top hats), Tristan Tzara declaimed one of his poems while mechanical birds flitted through the air, and the Fratellini brothers performed their circus tricks.

Everything — even the champagne bottles popped open by the bartender, Michel Larionov — was decorated. Paintings by Goncharova, Gris, Hélène Perdriat, and others covered the walls with a chaotic blaze of color. The artists who had been asked to design exhibition booths had outdone themselves: near Picasso's was Sonia Delaunay's, where the young painter and designer was selling modernist bibelots; Goncharova had decorated the Russian booth, which featured her striking handmade masks; and at the Japanese booth, the artist Tsuguharu-Léonard Foujita had constructed an entire kabuki theater, complete with live dancers. But even among these stars Gerald Murphy's contribution stood out: an extraordinary construction of skyscrapers topped with electric signs whose lights blinked on and off, the Great White Way transported to the banks of the Seine. It was monumental, futuristic, and thrillingly *American*, and it announced that this American artist had arrived.

That winter and spring of 1923 were so full of new people and new things that it was difficult, later, to remember what had happened when. When was it, exactly, that Gerald and Sara met Fernand Léger? Who introduced them to Gilbert Seldes, the American critic and editor of *The Dial* who had come to Paris to write the book that would become *The Seven Lively Arts*? Was it Rue and John Carpenter? (John had just created a ballet, *Krazy Kat*, based on the George Herriman cartoon strip that Seldes considered an example of the American sublime.) Or did they get to know him through Amy Lowell? It was all a wonderful blur of exhibitions, performances, and publications.

Gerald and Sara had returned from the Côte d'Azur at the end of the summer. They'd given up the rue Greuze apartment) and had resettled in the Hôtel des Reservoirs in Versailles, not far from the palace, where Sara delighted in prowling around the local antiques shops and the children could have a country atmosphere while still being close to the city. But Sara and Gerald wanted to be in the thick of things, and by the end of the year they had found an apartment on the top two floors of an old François 1er house on the corner of the quai des Grands-Augustins and a narrow street called rue Gît-le-Coeur. It was full of light, and from its windows overlooking the Seine you could see all the way from the Île St.-Louis to the Tuileries. But it was small, with only two bedrooms and a kitchen so tiny that food had to be stored in a *garde-manger*, a box hung outside the window. And it was dilapidated — probably its last face-lift had come just after the French Revolution — and there were rats on the stairs. It wouldn't do for a permanent family home, but they could use it as an in-town *pied-à-terre* while still maintaining a residence at Versailles. And they could justify the expense of remodeling it because they had decided to burn their New York bridges at last. They had sold 50 West 11th Street for $40,000 in February.

They began work on the apartment to make it habitable, but even before they were finished they gave their first dinner party in it, a soirée for the avant-garde Kamerny (Chamber) Theater, a Moscow troupe that was appearing in Paris that spring. The Kamerny actors were determinedly experimental: they did Racine's *Phèdre* in constructed faces (not masks), with the star, Alice

Coonen, climbing up a steeply raked platform, trailing a red cape as long as the set was wide; they did an adaptation of G. K. Chesterton's chase-thriller, *The Man Who Was Thursday*, on a three-story set featuring scaffolding, stairways, elevators, and slides and poles for quick escapes; they did a silly 1890s operetta called *Giroflé-Girofla* on the wings of a biplane. Gerald and Sara were wild about them, went to all ten of their performances, and at the end of the run threw a party that would have given Adeline Wiborg nightmares, but that their friends still remembered half a century later.

Inspired, perhaps, by the Kamerny's inventiveness, Gerald and Sara made their apartment's half-finished state into a virtue: they had no chairs or sofas, so they piled mattresses and pillows along the wainscoted walls and covered them with yards of brocade. Tables were improvised out of planks mounted on blocks. The lighting was provided by acetylene plumbers' lamps, and the bare plaster walls were hung with "found" sculptures made by their new friend Fernand Léger out of discarded bicycle wheels and other junkyard objects. There were mounds of couscous made by the Murphys' new Algerian cook, and plenty of wine to wash it all down; for dessert there was fruit and a chocolate mousse, molded into a suggestive shape and cloaked in *crème Chantilly*, called *négresse en chemise*. But the Russians, still not sated, invaded the kitchen and devoured the lemons they found there, skin and all. The rooms buzzed with laughter and singing and Russian and French conversation. The only mournful note was struck later, when the troupe's director, Alexander Tairoff, confessed to his hosts that the Kamerny's tour had not been a financial success. The company was, in fact, unable to meet its obligations, and would probably be stranded in Paris without the funds to get home.

It was the first time — though by no means the last — that Sara and Gerald exchanged the look that said, "We must Do Something." The something in this case was a draft on their bank for $3,000, an enormous amount of money, which they lent to Tairoff "with great difficulty." But they felt they had to come up with it: after all, Tairoff's company was doing such wonderful and important work. The Murphys didn't know that repayment was a chancy proposition at best. It was only later that they discovered that in Russia under the Bolsheviks "foreign debts were not honored and no money [was] allowed sent out of the country." Even if they had known, it might not have mattered.

Was it on the afternoon of the Kamerny party, or another day, that Gilbert Seldes's friend, Donald Ogden Stewart, came by the quai des Grands-Augustins with another writer he wanted them to meet, John Dos Passos? Stewart, a comic novelist and aspiring playwright from the Midwest, had gone to Yale a few years behind Gerald, and his Yale experience had been shadowed first by his father's disgrace in a fraud accusation, then by the father's death some time afterward. Always conscious of feeling like an outsider pressing his nose against the windows of those more fortunate than he, Stewart was dazzled by the Murphys' aura. To him they were figures in a fairy tale: "Once upon a time there was a prince and a princess," he wrote: "that's exactly how a description of the Murphys should begin. They were both rich; he was handsome; she was beautiful; they had three golden children. They loved each other, they enjoyed their own company, and they had the gift of making life enchantingly pleasurable for those who were fortunate enough to be their friends."

Dos Passos, a Harvard man who had served in France as an ambulance driver during the war, fancied himself too tough and street-smart to fall for a line like that. He had been hanging around with the Left Bank expatriate journalist crowd that ran with the *Toronto Star*'s young correspondent, Ernest Hemingway, and he was resistant to the Murphys' charm.

"Sara was obviously a darling," wrote Dos Passos later of their first meeting (which, it should be remembered, took place when the Murphys were preparing for a party), "but Gerald seemed cold and brisk and preoccupied." Put off by Gerald's sartorial splendor and the diffidence he sometimes had with strangers, Dos Passos declined the Murphys' invitation to stay for their party. But not long afterward he ran into Gerald again on the street, walking with Fernand Léger. Léger was a burly butcher's son from Normandy with dark eyebrows, a drooping black mustache, and a cigarette that seemed permanently affixed to his lower lip, who painted with the same vigor and passion with which he attacked life. He already had a considerable reputation for his bold, collage-like paintings, and his designs for the ballet *Skating Rink* — which showed fashionable women in the same pearls and turbans that Sara favored — had been lavishly praised. Gerald, who admired him intensely, found him "an apostle, a mentor, a teacher," and the two men frequently roamed around the city to explore railroad yards or shop displays or factories, any of which might be subjects for a picture, or merely interesting or provocative in their own right.

Gerald and Léger hailed Dos Passos and they walked along the quai together — Gerald tall and sandy-haired in his beautifully cut suit, Léger hulking and broody, Dos Passos peering shyly through his thick glasses. Gerald and Léger were *looking* at things in a way Dos Passos had never seen. "*Regardez-moi ça,*" Léger would say, his finger jabbing at a winch on a barge, wound about with coils of rope, or the shape of a tugboat's funnel; or Gerald would point out the way you saw only half of a woman's face behind the geraniums in the cabin window of her barge. Later, in his notebook, Gerald described the scene in his artist's shorthand: "tugs clustered, deck details, barges or barge, living quarters, lattices, painted woods, nautical form, 1 or 2 solid humans at table." Dos Passos was enchanted. "The banks of the Seine never looked banal again," he said.

Soon he was a frequent presence in the Murphys' lives, happiest to drop in on them when they were *en famille.* His shyness and his stammer made large parties difficult; and besides, he said, he "had never had a proper home life, and was developing an unexpressed yearning for it." The illegitimate son of a prosperous lawyer who would not divorce his wife to marry his mistress, Dos Passos had grown up lonely in the luxury hotels his father's money paid for, and he couldn't help feeling a pang when he saw the Murphys' obvious love for, and ease with, what he called "their three little towheads."

Who else did Gerald and Sara meet in that spring of 1923? Donald Ogden Stewart, who seems to have been treating the Murphys almost as a tourist attraction, brought the playwright Philip Barry and his wife, Ellen, to the quai des Grand-Augustins and rang and rang the bell downstairs. Suddenly a window flew up on the top floor and a head poked out. Ellen Barry, looking up, saw a smiling woman, her fair hair pinned into a French twist. "Come up, come up!" she cried, when they protested they were just passing by and didn't want to intrude.

Barry, another Yale man (he had entered in 1913, a year after Gerald's graduation), had just made a splash in New York with his boulevard comedy, *You and I,* and he and Ellen were in France to take possession of the villa in

Cannes that his father-in-law, a wealthy lawyer named Lorenzo Semple, had given the young couple. This was another link: the Murphys were planning a return to Antibes that summer and would be only a few kilometers away along the Corniche; they made plans to see one another again on the Riviera.

Ellen Barry, a dark-haired beauty in her own right, was struck by Sara's elegance — "she wore beautiful clothes," she remembered, "not the chic of the day, but wonderful flowing things that suited her perfectly" — and by the freshness and originality of the Murphys' apartment. The walls had been painted dead white, and the floors lacquered a glossy black, with white Mexican rugs scattered about; the floor-to-ceiling windows, with their picture-postcard view of the Seine, were framed in red antique brocade curtains. Apparently the Murphys' Empire chests and settees had been largely left in storage. "Sara was the first to have modern furniture," Ellen Barry remembered. There were chairs and sofas upholstered in the kind of black satin tailors used to line men's vests, little coffee tables with mirrored tops, and an ebony grand piano on which was displayed an enormous industrial ball bearing that looked like a piece of sculpture — which is what most visitors mistook it for. (Gerald said it was better than having a Rodin that could turn out to be fake.) The sitting room was filled with arrangements of flowers and — an innovative touch — stalks of pale green celery in black or white opalescent vases; but in the spare cubicle of a dining room Sara would place only a single rose in a vase against the bare wall. "Oh, la valeur de ça!" Fernand Léger exclaimed when he saw it — and put a single rose in a series of paintings afterward.

If their charming nineteenth-century house on 11th Street had been an expression of the Murphys' flair for the quaint and unexpected, this apartment was a statement about newness and originality. Unlike Cole and Linda Porter's grand residence on the rue Monsieur, which boasted platinum wallpaper, zebra-skin rugs, and priceless eighteenth-century furniture, it was not an advertisement for the Murphys' affluence. Instead it was a declaration of their own brand of unconventional modernism, an extension from canvas to life. To visiting Americans like the Barrys it had the excitement of Paris at that moment — and to Europeans like Léger and Stravinsky it symbolized the machine-age inventiveness of an America most of them could only dream of.

"The Murphys were among the first Americans I ever met," said Stravinsky once, "and they gave me the most agreeable impression of the United States."

That June all Paris was buzzing with curiosity over Stravinsky's new ballet, *Les Noces*, which Diaghilev would produce at the Théâtre Gaîeté-Lyrique to open the last week of his season. *Le Figaro, Le Gaulois,* all the papers bristled with front-page items calling it "this year's gift," "an aesthetic revelation," and more. The music, which Stravinsky had originally written for player piano and percussion, had been rescored for four pianos, a chorus, drums, bells, and a xylophone — a novel ensemble — and the choreography was singular in that it emphasized the movement of the corps de ballet over that of the principals. In fact, that was the idea: this primitivist wedding fable was intended to convey a sense of implacable social force in which the individual wishes of the bride and groom were meaningless. In addition, the traditional gender divisions of ballet had been abolished. Men and women performed the same steps, there was no support work — the ballet was as revolutionary sexually as it was musically.

Natalia Goncharova had been commissioned to do the sets and costumes for *Les Noces;* but a series of misunderstandings and disagreements with the choreographer, Bronislava Nijinska, had put her formidably behind an already tight schedule. Nijinska had persuaded Diaghilev to abandon Goncharova's literally folkloric costumes and décors in favor of stylized ones in tones of brown and white; as a result Goncharova was desperate to finish in time, and called on her henchmen the Murphys for help. Although Gerald was by now consumed by his own painting, he spent a week helping to spread brown and white paint on muslin flats. He also seized this opportunity to include John Dos Passos, who was passionate to know more about the Ballets Russes in its backstage life. Dos Passos found the conditions in Diaghilev's atelier hot (June in Paris can be brutal) and confusing (the cacophony of French and Russian, and the histrionics of the crew, bewildered him). But Gerald kept him going with frequent pit stops at the local brasserie, and they finished their task.

Gerald and Sara also invited him to one of the ten stage rehearsals *Les Noces* would receive before its opening (they themselves went to all ten), and when Dos Passos asked if another of his friends, the poet and novelist e. e. cummings, could come too, they were delighted. But at the theater cummings perversely and ostentatiously sat three or four rows behind the others — perhaps the Murphys' "well-laundered" elegance was off-putting to someone who often considered squalor a matter of principle — and although Dos Passos tried to make light of the incident he was reportedly deeply embarrassed.

The day before its official opening on June 13, *Les Noces* received a preview performance at the rococo *hôtel particulier* of Stravinsky's patroness, the Princesse Edmond de Polignac (née Winaretta Singer), the handsome lesbian heiress to the Singer sewing machine fortune. "Tante Winnie," as she liked to be called, was a fixed star in that affluent and sexually ambiguous universe that surrounded the Ballets Russes and, therefore, was a friend both of the de Beaumonts (who were there) and of Hoytie Wiborg, so it would have been natural for Gerald and Sara to have attended this private performance. But in addition they had decided they must make their own gesture of homage to the creators of *Les Noces*; and so — Gerald later recalled — they invited "everyone directly connected to the ballet, as well as friends . . . who were following its genesis" to a party in what they hoped would be "a place worthy of the event."

The first venue they thought of was the Cirque Médrano, the funky one-ring-circus-cum-vaudeville house that was home to the Fratellini brothers; nothing could have been farther from Winnie de Polignac's marbled halls with their José María Sert frescoes and busts of Louis XIV, and nothing could have been more Murphyesque. But the circus manager was not amused. "The Cirque Médrano," he told Gerald frostily, "isn't an American colony yet." Then they had a better idea: a converted barge tied up in front of the Chambre des Députés that, except on Sundays, served as the deputies' restaurant. Celebrating *Les Noces* there had a certain dadaist correctness: it was a bit like letting the lunatics take over the asylum.

The party took place on June 17, at 7:00 P.M., and was quickly transformed into legend. It almost began with disaster: Sara had forgotten that because it was a Sunday, the huge open-air market on the Île de la Cité would be selling birds instead of flowers, and she could find no fresh blooms for her center-

Top left: "My father wanted *boys*": Frank Wiborg in the 1880s

Top right: Adeline Wiborg and (*clockwise from upper left*) Hoytie, Sara, and Olga

Right: The Wiborg girls in fancy dress: Olga as a Pierrot, Sara as a Chinese empress, Hoytie as a Dutch girl

Top left: Gerald in one of his earliest disguises — a solemn, rather wistful child

Top right: Fred (*left*) and Gerald "always appeared to act as members of a royal family."

Patrick Murphy avoided all "close relationships, even family ones"; his wife, Anna, was "devoted, possessive, ambitious, Calvinistic, superstitious, [and] hypercritical."

Above: The drawing room at the Dunes.

Upper left: "The women all had tiny waists and they wore long fluttering eyelet dresses." *From left:* Sara Sherman, Olga, Hoytie, and Sara in East Hampton, about 1905

Lower left: The Lorelei — Sara steering her own course in Gardiners Bay

Below: Sara on the lawn, circa 1913: "Is *anything* so satisfying as to be picturesque? I am nearly dead with it."

Sara, circa 1910. "My own dear girl," Gerald wrote her,
"if you knew how I thought of you!"

Gerald as a man about town, circa 1915:
"The game in N.Y. . . . is not for me — is not *real*."

Sara's engagement photograph: "the face from *Town and Country*"

Sara, Honoria, and pearls

Gerald in the uniform of a private first class — perhaps one part for which he was not well cast

"They look so well laundered." *From left:* Baoth, Gerald, baby Patrick, Sara, and Honoria in Cambridge, just before they moved to France

Sara took an almost visceral pleasure in her children — here with Honoria and Baoth at Houlgate, 1922.

Sara (*foreground*) and Olga
Picasso

Left to right: Gerald, the de Beaumonts, an
Sara at La Garoup

Sara and Gerald
(and Picasso's hat
on the sand)

Picasso (*foreground*) and
Gerald

Sara and Picasso

"Some people even think
we started the summer season
on the Midi!"

Left to right: Honoria, Baoth,
Paulo Picasso (*partly hidden by hat*),
Gerald, and Patrick

Sara by Picasso.
Both portraits echo
photographs of Sara at
left, one in a turban,
with Picasso, the other
— clothed — at the
Garoupe.

Gerald's drop curtain and some of the characters (in costumes designed by Sara) from *Within the Quota*

Watch: Gerald was "struck by the mystery and depth of the interior" o this *instrument de précision.*

The picture that caused the sensation: *Boatdeck*, with its "huge almost vertical red-lead-colored smoke-stacks and dead-white mush rooming ventilators with black, gaping pure-circle mouths"

Top left: Cole Porter

Top right: Gerald and Sara at Étienne de Beaumont's "automotive ball"

Left: Archibald and Ada MacLeish were the Murphys' neighbors at St.-Cloud.

Bottom left: Easter party at St.-Cloud. *Front row, left to right:* Honoria, Baoth, Patrick; *back row, left to right:* Frank Wiborg, Patrick Murphy, Sara, Gerald, and Vladimir Orloff

Bottom right: Esther Murphy "looked exactly like Gerald but *moins jolie*," said a friend.

Villa America — the modest chalet transformed into a deco variation on a Mediterranean theme. Gerald is on the terrace, Baoth is driving a minicar on the patio.

Gerald's sign for the villa, which, like its owners, existed in two worlds at once: France and America, the real and the imagined

Robert Benchley (*left*) and Donald Ogden Stewart showing their mettle

At Antibes the day might begin with exercises on the beach. *Left to right*: Gerald, Baoth, Honoria, and Patrick

In the afternoon there might be a children's party for which the celebrant dressed specially — Honoria as an Infanta, Baoth as a knight, and Patrick as Charlie Chaplin

"The last unalloyed good time." *Left to right*: Dos, Ernest, Sara, Hadley, and Gerald at Schruns

Murphy beach parties
might feature Elsie de
Wolfe (*holding
parasol*), her husband,
Sir Charles Mendl
(*behind her*), or Monty
Woolley (*back row, far
right*)...

or Philip Barry,   Ellen Barry,   Zelda Fitzgerald,

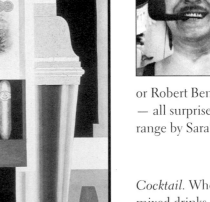

or Robert Benchley
— all surprised at close
range by Sara's camera

Cocktail. When Gerald
mixed drinks, Philip Bar-
ry told him, "You look
like a priest saying
Mass."

La Garoupe, summer 1926. "They have to like it," said one of Fitzgerald's characters about the Murphys' fictional counterparts, "they invented it."

All hands aloft. *Left to right:* Ellen Barry, Sara, Phil Barry (*partially hidden*), and Gerald

Pamplona, summer 1926. *Left to right:* Hadley, Ernest, Pauline, Sara, and Gerald

What might have seemed self-conscious on someone else
looked, on Gerald, somehow exactly right.

Gerald as an *apache*

On the terrace at Villa America

À *l'espagnol* at La Garoupe

In robes brought back from China
by Archie MacLeish

pieces. But she quickly recouped by going to a Montparnasse bazaar and buying quantities of cheap toys — trucks and fire engines, dolls, and stuffed animals — which she arranged in pyramids along the banquet table. Over it, suspended from the ceiling, was positioned a huge laurel wreath bearing the inscription *"Les Noces — Hommages."*

The guests gathered on the canopied upper deck for cocktails — all but Stravinsky, who first went below to the dining room to check the seating arrangements and rearrange the place cards to his liking. Diaghilev came, with his amanuensis, the devoted Boris Kochno, and the de Beaumonts and Winaretta de Polignac and Misia Sert. Although Gerald and Sara had wanted to invite all the dancers, the antiegalitarian Diaghilev disapproved: but his new favorite Serge Lifar was there, and the beautiful dark-haired Vera Nemchinova, and Léonide Massine. Larionov and Goncharova came, but not Nijinska — possibly the Murphys wanted to avoid a contretemps between her and Goncharova about the designs for the ballet. Rue and John Carpenter were there with their nearly grown daughter Ginny. So were the Porters, and Darius Milhaud, Walter Damrosch, Ernest Ansermet (who had conducted the ballet), Germaine Taillefer, and the "preferred pianist of *les Six,*" Marcelle Meyer. Scofield Thayer, the editor-in-chief of *The Dial,* turned up (someone said later that this was the last night before he went mad), and so did Gilbert Seldes and Lewis Galantière and his wife, Dorothy Butler. Tristan Tzara was there, and Blaise Cendrars, and Picasso and his wife, and Jean Cocteau, who, however, refused to come aboard until after the last *bâteau-mouche* had gone by because he feared the heaving from their wakes would make him seasick.

As the guests came down to the dining room Picasso, captivated by Sara's toy decorations, rearranged them into a giant assemblage that culminated in a stuffed cow atop a fire truck's ladder. The dinner went on and on: a great deal of champagne was consumed, Marcelle Meyer played Scarlatti on the piano, Goncharova read the guests' palms and promised them fame and fortune, and Cocteau — who had pinched the captain's dress uniform from his cabin — scurried around the deck with a lantern, sticking his head through the portholes to proclaim, *"On coule"* ("We're sinking"). Gilbert Seldes picked up one of the menus put at everyone's place and went about getting the guests to autograph the back of it; across the top someone wrote: *"Depuis le jour de ma première communion c'est le plus beau soir de ma vie"* ("Since the day of my first communion this is the most beautiful evening of my life").

As dawn whitened the sky over Notre-Dame, Kochno and Ansermet took down the laurel wreath from the ceiling and held it between them like a clown's hoop. Stravinsky, showing he had lost none of the form he had displayed in the pillow fight after the *Pulcinella* premiere, ran the length of the room and jetéd through the center. After that, everyone decided, they might as well go home.

11

"There is American elegance"

"On the pleasant shore of the French Riviera," Scott Fitzgerald wrote in *Tender Is the Night*, "about half way between Marseilles and the Italian border, stands a large, proud, rose-colored hotel. Deferential palms cool its flushed façade, and before it stretches a short, dazzling beach. Lately it has become a summer resort of notable and fashionable people; a decade ago it was almost deserted after its English clientele went north in April."

He has changed the name, but Fitzgerald is describing the Hôtel du Cap in Cap d'Antibes. It's wedding-cake white now, not pink, and the beach never was right in front of it. In fact, it's almost a half mile away. The hotel has a swimming pool instead, sunk into the rocks overlooking the Mediterranean. But the palms are still there, and the gigantic, primordial-looking aloe plants, and the Aleppo pines, their spindly silver trunks topped by tufty foliage. If you squint your eyes, obscuring the recent additions that have turned it into a *hôtel de grand luxe*, it looks almost as it must have on July 3, 1923, when Sara and Gerald, their three children, and Mademoiselle Géron arrived to spend the summer.

In past years the hotel would have been shut from May to September. But the previous summer's arrival of the Porters and their guests at the Château de la Garoupe, just down the road, had encouraged the hotel's owner, Antoine Sella, to think about keeping his establishment open this summer on a trial basis. When the Murphys proposed a return visit he agreed to keep a skeleton staff for them and for the family of a Chinese diplomat who, hearing the hotel would not close as usual, decided to stay on. After all, Sella rationalized, the weather was unseasonably wet and cold in the north that year, and perhaps other vacationers would come south for the sun.

At the time Antibes was a sleepy little port whose claim to fame was that Napoleon had been posted there when he was a loyal revolutionary soldier. There was a railroad station, and a pretty lemon yellow Romanesque church in the old town, where the narrow streets between the pastel stucco houses were bright with flower boxes. The tiny movie theater operated only once a week, and telephone service shut down for two hours at midday and altogether at 7:00 P.M. South of town a dozen modest villas were scattered on the piny slopes of the Antibes peninsula, but the shoreline was deserted except for fishermen's shacks, and the few roads crisscrossing the peninsula were unpaved.

This sense of remote tranquillity was exactly what the Murphys were seeking after the sometimes exhausting excitement of the past months in Paris. For Gerald, however, Antibes was a working vacation more than a real escape. Before he left Paris he had begun an enormous painting, which he hoped to complete for the Indépendents in February. Possibly inspired by a large model of the liner *Paris* which had been exhibited at the Salon d'Automne in the fall of 1921, it depicted in gigantic scale the funnels and smokestacks of an ocean liner. Gerald had taken more than sixty photographs on deck while making transatlantic visits home on the *Paris* and the *Aquitania* and that spring had started the painstaking process of transferring his preliminary sketches to a canvas the size of a billboard. Now, although he had left that project behind in his studio, he had other work to do, an exciting commission from Rolf de Maré, the director of the avant-garde Ballets Suédois.

A rich and aristocratic Swede, de Maré had set up the Ballets Suédois in 1920 as a Paris showcase for his male lover, a stocky blond dancer named Jean Börlin. Modeling his company on Diaghilev's Ballets Russes, de Maré had sought out those artists and composers considered to be on the cutting edge of fashion. Because de Maré's pockets were as deep as Diaghilev's were shallow, he had been able to pay not only for designs and music, but for costumes by the couturière Jeanne Lanvin, scenery executed by the Opéra's head scene painter, and the kind of full hundred-piece orchestra that Diaghilev could rarely afford. By 1923 he had seriously challenged Diaghilev's hegemony and was commissioning scores from Darius Milhaud, Arthur Honneger, Maurice Ravel, and Claude Debussy, and décors from Picabia, Bonnard, and Léger.

De Maré had scheduled a new African-inspired ballet, to be entitled *La Création du monde,* from Léger and Milhaud, with a scenario by the novelist and poet Blaise Cendrars. His intention was to include the piece in the company's winter 1923–24 American tour. But it was short, and he wanted an "American" ballet as a curtain-raiser, designed and composed by Americans, to give the box office a boost. Gerald's skyscraper construction for the Bal des Artistes Russes made him an obvious candidate to provide the ballet's décor, and his friendship with Léger, the artist on the other half of the proposed double bill, was a deciding factor. The commission was a considerable coup, and de Maré had done Gerald the additional honor of asking him to suggest a composer and outline the scenario.

Gerald, in his turn, had proposed his old friend and sometime protégé, Cole Porter. Porter's career had been languishing: after *See America First,* the show whose tryout Gerald had gone to see in New Haven in 1916, Cole had written only occasional songs, and Linda wanted him to concentrate on serious orchestral music. She had even asked Igor Stravinsky to come to Antibes the previous summer to teach him harmony and composition. (Stravinsky, after consulting with the Murphys, had declined.) But here was a chance for Cole to write an orchestral composition in the style of Milhaud's jazzy *Boeuf sur le toit,* to use his strength with popular idiom to good effect in a "classical" piece. And if he found himself over his head trying to score the piece, de Maré could certainly afford a first-rate orchestrator. Porter got the commission, and Gerald and Sara made plans to visit him and Linda in their rented palazzo in Venice later in the summer so that the two collaborators could work on the ballet.

In the meantime they luxuriated in the bright Provençal sun: Gerald raked seaweed from the deserted little Garoupe beach, the children splashed in the improbably blue water, and Sara — as had been her habit since East Hampton days — stretched out on a blanket in the sand, reading or writing or dreaming. Sometimes she wore some long white linen dress, sometimes a bathing suit, but always she wore her pearls, looped around her back like the duchess of Rutland's, so they wouldn't leave a white mark on her suntanned décolletage. She claimed the sun was good for them.

One day, not long after their arrival, the Murphys came down to the beach to discover they had company: Pablo Picasso, his wife, Olga, their two-and-a-half-year-old son, Paulo, and Picasso's mother, Señora Maria Ruiz, who had come to France for the first time in her life to meet her grandson. Picasso was no stranger to the area. The summer before Paulo's birth Pablo had dragged the unwilling Olga, who would have preferred the chic of St. Raphaël, to a villa in unfashionable Juan-les-Pins, just on the other side of the peninsula, and he had wanted to come back ever since. When the Murphys told him of their own summer plans in Paris that spring, he needed little encouragement to follow them.

Although Picasso ultimately rented a villa for his family in Juan-les-Pins, at first he and his household (including Paulo's *nounou*, or baby nurse) installed themselves in the hotel, and the two families had their meals together in the cavernous, nearly empty dining room, the children at one table and the adults at another. Señora Ruiz, according to Sara, "didn't speak a *word* of English," nor of French, and she tried in vain to teach the Murphys Spanish. Despite their lack of a common language they got on famously. Olga was harder to get to know. She was very pretty, except for a rather weak chin and a tight, thin-lipped little mouth, but she was, as the Murphys noticed, "entirely prosaic" and had no gift for small talk.

In the beginning the relationship between the couples was formal. "*Chère Madame Picasso*," wrote Sara in French, "our children are going to the beach at 9:45 and will return at 11:30 (they eat lunch at 12). We would be so happy if your baby could accompany them, with his nurse. Would you and M. Picasso come swimming with us later, at eleven? The beach is really very nice and we have an American canoe."

Soon, however, they were on more playful footing; and when the de Beaumonts and the Barrys appeared at their respective villas in Cannes later in the month, they all gathered regularly on the Garoupe beach.

Sometimes there were well-organized (if disorderly) diversions: The de Beaumonts planned a "*concours et costume de bain*" one Friday noon for which the invitees added fantastical elements to their usual swimming costumes. Count Étienne had a hat like a chef's toque trimmed at each temple with Aztec tassels, and the countess had a latticework of beads on her bathing suit and over her hair. Olga wore her ballerina's tutu and toe shoes, and coiled a twisted black and white scarf around her head. Sara put on a huge white top hat with a ribboned cockade at the brim; and Picasso wore his trademark black homburg over his white shirt and trousers. Señora Ruiz retained her Andalusian widow's black, and sat on the sand looking like a Buddha. They all clowned around and posed for photographs: Picasso supporting Olga *en attitude*, then stripping to his bathing suit and putting on Sara's white hat, and finally joining the others for a mock Victorian group portrait in the Murphys' canoe.

On other days Sara's Kodak captured just the four of them: Picasso and Gerald at the water's edge, Gerald tall and slender in his rolled-up trunks and white fisherman's cap, turning somewhat deferentially toward Picasso, who is wearing his homburg and standing on one foot, the other at his knee, like a ballerina's in *passé*, grinning hugely at the camera. Picasso and Sara, arms linked, she wearing a turban, he holding his hat in his hand — a photograph that he kept until the end of his life. Picasso alone, with a huge fig leaf pinned on the front of his bathing trunks. And a set of two pictures, one of Gerald and Picasso, the other of Olga and Sara, each in profile gazing at the horizon. Picasso is the figure in the foreground in one, Sara the figure in the foreground in the other. Gerald and Olga are each shadowy and indistinct.

Despite the air of tranquillity and holiday joie de vivre that pervades these photographs, all was not serene. Relations between Picasso and Olga had begun to cool imperceptibly by that summer. Olga's tension and anxiety, particularly around little Paulo, contrasted strongly with Sara's almost visceral delight in her children and her air of *luxe, calme, et volupté*. And increasingly, it seemed, Picasso was entranced by Sara. She had all the worldly and social experience that Olga only aspired to; but her directness and candor were the exact opposite of the flirtatiousness or *politesse* Picasso would have been accustomed to in European, and most American, women. ("She is never coy," Gerald said of her.) Picasso loved her habit of wearing her rope of pearls to the beach, and he found her unconventional gaiety contagious. One day she was arranging a picnic cloth on the sand with brightly colored plates and a straw-covered Chianti bottle, around which she had wound a garland of ivy. As she placed a little pottery vase of fresh flowers in the center of the cloth, Picasso said, in his idiosyncratic French, *"Sara est très festin."*

Gerald was fascinated by Picasso, by his "sense of the grotesque" and the absurdist anarchism that made him say, observing a chauffeur-driven car brought to a screeching halt when a sleeping dog refused to move until shooed away by the chauffeur with a lap robe, *"Moi, je voudrais être un chien"* ("I'd like to be a dog"). And Picasso seemed to appreciate Gerald's individual style. At the Opéra in Paris he had pointed out the younger man, who was wearing a high-crush opera hat, to Étienne de Beaumont by saying, *"There* is American elegance!" They rarely talked about art, though; about the closest they came was Picasso telling Gerald that he "resembled very much in face and body El Greco's model."

During those golden July weeks Picasso began working on a series of drawings and oils, done in the classical manner of Greek vase painting, of a fair-haired woman with slanting eyes. Many of the drawings show her seated on a beach that looks like La Garoupe. In three of the oils the paint is mixed with sand from the beach. Sometimes the woman is holding a child on her lap, her hair twisted lightly at the back of her head, as Sara's often was, then streaming loosely down her back. In some sketches she is shown in one of the long, classically flowing dresses that Sara favored. In one she is wearing the turban Sara was photographed in with Picasso. In others she is naked except for a rope of pearls.

Some of these pictures must have been openly drawn from life. Ellen Barry and Gerald both remembered that during their time in Antibes, Picasso had used Sara as a model or inspiration, and the painter's French biographers took it as a given. But what about the nudes? After all, painting your friend's wife is one thing, painting her naked with her trademark string of pearls is another. And scholars familiar with Picasso's methods now believe these drawings, and the obsessiveness with which Picasso returned to the same subject, indicate that his involvement with Sara went deeper than mere admiration.

"Picasso was in love with her," says the noted art historian and Picasso scholar William Rubin, adding that, although "nobody really knows," he believes Picasso and Sara might have had a "short-lived sexual adventure" that summer. John Richardson, the author of what is regarded as the definitive biography of the painter, concurs. "I would have thought that nothing was more likely," he says. "Picasso was tremendously attractive and charismatic, and very physical, and it would have been hard for her to resist." Rubin believes that the artist expressed his feelings for Sara by making her the subject of his neoclassical masterpiece *The Woman in White*, and by beginning a series of studies for a "mystic marriage" composition in which Sara assumed the role of Venus, and Picasso that of Venus's virile consort, Mars. In several of these, a group of pale, misty pastels, Mars holds a mirror up to Venus to reveal to her her true beauty — a metaphor for the artist's presentation of his subject — and he and Venus are flanked by a youth playing panpipes and a little Cupid holding a garland.

Oddly, the panpipes show up in another of that summer's creations, a play that Philip Barry was writing, but which he never produced or published. Called "The Man of Taste," it tells the story of Adrian Terry, "thirty-five, tall, of youthful figure. His face is unusually fine and sensitive. A man of wealth, education, and, above all, taste." A man, in other words, who was the same age as Gerald Murphy and looked very like him. Adrian's wife, Lissa, who is known for her beauty and her legendary rope of pearls, was "born twenty-eight years ago with a silver spoon in her mouth"; despite the deaths of her parents on the *Titanic* she has enjoyed a privileged if oversupervised transatlantic upbringing and "a debut party of more than the usual gorgeousness." Like Sara, she has married "a curiously tender, understanding [man with] a rare gift of enjoying life to the fullest and of making others enjoy it with him." But the marriage is threatened when a former lover of Lissa's, with whom she had a one-night affair during her engagement, shows up and plans to lure her into an elopement.

The catch is that Adrian knows what's happening, and he's planned a May eve party, "a dinner with at least the suggestion of the fiesta about it," for which the drawing and dining rooms will be transformed into "what is referred to as 'a sylvan grove.'" (The echo of Gerald's occasionally ornate speech is uncanny.) As entertainment during this "dinner fit for the gods, Pan and Bacchus," he has engaged an Italian boy to play panpipes, the flutes of love. But Adrian won't be there to hear them. He has arranged to be summoned away by a make-believe telegram, and he has also managed to turn away all the other guests by telling them the party has been canceled. Gambling on the principle that a move by the other man will offend and repel his wife,

Adrian has stage-managed things so that Lissa will be alone at the feast with her tempter.

The parallels between this play and Picasso's picture, and between the play and life, are unsettling. But art is art, and life is life. What really happened that summer?

In August the Murphys went to Venice, and Sara dashed off a farewell note to the "chers Picassos," dating it with a little drawing of a train. She promised to send them some American ties Picasso had admired, along with a present for Olga, and she looked forward to seeing them again at the end of the month. After saying that the Murphy family sent best wishes, she added, "We love you very much, you know — Sara."

The Murphys spent two weeks together with the Porters in the Casa Papadopoli on the Grand Canal, where Gerald and Cole were meant to work on their ballet. But there were distractions: Venice was *the* place to be for the roving European smart set that Linda Porter ran with, and so there were grand parties and trips to the Lido to swim and be seen. They posed like tourists in the Piazza San Marco — Sara and Cole and Gerald and Ginny Carpenter, Cole striking an attitude with his arms linked in the women's, Sara and Ginny smiling at the camera from beneath their hat brims, and Gerald, with his Panama hat and Norfolk suit and malacca cane, looking not at the camera but at Sara.

Despite the gaiety there was a sense of strain in the visit. Sara felt that Linda Porter disapproved of her and of Gerald, perhaps for different reasons. And Cole and Linda had increasingly begun to go their separate ways; Cole had discovered the city's homosexual netherworld and had begun seeking out gondoliers and other rough trade for pleasure. After two weeks Sara returned to Antibes, leaving Gerald to finish his work with Cole. The two of them went swimming at the Lido one day and Gerald swam far out past the buoys, causing the lifeguard to scream at him to come back — it was *pericoloso*. "So is love *pericoloso*," shouted Gerald in return, and went on swimming.

If Picasso and Sara had an affair, it would have happened then. In this version of that summer's events, Sara would have been responding not only to Picasso's animal magnetism but to her own frustration at being abandoned in favor of her husband's homosexual friend. But such a scenario seems unlikely.

As someone who was acquainted with them both pointed out, Cole was attracted to rather lowlife men, and Gerald was most emphatically not his type. More important was Sara's "sense of austerity" (as Ellen Barry described it) about extramarital relationships. "Sara," stated Hester Pickman's mother, Mrs. Winthrop Chanler, "is incorruptible." However attractive Picasso might have seemed, her unwavering integrity and her very real love for Gerald and her children made any long-term backdoor relationship impossible.

Love might be perilous, but it seems as if Gerald's gamble — if, like Adrian Terry, he *was* gambling — paid off. Some time after Sara returned alone to Antibes, Picasso painted over the composition he had been working on, the large oil we now know as *The Pipes of Pan*, eliminating the figures of Venus and Cupid, and leaving only the haunting, rather mournful image of two lonely men by the shore, one of them playing a double flute. Why? According to William Rubin, whose X-ray examinations of the picture revealed the ghost images beneath its painted surface, Picasso had planned *The Pipes of Pan* as a climax to his mystic marriage series, a way of consummating his love for Sara on canvas. When she put a halt to whatever was going on between them, he had to alter the painting.

It's difficult, as Gerald himself was later to acknowledge, to say what has gone in private between two people. But it appears that Sara had begun to master the art of balancing friendship and eros. In the years since her encounter with Walter Sickert she had learned to go beyond writing "Hate man not going back" in her diary. Whatever had or had not happened in Antibes, she managed to stay friendly with Picasso, but on her terms. "Will you come, both of you," she wrote to him and Olga in French later that year, "and have one of our orgies? We'll dance, we'll drink, we'll go a little crazy. . . ?" This note is signed "With *best wishes*" (underlined twice), and the words "from Gerald and me" have been added, like an afterthought — or a reminder? — in the margin.

This wasn't coquetry. It was a kind of chaste sensuality that was as new to Picasso as it was to others who would encounter it, a spirit that was mirrored in the Garoupe drawings, the sand paintings, *The Woman in White*. It's the spirit of unfulfilled desire and ineffable promise that has animated neoclassicism since Keats's "Ode on a Grecian Urn." As paradoxical as it seems today, perhaps it was Sara's withdrawal, rather than her surrender, that inspired the work Picasso did that summer.

Gerald and Cole Porter's ballet, entitled *Within the Quota*, received its premiere at the Théâtre des Champs-Élysées in Paris on October 25. The pre-opening buzz was considerable: The ballet had been originally planned as a curtain-raiser for Léger, Milhaud, and Cendrars's startling African-inspired *La Création du monde*. But after seeing the rehearsals Léger asked Rolf de Maré to change the performance order because he feared the Americans' ebullient jazz-inflected spoof would make the more serious pleasures of his piece seem like heavy going to the audience. On the day of the premiere there was a front-page story about the ballet in the *Paris Herald*, which of course would be read by all the members of the American colony in Paris and might very likely be picked up by the New York edition of the paper as well. The accompanying photograph was of Gerald, who told his interviewer that the ballet was "nothing but a translation on to the stage of the way America looks to me from over here. I put into the play all the things that come out of America to me, you see, as I get things into perspective and distance." The composer seemed to agree: The score, which had been orchestrated by Charles Koechlin, blended Milhaudesque jazz and Stravinskyan syncopation with the obbligato of a silent-movie piano. And Porter explained, "It's easier to write jazz over here than in New York . . . because you are too much under the influence of popular song in America, and jazz is better than that."

Within the Quota tells the story of a fresh-faced, clueless innocent from Sweden who arrives in New York with only a satchel, a hobo's bundle, and a landing card, and subsequently undergoes a series of picaresque adventures at the hands of a *dramatis personae* straight from central casting, circa 1923 — a Jazz Baby, a Cowboy, a Millionairess, a Colored Gentleman, a Social Reformer, America's Sweetheart. At the ballet's end he is improbably transformed into a movie star by a cameraman who "films" the action on stage.

This sort of burlesque bore more than a passing resemblance to parodic sketches like Fred's Maidstone Club triumph, *Mrs. Clymer's Regrets*, or the undergraduate reviews Gerald had seen at Yale. But it also had impeccable avant-garde antecedents in Cocteau's *Parade*, in which the characters are the

Acrobats, the Managers, the Chinese Magician, and the Little American Girl, and *Le Boeuf sur le toit,* with its Policeman, Barman, Negro Boxer, and Woman in a Low Cut Dress. *Parade* (the title refers to a sideshow or display) was a ballet about how the advertising image, the sideshow, comes to be more important than the real attraction inside the circus tent. *Within the Quota* was about how the image *becomes* the real attraction. For an artist who wanted to "represent" real objects as abstractions, the progression was obvious.

The power of the image was even emphasized in the costumes, most of which Sara had either designed or drawn, to Gerald's specifications. The Hollywoodish cast of characters was dressed in clothes from a semiotician's sign book: the Tom Mix–like cowboy wore furry chaps that might have been stolen from a grizzly bear and what looks like a twenty-gallon hat; the sheriff had a dinner plate–sized star for a badge; the gilt-haired Mary Pickford type was bedecked with roses, which Cocteau told Gerald were "the most powerful symbol in the world." Fascinatingly, Sara's sketch of the Millionairess, whom Gerald described as "a study of American women entering the Ritz," and who is wearing a rope of golf-ball-sized pearls, an ostrich-plumed cape, and a tiara, looks exactly like Hoytie Wiborg.

Gerald also struck a personal note in the designs for the décor. On an obvious level he was making a point about popular journalism as entertainment: The set was planned as a simple black and white backdrop (the monochrome influence of *Les Noces* may have been hard to shake) that reproduced in dadaist pastiche the front page of an American newspaper. But although some of the headlines simply parodied their real-world counterparts — "RUM RAID LIQUOR BAN" and "MAMMOTH PLANE UP" — others made sly fun of the establishment that his and Sara's families lived in and catered to.

"UNKNOWN BANKER BUYS ATLANTIC" screamed the main banner headline, in the best yellow-journalism tradition. Of course it was nonsense, but American millionaires had been buying everything else for the past few decades, and only a few months later J. Pierpont Morgan, Jr. (Gerald's host at Camp Uncas) would "buy" France when he bailed out the country with the $200 million Dawes Plan. Then there was the box advertising a story on "Ex-Wife's Heart-Balm Love-Tangle." It imitated the weird poetry Gerald often discerned in signs and slogans, but it also echoed a currently notorious lawsuit ("DANCER RENEWS HEART-BALM CASE") in which a showgirl, Evan Burrows Fontaine, was suing the Socially Registered New Yorker Cornelius Vanderbilt Whitney for $1 million in compensation ("heart balm") because he had jilted her to marry Marie Norton. (The marriage didn't last. Some seven years later Marie Norton Whitney married Gerald's Yale classmate, and Sara's old dance partner, Averell Harriman.)

In a certain sense, Gerald used *Within the Quota* to settle some old scores. In the scenario the immigrant — or "the European," as he is referred to — meets up with a slinky Millionairess with whom he dances a foxtrot, but she is frightened off by a Reformer. Then the European is diverted by the vaudeville dancing of the Colored Gentleman, who is driven away by a Prohibition agent. Finally "the Jazz Baby, who dances a shimmy in an enticing manner, is also quickly torn from him." They're all manifestations of the kind of patriarchal disapproval that had dogged Gerald in his youth and that, in part, had driven him from America. In the end the European overcomes that disapproval because he becomes a star. Perhaps Gerald hoped for the same thing.

It certainly seemed like a possibility at the Théâtre des Champs-Élysées on October 25, when "fashionable and artistic Paris," according to the *Herald*, "made up a brilliant first-night audience, with Americans much in evidence." Among those in the boxes were the Rudolph Valentinos, John Barrymore, and Elsie De Wolfe, along with her Anglo-Romanian diplomat husband, Sir Charles Mendl. As they leafed through their programs they must have admired Gerald's cover collage of New York City photographs — the Hudson River waterfront, the Battery, the Flatiron Building, the Woolworth Building — which the paper-doll Immigrant, in Sara's watercolor sketch, bestrode like a colossus. Only the most observant (and knowledgeable) among them would have noticed that the Mark Cross store on Fifth Avenue, with the company logo painted on the side of the building, had been planted between the Immigrant's legs.

They got all the other jokes, though. *Within the Quota* — the title made reference to a tide of pending anti-immigration legislation in the U.S. and Europe — "awoke laughter and applause." Reviews in both the French and U.S. press were unanimously enthusiastic. Gilbert Seldes praised it as "an

American ballet, the first . . . in which popular American music exclusively has been used in connection with an American theme."

In November the company took the ballet, along with the rest of its repertory, to the United States. But it was not performed at the invitation-only dress rehearsal at the Century Theatre (for which the publicist was the then underemployed critic Edmund Wilson). The audience, which included the sculptor and art collector Gertrude Vanderbilt Whitney (Cornelius Vanderbilt Whitney's mother) and John Dos Passos, seemed so mystified by the cutting-edge modernism of *Skating Rink* and *L'Homme et son désir* that Don Stewart, now back in America, offered to come before the curtain and provide humorous explanatory commentary on the ballets about to be performed. This tactic, shamelessly copied from a popular parodic Robert Benchley monologue called "The Treasurer's Report," puzzled the public even more deeply, and it was discarded after one performance.

The Swedes' prospects looked dim — but when *Within the Quota* joined the roster it received the equivalent of a hero's welcome. It was enormously popular, and was performed throughout the company's tour, from Washington, Philadelphia, Boston, and Buffalo, to Allentown, Scranton, Wilkes-Barre, Altoona, Rochester, Batavia, Utica, Dayton, Lima, and Columbus. In fact, it was the only "modernist" ballet retained on the program, *La Création du monde* and the rest having been dropped. And, whether through influence or noncausal synchronicity, ghost images of Gerald's striking design kept appearing long after the Ballets Suédois returned to France. There were John Dos Passos's newspaper-headline chapter headings in *Manhattan Transfer*, the novel he was working on when he went to the Suédois programs in New York; Stuart Davis's 1924 painting *Lucky Strike*, featuring a tobacco box, a packet of cigarette papers, and a pipe against the backdrop of an enormous newspaper; and nine years later Irving Berlin — who in the winter of 1923–24 was in New York supervising the early run of his *Music Box Revue* and would probably have attended at least one Ballets Suédois performance — created *As Thousands Cheer*, a musical entirely based on the concept and design of a newspaper come to life.

When he was interviewed by the *New York Herald* just before the premiere of *Within the Quota*, Gerald had said he believed that "Paris is bound to make a man either more or less American" — and the ambiguity was intentional. Although he had to be pleased by his American success, he had no desire to be a hometown boy who makes good; nor was he particularly interested in being lionized by the American community in Paris. At this moment, he had achieved considerable distinction as an American among Europeans, for which he was most proud.

But the balance was about to tip in the other direction. "RUSH OF TOUR-ISTS BEGINS IN EARNEST," the *Paris Herald* had declared, in type worthy of *Within the Quota*, on May 19: "Twenty-three Liners Bringing Thousands Are Due During Next Few Days." The *Herald* had interviewed one of them, a "Mr. Babbitt," at the Gare St.-Lazare; "I've come to Europe for three months of rum and fun," he said. You may print the fact that America is not dry, but it costs so much to get a glow over there that there isn't any fun left." At the other extreme, new American arrivals included the lawyer-turned-poet Archibald MacLeish, the returning expatriate newsman Ernest Hemingway, and the bestselling novelist Scott Fitzgerald. All of them were coming to Paris — not for the "rum and fun" — but because the favorable exchange rate allowed them to live on what Fitzgerald called "practically nothing a year," and because, as Gertrude Stein wrote, "Paris was where the twentieth century was." It wasn't long before their paths converged on Gerald and Sara Murphy's threshold.

12

"Very serious over trivialities and rather wise about art and life"

In early 1924, as *Within the Quota* was winding up its barnstorming tour of the minor cities of the Alleghenies, its designer and scenarist was making a sensation in Paris that rivaled the one created by the fictional hero in his ballet. On February 7, the day of the *vernissage* or installation for the 1924 Salon des Indépendents, four workmen walked into the Grand Palais carrying an enormous canvas stretched between two steel poles; more workmen followed, lugging an assortment of steel pipes and casing, which they began to build into a colossal frame. When the hanging committee for the Salon asked what was going on, they were told that this was the entry of M. Gerald Murphy, a painting eighteen feet tall by twelve feet wide entitled *Boatdeck*.

According to recent practice, work by Indépendents exhibitors was to be grouped by nationality; but the other paintings by American artists were hung in a room too small to accommodate the gigantic canvas. The only place for it was on the grand staircase leading to the American gallery in the Grand Palais's rotunda; but once installed there the picture not only dwarfed the other works in size, it overwhelmed them pictorially. On a canvas the size of a small house, Gerald had painted a closely cropped view of the smokestacks, steam pipes, and rigging of an ocean liner. As he wrote later, he had been "struck by the look (especially with the floodlights at night) of the huge almost vertical red-lead-colored smoke-stacks against the sky and the wires of the radio-telegraph, at their base the squat conglomeration of rectangular, ships-white-with-black-trim officer's cabins, dead-white mushrooming ventilators with black, gaping pure-circle mouths cut across with white rods spaced into six geometrical segments. Gray, white, black & red-lead: the whole."

Although there may have been a personal subtext to the painting — this was, after all, the sort of liner that was bringing his countrymen to France by the thousands — there was nothing personal about its presentation. The dark circles of the steam-pipe mouths, the hard white and gray cubes of the officer's quarters, were as abstract as any of the shapes that Gerald had drawn for Goncharova. In its monumentality, its vividness, its opaque, posterish simplicity, *Boatdeck* out-Légered Léger — and the polite little paintings by the other American artists chugging along in its wake seemed almost irrelevant.

Its hanging precipitated the kind of ritual crisis the French do so well: A contingent of disgruntled (and anonymous) artists claimed the painting's size and placement were an affront; the only reason for *Boatdeck*'s prominent position, they claimed, was some kind of pernicious inside dealing, and they wanted it moved, or removed entirely. An emergency meeting of the executive committee of the Indépendents was called; but the committee elected to keep the picture where it was, whereupon the president, Paul Signac, and another member, Carlos Reymond, resigned in protest. However, cooler heads prevailed upon the outraged duo to reconsider, and the following day they withdrew their resignations. In the meantime *Boatdeck* had become the talk of the show: on opening day, reported the *Herald*, "It could scarcely be seen, so great was the crush around [it]."

The crowds hardly thinned as the week went on, and the painting's creator got almost as much attention as his picture. He was photographed in front of it by the *Herald*, wearing a bowler, bow tie, and banker's pinstripes; another photographer caught him on his balcony overlooking the Seine, this time in a tweed Norfolk jacket, striped four-in-hand, and soft hat. You couldn't pick up a newspaper or magazine without reading about Gerald Murphy and *Boatdeck*. It was just like the publicity campaign in *Parade*; and if the profiles and news items seemed to focus on the sideshow rather than the real spectacle, it wasn't entirely the journalists' fault. They had help.

"If they think my picture is too big," Gerald told the *Herald*'s interviewer, with calculated grandiosity, "I think the other pictures are too small. After all, it is the Grand Palais." To the journalist from *L'Éclair* (who seems not to have been aware how thoroughly his leg was being pulled) he declared he was "truly sorry to have caused such a bother with my little picture." It was, after all, so much smaller than a *real* ocean liner — and smaller than the five huge billboards he said he had been commissioned to paint for a Pittsburgh freight terminal. Perhaps it was a good thing that Sara was nowhere in evidence for this interview; she could never have kept a straight face.

Even after the Indépendents exhibit was over and *Boatdeck* had been rolled up and put in storage, the sideshow continued. In the spring, when the Murphys went to Étienne de Beaumont's benefit gala, an "automotive ball" held at the Théâtre de la Cigale in Montmartre, Man Ray photographed them in their costumes: Sara in chauffeur's goggles and a dress of clinging silver foil, with her pearls wound around her neck three times; Gerald in tights and a metallic tunic that he had to be welded into, with a speakerphone fastened to the shoulder, and a towering headpiece bristling with hubcaps or headlamps. This double portrait had an emblematic significance: "To be done by Man Ray," said Sylvia Beach, the owner of the bookstore and expatriate headquarters Shakespeare and Company, "meant that you rated as somebody."

By now Gerald's celebrity had begun to resonate, not just within the world of the Parisian avant-garde, but in the growing expatriate American artistic community; he had, after all, already arrived where many of them aspired to go. Harry Crosby, cofounder with his wife of the Black Sun Press, met the Murphys through a mutual friend named Ben Kittredge at Ciro's — *the* nightclub of the moment — and was impressed by Gerald's reputation and Sara's indefinable allure. "Mr. and Mrs. [Gerald] Murphy were with us," he wrote to his mother, "he I liked a lot — very serious over trivialities and rather wise about art and life. You know he paints. . . . His wife very sphinx-like but knowing — particularly when she danced."

Crosby, the young, Harvard-educated nephew of J. P. Morgan, Jr., had stunned his Boston family by throwing over his job with the family bank in order to devote himself to the pursuit of culture and pleasure in Paris. Although he burned with a harder flame than the Murphys felt comfortable with — one of his parties featured a skeleton, with a black-bordered condom for a tongue, standing by the door like a butler — both Gerald and Sara liked him very much. He was dazzlingly handsome and vulnerable, in a Back Bay Byronic way, and the Murphys thought his eccentricities charming. Once they came to the Crosbys' tiny house near the Cimetière du Montparnasse to get a reference for a governess who had cared for Harry's stepchildren, and found him drinking champagne on the roof. It seemed the most natural thing in the world just to scramble up and join him. (They cared less for his wife, the self-named Caresse, whom they had known when she was Polly Jacob: "we always thought of her as a poseuse," Gerald told a friend, "affected and downright phony, tho' she was clever enough to go down with many people.")

Not all their new acquaintances were as congenial as Harry Crosby. Robert McAlmon, the writer and publisher of Contact Editions (which brought out Gertrude Stein's *The Making of Americans* as well as books by William Carlos Williams, H.D., Mina Loy, and the newcomer Ernest Hemingway), thought the Murphys "chic (which was unpardonable)." So he would try to horrify them by sprinkling his conversation with four-letter words, confiding intimate details of his sex life in mixed company, or shouting, "Where's the wotter clozit?!" in their quai des Grands-Augustins living room.

Sometime in May 1924 the Murphys met someone else who could, on occasion, be as maladroit as McAlmon, but who seemed to them infinitely more sympathetic. Scott Fitzgerald had made a reputation in America as the author of two novels, *This Side of Paradise* — the book that had defined the Jazz Age — and *The Beautiful and Damned*. His short stories, which appeared in all the glossy magazines, had established the stereotype of the flapper. He had married Zelda Sayre, "the most beautiful girl in Alabama *and* Georgia" (as he described her to Dorothy Parker), and the two of them had been painting New York City pink for the past several years. Their wading expeditions in the fountain in front of New York's Plaza Hotel — or was it the fountain in Washington Square Park? — were already the stuff of legend, but bootleg booze and night-long parties had taken a toll both on their finances and on Fitzgerald's creative output. So they had come to France to live more austerely while he tried to finish the novel that was to become *The Great Gatsby*.

In New York they had been friends of Gilbert Seldes and John Dos Passos and Esther Murphy — all of whom they invited to Christmas dinner in 1923 along with Edmund Wilson, a mentor of Fitzgerald's from Princeton. So when they arrived in Paris to live it was natural that they should seek out Gerald and Sara, who were so well established and well connected, and so much fun besides.

The two couples, outwardly so unalike, were instantly attracted to each other. Gerald saw their relationship as a kind of mystical symbiosis: "We four communicate by our presence rather than by any means," he told the Fitzgeralds later. "Currents race between us regardless: Scott will uncover for me values in Sara, just as Sara has known them in Zelda through her affection for Scott." But it wasn't entirely a friendship of equals: from the first it was also a bond between parents and children.

On their side, the Murphys found the Fitzgeralds' youth and golden, all-American beauty irresistible. And the Fitzgeralds, who had been acting out like undisciplined, unchaperoned adolescents, were attracted by the Murphys' unconventional maturity: their paradoxical mixture of spontaneity and settledness, and their ability to balance their family life with their role as friends. Gerald was more than eight years older than Scott, Sara thirteen years older; they belonged to a prewar generation, and with three children to the Fitzgeralds' one they had a shining aura of parenthood that the Fitzgeralds never managed to achieve. Zelda had had strained relationships with both her parents: her admired but distant and authoritarian father, Judge Anthony Sayre, and her mother, a somewhat fey woman named Minnie Machen Sayre who had seemingly never recovered from *her* mother's suicide. Scott's childhood hadn't been much more comfortable: his father, Edward Fitzgerald, had failed in business, and his overprotective mother, Molly, made young Scott the uneasy focus of her thwarted ambitions. As he wrote to his Scribner's editor and confidant, Maxwell Perkins, "My father is a moron and my mother is a neurotic, half insane with pathological nervous worry." In some important way the Murphys began to seem like glamorous parental substitutes for the younger couple. No wonder they, like Dos Passos, began to call Gerald "Dow-dow," the nickname that was Honoria's equivalent of "Da-da."

For Fitzgerald, the Murphys had an additional attraction: they seemed to be exactly the kind of cultivated, aristocratic easterner he had always worshipped. There was Sara, the millionaire's daughter who had been presented at court, who had her engagement photograph on the cover of *Town and Country*, and whose very voice, like one of his own heroines', was "full of money." With her beautiful, original clothes — she had dresses from Poiret and Nicole Groult, and suits Gerald ordered for her from a gentleman's tailor named O'Rossen in the Palais Royale — she was elegant without being fashionable, the same way her idol, Violet, duchess of Rutland, had been. And there was Gerald, who had been Best Dressed at Yale, a member of DKE and Skull and Bones, whose accent was so upper-class that he pronounced the word *first* as if it had an umlaut in it — and who was not only glamorous and (apparently) wealthy, but successful in a way Fitzgerald did not feel himself to be.

For although his books had propelled Fitzgerald onto the bestseller lists and into the gossip columns, they hadn't attracted the kind of critical acclaim he longed for; and on his arrival in France he was still smarting from the failure of his play, *The Vegetable*, which had self-destructed six months earlier during its out-of-town tryout. "It was a colossal frost," the chastened playwright said later. "People left their seats and walked out, people rustled their programs and talked audibly in loud, impatient whispers." The contrast with Gerald — whose photograph was in the rotogravure section but who also got praise from Picasso and Léger, and whose only foray into the theater had been a success on both sides of the Atlantic — was not lost on him. His admiration for the older man was tinged with envy, and something darker: "When I like men I want to be like them," he wrote. "I want to lose the outer qualities that give me my individuality and be like them. I don't want the man; I want to absorb into myself all the qualities that make him attractive and leave him out."

Shortly before the Fitzgeralds met them, Gerald and Sara had fallen in love with a beautiful old house in suburban St.-Cloud that belonged to the heirs of the French composer Charles Gounod. Three stories high, built of rosy brick with pointed gables, it was surrounded by green lawns and enormous oaks; a high brick wall went around the property, but from the upper windows one could see the Eiffel Tower far away across the river.

The Gounod family had fallen on hard times and wanted to rent the house;

and since the quai des Grands-Augustins was crowded and inconvenient for children, the Hôtel des Reservoirs too far from Paris to work as a family headquarters, the Murphys jumped at it. St.-Cloud had a true village character, with a cobbled main street and quaint old town hall; but it was only fifteen minutes by train from the center of Paris, and there were fifty-two trains a day back and forth. It seemed like a perfect place for the children, and by keeping the Paris apartment as a *pied-à-terre* Gerald and Sara ensured that they wouldn't settle down into suburban stolidity. Gerald, certainly, had some ambivalence about the materialistic drag a bourgeois existence could put on him: in his art notebook he outlined a surreal composition in which tiny people are seen "climbing seriously" onto gigantic furniture, or laboriously manipulating a "huge pencil to write notes on square feet of paper." Whether this represented "man's good-natured tussle with the giant material world" or "man's unconscious slavery to his material possessions," Gerald didn't seem sure.

By April the Murphys had moved into the Gounod house and were able to welcome both grandfathers, Frank Wiborg and Patrick Murphy, to a luncheon and Easter egg hunt, won by Baoth, then nearly five. Blond and sturdy in his shorts, Eton collar, and hand-knit pullover, he quickly filled his arms to overflowing with brightly painted eggs, easily outpacing his more tentative three-and-a half-year-old brother, who found only one and seemed unsure of what to do with it. Honoria, with the demure maturity of her nearly six years, disregarded the eggs entirely; instead she amused herself with a tin whistle that one of the grandfathers brought. The adults watched them as if they were at a play: Frank Wiborg in the formal morning coat, high collar, and four-in-hand he believed constituted proper church attire; Patrick Murphy, bald and bow-tied; Gerald and Sara, in their well-cut Sunday suits, she with her pearls looped around her throat.

There were no other family members at the party, although Hoytie was still in Paris and Fred Murphy was also living there. He had returned from the war a hero and in shattered health; and in 1920 he had married a friend of Esther's named Noel Haskins — a willowy blond beauty who was an aspiring lieder singer. They had settled at first in New York, but Fred had been unable to strike a balance with his father that would permit him to remain actively involved with Mark Cross. There was some kind of final rupture between them about which no one would say anything directly, and he and Noel had come to France; but because of Fred's congenital ill health they lived quietly and didn't frequent the vernissages and manifestations in Gerald and Sara's orbit, so the two couples saw little of one another.

On this particular Easter, however, Fred's health, as well as what Noel called "the trouble with his father" and the lingering effects of his war experience, had brought him to a critical juncture. He was in persistent pain from the thigh that had been shattered in the attack on the Somme; although the French government awarded him the Cross of the Legion of Honor for his wartime gallantry in October 1923, neither this decoration, nor surgery that winter, alleviated his increasing distress. In addition he had been losing weight steadily and suffering from what now would be diagnosed as post-traumatic stress disorder: sleeplessness and delirium in which, Noel reported, he was "*quite off his head,* but with no fever." Gerald and Sara, sensing he did not have much more time, had taken the children to see him. Honoria remembers him, barely, as a long-limbed form in a narrow white iron hospital bed, his red hair bright against the white linen pillowcase.

He had tried a cure at a spa called Divonne, but it had only minimal effect. In desperation Noel had written to Anna Murphy. Fred's doctors, she reported,

> all agree that overlooking the fact of who is to blame — (that's not the point) — the mental unrest — *(caused by the misunderstanding)* — & the pains go hand in hand.
>
> I wrote Mr. Murphy that several times but received no response.
> I don't care who is right or wrong — I only want Fred to get well.
> Have I made myself plain?

If this was the reason for Patrick's Easter visit, the reunion didn't do much good. Although the rift between father and son may have been patched over, Fred's condition worsened. In 1914, when Fred had been sent to the Mayo Clinic with his ulcer, Gerald had been the one to "take charge" and "step into command," but this time he could do nothing to help his brother. On May 23, 1924, Frederic Timothy Murphy died — whether from the aftereffects of his leg wound, a perforated ulcer, or some combination of the two was never entirely clear — and Gerald was left an uneasy only son.

It was during this spring that Gerald began work on two paintings whose family iconography gives them a painfully poignant edge. He made notes for some of his paintings now, a few words and sometimes a partial sketch in a schoolboy's *carnet*, and checked them off when he completed them:

> Picture: razor, fountain pen; etc. in large scale nature morte
>   big match box.

In the finished painting, which measures 32 ⅝ inches by 36 ½ inches, the safety razor and pen are crossed, like heraldic quarterings, in front of a gigantic box of matches that appears to be balanced on three other boxes or cubes. Although the picture seems straightforward and accessible, it's subtly unsettling. The perspectives in the painting are awry: the matchbox top is presented flatly, as if seen from directly above, while the section that holds the matches is done in receding perspective. The razor, as Gerald himself described it later, was shown "mechanically, in profile and in section, from three points of view at once." Even the pen is given a yellow highlight where a shadow should be.

It's a powerfully elegant painting, and at first glance it seems to fulfill Gerald's ambition to "*re*-present . . . real objects which I admired . . . along with purely abstract forms." But there's something monumental and brooding about the objects in the picture that seems to hint at a deeper personal significance. There's the pen, the instrument of office life that Gerald, and Fred, had left behind when they immigrated to France; and the razor, which Gerald had tried to patent for the Mark Cross Company. The model was even a Gillette, the kind that had beaten his own entry to the market. And there's the box, whose label, "Three Stars Safety Matches," could stand for the three Murphy children — Gerald's hope for the future, and his insulation against the hurts of the past.

The other painting he began at this time provides a kind of countervision to the picture he later called *Razor*. It is a nearly six-and-a-half-foot-square rendering of the inside of a watch, laid against a background of even more watch dials, stems, and wheels. Gerald said he was "struck by the mystery and depth of the interior of a watch"; and this mystery is heightened by his use of color, or noncolor. *Watch* is painted in more than fourteen shades of gray, with the merest touches of gold and ocher to highlight and shade the watchcase.

The image has obvious modernist connections: By his own admission Gerald was trying to do with paint what Poulenc had done in his *Mouvements perpétuels*, which the composer had played for Gerald and Sara on their piano at home; he may also have been stimulated by seeing Man Ray's 1924 rayograph silver print of the interior wheels of a clock's works. And there is no denying that the enormous wheels of this much-magnified watch make a powerful futurist statement about machine-age complexity. But there are even stronger personal undertones to this painting than there are to *Razor*.

The picture has two likely models for its literal inspiration. One is the gold pocket watch Sara had given Gerald as a present during their engagement — until then, he told her, he had "never had anything valuable of my own" — which he liked to keep propped on a table with its mechanism showing. The other is a larger "railroad" watch specifically designed for his father's Mark Cross Company. So the watch in the picture, however abstracted, seems to invoke Gerald's ambivalent feelings about his family (who had never given him "anything valuable"), and about his father and his father's business. In addition, the myriad dials and springs and levers in the painting, magnified to hundreds of times their normal size, have an overpowering quality, heightened by the placement of the enormous winding stem at the top of the canvas, where it looks like a crown. As one critic later pointed out, this placement seems to declare that time is king, or, as T. S. Eliot more memorably put it in *The Waste Land*, which was published in 1922 and which Gerald might easily have read, "Hurry up please its time." In this picture, time runs out for some: on the watch's main spring is embossed the initial "F," which could stand for Fred.

Both these pictures, which Gerald was working on in 1924, have the clean surface and the crisp edges of cubist paintings, portraying the shapes of things without the sloppy shading of sentiment. But they are far from contentless. For someone as eager for precision and control as Gerald was, the creation of overtly nonemotional works like *Razor* and *Watch* provided a way to make abstractions of feelings that otherwise might threaten his equilibrium. Gerald said almost nothing about his brother's death, and very little about the complicated relationship between himself, Fred, and their father. But he made two pictures in the year his brother died, and each of them tells more than he probably wished it to about how he felt. Perhaps it's no accident that in later years he used the words *instrument de précision*, usually applied to a high-quality chronometer, to stand for that hopelessly imprecise and unreliable thing, the human heart.

Spring brought the summertime expatriates back to Paris: John Dos Passos; Gilbert Seldes, with his fiancée, Alice Hall; Donald Ogden Stewart, who was working on a humorous novel about an Ohio couple called *Mr. and Mrs. Haddock Abroad.* Stewart became an almost nightly dinner guest of the Murphys, bringing each day's pages of his manuscript around to the quai des Grands-Augustins to read them aloud to his hosts, and sometimes to Seldes or Dos Passos. He found an appreciative audience, particularly in Sara, who had a wonderfully raucous laugh when she was really amused. Sometimes, Stewart recalled, they all went to Joe Zelli's nightclub in Montmartre, "where being a guest of the Murphys entitled one to 'the royal box.'" Zelli's had succeeded Le Boeuf sur le Toit as the hot club of the moment, and had "the best jazz band and the prettiest girls."

At some point that spring Stewart finally got the Murphys together with Archibald and Ada MacLeish. MacLeish — a lanky, sandy-haired, sleepy-eyed former football star from Glencoe, Illinois, whose father, a Scottish immigrant, had made a fortune with the Chicago dry goods firm of Carson Pirie Scott — had quit his job with a Boston law firm the day he made partner. He wanted to come to France to learn about poetry, and his wife, Ada, a pretty, plump, birdlike singer with a silvery soprano, wanted to pursue a concert career. They had arrived in Paris in the fall, and were living in a cold-water flat on the boulevard St.-Michel that they'd found through another couple the Murphys knew, Richard and Alice Lee Myers. Stewart, who had gone to Yale with Archie MacLeish, brought them around to the quai des Grands-Augustins; but at first Gerald and Archie circled one another warily, like young bucks in spring. Gerald, Archie said later, "was just instinctively leery of 'Bones' men"; and Archie and Ada were somewhat envious of and put off by the familiarity the Murphys so evidently had with the inner circles of the avant-garde. "We went . . . to the Strawinsky festival," MacLeish wrote sniffily to a friend early that summer. "Don Stewart was there with the Murphys & [they] proudly retired at the beginning of the second part of the program to miss Pachinella (?) & came back later for Noces."

Soon after seeing the MacLeishes at the Stravinsky festival, the Murphys returned to Antibes for the summer. They invited Dos Passos and Stewart to join them later at the Hôtel du Cap, and they encouraged Scott and Zelda Fitzgerald to think about coming south for the summer also. They knew how much Zelda loved to swim, and how much the Fitzgeralds wanted to econo-mize — and they were delighted when their new friends rented a villa in Valescure, about twenty-five miles away along the coast. Soon, however, the Murphys found themselves truly put to the test in their roles as surrogate parents.

At first Valescure seemed the ideal solution to the Fitzgeralds' needs: there was quiet and solitude for Scott to work on his novel, there was a nanny to look after two-year-old Scottie, and Zelda had the beach for a playground and a group of young aviators from the Fréjus air base a few miles away for play-mates. She and Scott befriended them, and he seemed glad of the distraction they provided for her.

When Gerald and Sara came over to Valescure from Antibes for the day, however, they noticed at once that something was going on between Zelda and one of the pilots, a golden-haired youth named Edouard Jozan. "I must say," remarked Sara, "everybody knew it but Scott." The Murphys saw Zelda on the beach with Jozan, and dancing with him at the casino. "I don't know how far it really went," said Gerald — but in her semiautobiographical novel, *Save Me the Waltz*, Zelda intimated that it went pretty far indeed. "He was bronze and smelled of the sand and sun," wrote Zelda of the blond, aquiline Jacques Chevre-Feuille, who plays Jozan's part in the novel; "she felt him naked underneath the starched linen. She didn't think of David [her hus-band]. She hoped he hadn't seen; she didn't care." When Scott finally did see what was happening, Gerald Murphy remembered later, "It did upset [him] a good deal. I wonder whether it wasn't partly his own fault?"

On July 13, according to Fitzgerald's ledger, there was a crisis. Whether Scott confronted her about Jozan, or she him; whether Zelda was "locked in my villa for one month to prevent me from seeing [Jozan]," as she later claimed; or whether Jozan was fortuitously transferred; Jozan and Zelda were suddenly no longer seen together. But the crisis wasn't over, merely shelved. Gilbert Seldes brought his bride to the Côte d'Azur at the beginning of August on their honeymoon. Driving to the beach with the Fitzgeralds he was alarmed when Zelda demanded that Scott give her a cigarette just as the narrow road made a hairpin turn. Scott, taking his hands off the steering wheel to rummage in his pocket, only barely managed to keep the car from plunging over the side of the road. On other occasions, Sara and Gerald noticed, the Fitzgeralds would leave parties and go to Eden Roc, at the tip of Cap d'Antibes near the hotel, where Zelda would strip off her evening dress and dive into the sea in her slip from thirty-five-foot rocks. Scott, terrified but unwilling to admit it, would take off his dinner jacket and pumps and follow her. When Sara tried to tell Zelda it was dangerous, Zelda merely fixed her with what Gerald described as her "unflinching gaze, like an Indian's," and said, "But Say-ra, didn't you know? We don't believe in conservation."

On one such evening the Murphys prevailed on the Fitzgeralds not to drive back to Valescure, but to stay the night at the Hôtel du Cap. In the small hours of the morning Gerald and Sara were awakened by a furious knocking on the door of their room. Outside stood Scott, clutching a candle and clammy with fright. "Zelda's sick," he said; and, as Sara and Gerald followed him to the Fitzgeralds' room, he added, "I don't think she did it on purpose." When she found out that Zelda had swallowed an overdose of sleeping pills, Sara tried to get her to drink olive oil to counteract the drugs. But Zelda protested, irrationally, "Sara . . . don't make me drink that, please. If you drink too much oil you turn into a Jew." So Sara and Gerald made her walk up and down until dawn to keep her awake. In the morning the Fitzgeralds went back to Valescure, and the incident was never mentioned again.

That summer there were forest fires in the hills behind the coast, and the air was perfumed with the smell of burning eucalyptus, the blue sky hazed over with smoke. But there was more than eucalyptus in the air. This sleepy stretch of coastline was beginning to be discovered. The owner of the Château de la Garoupe, where the Murphys had first stayed with the Porters in 1922, would come over to the Hôtel du Cap and ask Antoine Sella, "Who are all these people I don't know?" Rudolph Valentino, the film star whose slinky, slightly sinister sexuality had made him a heartthrob on three continents, came to stay in a château in Juan-les-Pins with his wife, Natasha Rambova (née, somewhat less exotically, Winifred Hudnut). Noel Murphy and John Dos Passos and Donald Ogden Stewart all came in Noel's old six-cylinder Renault on their way back from Pamplona, in Spain, where they had gone to see the running of the bulls at the Fiesta of San Fermín with their friend Ernest Hemingway. The nearsighted Stewart had two cracked ribs from a tussle with the yearling bull Hemingway had dared him to fight: he'd had to take his glasses off and he hadn't seen the bull come at him. But Gerald and Sara soon nursed him back to health with daily trips to La Garoupe and delicious Provençal meals eaten on the shady porch of the Hôtel du Cap, and all of them went to Nice to the bookshop where the expatriate literary magazine *the trans-atlantic* was on sale with a "Work in Progress by Donald Ogden Stewart" advertised on the cover. The Picassos came back to Juan-les-Pins, and the de Beaumonts, and the Barrys and the prince and princess de Faucigny-Lucinge returned to their villas in Cannes. (Johnny Lucinge, as everybody called him, claimed that the Murphys invented the Riviera in the summer.)

That was when, Gerald said, "we saw what was happening down there — the crowd of people that was coming in — and realized that if we wanted to live simply we would have to hit out and get our own villa." On the slope above Golfe Juan, between two dirt tracks called the Chemin de Mougins and the Chemin des Nielles, they found a 7,600-square-meter piece of property with a modest turn-of-the-century villa called the Chalêt des Nielles. The villa was nothing much, fourteen rather small rooms under a peaked chalet roof, but there were some tumbledown outbuildings on the property, including an old donkey stable, which could be made into a studio, and the view from the hillside was breathtaking: You could see Juan-les-Pins to the north, and the Cap to the south, and the blueberry-colored Mediterranean stretched away to the west toward the Îles de Lérins and Cannes. On a clear day, with the mistral blowing, the dark cones of the Esterel Massif behind Cannes looked close enough to touch. And the garden was spectacular: the current owner, a French army officer who had spent his career as a military attaché in the Middle East, was an enthusiastic amateur gardener, and he had brought back numerous exotic specimens from his travels. There were lemon trees, date palms, and genuine cedars of Lebanon; pepper trees, persimmons, and white-leaved Arabian maples; *Pittosporum coriacaeum*, desert holly, eucalyptus, and *Punica granatum*; olive and fig trees, mimosa and heliotrope, and a huge linden tree that shaded the terrace near the house.

"I think," Gerald had written to Sara during their courtship, "we shall always enjoy most the things we plan to do of our own accord — and together, even among others, but in our *own* way." Now they had found the "little farm" they had longed for since before their marriage, the plot of land on which they could nurture their family and become, at last, the people they had always planned to be, doing things in their *own* way. It took only a minute's hesitation before they agreed to pay 350,000 francs — about a quarter of Sara's yearly income — to buy it. On the deed, which they signed in September, Gerald listed his profession as *"artiste peintre."* By the time they left Antibes to go back to Paris, they had engaged a pair of Ohio architects named Hale Walker and Harold Heller to remodel the house. And they had given it a name. They called it Villa America.

13

"Our real home"

BACK IN ST.-CLOUD that autumn of 1924, Gerald and Sara found that Archie and Ada MacLeish had fled the high Parisian rents and were now their neighbors at 10 Parc Montretout. As Ada MacLeish wrote to a friend, "the Gerald Murphys, whom we like enormously, live near us, so we really haven't a want."

Between Archie and Gerald there now sprang up a friendship that — on Gerald's side at least — was perhaps the longest and most truly fraternal of his life. The two men shared a certain sense of dislocation articulated in MacLeish's notebook description of his poetic protagonist, L. T. Carnavel, who "had all his life from adolescence the conviction — at first merely sensed, that his consciousness of time & space, his individualness, his being himself, his detachment from conscious matter etc. — was the source of his unhappiness, or rather of his not-happy-ness. As a young man he tried to subject the universe to his consciousness (i.e. to annihilate the gulf between himself & the universe by translating the universe into terms of himself." Carnavel was meant to be MacLeish's self-portrait; but he could just as easily have been Gerald's.

In this friendship between brothers, however, Gerald had the advantage of the firstborn. Archie was spending long hours at the Bibliothèque Nationale and at Sylvia Beach's Shakespeare and Company bookshop, reading the books he hoped would help him to become the poet he wanted to be — works by Dante, Rimbaud, Laforgue, T. S. Eliot, Ezra Pound, whose absence from his curriculum at Yale made him feel his four years in New Haven had been wasted time. Gerald — who had become a voracious reader and copied out passages he liked in Pushkin or Shakespeare so as to memorize them — had similar feelings about their shared alma mater. But he had spent the past few years getting the real-life grounding in modern culture that MacLeish now aspired to. "Gerald was a remarkable companion," said MacLeish, "and very knowledgeable, not scholarly, but very knowledgeable."

He *knew* the composers Ada MacLeish was studying and whose works she wanted to sing: Satie, Poulenc, Stravinsky. He and Sara had sung Negro spirituals from his collection, as they used to do in Cambridge, for Satie after a dinner party, just the two of them at the piano; and Satie, after listening once, made them turn around and sing them again, a cappella. "Never sing them any other way," he said. And Satie, like Poulenc and Marcelle Meyer (who brought her baby to be admired), came out to visit "les Murphy" at St.-Cloud, turning down an invitation from Vincente Huidobro, the publicist for the Ballets Suédois, to do so; his rendezvous with these "useful and precious Americans," he said, was *"very important"* (underlined three times). Gerald was a friend of the modern French writers, like Cocteau and Radiguet, who interested MacLeish. Then there were the painters: Léger, who, on the strength of the Murphys' introduction became an intimate of both MacLeishes, and Picasso, with whom they never got quite so close. MacLeish was no rube, and he would have learned to appreciate these figures by himself. But he would not have known them in the same way. In February he wrote to a friend that he was "stirred by poetry by music now as I wish I might still be by my less elaborate desires. That is to say — I never more see beautiful women. I see lonely and uncapturable gestures, swift nuances of an arm, curves of a breast, a throat — lines, forms. . . . To write one must take the world apart and reconstruct it." It sounds like Gerald talking, or Goncharova speaking through him. And the immediate result of this thinking was perhaps MacLeish's most famous poem, begun in his notebook in March:

> A poem should be palpable and mute
> As a globed fruit,
>
> . . . .
>
> A poem should be equal to:
> Not true.

For all the history of grief
An empty doorway and a maple leaf.

For love
The leaning grasses and two lights above the sea —

A poem should not mean
But be.

Many years later Archie said that he had been friends with the Murphys "in French terms," by which he meant he knew them as Europeans in a European setting, not as Americans uncomfortably transplanted to an alien shore. It was an important distinction. Within this context, the MacLeishes soon developed a "very easy, hometown sort" of relationship with their new neighbors: "We would drop in or suggest that we would drop in, propose ourselves, and if they were going to be home we'd go out [and] see them." It was a profitable connection: through the Murphys, Ada became "very solid with Marcelle Meyer" — in fact, Ada wrote a friend excitedly, "She has asked me to share a program with her in the spring."

In April, Archie and Gerald took one of several long bicycle trips together, through the Burgundy countryside. Was it Gerald's painter's eye, and his appreciation of all things simple and sensual, that made MacLeish see everything in a new way? Archie's journal recorded "Stripes of mustard yellow, green, young green, the far blue hills, the cattle . . . luncheon by the rapid brook — the vague sun, the vague green trees, the white, lean bread, the cheese of St. Florentin, the Chablis (G.C. 1911) and the hunger to eat it with." In a road-mender's hut near Vézelay they found a message scrawled on the wall: "*La vie est un desert, la femme un chameau. Pour voir le desert il faut monter sur le chameau.*" ("Life is a desert, woman is a camel. If you want to see the desert you have to ride the camel.")

MacLeish would not quarrel with that — he had always had an eye for a woman. The preceding spring, MacLeish had an affair with Margaret Bishop, the wife of his friend, the poet John Peale Bishop. Ada had either not known of it or had chosen to ignore it, and the relationship had ended when the Bishops left Paris to return to New York. Now, like many a man before and after him, he found himself admiring Sara Murphy. In his notebook for 1924 to 1925 he began a poem, which he later revised and published, entitled "Sketch for a Portrait of Mme. G—— M——," perhaps not so coincidentally the same title Gerald had given to a proposed painting for which he had made notes. Whereas Gerald saw his wife in terms of objects — "lace, globe, black stems of wood coming at you at an > [he had drawn an angle], magnolia petals, snow flakes vertically falling, mirror, moulding tracery of crossed twigs" — Archie described her physical presence, "the curve her throat made that was not the curve / Of any other." More than that, though, he tried to capture the way she had of creating her own cosmology:

> Sara never lodged in a house. She lived in it.
> There was not one — & there had been as many
> As there were reasons to be somewhere else —
> Of all her houses that had not become
> The one house that was meant for her, no matter
> Whom it was meant for when the walls were raised —
> Even to furnished villas like the one
> Above the Seine that had belonged to Gounod. . . .
> And that was a strange house.

Not satisfied that he had got her right, MacLeish crossed out this draft and began again. At last he had it:

> "Her room," you'd say — and wonder why you'd called it
> Hers . . .
> . . . .
> Whether you came to dinner or to see
> The last Picasso or because the sun
> Blazed on her windows as you passed or just
> Because you came, and whether she was there
> Or down below in the garden or gone out
> Or not come in yet, somehow when you came
> You always crossed the hall and turned the doorknob
> And went in; — "Her room" — as though the room

Itself were nearer her: . . .

. . . .

. . . "Her room," as though you'd said
Her voice, Her manner, meaning something else
Than that she owned it; knowing it was not
A room to be possessed of, not a room
To give itself to people . . .
. . . It reserved
Something that in a woman you would call
Her reticence by which you'd mean her power
Of feeling what she had not put in words —

"Very sphinxlike," Harry Crosby had called her. Whatever her elusive magic, it was the same kind she had exerted on Picasso — and now also upon Scott Fitzgerald, who returned to Paris that spring from a miserable winter in Rome. He and Zelda had found a dreary, dim apartment in the rue de Tilsitt near the Étoile, and since he had finished and sent to his publisher the manuscript of *The Great Gatsby*, Scott was somewhat at loose ends. This was the spring he described as composed of "1000 parties and no work" — although, as Gerald recalled, the Fitzgeralds "weren't really party people. It was just that every night they wanted things to happen. It didn't take a party to start them." They would drop in and out of whatever was going on — at someone's house, in a nightclub — and then, often, they would drive out to St.-Cloud and honk their horn outside the Murphys' gate, shouting that they were leaving France the next day on the *Lusitania* (a neat feat, as the ship had been sunk by German torpedoes in 1915) and had come to say good-bye. Gerald and Sara wouldn't answer the door, but the Fitzgeralds kept coming back.

One of the reasons, Gerald believed, was that Scott was "sentimentally disturbed by Sara" — he was "in love with her. She fascinated him, her directness and frankness were something he'd never run into before in a woman." Sara, who wasn't attracted by Scott's pretty-boy looks, pooh-poohed this idea. "He was in love with all women," she told a friend many years later. "He was sort of a masher, you know, he'd try to kiss you in taxis and things like that. But what's a little kiss between friends?" In fact, his absorption with Sara was singular: he would stare at her when they were at the dinner table, and if he felt she were paying him insufficient notice, he would demand, loudly, "Sara, look at me." He would do the most puerile things to get her attention. Once, in a taxi with her and Zelda, he began stuffing filthy old hundred-franc banknotes into his mouth, and Sara — who used to wash coins before giving them to her children — was horrified.

He behaved just as badly with Gerald. One evening the Murphys took the Fitzgeralds and the Barrys out to a new alfresco restaurant near the Champs-Élysées that had a dance floor and a gypsy band. None of these features impressed Fitzgerald, who was uninterested in food and music and almost never danced. (When he did, Gerald recalled, he looked like a college boy of the prewar years.) They had drinks and dinner, but they rose to leave soon after. "Scott used to be very clever while sitting down," Ellen Barry remembered, "but when he got up he'd be staggering." Now, whether the cause was drink or sophomoric theatrics, he sank to his knees on the dance floor and clutched at Gerald's hand, sobbing, "Don't go! Take me with you — don't leave me here!" Gerald withdrew his hand, furious. "This is not Princeton," he said to Fitzgerald tartly, "and I'm not your roommate."

Despite such rebuffs, Fitzgerald continued to be fascinated by Gerald. He asked him for literary advice — the letters from Fitzgerald to Maxwell Perkins urging the latter to acquire Raymond Radiguet for the Scribner's list probably have Gerald as their inspiration — and he made Gerald repeat stories over and over: the one about seeing a factory somewhere that manufactured dolls' voices, the one about meeting the American Indian named John Spotted Horse at Mitchell Field during the war. He would beg him to demonstrate the trick he'd learned from his father, Patrick: to stand on his hands and then walk the length of the room upside down. Scott loved it because it seemed so unlike Gerald. And he persistently tried to discover what made Gerald tick. Eyeing his friend's exquisite European clothes, he asked, "Are you what they call a fop?" (Scott's own sartorial expression was more in the Arrow Collar–ad mode.) No, Gerald told him. As he later explained it, "I was a dandy, which is something entirely different. . . . I liked clothes that were smart, without having any interest in fashions or styles, and I dressed just the way I wanted to, always."

Occasionally — whenever, it seemed, Fitzgerald sensed the balance of their relationship tilting too far in the paternal direction — Fitzgerald's fascination with Gerald might be tinged with belligerence. Once Scott tore into Gerald for the rather orotund way he sometimes spoke: "I hear a pulsing motor at the door," he might say, and Scott would respond witheringly, "God, how that remark dates you!" He would even criticize, obliquely, Gerald's elegance. Because he hated to carry money in his pockets (it spoiled the line of the suit), Gerald had commissioned a saddler to make him a copy of the bag used by messengers at the Bourse, or stock exchange: it was made of black pigskin and had buckled compartments for 500-franc notes and another section for larger notes. One day he was coming out of the bank and met Scott, who said rather hostilely, "I've been watching you, and I've decided you're a masochist — you go to all that trouble with buckles and straps and little bags because you're a masochist." Nonsense, retorted Gerald, "I like buckles and straps."

If there was a kind of reductive ambivalence in this exchange, there was also attraction; Fitzgerald had what amounted to a case of schoolboy hero worship for his older, suaver compatriot, colored with something more complicated that he couldn't yet identify. No wonder that, as Scott and Zelda made plans for the summer, they inevitably found themselves drawn to the Riviera — and the Murphys — again. They took an August lease on a villa in Antibes, and Scott began to make plans for a new novel. It would be, he told H. L. Mencken, "about myself — not what I thought of myself in *This Side of Paradise*. Moreover it will have the most amazing form ever invented." He didn't tell Mencken — he may not yet have known — that it would also be about Gerald and Sara, what he thought about them, and how they affected him. When it was finally published, almost ten years later, it would be called *Tender Is the Night*.

With Scott and Zelda Fitzgerald — and, to a lesser extent, with the MacLeishes and John Dos Passos — a pattern was emerging in the Murphys' friendships, a kind of familial bond in which Gerald was the father, a focus for admiration, need, jealousy, and rebellion, and Sara was both mother and Mother, both nurturer and object of desire. Their friends weren't the only beneficiaries of this arrangement: for both Murphys, such an extended surrogate family filled a reciprocal need. They each felt remote, if not estranged, from their own families, even those family members who lived in Europe and might be presumed to share their attitudes and interests. Hoytie Wiborg, for instance, although she occasionally swooped down upon them, was too grand and socially preoccupied to be congenial, and matters had been sticky between them ever since Sara had refused to invite a houseful of Hoytie's international society friends over from Cannes to stay. (Hoytie thereupon left in a huff with all her luggage, only to find she had missed the single train out of Antibes that day; she had to return, trunks and all, to the uncomfortable bosom of her family, where she spent the next forty-eight hours without exchanging one word with her sister and brother-in-law.)

Noel and Esther, both living in Paris, weren't much closer. Esther had taken up with the lesbian circle that had Natalie Barney for its center and was celebrated by Djuna Barnes in her *Ladies Almanack*. There Esther, "noted for her Enthusiasm in things forgotten, . . . grand at History, and nothing short of magnificent at Concentration," appears as Bounding Bess. But her relationship with "l'Amazone," as Barney was called, was uneasy. Barney worshipped beauty in all forms and must have been somewhat put off by Esther's gaunt figure and her squint, to say nothing of her erratic personal hygiene; and she would have found Esther's brilliant but obsessional manner of discourse — an acquaintance likened her to "an idiot savant" — unnerving. Esther, on her side, was quick to ridicule Barney's erotic pretentiousness: she wrote a wicked satirical portrait of l'Amazone lying "on her back in bed, clad only in a silk shirt, . . . eating" while being read to by a female companion from a tome called "Classical Erotology." When, not surprisingly, she is overcome with indigestion, she must flagellate the poor companion to get relief. Amusing as this portrait may have been to a certain audience, it wasn't the kind of thing Gerald or Sara found funny, and they saw Esther infrequently. Noel Murphy, who was fond of Esther, found this distancing act inexcusable, which may have partly explained her own cool feelings about Gerald. In addition, a friend suggested, she had herself formed an attachment to Janet Flanner, the *New Yorker's* Paris correspondent, and she felt suspicious of someone like Gerald who, she thought, might not be entirely honest with himself about his own sexuality.

It was tricky sailing in these familial waters; but as Gerald and Sara would discover, the currents that raced between themselves and their friends held just as many dangers.

By July 1925 the renovations on the Villa America were completed, and Gerald and Sara were at last able to move their family into what Gerald called "our real home." The modest chalet had been transformed: it was now a sleek art deco variation on a Mediterranean theme. Its limestone walls had been stuccoed beige; a third story had been added; and the peaked chalet roof had been replaced by a flat Moroccan-style one that also functioned as a sundeck for luxurious and private basking. The dark little house had now been opened up with generous windows through which you could see the gardens and the glorious view; and striped awnings and yellow louvered shutters could be drawn against the midday Provençal sun.

The entrance, on the ground floor, led into a hallway off of which were a guest bedroom and bath, kitchen, pantry, and servants' rooms, as well as a dining room with a fireplace and French doors. These opened onto a flagged terrace, on which was an enormous linden tree. On the second floor, in addition to a study and sewing room, was a drawing room that ran the entire width of the house; like the dining room, it had a fireplace and French doors, which opened onto a spacious awninged balcony. A spiral staircase led to the third floor, where the children each had a large corner bedroom, and Gerald and Sara a suite with bedrooms and dressing rooms, a bath, and another balcony.

On this architectural canvas Gerald and Sara proceeded to lay down the elements of their personal style. In the main reception rooms they showed off the same modern panache they'd exhibited at the quai des Grands-Augustins, with mirrored fireplace surrounds, sculptural tables that looked as if Brancusi had designed them, white-upholstered, stainless-steel furniture — all of it slinkily elegant and minimalist. Whitewashed walls and waxed black tile floors completed the look, but Sara enlivened the deco black-and-white severity with the vibrant colors of the Côte d'Azur: table linens were blue or yellow, or both, or pink, or apple green; some of the china was green majolica, which looked like curly lettuce leaves, or pink and orange Provençal faïence; and for dinner parties there were handblown Venetian goblets shot through with

opalescent swirls. In the bedrooms and study some of the Murphys' cherished
nineteenth-century American pieces, sturdily crafted of curly maple, found a
new home. Throughout the house huge glass vases were filled with flowers
from the garden: peonies or roses or heliotrope or lilies, punctuated sometimes by sprigs of parsley that looked like green lace. And for the flagged
terrace, which they would use as an outdoor living and dining room, Gerald
had found what was then entirely original furniture: instead of the traditional
wicker or wrought-iron froufrou, he had bought simple iron café chairs and
tables, of the kind used in every little bistro on the Côte, from a restaurant
supplier, and had painted them with silver radiator paint. It was all fresh,
eclectic, unexpected, way ahead of its time.

The Murphys' special touch extended to the land outside the villa, which
ultimately covered almost seven acres of hillside. Around the house they
restored and replanted a series of terraced gardens that resembled outdoor
rooms full of fragrant nooks and crannies for reading, napping, or daydreaming. In July they purchased an additional parcel of land containing an old
Provençal *bastide* or farmhouse — which they turned into a guest house —
and put in vegetable gardens, giving each of the children an individual plot
for whatever crops might suit their fancy. Honoria's preference, copied from
her mother's, was for rows of pungent herbs. Sara wrote to her father's clerk,
Mr. Steinmetz, at Ault and Wiborg in New York and got him to send her
American seed packets so she could plant sweet corn — something unheard
of in France, where corn is only for cows, and tastes like it. She and Gerald
put in a citrus orchard — there were already enough productive olive trees for
an annual harvest — and a variety of nut trees; and they acquired two cows to
provide the children with fresh milk (with her fear of germs where the children were concerned, Sara was distrustful of the commercially purchased
variety). In the garden Sara constructed a playhouse for Honoria and furnished it with chairs, tables, beds, linens, and cooking utensils, all to scale; in
the afternoons she would give Honoria cooking lessons, making miniature
cakes and pots of cocoa, and when Ada MacLeish was visiting she taught
Honoria how to make tiny baking powder biscuits, which they ate with honey
and butter.

At the entrance to the villa, on the Chemin des Mougins, there were two cement gateposts, one topped by a glass-enclosed case in which the estate title could be displayed. For this Gerald created a fourteen-by-twenty-one-inch signboard that (anticipating Jasper Johns by several decades) was a fantasia on the Stars and Stripes in oil paint and gold leaf. The left-hand side of its bisected rectangle shows half of an enormous six-pointed gold star, with five smaller stars (for the five Murphys?) between its points, all on a field of intense cobalt blue. The right-hand side is composed of broad horizontal stripes of red and white. Across both star and stripes the words VILLA AMERICA are emblazoned, one above the other, in block capitals. The letters on the starry left-hand side of the picture are white, with black shading, those on the striped right, black with white. The effect is striking visually, but also metaphorically: somehow the villa, like its owners, exists in two worlds at once — France and America, the real and the imagined.

To manage this real and imaginary kingdom the Murphys had help: there was an Italian gardener named Joseph Revello and his wife, Baptistine; a cook, Celestine; Ernestine Leray, nicknamed Titine, the *bonne à tout faire*; two under-gardeners; the farmer, Amilcar; and a chauffeur, Albert. (Sara had tried to learn how to drive her family's car at the Dunes, but she kept swerving off the road into the high privet hedges that line East Hampton's lanes, and finally she gave up trying.) And there was Vladimir Orloff, the aristocratic young Russian émigré whom the Murphys had met at Diaghilev's atelier: he had originally come to work as Gerald's studio assistant, but his skills as a conversationalist, cook, and storyteller had turned him into a kind of Lord Chamberlain, sometime chef, and children's tutor as well. He kept Honoria, Baoth, and little Patrick spellbound with his account of his father's death at the hands of the Bolsheviks (the elder Orloff, who had been the czarina's banker, was shot before his cadet son's horrified eyes), or his tales of a boy called Mowgli who had been raised by wolves. These he recited as a serial, one segment at a time, and made them so much his own that the little Murphys never knew they had originally been written by a Victorian Englishman called Kipling.

In the enchanted world of the Villa America, life ran according to the rules Sara and Gerald had set — it was, truly, a place where they could "do the things we want to do of our own accord . . . in our own way." In the mornings they rose early: after breakfast, which might include the American muffins that were Sara's specialty, Gerald went to paint in his studio; the children did lessons with Mademoiselle Géron or Vladimir (if he wasn't helping Gerald prepare canvases or mix pigments); and Sara discussed the week's menus with Celestine, went over the family accounts in her study, and walked through the gardens with Joseph to tell him what needed to be done.

Sometimes the mornings would be interrupted by the arrival of Monsieur Trasse, the barber from Antibes, who came to the villa on his bicycle every ten days to cut Gerald's hair. He might also trim Sara's — for that winter, after years of wearing her dark gold hair in modifications of the Gibson-girl style of her youth, she had given in to prevailing fashion and had it cut in a crisp, ear-length bob whose soft waves framed her face becomingly. (Stella Campbell, visiting the Murphys on one of her ever more frequent furloughs from the stage, was devastated: "Think," she moaned stagily to Gerald, "all that tender weight, gone!")

Shortly before noon Gerald would emerge from the studio, and everyone — the children, Mam'zelle, any guests staying in the *bastide*, and Gerald and Sara — would pile into cars or make their way on foot down the winding road to the little beach at La Garoupe. There the children did exercises with Gerald — head and leg lifts, yogic plows, and toe touches. Everyone sunbathed and swam. The water, clear enough for you to see your feet on the sandy bottom, was salty and just cold enough to be refreshing. The grown-ups chatted and drank dry sherry and nibbled on what John Dos Passos called "recondite *hors d'oeuvres*" — probably the delicious little crackers called *sables* that Honoria still remembers — and then after a while everyone went back to the villa for lunch. They ate at the big table on the terrace under the linden tree — an omelette and salad from the garden, or poached eggs on a bed of creamed corn with sautéed Provençal tomatoes on the side, or a plain dish of new potatoes, freshly dug, with butter from the villa's cows and fresh parsley, and simple local wine to wash it all down. The sky would harden into an intense blue, the earth would give back the smell of bracken and eucalyptus, and the air would throb with the shrilling of cicadas.

The children would be set down for an hour's siesta. They were allowed to choose where they napped and often took their folding cots into the garden. Once when the Picassos had come to lunch, little Paulo enlivened the children's siesta hour by gravely instructing them on the different parts of the anatomy, with particular attention to the ways boys are different from girls. After their naps there would be some wonderful pastime, an expedition or a treasure hunt or a costume party. Or there might be a children's art show, which the Murphys called the Salon de Jeunesse, for which Picasso served as organizer and judge. After one such exhibition, Honoria sent him a note in her charming, haphazardly phonetic French: "*Chere mecie picaso,*" she wrote, "*vous vous lé que je vous décine une animal.*" ("Dear Monsieur Picasso, would you like me to draw you an animal?") At the bottom of the page is a hippopotamus-like horse with a rider on its back that comically prefigures the equine victims of Picasso's masterpiece *Guernica.* Picasso reportedly adored it.

Late in the afternoon Gerald and Sara would often take the children to the Hôtel du Cap to swim at Eden Roc, or watch Archie MacLeish — he and Ada had rented a villa in Antibes that summer — do showy dives from the highest point. Or they would drive to Cannes, to the flower market, for armfuls of fresh stock, stopping on the way to buy cheese wrapped in a grape leaf from the vendor near the railroad tracks. And later, back at the Villa America, the children would have baths and supper, and the grown-ups would dress for dinner.

Sara had a phrase, "Dinner-Flowers-Gala," derived from the notation carried on ships' menus for the captain's dinner: it was Murphy language for any special occasion, and there were many. Not grand contrivances, like the de Beaumont's balls or Linda Porter's musical evenings — for Sara had grown to detest big parties and called them "holocausts" — but usually dinners for eight or ten. First there were Gerald's special cocktails on the terrace, cocktails that he claimed contained "just the juice of a few flowers," sometimes a concoction of brandy, liqueur, and lemon juice in stemmed glasses whose rims had been rubbed with lemon and dipped in coarse sugar, or something called a "Bailey," which had also, Gerald said, been "invented by me as were a great many other good things."

Gin (Booth's House of Lords) ⅗ ths
Grapefruit juice ⅕ th
Lime juice (fresh) ⅕ th
Mint (fresh) 1 sprig per person
Ice (a great deal)

The mint should be put in the shaker first. It should be torn up by hand as it steeps better. The gin should be added then and allowed to stand a minute or two. Then add the grapefruit juice and then the lime juice. Stir vigorously with ice and do not allow to dilute too much, but serve very cold, with a sprig of mint in each glass.

These Gerald mixed, Philip Barry said, like a priest preparing Mass, and he served them ritually: you were only allowed two cocktails, and you were not offered anything else to drink before dinner. During cocktails the children would come down in their bathrobes and sing a song, or dance (Honoria practiced for hours in her bedroom to a jazz recording sent by the drummer in Jimmy Durante's band); afterward they would say good night and go up to bed. And then there would be dinner under the linden tree, by candlelight, the women in their beaded dresses and the men in their dinner jackets, with everyone so young and merry and clever.

This was the summer, Scott Fitzgerald reported, when "there was no one at Antibes . . . except me, Zelda, the Valentinos, the Murphys, Mistinguet [*sic* — his misspelling of the French cabaret singer who was Maurice Chevalier's partner, lover, and mentor], Rex Ingram, Dos Passos, Alice Terry, the MacLeishes, Charlie Brackett, Maude Kahn, Esther Murphy, Marguerite Namara, E. Phillips Oppenheim, Mannes the violinist, Floyd Dell, Max and Chrystal Eastman, ex-premier Orlando, Etienne de Beaumont — just a real place to rough it, to escape from all the world." Donald Ogden Stewart, newly arrived from another visit to Pamplona with the Hemingways, felt "ominous signs" that the Murphys' undiscovered paradise was on the verge of being invaded: there were "wealthy vacationers" at the Hôtel du Cap and on the Plage de la Garoupe. But Sara saw it differently: "Most of them (the intruders) were very dear friends," she said many years later. Or if they weren't at first, they became so, if they were interesting. And then the Murphys made sure they became friends of *other* interesting people they knew, because it gave them so much pleasure to bring such people together.

It was the Murphys who introduced the MacLeishes to the Fitzgeralds, and to the de Beaumonts; the Murphys who asked Picasso to bring his friend Manuel Ortiz de Zarate — a minor cubist painter but major avant-garde personality — to a soirée because he seemed so *interesting;* the Murphys who gave an enchanted dinner party for Scott and Zelda Fitzgerald and the violinist David Mannes and his wife and daughter, Marya. That night, as the Mediterranean moon rose over Gerald and Sara's fragrant garden, Marya Mannes, responding to a "sense of glowing peace," turned to Fitzgerald, her dinner partner, and said, simply, how *happy* she was to be there. In thanks for that evening, she wrote her hosts a poem; David Mannes said the only way he and his wife could repay the Murphys was to give them a private concert of Bach's four-hand piano pieces the next day. "I've never been so moved," Gerald said, remembering it years later.

The parties weren't always for the adults: there were costume parties for the children at the screenwriter and movie producer Charles Brackett's house, and Scott and Zelda staged a memorable battle of tin soldiers in front of a fairy castle in their garden that was guarded by a "dragon," a large beetle in a wooden cricket cage, who was allowed to run away when the good soldiers won. Perhaps most magical of all was the excursion to the Antibes lighthouse that Gerald planned for Scottie Fitzgerald. He had told her that the lighthouse was populated by fairies who made the light turn round and round, and one evening, dressed to the nines in spats, white Panama, and malacca cane, he took her there to see them. Scottie was afraid to approach the building, so Gerald said tactfully, "The fairies might be busy, so we'll watch from close by." The expedition was, of course, a complete success.

It all seems like fairyland now, like grown-ups playing children's games. But there was a kind of purpose in it. One evening that summer, in the garden at Villa America, Sara and Gerald sat talking long after dinner with Phil and Ellen Barry and Archie and Ada MacLeish at the table under the linden tree. ("Life gets a little denser chemically during talks," Gerald felt.) Their conversation, which was seemingly at odds with the ease and beauty of their surroundings, revolved around something John Peale Bishop had said about tragedy. Death wasn't a tragedy, Bishop had said: "it is the horror of evil, of unexpected, sharply contrasted depravity, of helplessness before one's own nature — *not death, but life and its terrible possibilities.*" At Villa America, life and its terrible possibilities seemed held at bay, at least for now.

That year Gerald, egged on by Vladimir Orloff, bought a little boat named *Picaflor.* Gerald himself had done little if any sailing since his youth, and not much of it then; but Vladimir had been an ardent sailor in prerevolutionary Russia, and had longed for the sea ever since. So in June, Gerald gave Vladimir carte blanche to purchase a small, eight-meter racing sloop, and he and Archie MacLeish came down from Paris to try her out. Although MacLeish, a son of the Great Lakes, was a stranger to ocean sailing, he was looking forward to another adventure with Gerald, like the bicycle trip of a month or so ago — but the voyage didn't turn out as planned. First they were becalmed; and as the boat rolled, gently and nauseatingly, Gerald became violently seasick. After a day and a half of this torture, during which he got horribly sunburned, a fierce mistral came up and blew them into St.-Tropez, an unplanned landfall. There Gerald, somewhat restored by doses of Vichy water, liberal applications of sunburn remedy, and contact with dry land, told Vladimir he was bailing out. "I'm going back to Paris tomorrow," he said. "Archie can do as he pleases. I'm leaving the boat with you — do what you want with it. But I'm never getting on it again, except to get my suitcase."

He did as he said; but somehow, eight days later, had a change of heart. He telegraphed Vladimir: "LIVED THROUGH MOST BEAUTIFUL ADVENTURE OF MY LIFE WITH YOU STOP UNDERSTAND CHARM OF SEA AND CRUISING STOP HOPE PICAFLOR NOT SOLD STOP WILL BE AT ST-TROPEZ IN JULY FOR NEW CRUISE STOP WILL YOU PARDON MY STUPIDITY." On second thought, it appears, Gerald wasn't about to let a little eight-meter boat defeat him, particularly in front of someone like Archie MacLeish, a former football star at Yale and Hotchkiss.

So sailing became a part of the life of Villa America, and Gerald — who, a friend later said, "always became a native of wherever he was" — adopted not only the craft but the uniform. In July, when he and Archie went out on *Picaflor* again, they returned with a collection of striped sailors' jerseys, and rope-soled canvas espadrilles, and knitted fishermen's caps, which Gerald had bought in the market at St.-Tropez and proceeded to bestow on Archie, Phil

Barry, and Don Stewart. None of them wore these things with quite the flair that Gerald did; what might have seemed self-conscious on someone else looked, on him, somehow exactly right. It was the difference between costume and disguise — a difference that Gerald, uncomfortable in his own skin, had understood instinctively all his life.

In December Gerald was asked to show two paintings, *Watch* and *Razor*, at the "L'Art d'aujourd'hui" exhibit, alongside works by Picasso and Léger. *Watch* had already been exhibited at the spring Salon des Indépendents and had earned glowing comments: it was, noted Florent Fels in *L'Art vivant*, "at first astonishing and then seductive," a painting that made machinery "as plastically exploitable as . . . Cézanne's apples." (No wonder Archibald MacLeish, who knew a thing or two about globed fruit, purchased *Watch* for himself.) Picasso (enclosing a review of "L'Art d'aujourd'hui" he thought Gerald might have missed) said "that he liked very much my pictures, that they were simple, direct and it seemed to him Amurikin — certainly not European," reported Gerald proudly to Philip Barry. Léger seconded the pronouncement: "Gerald Murphy," he proclaimed, "was the only *American* painter in Paris."

At the Indépendents *vernissage*, Gerald later recollected, he had met a young writer who was interested in one of the other paintings in the show, a modernist-folkloric picture by Joan Miró called *The Farm*. The writer, who was already a friend of other Murphy intimates such as John Dos Passos and Donald Ogden Stewart, was Ernest Hemingway; and although the Murphys had been hearing about Hemingway, and vice versa, for some time, he had avoided getting to know them. Possibly he was suspicious of their wealth; certainly, when he struck up a conversation about *The Farm* with Gerald, it was to confess that he wanted to buy the picture and couldn't afford it. But Gerald told him his instinct was right, the painting was wonderful — and Hemingway scraped together the $200 it cost by borrowing from friends and working as a stevedore in the market at Les Halles. Gerald was impressed. In December, at the "L'Art d'aujourd'hui" show, when the two men ran into each other again, this time Hemingway didn't shy away.

14

"The kind of man to whom men, women,
children, and dogs were attracted"

IN 1925 ERNEST HEMINGWAY was just twenty-six — ten years younger than
Gerald — tall, dark-haired, square-browed, with dazzlingly white teeth and a
newly grown mustache that gave his almost too handsome face a raffish,
buccaneer look. He was, remarked his wife, Hadley, "the kind of man to
whom men, women, children, and dogs were attracted." The son of a doctor
from Oak Park, Illinois, and his failed-opera-singer wife, he had left home
(and, in his parents' view, respectability) to come to Paris and write. He'd been
a correspondent for the *Toronto Star*, and his work was appearing in the
expatriate little magazines, where it had begun to stir talk among the café
crowd that hung out at the Dôme, the Rotonde, or the Closerie des Lilas.
Robert McAlmon had recently brought out Hemingway's *Three Stories and
Ten Poems*, and William Bird had just published the short story collection
in our time. Both had appeared in limited editions of no more than a few
hundred copies, but the quality of the work, in the words of at least one
contemporary literary handicapper, "promises to remove him from the three-
hundred-copy class of authorship." And he was more than just a paper war-
rior. He had been seriously wounded on the Italian front in World War I,
when only a boy of eighteen; and he had a penchant for activities involving
physical risk, like bobsledding, bicycle racing, and bullfighting, all of which
he either participated in or wrote about or both.

He and Hadley had a little boy, John (the Hemingways, who were fond of
fanciful nicknames for each other, like Waxin and Palty and Cat, called him

Bumby), and they lived on Ernest's small salary and Hadley's tiny trust fund in a solid, petit bourgeois apartment building in the rue Notre-Dame-des-Champs in Montparnasse. Down the street was James Joyce's studio, and only a few blocks away was the comfortable flat Gertrude Stein shared with Alice Toklas at 27 rue de Fleurus. There was a carpenter's shop on the ground floor, which made it noisy by day, so Hemingway often wrote at a table at the Closerie des Lilas, a few blocks away. But he found it hard to do so without being interrupted by one or another of his friends dropping by for a drink or a coffee, for the Hemingways had a wide circle of acquaintance among the American and English bohemians who lived in or passed through Paris: Sylvia Beach and her companion, Adrienne Monnier; Ford Madox Ford; Ernest Walsh; Ezra Pound; Stein and Toklas; Joyce; Dos Passos; the MacLeishes.

Gerald and Sara fell for Hemingway at once. To Gerald, who struggled to find the essence in things so as to paint them more truthfully, Hemingway's dictum that "a writer's job is to tell the truth" — his use of direct, natural, vernacular language — had the clarity of one of Léger's paintings, and his prose seemed like something entirely new and exciting. Beyond this, though, Hemingway had a kind of magnetic dominance, what Archibald MacLeish's son William calls his "alpha male" quality. As Gerald remembered it, "he was such an enveloping personality, so physically huge and forceful, and he overstated everything and talked so rapidly and so graphically and so well that you just found yourself agreeing with him." He was the complete opposite of Gerald, who won you over by charm, not domination, and so by the laws of physics Gerald was naturally attracted to him.

As for Sara, she adored Hemingway from the outset. His artistic sensibility, keyed to sharp glimpses and startling observations, matched her own rather off-balance perceptiveness; but perhaps it was his intense physicality, his macho swagger — tempered disarmingly by his occasionally self-deprecating grin — that struck her most. "Sara loved very male animals," recalled a friend; she had been preconditioned for it by Frank Wiborg, whose strong physical presence had dominated her youth. Other friends like Zelda Fitzgerald were skeptical of Hemingway's machismo — "nobody is as male as all that," she said — but Sara didn't care.

Although they were careful not to express it, or even to admit it, neither she nor Gerald felt the same way about Hadley Hemingway. She was "a nice, plain girl," said Sara years later, "very handsome. But a bit unrealistic, and not very bright." Gerald elaborated: "There was a kind of vagueness about her that worried you, because you felt that Ernest was having a hard time. They had very little money, and we were a little concerned to learn that he hadn't allowed her to know how poor they were; you somehow felt that she should have known, and been the one who helped to carry the burden."

Hemingway returned the Murphys' affection — they were "swell," he told Scott Fitzgerald — and he seemed to make some effort to share with them some of his own private passions. One of these was horse racing — he and Hadley used to spend the day at Longchamp or St.-Cloud or Auteuil whenever they felt flush enough — and shortly after the Murphys met him Gerald made the following entry in his art notebook: "Picture: — Finish of horse-race — horses head, profiled an inch apart in repetition, jockeys' heads, striped shirts, whips backward in air < 45°, legs, boots, heels. Structure of Judges stand as backing (+fencing, heads of onlookers)." In "My Old Man" Hemingway would describe the beginning of the race like this: "that big green infield and the . . . starter with his big whip and the jocks fiddling them around and then the barrier snapping up and that bell going off and them all getting off in a bunch and then commencing to string out." Where the picture ends and the story begins is hard to say.

Soon the Murphys and the Hemingways were planning a winter adventure together. They would go to Munich with John Dos Passos and charter a private plane loaded "with rich food, wine and condiments" and piloted by a World War I ace; then they would fly to the Silvretta glacier, high in the Austrian alps above Schruns, and ski down — the first time anyone had ever tried it. The Murphys were always thinking of intriguing and unexpected excursions that would interest their friends; they had toyed with the idea of going to North Africa with the Fitzgeralds in January, but Zelda had been in poor health and Scott was taking her to a spa in the Pyrenees for a cure instead. This new plan was even better, though: for Sara, it offered a thrill equivalent to sailing in a hurricane; for Gerald, a chance to revisit the kind of winter sport he had enjoyed as a young man in the Adirondacks, and to test himself against Ernest's skill. And for Ernest it was a glamorous, novel, and expensive adventure he now happily boasted about to his friends and family, and one which the Murphys were paying for.

Hemingway accepted their interest in his work with the same eagerness with which he fell in with their excursion plans. Certainly he didn't get the same support from his parents, whose disapproval of his louche subject matter and vulgar language were expressed in a cold ritual of passive aggression: they returned to him, unread, the copies of *in our time* that he had sent to them at home in Oak Park. Instead of writing them off as expendable philistines, though, Hemingway kept attempting to win their approval, his father's particularly. "You see," he wrote to Dr. Hemingway: "I'm trying in all my stories to get the feeling of the actual life across — not to just depict life. . . . You can't do this without putting in the bad and the ugly as well as what is beautiful. . . . So when you see anything of mine that you don't like remember that I'm sincere in doing it and that I'm working toward something." With Gerald and Sara, such entreaties were superfluous. "Those God-damn stories of yours kept me rooted and goggle-eyed all the way to Germany the other day," wrote Gerald. "My God, but you've kept your promise to yourself."

Soon Ernest was trying out other new work on them. The collection *in our time* had been taken on by the New York firm of Boni and Liveright (which would add capital letters to the title); the publishers had an option on Hemingway's next three books, one of which had to be a novel, but if they rejected whatever book he next offered them, the option would be broken and he would be free to submit his work elsewhere. He had, in fact, begun a novel about his previous summer's sojourn in Pamplona; but he'd started to feel dissatisfied by Boni and Liveright's efforts on behalf of the stories. And a number of other publishers (including Scribner's, to whom Scott Fitzgerald had been sending feverish scouting reports) were curious about this new writer's work.

It was at this point that he showed up on Gerald and Sara's doorstep with a new manuscript in hand. It was late, and the Murphys had been on their way to bed when he arrived; but they stifled their yawns and listened as Ernest read them *The Torrents of Spring*, a satirical treatment of "literary" life in the American boondocks, which he had thrown together in the past few weeks.

The book was little more than a rather heavy-handed parody of Boni and Liveright's bestselling author (and Hemingway's own onetime mentor) Sherwood Anderson, peppered with jocular potshots at other Hemingway boosters like Gertrude Stein and Scott Fitzgerald; but Hemingway seemed determined that it be taken seriously. He had already regaled friends — like Fitzgerald and Dos Passos and a pretty *Vogue* editor named Pauline Pfeiffer, who was a crony of Hadley's — with bits of the manuscript; now he proceeded to read the whole thing to Gerald and Sara in a single evening.

Sara dozed off during the reading (though her ramrod posture gave no clue), and Gerald was put off by the viciousness and pointlessness of the satire; but both he and Sara applauded its author. Whether they were party to the plan he now evolved, however, isn't clear. "I have known all along," Hemingway admitted, "that [Boni and Liveright] could not and would not be able to publish it as it makes a bum out of their present ace and best seller Anderson. Now in 10th printing." Because their refusal would free him to take the Pamplona novel elsewhere, he mailed the manuscript to Horace Liveright in December. At New Year's, Liveright rejected *The Torrents of Spring* by cable. "I'm loose," wrote Hemingway to Fitzgerald, and set off for New York (leaving Hadley and Bumby at Schruns) to formally extricate himself from Liveright and find a new publisher for both books. Before he left he discussed his plans with Gerald and Sara, promising to wire them about any developments and left a manuscript copy of his Pamplona novel with them to read. He seemed hungry for their continued approval.

"Gosh, what news of Transatlantic Charlie!" wrote Gerald to Hadley when he heard that Ernest had landed a contract with Scribner's for *The Torrents of Spring* and for the Pamplona novel, which was now entitled *The Sun Also Rises*. "It certainly broke prettily for him. . . . It is a great title 'The Sun Also Rises.' Some day he'll write 'Yet the sea is not full' — or its equivalent. We read it the other day & were blown out of the water afresh."

The rest of the letter contained a disappointment: Dos Passos had had to cancel plans for their glacier flight — a play of his was in rehearsal in New York, he said; or he was going to, or coming back from, North Africa — and when he scrubbed, Gerald and Sara had had second thoughts. Neither of them had any real skiing experience, and the trip down from the two-thousand-meter-high Silvretta would be grueling, and possibly dangerous, for novices. So now they, too, bowed out — although they "felt like skunks about" it. In the end, though, they couldn't disappoint Ernest entirely; in late March, accompanied by Dos Passos (who had miraculously materialized) they went to Schruns for a short ski holiday.

The snow in the valley was uneven so the Hemingways, Murphys, and Dos Passos took the little electric train up the mountain to the Hotel Zum Rössle-Post at Gaschurn, where the Hemingways had stayed in January with Pauline Pfeiffer, and Ernest proceeded to give the beginners skiing lessons. There were no lifts or tows in those days, nor any fancy boots and bindings: you just strapped heavy wooden skis to your feet and added sealskins on the bottom to give yourself traction, climbed up the slope, took off the skins, and skied downhill. Gerald "spent two days doggedly practicing and falling down, and learning the elements of the stem Christiana and the Telemark," but, he said, "Dos didn't bother . . . because his eyesight was so bad he knew it was no use."

Still Gerald felt himself somewhat at a disadvantage: "Dos has always had hugely powerful legs and tremendous restless energy, and Ernest was an expert climber," he recalled. But the same spirit with which he had conquered the elements in the *Picaflor* asserted itself:

> I struggled along, trying to keep up with them, and felt terribly ashamed that I was holding them up. . . . Ernest always gave you the sense of being put to the test, and he was an absolutely superb skier. . . . When we started down, Dos just decided to go straight and sit down whenever he saw a tree, with the result that his pants were not only torn to shreds but his backside had all the skin taken off it. I managed to get down the first part without falling. Then in the second part, we had to go through a forest. I managed that pretty well too, falling only once or twice. Ernest would stop every twenty yards or so to make sure we were all right, and when we got to the bottom, about half an hour later, he asked me if I had been scared. I said, yes, I guess I had. He said then he knew what courage was, it was grace under pressure. It was childish of me, but I felt absolutely elated.

The elation lasted all the way down the mountain to Gaschurn, where, in the evening, all five of them sat by the hotel's porcelain stove and ate *forellen im blau* and drank kirsch and told stories. Ernest got out the manuscript of *The Sun Also Rises* and read some of the parts he had revised, and Gerald and Sara said how much they would like to go to Pamplona and Ernest urged them to join him the next summer. Dos couldn't promise to be there, but Hadley's friend Pauline was coming. Why not Gerald and Sara as well? He showed them photographs of the bullfights — Gerald was so struck by the look of the dark bull's head that he made a note to use it as the "nucleus" of a painting. So they made their plans, and drank more kirsch, and slept under feather quilts while the stars shone on the snow.

One day they posed for a photograph, the five of them — Dos, the Hemingways, the Murphys — standing in the cold slanting sunlight, bundled in woolen caps and thick sweaters. Their faces were merry and brown; their bodies, as they stood touching one another easily, were relaxed. It was, said Dos Passos later, "the last unalloyed good time" they all had together.

That spring Gerald had two pictures in the Salon des Indépendents, *Laboratoire* and a still life — a third painting, meant to have been exhibited as well, never made it past the registration stage and must have been either withdrawn or damaged. *Laboratoire* was almost certainly the painting described in his art notebook as a "group of chemical retorts, — diaphanous, *white line profile shapes*, tender colors, sure, graceful forms, ghosted. *On glass, transparent paint* with colored papers background, laboratory table as setting." The *Nature Morte* might have been the painting also referred to as *Roulement à Billes* (*Ball Bearing*), now lost, which showed the sculptural machine part Gerald had so admired and placed on his piano like a work of art. Or it might have been any of a number of pictures outlined on the ruled pages of Gerald's notebook: a view of a drugstore window; a collection of sewing implements — needles, thread, scissors; a still life of *batterie de cuisine* with rattan rug beaters hung on the wall behind; a view of Gerald's black-and-white marble bureau top with a bunch of violets in a vase; "a table with real objects (glass) in foreground in front of a 'nature morte' of real objects in false perspective (treated)."

By any measure, Gerald had been prodigiously busy in the preceding months, the images crowding both his brain and the pages of his notebook.

And he hadn't limited himself to images: the notebook also held, in addition to a meditation on the difference between "'painting' forms and 'mechanical' forms," an idea for a play about a family breeding farm where "the regular life of 'sire-dam-service' talk" plays "against a running obbligato of prudery in human relations." What would happen, Gerald wondered, if a family devoted to an honest, animal expression of sex suddenly came across someone who used sex dishonestly, sophisticatedly, as a tool or weapon? "Is there dramatic material," he asked Philip Barry in a letter, "in the fact that intelligent people, taking a frank interest in the workings of sex and its results in animals, are at a loss and unable to see or act clearly as regards sex in the case of human beings"? There's no record of Barry's reply, if there was one. But soon Gerald got another kind of answer.

The spring of 1926 was cold and rainy in the north of France, and Sara and Gerald, mindful of how drafty and cramped the Hemingways found their Paris flat, were determined to bring them down to stay at the Villa America. Ernest wanted to go to Madrid to write and see the San Ysidro bullfights in May, and so Gerald and Sara proposed that Hadley leave little Bumby with them and join Ernest in Spain; then they could return to Antibes until Pauline Pfeiffer joined the party and all five of them went to Pamplona in July.

But Ernest and Hadley (unbeknownst to Gerald and Sara) had quarreled about Ernest's increasingly apparent partiality for Pauline. Under Hadley's questioning, he stoutly denied it, but in fact he and Hadley's friend had become lovers that winter in Paris, when he stopped over on his way back from New York. Now he went off to Spain by himself in a cloud of self-righteous indignation, leaving Hadley and Bumby, who had come down with a persistent cough, in Paris.

The Murphys persuaded Hadley to come with Bumby to Antibes anyway; it would cheer her up, they felt, and the MacLeishes and the Fitzgeralds were settled nearby, which would make things lively. Unfortunately, as soon as Hadley and Bumby arrived, the boy's croup was diagnosed as whooping cough and it was advised that he be quarantined. The Fitzgeralds were in the process of moving from their villa — the lease was up in June — to a larger one they'd taken for the remainder of the summer, so they offered the empty villa to Hadley, and Gerald summoned (and paid for) the Murphys' British doctor to care for Bumby. He wrote immediately to reassure Ernest: "Hadley seemed so tired when she arrived . . . [but] she's in great form now and resting finely. There's no doubt that Bumby's better off. We have the best doctor we've ever known: an Englishman. Hadley likes him. It's one of those crazy train of incidents which seems to lead to a situation somehow good. Don't worry — you."

That, to Gerald and to Sara, was the most important thing — that Ernest not worry, that he be able to do his work in peace. What they didn't tell Ernest (but Hadley later confessed) was that they were also paying for Hadley's grocery bills and other expenses, which galled Hemingway, who was both anxious and prickly about money and who resented (even while he accepted) the paternal role Gerald so often played in their relationship. As he did so often, Hemingway now used his fiction to get back at the object of his resentment: revising *The Sun Also Rises*, he put Gerald into the latest version as the rich dilettante hopelessly in love with, and ultimately humiliated by, the fallen angel who became Lady Brett Ashley. In his original draft, entitled *Fiesta*, the character has the same name as his real-life counterpart, Harold Loeb; in the final version he is Robert Cohn. But for a brief period Hemingway's classic portrait of a patsy — a man whose money the other characters spend, and insult him for the privilege — was called Gerald Cohn.

Neither Gerald nor Sara knew this, of course. They were busy planning a celebration for when Ernest rejoined his family and friends: they would give a party at the little Juan-les-Pins casino, which would help the casino's owner and make a fiesta for Ernest. And now, while they waited for Bumby to get better and Ernest to come back from Spain, they tried to keep Hadley amused. At "yardarm time" they would enlist the Fitzgeralds and Ada MacLeish (Archie was in Persia with the League of Nations Opium Commission until June) and drive over to the Villa Paquita, where they'd park just beyond the fence for a quarantined cocktail party — Hadley on one side, the Murphys and company on the other. "By the time we left," remembered Hadley, "that fence was covered with glass bottles artfully arranged. It was great fun."

The only one who didn't find it much fun was Scott Fitzgerald, who was beginning to feel a kind of free-floating hostility that he expressed in a variety of ways as the summer progressed. For the first time in a while he had no financial worries — a successful dramatization of *The Great Gatsby* and some healthy magazine sales had brought in money — and, as he later remembered it, "I made one of those mistakes literary men make — I thought I was a 'man of the world' — that everybody liked me and admired me for myself but I only liked a few people like Ernest and Charlie McArthur [the playwright Charles MacArthur, coauthor of *The Front Page* and husband of Helen Hayes] and Gerald and Sara who were my peers." But his feelings of self-confidence were undercut by uneasiness about Zelda, who had been acting strangely, and by a nagging jealousy about Hemingway, his friend and sometime protégé. Why were the Murphys, who had been *his* friends first, so crazy about Ernest? Why did they rave so about his writing, when they were so diffident about his own?

As often happens with insecure people, Scott transmuted his feelings of anxiety into belligerence, and when the drink was on him he got nasty. He ragged Gerald for the very thing that made him so irresistible to his friends: "I suppose you have some special *plan* for us today," he sneered when he met Gerald at the beach one morning. And he grew more and more demanding of Sara. A scene in the draft of the novel he was writing is telling: One of the characters, a promising composer ruined by drink, is talking to the beautiful Dinah Roreback, a woman so closely modeled on Sara that in this version of the manuscript the name "Sarah" is crossed out and replaced with "Dinah." "I've been in love with you for several years," says the composer. "In my imagination I sleep with you every night."

His infatuation has made him dislike her husband, Seth (originally called "Gerald" in this version); but she won't let him tell her why: "I can't discuss Seth with you," she says. Just as Sara, in a tart note written to Scott that summer, said, "It's hardly likely that I should explain Gerald, — or Gerald me — to you." Years later Gerald implied to a friend that Fitzgerald's portrait of a marriage in *Tender Is the Night* — not a "cooled relation," but "active love . . . more complicated than I can tell you" — was true of himself and Sara too. Whatever complications might have been caused by Gerald's own self-doubts, at this time the connection between himself and Sara was physical, and sexual, as well as emotional. But at this point Scott, perhaps willfully, could only sense the complications.

Hemingway's arrival in Antibes, welcomed by Gerald and Sara with champagne and caviar, made things worse. Fitzgerald wasn't a professionally envious man — his unstinting editorial and tactical support of Hemingway is proof of that — but he had fierce personal jealousies. And what he saw at the Juan-les-Pins casino made him deeply unhappy. It wasn't the grim minuet of Hadley, Ernest, and Pauline that caught his attention, though; it was the way in which Gerald and Sara — particularly Sara — hung on Ernest's every word. And perhaps there was something else. As Ellen Barry, who was there with her husband, Philip, later pointed out, Fitzgerald wasn't the only man at the party who was attracted to Sara. "So was Ernest," she recalled. Identifying with Gerald, as he often did, Fitzgerald had to feel uneasy about the danger Hemingway might pose to him. Anxious, hurt, and jealous, Scott proceeded to make a fool of himself and a shambles of the party with his behavior to Gerald and his moans that "Sara's being mean to me."

The Murphys were either ignorant of all these fault lines or chose to ignore them, as if they could ward off disaster with gaiety. When Archie MacLeish landed in Marseille on June 16 after his three-month trip to Persia, they made an occasion of it, bribing an officer of an ocean liner moored in the harbor to let the two of them and Ada watch his arrival from the liner's bridge, and then performing an Indian war dance on the pier. They organized morning beach outings for their friends and guests, all carefully chronicled in Sara's photograph albums: Scott and Zelda and little Scottie wading in the azure water and squinting in the sunlight; Ernest, tall and brown in striped bathing trunks, grinning at the camera, with Bumby on his shoulders; Hadley, fully dressed, kneeling by her son in the sand; "Ada of the Flying Fingers," as Gerald called her, knitting under a checked beach umbrella, with Sara beside her, glancing seductively over her shoulder at the camera, her pearls looping over her bare back.

There is another photograph, from July in Pamplona, the Fiesta of San Fermín. Sara and Gerald are sitting at a café table with Ernest, Pauline, and Hadley. On the table there are glasses and a soda siphon. It is hot; the sun glares in the foreground. Gerald is squinting beneath the brim of his cap;

Sara, with a cigarette smoldering between rigid fingers, eyes the photographer distrustfully. Ernest sits between Pauline and Hadley, wearing tweeds and a tie and black beret, smiling slightly at the camera. He looks, paradoxically, both uncomfortable and self-satisfied. Hadley, seated next to Ernest, is looking across at Gerald; she seems tired. Pauline, a slight, dark, crop-haired figure in the center of the group, sits with eyes cast down at her lap. She is smiling to herself.

They had arrived some days earlier, having left Bumby in Antibes with his French nurse. They had found the town filled with farmers and pilgrims who had come for the fiesta — many of them, unable to find lodgings, sleeping in the streets. Strange music played all day long and through the night — brass bands and men with drums and a plaintive reed pipe, like a short recorder — and itinerant vendors sold wine in wineskins, which they squirted into your mouth from a foot away. There were processions with banners and effigies and giants and dwarfs, and of course the legendary running of the bulls, who thundered through the streets on the first day of the fiesta with the young men of Pamplona racing alongside them. It was all strange, earthy, and exhilarating, but there was a peculiar undercurrent of tension.

The Hemingway party stayed in the bullfighters' hotel, the Quintana, on the main square, with two of the most prominent matadors at the fiesta, Villalta and Niño de la Palma, just across the corridor. Gerald was particularly struck by seeing them lying on their cots in the afternoon before the *corrida*, looking like effigies, their bullion-encrusted suits of lights draped across the chairs at their feet. Later he tried to put his reaction into words: "these men, living, as it seems to me in a region between art and life, . . . make you feel that you are as you find most other people — half-alive . . . They are a religion for which I could have been trained."

In fact, in Pamplona, Gerald felt very much the religious novice to Hemingway's father superior. Although he could still call Hadley and Ernest "you two children" and sign a postcard to them "dow dow," the balance in the relationship between the two men had begun to shift. Before they went to Spain, Gerald, who admired Pauline's gamine chic and her wit, had begun calling her "Daughter," his nickname for any young girl he liked; in Pamplona, Hemingway started doing it, too, and seemed annoyed when Gerald wouldn't relinquish the habit. And Ernest had started calling himself "Papa."

Gerald felt insecure enough to start worrying about what to wear, he with his unerring clothes sense and gift for disguise. Finally he settled on a pearl gray gabardine suit and an old golf cap of his father's — "I didn't want to wear a Panama hat," he recalled — and, to his relief, won Ernest's approval. The cap, Ernest told him, was just right: "it looks tough," he said. And, he reported to Gerald, the suit was a success with the townspeople: "They say you're called the man in the silver suit," Hemingway said. "Do they approve?" Gerald asked anxiously, and Ernest replied, "Yes, they think it's fine."

There was a tradition in Pamplona that in the mornings local aficionados could try their hands with the young bulls; it was at one of these sessions that Don Stewart had been tossed the year before. This time, with Hadley, Pauline, and Sara watching, Ernest put Gerald up to going into the bullring. Gerald had begged off running with the bulls — he hadn't wanted "to look or feel a fool" — but Sara had said, "I'm sorry you didn't run. It would have been a great feeling afterwards." So later he promised Ernest that next year he *would* run, "and I'll do it well, Papa." And now he took up Ernest's challenge in the ring. "He was watching me all the time out of the corner of his eye . . . to see how I would take it," Gerald recalled. When he saw Gerald execute an impromptu (and terrified) veronica with his raincoat, standing to one side as the bull brushed past, Ernest inevitably went him one better. With nothing in his hands to distract the bull, he waited until the animal charged him, then vaulted over its horns onto its back. His weight brought the animal to its knees, and, said Sara, "everybody yelled 'Olé.'"

Afterward, although he was already caught in a triangle with Hadley and Pauline, Ernest seemed compelled to flirt with Sara. Why did she never wear her diamond jewelry in the daytime, he asked; her diamonds would look so wonderful in the sunlight. Think how she would look at the bullfights with her jewelry blazing in the sun. So that afternoon, when they all went to the *corrida*, Sara put on "a little silk dress" and "all my diamonds" to sit beside Ernest in the *barrera* seats (paid for by Gerald), as close to the ring as possible. But when the *corrida* began, the slaughter of the picadors' horses by the bulls sickened and enraged her, and, she said in a recorded interview many years later, "I stamped out and walked back to the hotel," diamonds and all. "I wonder if anybody noticed," she mused. In the tape recording her husky voice, with its soft southern Ohio drawl, is regretful, almost plaintive. "I don't think Ernest ever knew that I'd left, did he?" she said. "He didn't notice."

She went back to the arena the next day, though, and the next, and sat through enough to tell Ernest that "no one has anything on me about liking bullfights — , even if I don't like seeing bowels — But *that* is just a woman's whimsey and does not count."

In the end she and Gerald were both disturbed and attracted by Pamplona's elemental quality. Perhaps it was the strangeness, or the sense of danger and sexual excitement. Whatever it was, Gerald told Ernest that their time there "kept unearthing and over-topping the best we've known together since we've known each other." They pillaged Pamplona's shops for gifts and memories — a guitar for Baoth, a drum for Sara herself — and they all ate the olives and wonderful roasted almonds and drank the very dry sherry. And one night there was a fireworks display and dancing in the plaza, and they all did the *sardana* and then a crowd of people, put up to it by Hadley or Ernest, surrounded the Murphys, clapping and calling out *"Dansa Charles-ton! Dansa Charles-ton!"* And Gerald and Sara, who had got a professional troupe from the Cannes casino to come to the Villa America and teach them the steps to the hot new dance craze from the U.S., rose and danced for the whistling, cheering crowd.

The Murphys arrived back in Antibes to find summer in full swing. Monty Woolley, who was teaching drama at Yale and had yet to make his celebrated appearance as *The Man Who Came to Dinner,* came to visit, and he and Gerald devised a sort of vaudeville routine, called "stomach touch," a parody of two old Yale alumni literally bumping into each other in a bar, full of hearty Bulldog banter. They also became fascinated with a visitor to the Hôtel du Cap, the Romanian-British diplomat Sir Charles Mendl. Sir Charles's impenetrable (and acquired) British accent — he pronounced "fire" as "fahhh" — entranced them, so they kept striking up conversations with him just to hear what he would say. One day Gerald asked him for his definition of a cad: Sir Charles struggled with the subtleties of this for some moments, then blurted out, to Woolley's and Gerald's intense delight, "Oh, hang it! A cad is someone who makes you go all crinkly-toes!" The expression became a by-word in the Murphy family, and Scott Fitzgerald drew heavily on Sir Charles for his portrait of the Englishman Campion in *Tender Is the Night.*

There were other visitors as well: Picasso brought Man Ray, who photographed Honoria in a harlequin suit with a matador's bicorne hat beside her (the same costume Paulo Picasso had worn in his father's 1924 portrait) and Sara and Gerald, separately, each dressed in white against the lush tangle of the garden, with the three children. The humorist Robert Benchley, a friend of Don Stewart's, came to stay, bringing his two sons and his wife, Gertrude, a Massachusetts girl whose Yankee vowels Gerald loved (he always spelled, and pronounced, her name "Gaytrûd"); Alexander Woollcott also visited; and eventually Don Stewart himself, newly married, with his bride, Beatrice. The Murphys greeted them at the station with Baoth's guitar and Sara's drum, and planned a party to welcome the newlyweds. They invited the Hemingways, who had just returned from Spain, and the Picassos, who were in Juan-les-Pins again; but Bea Stewart fell victim to what Sara tactfully referred to as a *crise de foie* and the party had to be postponed. "Brides, I find, just aren't as sturdy as they used to be," complained Sara to Picasso. "What is it they *all* seem to have??"

Suddenly there was a pervasive feeling of malaise in the air. Scott Fitzgerald, it was clear, was drinking more than ever; and although Zelda was in better physical health since an appendectomy in June, her behavior was exceedingly peculiar. Late one evening when the Murphys had joined the Fitzgeralds at the casino in Juan-les-Pins, all four of them were sitting at their table when Zelda suddenly got up and, lifting the skirt of her evening dress above her waist, began, slowly, hypnotically, like a dervish, to dance. "She was dancing for herself," Gerald remembered, "she didn't look left or right, or catch anyone's eyes. She looked at no one, not once, not even at Scott. I saw a mass of lace ruffles as she whirled — I'll never forget it. We were frozen."

Typically, neither Gerald nor Sara found this behavior reprehensible; they didn't judge Zelda, only appreciated her. "She had this tremendous natural dignity," said Gerald. "She was so self-possessed, so absorbed in her dance. Somehow she was incapable of doing anything unladylike." Not even when she hurled herself over a parapet at a restaurant in St.-Paul-de-Vence, a picturesque medieval village in the hills behind Antibes, where Gerald and Sara had taken the Fitzgeralds to dinner to escape the crowds now increasingly prevalent on the coast. La Colombe d'Or was a rustic inn, much beloved of the artists like Picasso, Léger, Signac, and Bonnard, who sometimes paid for their meals with drawings; the Murphys had reserved a table on the stone terrace overlooking the Loup valley, two hundred feet straight below, with Antibes and the Esterel visible in the distance. At the end of their meal, when the other diners had left, they were fascinated to discover Isadora Duncan seated at a neighboring table with three admirers. Although she was hugely fat and middle-aged and henna-haired, she still had enough of her old star power that Fitzgerald — when Gerald and Sara told him who she was — went to sit at her feet. Duncan was entranced by this blond, boyish acolyte and began running her hands through his hair and calling him her "centurion." That was when Zelda, without warning, stood up on her chair and leaped over the table — and over Gerald, who was seated with his back to the view — into the darkness beyond the parapet.

"I was sure she was dead," remembered Gerald, but moments later Zelda reappeared. She had fallen onto a stone staircase that ran down from the terrace, and now she stood at the top, her knees and dress bloody, but otherwise unharmed. Sara flew to her and tried to wipe away the blood with her napkin; as for Gerald, his first thought was "that it had not been ugly. I said that to myself over and over again."

To Fitzgerald, the contrast between his own fraying marriage and the Murphys' seemingly durable one had to be painful, and — as he worried at the manuscript he had begun, which was currently entitled *World's Fair* — he tried to analyze what it was that made them somehow different. One evening, when the Murphys had given a party for the Hemingways, the Fitzgeralds, and the MacLeishes, Fitzgerald started quizzing Gerald about his and Sara's relationship: Why did they seem so formal with each other? When they told each other jokes, he said, it seemed as if they were telling them to strangers. Had they slept together before they were married? Did they still sleep together? Sara was outraged. "Scott, you just think if you ask enough questions you'll know all about people," she said. "But you don't know anything about people." Goaded to repeat this remark by Fitzgerald, who was almost sick with fury, she did. And the evening, like others, ended badly. "Dear Scott," wrote Sara, with her usual haphazard punctuation, the next day,

> I've generally said what I thought. And it seems another of those moments.
> We consider ourselves your friends. . . . But you can't expect anyone to

like or stand a *Continual* feeling of analysis & subanalysis, & criticism — on the whole unfriendly — Such as we have felt for quite awhile. . . . It certainly detracts from any gathering, — & Gerald, for one, simply curls up at the edges & becomes someone else in that sort of atmosphere. . . . [L]ast night you even said "that you had never seen Gerald so silly & rude". . . . — and if Gerald was "rude" in getting up & leaving a party that had gotten *quite bad,* then he was rude to the Hemingways and MacLeishes too. No, it is hardly likely that you would stick at a thing like *manners* — it is more probably some theory you have, — (it *may* be something to do with the book), — *But you ought to know at your age* that you *Can't have Theories about friends.*

Although Scott wrote her an apology he couldn't seem to stop himself from making more and uglier scenes: getting drunk and pitching three of Sara's prized Venetian wineglasses out onto the driveway, one by one, so that Gerald banished him from the Villa America for three weeks; following two young Frenchmen around the dance floor at the casino and asking them, over and over, if they were "fairies," to the intense embarrassment of Ada MacLeish, who was dancing with one of them. Possibly the ugliest scene was the last: The Murphys were going to New York in October, and to celebrate the end of the summer they put on a "Dinner-Flowers-Gala" with a vengeance, inviting not only their American literary friends but all the gratin of the coast, including an aristocratic French neighbor, the Princesse de Poix, and her houseguest, the Princesse de Caraman-Chimay. Some time after the Fitzgeralds arrived Scott accosted another guest, a young, openly homosexual writer and pianist named Eugene McGowan, whom the Murphys liked because he was witty and charming. "Are you a homosexual?" Scott asked baldly, and — when McGowan said that he was — "What do you people *do,* anyway?" After this Fitzgerald subsided for a time, but when dessert was served he found his form again: plucking a ripe fig from a bowl of pineapple sorbet, he pitched it right between the bare, blue-blooded shoulder blades of the Princesse de Caraman-Chimay, who was seated at the next table. With impeccable sangfroid she pretended not to notice, but Gerald did, and asked Archie MacLeish to try and restrain Fitzgerald. Archie took Scott to the *bastide* and proceeded to give him a tongue-lashing, but Scott threw a punch at him and — as Gerald remembered it anyway — "Archie knocked him cold."

Things were patched up between them. As Fitzgerald rather churlishly put it in a note to Hemingway, who had returned to Paris at the end of August, "We saw the Murphys before they left, got stewed with them at their party — that is we got stewed — and I believe there was some sort of mawkish reconciliation. However they've grown dim to me and I don't like them much any more." The fact that the Murphys had lent the vacated Villa America to the Fitzgeralds for the remainder of the autumn seemed not to have abashed Fitzgerald in the slightest. He was much more interested in the news that Ernest had confided to him, and to Sara and Gerald before their departure: he and Hadley had decided to separate.

Fitzgerald said he was "depressed and . . . baffled"; on their side, Gerald and Sara were stunned. It was only weeks ago that they had written to the Hemingways as one person, literally: the letter began "Dear Hadern." But, although the Murphys had proclaimed Hadley and Ernest, together, to be "close to what's elemental," with their "values hitched up to the universe," when the crunch came it was with Ernest that their sympathies lay. Aware that Hadley had a private income but that Ernest was now living on $200 installments of his publisher's advance, Gerald quietly deposited $400 in Hemingway's Paris bank account. "When life gets bumpy," he wrote to Ernest afterward, "you get through to the truth sooner if you are not hand-tied by the lack of a little money. I preferred not to ask you: so Sara said just deposit and talk about it after." (Ernest had guessed they would do something of the sort, and even told Hadley not to worry about his finances as a result.) He and Sara both felt, Gerald went on, that "Hadley and you . . . are after two different kinds of truth in life . . . I hold in very sacred respect the thing that Hadley and you have enjoyed between you [but] your heart will never be at peace to live, work and enjoy unless you clean up and cut through."

Gerald offered Ernest the loan of his studio at 69 rue Froidevaux, as a temporary residence, and Ernest moved in there on his return to Paris. He didn't tell them that he was divorcing Hadley to marry Pauline, or that Hadley had made his divorce contingent on a hundred-day separation from her rival, who had returned to America. Perhaps he was afraid they would respond as his parents did when he finally announced his divorce and remarriage. His father attacked him with a harangue against "Love Pirates" and "persons who break up your home etc.," to which Ernest rather pathetically replied, "You would be so much happier and I would too, if you could have confidence in me. . . . You could if you wanted be proud of me sometimes — not for what I do for I have not had much success in doing good — but for my work."

Contrast Clarence Hemingway's reaction with the note Gerald wrote Ernest after an evening the Murphys spent with him at the end of September, just before they sailed for their autumn visit to America: "We said to each other last night and we say to you now that: we love you, we believe in you and all your parts, we believe in what you're doing, in the way you're doing it. Anything we've got is yours: somehow we are your father and mother, by what we feel for you." Sara's contribution, sealed in the same envelope, was less reasoned but no less emphatic: "Dear gros Patron [Big Boss, her nickname for Hemingway], We *certainly* believe in you as Gerald says — Thank you for talking to us — and don't think you were the only one helped by it! In the end you will probably save us all, — by refusing (among other things) to accept any second-rate things places ideas or human natures — Bless you & don't ever budge —"

15

"How can a wise man have two countries?"

"EVERYONE IN AMERICA is discontented, unhappy, or complaining," reported Gerald to Ernest Hemingway when the Murphys arrived in New York in 1926; but somehow he and Sara managed to insulate themselves from the prevailing angst. On a piece of hotel stationery Gerald copied out a verse from Genesis: "Therefore shall a man leave his father and his mother, and shall cleave unto his wife: and they shall be one flesh. And they were both naked, the man and his wife, and were not ashamed."

They couldn't leave their fathers and mothers totally: New Year's was spent with Frank Wiborg, or *"grang pere,"* as eleven-year-old Honoria called her grandfather. In her usual phonetic French, in her diary, she also wrote, *"mais ma tent n'etait pas la."* Hoytie evidently had other things to do. When Pauline Pfeiffer turned up in New York during her hundred-day separation from Ernest, Gerald and Sara took her to the senior Murphys' for Patrick's bootleg cocktails. Pauline's smart mouth and short haircut shone in the Murphys' drawing room like a good deed in a naughty world — and afterward the three of them went up to Harlem to listen to jazz in "three nigger hives," as Pauline described them. The Murphys, she told Ernest, were "adorable." Don Stewart, who was in between trips to the West Coast in search of film work, gave a party for the adorable Murphys, and for the Barrys and Dorothy Parker — the Algonquin Round Table's muse and Gerald's long-ago schoolmate at Blessed Sacrament Academy. The climax of this affair was a talk, given by Robert Benchley in his best ladies-club-lecture manner, on wildflowers, including his newest discoveries, "drovers wet lace or false goatsbeard."

Jazz and bootleg booze and snappy conversation weren't their only defense against gloom. For Gerald at least, there was work. Rocketing along Third Avenue on the elevated train, he saw his old city with a painter's eye.

Picture [he wrote in his notebook]: —
(1) from 3rd Av. El *down* into shops, lighted windows dressed, eggs in crates, kitchen utensils, drug store, — *across* at sills and windows, up at roof cornices: 3 perspectives
(2) electric signs (green gold yellow) topping buildings (in silhouette) against a sky darker than signs and lighter than buildings: use lighted windows

Everywhere he went that fall in New York, pictures suggested themselves: a view down the darkened canyon of Madison Avenue toward the golden space of Madison Square with the Metropolitan Life Insurance tower lit by the afternoon sun; viaducts and derricks and cranes slicing the Manhattan skyline; the rhythmic procession of rooftop water tanks, like miniature silos or Monet grain stacks, silhouetted against the sky. Unlike the tight close-up perspective of such paintings as *Watch, Razor,* and the recently completed *Roulement à Billes,* these notebook images have a kind of cinematic architectural grandeur, as if the artist were shooting them in long focus, then zooming in. Gerald even used the word *shot* in describing them.

Both architecture and film had begun to play a part in his artistic thinking, as if he were looking for new ways of saying the things he wanted to say with paint. During the last year he'd finished a painting entitled *Doves:* "Capital, ionic, corinthian, in large scale, with deep shadows (constructive), — with one or more pigeons clustered flat on it," was how he sketched it verbally in his notebook. It was a large (48 ⅝ inches by 36 inches) canvas in muted tones of slate, silver, rose, beige, and brown, in which segmented views of a variety of classical columns and cornices were intercut with three stylized images of a pigeon — in close-up, reversed in medium range, and in long shot. Gerald hated pigeons — a friend later recalled that he recoiled from their fluttering and cooing — but by distancing himself as if with a camera's lens he was able to make something almost beautiful out of them.

At the end of January the Murphys returned to Antibes — the children with newly acquired cowboy and Indian costumes, the better to disguise themselves for lightning raids on the kitchen. In mid-February, having hired a charming and sensible young woman named Yvonne Roussel to act as the children's tutor, Gerald and Sara set off on a two-week tour through eastern Europe with the MacLeishes. Sara and Gerald wanted to take their friends to Moscow to see what was going on in experimental theater — they hadn't forgotten the excitement they'd felt at the Kamerny's Paris performances — and they thought they would be able to float the trip with the rubles the Kamerny's director had borrowed from them four years previously. But by the time they secured their Russian visas, "the theatres had closed," said Sara, and "the snow started to melt not to mention the season for Executions." They consoled themselves with Sacher torte in Vienna and a trip to Berlin, where Gerald was electrified by Fritz Lang's Gothic expressionist film *Metropolis*, a moving embodiment of the picture proposals he had sketched in his notebook in New York. He was also intrigued by "a new opera (half revue half film — ballet — & moving abstract scenery, stern light etc.) by a guy 27 yrs," which sounds as if it might have been Bertholt Brecht's first experiment in "epic theater," *Mann ist Mann.*

During the course of their journey Ada and Archie confided to the Murphys their growing feeling that a return to the United States was inevitable — for all of them, possibly, and for the MacLeishes, certainly. The favorable exchange rate, which had made it so much cheaper to live in Europe than America, was evening out. Although Ada had begun to have some success in Europe — she had been asked to sing Debussy's Mélisande at the Opéra Comique and was to give a concert at the Conservatoire in May, where she would sing songs by their mutual friend Richard Myers as well as by Lully and Scarlatti — she hankered after an American career. Perhaps more important, Archie's father was in failing health and Archie felt the old pull of filial responsibility. And, said MacLeish later, "We wanted our children to be Americans."

The Murphys disagreed. They'd heard enough grumbling from Frank Wiborg about the Frenchified upbringing of his grandchildren. They had tried to mollify him by legally changing Baoth's name earlier that year to Baoth Wiborg, thus giving Frank a named descendant, something he desperately wanted. It was an extraordinary gesture, almost biblical; wasn't it enough? They'd had enough lectures about responsibility. They felt that the only responsibility you should have was toward your children and your art. As Archie huffily overstated it, "They really couldn't let anyone act as though anyone could ever have responsibilities toward anyone." There was a quarrel — at least, there was a quarrel between Gerald and Archie, one of "these damn school girl quarrels of Gerald's," as Archie put it in a letter to Hemingway, "that make it so hard for me to believe in his affection." And for a while matters between the two men were prickly.

For Gerald was still immersed in the cultural life of the Continent, and devoted, sometimes to the exclusion of personal commitments, to his work. It had become a small bone of contention between him and Sara: although she had encouraged him to go on a solo trip to Germany earlier in the year to paint, she found herself more and more carrying the burden of their complicated household alone and occasionally complained about it. But neither of them was ready to leave the freedom and ferment they had found in Europe. Gerald, for one, could feel changes coming in the artistic climate and was eager to experience them.

"You're right," he wrote Hemingway. "The ballet's as dead as the theatre. The world needs to know what it's looking at and listening to for a while." Not for him, anymore, the sort of project he'd proposed in his notebook around the time of *Within the Quota* and *Boatdeck*: a "ballet of *metiers*" in which goggled construction workers in overalls and young toughs in apache clothes dash about a set composed of girders and cranes and warehouses. Now he wanted to work in a new medium.

He had been talking with Fernand Léger about collaborating on a film. Léger had done a cinematic version of George Antheil's *Ballet mécanique*, featuring piano, airplane propeller, automobile horn, and other objects, in 1924, and followed it with other versions, either recut or reshot, and now he and Gerald made plans to begin shooting their project in May, in Gerald's studio. The movie, whatever it was, was never named, and Gerald never mentioned it again after the spring of 1927. But some time during that year, a version of *Ballet mécanique* that Léger made, featuring the same surreal collection of moving objects used in previous versions, appears to have been filmed in a large, light, bare interior that might have been 69 rue Froidevaux.

Hemingway had moved out of the studio just in time; his divorce from

Hadley had come through and he and Pauline were married on May 10, with a small luncheon afterward at Ada and Archie MacLeish's studio flat on the rue du Bac. MacLeish and Hemingway had become very close while the Murphys were in America that fall, taking bicycle excursions, going skiing in Switzerland at Christmas, and falling into the kind of boys' locker-room talk that Hemingway frequently seemed to call forth from his correspondents ("my testicles give me no end of trouble at these interseasonal periods," was the kind of thing MacLeish felt obliged to confide to Hemingway in this vein). But they, too, had had a falling-out. On an autumn trip to Zaragoza, in Spain, for the *feria* of Santa Maria del Pilar, they had a quarrel that MacLeish described in a poem, "Cinema of a Man":

> He walks with Ernest in the streets of Saragossa
> They are drunk their mouths are hard they say *qué cosa*
> They say the cruel words they hurt each other. . . .

Although the cruel words were occasioned by Archie's suggestion that Ernest might learn a thing or two from Joyce's fiction, the argument had begun as a kind of literary-historical shoving match over the sexual proclivities of Shakespeare, Julius Caesar, and various popes (Hemingway was in the process of becoming a Catholic in order to marry Pauline). MacLeish, Hemingway complained in a letter to Gerald and Sara, said they were "all Fairies." He reported this exchange jokingly, but only barely — for Ernest, Gerald later recalled, "was extremely sensitive to the question of who was and who wasn't."

The sensitivity spilled over into his fiction. In Gerald's studio, that autumn, he had written a story, "A Simple Enquiry," about an officer's homosexual come-on to his orderly. "You are quite sure that you love a girl?" asks the major in the story. "And that you are not corrupt?" "I don't know what you mean, corrupt," the orderly replies, evasively, although Hemingway leaves little doubt that both he and the major know what's being spoken of. Later, the major wonders if "the little devil" lied to him; at the story's end, the reader is wondering the same thing. A few months after he finished "A Simple Enquiry," Hemingway began a novel about a boy and his soldier-of-fortune father; the manuscript seemed to founder on a long digression about how to recognize and deal with homosexuals (who, according to the boy's father, make good interior decorators but lousy writers).

Hemingway's preoccupation with this subject matter was in part the inevitable obverse of his own compulsive maleness. But part of it also came from his exposure, in Gerald Murphy, to a man whose sexual persona was so troublingly different from anything he had experienced before. Gerald was athletic: he was a sailor and a long-distance swimmer. He had a beautiful wife with whom he had had three beautiful children. He had recently bought that manifestation of machismo, "a 4cv Terrot motocyclette" which, he boasted to Ernest, "does 90 kilos without losing a spangle." But on that "motocyclette" Gerald would sometimes ride tandem — in full evening dress, including top hat — with the red-bearded and flamboyant Monty Woolley, to the consternation of the Antibes shopkeepers who saw them whizzing by. Indeed, he dressed so exotically, in his brief bathing costumes or sailor's jerseys or beautifully pressed suits; he paid so much attention to decor and to other people's clothes, even to choosing dresses for Sara and Ellen Barry; he had so many sexually ambiguous friends, from Cole Porter to Cocteau to Étienne de Beaumont, that Hemingway didn't know how to pigeonhole him. And it made him uncomfortable.

Sometimes the discomfort showed. That spring the Murphys invited the Hemingways to a preview performance of *Oedipe Roi*, Stravinsky's new opera-oratorio to Jean Cocteau's text, at the *hôtel particulier* of Winaretta de Polignac, who had commissioned the piece. Predictably, Hemingway hated the whole thing, thinking it too effete and arty, and complained about it later to Gerald. His appreciation of the piece can't have been helped by having Cocteau (whom some wit had referred to as "the feminine of *cocktail*") twittering on Gerald's other side. "What a remarkable profile the Princesse de Polignac has!" Gerald remarked to Cocteau (who didn't like her). "She looks like Dante."

"*Oui,*" responded Cocteau. "*La Mère Dante,*" which, literally translated, means "Mother Dante," but which is also a vulgar pun ("*L'emmerdente*"), the equivalent of "pain in the ass." Hemingway, who (Archie MacLeish said) spoke French like a butcher, probably didn't get it, which would only have increased his feeling, when with Gerald, of being a bull in a birdcage.

Whether such feelings were the cause, a chill entered his relationship with Gerald during the spring of 1927. Hemingway complained about it to Archie MacLeish, who counseled him that "Gerald would get over whatever was

eating him the moment he saw" Ernest. "I didn't know for sure," he continued, "that you'd get over your irritation with Gerald ditto." The two of them
patched up their quarrel, and Ernest and Pauline came to visit at Villa America that summer. But between them and around them, all kinds of things had
begun to change.

At first only Sara seemed to notice. "People have now started to crowd onto
our beach," she wrote to Zelda Fitzgerald in Delaware, where the Fitzgeralds
had rented a house for a time:

> discouragingly undeterred by our natural wish to have it alone — However,
> by means of teaching the children to throw wet sand a good deal, & by
> bringing several disagreeable barking dogs & staking them around — we
> manage to keep space open for sunbaths. . . . The Old guard of last year has
> changed, giving place to a new lot of American Writers & Mothers. . . .
> We miss you and the MacLeishes dreadfully. . . .
> Is Scott working? And how's the book coming on? We haven't had any
> fights but then the season is barely opened — give us time.

In place of the Fitzgeralds and the MacLeishes, who were in Massachusetts
for the summer, a new, more social crowd had come to La Garoupe, people
who were less interested in painting or poetry and more interested in parties:
people like the Charles Bracketts and Harpo Marx (who asked the Murphys
how one arranged a trip to Pamplona). The Algonquin smart set, personified
by Woollcott, Benchley, and others, had made a permanent beachhead.
There were more and more distractions, and the relationships that had nourished the Murphys' sense of community and accomplishment were weaken-
ing. Dos Passos came to stay, as well as Pauline and Ernest; and they saw
Picasso at least once, but the old sense of intimacy had ebbed. At a Paris
concert the previous winter, MacLeish had seen Gerald cut Picasso dead.
Still, Gerald hoped to have Picasso come to his studio that summer — he was
particularly eager to show him the pictures he'd been working on — but it
wasn't possible. "*Hélas, alors,*" Gerald lamented.

The pictures Gerald wanted Picasso to see were, most likely, the ones he
also wrote to Hemingway about in June. "I'm working all the time," he said,
"and feel that I've knocked one or two things on the nose. Before I die I'm

going to do one picture which will be hitched up to the universe at some point. I feel it now and can work quietly."

One of these paintings seems to have been *Bibliothèque*, a composition in gray-blues, browns, and blacks showing objects from Patrick Murphy's study — a globe, books, a magnifying glass, and a bust of Emerson — arranged around a central column or pilaster topped with a classical cornice. The architectural forms of *Doves* are repeated here, but the addition of Emerson — and of the globe, which shows the continents of North and South America — gives *Bibliothèque* a strongly American flavor. Years later Gerald would say that in his paintings he was reaching for a kind of native classicism "such as the Greeks must have craved . . . what Emerson meant when he wrote, 'And we [Americans] shall be classic *unto ourselves.*'" But if Gerald was trying to celebrate this classicism in *Bibliothèque*, he did so with some ambivalence. The sober palette of *Bibliothèque* is far from the pearly tones he used in *Doves*. Rather, this painting carries with it the gloom of a Victorian town house. (In his notebook, Gerald proposed painting the base of the globe in "blk. fond" — *deep* black, as in the bottom of a well.) And although *Doves* had played with optical tricks of magnification and reduction, the magnifying glass here reveals only a blank, empty lens. Similarly, the title plates of the spines on the three bound books are blank, and the countries and continents depicted on the globe have no names. The New World, the world of his father, is an empty world, and it's not clear that he is ready to reenter it.

The other picture Gerald finished around this time, *Cocktail*, is altogether jauntier, a gleaming assemblage of cocktail glasses, corkscrew, crosscut lemon, and cocktail shaker, all surrounding an open cigar box whose painted lid has been replicated in photographic detail (the reproduction took four months to complete). Its inspiration, like *Bibliothèque*'s, was familial. In this case, it was Patrick Murphy's bar tray, the same one from which Gerald, Sara, and Pauline Pfeiffer had been served cocktails on their recent visit to New York. A gin-and-vermouth tang relieves the rigorous geometry of the composition and grisaille palette of the background: bright yellow lemon, yellow and gold cocktail glass, crimson cherry, and squiggly corkscrew.

But the center of the picture is the cigar box, within which rest five rather phallic cigars — that magic number five, standing, perhaps, for Gerald, Sara, and the three children, that crops up in so many of his pictures. On the box's lid, a woman in classical robes and crown points to a globe showing the continents of Africa and Europe; the woman's index finger rests where the Mediterranean should be. Also in the scene are a tiny schooner, a flywheel (like the ones in *Watch* and *Pressure*), and a painter's palette — all objects drawn from Gerald's personal iconography. If *Bibliothèque* represents the world of his father, the cigar box is Gerald's world — *on* his father's cocktail tray, but not *of* it. Sara may have sensed the climate changing at Antibes, but Gerald didn't seem quite ready to give it up.

He had ordered a new boat, a bigger, faster boat than the "faultily faultless, icily regular, splendidly null" *Picaflor*, in which he and Dos nearly came to grief that summer. They had been cruising to Genoa overnight when an epic Mediterranean gale blew them into the port of Savona under full sail. Not knowing the harbor, and unable to take in *Picaflor's* sails because the halyards were jammed, they miscalculated the channel and nearly smashed up on the breakwater, but just managed to drop anchor in time. The new boat, *Honoria*, was a "hot boat" in Gerald's words, a sixteen-meter sloop designed by Vladimir and custom-built in Bordeaux for racing as well as cruising; she had a motor for getting her skipper out of tight spots, and Gerald was already full of plans for racing her as soon as she was delivered, in the spring, when he hoped Archie MacLeish would join him.

The MacLeishes returned to France in the fall, but they had bought a farm in Conway, Massachusetts, and planned to move there permanently when the reconstruction on the house was completed. Ada was pregnant with her third child — "the child of my old age," she said in a letter to a mutual friend of the MacLeishes' and the Murphys' — and Archie's father was dying; they wanted to go home. They came to Antibes for a valedictory visit in February, but the cruel winter of 1928, in which snow fell on the Villa America, put paid to Archie and Gerald's plans for a maiden cruise aboard the new *Honoria*. In March the Murphys came to Paris for a series of farewells. For they were losing more than the MacLeishes: Pauline Hemingway was also pregnant, and she and Ernest wanted their baby to be born in America; they had rented a house in Key West and would sail there via Cuba in a few weeks' time.

When the Murphys saw them Ernest was looking particularly piratical: he had a thick bandage around his head where he'd cut himself on a skylight a few days before, after a dinner with the MacLeishes. Rather oddly, he struck up a conversation with Gerald about homosexuals: "I don't mind a fairy like X," he said, with studied casualness, "do you?"

"For some reason," Gerald later recalled, "I said 'No,' although I had never met the man . . . and he gave me a funny look. Afterward I almost wondered whether it had been a trap he laid for me. After that I always felt he had a reservation about me." Whatever the trap was, whatever its purpose might have been, nothing was ever quite the same between them.

The Hemingways left for Key West in March, and the MacLeishes sailed for New York in May. But almost at the same time the Fitzgeralds, who had been living an increasingly chaotic and unproductive life at Ellerslie in Delaware, decided to come back to France: "They were on their way to Paris," Zelda wrote in *Save Me the Waltz.* "They hadn't much faith in travel nor a great belief in change of scene as a panacea for spiritual ills; they were simply glad to be going."

Gerald and Sara were just as glad to see them. "We are very fond of you both," Gerald wrote Scott in anticipation of their arrival. "The fact that we don't always get on has nothing to do with it, Americans are apt only to feel fond of the people whom they see most or with whom they run. To be able to talk to people after almost two years is the important thing." And they seemed to pick up things right where they had left off the summer before. "We are friends with the Murphys again," Fitzgerald wrote Hemingway. "Talked about you a great deal + while we *tried* to say only kind things we managed to get in a few good cracks that would amuse you — about anybody else — which is what you get for being so far away."

The Murphys had recently given up their apartment on the quai des Grands-Augustins and had taken another at 14 rue Guynemer on the corner of the rue de Vaugirard, overlooking the Luxembourg Gardens; but they planned to be in Antibes for the summer and offered to lend it to Scott and Zelda. The Fitzgeralds didn't think much of the decor — "it looks like the setting for one of Madame Tussaud's gloomier figures," wrote Zelda to a friend — but they were glad to have a Paris base.

Zelda had started studying ballet in Delaware, and now she seemed driven to pursue her dancing even though, at twenty-eight, she was too old for a ballet career. Because of the Murphys' long-standing connection with the Ballets Russes, they were the logical people for Zelda to ask about possible teachers. Despite his misgivings about Zelda's potential ("There are limits to what a woman Zelda's age can do," he said) Gerald arranged for her to study with Lubov Egorova, a former principal for the Ballets Russes who was now head of its school, and the private teacher of Anton Dolin, Alexandra Danilova, and James Joyce's schizophrenic daughter, Lucia. "I had the feeling that unless one went through with it [arranging Zelda's introduction] something awful would happen," he explained.

Although the summer had begun hopefully, it was soon obvious that things were no more right with the Fitzgeralds than they had been. Scott was drinking, not just as an escape from work, but as an intended stimulus for it; and Zelda seemed to be lost in some alternative universe of her own. Sara Murphy went with her to a luncheon at which a number of people came up and introduced themselves, and as they did so Zelda took their hands, smiling, and muttered, under her breath, "I hope you die in a marble ring." "She was so charming and polite as she said it," Sara recalled. "Of course no one suspected that she was saying anything but the usual pleasantries; I heard her because I was standing right next to her."

One day Zelda invited the Murphys to come to Egorova's studio to watch her dance, an invitation they accepted reluctantly. The floor of the studio was raked to simulate a ballet stage, which caused spectators to look uphill at the dancers. "The view was not a flattering one," Gerald remembered, "for it made her seem taller, more awkward than she was. There was something dreadfully grotesque in her intensity — one could see the muscles stretch and pull; her legs looked muscular and ugly. It was really terrible. One held one's breath until it was over. Thank God, she couldn't see what she looked like." Gerald and Sara fled to Antibes with something like relief.

One morning, soon after their return, they called their children to a hasty and secret family conference. They said they had received anonymous instructions in the mail, telling them to dig up a map buried in their garden which would lead them to pirate treasure buried somewhere on the coast between

Antibes and the Spanish border. Being careful not to attract attention, the children raced to the garden and dug in the spot marked X; soon they un-earthed a small, rusty metal box, which appeared to be old and which contained a faded parchment map of the Mediterranean coast. On the map, remembered Honoria, was a cross drawn in some brownish substance that might have been blood; it marked a cove near St.-Tropez. The only way to get to it, Gerald told his now goggle-eyed children, would be to organize a sailing expedition: so food and tents and bedding and shovels were bought and brought on board *Honoria*, and two days later, with Vladimir navigating, they set off.

The treasure voyage was a long one. There were pauses for lunch, for swims in the limpid Mediterranean, and for dinner and the night in port at St.-Tropez; at last they arrived at a secluded cove where they dropped anchor, rowed ashore, and struck camp outside a small cave. But because they could see a man walking on a distant hill Gerald made them defer their excavations until morning. That night he told them ghost stories, and Sara played Stravinsky and Debussy's *La Cathédrale englouti* on the windup record player she had brought along. The next day they dug up another little metal box, this time with a key in it, and, at last, what seemed like a very old chest, its lock rusted from age and disuse. Sara fitted the key into the lock and opened the chest, and with gasps of delight the children saw that it was filled to the top with coins and jewels that dazzled in the brilliant sunlight.

It was years before any of them learned that the maps had been drawn by Gerald and Vladimir, who had also found the chest in a secondhand shop somewhere on the Left Bank in Paris, and that Sara had bought the costume jewelry at flea markets. But by then the treasure hunt had achieved mythic proportions. "It was such a success," said Gerald, "that sometimes I feel it didn't ever happen." Whether or not the treasure, or the pirates, were real had ceased to matter. Like a Fabergé egg, it was more wonderful *because* it was fabricated.

Some time before the treasure hunt, Gerald had entered *Honoria* in an extended ocean race from Marseille to Corsica called the Course Croisière de la Méditerranée. This was a very grand affair indeed, with twenty-three boats of different sizes and rigs, each with a handicap, and the contestants were all seasoned yachtsmen. Gerald's crew of four, including himself and Vladimir, set out on the first leg without ever having had *Honoria* under sail before. But after the first two stages, from Marseille to Toulon, and Toulon to Cannes, they had beaten all the other fancy yachts and were ranked first. Sara joined them at Cannes, bearing food and drink, which turned out to be a blessing because a thirty-hour dead calm off Corsica put them well back in seventh place. Sara kept them all going with cold beer, and with some skillful sailing by all hands they whisked into the harbor at Ajaccio in third. Gerald was jubilant — "I've never been exposed to an incessant excitement day AND night for twenty-one days before," he wrote to Dos Passos, who was in Russia — and he was looking forward to an August rematch with the boat that had beaten him for second place.

But events conspired to keep him from becoming a yachtsman along the lines of Sara's old friend Gerard Lambert; for before the August race something happened that, in unforeseen ways, would change the Murphys' lives forever.

In the summer of 1928 the American director King Vidor came to France to publicize the opening there of his film *The Crowd*, a picture much influenced by Fritz Lang's dark masterpiece *Metropolis*. Vidor himself was the first to admit this debt: he had, he said, consciously adopted the "shadowy effects" Lang invoked so tellingly in his film, and used "a lot" of false perspective, rather in the manner of Picasso, Léger — or Murphy. "[I]t was a time of the German Expressionist paintings, and the Picasso paintings were all with table tops tilted toward the painter, the viewer," Vidor recalled. He had been aiming at the same thing.

While he was in Paris, Vidor had read an article in *Variety* that announced a sort of Doppler shift in the movie industry: the phenomenal success of Al Jolson's *The Jazz Singer*, which had opened on October 6, 1927, had convinced studio executives that talking pictures were not a gimmick but the wave of the future; and now they were all paddling hard to catch up. If Vidor wanted to survive, it was clear he'd have to do likewise, so he quickly submitted a list of ideas to the MGM brass. At the top of his list was a musical drama called *Hallelujah!* a story of black sharecroppers in rural Mississippi featuring a love triangle gone wrong, a murder, a chain gang, a flood, and final redemption. Vidor wanted to use undiscovered black actors and explore expressionistic film techniques instead of producing "a classic country down south type of thing." And because he claimed to know and love Negro spirituals — "in my home town of Galveston," he said, "you could hear them down on the docks, pushing cotton bales around and singing songs" — he wanted an authentically African American score. Scott Fitzgerald, with whom Vidor had worked in Hollywood in the fall of 1927, told him he knew just the man to help him: Gerald Murphy.

On Fitzgerald's recommendation, Vidor came to see both Murphys at the Villa America. Vidor admired Gerald's pictures and seemed to be thinking about incorporating some of his work into the film; as he recalled later, "I thought that the type of painting he did would fit very well into the type of photography that I was going to use" in *Hallelujah!* On his side, Gerald had been impressed by Vidor's work, particularly *The Crowd*. His conversations with Léger had made him only more eager to explore the possibilities of film as an artistic medium, and he immediately understood what Vidor said he was after in *Hallelujah!* He and Sara ran through their repertoire of spirituals for him; and when Vidor invited him to come to Hollywood to consult on the photography and the score, Gerald immediately said yes.

Before he could leave, however, Gerald had to complete a canvas for a small show of his work which was to be held at the Galerie Georges Bernheim in Paris that winter. Even though it was conceived as a kind of appetizer to a larger exhibition of the paintings of Armand Guillaumin, it was his first one-man exhibition, and he was pardonably excited about it. "My latest things," he wrote John Dos Passos, "are a moving mass of looseness and liberation." Certainly, in the picture he was working on that summer of 1928, the rigid geometry and cubist displacement characteristic of his work after *Boatdeck* had begun to give way to something else.

Portrait is different in feeling from its predecessors. It's freer, less framed, and it seems not so much to deconstruct or refract reality as to *assemble* it. The painting had begun in the pages of Gerald's art notebook, not as a completed idea but as a series of images. "An eye," Gerald had written, "lashes, brow, lids, etc. big scale, — even pores, hairs." Elsewhere he added, "*(Use tracing of a foot in picture)." The picture that took shape from those notes was composed entirely of the *parts* of its subject — an eye, a footprint, three thumbprints, a mouth, a profile. All were presented as differently scaled objects on separate fields set off by rulers or measuring sticks, a device Léger had been experimenting with, although Gerald personalized it by his use again of the number five on the ruler. The eye, which was rendered in surreal, proto-pop detail, might have been a fragment of the advertising poster for the monstrous eyes of Dr. T. J. Eckleburg at the beginning of Scott Fitzgerald's *The Great Gatsby*. In fact, it was Gerald's own, magnified and reproduced on canvas. The foot, too, was Gerald's, a tracing from life, with its own inked imprint superimposed on top. The thumbprints were also his; he had taken three impressions on paper with ink, and then painstakingly reproduced them using a brush from which he had removed all but a single camel's hair. But the profile at the picture's bottom left-hand corner was an image he copied from the "conglomerate standard facial profile of the Caucasian Man, from the archives of the Bibliothèque Nationale."

Gerald was a meticulous craftsman who labored through countless preliminary studies and the process of recreating his thumbprints on canvas must alone have taken him months; so it's likely that he began work on *Portrait* early in 1928, when the MacLeishes were visiting Villa America before their return to the country Gerald wasn't yet ready to embrace. That September, as he finished *Portrait*, he received a letter from Archie — a letter in the form of a poem, which MacLeish later published, with some minor alterations, as "American Letter — For Gerald Murphy" in his collection *New Found Land*.

"Dear G," he wrote from Uphill Farm, his and Ada's new home in Conway, Massachusetts:

> . . . Why should I think of the dolphins at Capo di Mele?
> Why should I see in my mind the taut sail
> And the hill over St. Tropez & your hand on the tiller?
> . . .
> This land is my native land. And yet
> I am sick for home for the red roofs & the olives,

And the foreign words & the white of the sea fall.
How can a wise man have two countries?
How can a man behold the sun & want
A land far off, alien, smelling of palm trees,
And the yellow gorse at noon in the long calms?

. . .

It is a strange thing to be an American.

. . .

It is strange to sleep in the bare stars & to die
On an open land where few have perished before us.

. . .

It is strange to be born of no race & no people.
In the old lands they are many together. They keep
The wise past & the words spoken in common.
                                    . . . They eat
The same dish, their drink is the same & their proverbs.

. . .

They are many men. . . .
Here it is one man and the wind in the boughs.

. . .

Nevertheless this is our land & our people, —
This that is neither a land nor a race. . . .

. . .

Here we must live or live only as shadows.
This is our race, we who have known, who have had
Neither the old walls nor the voices around us —
This is our land, this is our ancient ground —

. . .

It is this we cannot leave though the old call us.

"American Letter" was MacLeish's answer to the question — implied between them ever since the quarrel last spring — "Who am I?" *Portrait* was Gerald's. Shortly after he completed it, on October 23, the five Murphys sailed from Marseille on the liner *Saturnia*, bound for the United States.

16

"A dismantled house
where people have once been gay"

ON NOVEMBER 1, 1928, the *Saturnia* docked in New York, and Gerald and
Sara maneuvered their considerable entourage from the pier to the Savoy
Plaza Hotel, on Fifth Avenue and 59th Street. This took some doing, for the
Murphys traveled in grand style. There were Sara and Gerald and the three
children; there were Mam'zelle Géron and Vladimir, who was acting as
majordomo and was going to help on the film; there were the dogs, who sailed
in the shipboard kennel and were walked on deck every day; there were the
portable gramophone and the favorite records; there was Sara's bottle bag, a
sort of doctor's satchel filled with bottles of alcohol, witch hazel, Dobell's
solution for gargling in case of sore throats, pastilles Vichy for upset stomachs,
and a variety of other remedies, including good bootleg whiskey decanted into
perfume bottles to evade customs. Then there were the trunks and valises,
made to order by Mark Cross and color-coded by owner: a red stripe woven
into the luggage fabric for Honoria, a blue one for Baoth, a yellow one for
Patrick, green for Sara, and brown, gray, or black for Gerald, to make it easier
to recognize and sort them all. "I'm afraid we traveled with an awful lot of
bags," Honoria says now.

Their rooms at the Savoy Plaza faced Fifth Avenue, Central Park, and
Grand Army Plaza, and from their windows the children could see Augustus
Saint-Gaudens's gilded equestrian statue of General William Tecumseh
Sherman being led southward by Victory in her tunic and laurel wreath.
"*C'est l'Oncle Général et Tante Hoytie*" ("It's our uncle the General and Aunt

Hoytie"), they assured one another. After all, as Saint-Gaudens had immortalized their famous ancestor, would he not have done the same for their tall and imperious aunt?

After the possibly mixed pleasure of watching Don Stewart make his acting debut impersonating Gerald — or the Geraldesque half of a couple described by the heroine as "the brightest, happiest people I've ever known" — in Phil Barry's new play, *Holiday*, the Murphys boarded the Super Chief for Los Angeles. The children were thrilled to see actual Indians and cowboys from the train, although they were somewhat anxious about the possibility of Indian raids and had to be assured by Sara that such things no longer happened. In fact, Gerald told them, most Indians had now been unfairly confined to reservations, something he condemned in no uncertain terms.

In Hollywood the Murphys moved into a stucco bungalow at 1737 Angelo Drive in Beverly Hills, where the children made friends with their nice black chauffeur, learned how to roller-skate and rode horses, and soon acquired a menagerie equal to the one they had left behind in Antibes: a turtle for Patrick, and a canary, named Dicky, for Honoria. They visited movie sets or went to elaborate parties — Marion Davies gave one at her faux-eighteenth-century Malibu "beach house" at which they met Charlie Chaplin. Or, dressed in Tom Mix Stetsons and pony-skin chaps, they played at cowboys and Indians ("Patrick," wrote Baoth mysteriously to Miss Roussel, "has become a babouni and a fighter of the Indians"). To them, Hollywood was a fragrant paradise; but Gerald and Sara hated it.

Everywhere they went they were bombarded with signs bearing egregiously cute or bathetically grandiose names like Hippedy-Hop Cake Shop, Oakwood Storknest Hospital, Holsum Wonder Bread, Rite Spot, Home of the Aristocratic Hamburger, or The Bedspring Luxurious. "My God what a place this is," wrote Gerald to Dos Passos in exasperation. "The whole works has gone quaint. . . . The kitchen utensils have enamelled handles in *pastel* shades. Bootblacks and barbers wear indigo and jade-green smocks at their toil. . . . Waitresses are costumed as Watteau Shepherdesses, Matadors, Holland Maidens (with wooden shoes), Sailors (the effect somewhat marred because of the prevalence of make-up and plucked eye-brows)."

Almost worse than the cuteness was the lack of authenticity. "I don't demand good art of a country," grumbled Gerald, "but when they can't cook a decent meal or sell a vegetable with any taste to it, then something's up. There is nothing to eat except when Sara cooks it." And even she was laboring under formidable handicaps. One day she went to the grocery store for a box of crackers and was told by the grocer that she must be looking for Cupid Chips. "In my time," she told the grocer, through gritted teeth, "they were called Saltines."

"Well, same thing, I guess," said the grocer — to which Sara tartly replied, "Not at all. A big man like you calling things Cupid Chips!"

In self-defense they spent as much time as possible in the Mexican quarter of Los Angeles ("It saves our lives, that place," said Gerald) and commiserated with a group of kindred spirits who helped them "cut the grease of Marion Davies and Mary Pickford": Edmund Wilson, who was writing a novel in a borrowed Santa Barbara beach house; Bob Benchley, who arrived in December to do three short movies for Twentieth Century–Fox; and Dorothy Parker, who was trying to make money writing scripts at MGM. Parker was so starved for company at the studio that she had put up a sign saying "Men's Room" on her office door — but perhaps no company at all was preferable to the company of the director who boasted to her that he owned "a $150,000 liberry with a first edition of *Edith* St. Vincent Millay."

"Now don't sit down and defend all this," Gerald admonished Dos Passos. "It would be all right if they weren't so smug. That combined with their ignorance. Their ignorance combined with their prosperity. The wealth of it all takes the heart out of you."

Gerald's view of things was possibly jaundiced by the permutations *Hallelujah!* was undergoing at the hands of the studio executives at MGM. The studio had always been skittish about Vidor's plans for a *real* all-black musical, but had green-lighted the project when Vidor agreed to underwrite it with his own money. The director proceeded to cast the movie under difficult conditions: although he hired some actors and singers from African American revues, such as Nina Mae McKinney from *Blackbirds of 1929*, he plucked others from the streets or from church choirs, or found them waiting on tables or carrying bags. In Chicago he had to rent an entire hotel for auditions because Jim Crow laws made it illegal for blacks to enter "white" hotel dining rooms in that city. But despite the fact that Vidor had as much invested in the film as the studio did, MGM's legendary Irving Thalberg kept Vidor on a short leash during the casting. One of his nearly daily telegrams to the director second-guessed Vidor's choice of an actress named Honey Brown for the part of the temptress, Chick: "SINCERELY HOPE THIS CAN BE ONE OF THE VERY FEW TIMES IN WHICH YOU ARE RIGHT. . . . MY CHIEF OBJECTION TO HONEY BROWN IS CERTAIN UGLINESS PARTICULARLY AROUND HER MOUTH HER FLAT CHESTEDNESS AND HER UPPER LIP HAS VERY OUTSTANDING HAIR LINE BEST REGARDS."

Thalberg's hand also weighed heavily on the choice of music for the film, one of the areas where Vidor, with Gerald's help, had hoped to maintain a certain authenticity. In the earliest stages the studio had not been entirely convinced that *Hallelujah!* should have sound, and even after the movie was cast and had gone into rehearsal the question had not been resolved. By the time it *was*, Gerald and Vidor might have wished it hadn't been. The first script, based on Vidor's conversations with Gerald, laid the movie's opening scene on "the small Johnson plantation" somewhere in the South, where the Johnson family is picking cotton to a voice-over of a spiritual called "Chilly Water." Close-ups of family members, with identifying subtitles, were to be synched with the verses of the song. By the time the project had become "Production # 394 Directed by King Vidor . . . Story by King Vidor, Continuity by Wanda Tuchok. Okayed by Mr. Thalberg Sept 25/28," however, some changes had taken place.

The opening was now to include "six typical scenes of picturesque cotton picking. The pickers are all . . . typical Southern negroes." The action was to be threaded through with songs that, the script said, "can easily be synchronized after the picture is finished. EXAMPLE: 'Old Black Joe' — 'Carry Me Back to Ole Virginie' — 'My Old Kentucky Home' — 'Swanee River' — 'In the Evening by the Moonlight'." Somehow Stephen Foster had replaced the authentic race music that Vidor and Gerald had envisioned, and worse was to come.

Possibly the penultimate straw was the comic bit of business involving a watermelon that was added for three little boys called Sears, Roebuck, and Coe; or the dialogue between a parson and two characters named, improbably, Adam and Eve (Parson, after Adam and Eve have asked him to marry them: "Ain't these kids yourn?" Adam: "That's jes it — we think it's bout time to make it permanent"). Whatever the cause, Gerald was disgusted. "[I]n two weeks," he recalled, "they had it so full of scenes around the cabin door, with talk of chittlin's and corn-pone and banjoes a-strummin', that it was about as negro as Lew Dockstader's Minstrels."

Then, in early December, after location shooting in Memphis, Tennessee, and more filming on the MGM lot, the studio began recording the sound sequences — which, since portable sound equipment had yet to be invented, had to be produced on the lot and synchronized with the existing footage. When Thalberg heard the sound track, he was not pleased: it was too depressing, it was too strange; the audiences that had packed theaters for *The Jazz Singer* would stay away from this picture in droves. To lighten things up a little, Thalberg added two songs by Irving Berlin to the score, "The Swanee Shuffle," for which a whole scene involving singing waiters was created, and "Waiting at the End of the Road," an uplifting finale. And — for Gerald, the coup de grâce — Thalberg hired "LIONEL BARRYMORE to coach these negroes in the use of dialect." Gerald resigned. As he reported it to Dos Passos, "to see what I have seen, hear what I have heard. Zowie."

Despite their feelings about California, the Murphys stayed on after Gerald left *Hallelujah!* Vladimir, however, whose role as production assistant had now evaporated, departed for France almost immediately. Henriette Géron had developed a crush on him, which made him horribly uncomfortable, so Gerald deputed him to go to Paris and supervise the installation of his show at Galerie Georges Bernheim, which opened on January 15. After his departure Sara, Gerald, and the children went to Carmel briefly to visit Olga and Sidney Fish. Sidney had been very ill with pneumonia and had been advised to leave New York for a more temperate climate, so he and Olga had just bought the Palo Corona ranch outside Carmel and planned to move there permanently. It was still quite wild — there was only a cabin on the property, not a proper ranch house — but the Murphy children adored it, and when they weren't doing perfunctory lessons with Mam'zelle they spent all day riding and picnicking.

Possibly as a result of conversations about Sidney's illness, Sara determined to have all three children's tonsils removed while they were still in California. "It seems the most favorable time — in a mild climate like this," reported Sara to her father, "and it's really most necessary — They have glands and things — which would only make trouble later." All three spent the night in the hospital and were driven home to Angelo Drive afterward by the chauffeur, who carried each child tenderly from car to house. Although there was an anxious moment when Honoria suffered a postoperative hemorrhage, the children quickly recuperated, and were soon ready to travel eastward. Sara wanted to discuss some financial matters with her father — she was eager to take more control over her money, and hoped to persuade him to relinquish his power of attorney over her investments. Rather than "letting everything lie" in the hands of the Guaranty Trust she wanted to get into the market with a more aggressive broker, as Olga had done, and couldn't understand why Frank Wiborg had been carefully getting *out*, selling some of her shares in addition to his own. Every day, it seemed, the stock market posted ever higher gains, and only a few people like Frank Wiborg understood that there was a reckoning ahead. But by the time it happened, in October, Sara and Gerald would have other things on their minds.

Photographs taken before a cataclysmic event have a strange power: the viewer scans them, looking for clues to the events that will soon overtake the subject, but fate rarely shows its hand that way. When it does, the viewer wonders how much of what is visible is only hindsight. What, for example, can be read in the photograph of the Murphys on shipboard as they were on their way back to France in March 1929? All are bundled against the cold, the children in identical brass-buttoned, double-breasted navy peacoats and dark berets, Gerald in a sleek dark overcoat and jaunty cap, Sara in leopard with a turned-up collar, her beret pulled vampishly down to her eyebrows. Gerald looks both dreamy and withdrawn, as he often does in photographs; Honoria pensive. Baoth, already taller than his older sister, grins into the sunlight, his chin thrust out confidently; at his side, Patrick smiles shyly, his features delicate beneath his thatch of white blond hair. Behind him, Sara is also smiling, but only barely. She looks wary, slightly mistrustful, as if she were waiting for something to happen.

Shortly after the Murphys arrived home at Villa America, the Fitzgeralds — frayed by their attempts to make a life in the United States — joined them briefly. They were on their way to Paris, where they planned to settle indefinitely, and they were not the best of company: Scott was frustrated and guilty about his lack of progress on his novel, and hoped to get back on track in France; and Zelda could think only of returning to her ballet studies with Egorova.

The Hemingways were back in France, also, with their baby, whom they had named Patrick; when Gerald heard the news he had written tetchily to Dos Passos that "Ireland is doomed if *that* name is going to take on literary values. . . . I thought it was foolproof." Apparently he felt that Ernest was straying onto his turf: for although Sara remained as fond of both Hemingways as before, and although Gerald liked Pauline enormously, relations between him and Ernest had taken on the chancy quality of March weather, promising one day, frosty the next. They weren't helped by the suicide, in December, of Ernest's father, for whom Ernest had long felt the greatest ambivalence. In the winter before he and Pauline married — when he was writing his father that "You would be so much happier and I would too, if you could have confidence in me" — he was also symbolically destroying his father's most treasured possessions. In a story called "Now I Lay Me," the protagonist, named "Ernie" in the first draft, helps burn his father's collection of Indian arrowheads. Later, in another story, "Fathers and Sons," Hemingway acted out a symbolic parricide in which his protagonist sits in the woodshed cradling a rifle, looking out at his father, who is on a porch a few yards away, and thinking, "I can blow him to hell. I can kill him."

Gerald Murphy, of course, had been playing father to Hemingway ever since they had met: writing letters to "My Dear Boy" from "daow-daow — (french spelling)"; giving Ernest money; paying his son's doctor bills; admiring his work; supporting his divorce and remarriage. Ernest's real father had done none of these things; and after his death Ernest could barely bring himself to acknowledge how he felt about that. Writing to Dos Passos from Key West, he maintained a dismissive flippancy: "Every other day we shoot snipe for the day after. My old man shot himself on the other hand (not in the other hand. In the head) as you may have read in the paper." But Archie

MacLeish understood what was going on in Hemingway's mind; in a condolence letter he sent that December, which Hemingway never opened, he wrote: "I know how the death of your father changes him in your mind . . . You must not let your mind work over and over the way it happened. I know the way your mind works round and round your pain like a dog in cover going over and over the same track."

Working around and around, it was inevitable that Ernest would manage to displace much of the pain and resentment he felt about Clarence Hemingway to his surrogate father, Gerald. How else could he use those feelings in his fiction? So when Gerald asked Ernest to join him in another Course Croisière that summer, from Cannes to Barcelona by way of Marseille and Majorca, Ernest excused himself. He was going to Spain, and said that the proofs of his new novel, A *Farewell to Arms*, would keep him too busy to join *Honoria*'s crew.

Despite Hemingway's defection, the Murphys had a full house. At the end of April, Gerald's sister Esther had surprised everyone by suddenly marrying John Strachey, an English economist and recently elected member of Parliament. Strachey came from a distinguished Bloomsbury family (Lytton Strachey was his cousin, as was James Strachey, the psychiatrist and translator of Freud) and had political ambitions without the funds to implement them. On his insistence, the elder Patrick Murphy paid him a handsome dowry. After their wedding, at which Oswald Mosley, not yet a Fascist, was best man, the Stracheys came to France on holiday and stayed at Villa America. The visit was not entirely pleasurable: Strachey was already confiding to an old girlfriend that the marriage "is not going well," and he seemed to regard all Americans as bad-mannered parvenus. Esther, possibly under provocation, was polishing off a bottle of gin a day by herself.

In June, Robert Benchley and his family drove down from Paris accompanied by Dorothy Parker, who had been working on a novel and was recovering from a failed romance with a New York banker named John Garrett. They all arrived hot and cross: both Benchley boys, Nat and Bub, had quarreled energetically throughout the journey; Parker's dog Timothy had kept up a migraine-inducing continuo of yapping from Paris to Antibes; little Bub had been stung by nettles when he got out to relieve himself by the side of the road; and Bob and Gertrude Benchley were barely speaking to each other, much less to Parker. The Murphys set everything to rights at once: they put the Benchleys in the Ferme des Orangers (which Benchley referred to as "La Ferme Dérangée") and gave Parker the *bastide* so she would have a quiet place to work. But, although the little stone cottage was exquisitely decorated and idyllically peaceful, it was surrounded by fig trees and, Parker said, "I hate figs in any form." Still in mourning for her affair with Garrett, she spent much of her time smoking solitary cigarettes in the garden, where the children's tutor, Yvonne Roussel, found her sitting with a "lost" look on her gamine countenance. In an effort to cheer her up Gerald and Sara took her to the beach and got her to swim, with Gerald, two kilometers a day, which did wonders for her sometimes overly voluptuous figure, and the children begged her to join their games. Baoth went so far as to name his pet hen after her; when it was later discovered that Dorothy the hen was, in fact, a rooster, he was unfazed. "What is that of difference?" he asked, in the children's translated-from-the-French patois. As Scott Fitzgerald reported to Ernest Hemingway, "the Murphys have given their whole performance for her this summer and I think, tho she'd be the last to admit it, she's had the time of her life."

Trying to touch the sources of their old magic, the Fitzgeralds had also come south for the summer, but so far the magic seemed to have eluded them. From their rented villa in Cannes they made forays to La Garoupe or the casino or Villa America, Scott unearthly pale and given to drunken displays of maudlinity, Zelda more and more distant. She seemed to care only about her dancing — and although he privately despaired of her chances Gerald, at least, did what he could to help her, trying to get her together with Diaghilev's prima ballerina Vera Nemchinova, who was staying in Antibes that summer. One day the Fitzgeralds and Murphys took their children to the poky little movie theater in Antibes to see a documentary about underwater life, and Zelda became terrified by the sight of an octopus moving diagonally across the screen. "What is it? What is it!" she screamed, burying her head in Gerald's chest and clinging to him like a drowning victim.

"It's been gay here," commented Scott with unintentional irony to Hemingway, "but we are, thank God, desperately unpopular and not invited anywhere." The only people willing to put up with them for any length of time were the Murphys, whom they saw "once a week or so," he said. "Gerald is older, less gay, more social, but not so changed as many people in five years."

Although old friends like Don and Bea Stewart came to stay, the Riviera that summer was overrun with showbiz types and international millionaires: Peggy Hopkins Joyce and Rosie Dolly, one of the famous Dolly sisters; the matinee idol John Gilbert and his bride, Ina Claire; "Laddie" Sanford, the polo-playing, horse-racing heir to a carpet fortune; assorted playboys and minor royalty; the duke of Westminster and Coco Chanel. Bob Benchley literally bumped into a former mistress on the street in Cannes, where only two years previously it would have been rare to find an English-speaking person in summertime; he was so unnerved by the experience that he made Dottie Parker come out with him that afternoon and get "absolutely blotto." Another day, driving in Nice, he collided with the chauffeur-driven limousine of a Georgian prince; but he thought the prince had agreed there was no harm done, and was furious when a *huissier* — a court bailiff — arrived at the Villa America to impound his car. Gerald, most unusually, lost control: he went into a towering rage and threw the bailiff out, calling him a *sale voleur* (dirty thief). Whether, as he later claimed, he thought the bailiff was just one of the prince's minions trying a touch of extortion, or whether he was infuriated to find himself, unfamiliarly, on the wrong side of French bureaucracy, Gerald was convicted of "outrageous conduct to a public official" by the Criminal Court of Nice and sentenced to fifteen days' imprisonment. He remained free on appeal, and by the time the matter was resolved other circumstances had claimed his attention. But more and more it must have seemed to Gerald as if their formerly Edenic garden was full of the thing he had so decried in Hollywood: "Green fruit softening in the sun off the tree but no ripeness yet."

During those summer mornings, before gathering the Benchleys and Parker for their noontime forays to La Garoupe, where he would rake the sand and sweep out the cabanas as usual, Gerald went to his studio to paint green fruit. He called the picture *Wasp and Pear*, a composition he had outlined, in his notebook, as "hornet (colossal) on a pear, (marks on skin, leaf veins, etc.) (*battening* on the fruit, clenched)." In the margin he sketched two pears, one in profile, the other in seeming cross section, seen from below. If the language he used to describe it seemed predatory, the finished picture itself was more so: the wasp "battening" on the pear is terrifying. Enormous, its hooked proboscis poised over the pear like a weapon, its horny leg shown in microscopic enlargement that reveals its cruel spikes, it is a paradigm — almost a parody — of male sexual aggressiveness. And the swelling shape of the pear, with its curved waist and round bottom that recall Man Ray's (and Ingres's) odalisques, its womblike cross section revealing a tiny seed, is lushly, almost embarrassingly female. It is as if — in this painting that uses Sara's green, Patrick's yellow, and his own browns, grays, and blacks — Gerald were depicting the corruption of all that is fruitful in desire.

When he had started painting in Goncharova's atelier, Gerald had wanted to represent real objects as abstractions; but what had begun as an exercise in formalism had become a means to put distance between himself and images that carried a heavy load of personal connotation. *Watch, Razor, Bibiliothèque, Cocktail, Portrait* — all these successfully transformed a personal iconography into shapes and patterns that are pleasurable in the abstract. *Wasp and Pear* is much more disturbing. Gerald later claimed that the images in the picture derived from "the large technically-drawn and coloured charts of fruits, vegetables, horses, cattle, insects (pests)" he had seen as a cadet at Ohio State University. But the painting has none of the blandness of such art. Its vision is closer to that of one of Archie MacLeish's favorite poets, William Blake, who wrote of a rose whose "bed of crimson joy" has been attacked by an "invisible worm." Like Gerald's wasp, the parasite destroys its prey with a "dark secret love" — battening it, clenched, in a sickening parody of procreation.

Shortly before the Benchleys and Dottie Parker arrived at Villa America, Gerald had had to cut short his June Cannes–Barcelona race: Sara wired him that Patrick wasn't well and that "it was his duty to come back and be with his children." Always a delicate child, Patrick had had some kind of intestinal complaint in May and now seemed listless and feverish. But the doctor couldn't find anything wrong, and Sara and Gerald made plans to go to Venice with the Benchleys in August, and to Spain to visit the Hemingways in early September. They never got there: on September 4 Hemingway wrote

Scott Fitzgerald that "a wire from Gerald yesterday says Sara has had to go to the mountains with Patrick . . . believe their Spanish trip off."

The doctors in Antibes had concluded that Patrick was suffering from bronchitis, and Sara had taken him to Villard-de-Lans in the Cévennes *massif* of southern France — a place, Gerald reported to Hoytie and her father in New York, "at an altitude of 1,050 metres and surrounded by glaciers," where the air was thin and pure and the boy would regain his strength. "The food is not very good," said Gerald, "but Sara is able to scout through the country with the car and forage for milk, cream, fruits, etc." After three weeks of fresh air and trout fishing, however, Patrick had not improved. After returning to Antibes to welcome Pauline Hemingway's sister Jinny Pfeiffer, Sara and Gerald took the boy to Paris to see the specialist Armand De Lille.

The diagnosis was devastating: On October 10 they learned that Patrick had tuberculosis, which he had probably contracted from their Los Angeles chauffeur — they remembered now that he had had a persistent cough. The disease was firmly entrenched and had severely compromised one lung; Patrick would have to begin painful pneumothorax treatments and enter a sanatorium immediately if he were to have any hope of survival.

"He's taking the injections of gas like that brick," Gerald told the Hemingways: "He gets 300 cub. centimetres of it each time through a thick needle under his arm between the ribs. It surrounds and collapses the lung, immobilizes it, stops the spread. He's living on the good lung. They hope to keep it good. Altitude and sun treatment will help. Injections — one every 15 days to keep up the gas pressure, — for two years." On October 18, Gerald and Patrick left by train for Montana-Vermala, a health resort in the Swiss Alps one thousand meters above sea level on the Plaine Morte glacier, where the Murphys planned to remain indefinitely. It was Patrick's ninth birthday.

Sara stayed behind briefly in Paris to take Honoria, whom Jinny Pfeiffer was bringing up from Antibes on the Train Bleu, to the doctor as well, because her "bronchials showed speckly" when she was given a precautionary X-ray. De Lille could not say for certain whether she, too, was infected — she was running a fever and the X-rays were problematical, although she had no trace of TB bacilli — so he advised that she be given three months' bed rest. Numb with shock, Sara took her back to Villa America to pack up the family for the journey to Switzerland. The Hemingways offered to have Baoth come to them, but Sara could not bear to part with him: "My mother wants me to stay with her this winter," wrote Baoth, "but I'd like very much if you invite me some other time for she says that time I shall go with you to America."

It was at this point that Dottie Parker, who had gone to Paris herself on business, returned to discover that the walls had come crashing in on the Murphys' paradise. Sara, uncharacteristically thinking of herself first, begged her to help close up the villa and then come with them to Montana. But Parker, who had gone to Paris to talk about her progress, or lack of it, with her publisher, needed desperately to work on her novel. She cabled Bob Benchley for advice; when he didn't respond, she acceded. It was, her biographer said later, the worst decision she could have made; it was also the kindest.

"Sometime you must try that trip up from the Midi with three dogs, two of them in high heat, and the baggage the Murphys left behind, which consisted of eleven trunks and seventeen handpieces," she told Benchley later. It was a horrendous journey, including three changes of train, the last to a funicular which led from Sierre to Crans, a mile to the east of Montana, "as long as it takes to get to Stamford, going absolutely vertical, with nothing between you and your Maker but a length of frayed cable!" But as bad as the trip was, closing Villa America was even worse, "because what is more horrible than a dismantled house where people have once been gay?"

In Montana the Murphy entourage settled, with Patrick, into a suite of six rooms opening off a balcony on the second floor of the Palace Hotel, which in those days functioned as a kind of residential sanatorium housing the tubercular and their families. Doctors — most of whom were also tuberculosis sufferers — and nurses scurried about the halls, which were kept antiseptically clean. Because the only known cure for tuberculosis involved rest, sun, and fresh air, the "guests" had to observe quiet hours from two to five in the afternoon and after eight at night, and the hotel was well ventilated with chill Alpine breezes. As Parker described it, only half hyperbolically, "what you wear for dinner is a tweed suit, a coat over it, a woollen muffler tied tight around your neck, a knitted cap, and galoshes. When you go outdoors, you take off either the coat or the muffler."

Ernestine, Yvonne Roussel, and Clement the chauffeur had accompanied the family to Switzerland. Ernestine took care of the household tasks, Miss Roussel tried to keep up all three children's lessons, and, because the Murphys' Chrysler was next to useless on Montana's narrow, twisting roads, Clement helped to amuse Baoth during the day. Sara had already transformed their dreary suite of rooms with touches of Swiss kitsch (which in her hands wasn't kitschy at all), but Gerald "isolated himself" with Patrick, serving his meals, taking his temperature, giving him medicine, changing bedpans. "He works every minute," Parker said; "[A]ll the energy that used to go into compounding drinks and devising costumes and sweeping out the bath houses and sifting the sand on the plage has been put into inventing and running complicated Heath-Robinson sick-room appliances, and he is simply pouring his energy into Patrick, in the endeavor to make him not sick."

In an effort at gaiety — "they are so damn brave, and they are trying so hard to get a little gaiety into this, and it just kills you," Parker continued — Gerald and Sara had fixed up the salon as a *Glühwein* parlor, where they mixed hot mulled wine for their little party before they all went to bed at nine each evening. They kept on their mufflers and woollies against the cold, and they had to whisper so as not to disturb Patrick or Honoria or the other, sicker patients coughing in rooms farther down the hall, but they drank their *Glühwein* and toasted absent friends with their thick hospital tumblers. "Their families, of course," Parker went on, in a long epistle to Benchley which must rank as some of her best work, if not as one of the best letters ever written,

have been of enormous assistance. Mrs. Murphy [Gerald's mother] writes that all they have to do is act and think as if Patrick were twice as ill as he really is, and then everything will be all right with God's help. (Gerald got that letter just as he was about to stagger out of the room with four laden trays piled one on another. "With God's help," he kept saying, when he resumed his burden. "With God's help. Oh, my *God!* with God's help." Mr. Wiborg points out that this doubtless would never have occurred if the children had not been brought up like little Frenchmen. And Hoytie, good old Hoytie, cabled: "Dont be forlorn I will be over after Christmas". When he heard that one, Dow-Dow's face lit up just like the Mammoth Cave.

Back in New York, on October 29, the stock market had imploded like a quasar. In Venice, in August, Serge Diaghilev had died of the complications of diabetes, and the Ballets Russes was disbanded. In December, Harry Crosby, who had just arranged to publish Archie MacLeish's *Einstein* for his Black Sun Press, shot himself in a suicide pact with his lover, Josephine Rotch Bigelow, in New York. Up on their "God damn alp," the Murphys and Dorothy Parker knew hardly any of this — magazines and newspapers were hard to come by in the Palace Hotel. But on Sara's birthday, November 7, they had a party. "Everybody gave everybody presents — not just Sara. Even the dogs — the complete five are here — and the canaries and the parrot had things. We had a cake, and Honoria was carried into Patrick's room for the event. . . . And we had champagne, and when Sara's health was drunk, Gerald kissed her, and they twined their arms around — you know — and drank that way. . . .

"Poor Gerald," commented Parker, "(and those lights are out in the Hippodrome, Mr. Benchley, when you think of Gerald Murphy as 'poor Gerald')." But she did, and they were.

17

"The *invented* part, for me, is what has meaning"

THE MURPHYS KEPT TRYING. At Christmas they invited the Hemingways and Jinny Pfeiffer to Montana, along with John Dos Passos and his new wife, Katy Smith, the sister of Ernest's old friend Bill Smith and also a long-ago girlfriend of Ernest's; they had met in Key West and had been married in August. Katy was a slender, green-eyed woman with a mobile, rather simian face and a sharp wit — and she and Pauline and Jinny and Dorothy Parker, who was still in residence, kept up enough fast talk to fill the painful silences. Everyone pretended to be having a marvelous time eating fondue and drinking local Riesling and skiing and "laughing our heads off," as Dos Passos later described it. For Christmas dinner Ernest, almost too predictably, shot a goose, and Sara roasted it and made chestnut purée and flaming plum pudding with a holly sprig stuck on top, and they all sang Christmas carols.

The spirit of forced gaiety began to tell on Parker, however, and when the Hemingways and Dos Passoses left after Christmas she went with them, returning to New York for some rest and relaxation. But Sara and Gerald and the children were never far from her thoughts: when she met the MacLeishes at a "big arty rout" thrown by Hoytie Wiborg, it was the Murphys they talked about. In the meantime Bob Benchley, probably under the influence of her lengthy and tearstained account of the Murphys' tribulations (and possibly also motivated by guilt over the *huissier* contretemps), had sent Sara a check for $320. She promptly sent it back with the words "an *impossible* sort of cheque" scrawled across the face of it. "*Don't* be mad at us," she implored.

"Can't you — with this horrid bit of paper, buy a nightclub evening, — a grandfather clock — a Saks bill or ½ an ocean voyage? . . . Any time you feel you could come over & join us — (with a stout cane & a pr of galoshes) a lot of people at least 3 — or 6 — would give you a *warm welcome* — & we could have great fun in the eternal snows."

Although Patrick had had a slight relapse just before Christmas, by February, under a cure regime that emphasized nutrition, rest, and exposure to fresh air and sunlight, he seemed to be slowly improving. He would sit for hours in his "cure chair" on the balcony, bundled up in steamer rug, coat, cap, and muffler, and work at etching, which had become a passion, or talk with Sara or Miss Roussel or Gerald. Honoria had been pronounced healthy and was allowed to resume normal activities around Christmas, and in February she went with Gerald, Sara, and Baoth on a flying visit to Antibes so that Gerald could appear before the Nice Correctional Court. Gerald cabled the outcome to Benchley: "DEUX CENTS FRANCS D'AMENDE [TWO HUNDRED FRANCS FINE] AND LAST WALTZ OF THE EVENING WITH THE JUDGE SARA LOOKED LOVELY IN BLACK LACE BAOTH WAS MY MATRON OF HONOR . . . WE MISS YOU STILL, MURPHYS."

Later in the spring Gerald and Sara went briefly to Paris to revisit old friends and old haunts, but it was a disturbing trip. During their anxious fall and winter they had heard next to nothing from the Fitzgeralds, who had been undergoing difficulties of their own. Zelda was volatile, Scott persistently drunk and seemingly unable to work. A trip to North Africa, meant as a restorative, had done nothing for either of them. And they had returned to Paris in a kind of armed truce, interrupted every now and then by Scott's disparagement of Zelda's obsession with ballet, and Zelda's suspicions (fueled by a canard put about by the expatriate litterateur Robert McAlmon) that Scott was a closeted homosexual who was having an affair with Ernest Hemingway.

Although Gerald and Sara knew nothing of these developments, they could see at once that something was very wrong. One day they made arrangements to take Zelda to an art exhibit, and arrived at the Fitzgeralds' apartment to find her, Scott, and John Peale Bishop standing on the pavement outside. The three of them had been having lunch, and inexplicably Zelda had been overtaken by some kind of paranoid frenzy. Now, although she barely spoke to the Murphys, which was most unlike her, she turned on Scott and Bishop. "Were you talking about me?" she demanded suspiciously. Gerald was stunned: how *could* they have been talking about her without her knowledge? "I mean, she was sitting right there with them!"

Deeply concerned for Zelda, they returned to Switzerland; it wasn't until later that they heard she had had a breakdown on April 23, and had been admitted to the Malmaison Clinic outside of Paris. By the time they learned all this, Zelda had been diagnosed as schizophrenic and had come to Switzerland herself, to Dr. Oscar Forel's asylum at Prangins, on the shores of Lake Geneva.

Meanwhile the Murphys, desperate to move from the gloomy confines of the Palace Hotel, had leased a large chalet, called La Bruyère, on the winding road from Montana to Vermala. It was a tall, half-timbered stucco building, four stories high, perched on a steep incline with a spectacular view of the forested slopes above, the Rhone valley below, and the cold majesty of Mont Blanc in the distance. Patrick, who preferred the fragrant Aleppo pines and mimosa and blue seascapes of his beloved Antibes, pronounced it "melancholly skenery"; but Honoria quite liked it, reporting cheerfully to Yvonne Roussel, who had returned to Antibes, that "there is no more snow here, some little flowers are coming out."

The renewing force of springtime was elusive, however. Just as the Murphys were preparing to move into their new house, Sara was summoned to New York: Frank Wiborg had come down with pneumonia and was not expected to recover. She took Baoth with her, but they were too late. Frank died on May 12, and Sara and Baoth stayed only long enough to go to the funeral and hear the will read before returning to Switzerland. Rather surprisingly, Frank had named Gerald as coexecutor of his estate along with Hoytie.

When Sara and Baoth sailed back to Europe they brought Dorothy Parker with them to help the family get settled in La Bruyère. In addition, they had a new project, one that sounds as if it had been cooked up over Christmas with the Dos Passoses and Hemingways: they took over a house in the village and turned it into "Harry's Bar," naming it after the famous watering hole at the Ritz in Paris. It was a real bar, with mirrors and rattan furniture and

red-and-white-striped awnings and printed matchbooks and tiny morocco-
bound pocket diaries as giveaways, and Sara had hired a first-rate chef and got
a Munich dance band to come and liven up the Alpine evenings. Sometimes,
at the end of a set, she and Gerald would sit down at the piano and sing. It
was the most exciting thing that had ever happened in Montana-Vermala,
Honoria noted proudly: "My father holds a bar now called 'Harry's Bar,' and
he has great success." There were family visits from Hoytie and Frank Wiborg's Cincinnati sister Mary (Aunt Mame). In July, Robert Benchley came to
see them — Sara had tried to send him passage money, but he refused it —
and, fortified by Cinzanos at Harry's Bar, Dottie drove down to Sierre to meet
him at the train. Because of the potency of strong liquor at high altitudes, she
had really tried to stay on the wagon in Montana; but the presence of her old
Algonquin crony proved too much for her, and the two of them stayed up late
drinking at Harry's Bar almost every night. Then they'd lurch home through
the silent streets, with Benchley bellowing "With the Crimson in Triumph
Flashing" in case some lonely tubercular Harvard men needed bucking up
— and the next day they'd repair to Harry's for a dose of hair of the dog.

Patrick was steadily improving, as Honoria breathlessly reported to Yvonne
Roussel: "I have a great surprise to tell you, guess what? *Patrick gets up now!* he
goes and plays in the fields (for there are beautiful fields in front of our house)
and he goes out for walks. . . . In about a month we are going on a trip with
Patrick, we are going to a place called bushy [Bussy], near Lausane it is just on
the lake Leman, so you can imagine how well he is to take trips now! Patrick
eats at table now too with us. We are all very happy that he is well."

While not recovered, he was indeed well enough for Sara and Gerald to get
away together, with Benchley and Parker, for what was meant to be a real
holiday — to Venice for coffee at Florian's and the Titians in the Accademia,
and trips to the Lido and the Murano glass factories. From Venice they went
on to Munich, where they saw a film that electrified Sara and Gerald, *Der
Blaue Engel*, featuring the then unknown Marlene Dietrich in her elegant
drag. Gerald spent the rest of their visit scouring the record shops for her
recordings; and Parker bought a dachshund puppy whom she named Robinson, as in Swiss Family Robinson — a nod to Gerald and Sara and the children, whom she had dubbed "The Swiss Family Murphy."

Benchley went home from Munich to the United States, but toward the end of August another Villa America regular reappeared: Scott Fitzgerald, who was living in Geneva in order to visit Zelda at Dr. Forel's asylum in Prangins, midway between Geneva and Lausanne. (Poor little Scottie was in Paris, where she was being partially looked after by Richard and Alice Lee Myers.) Scott was devastated by Zelda's descent into madness and by the wreck it had made of his family; and he was struggling with his defensiveness over the accusations Zelda made to Dr. Forel — that he drank too much, that he was a closeted homosexual who could never really love her. Sara and Gerald shared his grief — they loved him and Zelda, after all, and mourned the good times they had all had together — but they were incredulous when, self-centered as always and maudlin after a drink or two, he turned to Sara and said, "I don't suppose *you* have ever known despair." Parker gave him a tongue-lashing, but Sara for once was speechless.

When Don and Bea Stewart came to visit soon after they sensed (as Don rather portentously put it) that "even though Patrick was 'improving,' . . . Death seemed to be waiting mockingly in the cold clear air outside [for] the two people who had been our models for the Happy Life." You had to look hard to see this: on the surface Sara and Gerald had made real efforts to create the same kind of enchanted realm in Switzerland that they had achieved in Antibes. La Bruyère was exquisitely decorated and pulsing with Murphy life, with fresh flowers and the latest phonograph records; as he had done in Antibes, Gerald rented current films — features like *La machine infernale* as well as newsreels and short subjects — to show on Saturday nights; and underfoot there was the usual menagerie of pets. In addition to the Murphys' Scottie and Sealyhams, there was a rabbit, and Dottie Parker's dogs Timothy and Robinson, and Honoria's canary, Dicky — who narrowly survived having his cage dropped when Dottie, somewhat the worse for drink, insisted on cleaning it. She had also bought Gerald a parrot named Cocotte (French for "trollop"), of whom he was terrified, although he carried her around on his shoulder everywhere. When they went to Paris Gerald and Sara had brought back a monkey, named Mistigris, "and two enormous turtles and a male parrot for Cocotte," reported Honoria to Miss Roussel.

But La Bruyère was almost a parody of Villa America, right down to its cuckoo-clock kitsch; and the presence of all the friends from their old life only made them realize how thoroughly that life was lost. After a year in the anxious and extreme climate of their Magic Mountain, Gerald was disintegrating. "The Black Service" — his old nemesis, what Dorothy Parker called "that morbid, turned-in thing" — had made its reappearance, and with it a barely controllable volatility. One day he became enraged over some misbehavior of Baoth's, which was compounded by the boy's adolescent feistiness: unable to control his temper, he slapped Baoth with a slipper. Dottie Parker and he had a blazing row afterward: he should not have hit the boy, she shouted; he told her to mind her own business, whereupon she announced her intention of leaving. They patched things up, but it just wasn't the same.

There was another row, this time with Sara, over a trip Gerald had to make to New York in September. Of course you'll cable the MacLeishes that you're coming, said Sara — but Gerald refused. They fought for an hour. *Why* wouldn't he want to see them? what was the *matter* with him? Finally she burst out, "I think you are *afraid* to have people *like* you." But Gerald was not to be moved. In the end Dottie Parker cabled Benchley of Gerald's arrival and Benchley met him at the dock, to Gerald's intense discomfort. He managed to avoid everyone else. "Gerald is here," wrote Archie (who of course had found out) to Scott Fitzgerald, "but no one has seen him. Skulks like a shadow. Why I can't think. He likes us all. But he has deflated the world so flat he can't breathe in it."

Gerald himself tried to explain this withdrawal some months later in a letter to Archie. Typically elegant, extremely careful, it was the closest thing to a confession he ever wrote.

> After all these years — and in one sudden year — I find myself pried away from life *its*elf by the very things that make up *my life*. . . . I awaken to find that I have apparently never had one real relationship or one full experience. It would seem that all my time has been spent in bargaining with life or attempting to buy it off. . . . [I]t is never quite possible to believe that *all* that one does is unreal, or that one is *never* oneself for a moment — and that the residue of this must needs be a sense of unreality, all-pervading. I don't think I hoped to beat *life*. Possibly I thought that mine was one way of living it, among many thousand ways.

My terms with life have been simple: I have refused to meet it on the grounds of my own defects, for the reason that I have bitterly resented those defects since I was fifteen years of age. (I once tried to tell you that I didn't believe in taking life at its *own* tragical value if it could be avoided. It was this I apparently meant.) You of course cannot have known that not for one waking hour of my life since I was fifteen have I been entirely free of the feeling of these defects. In the vaults of the Morgan Museum on Madison Avenue I was shown once when I was twenty the manuscript of Samson Agonistes, and while I was listening to a recital of its cost I read "O worst imprisonment! To be the dungeon of thyself." I knew what it meant, then. Eight years of school and college, after my too willing distortion of myself into the likeness of popularity and success, I was left with little confidence in the shell that I had inhabited as another person.

And so I have never felt that there was a place in life as it is lived for what I have to give of myself. I have doubtless ended by trying, instead, to give of my life as I lived it.

My subsequent life has been a process of concealment of the personal realities, — at which I have been all too adept. . . . The effect on my heart has been evident. It is now a faulty "instrument de précision" working with accuracy in the direction of error. It makes a poor companion, I assure you.

Thus I have learned to dread (and avoid) the responsibilities of friendship (as being one of the realities of life), believing, as I do, that I was incapable of a full one. I have *become* unworthy of one.

I have never been able to feel *sure* that *any*one was fond of me, because it would seem too much to claim, knowing what I did about myself. I have been demoralized by coming under the banner of what Sara gives to people and what she demands of them in the way of affection. This seems to have deceived even you and Ada. It is she who has floated our friendships on the flood of her very deep and very real feelings. You *know* that you have always known that Sara has given you what she was and is. You have never known that I have given you what I was not, — am not. You have *felt* it. That I know.

. . .

Have I made myself clear enough to have you see why I could come to America and dread the possibility of seeing you and Ada, and risk disfiguring one of the few phantom realities of my life, my friendship with you both? I preferred to skulk it and take the consequences. . . . It was rude, unkind and selfish of me. Please pardon it, if you can.

So this is what was at the root of "those damn schoolgirl quarrels of Gerald's," and behind the smoke screen of his phrasemaking and the disguises, from the bespoke suits to the sailors' jerseys and apache trousers: a sense of profound unease, of unreality, about who he was. It went beyond a fear that he was incapable of affection, although that, too, was part of the problem. As a young man he had been haunted by feelings of otherness, of difference, either social, or sexual, or personal; but his very real love for Sara, which she had so frankly returned, had overwhelmed them. She had encouraged his decision to live where he would not constantly be held to standards by which he would be found wanting; and for nearly ten years the two of them, and their marriage, had flourished creatively. For a time it seemed as if he had beaten back the demons. But all that was over now. His creations — his paintings, his marriage, the children who embodied his and Sara's fondest hopes, the "loaded and fragrant" way of life they had invented together — had all been corrupted.

What he was left with was his own uncertain nature — a nature he had never been taught to value, and which he feared would revolt the people he most cherished if it were ever revealed to them. "I hope," he added in a poignant postscript to Archie, "this letter does not offend your taste, — or whatever that thing is that gets offended — and you can never feel the same about the person afterwards. I *know* I could have told you this without offending you."

It was during this trip to America, apparently, that Gerald sat for a strange photographic portrait — a multiple exposure in which five Gerald Murphys, in the same overcoat, starched white collar, and elegantly tilted homburg, stare at one another across a table. It is as if Gerald's many selves were playing poker together, none willing to let on to another how strong a hand he holds.

Returning to Switzerland that winter, Gerald tried desperately to regain his emotional equilibrium: and as he increasingly did in times of crisis he quite simply withdrew. Honoria remembers his taking "a long hike to a monastery where he stayed overnight." The monastery kept rescue dogs, one of whom

(Gerald claimed) had recently turned on a lost traveler and killed him. Whether this was truth or invention — he was, after all, telling the story to his children — it was a fitting metaphor for what had happened to Gerald Murphy. The monastery was probably the famous hospice of St. Bernard, on the main ridge of the Alps at nearly ten thousand feet, which had been a refuge since medieval times for travelers who had lost their way, as Gerald arguably had in the middle of his life's journey. According to Hester Pickman, "he'd had a kind of breakdown. He retired to think all by himself. He painted that clock while he was there" — a puzzling reference, because there is no record that Gerald painted anything while he was in Switzerland. In fact, after Patrick was diagnosed with tuberculosis, Gerald rolled up most of his canvases and never, so far as anyone knew, picked up a paintbrush again.

A long time afterward he told the playwright Lillian Hellman that he had stopped painting "because I never believed I was any good." But coming from the man who in the year before he stopped said he felt confident of producing "one picture that's hitched up to the universe," this sounds like a case of protesting too much. His career, despite the meticulous snail's pace with which he had pursued it, was on an upward trajectory. *L'Intransigeant,* in its review of his Bernheim show the previous January, had praised his paintings' "authenticity," their "objectivity, precision, and absolute clarity of execution," the "perfect order of their composition." Gerald Murphy, *L'Intransigeant* proclaimed, "gives a future consciousness to American art, and gives us a new perspective on its prospects." Gerald had high standards, and may not always have felt himself capable of satisfying them. But when he put away his brushes and pigments he wasn't abandoning a faltering career as a painter. He was relinquishing a bright one.

From the first he had painted "real objects which I admired," and which often had personal resonance for him, in a way that abstracted their specific emotional content; he had tried to impose his own order and discipline on a world he distrusted. But when he couldn't hold that world at bay with his brush, he exacted from himself the penance of giving up the one thing that had ever made him completely happy.

Sometime during the fall of 1930, in circumstances of extreme secrecy, Gerald went to Basle to consult a Jungian analyst, Dr. Schmid-Guisan, who

(Gerald said) "specialized in Anglo-Saxons. You went and lived in a hotel in Basle, completely unidentified, and went out by trolley to Schmid-Guisan's villa every day at a fixed time, and waited in the garden so that you never saw anyone else coming out." He left no record of what he discussed with Dr. Schmid-Guisan; but he did talk about his analytic sessions with Scott Fitzgerald, whom he continued to see frequently, and a clue to their substance may lie in alterations that Fitzgerald made to his current manuscript.

Gerald later recalled that in one of these conversations he'd told Fitzgerald: "for me only the invented part of life is satisfying, the unrealistic part. Things happened to you — sickness, birth, Zelda in Lausanne, Patrick in the sanatorium, Father Wiborg's death — these things were realistic, and you couldn't do anything about them. Do you mean you don't accept these things? Scott asked. I replied that of course [I] accepted them, but I didn't feel they were the important things really. . . . The *invented* part, for me, is what has meaning." It was the corollary to what he had told Archie MacLeish — and for perhaps the first time, Gerald seemed to feel that Scott understood what he was trying to say. "He talked thoughtfully and with a kind of tenderness of all of us," he told Sara. "I had the sense of coming on undiscovered gold."

Gerald was less happy when Fitzgerald chose to play go-between for him at Harry's Bar with a young South American named Eduardo Velasquez. Fitzgerald had met Velasquez in Lausanne, where the young man had been undergoing psychoanalysis in an effort to "cure" his homosexuality; and for some reason Scott told him to go to one of the weekend dances at Harry's and introduce himself to Gerald.

Gerald, probably remembering Scott's homophobic antics in Antibes, later told a friend he suspected Fitzgerald of playing some kind of practical joke. But Scott's gesture seems more like one of his gauche and misguided attempts at empathic behavior, as when he told Edith Wharton a racy story in a disastrous effort to establish a rapport with her. Whatever signal he was trying to send Gerald, however, it was garbled, and the encounter was "very painful." The young South American insisted on giving Gerald a cross that had belonged to his mother, perhaps as a talisman for Patrick. Then he left, and if he ever saw Gerald again there's no record of it. But he made a telling reappearance in the novel ultimately entitled *Tender Is the Night*, as Francisco, "the

Queen of Chili," who makes it possible for the novel's hero to understand "the courageous grace" and "charm" of someone he would previously have dismissed as "pathological."

Fitzgerald had been stalled on his manuscript all through the autumn, but around this time he made a crucial change in it. The book had gone through a number of false starts already, and would metamorphose even further before he finally completed it. The title had been, variously, *World's Fair* (the allusion to Thackeray's *Vanity Fair* was intentional), *The Boy Who Killed His Mother,* and *Our Type.* Originally Fitzgerald had intended to tell the story of a young man, a film technician named Francis Melarkey, who is hopelessly under the thumb of his domineering mother (a familiar theme to both Scott and Gerald) and comes to the south of France hoping to find work in the nascent Nice movie industry. There he meets an American couple, Seth and Dinah Roreback (or Seth and Dinah Piper, depending on the version of the novel); he is enthralled by them both, but falls in love with Dinah, with whom he has a brief affair.

Francis, who shares Fitzgerald's given name, was also his alter ego. The Roreback/Pipers, who until recently, another character tells Francis, "were the only other Americans on the whole Riviera," were clearly modeled on the Murphys. There were details that came straight from the Villa America to the page, such as the description of Seth and Dinah singing for their guests "things from a bundle just over from America. Seth played and sang the air in his clear, arresting voice, and Dinah standing beside him, sang a soft, huskily accurate contralto." There were observations from Fitzgerald's notebook, like "Gerald's Irishness: face moving first," which made it into the manuscript as "Seth is quite amusing — but so Irish — his face begins to move before he says anything in that Irish way." And there were other things.

At one point Dinah — the name has been written in here, above the typed, crossed-out "Sarah" — meets Francis in Paris. The two of them kiss in a taxi and go to her apartment, a top-floor walk-up like the Murphys' flat on the quai, for more amorous byplay. Afterward, as Francis is walking away, he sees Seth — "Gerald" in earlier pages — returning home. The description is Gerald Murphy to the life: "[A] taxi drove up and Seth got out and went into the house. His step was quick and alert as if he had just come from some great doings and was hurrying on toward others. Organizer of gaiety, master of a richly incrusted [sic] esoteric happiness. His hat was a grand hat and he carried a heavy stick and thin yellow gloves. Francis thought what a good time everyone would have who was with him."

It seems highly unlikely that Fitzgerald was portraying, in fictional terms, an affair, or even a two-way flirtation, with Sara Murphy. Although Sara admitted that "he'd try to kiss you in taxis and things like that," she had never encouraged his infatuation. Mostly she managed to deflect it, possibly by saying, as Dinah does elsewhere to Francis:

> "I don't kiss people. I'm just before that generation. We'll find you a nice young girl you can kiss."
> "There aren't any nice young girls — you're the only one I like."
> "I'm not nice. I'm a hard woman."

That sounds like Sara. The scene at the Pipers' apartment sounds like wish fulfillment. But although wish fulfillment isn't inconsistent with successful fiction, the novel as Fitzgerald had been trying to write it was unsuccessful. One reason was that he had planned for the plot to turn on Francis's murder of his mother. The matricidal theme — which Fitzgerald abandoned in 1930 — was clearly a dead end. But there was something else in the plot that was a dead end as well, something Fitzgerald carefully altered as he reworked his manuscript. In the published version of *Tender Is the Night*, he gave the love scene at the apartment to the young actress, Rosemary Hoyt, and Gerald/Seth's avatar, the psychiatrist Dick Diver, not to Francis and Sara/Dinah.

Fitzgerald belonged to a generation that was sensitive about sexual orientation in a way that bordered on paranoia. His and Hemingway's and MacLeish's comments about "fairies" revealed a kind of sexual absolutism — either you were or you weren't — that precluded *any* kind of attraction to someone of the same sex. Drunkenly crossing the street in Paris the year before Zelda's breakdown, Fitzgerald had resisted taking the offered arm of a friend, the journalist Morley Callaghan, because, he told Callaghan, "You thought I was a fairy, didn't you?" Such feelings made authenticity impossible. The story he had been trying to tell in his stalled novel was the romance between himself and Sara Murphy, a story he could not tell because it led

nowhere. The story he was *afraid* to tell was the story of his own romantic —
not sexual, but romantic — attraction for Gerald Murphy, a story he was only
able to tell by transforming himself into Rosemary Hoyt.

Once he had managed that metamorphosis, another took place: the emer-
gence of Gerald/Seth as the main character, instead of the callow Francis. In
his "General Plan" for this revision, Fitzgerald proposed that "The novel
should do this. Show a man who is a natural idealist, a spoiled priest, giving in
for various causes to the ideas of the haute Burgeoise [*sic*], and in his rise to
the top of the social world losing his idealism [and] his talent. . . . Background
one in which the liesure [*sic*] class is at their truly most brilliant and glamorous such as Murphys." His new central character, now called Dick Diver,
shared some of Fitzgerald's qualities, notably his alcoholism and his wife's
insanity. But these elements were arguably less essential to the real theme of
the novel as it now presented itself to Fitzgerald: the story of Dick Diver's
feelings of emptiness and imposture, his betrayal at the hands of a world he
thought he could manipulate, his struggle to come to terms with the renun-
ciation of his idealism and talent. These feelings, this betrayal, this struggle —
Fitzgerald now saw — all were Gerald Murphy's. As everyone knows, Dick
Diver would lose his battle. For Gerald Murphy, during that autumn in
Switzerland, the issue was still in doubt.

18

※

"The geodetic points of our lost topography"

CONTENDING WITH HIS OWN DEMONS, Gerald seemed not to notice that Sara's health was showing the strain of the past year. In October, though, she was admitted to the American Hospital in Paris for tests. Doctors diagnosed a gallbladder disorder. She and Honoria, accompanied by Dorothy Parker, went to Cannes for a rest and change of scenery, and then Dottie, who by this time was suffering acutely from cabin fever, returned to the United States. Baoth was sent off to boarding school in Germany — an establishment called Rosenheim, near Munich, which the Murphys had learned about from their old friends the Pickmans. "The orderliness, organization and simplicity of the life is just what he needs," said Gerald, managing to repress his and Sara's miserable boarding school memories.

Sara spent October sailing on *Honoria*. When she returned to Switzerland she and Gerald, for perhaps the first time since they had come to Montana, took inventory of their lives. They could see they'd have to make changes. The stock market crash and ensuing depression had weakened their financial situation, and the continuing drain of Patrick's medical expenses, not to mention the upkeep of three residences, had to be reckoned with. Because the favorable exchange rate that had floated their expatriate existence had flattened out, it was now cheaper, and maybe safer, to live in the United States.

The Murphys also had to come to terms with profound changes in their personal geography: the avant-garde they had known in Paris in the early twenties had disbanded or grown bourgeois, their idyllic undiscovered paradise in Antibes had become a millionaire's playground. So Gerald and Sara decided to let the Paris apartment go, and they rented the Ferme des Orangers. They also sold *Honoria*, to a young Englishman who was apparently attracted by the powder blue enamel plates in the galley which Gerald had found at Girl Scout headquarters in New York. Finally, and most reluctantly, they made up their minds to sell Villa America. It was unclear whether Patrick would ever be well enough to return there to live, and now the place was haunted with the spirit of might-have-been. They had given Léger a commission for the villa: a series of panels for a screen, showing white comets on a black background, which would echo their black-and-white decor. The comets looked more like ghostly apparitions, though, and because they planned to sell the villa they let the panels go to another collector.

But, being the Murphys, they couldn't live in a state of total retreat. "In spite of thunder," wrote Gerald to Archie MacLeish, they planned to build a new, spacious, seagoing schooner, twenty-seven meters long, with both regular and marconi (or racing) rigging, a big deckhouse and plenty of room below for living and sleeping quarters. They planned to use her as a floating villa and living classroom in which the children would soak up lessons in history and geography as they sailed the Mediterranean coast. They drew an outline of the boat on the lawn outside Patrick's window, so he could get an idea of her size; and when she was still in the dry dock at Fécamp in Normandy they sealed into her keel a recording of Joe "King" Oliver's song "Weather Bird," played in jaunty, swinging counterpoint by Louis Armstrong and Earl "Fatha" Hines. Naturally, they named the boat *Weatherbird*.

The new year of 1931 brought what seemed like better times: Vladimir Orloff arrived in January to help plan the specifics of *Weatherbird* and, incidentally, to build a cage for Mistigris, the monkey, who had recently managed to fingerpaint one of La Bruyère's rooms with ink; the MacLeishes came to visit in February and taught Honoria how to ski; Helen Stewart, who had been baby nurse to all three little Murphys in America, came to take care of Patrick. He soon seemed improved enough to start ice skating lessons with Honoria, and when Baoth came home for his Easter break the two boys went skiing before Gerald and Sara took Honoria and Baoth to Venice. In fact, Patrick was now considered sufficiently recovered to leave Montana for the summer — not for sea level, which the doctors still thought dangerous, but somewhere in some other mountains.

Gerald and Sara found a hunting lodge called Ramgut for rent in the Austrian Alps, at Bad Aussee, and the family moved there in July. It was a beautiful old house, large but simple, with whitewashed walls and scrubbed pine floors, set in the middle of ripening wheat fields. The cook, Frau July, made delicious Austrian meals, and the children, even Patrick, rode their bicycles all around the lovely rolling countryside. Honoria remembers Ramgut with pleasure, and certainly Gerald and Sara were making an effort to enter into the spirit of the place: a local photographer captured the whole family, outfitted authentically in lederhosen and dirndls and Tyrolese hats, for a formal portrait. But the gay costumes, and the jaunty bouquet of flowers in Sara's hands, belie the glum expressions on all their faces.

Sara's guest book recorded a number of visitors that summer: The Pickmans came to stay, as did Léger, who was struck by the regulated quality of the Murphys' household. It was almost as if Time were a member of the family, he wrote to his mistress Simone Herman: "someone who is always consulted and who dominates everything." And in August, Scott Fitzgerald asked if he could bring Zelda, who was better and was gradually being given more exposure to the world outside the asylum. She had been allowed visitors in the spring, and the first person she asked to see then was Gerald. "Absolutely terrified," he had nonetheless gone to Prangins, and had made charming inconsequential small talk with her about the basket she was weaving. "I said that all my life I had wanted to make baskets like hers, great heavy, stout baskets." Now, although he and Sara were "petrified at the idea," they wrote Scott to say it was "great . . . that you all can really come here." The Fitzgeralds brought Scottie with them, and although Scott confided to Alice Lee Myers that "Scotty + the little Murphys begin to glare as soon as they're in a radius of a hundred yards from each other," everyone was for the most part well behaved. Zelda seemed to find the Murphy ambiance healing, and the only difficulty occurred when the children's nurse put bath salts in Scottie's bathwater. Scottie thought the cloudy water had been used to bathe all the Murphy children and ran to complain to her parents. Scott, afraid that Patrick had used it first, made a scene. The incident turned up later in *Tender Is the Night* — without, however, the undertone of terror that came from Scott's fear of tuberculosis.

Hoytie Wiborg descended on Ramgut for a visit on her way from some fashionable watering hole to Paris, and Scott and Zelda left soon after — but not so soon that Scott wasn't exposed to a dose of both Hoytie's grandeur and her solipsism, which would reappear in his portrait of Baby Warren in *Tender Is the Night*. Shortly after the Fitzgeralds' departure the Murphys packed up also. Baoth had to return to Rosenheim, and Patrick, Honoria, and their parents were headed for Paris with Miss Stewart. As a treat, Honoria rode with godmother Hoytie in her smart chauffeur-driven car; but on the road they got into a minor accident with another motorist, which so infuriated Hoytie that she rolled down the window and shouted *"Jude! Jude!"* ("Jew! Jew!") at the driver of the other vehicle. "She was terribly anti-Semitic, and it was the worst name she could think of," remembered Honoria. Sara and Gerald were appalled. "This is typical, just typical," Sara muttered. Whether she meant it was typical of Hoytie, or typical of what was starting to happen all over Europe, she didn't say.

Although Gerald continued to find American society stultifying — "My God, what a race of people!" he had written to Archie MacLeish after his last visit — he and Sara continued to think about reestablishing a base in the United States. There was a small farmer's cottage on the Wiborg land at East Hampton, on the parcel that Sara had inherited, which could be remodeled for their use. In September, leaving Patrick in Paris with Helen Stewart, they took Honoria with them to New York while they began construction and attended to other business, including a trip to Massachusetts to see their three-year-old godchild, Peter MacLeish, for the first time. They also brought Fernand Léger along on his first visit to New York, putting him up with them at the Savoy Plaza and taking him to what he called "Broderie" (Broadway) and Times Square, where the lights and garish billboards "delighted him."

Now that it seemed Patrick was on the mend, Sara could not bear to return full-time to Montana. It was too full of horrors for her, and too lonely. Although she and Gerald had given up their rue Guynemer apartment, they decided that on their return to Europe Gerald would accompany Patrick back to Switzerland; Honoria and Sara would remain in Paris, at the Hotel Prince de Galles, where something could be done about the state of Honoria's education. Miss Roussel had returned to Antibes and because Montana had few teachers — people who went there weren't seriously expected to survive

— Honoria's schooling would have to take place elsewhere. Baoth was thriving at Rosenheim, although his academic performance wasn't stellar — he was ranked only thirty-eighth in his class, with a 78.9 average. But Sara resisted sending Honoria away as well. Instead she and Gerald engaged a down-on-her-luck German aristocrat whom they had met at Rosenheim, Countess Lieven, to give Honoria lessons in Paris, where she would have the added bonus of being close to her favorite friend, the Myerses' daughter Fanny.

Bob Benchley sailed with the Murphys and kept Sara company in Paris, squiring her to Zelli's in Montmartre and elsewhere. Sara went shopping and to the theater and had fittings with her *vendeuse*, Mme. Hélène, at Groult. Ellen Barry, who was in Paris at the same time with her husband, remembered her buying a "gorgeous" black evening dress, "a Madame Bovary dress," Barry called it. (She must have forgotten that Emma Bovary, overwhelmed by the pettiness and frustration of her provincial life and adoring but unsatisfying husband, committed suicide.) Honoria, a wistful thirteen-year-old with a watercolor prettiness, used to sit on Sara's bed and watch her mother dress and put on her make-up in the evenings: "She used Helena Rubinstein make-up, or Cyclax, and she kept her lipstick, a pinkish red lipstick, sort of a geranium color, in a little round case — she'd dab in her little finger and then put two or three spots of color on her lips, and then rub her lips together. And then she'd wipe off her finger." After that, Honoria remembers, she'd put on powder, a touch of her favorite Lanvin perfume, and the pearls; then, over her dress, a black fox fur piece. Finally, a last glance in the mirror and she was ready — with a face prepared to meet the faces she would meet.

In the end the Paris experiment didn't work: the countess was more interested in the Almanach de Gotha (and her place in it) than in Honoria's education, and the Prince de Galles was ruinously expensive. So after an extended Christmas holiday at Montana, Sara took Honoria to Villa America, which remained unsold. Honoria was enrolled in Mademoiselle Fontaine's day school in Cannes until the end of the school year, when the Murphys planned to leave for America.

In the meantime, however, another unforeseen event had taken place. In November Gerald's father went on a business trip to the Kodak laboratories in Rochester, New York. As usual, he wore no overcoat, but this time his iron will could not prevail over the blustery weather. Coming from the overheated lab to the train he had caught a chill that settled in his lungs and turned into pneumonia. As soon as Gerald heard the news he sailed for New York with Esther; but before they could reach him, on November 23, Patrick Murphy died. Neither of his surviving children was present at his enormous funeral at St. Patrick's Cathedral, which was attended by several hundred people, including the political cartoonist Finley Peter Dunne, creator of "Mr. Dooley," and Senator Robert F. Wagner. But they arrived for the burial and the reading of the will, in which, Gerald later said, "my father left a company, not an estate." The Mark Cross Company's assets, at the time estimated at $2,000,000, were left to Gerald and Esther (Anna Murphy was otherwise provided for). But control of the company, and therefore of their inheritance, was left to its new president, Patrick Murphy's former secretary and longtime mistress, Lillian Ramsgate.

Gerald was outraged. Not because he had been passed over in the corporate succession — after all, he had left the company in no uncertain terms more than a decade ago — but to be placed in a position of subservience to his father's paramour was more than he could stand. Although his mother wailed that he must "take care of Esther," whose marriage to John Strachey was foundering, he resigned his position as vice president and left Miss Ramsgate to run the company by herself.

Sailing back to France on the *Europa*, Gerald sought out Shakespeare's classic work on inheritance, *King Lear*, in the ship's library. As he sometimes did in times of stress or reflection, he copied out some passages that give a clue to his resentful and conflicted state of mind:

> He cannot be such a monster
> To his father who tenderly and entirely loves him

But then:

> And the noble and true-hearted Kent banished! his offense honesty!

And again:

> Is it the fashion that discarded fathers
> Should have thus little mercy on their flesh?

His conclusion was bitter:

As flies to wanton boys, are we to the gods.
They kill us for their sport.

Soon after Gerald's return to Switzerland, Anna Ryan Murphy had a stroke and never recovered her faculties. She died in April; Gerald did not travel back to New York to see her. By then Sara and Honoria were in Antibes, which — after Montana's "melancholly skenery" and the gray drizzle of Paris in the winter — they found "a paradise: mandarines, lemons, oranges, camellias, anemones, mimosa, & lunch on the terrasse." Sara made a ceremony of throwing out all the medicines in her traveling case — prematurely, as it turned out, for at the end of March her old gallstone trouble returned and kept her in bed off and on for a month.

She wasn't too ill, however, to enjoy the arrival of *Weatherbird*, which Vladimir had sailed from Normandy to Antibes through the Bay of Biscay and the Mediterranean in a series of howling gales. "A thing of great solid beauty" was how Sara described the boat to Gerald: not just seaworthy and sturdy but gracious. The deckhouse had windows on all sides, with benches beneath covered with navy blue cotton, and was spacious enough to accommodate a long table at which everyone could eat above decks, even when the weather was bad. Below decks were the cabins: Honoria's decorated in pink, Sara's and Gerald's in green, another for the boys to share; Vladimir Orloff and a crew of five had quarters on board as well. The saloon, which held four bunks for guests, was also furnished with comfortable upholstered chairs, a long table, and an upright piano, painted white, for convivial evenings. The galley had a refrigerator — Ada MacLeish called *Weatherbird* a *bâteau à Frigidaire* — and there was also a bathtub on board, although it was rarely used because it took so much water to fill it.

Gerald and Baoth came down for an inaugural cruise at Easter, but "poor little Pook" had to stay in Switzerland. The doctors felt the air and heat at Antibes would tax his still fragile lungs. "O — I wish I had another sickness!" Patrick lamented to Gerald, in a rare outburst. At last, however, the doctors gave him permission to leave, and in mid-May he and Miss Stewart arrived at Villa America to find the garden alight with lanterns to welcome them.

Finally the whole family was reunited, for — alarmed by the rising tide of Nazi sentiment in Germany, and mindful of their impending departure for the United States — the Murphys had removed Baoth from Rosenheim in March.

The spring and early summer passed in a kind of valedictory haze: there were visits from the Barrys and the Myerses and from Stella Campbell; cruises to Port Cros and St.-Tropez and Portofino; evenings at the casino, where Sara and Gerald took Caresse Crosby; or at the ballet in Monte Carlo to see Balanchine's *Cotillon* and *Concurrence*; the children swam at La Garoupe and had parties in Honoria's playhouse and went fishing. At the end of May, Patrick went to Canada with Helen Stewart; and Mistigris (who bit everybody but Sara, whom he adored) was left with the Légers. Fernand Léger later sent Sara a photo of him, along with the news that he was behaving perfectly; Jeanne Léger's postscript, however, added that Misti was betraying Sara: "he kisses me on the mouth with his tongue, it's true love," she said. At Villa America trunks were packed, linens and china laid away, books and records crated. On July 5 Honoria wrote in her diary, "Put away my house in the afternoon." Eight days later, having put away not only their house but a chapter of their lives, the Murphys sailed for New York on the *Aquitania*.

At first — even though Sara had started to refer to their years in Paris and Antibes as "the era" — they didn't see the chapter as finally ended. Their closest friends — the Hemingways, the Fitzgeralds, the Dos Passoses, the MacLeishes, Dottie Parker — were all in America, and to maintain those friendships in their customary way meant doing so on American soil. "Some day we'll all be together again," Gerald had written Archie in February; and their voyage that July fulfilled that promise.

Almost immediately, however, they were reminded of at least one of the reasons they had left America in the first place. Hoytie met them at the dock and, before they were through customs, she began filling them in on her financial and legal vicissitudes. As she'd already informed them, she'd "lost [her] shirt in the stock market," and in addition had invested heavily and unsuccessfully in New York City real estate, attempting to buy and develop a large property at Park Avenue and 72d Street. Her stock market losses had left her unable to meet the payments, and she had other obligations as well. Like many another developer before and since, she thought she could seek refuge in personal bankruptcy. But to do so she had to protect, or dispose of, her share of the East Hampton property she had inherited from Frank Wiborg. In October she had bullied Frank's elderly sister, Aunt Mame, into buying all twenty-seven oceanfront acres, plus the house, for a token $1. Then she'd set up a shell corporation to receive the property and had Aunt Mame transfer the deed to it.

Now, however, she owed money to the government for unpaid taxes. The bank had foreclosed on her 72d Street property; and to avoid liens and creditors she was, as Sara put it, "living here and there under assumed names." Borrowing to cover her obligations wouldn't help; she needed a large infusion of cash into her shell corporation, called Trex, where her creditors couldn't get at it, but she could draw on it for her needs. What she proposed was that someone should buy the East Hampton property from Trex and pay the money, in cash, into that account; but in July 1932 the country was sliding toward the deepest part of the Depression, and the amount she needed, $25,000, was serious money. She had already approached friends and family members, such as Sara Sherman Mitchell and her husband, Ledyard, and Olga and Sidney Fish, and they had all turned her down: now she turned to Sara and Gerald.

It was the same old story: Hoytie and her "unsound, headstrong" behavior, as Sara described it, "always a problem to the family." Sara had run away from it before, but it had caught up with her. This time sentiment made her vulnerable: her parents had loved the Dunes, and her children did also. And wouldn't it be better, she rationalized, to save Hoytie from disaster *now* instead of having to bail her out later, without any property to show for it? So Sara called nice Mr. Copley Amory at Loomis-Sayles in Boston and had him sell some of her stock (at a terrific loss, of course) and paid Hoytie $22,500 in cash, with another $2,500 check to the government for taxes due on the property, and she lent Hoytie an additional $1,000.

So now the Murphys owned a semistaffed villa on two and a quarter acres in Antibes, which they hoped vaguely to sell but couldn't seem to; a twenty-seven-meter schooner requiring a crew of five; and a cottage, twenty acres, and an enormous, unheatable mansion on the dunes at East Hampton. All this, along with Patrick's medical bills and the other children's tuitions and other expenses, was in the debit column. On the credit side were Sara's capital (already reduced in value by the fall in stock prices) and the expectation of income from a struggling Mark Cross Company. Somehow, by renting the Dunes and some of the Antibes property, they managed to offset some of the damage, but the next years would be trying ones for them financially.

They were, of course, difficult years for everyone, and the Murphys' circle of friends was no exception. Archie MacLeish's patrimony, his stock in the Carson Pirie Scott Company, had stopped paying dividends, and Archie was working as a journalist at *Fortune* to pay the bills; Dick Myers lost his job at the Paris bureau of *Ladies' Home Journal* and had trouble finding a new one; John Dos Passos was making little from his writing and was suffering from health problems, particularly rheumatic fever. Worst off were the Fitzgeralds, who had come back to the United States soon after their stay with the Murphys in Bad Aussee. They had settled in Alabama, near Zelda's family, but in February 1932 Zelda had had a relapse and had been hospitalized at the Henry Phipps Psychiatric Clinic at Johns Hopkins University Hospital in Baltimore. Scott had found a house in the vicinity, named, with cruel irony, La Paix, and once Zelda regained sufficient composure to become an outpatient she moved in with Scott and Scottie. But Scott — beset by Zelda's heavy medical expenses, the cost of constant relocation, and his own inability to finish his long-overdue novel — had begun to drink heavily again and was himself seeing a psychiatrist at Phipps.

Not surprisingly, he was in only perfunctory touch with the Murphys that summer, but other friends helped them pick up some of the threads of the past: John and Katy Dos Passos, whom they hadn't seen since that grim Christmas in Switzerland, came to stay at Hook Pond Cottage, as did the MacLeishes, and Dottie Parker was a frequent guest on weekends. And at the close of summer they went to stay with Ernest and Pauline Hemingway at a hunting and fishing ranch that Ernest had discovered, the L Bar T, located in southwestern Montana, not far from Yellowstone Park.

Although Patrick had to remain behind with Miss Stewart, the older children "adore[d] it," Gerald reported to Archie MacLeish. "Ernest [was] an angel about arranging their lives." They rode all day through the glorious mountains, and Ernest took Honoria fishing. He overcame her squeamishness at killing the trout she caught by showing her its lacy fins and beautiful gills; she was mesmerized, and proud to have "performed well for Ernest."

Sara and Gerald, on the other hand, had mixed feelings about the visit. They were both delighted to see Ernest and Pauline again, and Sara enjoyed riding over the "lovely trails" and "com[ing] back at night [to] have those Dainties Pauline used to whip up with the moon cocktails." But other aspects of their stay were less delightful. It was the custom of the owner, Olive Nordquist, to take the game and fish caught by the guests and turn it into the equivalent of Spam, flouring it and frying it and then packing it in Mason jars to steam for three hours — and the Murphys' reactions were to be expected. Sara, who had an instinctive sense of how far she could go with Ernest, dared to make fun openly of the first course one evening: a pillow of iceberg lettuce with canned fruit salad plopped over it, topped by a dollop of mayonnaise and a maraschino cherry. Ernest told her it was "good for her." Gerald kept his feelings about the ranch-killed beef ("tasteless, without variety — and indifferently cooked") and the fresh trout ("neutralized") to himself, but he was troubled by what he thought of as a lack of authenticity about the whole experience, which was light-years away from the thrill of discovery he had felt with Ernest in Pamplona. "I suspect," he confided to Archie MacLeish, "that just as the vastness of our industry and amassed fortunes in the East seems to have dulled our people spiritually, — so here in the West the reaction of the people to their vast and spectacular Natural surroundings and resources is not as fine as one would expect."

But Ernest had bought into this Western mythology — he had given one of the "indifferent" colts bred on the ranch to Pauline with the sort of ceremony befitting the bestowal of a purebred Arabian by a royal sheik — and Gerald could no longer talk to him about things that were hitched up to the universe. He had noticed a change in his old friend. "I find him more mellowed, amenable, and far more charitable and philosophical than before, — more patient also," he wrote Archie. But that was because "he is never difficult with the people he does not like, the people he does not take seriously. He has crossed swords with Sara and Ada, with you, with Dorothy (whom he likes), with Dos. But he will never do it with me, [and] there has been no real issue with Don or with Scott whom he no longer respects."

Ernest still loved Sara, but Gerald was increasingly closed out. In the photographs Sara saved from those three weeks, Ernest is shown with his arm around Sara, or around Pauline, but Gerald stands apart.

That fall Baoth was enrolled in the Fountain Valley School in Colorado, where Sara and Gerald dropped him off before returning east, and Honoria also went away to boarding school, to the Convent of the Sacred Heart in Noroton, Connecticut, where the Pickman girls, Jane and Daisy, were also students. Despite Gerald's still profound mistrust of Catholicism and his and Sara's dislike of the boarding school environment most of their class thought essential to a proper upbringing, they recognized Honoria's need for regular study and the companionship of children her own age. Gerald and Sara and Patrick, who was still delicate, would divide their time between Hook Pond Cottage and a house they had rented in the rural Westchester village of Bedford. It was about an hour's journey by train from New York and only a short distance from a cottage the Barrys owned — and were currently lending to the Myerses — in nearby Mount Kisco.

After a brief trip to Paris in November with Dottie Parker, whom they were trying to console for the sudden death of her little dachshund, Robinson, Gerald and Sara spent Christmas in Conway, Massachusetts, with the MacLeishes. It was a holiday from a Currier and Ives print: Baoth and Patrick and Honoria sledded and skied with the MacLeish children, Archie put up clay pigeons for the boys to shoot at, and everyone went for a ride in a horse-drawn sleigh. Ada and Sara cooked "a goose with all its accessories," giblet sauce and sweet potatoes, and Gerald ransacked the 1916 Manhattan Club cellar he had inherited from his father for the very best wines and liqueurs. They laughed and sang and generally carried on; as Archie wrote to John Peale Bishop, the Murphys' reappearance in his and Ada's lives "restor[ed] a few of the geodetic points of our lost topography."

The Murphys were trying to retrieve some of their own lost topography. That winter Gerald had surgery for a bony growth in his sinus cavity, a "nasty mean operation" from which "he suffered agonies," reported Richard Myers to Alice Lee, who was in Paris. Although "rather rickety and looking too much like the Phantom of Crestwood for Sara's comfort," he wasn't so consumed by his own distress that he couldn't spare a thought for the Myerses, who were struggling financially. He and Sara wrote them a check for $3,000, with the promise of more if need be. By springtime Gerald was recovered enough for the Murphys to make two more trips to Europe: in March they cruised the Mediterranean with the MacLeishes, and in June they sailed around the coast of Spain with John and Katy Dos Passos. The Dos Passoses, who were living in Katy's house in Provincetown, Massachusetts, had had their own health emergencies that winter: Katy had been suffering from persistent tonsillitis, and Dos, more seriously, had had another bout of rheumatic fever. Gerald had sent him $300, "a chip of a little legacy that mother left me and which I'd like you to use for something you shouldn't"; he and Sara paid for Dos and Katy's steamer tickets to Europe as well.

Dos Passos had recently completed a group of three plays — *The Garbageman*, *Airways, Inc.*, and *Fortune Heights* — and he and Gerald were thinking about trying to produce one of them. Although nothing came of this effort, Gerald clearly wanted to reconnect with the world of art and artists he had once moved in so confidently; and in the spring of 1934 he had a chance. Archie MacLeish had been approached to do a ballet libretto by a Russian émigré composer named Nicholas Nabokov who was desperate to make a living in America and saw a collaboration with a prizewinning poet (MacLeish had been awarded the Pulitzer Prize that spring for *Conquistador*) as a meal ticket. Although MacLeish had no experience with such a project, Nabokov pressed him to come up with a story line; and MacLeish thought of some research he'd been doing for *Fortune* about the building of the Transcontinental Railroad. He could, he thought, carve a good story out of that, but he realized that "Nick had no idea about America. He was here just because he had to get out of Europe [and] he didn't know where to turn." Remembering that Gerald Murphy had an unparalleled collection not just of Negro spirituals, but also of nineteenth-century American sheet music, MacLeish sent Nabokov to Gerald. "Gerald's collection was invaluable to him," MacLeish remembered, "and he used that music, which is incredibly exciting and foot-twitching," as the basis of his score.

Gerald's involvement didn't end there. He also helped to put together the financing that made production possible. Nabokov had approached Colonel Vassily de Basil, a "white Russian crook" (as Archie described him) who had taken over the remnants of Diaghilev's Ballets Russes, about mounting the ballet. As choreographer, Nabokov proposed Léonide Massine, later to achieve celluloid fame as the warped ballet master in the film *The Red Shoes*. But the wily de Basil took on no projects without backers: so Sara Murphy, Hoytie Wiborg, Lila Luce (the wife of MacLeish's employer, Henry Luce), and several others wrote him checks for $1,000 apiece, with the promise of more money from solicitations by Esther Murphy Strachey. It felt a little as if the sweat-equity philanthropy of the old Diaghilev days had returned. In March, after a song recital by Ada MacLeish, Gerald and Sara celebrated by giving a dinner party to which they invited Nicholas Nabokov, the Barrys, the Myerses, the Stephen Vincent Benéts, Aaron Copland, and Virgil Thomson, who distinguished himself by speaking to no one, standing at the buffet table and devouring an entire serving bowl full of strawberries and cream, and leaving immediately afterward.

In early April the ballet, now called *Union Pacific*, opened at the Forrest Theatre in Philadelphia to huge acclaim, and it played to packed houses in New York, Chicago, Paris, and London that spring and summer. "What carried that ballet," said Archie years afterward, "was not my idea and not the dancing of the ballerinas of the Ballet Russe de Monte Carlo, it was Gerald's music." But Gerald's name and contribution were nowhere noted on the program. Nor were Sara, Hoytie, Mrs. Luce, or the other investors ever repaid by de Basil, even though Hoytie, who still thought of herself as a businesswoman, had supposedly engineered an agreement that would have paid them out of the first night's proceeds. The whole experience seems to have precipitated another of Gerald and Archie's fallings-out. "Archie has hurt him very deeply," commented Alice Lee Myers later, "and it seems too bad for that long devotion to be dissipated — however, Gerald's reaction is based on emotion and no one can change that." Archie, for his part, was aware of the alienation Gerald felt: "He's a pretty lonely guy you know," he wrote to a mutual friend that summer. "He knows it now."

In April, though, Gerald was still wrapped up in the business of *Union*

Pacific's premiere, and so decided not to accompany Sara on the first of what would become nearly annual visits to the Hemingways in Key West. For obvious reasons Archie didn't go, either, although Ada did. She and Sara stayed with John and Katy Dos Passos in their rented house on Waddell Avenue, thus earning the nickname the "Waddell Girls."

The weather in Key West was bad, but the Waddell Girls made light of it: they went fishing with the Dosses and Ernest and Pauline and concocted lime juice cocktails and played Sara's records. Ada and Sara and Ernest got tight and danced after dinner in the Hemingways' living room, where the kudu and impala heads he had shot on his African safari that winter stared down at them. Afterward Ernest sent Gerald an oddly polite note enclosing some money he owed: "It was lovely having Sara here," he said, "but we missed you very much. You would like it I think." To Sara he wrote rather differently: "Dearest Sara," he began: "I love you very much, Madam, not like in Scott's Christmas tree ornament novels but the way it is on boats where Scott would be sea-sick."

The "Christmas tree ornament novel" was *Tender Is the Night,* which had been appearing in *Scribner's Magazine* in installments, the last of which came out while Sara was in Florida. The book itself was published in April, and Hemingway's sideways shot at its author is an indication that it had been an item of table talk in Key West. Certainly Sara was both outraged and shaken by Fitzgerald's portrayal of the Divers and their world: more than twenty-five years later she couldn't speak of it without indignation. But was she angry because Fitzgerald had missed the mark — or because he had come too close?

There were obvious parallels between Fitzgerald's characters and his friends, evident to anyone who knew the Murphys: the seductive figure of Nicole Diver on the beach with "her bathing suit . . . pulled off her shoulders and her back, a ruddy, orange brown, set off by a string of creamy pearls, [shining] in the sun"; the description of Dick Diver "mov[ing] gravely about with a rake, ostensibly removing gravel" from the beach; the picture of the villa and its spacious gardens; the conversations and witticisms that Fitzgerald had reproduced; the portrait of Baby Warren, Nicole's sister, "a tall, fine-looking woman" with Hoytie Wiborg's imperiousness. But none of this should have upset Sara. After all, she hadn't been upset by Picasso's pictures of her wearing nothing but her pearls on La Garoupe. What bothered her?

Ernest, who had told Gerald that "Scotts book, I'm sorry, is not good," finally wrote to Scott in May to say, "I liked it and I didn't like it." The problem, he maintained, was that

> It started off with that marvelous description of Sara and Gerald. . . . Then you started fooling with them, making them come from things they didn't come from, changing them into other people and you can't do that, Scott . . . You can take you or me or Pauline or Hadley or Sara or Gerald but you have to keep them the same and you can only make them do what they would do. . . . You could write a fine book about Gerald and Sara for instance if you knew enough about them and they would not have any feeling, except passing, if it were true.

That they *did* have a feeling about it, Ernest believed, stemmed from Scott's melding of Sara's and Gerald's histories with Zelda's and his own — Nicole's madness, Dick's drinking and brawling. What he implied — and what later readers have generally believed — was that Fitzgerald used the Murphys as models only for the glamorous parts of Nicole and Dick; that the wounded or wayward aspects of them were inspired by Zelda and Scott himself. And that this combination of disparate characters violated the integrity of his novel.

But Sara knew, and Gerald knew, how much else came from their own lives — not only as they were, but as they might have been. It was this airing of truths she could barely admit, or possibilities she couldn't bear to imagine, that frightened Sara. How could she stand to read about Nicole, who shared so many of her characteristics and secret thoughts, leaving her husband for a dark, swashbuckling man who, like Ernest, "look[s] like all the adventurers in the movies"? Sara loved Ernest, even felt the pull of his sexual attraction, but the idea that she would betray her husband with him would have both scared and repelled her. And how could she endure the novel's ending, in which the ruined Dick, stripped of his vocation and his family, about to leave forever the world he was once so happy in, makes a papal cross over the beach the way Gerald used to "say Mass" over his cocktails? The implications were too much for her, and it was a long time before she could be civil to Scott again.

That spring she sent him the kind of epistolary dressing-down she so often let him have when she was angry:

Dear Scott: —

We were sorry not to see you again — but it seemed, under the circumstances better not to —

Please don't think that Zelda's condition is not very near to our hearts — . . . and that all your misfortunes are not, in part, ours too — . . . We have no doubts of the loyalty of your affections (& we *hope* you haven't of ours) — but consideration for other people's feelings, opinions or even time is *Completely* left out of your makeup — I have always told you you haven't the faintest idea what anybody but yourself is like — . . . You don't even know what Zelda or Scottie are like — in spite of your love for them. It seemed to us the other night (Gerald too) — that all you thought and felt about them was in terms of *yourself* — the same holds good of your feelings for your friends. . . .

Please, please let us know Zelda's news. . . . I think of her all the time —
. . . .

When Sara wrote this letter Zelda was back in Baltimore, at the Sheppard-Pratt sanatorium. She had been getting more and more unstable all spring, possibly as a result of reading the serialization of *Tender Is the Night*, with its liberal borrowings from her own correspondence, and at the beginning of March had been admitted to the Craig House sanatorium in Beacon, New York. She seemed to be improving; then, in April, she had another breakdown and returned to Sheppard-Pratt.

While she was at Craig House, however, there was a one-woman show of her paintings at Cary Ross's gallery in New York. Zelda had painted for years as an avocation — mainly drawings and elaborate paper dolls for Scottie — but since her illness she had produced a substantial number of works in oil and gouache. They were, for the most part, strange, distorted images of the human figure, painted in vivid colors, something like Reginald Marsh on acid, or floral still lifes reminiscent of Georgia O'Keeffe. But they had great expressive power, and Scott, hoping to encourage her, had arranged this exhibition. It was covered by *Time* and *The New Yorker* and the *New York Post;* but the tone of their notices had the dusty sound of history: "Jazz Age Priestess Brings Forth Paintings"; "Paintings by the almost mythical Zelda Fitzgerald."

Just before Sara went to Key West she and Gerald went to see the pictures, and Sara bought one — the only oil, in fact, to sell. *Time* described *Chinese Theatre* as "a gnarled mass of acrobats with an indicated audience for background." Sara paid $200 for it, the largest sum Cary Ross took in. Gerald seemed almost revolted by the picture: "Those monstrous, hideous men," he said later, "all red with swollen, intertwining legs. They were obscene — I don't mean sexually. . . . they were figures out of a nightmare, monstrous and morbid." Anything further from his own cool precision, his covert, almost hermetic iconography, would have been hard to imagine — and Zelda, with that intuitive flash of sympathy that had so often characterized their friendship, understood. "I am going to paint a picture for the Murphys and they can choose," she wrote to Scott, "as those acrobats seem, somehow, singularly inappropriate to them and I would like them to have one they liked. Maybe they aren't like I think they are but I don't see why they would like that Buddhistic suspension of mass and form and I will try to paint some mood that their garden has conveyed."

There's no evidence that she ever did offer them an alternative, but she painted a still life that might have been intended for one: *Mediterranean Midi*, an undated oil of two wineglasses, a decanter, and fruit on a white table, shaded by a huge tree, with a view of the sea in the background. The picture is both precise and luminous, suffused with the golden light of Provence (the Midi) at noon (*midi*). And the glasses, globular and iridescent, bear a certain resemblance to the Venetian goblets that Scott had pitched over the wall at Villa America a seeming lifetime ago.

During that spring of 1934 Gerald and Sara gave a small dinner party for Ernest Hemingway, who happened to be in town, at the apartment to which they'd recently moved at 1 Beekman Place, on the East River. The other guests were Dottie Parker and her new young man, a heart-stoppingly handsome actor and writer eleven years her junior named Alan Campbell, and John O'Hara, whose novel *Appointment in Samarra* was just then making a sensation for its brutally unpleasant portrait of contemporary American life.

O'Hara was a journalist and screenwriter who had been taken up by their

friend Adèle Lovett, the wife of Averell Harriman's partner and Archie Mac-
Leish's Harvard Law classmate Robert Lovett; and although he was eager to
break into the circles the Lovetts and Murphys moved in, he was defensive
about his lack of background. (The joke was that his friends were getting
together a collection to send him to Princeton.) As a newcomer to the Murphys', he felt prickly in their presence; the small talk and funny-names games
that Gerald liked to play with Dottie, and which Alan Campbell so gladly fell
in with, left him cold. Ernest was late, and Dottie had made the mistake of
bringing with her her two new Bedlington terriers, replacements for the much
mourned Robinson, who got as restless as O'Hara, with predictable results: "I
had the pleasure," O'Hara wrote to Ernest afterward, "of watching first one
dog, then another taking a squirt on Mrs. Murphy's expensive rugs." Mrs.
Murphy, of course, didn't care. But somehow Mr. O'Hara never quite caught
on with her.

Not long after this evening Gerald and Sara got good news: Patrick's doctors
felt him strong enough to go to France that summer, where the Murphys
would stay at the villa and go cruising on the *Weatherbird* with the Myerses; if
all continued well in the fall he could go off to the Harvey School in Haw-
thorne, where Baoth had transferred that year, and resume his interrupted life
as a healthy boy. After nearly five years of holding their breath, the Murphys
must suddenly have felt that they could exhale cautiously. The only difficulties bedeviling them at the moment were the struggles of the Mark Cross
Company and Hoytie Wiborg's recently announced conviction that Sara's
purchase of the Dunes had been only a loan, secured by the property, which
she now wanted assurance of repossessing. However, as Mark Cross was in
Miss Ramsgate's hands and not Gerald's, and as Hoytie would surely come to
her senses after talking to the family's lawyer, there didn't seem much point in
worrying about either of these problems.

So they said their good-byes and packed their innumerable trunks for a
June 9 departure on the *Conte di Savoia*. Just before they sailed they received
two telegrams. One was from Dottie Parker: "THIS IS TO REPORT ARRIVAL
IN NEWCASTLE (PENNSYLVANIA) OF FIRST BEDLINGTON TERRI-
ERS TO CROSS CONTINENT IN OPEN FORD. MANY NATIVES NOTE
RESEMBLANCES TO SHEEP. COULDN'T SAY GOODBYE AND CAN'T

NOW BUT GOOD LUCK DARLING MURPHYS AND PLEASE HURRY BACK
AND ALL LOVE."

The other was from Hoytie. "YOU WILL NOT HAVE A LUCKY JOURNEY
FOR WHAT YOU HAVE DONE IN BREAKING FATHER'S PLANS FOR US.
ALL HIS REPROACHES WILL BE WITH YOU." She had signed it with only
her initial, "H."

19

"We try to be like what you want us to be"

IN THE HOME MOVIES they filmed that summer the sun is always shining. The wind bellies out the sails of the *Weatherbird* and flutters the flag Gerald designed for it, which Picasso so admired, a stylized eye in black, white, and red on a yellow ground that appears to wink as it waves. Sara squints into the sunlight or lifts her glass to toast the company. The boys, in striped jerseys that match the crew's, shinny up and down the masts — Baoth sturdy and strong, Patrick wiry and quick — or have toe-wrestling matches with their bare feet, or swim naked in the crystalline water. Honoria, looking more like a Renoir than ever, smiles demurely from beneath her hat brim or giggles with her friend Fanny. Gerald, his white shirt open to the waist of his white trousers, a white kerchief around his neck and a white slouch hat on his head, points toward some wonderful destination.

In one sequence Baoth has stuffed something into the front of his jersey to give him a voluptuous, Mae West profile, which he exhibits proudly to the camera; in another some of the sailors put him into a canvas bag, like the count of Monte Cristo, and dunk him in the ocean. He emerges laughing moments later. In still others Patrick deftly receives the American flag when it's taken in at day's end, folding it carefully into a regulation triangle, or sits with his fishing rod in hand, intently waiting for a bite. The girls show off their swimming strokes and clamber up the floating stairs at the side of the boat. The camera pans slowly along the rocky coastline, past *calanques* and fortresses and picturesque fishing ports, or lingers lovingly on the sleek hull of the *Weatherbird* itself, low and dark in the water.

The country is beautiful: "260 kilometres of wheat, sun, mules, threshing, oxen drawing, hats, Tio Pepe, — well, you know," writes Gerald on a postcard (with a little drawing of a hat) to Pauline and Ernest Hemingway. And "the boat (& the sea) were never so nice (or so blue)," adds Sara. It is a perfect summer.

Léger — bringing prints of *Ballet mécanique* and *Entr'acte* to screen — met them when they reached Gibraltar on the *Conte di Savoia*. He had sailed from Antibes with Vladimir and the crew, and as a thank-you to the Murphys he had made them a book of watercolors to commemorate his voyage, signing it, "A *Sara à Gerald, leur mousse très dévoué*" ("To Sara, to Gerald, their very devoted cabin boy"). He had reason for his devotion, for in addition to the cruise and the trip he had made to America in 1931 under their auspices, they had been sending him numerous "small checks" over the past year to help him out.

Villa America was lovelier than ever. Gerald (as he had done with Sara and Ellen Barry years ago) took Honoria and Fanny to Madame Vachon's fashionable boutique in St.-Tropez to outfit them with dresses and crocheted sandals, scooping up other pretty things by the dozen to take home as presents. One evening he and Sara accompanied the girls to the casino in Juan-les-Pins for dinner and dancing, an outing for which Sara made sure they were both wearing stockings. She herself — she told them — had once been denied admission to the Monte Carlo casino because she was bare-legged; but she'd outwitted the fashion police of the Société de Bains de Mer by going outside, where she resourcefully pulled a brown eye pencil from her evening bag and drew a line down the backs of her legs to look like a seam. No such ruse was required on this occasion, though; and inside the casino Gerald swept them around the floor, just like the dancer who was making such a sensation in the movie of Cole Porter's *Gay Divorcee*, Fred Astaire. Fanny Myers, a dark young beauty of considerable height who was wearing her very first evening dress, was horribly self-conscious to discover that her adolescent growth spurt (and her new high heels) had made her slightly taller than Gerald. In an effort to minimize the difference she slouched down when he led her onto the dance floor, but Gerald admonished her. "Stand up straight," he told her. "I know I'll be shorter than you, but *you* will look more beautiful if you stand tall."

The Murphys sailed back to New York on the *Aquitania* the first week of

September, and went directly to Hook Pond to get the children ready for school. There were new shoes to buy, routine doctor's and dentist's visits to make, trunks to pack — the familiar parental rituals of autumn. Meanwhile the children tried to catch the remnants of summer and make them last. One afternoon Baoth and Honoria were lying on the beach after swimming when Gerald came over the dune and walked slowly down to them. Honoria knew at once that something was wrong. "Children," Gerald said, "I have some bad news for you. Patrick has had a *rechute* [relapse]."

A routine checkup had revealed a spot on Patrick's "good" lung, the one he had been "living on," in Gerald's parlance. Almost immediately there followed the dreaded sequence of fever, loss of appetite, and difficulty breathing. Instead of going off to the Harvey School as he had dreamed of doing, Patrick was admitted to Doctor's Hospital on East End Avenue in New York, where he was confined to bed and only occasionally allowed to sit up in order to use his beloved etching tools or paints. Honoria came to visit him on weekends home from her new school, Rosemary Hall, in Greenwich, Connecticut, and was struck by his pallor as he lay against the white pillows. He had always been a delicate-looking child, but now he seemed practically transparent.

"Isn't it *horrid?*" wrote Sara to Ernest and Pauline: "And what a fool's paradise it is ever to think you have won a victory over the White plague!! — Well, he *is* going to be alright ultimately, & all our fighting blood is up again . . . but at times it *does* seem too much, — Especially as he himself is so decent about it all." The rest of the letter is cheery and gossipy; only in the hastily scrawled postscript did she let her anguish show. Under the message "Dow dow sends best love," she wrote a single line, without closing punctuation: "I wish I knew some more words"

Sara's fighting blood didn't fool any of the Murphys' friends, who saw — even if the Murphys could not bring themselves to admit — the seriousness of Patrick's condition. Esther Murphy Strachey confided to a friend that "the doctors have told Gerald he cannot live through the summer." Alice Lee Myers and Katy Dos Passos wrote to express their concern; and Ernest managed to go them one better by offering to send "either a Grants Gazelle or an Impalla" head to Patrick — whichever he'd like — They are really no trouble — (housebroken) very clean and light and quite beautiful to look at when you're in bed — Impalla is the most beautiful I think and I have a record one he would like. . . . Tell Patrick they are the ones that float in the air when they jump and jump over each others backs."

But it was Archie MacLeish who most perceptively, and poignantly, caught the meaning of what was happening to his friends, and to his friends' son. He wrote Patrick a letter, detailed and enthralling, about finding an injured animal in the leaves:

> I thought as I carried it that it was very hot in my hand but then I thought too that small animals always feel hot to us. When I came to the kitchen under the bright light over the sink I saw what it was . . . a young flying squirrel. . . . I . . . went back into the woods and put it into the bole of a great maple covered with leaves. It lay still there. All night under the brilliant moon I thought of it there and wondered about it. Somehow it had fallen and been hurt or perhaps some hunter had hit it. Its fur was softer than any squirrel. My love to you.

The young animal, flightless now, beautiful and vulnerable, tore at his heart.

In addition to the terrible anxiety they faced because of Patrick's illness, Gerald and Sara now had the additional burden of financial worries caused by renewed medical expenses and by a crisis within the Mark Cross Company. By the autumn of 1934 the Depression had made serious inroads in sales of the luxury goods for which Mark Cross was known: matched sets of luggage, from steamer trunks to handgrips, were not in great demand if the prospective purchasers could no longer afford the steamer tickets and grand hotels that went with them; nor were sumptuously outfitted picnic hampers or engraved thermoses or noncrushable cigar cases for the finest Havanas. Worse, in her role as president, Lillian Ramsgate had spent down the company's capital so that by the beginning of 1934 Mark Cross stood on the brink of bankruptcy. The other tenants at 37th Street and Fifth Avenue had already gone under and defaulted, leaving Mark Cross solely responsible for payments of $100,000 yearly to the landlord, Robert Walton Goelet.

Miss Ramsgate decided that the only course was to liquidate the company, and called a meeting of the board of directors in December. Gerald had remained a director even after his resignation as vice president, and his approval was necessary for Miss Ramsgate's plan; she told him if he didn't attend the meeting she would resign. He didn't, and she did. And now the company he had run away from in 1919 was his responsibility.

On December 19 Gerald became president of Mark Cross. In a speech to the employees he said that "I didn't know one thing about the business but it was all my sister and I had to live on, and so I would have to make a go of it." Not strictly true, perhaps, but close enough. His first act was to allow Goelet to buy fifty percent of the company as compensation for unpaid rent; his next was to move the business to smaller but more fashionable quarters on Fifth Avenue and 52d Street. He set about a stringent recovery program with the help of a younger Yale man named Ward Cheney, who joined the company as chief financial officer, and he began to redesign the store and its merchandise to bring it into line with market demand. He hired Tomi Parzinger, a chic leather-goods designer, to help give the accessories a more contemporary look; and he retained the services of Alice Lee Myers (whose eye he trusted as he did his own and Sara's) to seek out elegant European household goods. He even started a line of men's colognes — there was one called "Cross Country" and another, with a *cuir de Russie* base, called "Leather."

Some months after Gerald took up the reins at his father's company, Dos Passos told Hemingway that "spend[ing] all his time on Mark Cross and the Fifth Avenue Association [a merchant's group]. . . gives [Gerald] something to use his brains on — he's like he was years ago when he was painting." This was wishful thinking on Dos Passos's part. Even though the work allowed him to indulge, for a profit, his unique penchant for discovering recherché country pottery or clever dime-store key cases (which he replicated in the finest leather); even though he could showcase his design sense by putting Mark Cross evening purses together with semiprecious clips from the fashion jeweler Seaman Schepps to create a completely new kind of accessory — this wasn't art to him. "'Trade,'" he said to Scott Fitzgerald, was "an efficient drug — harmful but efficient." He told a friend in later life that his time at Mark Cross felt like sleepwalking.

He and Sara were trying, as usual, to carry on as if nothing cataclysmic were happening, while also trying to support and nurture the friends who meant so much to them. In November — in a letter in which he commissioned Gerald to buy him a batch of new records "to the value of the enclosed check" — Hemingway asked the Murphys to visit and "make a fuss about" an exhibit of paintings by an imprisoned Spanish friend of his and Dos Passos's. "If you wanted to buy one or a couple it would be swell, but I know with Patrick ill you must have God awful expenses," he wrote. Gerald and Sara responded: "YOUR RECORDS SHIPPED PARCEL POST YESTERDAY WOULD LOVE TO SEE YOU LISTENING TO THEM QUINTINILLA SHOW SUPERB SPLENDIDLY HUNG GOOD GALLERY INTELLIGENT MAN IN CHARGE FINE ATTENDANCE FOUR SOLD FIRST DAY TRYING TO SCARE UP SOME WRITEUPS SARA SURE YOU NEED CLIMACTIC CHANGE PLEASE COME STAY WITH US. . . . LOVE = MURPHYS."

They also managed to subsidize the Dos Passoses' need for a warm-climate base during the winter. Dos's siege of rheumatic disease the previous summer was dangerous enough that his doctor forbade him to come north during the cold months; but money was as chronic a problem for him and Katy as his health, and lack of both was making it hard for him to work sustainedly on *The Big Money*, the third part of the *U.S.A.* trilogy that had begun with *The 42nd Parallel* and continued with 1919. So in addition to a Christmas check — which, Dos reported from Jamaica, "turned into various things notably a bottle of Madeira . . . the rent of a car driven by a brownish smoke with an oxford accent — and into a small rowboat" — the Murphys proposed to rent a house in Key West which the Dosses could use until summer. Perhaps they would be able to visit themselves, they told Katy, if Patrick's health and the state of Mark Cross permitted.

That fall they had moved to a new apartment, at 539 East 51st Street, whose windows overlooked the East River — the same view that Patrick looked out on from his room at Doctors' Hospital two miles farther uptown. At Christmastime, when Baoth came home from his prep school, St. George's, in Newport, Rhode Island, he and his friends traveled on the Fall River steamer. As it came abreast of the Murphys' apartment they saw that Sara had hung out a sheet from the window with the words "Welcome Home, Baoth" emblazoned on it.

After Christmas, showing the strain of her worries about Patrick, Gerald, and Mark Cross, Sara was persuaded to go south to Key West for a brief winter holiday, joined by Ada MacLeish. Both "Dos and Ernest are very anxious for Gerald to come down," wrote Katy Dos Passos. But Patrick had been running a troublesome fever and the Mark Cross lease negotiation was at a crucial stage, so Gerald stayed behind.

Key West was gay, though unfortunately crowded with what Katy called New Dealers or Old Bohemians, many of them literary groupies hoping to get a glimpse of Ernest, who — with the success of *Farewell to Arms* and his short story collection *Winner Take Nothing* — had become a celebrity, and a somewhat self-impressed one at that. (Katy described it as "a tendency to be an Oracle . . . [he] needs some best pal and severe critic to tear off those long white whiskers which he is wearing.") In fact he had no white whiskers, no beard at all: he still looked like the Ernest of Pamplona and Schruns, a little burlier, perhaps, and needing to wear his glasses more often; but full of fun, always ready to sweep up Pauline or Sara in his arms and swing them around to "You're the Top" or the new Fats Waller records Gerald had sent. His new boat, named *Pilar* (Pauline's code name in the days of their affair), was a real working fishing boat that slept eight, and he and Pauline, the Waddell Girls, and the Dosses took her out almost daily. And the Hemingways' new house, a big Victorian stucco affair, was grand, with a peacock strutting on the lawn and palm trees all around.

Back in New York, Gerald had had a visit from his sister Esther, who had finally divorced John Strachey in 1933. The marriage was probably doomed from the start: although Strachey had embraced her leftist politics and her money, he had stuck at her drinking, her talkiness, and her lesbianism; and he had maintained throughout his premarital relationship with his mistress, Celia Simpson. As Esther's sister-in-law, Fred's widow, Noel, put it, "John was very dishonest with her — and Esther got mad and divorced him and was very sorry, because they had a wonderful mental relationship." But Esther hadn't been in love with him. "I don't think she ever loved anybody," said Noel, "except at a distance — actresses and so on. And she couldn't keep house. I went to see them once and it was dreadful — dirty sheets and everything."

About the closest Esther ever came to a long-term romantic attachment was her friendship with Muriel Draper, the interior designer and estranged wife of the composer Paul Draper. But now, she announced to Gerald over the telephone, she was planning to be married again, to Chester Alan Arthur III, a grandson of the twenty-first president who shared her Utopian political ideals and had been a member of the Irish Republican Army. He, too, was divorced. "[A]pparently," wrote Gerald to Sara, "they've both had the same sort of bad time and are most sympathetic. I can't say I'm sorry because Esther's life is so dreary. . . . I do hope she gets some happiness out of it. . . . She's asked me to announce their marriage (at City Hall) in about a month's time. I think they know what they're doing." Whether he gave any thought to the effect of Esther's sexual preferences on her marriage, whether he thought they even mattered, he didn't say. In sexual matters, silence, and its cousin denial, were familiar members of the Murphy family.

Most of Gerald's news, inevitably, concerned Patrick. The boy's temperature had subsided, but he still could do little more than sketch or fly paper airplanes or listen to the radio, currently a source of considerable stress for him because the airwaves were dominated by news of the trial of Bruno Richard Hauptmann for the kidnapping and murder of Charles Lindbergh's infant son. When the guilty verdict was finally handed down it was "an actual relief to him," said Gerald. "He now avoids any such programmes." The other children, he reported, were doing well. Baoth had come down with measles, but with his usual resilience he was convalescing in the school infirmary — a jokey letter he wrote was signed "The leaning tower of Baoth." The only troublesome note was that, as Gerald told Sara, "We *are* still behind on our bills. . . . Think a long time before you decide to make a gift (45.00 dollars) of the phono [to Dos Passos], — as it looks as if the *only* actual thing we *can* cut down for *some* months is gifts to people. Of course if Dos does seem to lack one, — why — "

About a week after Sara received this letter, Gerald telephoned her in Key West with frightening news: Baoth's measles had metamorphosed into double mastoiditis, the same potentially fatal infection that had once rushed Fred Murphy to the hospital. Baoth was to be operated on in Boston; Sara would have to leave Key West and join Gerald at once. There was no overland connection to the mainland, and the only way to get there was by car ferry to

Havana and thence by air to Miami, a trip that would take at least a day and a half. Instead, that very night, Ernest took her and Ada on board the *Pilar*, the three of them roaring along the Keys in the darkness; the next morning Ada flew with Sara to Boston. There the worst happened: as a result of Baoth's surgery, bacteria contaminated his spinal fluid and he developed meningitis, an inflammation of the brain and spinal column which can result in brain damage, blindness, or death.

What followed was, as Esther Murphy described it to Muriel Draper, "ten days of hideous suspense and five operations on the brain entailing the cruelest suffering." Friends and family flocked to Boston — Honoria from Rosemary Hall, Sara's cousin Sara Sherman Mitchell, Archie MacLeish, Dick and Alice Lee Myers — and Gerald and Sara were comforted to have Edward and Hester Pickman close by on Beacon Street. Significantly Hoytie — whose telegram of the previous summer Sara had come to believe was a curse — was absent. Archie could not stay — his verse play, *Panic*, a quixotic anticapitalist drama about the 1929 Crash, was to begin a two-night run on March 16 as the first production of the Phoenix Theatre, with Orson Welles in the lead. Ada followed him to New York on March 14, accompanied by Dick Myers, but Alice Lee stayed behind. Finally Baoth's condition became critical — he was in and out of consciousness and burning with fever — and Gerald, Sara, and Honoria moved into the hospital to be with him. Hester Pickman and Alice Lee joined them. Sara, refusing to believe her boy would not recover, sat by his bedside, holding his hand. "Baoth, *breathe*," she said, over and over for four hours, as if she could stave off the inevitable. "Breathe, Baoth. Please breathe." Over and over — even when, at last, he stopped. It was 10:30 in the morning of Sunday, March 17, 1935, St. Patrick's Day.

The doctor gave Sara an injection of a sedative and sent her to lie down in another room. Gerald turned to Honoria. "You watch out for your mother," he told her. "Do not leave her side. Sit by her bed, because when she wakes up and has to face what has happened, it's going to be rough." Gerald went to the telephone to call Doctors' Hospital and break the news to Patrick — who had been told that Baoth was ill but not how seriously — that his brother was dead. On her borrowed hospital bed Sara "slept for an hour or so," Honoria remembers, "and then she cried and cried."

"Darlings," wrote Katy Dos Passos when she heard, "we cannot help you in this disaster but you are so brave you will master it somehow and go on with your good and beautiful lives, so dear to us all." Dos echoed her: "You've been so brave throughout all this horrible time that it seems hard to write that you must go on and be brave." Even Ernest, who wrote perhaps the kindest and most perceptive letter ("It is not so bad for Baoth," he said, "because he had a fine time, always, and he has only done something now that we all must do"), fell into the trap: "It is *your* loss: more than it is his so it is something you can, legitimately, be brave about." And so did Archie MacLeish, paying tribute to "courage & grace & nobility such as yours," which, he told them, created "a new justification for all suffering, a new explanation of the mystery of pain." It was all cold comfort, being brave and wonderful. It would have been better, probably, for Archie to have said to them what he said to the Dos Passoses, that the taking of Baoth, the Murphys' healthy son, was "fancy. *Fancy*. There's no other word for it. They could have thought & thought for a million years & they wouldn't have been able to think of one like that."

On March 21 Sara and Gerald wired the Hemingways and Dos Passoses in Key West: "BAOTHS ASHES STAND ON AN ALTAR IN SAINT-BARTHOLOMEWS UNTIL SUNDAY WHEN THEY WILL BE LAID BESIDE HIS GRANDFATHER AT EASTHAMPTON OH THIS IS ALL SO UNLIKE HIM AND ALL OF US WE TRY TO BE LIKE WHAT YOU WANT US TO BE KEEP THINKING OF US PLEASE WE LOVE YOU ＝ SARA GERALD."

In the taxicab on the way to Baoth's memorial service Gerald broke down for the first and only time, grieving for the moments when he had lost his temper with his high-spirited son. Sara sat in frozen silence, but during the service, unable to bear it anymore, she rushed out onto Park Avenue. Archie MacLeish ran after her. As the two of them stood on the pavement Sara raised her fist to the sky and shook it, cursing God.

They were numb with the shock of Baoth's death, but, Gerald and Sara thought, they had to keep going for Patrick. (They seem almost to have lost sight of the idea that they had to cherish Honoria, too. "The news," remembers their godson William MacLeish, "was always about Baoth and Patrick.") Their friends thought about Patrick, too. Alexander Woollcott had an enormously popular radio show called "The Town Crier," which every week profiled a different person, usually a celebrity, and played that person's favorite song. One Sunday his featured personality was someone few in his audience had heard of — Patrick Murphy. After playing his subject's signature tune, Percy Grainger's prim little gavotte "Country Gardens," the Round Table pundit said, over the airwaves, "Good night, Patrick. I hope you're feeling better." And Ernest wrote Patrick a wonderful newsy letter about a tuna-fishing expedition he had planned — where he would go, who would be with him, and how he would take films of the expedition and send them. "The difficulty will be," he said, in one of his man-to-man asides, "to get Dos to take the movies with the camera pointed away from him and toward the tuna instead of away from the tuna and toward him. But he is full of confidence and already thinks of himself as a big camera man and is starting to wear his cap with the visor on backwards."

Although there had been some thought of taking Patrick out west to Santa Fe or Tucson in hopes of a cure, Gerald and Sara decided on somewhere nearer home, the town of Saranac Lake, New York, where in the 1880s Dr. Edward Livingston Trudeau had established a "Cottage Sanatorium" devoted to what he called "the Outdoor Life." Unlike many tuberculosis treatment centers, Saranac did not have a large-ward hospital; treatment was carried on in "cottages," or lodging houses, where patients could lead more homelike lives, attended by nurses and visiting physicians. Saranac was located in the Adirondack Mountains, not far from Raquette Lake, where Gerald had gone to stay with the Morgans in the heady days following his secret engagement to Sara. But although there were numerous millionaires' "camps" on the neighboring lakes, the town itself was no getaway paradise. In the days before antibiotic drugs, Saranac had a population of two thousand actively tubercular people. In addition, hundreds of tentatively cured sufferers remained in the town, and there was virtually no one there whose livelihood didn't depend in some way on the disease and its treatment.

The success of the tuberculosis industry had led to a turn-of-the-century building boom in the tiny wilderness hamlet, and so the hills around Lake Flower in the center of town were covered by Queen Anne–style frame houses sporting "cure porches," enclosed glass or open porches for living and sleeping where TB patients could have maximum fresh air and sunlight while being sheltered from the elements. But there was little industry other than the cure, and less amusement. The town was very quiet — even the local radio station went off the air during the two-to-four-P.M. "rest hour" — and, in wintertime, when the wind swept down from the dark Adirondack peaks surrounding it, very cold.

But it was close enough to New York for Gerald to spend time with his family while he struggled to get Mark Cross out of the red, and for Honoria to come for weekends away from school. Sara found a property for rent, called Steele Camp, near the Trudeau Institute on Lower Saranac Lake: a classic Adirondack house made of whole weathered logs with gables and fretwork under the eaves, set in a clearing among enormous old pines and hemlocks, with a detached boathouse and guest quarters across its sloping lawn. The house was full of rather self-consciously rustic touches: one bedroom, which had a screened porch, was paneled in planking made from old railroad ties; others had oak paneling or were walled in barn siding; and the spacious living room, whose windows overlooked the lake and a pair of small islands, had a stone fireplace large enough to stand in. But it was comfortable and had a sandy beach for swimming when the weather got warm enough, and when Patrick's condition stabilized sufficiently for him to travel he and Sara — and Honoria, who was on her summer vacation — moved in, with Gerald ("the Merchant Prince," he self-mockingly called himself) making the seven-hour train journey to Saranac every other weekend.

The MacLeishes and John Dos Passos came to visit in July (Katy was in New York on magazine business). Dos had been working on *The Big Money*, the third novel in his trilogy *U.S.A.*, in which a character named Eveline Hutchins Johnson, who "gives the most wonderful parties," attended by "all the most interesting people in New York," and has a "teasing singsong voice" like Sara Murphy's, swallows a fatal dose of sleeping pills because her life has collapsed from the inside. So Dos was relieved to find "Sara very thin and pretty and in better shape than I expected," or so he wrote to Ernest. Also in July, after a long silence, the Murphys heard from Fernand Léger, who, ignorant of Baoth's death, imagined they had been out of touch because of their worries about Patrick. It had been a difficult year for him financially, he said, but he had hopes of an upturn because the Museum of Modern Art in New York, the Art Institute of Chicago, and the San Francisco Art Museum planned exhibitions of his work in the fall. All his big canvases would be there, he wrote, and all his friends were telling him he had to go to New York, if only just for the Modern's exhibition . . . If he could stay with the Murphys on Long Island, he said, he thought he could manage the trip: "Dear Gerald, and dear Sara, do everything in your power to help me with this. If you could advance me 1500 francs . . . you would be my 'guardian angels' and I would be your 'cabin boy' for all eternity."

They did, of course — when had they said no to someone they loved? — and the trip turned out to be a success, with ten thousand viewers coming to the MOMA show in twenty days. Sara was able to get to New York for the *vernissage*, and Léger, with his usual playfulness, told her and Gerald that one of the paintings on view belonged to them — if, that is, they could pick it out. They walked through the crowded galleries until, at the foot of some stairs, Sara saw a picture called *Composition à un profil* — a stark, surreal rendition of tubular forms reminiscent of the primordial aloe plants that grew on the Côte d'Azur; its predominant color was brown, Gerald's favorite, but one Léger used infrequently. They were standing in front of it when Léger came up behind them and said, "I see you found it." Turning the picture around, he showed them what he had written on the back of the frame: *"Pour Sara et Gérald."*

It was a fitting gift, for despite being beleaguered with Mark Cross's affairs, Patrick's illness, and his grief over Baoth, Gerald was putting Léger up at the Hotel Russell, and acting as a nearly full-time artistic, business, and personal adviser to him. Who to see, what to say, how to treat this potential buyer — all such questions were addressed to Gerald, along with requests for funds to tide Léger over when promised sales didn't come through or checks were slow to arrive. At one point, Léger hoped to enlist Mark Cross as a corporate patron and went so far as to suggest the architect Le Corbusier (whom Gerald had known as the painter Jeanneret in Paris) as a potential designer for the store's new premises on 52d Street. He himself would create murals for it. "We're both at the complete disposal of Mark Cross, if you wish," he wrote, but unfortunately this grand project never got off the ground. On a smaller scale, at the beginning of his stay in America, in order to encourage Marie Harriman, who was acting as his dealer, Léger asked Gerald to buy a small drawing for $100 — "the price isn't important; it's the fact that I have a *'sale.'*" Later on, when he needed $1,000, it was again to Gerald that he came. "We don't buy pictures to own," rationalized Gerald to Sara, so "I'd rather *give* him what we can afford. . . . He is *giving* us in return a toile [canvas], which is all right." Thus the Murphys acquired another Léger, *Nature morte, tête et grande feuille* (Still life with head and leaf). Léger wrote them that it was "thanks to you two that all this" — his exhibitions, his contacts with and sales to museums and collectors from coast to coast — "has been made possible, and I am eternally grateful."

Léger had always had a tenderness for Patrick, and made sure to send him a telegram on his fifteenth birthday, October 18. He also came to visit him in Saranac Lake, when each did a drawing of the other. Patrick's portrait of Léger, a strong, sure likeness whose firm lines have something of the subject's own forceful character, is a testament to the youthful artist's gift. Léger's drawing, which shows his young friend reading in a white iron bed, is less straightforward, more unsettling. The bedside table, with its sickroom paraphernalia, is at the center of the composition, while Patrick — who is shown engulfed in heavy sweaters and a knitted cap against the winter chill of his screened porch — is off to one side, marginalized by his illness.

When he got Léger's telegram, Patrick was still very sick indeed. He weighed only fifty-nine pounds, about half what a healthy boy of his age would, although Sara courageously maintained that he was "on the mend, — definitely." Gerald knew better, and he knew, too, that Sara was suffering — not just from loss but from loneliness. He asked for help from the only person he knew who might understand.

Dear Scott: —
  . . . It has occurred to me in all this that you alone have always — known shall I say — or felt? — that Sara was — that there was about Sara — something infinitely touching, — something infinitely sad. . . . Life begins to mark her for a kind of cumulous tragedy, I sometimes think. . . . She needs nourishment — from adults — from those who are fond of her.

Fitzgerald was shuttling between Baltimore — where Zelda stayed, unimproved, at the Sheppard-Pratt sanatorium — and Asheville, North Carolina, with short visits to New York. He was currently struggling with the painful self-examination involved in writing the essays that would form *The Crack-Up*, and he had to be smarting from Sara's tart disdain of *Tender Is the Night*. But he found time to write Sara a letter to tell her not just what she meant to him, but what she meant to anyone whose life she had touched. Typically, for in their relationship they had never beaten about any bushes, he went straight to the subject that had been the latest source of friction between them:

Dearest Sara:

. . . In my theory, utterly opposite to Ernest's, about fiction i.e. that it takes half a dozen people to make a synthesis strong enough to create a fiction character — in that theory, or rather in despite of it, I used you again and again in *Tender*:

"Her face was hard & lovely & pitiful"

and again

"He had been heavy, belly-frightened with love of her for years"

— in those and a hundred other places I tried to evoke not *you* but the effect you produce on men. . . . And someday in spite of all the affectionate skepticism you felt toward the brash young man you met on the Riviera eleven years ago, you'll let me have my little corner of you where I know you better than anybody — yes, even better than Gerald. And if it should perhaps be your left ear (you hate anyone to examine any single part of your person, no matter how appreciatively — that's why you wore bright clothes) on June evenings on Thursday from 11:00 to 11:15 here's what I'd say:

That not one thing you've done has been for nothing. . . . The people whose lives you've touched directly or indirectly have reacted to the corporate bundle of atoms that's you in a *good* way. *I have seen you again & again at a time of confusion take the hard course almost blindly because long after your powers of ratiocination were exhausted you clung to the idea of dauntless courage.* You were the one who said:

"All right, I'll take the black checker men."

I know that you & Gerald are one & it is hard to separate one of you from the other, in such a matter for example as the love & encouragement you chose to give to people who were full of life rather than to others, equally interesting and less exigent, who were frozen into rigid names. I don't praise you for *this* — it was the little more, the little immeasurable portion of a millimeter, the thing at the absolute top that makes the difference between a World's Champion and an also-ran, the little glance when you were sitting with Archie on the sofa that you threw at me and said:

"And — Scott!"

taking me in too, and with a heart so milked of compassion by your dearest ones that no person in the world but you would have had that little more to spare.

Well — I got somewhat excited there. . . .

It's odd that when I read over this letter it seems to convey no particular point, yet I'm going to send it. Like Cole's eloquent little song.

"I think it'll tell you how *great* you are."

> From your everlasting friend,
> Scott

20

"Life itself has stepped in now"

IN SARANAC LAKE, alone in her huge Adirondack lodge except for the company of a sick child and his nurse, Sara was, as she wrote to Scott Fitzgerald, "raw to the feelings toward me of my friends (like the man who scraped his fingers to feel the combinations of safes)." So Scott's letter to her "did me a lot of good," but it wasn't enough. Archie MacLeish noticed that Sara was "very unhappy . . . [with] the kind of unhappiness you can't reach because it is not only about Patrick but about another winter at Saranac and about the headaches she has so much of the time and about a lot of other things she won't talk about." As autumn drew on, the undertone of panic in her voice became more and more noticeable.

My Dearest Scott, —

. . . . I hope you *are* coming up to see us in Sept.? Gerald thought you would & we are delighted. Would you like to bring Scotty? There isn't the least danger . . . we have had lots of guest-children & so take infinite precautions.

My *Dearest* Hemingways, —

. . . . *Is* there any chance of your coming up to these parts? Really? Because I am pining to see you. I have *such* a good wine cellar, & a good cook, & lots of new music — Room for the children too, if you want to bring them — Our guests are in a separate guest-house apart — & all Patrick's dishes — silver laundry etc etc are separate so there isn't the slightest danger about that, & people have been confiding their children to me all summer — oh we sleep under piles of blankets and have a roaring wood fire most of the time — and we love you so much.

My Dearest Pauline, —

I sent you off a wire today to please all come. . . . My dears, *do, do* come here — and just *sit* for a spell until you can find & arrange what & where you want to be — & I shall — & it will be my pleasure — to cozen & feed you & make you little drinks & what not (& wrap your feet in a red blanket) — I am fixed up *so* well here! With a good cook, a heated camp, a licensed guide (*how* that man talks!) — all alone, mind you, all alone — Honoria is off to school on the thirtieth & my Merchant Prince Dowdow only comes every two wks & sometimes not that — Here Patrick & his nurse & I live in solitary state & he P. is off in isolated quarters & on his porch, so I roam the place in desolate grandeur.

I can't go away to New York to live too — P. counts on me to be here & tell him jokes & bully him. . . . So please darlings, come along & cheer me up & I have such a lot of new music & wines & spirituous liquors, & a boat & hunting. . . .

So I don't see how you can not come, unless it was just wilful — & God knows you aren't that — . . . .

My dearest Ernest, —

Just by a curious coincidence — Some of my mother's estate has *just,* this month, been settled up. . . . and so I have some *Cash.* Quite a lot of cash — (It nearly *never* happens!) Before it is re-invested — ugh — Will you (& I *hope* you aren't furious?) — do me the greatest compliment one friend can do another, & take some?

Please, *please* don't say no right off like that without thinking — now listen: we have plenty — we don't need it. — We have no boy to put through school — Our friends are the dearest things we have (after the daughter, & she is fixed up). . . .

I enclose a small amount which would get you all North . . . (I sent some to Dos & Katy too) . . . It *is* just a short cut, if you really want to start your book & get settled, where it is cool. . . .

Neither Ernest nor Pauline needed money — she was independently wealthy and he was by now extremely successful — but they responded to her tone of desperation, and came to visit her and Patrick that fall, most likely in September. And in October, around the publication date of *Green Hills of*

Africa, galleys of which Ernest had specially sent to Sara, he saw her again. What he saw worried him enough that he hounded John and Katy Dos Passos to go cheer her up, "even though I knew you couldn't and shouldn't," because "Sara seemed so dismal about nobody coming."

Not the least self-centered of men, Hemingway had come to feel uncharacteristically tender, almost sentimental, about Sara. One of his biographers says he had developed what amounted to "a crush" on her. He'd always been good at making grandstand plays for her and Gerald's sympathy, but now this talent was expended only on her. In September he had told her that "maybe I am bad luck and . . . should not have to do with people"; to which she protested, "It isn't true — it's a lie — When have you been anything but good for people?" Now he complained to her of feeling like a "skyzophreniac" — on the one hand a workaholic, on the other a hard-partying all-around guy. "Only place these rival skyzophreniacs agree is do not like to sleep alone," he added suggestively. He had (he did not mention) taken steps to prevent this. From 1932 to 1934 he had been carrying on an intermittent flirtation or affair — his biographers differ over its extent — with a blond, Havana-based New York socialite named Jane Mason, which had placed a strain on his marriage to Pauline. By the winter of 1935–1936 the relationship had cooled, however, and Hemingway may have been feeling as sorry for himself as he did for Sara. He was especially sorry that it seemed as if she would not be coming to Key West that winter and hoped she would reconsider. He signed his letter "With very much love much love and love also with love, Ernest."

The Murphys had given up their New York apartment and had taken a small flat for Gerald only, first in the Hotel Russell on Park Avenue, and then at the New Weston on 52d Street. There Gerald occasionally saw New York friends like the Myerses, Benchley, and Alexander Woollcott, who had begun to play an increasingly prominent part in Gerald's life. Woollcott was that dangerous thing, someone who really was a legend in his own time: a 250-pound gourmand whose flamboyant clothes (he was known to wear a scarlet-lined cape flung about his shoulders) and acid wit were currently being immortalized by his friend George S. Kaufman in the eponymous *The Man Who Came to Dinner*. (Gerald did his part to burnish the legend by using Woollcott's radio show as the inspiration for a Mark Cross "Town Crier" cocktail shaker in the shape of a bell.) As a youth Woollcott had been photographed in Victorian drag, but he was far too frightened of the idea of sex to give in to any homosexual impulses. He sublimated by giving himself nicknames like "She-Ancient" and "Pretty," which he asked other friends to adopt; but here Gerald drew the line. He called him "Alexis," "Alexis, Prince of the Heavenly Flocks," "Alexis lunaire," "Alexis borealis," or "Great White Heron." If their banter ever took on overtones of flirtatiousness ("You show signs of being embarrassed by my material attentions," wrote Gerald after sending him a gift, "or is it that you were brought up never to accept gifts from strange gentlemen?"), it was always demure. The two of them frequently went to the theater together while Gerald was alone in New York, and Gerald saw in Woollcott what few could discern behind his smoke screen of bombast and punditry: a "gift . . . to make the people he loved feel valuable." During the next few years, during which he and Sara frequently led separate lives, he would confide some of his most painful and vulnerable feelings to this outwardly outrageous man.

Sara and Patrick had left Steele Camp and had moved for the winter into the town of Saranac Lake, to a lofty barn of a house at 129 Church Street, within range of the bells of four different churches. Dick and Alice Lee Myers came with Fanny to the Winter Olympics in nearby Lake Placid in February, and Sara had made friends with the family of Dr. Trudeau, with whom she sometimes went bobsledding. But there may have been an edge to these amusements. Honoria remembers her mother hurtling down the most difficult slopes, laughing and laughing, whether from gaiety or desperation she doesn't try to guess.

Sara and Gerald were going through a difficult time — more difficult, perhaps, than their years at Montana-Vermala. The death of their *healthy* son, on Gerald's watch (although Sara would never put it that way); the cumulative sense of time passing, for themselves and for their friends, what Archibald MacLeish, in "You, Andrew Marvell," had called "the always coming on of night": all this made things worse. And their physical separation, which had become almost a constant with Sara's move to Saranac, merely underlined the isolation each had begun to feel. December 30 was their twentieth wedding anniversary, a date that in the Antibes days would have been celebrated by the three children, in festive clothes, bringing them flowers on their balcony. In Saranac, on December 31, this is what Gerald wrote to Scott Fitzgerald:

> Of all our friends, it seems to me that you alone know how we felt these days — still feel. You are the only person to whom I can ever tell the bleak truth of what I feel. Sara's courage and the unbelievable job she is doing for Patrick make unbearably poignant the tragedy of what has happened — what life has tried to do to her. I know now that what you said in "Tender is the Night" was true. Only the invented part of our life, — the unreal part — has had any scheme any beauty. Life itself has stepped in now and blundered, scarred and destroyed. In my heart I dreaded the moment when our youth and invention would be attacked in our only vulnerable spot, — the children, their growth, their health, their future. How ugly and blasting it can be, — and how idly ruthless.

At the beginning of February, Gerald left for a six-week European buying trip for Mark Cross, his first. And it seems as if Sara, unnerved by the prospect of so solitary a winter, wrote the Hemingways to ask them to return to Saranac. They couldn't. "Damn I wish we could come there for the winters sporting," wrote Ernest, "but I have to work like the devil the rest of the winter." Then the inflection of his voice changed: "How are you dear beautiful Sara?" he asked. "I had a gigantic dream about you about ten days ago and woke up determined to write you a long letter (longer than this one) and tell you how highly I thought of you. . . . There are about three records that I never hear without think of you. I wish you were here, Sara."

Her next letter to him is missing. From his response, it seems to have been concerned not only with her own sense of isolation and despair, but with her feelings about Gerald and her marriage: "Poor Sara," said Hemingway. "I'm sorry you had such a bad time. These are the bad times. It is sort of like the retreat from Moscow and Scott is gone the first week of the retreat." (Although in this case it was Gerald who was gone, in Europe, Ernest never could resist a jab at Fitzgerald, especially in front of Sara.) The last half page, or more, of this letter is missing; what is left cuts off after a description of the paternal qualities of a mutual friend. It doesn't take a huge leap of the imagination to wonder if the rest of the letter dealt with the father of *her* children, and if it was Sara who scissored it off so she could save the remainder, as she did everything else, for a keepsake.

Gerald returned to America in mid-March, but the difficulties between them that might have seemed implicit before he left became harder and harder to ignore. "There is one thing that has always surprised me," Gerald wrote to Sara from New York in April, answering "2 type-written and rare semi-philosophical letters" from her, which have not survived:

> and that is one's tendency to feel that just because two people have been married for 20 years that they should need the same thing of life or of people. You are surprised anew periodically that "warm human relationship" should be so necessary to you and less to me. Yet nothing is more natural under the circumstances. You believe in it (as you do in life), you are capable of it, you command it. I am less of a believer (I don't *admire* human animals as much), I am less capable (for a fundamental sexual deficiency, like poor eyesight), I lack the confidence (quite naturally) to command it — or to keep it in its proper relationship to me. Certainly feeling exists in people or it doesn't. No two people show it in the same *degree* or *manner.* Hence the inadequacy of most relationships which are supposed to be kept at a *constant* emotional pressure.

Two days later he wrote again:

> Dear Sal: —
> Addenda: I suppose it's downright tragic (if things in life *are* tragic, — or just life —) when one person who *lives by communicated affection* should have chosen a mate who is (damn it) deficient. I have always had (as early as I can remember) the *knowledge* (conviction, feeling) that I lacked something that other people had, — emotionally. Whether this is due to the absence of degree and depth of feeling, or the result of trained suppression of feelings, distrust and fear of them, I don't know.

It's fashionable now to pigeonhole people, as Hemingway (and to a lesser extent Fitzgerald) tried to do, by either/or sexual preference. But Gerald belonged to a less arbitrary generation, and to a class and milieu — the New

York of Stanford White and the polymorphous Paris of Cocteau and de Beaumont — in which ambiguous or bisexual behavior was, if not accepted, at least ignored. He himself maintained to Sara that "nothing which I *believe* in . . . should cause this lack [of feeling]; — nothing against Nature," and he meant it. He didn't think of himself as homosexual in an exclusive sense. "Outside of a man and a woman, and children and a house and a garden, — there's nothing much," he wrote. But his old feelings of ambivalence, imposture, and diffidence, the ones he had written to Archie about in 1931, had been exacerbated by Sara's evident need of emotional, and probably sexual, warmth. And although in 1926 he might have told Scott Fitzgerald, as Dick Diver told Rosemary, that his love for Sara was "active love," by 1936 this was less and less true. At lunch one day with Phil Barry and Archie MacLeish, Gerald responded to their off-color stories about their sexual exploits by exclaiming, "Thank God all that is behind me!" This may have been a pose, adopted to distance himself from his friends' self-conscious machismo, or it may have been an overstatement. But to Sara he admitted that his "deficiency" must make her feel "rotten."

Shortly after Sara got this letter, and despite having said earlier that she couldn't get south that winter, she drove to Florida with John and Katy Dos Passos and flew by seaplane to join Ernest in Havana. (Pauline, who was visiting her family in Arkansas, wasn't with them.) Although Dos was correcting proofs of *The Big Money* and barely looked at a fishing rod, the rest of them went out on the *Pilar* nearly every day. After an inauspicious beginning in which Ernest raised only one marlin which "Dos blew" (as Ernest sourly put it in his ship's log), Sara managed to catch three dolphins, one barracuda, and one arctic bonito within two days. In the evenings the *Pilar* chugged back to Havana harbor with a "fish flag" flying if they'd caught anything, and Dos and Katy and Sara and Ernest had dinner together in the Ambos Mundos Hotel. Very possibly they talked about their absent friend Scott Fitzgerald, whose three autobiographical essays about his professional and personal breakdown, later published as *The Crack-Up*, had just appeared in *Esquire*. Ernest, predictably, hated them — "whining in public," was his comment. When Sara read them she had written to Scott: "Do you *really* mean to say you honestly thought 'life was something you dominated if you were any good — ?' Even if you meant your *own* life it is arrogant enough, — but life!" It's easy to imagine her saying the same thing to Dos and Katy and Ernest, over dinner at the Ambos Mundos, and adding (as she did to Fitzgerald), "If you just won't admit a thing it doesn't exist (as much) . . . [but] rebelling, dragging one's feet & fighting every inch of the way, one must admit one can't *control* it — one has to *take* it, — & as well as possible — that is all I know."

After dinner, when Dos had gone up to his room to work on his galleys, they would sit with their drinks and listen to the three straw-hatted Cubans who played rumbas and Latin versions of "There's a Small Hotel" for them. One day, after a long night, Sara "breakfasted" Ernest on Bromo-Seltzer and whiskey sours where the *Pilar* was anchored in a secluded cove. And sometime during this week in Havana, Sara and Ernest dug rather deeply into what each of them had made of their lives.

"Some people," Hemingway's son John acknowledges, "say that Father had some kind of secret thing going on with Sara. Although he "can't imagine it," the rumor has never entirely disappeared. The reasons aren't hard to determine. Like Picasso, Hemingway was the sort of man Sara invariably responded to, magnetic, male, and physical, but with an artist's intuitiveness; she had always been attracted to him — certainly Scott Fitzgerald had noticed — and at this point in her life she was hurt and needy. And Hemingway, the man who didn't like to sleep alone, *was* alone, his marriage to Pauline tacitly on the rocks.

So what happened next? John and Katy Dos Passos and Sara left Havana after a week. In Miami they telephoned Pauline, who had just returned to Key West, and begged her to see them, if only for an hour, in the Miami airport. Pauline duly arrived, on her way to rejoin Ernest in Havana, looking, Sara said, "like a delicious, and rather wicked little piece of brown toast." (Pauline, for her part, thought Sara looked "beautiful. . . . She met me at the Pan-American station in pearls and one of her hats and I thought who or whom is that lovely woman expecting and it turned out to be me.") And when Sara got home to the Adirondacks she wrote Ernest a letter whose lines beg to be read between.

"About being snooty," she said: "You don't REALLY think I am snooty do you? Please don't. It isn't snooty to choose." There's just the faintest echo here of the old Sara — the Sara of Picasso's pictures, the Sara who Scott Fitzgerald complained was being "mean to me," the woman who had chosen one man and was going to stick with him. "Choice, and one's affections," she said now to Ernest, "are about all there are." And, as if to remind him of the choices *he* had made: "Oh Ernest, what wonderful places you live in and what a good life you have made for yourself and Pauline."

Hemingway wasn't used to people saying no to him — if indeed "no" is what was said — and he doesn't seem to have risen to the challenge of these choices. Ever since *The Sun Also Rises*, he had used his fiction as a weapon. Now, in a story he was calling "The Happy Ending," but which would be published as "The Snows of Kilimanjaro," he seems to have turned that weapon on Sara. "Snows" takes place on the slopes of Mount Kilimanjaro, where the writer Harry Walden is dying of gangrene, literally corrupted by his relationship with a wealthy woman. He is lamenting the lost chances and lost loves of his life, the good times he had in Paris and in the Vorarlberg when he and the century were young. And he is musing on the pernicious influence of "the very rich," about whom he has had an argument with "poor Scott Fitzgerald" — the argument sparked by the now mythic exchange about the very rich being different from you and me because (in Hemingway's view) "they have more money." Poor Scott (Hemingway grudgingly changed the name to "Julian" in later published versions of the story) "thought they were a special glamorous race and when he found they weren't it wrecked him just as much as any other thing wrecked him."

Although Hemingway had berated Fitzgerald for creating composite characters, he had done it himself (*A Farewell to Arms*'s Catherine has trace elements of Pauline and Hadley, as well as Hemingway's lost love Agnes von Kurowsky); and "Snows"'s Helen, while she owes something to Pauline and Jane Mason, bears other marks as well. Like Sara (and like Fitzgerald's Nicole Diver), she is the heiress to a midwestern industrial fortune; even more like Sara, she has suffered the death of a child. As Harry is waiting for the end to come she says to him — like Sara imploring Baoth to breathe in that hospital room in Boston, or arguing with Fitzgerald about not admitting defeat — "You can't die if you don't give up." But he does die, and before he does he feels death's presence inextricably linked with hers: "She looked at him with her well-known, well-loved face from . . . *Town and Country* . . . and he felt death come again." Although Jane Mason had posed for a face cream ad in *Ladies' Home Journal* which Hemingway kept in his files, it was Sara Murphy, when she was engaged to be married to Gerald, who had had her face on the cover of *Town and Country.* And apparently it was Ernest who, hiking or hunting in the Rockies, had found that photograph tacked to the wall in a deserted mountain man's hut, and had torn it down and sent it to her.

Hemingway had once written Archie MacLeish a letter — one of those rather gratuitously cruel letters he occasionally sent to male friends to show how tough he could be — in which he said that "Every woman's husband is, in a way, after a certain time, her own fault. All women married to a wrong husband are bad luck for themselves and all their friends." In case Archie didn't catch his drift, he added: "Cf. Mr. Benchley's pal and Mrs. Parker's confidante," surely a reference to Gerald and Sara. But whatever Sara might have confided to Hemingway about her marriage, she would never think of it as causing "bad luck" for her; she knew where her heart truly lay. She had chosen, and so had Gerald. Later that spring, after she returned from Florida, Gerald told her that, although his "defect" made him "terribly, terribly sorry that I am as I am . . . only one thing would be awful and that is that you might not know that I love only you. We both know it's inadequate (that's where 'life' comes in); — but such as it is it certainly is the best this poor fish can offer, — and it's the realest thing I know. Who knows but that the good Lord may let it make up for its defect in some other way?"

That summer Sara — in a show of optimism and commitment that she hoped would ensure Patrick's recovery — bought a camp on Lake St. Regis near the hamlet of Paul Smith's, the site of Dr. Trudeau's own original cure, and moved Patrick out there. Camp Adeline (she renamed it after her mother) had a boathouse with a wheelchair-accessible dock, which permitted Patrick to fish, and residents were housed in eight different cottages — including a guest house, servant's cottage, girls' bunkhouse (for Honoria and her visiting school friends), and main living quarters — all filled with bright painted and slipcovered furniture, white rugs, Mexican metalware, and potted plants and flowers. As proof that she and Patrick intended to have many summers there, Sara ordered writing paper with "Camp Adeline" engraved on it; at the top, tiny logos of an envelope, a telephone, a telegraph key, and a locomotive indicated the mailing address, phone number, telegraph address, and railroad station outsiders needed to use to reach it.

Gerald had been having some trouble with his tonsils, and after having them out in July he was persuaded to take a real vacation, for the first time in a long time. A camera caught the two of them, Gerald and Sara, sitting on a bench by the boathouse, Sara's brown Pekingese, Puppy, at their feet. Gerald is wearing one of his trademark abbreviated bathing suits and a knitted French sailor's cap; although his hairline has receded, his body is still taut and athletic, and he appears to be reading a postcard, or looking at a photograph, with a slightly quizzical expression on his face. Next to him, Sara has wrapped a thick terry cloth robe over her bathing suit against the Adirondack chill; a broad-brimmed hat nearly covers her eyes. Her long, pretty legs are stretched out in front of her, her feet in the high heels that Ellen Barry said she wore even on shipboard. She looks tired but defiant. She is smoking. She and Gerald sit close together, shoulders touching; they do not look at each other. Probably they don't need to.

It was a summer full of superficial gaiety: the Murphys' home movies show Fanny Myers and Honoria aquaplaning; Dick Myers doing the shimmy on the dock, dressed in a voluminous bathrobe that makes him look like an animated Buddha; Honoria chasing Puppy up and down the little beach. Gerald was more "like his old self — swimming twice a day — singing and even playing the piano," reported Dick Myers to Alice Lee. One after-supper musicale got so out of hand that Sara jumped on the table to dance the fandango. Gerald bought a car, "a black and chromium mechanical panther," which was intended for "a good bit of junketing," and he and Sara drove it to Conway for the MacLeishes' twentieth wedding anniversary — a party like one of the old parties, with square dancing and a caller, and everybody dressed up in improvised peasant costumes, and lots of wonderful food and drink. They spent a few days with the Dos Passoses on Cape Cod and saw Phil Barry's new play, *Bright Star*, which was having a tryout in Dennis; later in the summer they went to Maine. Back at Camp Adeline they heard that Dottie Parker and Alan Campbell had quit Hollywood for a farm in Bucks County, Pennsylvania, and that Don and Bea Stewart had built a house in Ausable Forks, just miles away in the Adirondacks, which meant that some of their old friends, at least, were no longer so very far away.

That summer Gerald did something he hadn't done in seven years: he opened the little composition book he had used for an artist's *carnet* and made notes for a series of projects. The first, dated "July 14, '36," was for a painting he provisionally entitled *State Fair*, in which the chief elements were "a prize hog (animal husbandry chart)"; a squash, "(1st prize) bot. [botanical] study stem, leaf, tendril"; an ear of corn with its silk magnified, "(inset of it in black & white"); and a "burlap fertilizer bag." Surreally inset into the hog's side would be a window — "edges flous" (French for "blurry") — with curtains, a potted geranium, a "brilliant blue sponged sky." A strange picture indeed — considering that any prize hog is destined for the slaughterhouse.

The second project he outlined was dated "August, '36": a "construction in frame" using a rattan rug-beater, a sickle, and parts of various household tools. He had always loved gadgets — he was famous for being unable to pass a hardware store without going in — and he had thought of doing such an assemblage before, in the twenties; but there was something macabre about the mutilated objects — "a hammer (handle sawed 1/2 off?)" — that engaged his imagination now.

Why, given all that had happened in the years since he closed his studio in Antibes, did he even think of taking up his painting again this summer? He had been working nonstop at Mark Cross since the beginning of Patrick's most recent illness, and although the business *had* been an "effective drug," it had fatally compromised his creative life. But during these summer months he had the leisure to see and think, and the company of friends who stimulated him artistically. Why not just *try*, and see if he could still do it? So he made those first tentative, secret steps — only to find a *memento mori*, a butchered hog, a mangled hammer, lurking in every composition like the skulls medieval painters put in their pictures as a reminder of their mortality. It was too much; he never executed either of these projects, and never took up painting again.

Behind all their activity that summer was the inescapable reality of Patrick's illness. Sara had fixed things so he could fish from his reclining wheelchair; he had a room full of fishing paraphernalia, trophy heads from Ernest, and his own and Baoth's guns; and to the extent that it was possible he was included in all the family's plans and discussions. Honoria even asked him for romantic advice about a boy she admired who was a budding yachtsman. "Honoria, I think you will have to learn to sail," said Patrick gravely. But he was a very sick boy. He was still running a fever — after nearly two years in bed — and he had no appetite; he was anemic and needed transfusions; he still weighed less than a hundred pounds. His doctor told Gerald in August that "it is still a very doubtful question as to when and if he gets well."

Sara was in denial. Although "everyone remarks on her gaiety and becomingness," Gerald wrote to Scott Fitzgerald, "[s]he refuses to release her tense grip and is burning white. . . . Even her loneliness I cannot reach. She is gay, — energetic, — but is not well." She told the Hemingways that she was pining to go to Paris in September:

> I want new clothes & new ideas (in order named) & Hellstern shoes & perfumery & trick hats, & linge [underwear], not to mention THE eve. dress & to sit hours with Léger & his friends in cafés, & haunt rue la Boétie, & see every good new play & all music if any, & be back here in about three days & eleven hrs. twenty-seven mins. . . . I'd also like (how I do run on) to dance late at Boeuf or somewhere & go to the Halles. Dark dawn in Sept. What's in season? Des chouxfleurs, ma petite dame, des reines marguerites [cauliflower, little lady, and Chinese asters].

She didn't get to Paris. Patrick had a setback in October, around the time of his sixteenth birthday, and the Murphys moved into winter quarters in town, a huge half-timbered "cottage" glowering down from a hill above Lake Flower. It had been built in 1928 — many locals suspected it was meant to be a speakeasy — and Dr. Francis Trudeau, son of Edward Trudeau, was a neighbor, as was Patrick's chest specialist, Dr. John Hayes. (The previous summer a Princeton professor, Albert Einstein, had stayed down the street — and had plunged his house into darkness by overloading the electrical circuits. He had had to get his neighbor's son to change the fuse.)

Honoria, who was boarding at the Spence School in New York with Fanny Myers (the Murphys were paying Fanny's tuition and board), telephoned anxiously every few days for bulletins; she came up every weekend she could,

Above left: Scott Fitzgerald during the spring of "1000 parties and no work"

Above right: *Wasp and Pear*, Gerald's painting of "green fruit softening... but no ripeness yet."

Right: Before the diagnosis: Honoria, Gerald, Baoth, Patrick, and Sara on shipboard, returning to France in 1929

Dottie Parker on the "Goddamn Alp," photographed by Honoria on the porch of the Palace Hotel, Montana-Vermala

Below: The Swiss Family
Murphy: one of Sara's collage
New Year's cards showing (*left
to right*) Patrick with his etching tools, Honoria, Baoth

Bonne et Heureuse
Année!

Above: In Austria the
Murphys made an effort to
enter into the spirit of the
place, but their glum
expressions belie the festive
air of their costumes.

"My life has been a process of concealment of the personal realities"
— Gerald in 1930

Above left: Léger and unidentified woman at Ramgut

Above right: Sara and Mistigris the monkey

"Ernest was an angel about arranging their lives": the Murphys and Hemingways at the L Bar T Ranch. *Clockwise from upper left:* Pauline, Sara, Gerald, ranch hand, Ernest, and Baoth

Right: Vladimir and Patrick at the helm

Below: Weatherbird: "the boat (& the sea) were never so nice (or so blue)."

Katy Dos Passos on the *Weatherbird*

Archie MacLeish (*in tartan waistcoat*) flanked by two of "the Waddell Girls," Sara (*left*) and Ada. Dick Myers is at the far right.

Ernest on the *Pilar*

Steele Camp. "God, it's dreary on those Adirondack lakes!" wrote Dos Passos.

Right: Sara and Gerald on the dock at Camp Adeline. "One thing that has always surprised me . . . is one's tendency to feel that just because two people have been married for 20 years . . . they should need the same thing of life or of people."

Patrick Murphy by Fernand Léger, and *Fernand Léger* by Patrick Murphy

Top left: "Alexis, Prince of the heavenly flocks" — Woollcott and Gerald, in Amish disguise, at Lake Bomoseen

Top right: Marc Platt — "a very good dancer, and very handsome" — the choreographer of Gerald and Richard Rodgers's ballet, *Ghost Town*

Right: Frederic Franklin as Ralston, the young miner, and Mia Slavenska as his sweetheart, Eilly Orrum, in Karinska's costumes for *Ghost Town*

Upper left: Fanny Myers and Alan Jarvis

Lower left: Honoria's wedding to John Shelton left the Murphys' nest definitively vacant.

Bottom left: John Dos Passos in the 1950s

Bottom right: Dawn Powell

"Dear Mrs. Puss" —
Sara in the 1940s

Gerald at East Hampton in the 1950s, still raking the beach

and Gerald rearranged his schedule to give him more time in Saranac. "I spend three intensive days (and evenings) a week at the office — the rest here," he wrote to a friend that autumn; "every two weeks I force Sara from here overnight in an effort to break the back of her anguish; she has a few hours with Honoria who is at school in New York. Of the three golden children you saw on the sand at Antibes, but one has been spared us — so far. The miracle may yet happen, but the doctors are uneasy."

Everybody but Sara knew what was going to happen. Gerald tried to persuade Alec Woollcott, to whom he had become quite close, to visit Patrick even though Woollcott was famously nervous around children: "Patrick is an adult," said Gerald. "Eight years have made him so. . . . He will expect nothing of you, but will get a great deal." Woollcott, who agreed that "Patrick is no more a youngster than the Panchin Lama," came at once. So did the Dos Passoses, at Christmas, which, Dos wrote to Ernest, was "pretty horrible": "Gerald and Sara [were] both behaving so well in their separate ways that it's heartbreaking."

For Christmas, Patrick was given a five-year diary, bound in red morocco and stamped in gold:

> *Jan 1* [wrote Patrick, carefully, in pencil] New Year's day was one of the dreariest that I ever spent. Muggy, cloudy, no snow to be seen anywhere in Saranac Lake! I woke up in a wretched mood, took hours for my nourishment, and listened gloomily to the merrymaking of my family and their guests. During the afternoon they were allowed to come in for a few minutes. We pulled some little gifts out of a paper Santa Claus. I am greatly inconvenienced by having to breathe out of an oxygen tank, due to breathlessness.

Ada MacLeish and Alice Lee Myers had come to stay; Ada went walking in the snow with Gerald, and Alice Lee ran interference between Patrick, who had no appetite, and Sara, who kept trying to cajole him into eating. Patrick had to have his throat cauterized and was receiving frequent painful injections, which left him groggy; as the days wore on he could not even keep up the entries in his diary — he wrote on tiny scraps of paper that were later pasted into its pages, and his usually neat handwriting dissolved into a sick, wobbly scrawl. Ernestine Leray, their faithful "Titine," arrived from Antibes;

she had brought a basket of oranges from the garden at Villa America for her little Patrick, but the customs agents impounded it.

On January 16, Ernest Hemingway, Jinny Pfeiffer, and Ernest's friend Sidney Franklin — "noted and only american bullfighter," as Patrick described him, shakily, in his diary — drove up from New York for a few days' visit. "Ernest came in to see me for a few minutes before I went to bed. He is giving me a bear-skin for a Christmas present but it is not ready yet." When Ernest emerged from Patrick's room, Honoria remembered, he was weeping openly: "He looks so sick," he said. "I can't stand seeing that boy look so sick." Although Gerald recognized what a tonic the visit was for Sara ("mother's milk" was how he described it in a letter to Pauline), he found Ernest's "animal magnetism" and his "steam-roller" put-downs wearying, especially as he was facing the loss of the son he had tried so hard, for so many years, to save.

On January 29 he wrote to Alexander Woollcott, using the imagery of the *instrument de précision* that he'd first explored at the time of Fred's death: "I feel as if we were all caught in some vacuum of timelessness . . . the days are like the tick of a clock." Honoria and Fanny Myers, released from school by their sympathetic headmistress, Dorothy Osborne, had come to Saranac by train the previous week; they, and all the household, had to wear surgical masks when they visited Patrick because the danger of infection was by now so acute.

On the morning of January 30 Patrick went into a coma from which the doctor said he would not awaken. Gerald and Sara sat by his bed, each holding one of his hands. "You're just fine, Patrick," they said to him. "We're right here with you." Gradually his breathing became fainter and fainter; finally it stopped. Their long fight was over.

The next day the front doorbell rang: it was John Dos Passos, who had come straight from an assignment in South America. Putting his arms around Sara, he told her, "I just wanted to be with you." And with the afternoon mail there was a letter from Scott Fitzgerald: "Fate can't have any more arrows in its quiver for you that will wound like these," he said. "The golden bowl is broken indeed but it *was* golden; nothing can ever take those boys away from you now."

21

"Not on the same course, nor for the same port"

"THERE IS SOMETHING about being struck *twice* by lightning in the same place," Gerald said many years afterward to a friend, the writer Calvin Tomkins. "The ship foundered, was refloated, set sail again, but not on the same course, nor for the same port." He knew, and Sara knew, that Scott Fitzgerald had been wrong to say that there were no second acts in American lives: the audience and the critics might leave the theater, and the actors had no choice but to play out the drama until the final curtain was rung down.

There was a memorial service for Patrick in the nearly empty Church of St. Luke, the Beloved Physician, in Saranac Lake; afterward Alice Lee Myers helped pack Patrick's belongings, and at Sara's request she sent his gun racks and stuffed animal heads to the Hemingways. Sara simply gave away Camp Adeline, deeding it to the Kip's Bay Boys Club of New York, which she hoped would use it as a summer camp for inner-city boys. Gerald had a more delicate task to perform: sending to Scott Fitzgerald the cross that had been given him, years ago, in Switzerland, by Eduardo Velasquez. "Dear Scott," Gerald wrote, "This cross was given to me against my will by Eduardo Velasquez — under very painful circumstances. It belonged to his mother. She should have it. Can you get it back to him or her, — for me? He should not — nor has not for years — hear from me. Aff'y, Gerald." Whatever the purpose of Velasquez's talisman, its usefulness was over now.

Sara and Gerald moved back to New York. They rented an apartment at the New Weston, a penthouse with sweeping views of the city, including the rooftops of St. Patrick's, where archiepiscopal laundry — "choir-boys' gowns, lace chasubles, priests' cassocks and surplices" — danced incongruously on the washline. It was a chic urban flat for the chic urban couple they had to be now; but, Archie MacLeish noticed, "Gerald threw everything out of his room but the bed and the chair — white plaster walls, a white bed and chair." It was a monk's cell, a sensory deprivation chamber. "He was a painter," says Archie's son (and Gerald's godson) William MacLeish. "And what he was doing was forcing himself to live in something in which there's a total absence of color. Now that's torture — it takes a real masochist to do that." He took to wearing only gray and black, lit by touches of white.

Honoria became a day student at Spence so she could live with her parents, but no sooner had they reestablished themselves as a family than there was more sad family news: Sara's beloved little sister Olga was dying of cancer in California. Sara flew to be with her but had to be taken off the plane with acute and immobilizing neck spasms; and when she was able to travel again she arrived too late, landing in San Francisco the day Olga died.

For some of the Murphys' contemporaries in the grim 1930s, political action became a means of self-assertion in the face of despair and difficulty; but Sara's early advocacy of Mary McLeod Bethune notwithstanding, neither she nor Gerald had ever been particularly *engagé* politically. The protests surrounding the execution of the anarchists Sacco and Vanzetti in 1927 had interested them far less than Charles Lindbergh's landing at Le Bourget the same year ("It tightens the main-spring," Gerald had said of Lindy's accomplishment.)

But while they had been preoccupied with their personal tragedies, the Nazis had taken over Germany and marched into the Rhineland, war had broken out between the Loyalists and the fascist Nationalists in Spain, and these conflicts, as well as the continuing effects of the Depression, had stimulated the American left to act. Soon, after their fashion, the Murphys followed.

For not only that old Marxist Dos Passos but Dottie Parker and Don Stewart and even Ernest Hemingway and Archie MacLeish were expressing their consciences in public ways. Don Stewart, whose wife, Bea, had recently left him for Count Ilya Tolstoy (grandson of the novelist), had gone so far as to get romantically involved with Ella Steffens, the "grimly socio-politico-economic" widow (as Gerald described her) of the celebrated muckraker Lincoln Steffens. Such politicization had begun to drive a wedge between some of the Murphys' circle: Dottie Parker, in particular, had stopped speaking to Bob Benchley over "some labor issue," although she claimed it was because "I told her not to make those ingenue eyes at me as she was no longer [an] ingenue," Benchley reported to the Murphys. Benchley wasn't the only one to feel the chilling effect of Parker's cold shoulder. She cut Adèle Lovett and made jokes about her other rich friends — but (writes her biographer) "she never joked about the Murphys, because she loved them."

During 1936 Dos Passos and MacLeish had decided to make a motion picture about the Spanish civil war which would give Americans a "clear, objective statement of the facts" about the origins of the conflict; they'd enlisted the services of the rising young playwright Lillian Hellman to collaborate on the screenplay, and a prizewinning Dutch filmmaker, Joris Ivens, to film it. In February 1937 Hemingway joined the group, which had now incorporated under the name Contemporary Historians, and went to Spain with Ivens and Dos Passos to shoot footage. In the meantime Gerald was persuaded to pitch in as well, investing a substantial amount of money and — as he had for Archie's *Union Pacific* ballet — his musical expertise in the movie they were now calling *The Spanish Earth*.

The film was to have a score by Marc Blitzstein and Virgil Thomson, but the composers were having difficulty coming up with authentic music for background. Dos Passos remembered that Sara and Gerald had a fine collection of traditional Spanish records that they'd amassed on their trips along the coast. So Thomson came up to the New Weston one afternoon (no strawberries this time) and listened to sardanas on the Murphys' phonograph, and went away with his arms full of records, many of which found their way into the score for *The Spanish Earth*.

Despite his contributions to the film and his devotion to its principles, Gerald's diffidence kept him from becoming very deeply enmeshed in political activism. He had been mistrustful of groups since his Yale days, and had resisted being a part of any "isms" in Paris in the twenties. Don Stewart and Dottie Parker could join the Hollywood Anti-Nazi League; Archie and Ernest could speak at the League of American Writers Congress in New York, with American Communist party secretary Earl Browder on the platform with them; but even though Gerald was searching for a new direction to sail in, this was not to be the one. He did, however, go to the League of American Writers meeting that spring, as did Sara. They heard and applauded Ernest's speech — "if there was a fascist hair in the hall it must not only have whitened, but singed as well," wrote Sara to Pauline Hemingway — and felt it "was a terribly interesting meeting, & a most intelligent audience."

Shortly after this Sara and Honoria set off for Europe. It was not the gay trip that Sara had dreamed of the autumn before Patrick died; it was a journey made without definite plans other than to get away. "The future," Sara remarked to Pauline, "is a clear jelly, & about as interesting. However I persist in believing . . . that all will seem better in the deceptive light of Europe. Lights OUGHT to be deceptive, and by god, mine shall be." Holding herself together with difficulty — Dick and Alice Lee Myers agreed that she was "pitiful," and seemingly "dissatisf[ied] at everything" — she forced herself to go from Paris to London, then for a cure in Karlsbad, at which Gerald joined her, Honoria having gone on a graduation trip around Europe with Alice Lee Myers, Fanny, and Scottie Fitzgerald. "We get up at seven, drink at the fountain ½ mile away, walking up and down under arbors of clematis for an hour," reported Gerald to Honoria:

> then Kaffee, Milch und Schlagobers, ein Grahambrot, ½ Butter und Honig. A rest then at ten exercises in the Gymnasium for all parts of the body — on special machines — then massage, electric treatments, steam or *mud* baths and rest then luncheon. Delicious food, only graham starch, grape-sugar, no alcohol (two small glasses red wine at night). Sometimes we walk up the mountain to breakfast, orchestras start at 9:30 (very good), in the P.M. rest, walk to tea (fruit-juice or Yogourt) in the evening to the fountain to drink, dinner outdoors, orchestra too, walk, bed at 10 P.M.

Sara submitted only reluctantly to the tyranny of the *Kur* regimen. "I know that it doesn't seem very important in the face of what's happened whether we take care of ourselves or not," Gerald told her. "But as long as we *must* live we might as well feel as well as we can. It probably helps to give others a better time."

Returning to Paris in August, they managed to avoid Hoytie, who was ensconced in her Paris flat; friends reported sighting her at various *haut monde* parties "with fantastic hats and looking like something pulled out of a scrap-bag." They did, however, rendezvous with Ernest Hemingway, who was on his way to Spain to cover the civil war for the North American Newspaper Alliance, as well as Dottie Parker and Alan Campbell and Lillian Hellman, who had sailed with the Campbells on the *Normandie*. According to Hellman, Archie MacLeish had urged her to become acquainted with the Murphys; "they now need new people around them," she recalled him saying to her. "You're young and they'll like you." Like many of Hellman's memories, this one seems designed for maximum self-promotion: charming, energetic Lilly lighting up the lives of a sad old couple. In fact, the shoe was somewhat on the other foot. Hellman was on her own in Paris and knew no one, and the Murphys and Campbells introduced her to Hemingway, Fernand Léger, and other friends.

Hemingway (although he was careful to disguise the fact around family friends) was engaged in a new liaison with the journalist Martha Gellhorn, who had met him in Key West and attached herself as firmly to the Hemingway *ménage* as Pauline had once attached herself to Ernest and Hadley. She had been to Spain with Ernest in the spring and had come to his Writers Congress speech — where a friend of Dos Passos's, the novelist Dawn Powell, described her as Hemingway's "private blonde . . . who had been through hell in Spain and came shivering on in a silver fox cape chin-up." Although Gellhorn was not on display in Paris (she doesn't recall ever meeting the Murphys), her influence had bred animosity between Hemingway and many of his old friends, or so he later implied when reminiscing about "my great 37–38 epoch when alienated all my friends (who I miss like hell)." He was feuding with both Archie and Dos — with the former he quarreled over repayment of money he had lent to Contemporary Historians to make *The Spanish Earth,* and the latter he had savagely satirized as the sexually impotent phony-radical Richard Gordon in *To Have and Have Not.* These quarrels upset Sara, who wanted all her old shipmates to be easy with one another, and she begged Gerald, when he returned to New York in early September, to try to make peace among them. "Never having been in his field (as Archie and Dos have been — are . . .)," responded Gerald, "he has never done anything violent to me (and tho' I've been terribly critical and think that at times he's been pretty nearly a cheap sport) I find it easy to revive my affection for him. Don't worry about what I'll say about him to Dos and Archie. I'd like to try (as I did with E.) to fan the embers of an old affection even if it comes to nothing."

But Sara still fretted over Ernest's well-being. Since he was now in Valencia among the falling bombs, far from the bistros of Paris, she and Dorothy Parker sent him a food hamper containing tins of roast chicken, ham, salmon, preserved goose, Welsh rabbit, antipasto, and *tripe à la mode de Caen*, as well as bouillon cubes, sugar, and malted milk. With it went a chatty note adjuring him to wear warm clothes and enclosing news from home. The mask of nurturing good cheer slipped only slightly at the end, where she noted poignantly: "Baoth would have gone to college this autumn."

Back in New York that fall, Sara went through all the motions: dinners and cocktails and lunches with the Barrys and Myerses, the MacLeishes and the Stephen Vincent Benéts, or new friends like Dorothy Parker's publisher Harold Guinzburg and his wife; concerts and plays, including Thornton Wilder's *Our Town*, which, with its theme of death and reconciliation, must have been a painful evening; a croquet party for her birthday in November. But Gerald was careful never to leave her alone in the evenings; she was still too fragile.

Grateful for the supporting presence of cherished friends, she and Gerald continued to make them a steady stream of gifts: furniture and clothes to the Dos Passoses; a car for the Myerses, and an annuity in honor of Baoth; rent checks to Stella Campbell, who had "given up being a jackanapes in Hollywood" and was now ensconced in the Hotel Sevillia on 58th Street. Truth to tell, Stella hadn't been able to make it in Hollywood. She was too old, too dumpy, and too imperious, and she had not endeared herself to MGM's supremely important Irving Thalberg, who was married to the actress Norma Shearer, when she approached him at a party and said throatily, "Dear Mr. Thalberg, *how* is your lovely, lovely wife with the tiny, tiny eyes?" Now she nominally repaid the Murphys' generosity by giving acting lessons to Honoria, who was trying to launch herself in a career on the stage and had got a job with the French Theatre of New York; and she introduced the starry-eyed girl to John Gielgud when he came to Broadway with his celebrated production of *Hamlet.*

Sara had hoped that perhaps Gerald could leave his post at Mark Cross that winter and they could go take a flat in London, where the only ghosts were those of her parents and sisters and herself as a girl. But it never happened. Instead they threw themselves into a new construction project, moving an old dairy barn on the Wiborg estate to the edge of Hook Pond and remodeling it for their use. Hook Pond Cottage belonged to the old life, the life of Patrick and Baoth, and they needed a new place.

Swan Cove, as the new house was called, was named for the swans that glided over the waters of the saltwater pond next to the house. A rambling, gracious building walled in faded pink stucco, it had a garden room verdant with tropical plants and an enormous living room lit by seven windows and full of rococo furniture and *objets* the Murphys had found in Czechoslovakia the previous summer. The gardens and flagged terrace had a European formality. There was classical statuary set among the flowers and vines and an *allée* of ailanthus trees going down to the water. Katy Dos Passos called it an "Arabian Nights house." Perhaps she didn't intend the allusion to Scheherazade, who kept death at bay with her thousand-and-one nights' tales; but when the house and garden were completed Gerald described them as "an oasis of comfort" for Sara, and "the spectacle of her enjoyment *for the first time*" since the boys' deaths affected him powerfully. "I had not thought she could forget for a moment what haunts her continually," he confided to the house's designers, Hale Walker and Harold Heller, who had also worked on Villa America. But even at Swan Cove, he realized, she "is — and always will be — inconsolable. As time goes on she feels her bereavement more and more and understands less why the boys were taken away, — both of them."

At Christmastime Gerald and Sara heard from Scott Fitzgerald, who had been living in Hollywood and trying to make enough writing for the movies to keep Scottie in college and pay Zelda's medical expenses. He had recently become involved with Sheilah Graham, the syndicated Hollywood columnist for the North American Newspaper Alliance, who was making a trip to New York in late January; he very much hoped that the Murphys would welcome her — he himself was taking Zelda to Miami — but Sara simply could not face it. It was the anniversary of Patrick's death and "her mind [was] far afield," Gerald explained. But she was also fiercely loyal to Zelda and might have felt that seeing Graham would be a betrayal of her friend. As Ellen Barry had noticed, "Sara had a sense of austerity about these things." It was one thing to countenance Léger's mistresses — Jeanne Léger knew about them too, and had lovers of her own; it was another thing to have Scott's girlfriend to tea when Zelda not only didn't know anything about it, but was confined to a lunatic asylum. In the end Gerald asked Sheilah Graham to cocktails at the New Weston with Honoria — Graham drank cocoa — and commented tactfully to Scott on her beauty and charm. Thanking him, Fitzgerald wrote that "you were awfully damn kind, in any case, and as a friend, you have never failed me."

In May, after a farewell visit to the boys' graves in the little East Hampton churchyard, Sara left with Honoria for another European summer. There were dinners and lunches with Léger and his girlfriend Simone Herman or with Marcelle Meyer, Stravinsky concerts, evenings at the ballet and the theater. Everywhere there was a sense that this *might* be the last such trip for many years. The Nazis had taken over Austria and were making noises about annexing Czechoslovakia, Europe was moving closer and closer to war, and — as Katy Dos Passos had commented to Sara earlier — "Pears like nobody gits to carry out his plans but that ole Hitler."

Gerald arrived in June, and in July the Dos Passoses joined the Murphys for a cruise in the *Weatherbird* around Sicily and the Italian coast. It was not an unalloyed delight. Sara's health was shaky — she was briefly admitted to the American Hospital in Paris with gallbladder problems — and Gerald, despite having had his tonsils out, was suffering from a painful and persistent sore throat, and seemed distracted. The ruins at Paestum and the frescoes at the Villa of the Mysteries in Pompeii were splendid; the whirlpools at the site of the Homeric Scylla and Charybdis were awe-inspiring; and their simple picnic lunches of wine, bread, cheese, tomatoes, and a little *friture* were as delicious as ever. But there were other sights, like the ominous nationalistic "MARE NOSTRUM" graffiti they saw scrawled on a wall, and the occasional unfriendly knot of onlookers they encountered, that were less pleasant.

At Siracusa the Dos Passoses disembarked, and at Messina, Gerald, who had been suffering with his throat and was mysteriously "out till late" one evening in Sicily, decided to leave the boat to attend to business in Florence and elsewhere. Sara rather forlornly saw him off, and she, Honoria, Honoria's friend Louise Dowdney, and the little Pekingese Puppy continued on, returning to Naples on August 18. There was a bittersweet parting from Vladimir, the crew, and the *Weatherbird:* "Very sad leaving boat. Champagne. Bed early," wrote Sara.

Returning to New York in September, Gerald and Sara left Honoria behind until Christmas to study French theater with Madame Darius Milhaud, but they took Scottie Fitzgerald home in her stead. Scottie was met at the dock by Zelda, who had been allowed by her doctors to make a supervised visit to New York for the purpose. Zelda hadn't seen the Murphys since before the boys died, and she found them "very engaging; age and the ages leave them untroubled and, perhaps, as impervious as possible." With allowances for Zelda's peculiarly overdecorated diction, and the Murphys' self-abnegating good manners, this observation seems almost willfully unperceptive. She was closer to the mark a few weeks later when, in a letter to Scott, she mused wistfully that "It fill[s] me with dread to witness the passage of so much time . . . Do you suppose [one] still cook[s] automobiles at Antibes, and still sip[s] the twilight at Kaux, and I wonder if Paris is pink in the late sun and latent with happiness already had."

The Murphys must have wondered how much of their own happiness was "already had" that fall. In Paris, before they sailed for New York, Sara had taken Honoria and Fanny Myers to lunch at the Brasserie Lipp (Gerald had made a quick trip to London on business). They were seated at a table in the center of the room when Fanny noticed Picasso at a table along the wall, facing them. "Look," she said to Sara, whose back was to him, "there's Picasso." Sara paid no attention; and Picasso gave no sign that he had recognized the woman he had loved and painted in sand so many years ago in Antibes. They left without speaking to each other.

Now, returning to Swan Cove, the Murphys found the house exquisite, the gardens blooming with tuberoses, heliotrope, nicotiana, bamboo, and elephant ear, and lit with fairy lanterns for their homecoming the way that Villa

America's garden used to be for "dinner-flowers-gala." Sara bustled happily from room to room, laying out swatches of brocades she'd bought in Europe and folding away in her cupboards the antique lace and linens she'd found on the trip. Eleven days later a hurricane struck Long Island, leaving two to five feet of water in the house and five-inch bass flopping helplessly in the orchard. "Hurricane — garden gone," Sara noted bleakly in her trip log.

So they started over yet again. Sara had a quiet birthday in East Hampton with Alice Lee, Pauline Hemingway (who had taken her own apartment at the New Weston while Ernest was in Spain), and Pauline's sister Jinny; two days later there was a larger, braver party in their New Weston penthouse for which Gerald ordered a cake made to look like a telegram. It read "SARA PENT-HOUSE 34 EAST 50TH STREET NEW YORK NY BEST OF HEALTH AND VERY MUCH LOVE FROM EVERYONE." The Barrys were there, and Pauline and Jinny, and Ada MacLeish (Archie had just been asked to direct the Nieman Fellowship journalism program at Harvard and couldn't join them) and Léger and Simone Herman and the art critic James Johnson Sweeney and his wife, and the novelist Dawn Powell. They all had champagne and danced to the Murphys' records, and everyone felt brilliant and amusing, for a few hours at least.

In February, Gerald and Sara went to Baltimore with Dottie Parker and Alan Campbell for the out-of-town tryout of Lillian Hellman's new play, *The Little Foxes*, which starred Tallulah Bankhead; they stayed in the same hotel with the company and came to Bankhead's party after the opening. It was a pretty dreadful evening, the kind of thing Dick Diver had in mind in *Tender Is the Night* when he said he wanted to give "a really *bad* party . . . where there's a brawl and seductions and people going home with their feelings hurt and women passed out in the cabinet de toilette." Tallulah quickly got drunk and began arguing with Dashiell Hammett (Hellman's lover of nine years) and Gerald about her drug habits. "I'm not going to listen to you about cocaine," she said. "I've used it *all* my life and it is *not* habit forming" — a statement that caused Gerald to roar with laughter. Then she made a pass at the waiter — who, being black, might have gotten into trouble with Maryland's antimiscegenation laws if he had responded — and protested when Hammett spirited him out of the room. *Then* she had a drunken lovers' quarrel with her female secretary. In the meantime her father, the former Speaker of the House of Representatives, began to serenade the guests loudly and unstoppably, until Gerald managed to quiet him by suggesting, soothingly, "Mr. Speaker, why don't you rest your beautiful voice?" Hellman, and Hellman's play, were unfortunately not the center of attention, and after a time she went to bed; the next day she and the Murphys hid from everybody else in the hotel dining room, "ordering endless dishes from the kitchen in order to mix them together, or to add to them what we thought would be of interest."

Perhaps it was these concoctions that proved to be Sara's downfall, for shortly after she got back from Baltimore she went into the hospital for gallbladder surgery. Dick Myers wrote a charming piece of doggerel to speed her recovery:

> I've got a favorite lady
> Whose familiar name is Sadie
> And whose talents have excited many blurbs.
> She's not so very staid-y
> And sings songs a little shady
> And her plats du jour are full of fancy herbs.

And so on for six verses, which were not, perhaps, as elegant as Archie MacLeish's "Portrait of Mme. G—— M——," but more affectionate.

Pauline Hemingway invited her to come to Key West to convalesce. Although Pauline would never have admitted it, she and Ernest had reached that point in a marriage's endgame when neither party can stand being alone with the other and relies on old mutual friends to keep conversation going. Ernest had spent the month of February in Cuba, but he did intend to stay on in Key West long enough to see Sara before he returned to Cuba, where Martha Gellhorn was waiting for him.

Sara drove down with Jinny Pfeiffer and Honoria — who had returned to New York at Christmastime — on April 1; they stayed three weeks. After Sara and Ernest had both gone, Ernest wrote her a letter whose tone of slightly inebriated melancholy veers perilously close to elegy. "Dearest Sara," he began, "How are you and how goes everything and all of it? Here it's blowing a huge storm — close to a hurricane — and the royal palms are bent over in it." Then he began again: "Dear Sara how are you and how is everything? It must be lovely there now and where are you and Honoria and how do you feel and how is everybody?" He told her how hard he was working, how he had gone to the cove where they'd picnicked together, how to recover from working so hard he had partied hard too: "It was a fine party and many times and all the time I wish you were here for the fine good jolly times. I never did thank you for the lovely records and I never could thank you for how loyal and lovely and also beautiful and attractive and lovely you have been always ever since always. . . . I wish we were killing this rainy afternoon together. It is a beautiful storm. I love you always and please always count on it."

Six months later, when he and Pauline were finally separated and he was planning to marry Martha Gellhorn, he bade Sara what seems like a final farewell. He had been alone with his son Patrick in Havana for Christmas; they'd had suckling pig at the Ambos Mundos, and "I had that orchestra play No Hubo Barrera en el Mundo for you," Sara's signature tune from her visit to him in Cuba. And now he was saying good-bye. "Much love always," he wrote, "from your old friend who will be your good and old friend as long as he lives and afterwards will think of you with considerable affection, good kind beautiful lovely Sara."

Ten years later, in one of those boys-together letters he used to write to one friend about another, he confided to Archie MacLeish: "I liked Gerald and appreciated his leather and his chromium and his semi-impeccable taste but always felt about him the way people who do not like cats feel about cats." But, he told Archie, "I love Sara."

22

"Enough to make the angels weep"

WHEN SARA RECEIVED Ernest's June letter she had fled with Honoria to Europe again. Everyone suspected that war was coming, and the mood in Paris was expectant and valedictory, perhaps nowhere more so than in an exhibit at the Louvre of the décors and costumes of the Ballets Russes, some of which Gerald and Sara had painted at Diaghilev's Belleville atelier. Noel Murphy's companion Janet Flanner, writing in *The New Yorker* under her pseudonym of Genêt, sounded the right elegiac note:

> A list of the painters who made curtains or costumes during the Ballet's twenty years' utilization of the talents of all Europe contains what are now the most famous, and were then some of the least-known, names on earth. . . . More than any other spectacle, Diaghilev's Ballet has come to symbolize what are now called *les beaux jours*, the days of civilized, uncensored pleasures, of new musicians and artists . . . — the days of the early nineteen-twenties, when politicians as well as hedonists thought a permanent, peaceful age had been born.
>
> With such memories in mind, it's not strange that balletomanes were saddened by the show. It was enough to make the angels weep.

Sara didn't stay in Paris long: Fanny Myers had engineered invitations for herself and Honoria to the commencement ball at University College, Oxford; so after outfitting both girls with organza evening dresses from her *vendeuse* at Nicole Groult, Sara accompanied them to England.

The two young men who were to escort the girls, Lloyd Bowers and his friend Alan Jarvis, earned Sara's approval at once. Bowers, an American and Yale graduate "with *Manners*," was a "nice, well-brought-up boy." Jarvis, a "very tall blond, nice-looking" Canadian who "sculps and likes the stage," was, Sara reported to Gerald, "very attractive and no feathers anywhere." Although there was lots of wild partying in students' rooms — during which Bowers, "momentarily maddened by her appearance and champagne," bit Honoria on the arm so passionately that he left a sizeable bruise — Sara turned a tolerant, even amused eye on the proceedings. ("I told her she must consider it a compliment," she said, adding — a little ruefully? — "No one ever bit me, even in my heyday.")

She invited both young men to accompany her and the girls on a *Weatherbird* cruise to Corsica the next month, and although Jarvis had to beg off, Bowers came along, only once getting on Sara's wrong side. While the *Weatherbird* was anchored at Monte Carlo, he accompanied Honoria and Fanny and a friend of his on a midnight reconnaissance of Juan-les-Pins and Antibes which kept them out until six in the morning. The young people had gone to the Juan-les-Pins casino, where their parents had once been so gay, and afterward had driven around Villa America in the dark, peering at the deserted buildings behind the garden walls. Arriving at the dock as the sun came up they found Sara in a fury of anxiety, which hardly abated when she found out where they had been. She could not bring herself to visit the villa, although it was only forty-five minutes' drive away.

They left port a few days later and spent the next month cruising around Corsica and Elba — Sara compared the scenery to de Chirico paintings, or Picasso's backdrops for *Pulcinella*. Despite some heavy weather they had a fine time: "The girls, I *hope*, are enjoying themselves," Sara wrote to the Dos Passoses, whom she missed. "They chatter along & play the Victrola, & read endless movie magazines with some light manicuring in between, — so think they'll be alright — although Honoria always wishes the boat were run more along the lines of the Ritz." But Sara was concerned and "disappointed" that she had heard so very little that summer from Gerald, normally such a good correspondent.

He had been spending more and more time at Mark Cross during the past year; the economy had finally rebounded from the Depression and the store was often full of customers. At Christmas he had telephoned Sara to tell her that there were 3,300 people in the building at the time, "all milling." He was working hard to stay ahead of the curve of fashion: from his second-story office windows he would "rake the Avenue with my aviation binoculars, learning how bags are carried and who wears gloves or no." And he and Alice Lee Myers had made some delicious European purchases, from Czechoslovakian stemware to elegantly relaxed men's shirts to French country plates decorated with hand-painted explications of the language of flowers. He had evolved a number of signature designs, too: There was a leather drawstring bag inspired by the feed bags used by the grooms at Longchamp racetrack. Robert Benchley, who had one of the first models, called it a "Noah" bag because you could put everything in it you would need on the ark, and the name stuck. And there was a smart, boxy purse like a small version of a man's attaché case, which was such a symbol of elegance that Grace Kelly carried one in Alfred Hitchcock's movie *Rear Window* to show how chic she was.

But despite these items' seemingly limitless cachet, the company still wasn't making a sufficient profit; and loans from Gerald, Esther, and the landlord, Goelet, would soon have to be renegotiated if Mark Cross were to survive. In addition, and more pressingly, the Murphys' investment adviser Copley Amory informed Gerald in July that — what with the expenses for Swan Cove's reconstruction and the effects of their withdrawals for Patrick's care — their personal capital had been reduced to a not very robust $201,000. They had never been as wealthy as Scott Fitzgerald thought, and now they were even less so.

But Gerald's attention to work and finances played only a small part in his lack of communicativeness that summer. He had also become involved in a new project that — while it promised no financial remuneration — helped him to forget the anxious present and the anguished past, and to imagine himself in a time that preceded them. Back in February the Ballet Russe de Monte Carlo (now styled in the singular) had initiated plans for a new production with American music, choreography, and subject matter that the company's current director, the Moscow-born banker who went under the name Serge Denham, hoped to make the centerpiece of his 1939 season. With Europe almost certainly about to be engulfed in war, it looked as if the Ballet Russe would make an extended visit to America, and Denham felt that the American box office would respond most enthusiastically to an American ballet on the lines of Eugene Loring's recent and successful *Billy the Kid*.

He thought first of approaching Cole Porter to compose a score, but a check with Porter's longtime friend and former Yale classmate Leonard Hanna revealed that Porter was in Havana, unreachable and uninterested. Denham's next choice was the quintessentially American Irving Berlin, then in Hollywood working with Fred Astaire. Berlin was flattered, though ballet was "completely out of my field." At the end of February he sent Denham a list of his songs that he thought could be orchestrated for dancing, arranged into the categories of "Ragtime," "Production," "Ballads," and "Jazz": among them were "Alexander's Ragtime Band," "Always," "A Pretty Girl Is Like a Melody," "Everybody Step," "Everybody's Doin It," "What'll I Do," "Easter Parade," and "Top Hat." This revue format, which George Balanchine so artfully used later in his Gershwin ballet, *Who Cares?* may not have seemed sufficiently surefire to Denham, and he was certainly made apprehensive by Berlin's price and his near mania for creative control. So without telling Berlin, Denham quietly explored another option, that of using Lorenz Hart's collaborator, Richard Rodgers, to write a full-length dramatic score. The person who suggested Rodgers was Gerald Murphy, who knew the composer and knew that he'd already done a ballet in miniature, the "Slaughter on Tenth Avenue" number in the 1935 musical *On Your Toes,* choreographed by Diaghilev's old ballet master, Balanchine.

Rodgers, as it happened, was interested, and Denham quickly signed a contract with him, waiting until that deal was done to wiggle tactfully out of his understanding with Berlin. Shortly thereafter Denham and his adviser, the Russian émigré-cum-café-society-fixture Baron Niki de Gunzbourg, tried to enlist John Dos Passos as librettist — their heads evidently turned by Dos's recent appearance on the cover of *Time* magazine after the publication of *The Big Money.* They offered him a $250 flat fee and on March 22 sent their contract to him at the Murphys' New Weston penthouse, where he often stayed while in New York.

For some reason — possibly disinclination to pursue the project, possibly a desire to involve his friend in something besides commerce — Dos seemingly passed this baton (though not, it appears, the check) to Gerald, who was already peripherally involved because of his nomination of Rodgers. And at the end of March the notoriously tightfisted Denham paid a week's salary to one of his young dancers, an aspiring choreographer named Marc Platt, so he could come to New York and discuss the evolution of a ballet with a Western theme with Rodgers and with Gerald.

Platt had been a leading character dancer with the Ballet Russe for several seasons and, as was de rigueur in the ballet world at the time, had taken a Russian stage name, Marc Platoff. But he was a nice, red-haired American kid from Seattle with a winning smile and a big jump; "he was a very, very good dancer," remembers Frederic Franklin, the English *danseur noble* who was to dance the lead in the ballet, and "very handsome. And he was the first American I met who had a sense of humor." He charmed Gerald and the Murphys generally. "We all had crushes on him," Honoria recalled. "He was so handsome — he said I had a sexy lower lip, and he liked Fanny's looks, too. But he really wasn't interested in us in that way."

Honoria thought that possibly her father saw in Platt a kind of surrogate for his lost sons, as inevitably any young man must have seemed to him. If he saw anything more, there is no record of it, other than a puzzling postscript he added around this time to a letter to Woollcott, in which he quoted the lines from Milton's *Samson Agonistes* which had haunted him from his youth: "O worst imprisonment — To be the dungeon of Thyself!" But certainly Platt was also a means to rediscover a world Gerald must have thought lost to him during the past decade. It was no accident that the scenario Gerald developed for Platt's choreography was called *Ghost Town*, nor that it concerned the awakening of memories for an old miner, left behind by fortune and his sweetheart when the vein of ore he had been working was exhausted.

He threw himself into the project, lending his extensive collection of "notes, records, books, and music" to Platt, Richard Rodgers, and the designer Raoul Pène DuBois, and drawing on his own knowledge of popular nineteenth-century culture to create a meticulously detailed scenario that mapped out characters, setting, costumes, action, even dances. It seemed to him at times that he was back in the golden days of *Within the Quota:* "it was so exciting," remembers Honoria, "that my father had gotten involved in the arts again." Honoria was so taken with Platt that she asked him to join the *Weatherbird*'s cruise that summer, which for some reason made Sara "furious." She insisted that "he can stay for 3 days and that is all." In the event he never went. But he did develop a close relationship with Gerald; it's easy to picture the younger man listening, enthralled, to Gerald's tales of Diaghilev and Stravinsky and Picasso in Paris in the twenties.

Annoyingly, however, Gerald couldn't seem to achieve the same rapport with Denham or even Rodgers; when he asked to hear recordings of *Ghost Town's* score he was told they'd been sent to Léonide Massine, the company's Russian artistic director, in Monte Carlo, and were unavailable — even though Rodgers, and his music, were in New York, and Gerald could easily have been allowed to sight-read through the score himself. What he didn't realize was that for reasons known only to themselves (but which may have had something to do with money and copyrights, areas where Denham was a notoriously sharp operator) Denham and company were energetically cutting him out of the picture.

First Denham seemed to attack the scenario. In Gerald's script a diversion is created when a stagecoach full of historical characters — including the soprano Jenny Lind, the English poet Algernon Charles Swinburne (on tour in America), and the boxing champion "Benecia Boy" Heenan — arrive in town. The scene allows several corps numbers as well as solos for the Ballet Russe's notoriously top-heavy company roster, but instead of being grateful Denham seized on it as an excuse to dump on his librettist. "The . . . story . . . is too overcrowded by useless incidental characters," wrote the Russian Denham in English (and for the record?) to the Russian Massine in Monte Carlo: "I spoke to Rodgers about it and he feels the same way. Murphy, apparently a capable man in writing a story, does not visualize the imperative simplicity of a ballet and although he was of very great help to us with all his materials I still feel that we have to curtail some of the details and bring it into a much simpler form."

The tactful tone didn't last. Soon Denham was instructing Platt not to "complicate our work" by "unnecessary loose conversation" with the troublesome Mr. Murphy,

who . . . is inclined to consider himself a prominent figure in the whole matter, whereas his work, according to our judgment, was merely to restore the historical research data.

Please tell Platoff [this letter, also in English, was addressed to his Russian associate Jacques Rubinstein] that the less he writes to Murphy the better it is from all points of view, because I presume that with every letter the estimate of Mr. Murphy's self-importance in the matter will be on the increase.

Denham's snide dismissal of Gerald's contribution to *Ghost Town* seems not only gratuitous but ludicrous on its face: for the Ballet Russe used Gerald's scenario exactly as it came from the typewriter, reproducing it, verbatim, in the company program as well as in a popular ballet reference book. Despite Denham's apparent objections to "overcrowding," no characters were ever cut. The cast list Denham sent to Barbara Karinska, who designed and built the costumes, contains every name from Gerald's original, with the name of a dancer beside it.

Whether Gerald was aware of this behind-the-scenes backstabbing, his preoccupation with *Ghost Town* was one reason he was such an indifferent correspondent that summer. Another was business — there were problems with overseas production for Mark Cross — and some tricky maneuvering he had to go through to avoid losing his driver's license for a fourth speeding offense. And still another reason may have been the intensification that summer of his friendship with the unfathomable Alexander Woollcott, to whom he confided the persistent feelings of loss he could scarcely bring himself to mention to anyone else.

"Thanks for the film," he wrote to Woollcott, referring to who knows what movie they had attended:

what shadows passed thro' it . . . and what a strange reecho of a night years ago when an unguided voice said to me "What are you doing now?" . . . as I sat and waited for further news of Baoth . . . before starting out. From that moment on — as I've come to a corner — I've felt the thing which you give by your presence *somewhere*. In a world in which almost no communication between human creatures is possible it is *strange* to feel as I do — and to know — that I owe you so much,

Aff'y.
Gerald

Whatever corner Gerald felt he had come to at this point, he seemingly could discuss it only with Woollcott, this flamboyant but reclusive nonpracticing homosexual, and not with Sara, his confidant of so many years. She didn't know this, not in so many words, but she felt the redirection of his attention.

In addition to his outings to the theater with Woollcott, Gerald had agreed to landscape his friend's island retreat, Neshobe, on Lake Bomoseen in Vermont, an undertaking that would last through the succeeding winter and spring and consume a considerable amount of time. But despite his distractions he began to be concerned for Sara and the girls as the news from Europe worsened.

For during the course of that summer, Spain fell definitively to the fascists, Italy annexed Albania, and (Gerald exclaimed to Sara) "the English . . . sold China down the river to the Japanese!" By the time Sara and the girls landed at Monte Carlo on August 16 it seemed only a matter of days before Germany would make its next move, but, reluctant to leave behind their Mediterranean dream, they postponed their departure for a few more days, sailing to the Îles des Lérins off Cannes, sleepy, pine-scented islands shimmering timelessly in the blue sea. "Very lovely," wrote Sara in her log. "In bathing — cocktails, dinner — music on deck — all fell asleep." The trip back to Paris provided a rude awakening.

> Paris is on a wartime basis [wrote Dick Myers, who was in the city on business, to Alice Lee] — no telephones from hotels — only private houses — nobody is allowed to communicate — either by phone or mail inside the country except in French — all mail and cables censored. . . . Children are being evacuated — people are leaving — and of course at night the city is black. . . . Most of the younger men are mobilized — and older ones gradually going — and the cafés are crowded at night with people simply seeking the solace of one another's society.

At Maxim's for dinner — which in the blackout Sara said "looked like Prohibition days in N.Y." — the first person they saw was Hoytie, to whom Sara had refused to speak since Patrick's last illness. "Here she comes," muttered Sara. "Let's all behave perfectly normally." Striding up to their table, Sara remembered, Hoytie "gave us advice in [a] strangled voice," offering the loan of her apartment in case they couldn't get out of Paris. Sara declined. The next day Noel Murphy sent Sara a hasty note, scrawled at the bank during an air-raid drill: "For heaven's sake, get Honoria home. Go to Cannes and stand up on an Italian boat . . . Good luck and come back." In fact Sara fully intended to do so: she'd conceived a wild notion of opening a soldiers' canteen in Paris and running it for the duration of hostilities, and she was dissuaded only when Honoria refused to leave Paris without her mother.

War was declared on September 3, a "very *angoissante* day." Everyone was rushing about trying to get luggage to escape points (Sara had twenty pieces, which Léger helped her transfer to the Gare St.-Lazare), make sailing reservations, or exchange money. The Guaranty Trust was a scene of pandemonium, with Léonide Massine trying in vain to persuade the bank to store a metal box full of irreplaceable Ballets Russes films (he ended by carting it around with him). Sara, Honoria, and the Myerses had long ago booked passage on the *Normandie* for September 6, but the *Normandie* was a French boat and would be fired on once hostilities began; so they tried to make alternative arrangements. Finally they managed to get passage on the United States ship *George Washington*, which left four days later. After lying low at the Normandy house of her cherished Madame Hélène, Sara, Dick Myers, and the girls got to Le Havre, from which the *George Washington* sailed on September 10, bound for Southampton and New York. To deter bomber pilots the deck had been painted with a huge Stars and Stripes, reminiscent of Gerald's Villa America sign, which gave the ship an air of improbable, Murphyesque festivity. There were nearly two thousand people on board in space meant for half that number, and Dick Myers had to sleep in the (drained) swimming pool, but they made the trip safely. "I feel like sitting under a tree in the sun and holding someone's thumb," wrote Gerald, in relief, to John and Katy Dos Passos.

On November 12, Gerald, Sara, and Honoria attended the premiere of the Ballet Russe's *Ghost Town* at the Metropolitan Opera House. Gerald hated first nights, in particular the audience's "greedy sense of being included at the only spectacle worth going to," and the stakes this evening were high. There had been considerable advance publicity for the production, including a photograph in the *New York Times*'s rotogravure section for Sunday, October 22: "Three young American members of the cast try on the voluminous frills they will wear in the new American ballet, 'Ghost Town,' which is patterned after a story by Mark Twain." (Twain, of course, was safely dead, unlike Murphy, whose name was nowhere mentioned.) Gerald had attended only a few rehearsals, so this premiere was one of his first glimpses of what Rodgers, Platt, and Raoul Pène DuBois had done with his plot and characters. Opening the program, he could see that the young miner, Ralston, was played by Frederic Franklin; his sweetheart, Eilly Orum, was Mia Slavenska; the Mormon preacher Orson Hyde was Roland Guérard; Jenny Lind — in Karinska's pleated pastel organza, with a wig of golden ringlets reminiscent of America's Sweetheart in *Within the Quota* — was "the Danish-Javanese dance sensation" Nini Theilade, offstage a sultry-lipped brunette with a very luscious figure. But the scenario — which at one time Denham had grudgingly proposed should be credited to "Richard Rodgers, in collaboration with Gerald Murphy, who supplied the historical research" — was now listed as the work of Marc Platoff.

Although later critical reaction was mixed, the ballet scored an enormous hit with the audience. There was tumultuous applause: Rodgers and Platt came on stage to take six curtain calls. Gerald, however, was left in his seat. He and Platt, who left the Ballet Russe soon after for a career on Broadway, continued their friendship into the 1940s; but Gerald never tried his hand at the ballet, or indeed at any art form, again.

In September, shortly after Honoria and Sara returned from Paris, Gerald received a disturbing telegram: "WAS TAKEN ILL OUT HERE LAST APRIL AND CONFINED TO BED FIVE MONTHS AND NOW UP AND WORKING BUT COMPLETELY CLEANED OUT FINANCIALLY WANT DESPERATELY TO CONTINUE DAUGHTER AT VASSAR CAN YOU LEND 360 DOLLARS FOR ONE MONTH IF THIS IS POSSIBLE PLEASE WIRE ME 5521 AMESTOY AVENUE ENCINO CALIF=SCOTT FITZGERALD."

Naturally the answer was yes; and Fitzgerald's gratitude, when he was able to write, was profound, if slightly less than candid. "What a strange thing that after asking every other concievable [sic] favor of you at one time or another I should be driven to turn to you for money!" he said. "The story is too foolish, too dreary to go into." Or, he didn't say, too embarrassing. His screenwriting contract at MGM had been terminated the previous December, and when

Walter Wanger hired him to write a script about the Dartmouth Winter Carnival with Budd Schulberg, he had gone on a week-long bender while on location in New Hampshire: so he was fired from that job, too. He had been unable to find work and although he told his agent Harold Ober and his editor Maxwell Perkins that he had a number of fiction projects in mind, the entire year had passed in a haze of alcohol — which in his letter to the Murphys was described as "a temperature of 102°" — and no novels or saleable stories resulted. Finally Ober had refused to advance him any more money, and Fitzgerald had been desperate. Gerald's loan, he said, "saved me — Scottie and me — in spite of our small deserts. I don't think I could have asked anyone else & kept what pride it is necessary to keep."

Gerald never knew — and probably wouldn't have cared — that Scott *did* ask someone else: his old Minnesota friend C. O. Kalman, in a telegram that duplicated the wording in Gerald's. Kalman was in the hospital, though, and couldn't reply, as Gerald did: "Please don't keep us ignorant ever again. Please take care of yourself. Please don't worry about the money. If you knew how *fond* we are of you I think you'd believe this. One is fond of so few people." Although he suspected Fitzgerald was dramatizing his ailments and covering up for his drinking — "I do not like to feel that you *consider* yrself ill. I can't believe you *are*," he said later — it didn't really matter. As Sara had told Scott in 1935, "I don't think the world is a very nice place — And all there seems to be left to do is to make the best of it while we are here, & be VERY grateful for one's friends — because they are the best there is, & make up for many another thing that is lacking."

The friends were widely scattered now, many battered by the events of the past few years. In May 1939 Archie MacLeish had been offered the post of Librarian of Congress. Because it would seriously interfere with his poetry, wrote Gerald to Woollcott, "He was against accepting so were we his doing so." But President Roosevelt persuaded him to say yes. Commented Gerald: "4,000 volumes! (and *all* sons of bitches) He'll never get thro' his dusting mornings." Gerald had traveled with the Dos Passoses to Conway for a farewell clambake while Sara was in Europe, an occasion that imprinted itself indelibly on the memory of his godson Peter, now rechristened William. It was an enormous alfresco feast, with bonfires and music and laughter, and

Gerald had brought a red, white, and blue beribboned jeroboam of champagne. Even the children partook. "We ate a very great deal," says William
MacLeish, "and I remember going to sleep with my head on my pa's chest,
and *he* went to sleep, and we all just snored for about an hour."

In October, Sara and Gerald went with Dottie Parker and Alan Campbell
to see the opening of Moss Hart and George S. Kaufman's play, *The Man Who
Came to Dinner*, in which an arrogant, acid-tongued, but perversely lovable
world-famous lecturer named Sheridan Whiteside — who seemed to Gerald
only a pale simulacrum of Alec Woollcott — is stranded by a broken leg in the
home of his small-town Ohio hosts. Monty Woolley, playing Whiteside in
only his third Broadway appearance, made a huge personal triumph; but the
somewhat collegiate humor that had amused Gerald in the days when he and
Woolley played "stomach touch" in Antibes no longer seemed terribly funny.
"The play depressed me," he wrote to Woollcott afterward; "it doesn't even
succeed in being incisive. . . . I wonder if any of all those people you know
know what you're like. I'm not saying I do, — but I am saying that the play
showed me (by what it lacks essentially) how fond I am of you."

Woollcott didn't seem to share Gerald's rather dour opinion, and in the
spring consented to star (as "himself") in the West Coast touring company of
the play. But during one performance he suffered a severe heart attack; after
spending time in a California hospital he returned to Neshobe, where he
recovered slowly. This latest intimation of mortality, along with the death of
Sara's adored Puppy ("the last tie to the boys"), shook Gerald badly. In his
dreams, night after night, the boys were dying over and over again, first Baoth,
then Patrick. "Will one's heart never touch bottom?" he asked Woollcott. "Is
there a point beyond which impotent rage can carry you? By noon of every
day the brain has reached saturation." He could no longer share these feelings
with Sara; she was too wounded herself to bear his losses too. And so he turned
to Woollcott. "I probably shouldn't have written this letter," he said, "but I
wanted to talk to you."

He and Sara were both concerned with helping Pauline Hemingway
weather the irretrievable wreck of her marriage. During the previous autumn,
when she was living in New York, Gerald had done his best to act as a
surrogate father to her boys, buying Patrick and Gregory the puppy they

craved and taking Bumby, who was now at boarding school, to grown-up treats like lunch at Gallagher's Steak House or the King Cole Bar at the St. Regis, followed by a matinee — John Hemingway remembers a performance of the musical extravaganza *Hellzapoppin* with particular enthusiasm. Back in Key West that spring of 1940, though, Pauline seemed, Gerald reported to Scott Fitzgerald, "forlorn. . . . I guess women who really love have always been."

She sent up an SOS to the Murphys — "would like to be a little bitter about the way you haven't come down here," was how she put it — and so he and Sara traveled to Florida with the Dos Passoses in the spring. After stopping on the way to see Bea Tolstoy (formerly Stewart) and the Barrys, they took Pauline with them on a tour of the back country that included a moment that only the Murphys could have devised. Their trip coincided with a solar eclipse, and near Kissimmee they stopped to watch it: pulling over to the side of the road, they poured cocktails from a thermos and tuned in the car radio to Carnegie Hall, where the New York Philharmonic was playing Stravinsky's *Sacre du printemps*. Gravely sipping their drinks to Stravinsky's throbbing dissonances, they stared upward as darkness covered the earth.

That summer Pauline went to San Francisco to live, and Sara, trying to hold together the threads of all their old friendships, asked Ernest to come and stay in East Hampton. She signed her letter "Yr old shipmate, Sara." But she never heard from him. It wasn't until the following December — after he had married Martha Gellhorn and they had honeymooned in New York without seeing the Murphys — that he replied. "I felt sort of strange about the honeymoon business," he wrote: "So I didn't go to see Ruth Allen nor you nor other oldest friends (I have no closer friend than you) because it seemed sort of vulgar. . . . I didn't want to strain your loyalties although I always marry good wives as you know. But I think you and me felt about the same and I love you the same as always."

By the time she got this letter, Sara and Gerald were coping with another loss. In September, Scott Fitzgerald had repaid $150 of the $360 they had sent him to cover Scottie's Vassar tuition. He'd been writing a series of stories for *Esquire* about a failing alcoholic screenwriter called Pat Hobby, and he had sold his long-ago short story "Babylon Revisited," in which the little-girl heroine is named Honoria, to the movies. His secretary, Frances Kroll, recalled later that he wanted to repay out of first moneys "the people he spoke of most warmly." Gerald remonstrated with him that "Yr cheque gave me a turn somehow. I wish we could feel that we'd done you a service instead of making you feel some kind of torment. Please dismiss the *thought*." It was their last communication: On December 21 Fitzgerald suffered a fatal heart attack at Sheilah Graham's apartment in Los Angeles.

"How cruelly the world needs the beauty of his mind," lamented Gerald to Woollcott. But only thirty people, including Gerald and Sara and Maxwell Perkins and Harold Ober, came to stand in the rain at his graveside on December 27. Because the Catholic Church considered his books immoral, and he had not received last rites, Fitzgerald was denied a Catholic burial in St. Mary's Cemetery alongside his Maryland ancestors; the interment was held at Rockville Union Cemetery with an Episcopal priest officiating. Zelda wasn't allowed to attend, but her letter to the Murphys afterward was a poignant farewell to the four-pointed star that their friendship had been since 1925: "Those tragicly ecstatic years when the pockets of the world were filled with pleasant surprizes and people still thought of life in terms of their right to a good time are now about to wane," she wrote. "That he wont be there to arrange nice things and tell us what to do is grievous to envisage."

"Poor Scott," said Ernest to Sara. "No one could ever help Scott but you and Gerald did more than anyone."

23

"One's very Life seems at stake"

"WHAT SAD DAYS," wrote Gerald to Archibald MacLeish in August 1940, when German soldiers were goose-stepping down the Champs-Élysées and sitting in the Deux Magots, putting an end definitively to the world the Murphys and their friends had loved. Now, with the same energy with which they had then painted backdrops for Diaghilev, Gerald and Sara threw themselves into war work: William Allen White's Emergency Rescue Mission, an organization devoted to obtaining U.S. visas for European artists and intellectuals, "take[s] all our time & $," Gerald wrote Archie. In addition Sara was acting as a virtual one-woman aid mission, procuring and shipping to Europe nine tons of powdered milk, and she was raising additional money for war relief. Said Gerald: "One's very Life seems at stake: *all* one cares for, finally."

When the war broke out Stella Campbell had been living in France, most recently in the Murphys' Ferme des Orangers, unable to return to England because of the quarantine laws that would have imprisoned her beloved Pekingese, Moonbeam. In the spring of 1940 Gerald received news from her nurse-companion, Agnes Claudius, that Stella was in the Pyrenees, ill and destitute. She needed medicine but couldn't afford it; she had to be hospitalized, but the war had made the local hospital uninhabitable. As they never failed to do when they were needed, the Murphys responded, wiring funds immediately to her and to Claudius; but it was too late. On April 9 came the news that Stella had died. Claudius used the money they had sent for medicines to buy her a burial plot in the Cimetière Urbain at Pau. Sad days indeed.

One of the Murphys' strongest links with the Europe of their past remained Léger, who had been characteristically pragmatic and sardonic in the early days of the war, when it seemed as if the declaration were just a formality and, he complained, "Everything goes so slowly!" He urged Gerald to come back to France and start a new line of luggage: "You can do amazing things with 'German hide' — the 'Siegfried valise' or something like that," he said.

In the summer, he wrote the Murphys that he had been invited to give the Harrison lectures in art at Yale University, and thus had been granted a visa to the still neutral United States; but he was reluctant to desert his country because "a Frenchman could not do that." Then, however, the Germans marched into Paris: with half of France under German control and the remainder "self-governed" by the accommodationist Vichy regime, Léger was desperate to get out. He had been in a German prison camp in the last war and had no desire to repeat the experience. To Gerald, a fellow artist, he painted a grim picture of the present and future: "Everything is hard, and will get harder and harder. . . . We know what it is because we've already seen it in all its colors — only the colors change. The grays darken — they will deepen to black, broken only by a few rays of light." Léger saw a terrible inevitability in what had happened. "We have paid a dreadful price for our taste for Impressionism, for the unfinished, the seductive, the charming. Our bour-geois culture hated anything that was too constructed: . . . [it preferred] the inspired sketch, the adorable, lightly-sketched indication. Unfortunately for us Hitler's tanks aren't sketches."

His next letter to the Murphys described an arduous journey to the south, during which one of his suitcases, containing the bulk of his travel funds, was lost. At Bordeaux there were air raids, and the city's prominent Jews were fleeing en masse; in the unoccupied zone there were discreet signs posted in the train stations for all trains whose destination lay in the Nazi-occupied north: NO NEGROES, NO JEWS. "They're whispering in Vichy that Hitler is going to make us a present of all the Jews in the Occupied Zone — and some people say they're all going to be sent to a colony." Whatever apologists for America's neutral stance might say, the sharp-eyed Léger saw what was up; and so, through him, did the Murphys.

From Marseille, Léger cabled Gerald and Sara to ask them to wire U.S. dollars to his account so he could pay for his passage; Gerald sent them that very day. And when the Murphys heard that Jeanne Léger (who had no visa and had to stay in France) had been dispossessed by German officers occupying the Légers' Normandy farm and Paris apartment, they gave her shelter at the Villa America, which lay in the unoccupied south. "You have always been 'my mighty refuge' in difficult times," Léger wrote, rather biblically, "and your great friendship pervades every part of my life."

These gestures cost the Murphys considerably at a time when they could ill afford it. Poor Copley Amory, their Boston Brahmin man of business, kept up a futile chorus of protest about their expenditures all through the forties, but Gerald would just sniff, "*Anyone* can live on his income," and then do exactly as he pleased. Doing as Gerald pleased meant keeping up a certain style — but, perhaps more important, it meant helping friends whenever generosity dictated, or when, as in Léger's case, "one's very Life is at stake."

Léger's letters made the newspaper headlines real, and as the conflict in Europe accelerated from phony war to blitzkrieg with no sign that America would intervene, Gerald grew increasingly unhappy. He went to work against inaction in the best way that he knew how: at the Mark Cross Company, which had an English factory since Patrick Murphy had established it in 1892, and thus had unique ties with beleaguered Britain. During one week in 1941 (he reported to Archie MacLeish) he removed the luxury leather goods from Mark Cross's Fifth Avenue windows and substituted photographs of where they came from: the blacked-out factory in Walsall, four miles out of Birmingham, and the air-raid shelter that protected the factory workers from German bombs. These displays excited so much comment that he came up with another idea: that of asking his fellow members of the Fifth Avenue Merchants' Association to join him in creating a week's worth of windows "calculated to stop the passer-by in his tracks and make him *think* about what he stands to lose *right now*" from the advance of fascism.

The Fifth Avenue merchants declined — they were afraid of offending clients who didn't care what happened elsewhere as long as they were free to shop — but Gerald went ahead with the plan anyway. For a week Mark Cross's six windows were each filled with five-foot-high white posters lettered with black type large enough to be read at thirty feet (shades of the *Within the Quota* backdrop!): On one was Patrick Henry's "Give me liberty or give me death!" speech ("Our brethren are already in the field! Why stand we here idle?"); on another, Thomas Paine's words about the times that try men's souls; on another, Daniel Webster's "God grants liberty only to those who love it, and are always ready to defend it" — on the others quotations from George Washington, Samuel Adams, Benjamin Franklin, all elaborating on the theme that the only way to preserve freedom at home was to defend it anywhere it was attacked.

The displays were a sensation. An average of three thousand people a day stopped to read every word; sometimes there were seventy to eighty people clustered at a window at one time, and foreign-language speakers were overheard translating them for those who couldn't read English. It's impossible to know whether they ultimately had the public impact Gerald was aiming for; but they *did* have a powerful effect on the man who put them in place. Delving into the writings of these bygone Americans had reawakened Gerald's "sophomore predilection for reading from Ralph Waldo [Emerson] and Thoreau"; writing to Archie MacLeish to tell him all this, he closed with a quotation from Emerson: "This pale Massachusetts sky, this sandy soil and raw wind, all shall nurture us. Unlike all the world before us, our own age and land shall be classic to ourselves." It was another answer, a decade later, to Archie's "American Letter." For Gerald, it was the beginning of a new direction.

The Murphys had by then moved from their New Weston penthouse, impelled not only by the nomadic custom of New Yorkers at the time, but by some deeper need to reinvent themselves — or if not themselves, their surroundings. After a year's stay at an apartment on West 54th Street behind the new Museum of Modern Art, they installed themselves in a duplex at 131 East 66th Street, one of a pair of Doric-pedimented limestone buildings designed at the turn of the century by the eminent architect Charles Platt. Grander in scale than their most recent apartments, it was a house for people who wanted to fill their lives with other people — old friends, certainly, but also new ones like Dawn Powell and Edmund Wilson and Lillian Hellman, the poet and translator Jacques LeClerq, the lyricist and translator John La Touche, and various contemporaries of Honoria.

Their visitors came up against the Murphy style immediately: in the entry hall was a built-in glass utility cabinet filled with fireman's tools, including a coiled hose and a handle that bore the label "Pull in case of emergency." Most tenants would have covered up this eyesore with an Oriental screen or some other elegant camouflage, but the Murphys not only left it out in plain view, they treated it as if it were serious art. Léger, only half joking, called the installation the best picture in the house. And everyone remembered it, as they remembered the huge double-height living room, which, the writer Brendan Gill recalled, was "more than simply odd and amusing; some true emotion — an emotion beyond the desire to please — had gone into its creation." It was a room for entertaining, and for display: on the vast expanse of one wall there was finally space for one of Gerald's pictures: *Watch*, which Archie MacLeish had exchanged for *Wasp and Pear* because the former wouldn't fit comfortably in his Alexandria house. From the living room a staircase led up to several bedrooms, including one in the back of the house which looked out on the wall of a neighboring apartment building; Dos Passos, who frequently occupied it when he came through New York, called it "the inside cabin." Gerald, however, continued to occupy a white-painted monastic cubicle with a tiny window overlooking the living room, like a priest's hole in a Reformation house. Although outwardly he had reassumed the role of "organizer of gaiety," he was more and more an ascetic at the bone.

Not that he turned away from the world around him. Just before the war he had been called to serve on the Grand Jury of New York County, where the usual menu was larceny, second-degree rape, sodomy, and assorted drug-related crimes. His collector's appetite — for people, for strange stories, for peculiar names or speech patterns — was whetted, and he wrote down in his notebook fragments of particularly evocative dialogue ("They started ransackin' thro his pocket"; "Tell Reuben his ass belongs to me"; "he made 'em all lie down on top of me on the bed face down"; or, from the district attorney, "Don't tell us what you said to yourself, tell us what you did").

From the court he went on to a new enthusiasm. Always something of an autodidact — who had made lists of vocabulary words in his school notebooks at Andover, and learned everything there was to know about Napoleon during the years he was in Antibes — Gerald had begun taking classes in the fall of 1940 at the New School for Social Research, a combination of graduate and extension school staffed by notable intellects — Theodor Adorno, Walter Benjamin, and Thomas Mann, among others — who had fled Nazi tyranny. One of them was Hemingway's friend, the Spanish artist Luis Quintanilla, who had settled in New York and East Hampton, where he often saw the Murphys, and was teaching a course in art appreciation in which Dawn Powell was enrolled. Gerald made up for what he thought was time wasted in college by taking a survey course on "Ideals of Western Civilization," which swept from Plato and St. Augustine to Machiavelli and Voltaire to Darwin, Nietzsche, Marx, and William James, with stopovers at John Dewey, Jakob Burkhardt, and Oswald Spengler. During the 1940–41 academic year he also took "Introduction to Modern Politics" (the French Revolution, Lenin, Mussolini, Hitler); Latin American history; "Japan and the New Order in the Far East"; a course on international politics based on a reading of quarterlies like *Foreign Affairs*; a study of Bach; and a course on American literature — which covered work by Hemingway, MacLeish, and Dos Passos, in addition to the more predictable Howells and James — taught by Alfred Kazin. The Bach and Kazin's course, it seems safe to say, were a personal indulgence; the rest of Gerald's curriculum was a kind of immersion in the context of the time that, like all Gerald's enthusiasms, sometimes verged on the obsessional.

Such zeal made him an easy mark for cynics: according to Lillian Hellman, it set him up for one of Dorothy Parker's rather prickly jabs. She was having dinner with the Murphys one evening after not having seen them for some time, and Hellman — who had met them on their rather shell-shocked 1937 visit to Europe — was asked also. On the way to dinner Dottie bet Hellman that she could guess "who Gerald will have discovered this time — what writer, I mean." Parker made three guesses: Madame de Staël, Gerard Manley Hopkins, and "Philippe de Swartzberger . . . [an] Alsatian who moved to Tibet. Born 1837, died 1929, or so it's thought. A mystic, most of whose work has been lost, but two volumes remain in Lausanne under lock and key, and Gerald invented him this afternoon." Hellman took the bet; after dinner, unaware of this conversation, Gerald produced a slim volume along with the cognac and asked if he could read a few poems from it. Hellman and Parker looked at each other meaningfully. It was Hopkins. Or that was the story Hellman told.

In fact Gerald had become fascinated with Hopkins, a Victorian Jesuit whose dense, alliterative, highly charged language would seem the antithesis of Gerald's cool artistic expression. He memorized whole stanzas of Hopkins's poems by copying them out — as he had with passages from Shakespeare that he found beautiful, moving, or to the point — and taping them to his shaving mirror. "Poetry doesn't become your own until you've memorized it," he said. So, trying to make Hopkins his own, he would stand with lather on his face declaiming, "Glory be to God for dappled things" in his ringing, dramatically tuned tenor. Not just for the pleasure of the sound the lines made, but for the substance of them.

Gerald had turned his back on his Catholic upbringing; he had buried his two sons, who were baptized Catholics, in the Episcopal Church; and he was still seething over the affront of the church's refusal to allow Scott Fitzgerald eternal rest next to the bones of his ancestors. But something in Hopkins's faith — his belief that despite pain and tragedy "God's grandeur" can still be discerned in nature, and that suffering and loss can be a means to greater understanding — spoke to him. David Pickman remembered how he would recite "yards and yards of 'The Wreck of the Deutschland,'" Hopkins's tortured elegy to five Franciscan nuns killed in a shipwreck:

> Thou mastering me
> God! giver of breath and bread;
> World's strand, sway of the sea;
> Lord of living and dead
> Thou hast bound bones and veins in me, fastened me flesh,
> And after it almost unmade, what with dread,
> Thy doing: and dost thou touch me afresh?

"Thou mastering me" — it was a hard lesson for someone who "refused to meet [life] on the grounds of my own defects." He would have to be "touched afresh," though, and made to suffer again, before he learned it.

In 1940 Fanny Myers had returned from France and was visiting the New York World's Fair when, in one of those truth-is-stranger-than-fiction coincidences, she spied a familiar figure making his way between the exhibits. It was Alan

Jarvis, one of the two young Rhodes Scholars who had given her and Honoria such a good time at Oxford the previous summer. After they had caught up with each other's news she told him that Honoria was in New York as well, working in the theater, and she encouraged him to call on the Murphys, who she knew would be delighted to welcome him.

Jarvis was, as Sara had described him, tall and blond, with a Byronic lock of hair that occasionally tumbled across his forehead; he would sweep it back with what Fanny called "a Noel Coward gesture," index finger beneath the curl. He was a sculptor and art historian, currently working on a book in which he hoped to interest publishers. And he would go on to a distinguished career as a museum curator in Canada after the war. Despite Sara's assertion that he had "no feathers anywhere," he was, in fact, homosexual and deeply conflicted about it; he had turned down her *Weatherbird* invitation because he was undergoing psychoanalysis in London in an effort to "cure" himself. He kept this turmoil hidden, however, and to the world was the very model of a charming, erudite, witty, and attractive bachelor, the sort of young man any parent would be thrilled to have for a son-in-law.

Very soon he and Gerald discovered their mutual passion for Gerard Manley Hopkins, and for T. S. Eliot and Johann Sebastian Bach; and they began spending more and more time together. As he did for so many other surrogate sons — as he could not for his own boys — Gerald became a sort of mentor. Gerald's godson William MacLeish recalls that "Dow used to advise me in spiritual matters — which means he would point out the benefits of these wines against the other wines. And he introduced me to oysters vinaigrette, which absolutely blew me away." To Jarvis, in addition to giving enological and gastronomical advice, Gerald could be more practically helpful: he put him together with several prospective publishers and wrote him a letter of introduction to Archie MacLeish.

But as 1940 gave way to 1941 the friendship became something deeper — what Jarvis's biographer called "a fierce and joyous relationship centered on their love of poetry," and expressed through a series of letters that said what could not be spoken between them. In some of them Gerald addressed Jarvis as "A. amatus," Latin for "beloved." He had always had a penchant for nicknames: "Oiness" for Hemingway (who couldn't pronounce R's), "Sal" or

"Sadie" for Sara, "Fanita" and "Scottina" for Fanny Myers and Scottie Fitzgerald, "Alexis" for Woollcott; but this one was more than an affectionate furbe-
low. It was a declaration. Jarvis, he said, was the soul mate he had been
searching for in vain since he was fifteen — that watershed year when (as he
had written to Archie MacLeish) he had become aware of, and started to
conceal, the "defects" in that "faulty 'instrument de précision,'" his heart.

It wasn't that he discounted or repudiated the uncanny closeness that he
had always had with Sara — a closeness that Scott Fitzgerald had acknowledged when he told her, "I know that you and Gerald are one." But their crisis
in 1936, when he had spoken of her need for *"communicated* affection" and
his inability to provide it, had made it clear that there were aspects of himself
he could not speak of to her without causing her pain, and he loved her too
much to do that. He had given some account of himself to Archie MacLeish,
in his January 1930 letter, and to Fitzgerald, in their talks in Switzerland; but
with each of them he felt a certain reticence. To Jarvis, who was struggling
with his own feelings, he could confide it all and know that it would be
understood.

In later life Alan Jarvis used to call Gerald the ideal father he had never
had; he would say he thought of him as the father of two dead sons who would
never see his boys grow up. He never referred to him as a lover. Whatever
either of them might have wanted from this relationship, it seems not to have
been physical. But on Gerald's side at least it was intense, it was consuming,
and apparently it was noticed: Sara, who had been so welcoming to Jarvis at
first, began to send out little signals of disapproval. "She was rather edgy about
him," Fanny Myers noticed, though Fanny didn't know *why.*

There was never any confrontation: there was no need. Sara went away for
an extended southern trip in the spring of 1941, and while she was gone
Gerald developed a painful abscess in his throat which required hospital
treatment. But after his release from the hospital he joined her in Warm
Springs, Virginia, for the weekend: her journal records long drives in the
country, swimming, and walks through fields carpeted with violets and woods
bursting with dogwood and lilac; at night they picnicked in front of the
fireplace in her room and toasted each other with sparkling Burgundy that
Gerald had bought to go with their steaks. Whatever his relationship with

Alan Jarvis, whatever Sara might have thought about it, nothing was said; if it had been, it might have upset the delicate equilibrium of his marriage. As it was, the relationship did unsettle his own internal balance.

As England battled on alone against Hitler, Jarvis began to wonder if he had shirked something by coming to America; he felt he had to go back. Although "Gerald agreed that Alan should go," said Jarvis's biographer, "he express[ed] great pain at their separation": he couldn't bear to lose Jarvis when he had only just found him — it was like suffering through the boys' deaths all over again — and he could not fully express his grief. But he helped arrange the "difficult" return to England in the days after Pearl Harbor, when America had also entered the war, and he accepted a cache of Jarvis's papers for safekeeping, which he stored in the Mark Cross safe "in a concrete container, zinc-lined."

And there matters rested, as if encased in that same zinc-lined concrete container. Jarvis was in England, and spoken of — when his name came up — as a friend of Honoria's. But his and Gerald's interlude had a curious sequel. Not long after his departure, Dorothy Parker's husband, Alan Campbell, took the astonishing step of enlisting as a private in the U.S. Army. Although younger than his wife, Campbell was hardly in the spring of youth; nor was he the Hemingwayesque soldier-of-fortune type from whom such a gesture might be expected. Gerald was much moved by his decision: he gave Campbell a watch engraved with the rather melodramatic encomium QUI SENSAT ACET ("He who feels, acts"). But Bob Benchley, whose irony got in the way of such lofty sentiments, cracked that the inscription *should* have read WHOSE WIFE FEELS, ACTS — because Campbell was responding as much to the goad of Dottie Parker's criticism as to his feelings of patriotism.

Parker's political and social conscience had been stirred up by the war, and her and Campbell's conviviality, based on a shared appreciation for dogs, drink, and bad housekeeping, had been severely strained. She had begun to resent Campbell's love and dependence — often she seemed to prefer men who mistreated her — and, more hurtfully, she had begun telling anyone who would listen that her husband was "queer as a goat." Enlisting was his response; and Gerald's *Beau Geste*-ish support of it seems to have made Parker suspicious of him as well.

For around this time, Lillian Hellman remembered, Parker "flatly stated" that Gerald was "sexually confused." Hellman herself was quick to disavow any personal knowledge: "I never saw any signs of it," she recalled, "but Dottie says she crossed over on a boat with him once and there were definite signs of it with a young man." By the time Hellman spoke these words, Parker was dead and unable to clarify or confirm them, and Honoria (to whom she said them) denied their merit. Bearing in mind Hellman's own penchant for invention and embroidery, it's possible that her account tells more about Parker's state of mind at the time than it does about Gerald. In the course of it, however, Hellman did make one unarguable assertion. Gerald, she said, was "a very brilliant and complicated man. To make definite statements about him would be a sin."

Sara spent New Year's 1942 with the Dos Passoses; Gerald, for some reason, was absent. "We all talked about and wished for the presence of our old Gaelic cormorants," wrote Dos to Archie MacLeish. (Archie was in Washington, where he had recently been named head of the new Office of Facts and Figures.) It was to be a trying year for Sara, for — whatever other anxieties she suffered — after a lifetime of discomfort, her long-standing difficulties with her surviving sister flared into open animosity. Except for the few words that passed between them at Maxim's at the outbreak of the war, Sara and Hoytie had not spoken since — as Sara believed — her sister had put a curse on Patrick and Baoth: one of their few communications had been a barrage of letters from Hoytie's lawyer, a Mr. Zimmerman, which began less than a month after Baoth's sudden death. Now Hoytie was in America — her apartment on the quai de Conti had been commandeered by an S.S. colonel — and almost exactly ten years after she had first confronted Sara at the dock with her tale of financial woe, she initiated a lawsuit against her sister for unlawfully appropriating her property in East Hampton.

The ten-year statute of limitations had run its course and Hoytie was free of legal repercussions from her failed real-estate deals; she could now own property again, and she was determined to do so. The fact that she had sold the Dunes of her own volition, and that she had been paid her own asking price, simply didn't register: in Hoytie's cosmology, *her* needs and wants lay at the center of the universe, and anything else was irrelevant. It was her old complaint of "It's raining on *me*" raised to a new level; but what could be overlooked in a nursery squabble was unbearable as litigation. The Murphys' friends, many of whom had felt the sting of Hoytie's snubs, were outraged: "What you write about Sara and Gerald makes me feel so bad; the wicked Hoyty," growled Hemingway to MacLeish, "that I can't write about it."

The court ultimately found in Sara's favor — and commented that Hoytie had sought "the aid of a court of equity to enforce a transaction, which, if it ever existed, was conceived in fraud and bad faith on her part." But it was two years before it did so, and defending herself against her sister's suit — as well as against a subsequent flurry of frivolous actions — cost Sara $5,200, and considerable anguish.

Ironically, the house itself, the Dunes, had been pulled down by then. Unable to find tenants or buyers, unhappy at the size of its fuel bill, and unwilling to pay taxes on the "improved" land, Sara had regretfully ordered that her girlhood home be burned to the ground in July 1941. She couldn't bear to watch that happen, instead deputizing Gerald to oversee the job; but now — just as she used to pull up all the dead annuals in the Dunes's flower beds at summer's end — she tore up the last of her sisterly feelings by the roots. "I have contributed to [Hoytie's] support every month, for my parents' sake," she said in an affidavit for the state Supreme Court in August 1942. "However, nothing can force me to jeopardize the future of our only remaining child — our daughter — to benefit a woman who has continually insulted me and my family — and whom I do not like or admire."

In January 1943 Alexander Woollcott died of heart failure, to Gerald's great sadness. He had been in declining health but had nonetheless managed to have dinner with Gerald and Sara almost weekly, sometimes alone and sometimes in company. On one occasion Gerald offered him a choice of other guests:

1) dinner Tuesday at 7:45: Cole & Linda Porter are coming. He dresses . . .
2) dinner Thursday at 7:30. Professor Kazin & his wife are coming. We don't dress . . . I've just finished his brilliant series of lectures at the New School.

Later Gerald scolded Woollcott for ducking dinner with the Kazins "(just because they're not in your set)." Parochial Woollcott might have been, but, said Gerald to Archie MacLeish, "His gift was to make the people he loved feel valuable." Gerald himself had begun to wonder more and more about his own worth.

He saw other men going to war — Alan Campbell, Jarvis, even the alcoholic forty-eight-year-old formerly tubercular Dashiell Hammett — and he asked MacLeish, who was now the director of the Office of War Information, "what kind of service" he could be eligible for "when the moment comes." He wrote, "Granted my age (55 this March) am I fitted for anything in which I would be of value? Physically I'm in pretty good condition, although Sara and I do notice that we have recently been pretty much slowed up due to the wallop that bumpy period of Baoth's and Patrick's illnesses took out of us."

There was no response to this query, and Gerald spent the war years at "that monument to the inessential, the Mark Cross Company," putting away forever his hopes, unrealized in two wars, of doing something substantive for his country. When he saw Archie he realized it might be for the best: for his friend was entirely consumed by the bureaucracy he was charged with running, and had written hardly a line of poetry since the war began.

Not that the MacLeishes were living in a philistine desert. On the contrary, when the Murphys visited, there were dinners with the Dean Achesons (Archie's old Cambridge crony was now assistant secretary of state) and Supreme Court Justice Felix Frankfurter (who thought Gerald "charmingly civilized"), or an arts festival with a "first Stravinsky performance, a first Piston performance, and three brand new ballets," or simply at-home evenings when Gerald played songs from Richard Rodgers's new hit musical *Oklahoma!* and Ada sang. But at the heart of all this gaiety, Gerald could see, was the dutiful emptiness of service. "Archie is being pulled thin over what he calls this 'blood and disaster,'" he had written to Woollcott earlier. "His skull shows through and his eyes are farther away."

In March 1945 the MacLeishes and Murphys went together to the Homestead, a grand old resort hotel in Hot Springs, Virginia, for a short spring holiday. Archie had left OWI — and the Library of Congress, to which he had briefly returned — to become assistant secretary of state for cultural and political affairs. He had survived a bruising confirmation battle (a group of conservative senators were alarmed by the elevation of the author of *Frescoes for Mr. Rockefeller's City* to a position of public trust), but now felt conscience-stricken at taking even a week away from Washington. His vacation worked on him "like a stone bruise on the heel," he wrote his mother.

As if in compensation, Gerald exerted himself to amuse his godson William, taking him riding every day and drawing him out, as he was so masterly at doing, on any number of subjects. Gerald was still reading and memorizing Gerard Manley Hopkins, and one morning, during breakfast, he came to stand behind his godson's chair and recited the sonnet "The Windhover" from start to finish:

> . . . My heart in hiding
> Stirred for a bird — the achieve of, the mastery of the thing!
> Brute beauty and valour and act, oh, air, pride, plume here
> Buckle! AND the fire that breaks from thee then, a billion
> Times told lovelier, more dangerous, O my chevalier! . . .

The tenor voice rang on, declaiming Hopkins's hymn to the unfettered beauty of the wild hawk, his symbol of poetic inspiration. "I thought I was going to cry," says William MacLeish, remembering it, "and I looked at my pa, and realized that *he* was going to cry. He hadn't been writing any poetry for years and it was driving him crazy. So that was one of the great, great times with Dow." It was Gerald's present to Archie: a reminder of his essence, a reminder that he had to return to it to survive.

24

"Isn't it strange how life goes on?"

"PEOPLE SHOULD NEVER be themselves, least of all their *old* selves," Gerald once remarked, rather sardonically, to John Dos Passos; and although the war ended in August 1945, life didn't pick up where it had left off in 1939. In 1946 Alan Jarvis returned from England to America, but there was no reunion with Gerald, who wanted to avoid "the revisitation of scenes of the past." As he told Jarvis, "the reopening of relationships (even after a three day absence) are more trying than termination, — commensurately with one's affection. . . . I've felt we would see each other one day, — but par hasard [by chance]." Whatever their friendship had been, it could go nowhere — or nowhere that Gerald could imagine. And so he renounced it. But it had marked him ineffably, and its loss left him with a feeling of real desolation: "I think it's only fair to tell you," he wrote, "of that wake which was left in a trackless sea. I hope you agree. You've sensed it I know." He signed the letter "Love . . . Gerald."

Before Jarvis left New York for Canada, however, he defied Gerald's proscription and stopped at the Murphys' one evening; Gerald, returning at six from the office, entered the apartment by the upstairs entrance and thus didn't see him in the living room below. He heard his voice through the little monastic window, though, sounding "grave but harmonious . . . You laughed and sounded well. I was very glad of it." But Gerald didn't — couldn't — come downstairs: "the shock of recognition seemed too much. . . . Albeit I've found my heart to be a somewhat faulty instrument of precision, all at once I was constrained to protect the past from the present. Life may one day allow of my being proven right. I hope so. It all seems to me so sad. Unutterably. I feel it . . ."

There it is again — the *instrument de précision* about which he had written to Archie MacLeish in 1930; the one he had painted in the year of Fred's death, which now hung in his living room downstairs. A watch, his heart, measuring out the empty days. He sent the packet of letters that he had stored at Mark Cross during the war back to Jarvis, and they never saw each other again.

And what about Sara's empty days? In 1943, to her, and Gerald's, delight, Honoria had met and married a young English naval officer named John Shelton. The wedding took place in the East Hampton church, and Phil and Ellen Barry, who had a substantial house nearby, lent it for the reception. Afterward Honoria returned to live with her husband in England, and the Murphys' nest was finally, definitively vacant.

Possibly to fill the emptiness, Sara had become a volunteer at the Wood Memorial nursery, a day-care center on "the Polyglot Rim of Harlem" for thirty children whose "daddies have gone off to war and [whose] mothers are obliged to work," in the words of a fund-raising brochure. The children were a diverse group but all were living in considerable poverty and suffering from a variety of greater or lesser illnesses. Every morning, when they arrived at the nursery, they lined up to have their throats looked at and their scalps inspected for lice, and afterward they were dosed with cod liver oil and given a snack of fruit juice and crackers. During the course of the day there were games and stories; art classes and trips to the park; a "nutritious luncheon"; naps and more snacks; most important, the children were listened to and cuddled and cared for.

Sara took to this work with almost frightening enthusiasm, eventually becoming president of Wood Memorial's board as well as a caseworker. She attended psychology seminars, keeping careful notes of the nursery's structure and personnel, and followed a full load of cases (she had to do an early evaluation of each child in her dossier as well as follow-up in three and six months). She also edited the nursery's fund-raising brochure and helped to refine its mission statement. But these executive functions weren't as important to her as the children themselves. Singing "Au clair de la lune" with them, she might have been with Baoth and Patrick in the garden at Villa

America. One day Honoria — who had returned to the United States when her husband was posted to the Pacific — came to visit Sara during a music class and was so moved by the experience that she left the room in tears.

Sara even brought two of the children — brothers named Charlie and Toopie, who she suspected were being mistreated at home — to East Hampton for weekends; and although she and Gerald were both by now in their sixties and out of training as playmates for anything larger than a small dog, she made an attempt to adopt them. Honoria thought it was "touching — wrenching might be a better way to describe it — to watch her being a mother of sons again"; but her effort to turn the clock back (if that's what it was) was doomed to failure. The boys' grandmother, their legal guardian, opposed the adoption; when Sara's term as president ended not long afterward she stepped down from her post, and her involvement with Wood Memorial seemed to end. At the same time, Honoria's marriage, like many wartime romances, was coming apart; she returned to America permanently, and although she set up her own apartment, the Murphys were parents again.

Others in the Murphys' circle of friends seemed to be having a hard time finding a new rhythm for their lives in the days after the war. Katy Dos Passos remained in Provincetown, in the house that Gerald had likened to a ship's cabin with its view of the water. She wrote Sara long, funny reports of quotidian Cape Cod life; but her husband was still overseas, filing stories for *Harper's* from the Philippines, fortifying himself with vitamins that Sara had given him against "the constant aeroplane hopping, jeep and truck riding and the heat and the dust and the mud and the general carnage."

Archie and Ada MacLeish were stuck in Washington, where Archie was working — in the aftermath of the death of the president who had given him the job — to establish the United Nations and sell it to the American people. In July their daughter, Mimi, was married to Ensign Karl Grimm in their house in Alexandria, and Sara lent the bride her own pearl-encrusted satin-and-lace wedding dress for the occasion. "Mimi looked like a picture out of *Vogue*," recalled her aunt Ishbel. But with every step she took "the pearls went crunch," and, Mimi said, "I couldn't wait to take the damned thing off." Archie felt the same way about his government duties, but he wouldn't return to civilian life, or to the little stone house in Conway where he wrote his poems, for more than a year, after a stint as chairman of the first UNESCO conference; and when he did he found it hard to follow Gerald's advice and reignite the Windhover's lovely and dangerous fire. One day, struggling to put a match to a pile of damp wood outside the house, he thought despairingly, "It's just like me, I'm that way inside, I just won't burn inside."

Hemingway wrote Sara from Cuba to tell her of his exploits in the closing days of the war in Europe, which he had been covering as a correspondent for *Collier's*. Typically he felt it necessary to cast his participation in the most combative, macho light possible: "went with an infantry division for the St. Lo breakthrough, and stayed with them, or up ahead with the French Maquis, in the fighting through Normandy. . . . We assaulted the Siegfried line on Sept. 14th. From then on it was a terribly tough fall and winter . . . terrible fighting, Sara, all winter long."

He also informed Sara that he and Martha Gellhorn had broken up. "I need a wife in bed," he wrote, "and not just in even the most widely circulated magazines." But, he reported, in a typical combination of braggadocio and camaraderie, he was marrying someone else, "a girl named Mary Welsh . . . [who] is a great believer in bed which I believe is probably my true Patria. . . . Also she is the only woman ever knew besides you who really loves a boat and the water: which is a break for me."

But he wasn't doing any writing. "As you know I was out of business as a writer except for 6 Colliers pieces and the poems . . . from early 1942 to 1945," he told a critic some years later. And the two novels he worked on in the years after the war — his exploration of androgyny, *The Garden of Eden*, and an ambitious multilayered epic that was planned as part of a trilogy — proved intractable. Neither one was published (or publishable) in his lifetime. His fire was proving just as hard to rekindle as MacLeish's, but he was reluctant to admit it. All of them, it seemed, were waiting for a signal to move on to the next chapter of their lives.

Just before the war Gerald and Sara had made the acquaintance of Dawn Powell, a commercially underappreciated but critically esteemed novelist (she had published nine books by 1940, when her friendship with the Murphys really began) who was ten years younger than Gerald. A plump, rather dowdy woman with a paradoxically sharp eye for elegance and style, she had been married since 1920 to an alcoholic, occasionally successful advertising man named Joseph Gousha, and they had a mentally handicapped son who was in and out of institutions. Despite this strain, however, and the Goushas' near constant money troubles, Powell managed to keep her wit dry and her perspective bemused, at least in public. Being themselves practiced in keeping up the same sort of appearances, Gerald and Sara took to her at once; they not only relished her cleverness and her talent, they also responded to her aura of wounded gallantry. "Darling Dawnie" was asked to dinner, showered with presents — from bunches of flowers to dresses to occasional infusions of cash — or invited for the weekend. Sara managed all this in an almost distracted way, as if it weren't really happening. "I enclose a bit of cash," she'd say, "which never hurt anybody." Gerald made more of a production: "I don't really know whether you cared for that bag and those gloves or whether you were partly insulted," he wrote Powell early in their friendship, on a hilariously tacky postcard of a "Penguin Duck" whose white pom-pom crest makes her look very like Dawn Powell in a hat: "Maybe the whole thing was just a sordid assignation that I would boast about at my club later. Or maybe life as the Belle of the Latin Quarter has made you accept as your lot the gifts that men vie to lay at your feet. As for me, what I expect is a little goddam civility and that of the most expensive kind. No Yale 1912 man is designing and making bags for his health & you can go to our 30th reunion (I'm not) this year & ask. Love, G."

Powell wrote the ending of her novel *My Home Is Far Away* during a stay at Swan Cove; later, she started another, *The Wicked Pavilion*, as the result of conversations she'd had with Gerald about a book he was reading, a collection of eighteenth-century family letters called *The Creevey Papers*. During another "wonderful weekend of restoration" with "these miraculous two people" Gerald taught her to confront the Atlantic surf by diving through the first two breakers, as he did, until she could float serenely on the far side. "This conquering of the deep is something," Powell confided to her diary; in fact it enabled her to throw off a paralyzing case of writer's block.

Something else happened during that weekend, too, something so strange that Powell could articulate it only later. Talking to Gerald, she said, she felt they each became aware of some other presence, what she called "the finger of death." It was pointing at him.

"Sal dear," wrote Gerald to Sara a week later, from a Pan Am Clipper nine thousand feet over Long Island Sound, "we're veering over Connecticut and Montauk goes out to sea with a line of fleecy torn clouds over it . . . over Boston now and I think of dear Dos lying there below . . . And of the anguish in his mind when he wakes."

For the finger of death that Dawn Powell had seen on Gerald had, Powell believed, been "deflected to Katy." On September 12, driving from Cape Cod to Connecticut in the late afternoon, Dos had been momentarily blinded by the setting sun and the Dos Passoses' car had collided with a truck parked by the side of the road. Katy was killed outright — the top of her head sheared off by the windshield — and Dos lost an eye. "Where can he put this night- mare?" Gerald asked. "I keep wondering what he'll do." Taking a cue from his own experience, he added, "Stand it, I guess."

When the call came, Gerald was just leaving for a business trip to London during which he was to discuss arrangements for a possible partial sale of the Mark Cross Company, so he could not go to comfort his friend; but Sara went to Boston at once. As Ada MacLeish and Alice Lee Myers had done for her, she organized visitors to the hospital, helped make arrangements for the funeral in Truro, and urged Dawn Powell to take her place at Dos's side when she had to return to New York. Then, because he couldn't bear to stay in Provincetown where he and Katy had been so happy, she invited Dos to come to New York and then travel out west with her and Honoria and two mutual friends of the Murphy and Dos Passos families, Lloyd and Marion Lowndes.

"We have all come to the part of our lives when we start to lose people of our own age," Ernest Hemingway had written the Murphys when Baoth died; now it was really true. First Scott Fitzgerald and Alec Woollcott, then, in 1945, Bob Benchley. Now it had happened to Katy, from whom there would be no more chatty letters addressed to "Dear Mrs. Puss," with whom there would be no more Waddell Girls jokes or cruises on the *Weatherbird*. And in December 1949, very suddenly, Philip Barry was killed by a massive heart attack. The smell of death, and age, seemed to be in the air: in a time that should promise renewal, there seemed little to hope for. "[Y]ou & I alike feel it," wrote Archie MacLeish to Gerald in the fall of 1948. "'A kind of boding' you say. It is true. Or at least it is true for you & me. But why, unless because autumn is the time for change & we await it, our hearts beating faster than the season, I do not know." A year after Katy's death Sara sent flowers to her grave in the Truro cemetery. Dos, who had gone to Havana, spoke for all of them when he told her, in thanks, "I cant yet find words to write. After a year the void is as deep as ever."

Gerald and Sara continued to fuss over Dos Passos like a pair of mother hens. For his birthday in January 1949 Gerald organized "an old-fashioned theatre party" (as he described it) of the kind they had enjoyed so many years before to mark the occasion. First, dinner at Sixty-sixth Street with Lloyd and Diddy Lowndes: very dry martinis, followed by hot clam broth, squab, new potatoes, Brussels sprouts, salad, iced shredded pineapple, and a birthday cake with one candle, all washed down with Château Carbonnieux champagne, "really cold." Then tickets to Cole Porter's hit musical *Kiss Me, Kate*. Dos was terribly moved. "Nobody's ever done anything about my birthday before," he kept saying.

The Lowndeses lived in the Rockland County hamlet of Sneden's Landing, a sleepy collection of eighteenth- and nineteenth-century houses on the banks of the Hudson River. Shaded by huge old trees and bounded on one side by the majestic expanse of the Hudson, Sneden's (as its residents call it) has the air of being in the middle of nowhere instead of just twenty-five minutes from midtown Manhattan. When Sara and Gerald came to visit, they were predictably entranced. In fact, while out on a walk with his hosts along the river, Gerald saw a house that so caught his fancy that he wanted to buy it. It was a beautiful, pre-Revolutionary Dutch stone house with a pillared second-story porch running the length of the building and wide dormers overlooking the broad expanse of the Hudson; but it was owned by an old woman who, Diddy Lowndes said, would never sell it.

"Don't worry," Gerald had replied. "The house will be available in a year." By coincidence or, Diddy Lowndes believed, some Celtic kind of second sight, his words came true: a year later the old woman died and the house was for sale.

By an even greater coincidence, in 1941 Vladimir Orloff had sold the *Weatherbird* (the boat they had built "in spite of thunder") to a Swiss named Gérard de Loriol, whose "highly marginal and equally lucrative" activities during the war enabled him to pay for her in gold and thus save her from being impounded by the authorities. Vladimir had managed to hang onto this sum all through the war and contrived to send it — via Fanny Myers and her fiancé, Francis (Hank) Brennan — to Gerald in 1945. So despite a continuous leakage of funds from the Murphys' accounts they had enough to respond to the opportunity the Sneden's property presented. Researching the title, they discovered that the house had been built in 1700 by the then mayor of New York, William Merritt, who had given it the rather Dickensian name of Cheer Hall. After two decades of loss and accommodation, they may have felt that they could use some cheer themselves, and by the beginning of 1949 the house was theirs.

Having a new house to conjure with, a new life to invent, always stimulated the Murphys. At Sneden's they ripped out rotting boards, replastered walls, built in bookshelves, sanded and stained floors ("dark seal brown" was how Gerald described the color). They added a small wing on one side, but before starting construction Gerald researched where the original stones had been quarried, got the quarry reopened, and ordered new stone for the addition. Although the Murphys still kept two in help, including the faithful Ernestine, Gerald had been taking classes at the Cordon Bleu school and had begun doing much of the household's cooking. At Cheer Hall he put in a state-of-the-art kitchen that included space for that new invention, a dishwasher, as well as a separate bar area where he could mix his specialty concoctions: sometimes Black Velvets, sometimes glögg, sometimes planter's punch served in a hollowed-out coconut. He still made a production out of mixing drinks, and also out of drinking them. A neighbor remembers Gerald instructing him that the only way to sip champagne was to do it while "looking up into the branches of a tree."

Sometimes there were parties, particularly in summer, when Sara would light the grounds with candles placed in little paper bags — a charming and unusual idea in 1950, before Martha Stewart came on the scene; but both Murphys preferred intimate dinners with a few friends or houseguests. These would be preceded by apéritifs and hors d'oeuvres — the *sablés* of La Garoupe had given way to squares of whole-grain bread (with the crusts removed, of course) topped with a slice of peeled, seeded tomato and a dollop of whipped cream spiked with very hot horseradish — and there would be pheasant with bread sauce, perhaps, or veal poached in broth. Afterward Gerald and Sara would sit at the piano and sing as they used to do, or play their now priceless old records of *Le Boeuf sur le toit* or Louis Armstrong or Marlene Dietrich or Fats Waller; or Gerald would indulge in his latest enthusiasm, the harpsichord. Finally, as Dawn Powell said, they would all sink into "wondrous black hushed sleep."

Powell described Cheer Hall as "curiously beautiful and still — like Arlington in fact — like a beautiful mausoleum in a private cemetery." Her words reflect the hypnotic effect of the stately river winding by its lawn, but also the fact that if the Murphys' previous houses had been adventures in forward-looking flair, exercises in the modern, this one was almost a retreat into the past. Not just the house itself, but its surrounding area, which was rich in Colonial and Revolutionary history. Having become a property-holder, Gerald now began to immerse himself in the "native classicism" of the Hudson valley. And he would regale anyone who would listen with stories of patroons and patriots, Colonial schools, shad fishing, and Hudson River steamboats. In 1950, the year Cheer Hall's restoration was finished, the Murphys celebrated Washington's Birthday with a grand fête for which Gerald appeared as the Father of His Country, in powdered wig and Continental uniform with knee breeches and buckled shoes, to ladle out the punch; his costume was a surprise even to Sara, and Dawn Powell was "still reeling" from the effect of it when she wrote "Dear George and Martha" to thank them.

The eighteenth century must have seemed a welcome refuge from the clamor of what increasingly filled the newspapers and the radio waves in the late 1940s and early 1950s — the ever rising pitch of anti-Communist hysteria in America, and the deepening silence from behind the Iron Curtain. Gerald found himself increasingly compelled to take a stand. What he did wasn't radical, or even, by the standards of Dorothy Parker or Don Stewart, particularly *engagé*: in 1946 he joined the Independent Citizens Committee of the

Arts, Sciences, and Professions, a political action committee dedicated to electing legislators opposed to "the increasing growth in our country of anti-democratic forces." But even being associated with such a group could be thought questionable in the paranoiac atmosphere of the time.

In 1947 the Un-American Activities Committee of the House of Representatives had held the Hollywood hearings that resulted in the blacklisting of ten "suspected Reds" — the Hollywood Ten — and their associates. Increasingly people like Parker and Stewart could no longer find work in the studios because of their political beliefs; but the Red-hunting juggernaut was only gearing up. By the early 1950s HUAC took on the aspect of Robespierre's Committee of Public Safety, and at that point its reach came closer to home.

Gerald and Sara had been seeing quite a lot of Lillian Hellman, who by her own account came to stay at Sneden's "any number of times," and their relationship had already survived at least one challenge. Hellman had invited the Murphys to her farm in Duchess County and, in a fever of historic authenticity, had cooked them a meal composed entirely of foods the local Indians had eaten, including skunk cabbage; afterward Sara had become "deathly sick."

"What shall I do?" wailed the rarely-at-a-loss dramatist, to which Gerald replied, "I don't think you'd better do *anything*. You'll kill her." He had gone to the pharmacist in town and said, with great tact and gallantry, "I don't like to mention Miss Hellman's name in such a context, but she has poisoned my wife. Can you give me anything to make her throw up?"

A different and more serious test of their friendship came in July 1951, when Dashiell Hammett, Hellman's longtime companion, was arrested for refusing to provide the names of contributors to the bail fund of the Civil Rights Congress, a group of which he was a trustee. The fund had provided bail for four Communists, convicted of antigovernment activity under the Smith Act, who had then disappeared. Now the judge in the case, Sylvester Ryan, and the assistant U.S. attorney, Roy Cohn — soon to become a byword as Senator Joseph McCarthy's counsel — wanted to indict the bail fund contributors for aiding fugitives. Hammett didn't know who the contributors were; but he refused to cooperate in what he felt was a witch-hunt. So the judge put him in jail for contempt.

The talk on the street was that the judge would set Hammett's bail very high — the figure Hellman remembered was $100,000; but Hammett was in frail health and Hellman was desperate to spare him the rigors of imprisonment. She didn't have the money; she couldn't mortgage her brownstone quickly enough; and even after she pawned all her mother's jewelry she had only $17,000. The rich friends she called for help weren't home. She called the Murphys, and Gerald told her to come down to Mark Cross. He said he would give her everything in the store's safe that day (it was a Saturday), and he wrote her an additional personal check for $10,000. Hellman always maintained that the Mark Cross contribution was a fiction, "made up to save my feelings," and that that money was Gerald's, too. Whatever it was, it was typical. "Gerald Murphy was always a champion of victims," said another blacklisted artist, the dancer Paul Draper, Muriel Draper's son, who also ran afoul of the Red hunters at this time.

But Draper had it only half right. Gerald, and Sara, were motivated by friendship, not charity, and they were never limousine liberals who supported underdogs out of some kind of *nostalgie de la boue*. In 1939 Dorothy Parker had asked Gerald to a power lunch at the Bayberry Club — an elite midtown watering hole full of gold leather banquettes and black glass tables shaded by jade faux-bayberry trees — with Donald Ogden Stewart, his recent bride, the "formidable and far from alluring" Ella Steffens, and one of the editors of *The New Masses*. Gerald found the whole setup incongruous: "The talk was violent and technical," he told Sara, "and the check very high. Being a guest I did not pay, but Don insisted on paying himself and everyone told him he should save his money for his children, etc. etc. Why didn't we go to Schrafft's then? I have luncheon there every day." Needless to say, *The New Masses* didn't get any money out of Gerald.

In 1953, after the Iron Curtain had descended with a clash, Gerald had one of those fallings-out with Parker which punctuated so many of her friendships; this time, Gerald concluded, "To be anti-Communist is to be anti-Dottie, apparently. Too bad!" But if he was, or became, anti-Communist as the fifties went on, he was still a liberal. In the late forties or early fifties, on one of the slips of paper that served as his unbound commonplace book, he jotted down — because he liked it or wanted to repeat it in company — a comment about congressional investigating committees, calling their actions "a pernicious nonsense and a direct denial of the principles of the Constitution." And there's another scrap, even more expressive, bearing a quotation from Shakespeare's *Coriolanus*, that eternally pertinent political commentary adapted in the 1950s by Bertholt Brecht (whose flight from the United States when under investigation had turned the Hollywood Eleven into the Hollywood Ten): "You fragments! You shames of Rome, you!" cries Caius Martius Coriolanus to his craven fellow citizens. "You souls of geese, that bear the shapes of men, how have you run from slaves that apes would beat! Pluto and Hell! All hurt behind, backs red and faces pale with fright and agu'd fear!"

It was all so unlike the way things had been after that other war, in that other city — or so the Murphys seemed to think. "By and large what we did had a kind of personal style," grumbled Gerald to Ellen Barry. "I don't see its like around anywhere today." In fact, New York was at the center of what was new and exciting in the cultural avant-garde, just as Paris had been after the end of World War I. Between Jackson Pollock and Mark Rothko, George Balanchine and Martha Graham, Leonard Bernstein and Arthur Miller and the Beats, everything was happening there. But although the Murphys picked up the threads of a friendship with Alexander Calder, whom they had barely been aware of in Paris (he made Sara a zigzag silver bracelet that she wore constantly, and she was enormously fond of him, although she complained that he "always smelled of wet tweed"); although they admired Calder's mobiles and sculptures; although Gerald was so riveted by *Death of a Salesman* that he went to see it twice; and although he found John Cage and Robert Rauschenberg, for instance, both "provocative and sympathetic," he and Sara seemed to watch these phenomena from the sidelines, as observers, not participants.

They had begun to find refuge in the familiar, so their new Sneden's circle contained old faces — along with Katharine Cornell and Agnes de Mille and her husband, Walter Prude, there was Helen Hayes, the widow of their old Antibes friend Charles MacArthur, and the Lowndeses. Despite their dismay at his increasingly conservative politics, they kept up their close connection with Dos Passos and — after his remarriage in 1949 — his new wife, Eliza-

beth Holdridge. And during these postwar years they reanimated their friendship with Cole Porter, which had languished during the latter twenties and
thirties.

Cole had suffered a crippling riding accident in 1937 that left him without
the use of his legs: the blow to his vanity, not to mention the often excruciating
pain and the anguish of immobility, had softened him somewhat. Linda was
also in somewhat frail health, suffering, Honoria remembers, from emphy-
sema, and she seemed glad to be with old friends with whom she did not have
to try so hard.

Now the two couples often had dinner together at the Waldorf-Astoria,
where Cole and Linda had adjoining suites; sometimes, though not always,
they went on to the theater. Even with this renewed rapprochement, however,
there was still the slightest hint of reserve between the two men. Although
Gerald had thought Porter's 1949 hit, *Kiss Me, Kate*, was "Very stunning,
stylish, sophisticate. Cole at his best with all its limitations. . . . Clever idea,
brilliantly staged," he couldn't help adding: "I wish I didn't know Cole. It
would have more freshness for me."

In the summer of 1950 Honoria, who had been living on her own in New York
since shortly after her divorce, made a trip to California where she met and
fell in love with a World War II veteran, William Donnelly. They were
married in November in the chapel of St. Patrick's Cathedral — Donnelly
was a Catholic, and Honoria, though she had never practiced the faith Anna
Ryan Murphy had insisted she be baptized in, had decided to embrace it as
well. This presented a difficulty for her parents. Gerald, recalled Archie
MacLeish's daughter, Mimi, "never set foot in a Catholic church as long as I
knew him." But, Honoria says, "they realized it was what I wanted to do, and
that was that." Although they delighted in her happiness, they were inevitably
a bit wistful; and their feelings were compounded by their decision that same
summer finally to sell the Villa America, which had languished without a
buyer since the 1930s.

Although Gerald had been back to Europe on business since the war —
and had been saddened to find so much of it devastated or still in the grip of
postwar privation — he had resolutely avoided their former home. It was

increasingly clear that they would never go back; it was time to let it go. With the war's end the south of France was again a possibility for traveling Americans and Europeans with money; and keeping an unused property there, even only partially staffed, was a potentially fatal drain on the Murphys' finances, already strained by the acquisition and renovation of Cheer Hall. A price tag of $40,000 was put on the villa and it wasn't long before a purchaser materialized. But before a sale could go through, Gerald, who was in Europe on another buying trip, had to make the journey to Antibes to put everything in order.

Imagine him then, driving along the Corniche from Nice to Antibes, past all the new villas, the postwar hotels and marinas, everything that, as Vladimir has warned him, has "spoiled the Côte d'Azur." He turns onto the Boulevard du Cap, drives past the Jardin Thuret and the Chemin des Mougins. His car goes in at the gate:

> Immediately one is caught up by the compelling beauty of it [he writes to Sara] — that shining *transparent* sea, the high healthy palms, the mixed smell of watered parks with oleander dominating (laurier rose just at its height). The stillness and peace and the air stirred constantly by the sea. I had come with misgivings, prepared to be saddened, but no! The villa *is* untended in appearance, but the garden no! The palms, the large conifer, the linden, the eucalyptus (like a tower) have now eclipsed the view of the water, so that it's a secret garden.

Somehow the ghosts — of himself, painting or "saying Mass" over his cocktail shaker, of Sara in her long filmy dresses, of Scott and Zelda and Picasso and Ernest, of the children in their sun hats and "Patrick at his little garden" — were all exorcised by his return; or not exorcised, but transfigured, so that they no longer haunted, but instead blessed him.

In June 1951 Honoria gave birth to a son, John Charles Baoth Donnelly, in Carmel, California. Gerald and Sara, who had just returned to Cheer Hall from a trip to Europe together, were ecstatic: Sara ran from room to room when she heard the news, crying out to the dogs and Theresa the cook and their neighbors the Lowndeses that Honoria had a baby. "Isn't it strange how life goes on?" she said to Gerald when she could speak coherently. "My mother had me. I had Honoria, and now Honoria has her child." Two years later Honoria had a second boy, William Sherman Donnelly, and Sara flew to Carmel to be with her at the birth. "How different a dawn than the one we saw in a hospital eighteen years ago," wrote Gerald to Sara afterward. "I guess that's how it is. Two boys went out from our family and now two other boys have come into it."

25

"Back there where they were"

No one was quite sure what set off the last of the "damn schoolgirl quarrels" between Gerald and Archie MacLeish, but everybody knew where it happened. MacLeish had taken the post of Boylston Professor of Rhetoric and Poetry at Harvard University and was dividing his time between Cambridge and Uphill Farm in Conway; but he and Ada spent the winter months in the Caribbean, and the Murphys sometimes came to visit them at the Mill Reef Club in Antigua.

Either Gerald had tracked sand into the MacLeishes' beach house and had been insulted when Archie reproved him, or Ada and Archie had been insufficiently sympathetic to a bout of flu that Sara suffered while she was visiting, or Sara and Gerald were put off by what they privately considered to be Archie's too assiduous cultivation of the rich and socially powerful club denizens. Whatever the cause, a pall descended on their friendship. The Murphys even declined to attend the MacLeishes' fortieth anniversary party in Conway in 1956 — although both Gerald and Archie tried strenuously to deny that either was really sore at the other. Paradoxically, however, it was during this period of estrangement that MacLeish drew most heavily on Gerald and Sara for what turned out to be one of the great, and final, successes of his career.

In the days just after the war Archie had traveled to Europe and was saddened, as Gerald had been, by the pervasive destruction, its purposelessness, its capriciousness. Asked to give a guest sermon at the Congregational First Church of Christ in Farmington, Connecticut, in 1955, he explored "the question of belief in life," using as his departure point the biblical story of Job. How was it possible, he asked the congregation, to "believe in the justice of

God in a world in which the innocent perish in vast and meaningless massacres, and brutal and dishonest men foul all the lovely things?" But the sermon didn't say all he wanted it to say, and in 1957 he began to turn the material into a verse play that was published in 1958.

J.B., as the play was called, begins in a circus tent where two unemployed actors, Mr. Zuss and Nickles, take on the respective roles of God and Satan. Nickles offers Zuss the same wager his counterpart offered God in the Bible: that when misfortune visits a man whom God has blessed with wealth and happiness, he will lose his faith, will turn on God and curse him. MacLeish's Job, or J.B., is a rich and successful New England businessman with a loving, beautiful wife and five children, but his charmed life is ended by Zuss and Nickles's wager: a son is killed in a military accident; another son and daughter are victims of a fatal car crash; another daughter is murdered; the youngest daughter dies in an atomic bombing; J.B.'s bank is destroyed and his fortune lost; and he is plagued with boils that cover his body.

Although the afflictions are different in number and in kind, in effect they mirror what Archie MacLeish saw happen to his friends Gerald and Sara Murphy: the loss of their children, their way of life, and, in Archie's view, their fortune. As he said later to an interviewer, to him the Murphys "had never been 'rich' by American standards but they had always spent money as though they were, having a blithe contempt for money as such — a healthy conviction that money should be used for the purposes of life, the living of life, the defeat of illness and death. One has to pay for faith like that and Gerald and Sara paid without a whimper."

Years before, on one of his ocean crossings, Gerald Murphy had copied out six pages of verses from the Book of Job, line after line of beautiful, agonizing poetry. All alone on top of one page is this verse: "Then said his wife unto him: Dost thou still retain thy integrity? Curse God and die." That, of course, was what Sara herself had done on the day, more than twenty years ago now, when she had rushed out of St. Bartholomew's Church with Archie at her side and had shaken her fist at heaven. And Archie had never forgotten it. In the Bible, Job's wife has no name, and after this one expostulation, she is silent and unmentioned. So in MacLeish's play, as he himself admitted, the character had to be "an almost total invention."

MacLeish made her beautiful, and not only beautiful but famous, in the way great beauties of the Edwardian era were famous: "Pretty," is how one of the characters, a Mrs. Lesure, describes her, to which another, Mrs. Botticelli responds, "Ain't she. / Looks like somebody I've seen." But another character, Mrs. Adams, clarifies: "I don't believe you could have seen her. / Her picture possibly. Her picture was published" — just as Sara Wiborg's picture was published, over and over, in the rotogravure and on the cover of *Town and Country*. When MacLeish came to give Job's wife a name, it was almost inevitable that he called her Sarah. "There is no such name in the *Book of Job*" — even though, as he admitted later, "She is never called Sarah."

MacLeish had had the parallels between Job's miseries and the Murphys' misfortunes in mind ever since Patrick Murphy's death — reminiscing about it later he compared the silences at the boy's memorial service to "the confrontation with the Voice out of the Whirlwind in the Book of Job." But his feelings had been essentially private. Now, however, they became undeniably public: for in addition to the published text of the play, which appeared in March 1958, the Yale School of Drama put on *J.B.* in April for a limited run of six performances. Surprisingly, even though Yale was still a decade away from the quasi-professional hothouse it later became, these performances were reviewed by the *New York Times*'s drama critic, Brooks Atkinson. And Atkinson's rave, which called *J.B.* "the fable of our time in verse that has the pulse and beat of modern living," attracted the attention of the producer Alfred de Liagre, Jr., who enlisted the director Elia Kazan to bring the play to Broadway.

J.B. opened at Broadway's ANTA Theater on December 11 during a newspaper strike that, it was feared, would sink the play in oblivion; as it turned out, it was a sensation, with newspaper reviewers taking to the airwaves to proclaim it "brilliant," "the best play of this, or, perhaps, many seasons," "one of the memorable works of the century." There was a line around the block for tickets the day after the opening, and the play ran for a year (a healthy life span in those pre-*Cats* days); it won a Tony Award for best play, and it gave Archie MacLeish his third Pulitzer Prize.

Gerald and Sara didn't attend the opening of *J.B.* that December; in fact they didn't see the play until the following spring, when they took Dawn Powell with them to a performance on March 18. Powell's reaction was derisive: "If Hamlet was your Omelette, this is your Jambalaya," she wrote to Edmund Wilson (the pun was on his long-ago review of Archie's *The Hamlet of A. MacLeish*, a review which bore the title "The Omelette of A. MacLeish"). Possibly predictably for someone whose ironic fiction was at such distance from her painful life, she thought the play pompous, facile, a trivialization of tragic possibilities. What Gerald and Sara thought is harder to discern. "Gerald said he feared Archie was now going to be King of Broadway, and was in fact on the sands of Antigua right this minute with Kazan cooking up another big cookie," Powell told Wilson. Making allowances for Gerald's frequent reflexive irony, this comment still has the sound of hurt and bitterness in it. If Gerald and Sara had been upset by the use Scott Fitzgerald made of them in *Tender Is the Night* (at least he dedicated the book to them in gratitude), what can they have thought of MacLeish's presentation of their private agony?

For at the climax of the play is an important departure from the biblical story that may have said more than either Gerald or Sara would have wanted known about the toll that tragedy had taken on their marriage. In the Bible, Job's nameless wife makes no further appearance after she cries out, "Curse God and die!" Presumably she suffers on at Job's side so she can bear him the seven sons and three daughters who bless his life at the end of the story. But Sarah in the play is so outraged and bereaved by what has happened to her family and by what she sees as J.B.'s passivity in the face of suffering that she leaves her husband. Sara hadn't left Gerald in 1936 — to use one of her own expressions, it would have been *unlike* her to do so. But William MacLeish says that in the years after Patrick's death "Gerald was going into himself, and no one was there for Sadie. They were moving in opposite directions. They had a very, very bad patch there." For Sara and for Gerald — who once cautioned Honoria, when she was speculating about the marriage of a couple they knew, "You can never know what goes on between two people" — this twist in the plot of *J.B.* must have been both painful and invasive.

In the play's final moments, however, J.B.'s wife returns to him, and the speech Archie wrote for her has the ring of the old songs Gerald and Sara used to sing:

> Blow on the coal of the heart.
> The candles in the churches are out.

The lights have gone out in the sky.
Blow on the coal of the heart
And we'll see by and by . . .
We'll see where we are.
We'll know. We'll know.

"Wait till the clouds roll by, Sally," Gerald had written to her when they were secretly engaged — *wait till the sun shines, Nelly, by and by*. Archie may have given this speech to Sarah/Sara, but it was she and Gerald who had given him the answer to his question, "the question of belief in life." Whatever they thought of *J.B.* as they sat in the darkness of Row C on that March day, they must have understood that.

In the fall of 1958 Richard Myers died, and at his funeral Archie MacLeish "sat between Gerald and Sara," as he wrote to Ernest Hemingway,

> whom haven't seen for maybe two years, Gerald having written me off. And for good reason. Didn't behave well. Numerous occasions, as you know, I haven't. Anyway I felt very sad and far off somehow sitting between them with no relationship anymore except of Sarah's warmth and generosity and thinking about the years when I knew Dick and everything off at the back of those years. The only friends you make really are the ones you make when you are young — or so, anyway, of my life — and you keep them but don't keep them. I mean they are always anyway your friends because they once were but only in memory. When you see them again you go back there where they were.

Archie and Ada and Gerald and Sara *did* go back there: Myers's death, and the passage of time, made them conscious of how precious their continuing friendship was to each of them. Acknowledging that he had felt "that nuisance — one's amour propre raising its head," and heard "the low whine of hurt feelings," Gerald told Archie that nonetheless "I cannot see life — either past or future — without in it an enduring affection for you and Ada."

Hemingway, however, didn't seem to have such feelings for his old friends the Murphys — or at least not for Gerald. He had kept in touch with their news since the war, and sent messages to Sara through intermediaries like

MacLeish and Dos Passos, but he was personally unreachable. "I always loved to watch Gerald like a snake is fascinated by a brilliant young Gopher," he told Dawn Powell, "and I loved Honoria and the dead kids. Sara I [c]an't even kid about." The passage of time hadn't changed things: "Poor Sara and Gerald," he wrote to MacLeish after Dick Myers's funeral, "let's not write about it. I loved Sara and I never could stand Gerald but I did." When he was involved in two separate plane crashes on safari in Africa in 1954 some newspapers erroneously reported him dead, and Archie MacLeish, for one, worried that Sara might have "heard of his death before she heard of his undeath." Ultimately she found out the truth, but not because he bothered to enlighten her.

The 1950 publication of Arthur Mizener's biography of Scott Fitzgerald, *The Far Side of Paradise*, set off a revival of interest in the literature and culture of the 1920s, which focused not only on the familiar players of the time, but also on those, like Gerald and Sara Murphy, whose role was subtler and less known. Gerald seemed rather to enjoy his new role of twenties raconteur, telling Dawn Powell, who had just read Mizener's book, about how he and Sara had visited Edith Wharton, or entertained Rudolph Valentino. Sara seemed less comfortable, more private, about such anecdotes: "I don't consider the story worth repeating," she said once, interrupting Gerald's description of what really happened when Scott Fitzgerald disrupted one of their parties. "Scott was always throwing ripe figs at people."

One person who did feel the story worth repeating was a Sneden's Landing neighbor, Calvin Tomkins, who made the Murphys' acquaintance when his two young daughters marched up to the door of Cheer Hall and introduced themselves. The Murphys were entranced with these gregarious children and soon counted them and their parents as friends; in fact, they adopted them, as they had adopted the Hemingways and the Fitzgeralds and others. Their empathy and concern for their new young friends was total — and when the Tomkinses decided to separate some time later, "they were a great source of comfort and strength for both of us," Tomkins remembers. Tomkins, for his part, was smitten with Sara — "I'd never met an older woman, as she seemed to me at the time, who was so *attractive*" — and mesmerized by Gerald's stories. He wanted Gerald to write his own book about his Paris years, but

Gerald demurred. "I have too much respect for the craft of writing to take it up as a second-rate practitioner," he said.

But Tomkins wouldn't give up. Eventually it was proposed that *he* tell the Murphys' story of their part in the flowering of what was increasingly called the Lost Generation; armed with a reel-to-reel tape recorder and a notebook he would sit by the Murphys' fireplace while the pugs, Edward and Wookie, snored on the hearth rug and Gerald and Sara talked about the past. Sara's contralto drawl was by now husky from too many cigarettes, but Gerald's tenor still had the bright barking sound of a particularly well bred seal, and the two of them seemed to luxuriate in memories they had suppressed for far too long. By tacit unspoken agreement, however, two subjects remained essentially out-of-bounds — the boys' deaths and Gerald's pictures.

Not that these were hidden from view; they just weren't discussed. Everyone knew about Baoth and Patrick, but no one talked about them. And similarly, most people knew, if they cared to ask, that Gerald had painted in the 1920s. But the news often came as a surprise: John Hemingway, for one, had been "absolutely shocked" by it ("he didn't seem the type"), and Jane Pickman, who said she "thought I knew Gerald well as a person . . . never knew he had painted. He never talked about it." And of course he had left all his pictures except for *Watch* and *Wasp and Pear* in France. After the war's end he had asked Vladimir Orloff to gather them together and ship them to America via Archie MacLeish, who was in Paris on UNESCO business; but the arrangements got bungled and eventually it was Alice Lee Myers who retrieved the paintings from UNESCO and brought them over in September 1947. There were, as it turned out, only four canvases: the enormous *Boatdeck* was supposedly still in Paris at the warehouse where it had been since the twenties; *Portrait* had been given as a gift to Vladimir and so was not among the paintings shipped; and *Turbines, Pression,* and *Roulement à Billes* — not to mention the forgotten *Laboratoire* — were nowhere to be found. Gerald seemed not to care: of the paintings that did arrive, only two were framed and hung, and they were consigned to the guest suite at Sneden's Landing (one in the bathroom). The other two canvases were rolled up and put in the attic.

And there they might have stayed had not a writer named Rudi Blesh learned about Gerald's work and decided to include a discussion of it in his book *Modern Art USA*. "A series of semi-abstract canvases . . . complex in design . . . meticulous in craft, and . . . heroic in size" was how Blesh characterized them. Although he saw resemblances to the work of American painters like Demuth and Sheeler and "the French purists Ozenfant and Jeanneret," Blesh considered that the Murphy paintings "strike an original note of their own, particularly in their complex design and in their wit." Blesh's comments — his book was published in 1956 — attracted the interest of Douglas Mac-Agy, then curator of the Dallas Museum for Contemporary Arts, who was planning a show on neglected American artists of the twentieth century. Would Gerald agree to exhibit some of his paintings in Dallas? Somewhat surprisingly, Gerald said yes.

According to family legend, Gerald announced this development at the luncheon table with a flourish: "I've been discovered," he is supposed to have said. "*What* does one wear?" Calvin Tomkins, who was then a nearly constant presence in the Murphys' house, felt this was less delighted swaggering than "ironic distance." Or perhaps it was a disguise, like the apache clothes or the fisherman's jersey, a way of hiding what was really important. When Blesh had asked Gerald about his exhibition history he told him that he had a one-man show at Bernheim Jeune in 1935, a statement that was doubly misleading because the gallery had been *Georges* Bernheim (a much more "modern" dealer) and the date had been 1929. But he wasn't indulging in conscious misrepresentation, nor making a postdadaist spoof of artistic grandiosity, as later critics suggested. This was something much more poignant. Gerald had been denying his artist self for so long that he had forgotten the details. He was even unable, when asked, to supply correct titles and dates for the paintings, or to recollect all of them. The Salon des Indépendents *Turbines* of 1924, for instance, and the 1926 *Laboratoire* simply slipped from his memory. Faced with these inevitable lacunae, he covered up with bravura and fake self-assurance.

In preparation for the Dallas exhibit, the paintings in the attic were taken out, unrolled, and framed, and Gerald made an effort to recover the paintings he knew he had left behind in France: *Boatdeck*, which had been stored at the artists' supplier Lefebvre-Foinet in Paris, and the self-abstraction *Portrait*. To his and Sara's dismay, neither could be found. Perhaps it was naive to expect that *Boatdeck* could have made it through the war unscathed in Paris; but the disappearance of *Portrait* was hard to fathom. Vladimir Orloff maintained that it had been destroyed when his hut in the hills was bombed during the war — but there were no bombardments on that part of the coast. It appeared that Vladimir was being less than truthful, and that hurt. Had he sold the painting, or bartered it during the war for food or fuel? Had he simply mislaid it? Resignedly, Gerald told Tomkins, "There's nothing more to be done."

MacAgy's show, "American Genius in Review," opened in May 1960, and included — alongside work by four other artists, Tom Benrimo, John Covert, Morgan Russell, and Morton Schamberg — five canvases by Gerald Murphy: *Watch, Razor, Wasp and Pear, Doves,* and *Cocktail. (Bibliothèque,* rolled up in a corner of the attic, wasn't even discovered until later.) The exhibit was warmly received, and Gerald was so grateful to have his work treated seriously at long last that he donated two of the pictures, *Watch* and *Razor,* to the Dallas Museum for Contemporary Arts. He was even more gratified by MacAgy's determination, which predated the exhibition itself, to write a long critical appraisal of his *oeuvre* for the journal *Art in America.*

This necessitated a series of exchanges between the two men about Gerald's creative life in the 1920s — exchanges in which, for the first time in years, Gerald allowed himself to revisit his apprenticeship with Natalia Goncharova, his artistic method, and his aims and aesthetic. At the same time he and Sara were also recollecting, for Calvin Tomkins, their lives in Paris and Antibes and their friendships with Picasso and Léger, Fitzgerald and Hemingway. It was as if they had each turned a corner and suddenly come upon their old selves; and if they couldn't or didn't wish to *be* those old selves, at least they now accepted them. Gerald even considered, very cautiously and diffidently, whether it might be possible to pick up a brush once more: "O to be young again!" he told Tomkins, surveying the very American art being produced by Rauschenberg and Rosenquist. "And yet Ucello, a mathematician, started painting at 60!" He knew that Ucello had *given up* painting for mathematics, "but returned to painting after a long lapse." Why couldn't he do the same? Possibly he was toying with this idea when he took his young grandson, Sherman Donnelly, down to his ground-floor workroom at Sneden's Landing to show him how he'd painted the cigar box label in *Cocktail,* which hung on the wall. Pointing out the label's tiny train to the boy, he told him how hard it had been to get the smokestack right: "he had to keep scraping off that plume of smoke and painting it again, but he said the beauty of oil paint was that you could keep doing that, over and over, until you had it the way you wanted."

The following spring Gerald and Sara had news of Picasso, whom neither had seen since Sara's nonencounter with him at the Brasserie Lipp in Paris before the war. Reinventing himself, as he often did, with a new woman, he had married Jacqueline Roque, his companion of the past few years, in March. Sara had a sudden impulse to write to him in congratulation. Her letter, though, has more of the ring of an elegy. "One remembers so well," she mused — in French, with its useful impersonal pronoun —

(and one is sure you remember also) the beautiful days we all had together back then at Antibes — on the beach at La Garoupe and also at the Hotel du Cap — with your wife, your mother (such a dear), and Paullo — Some people even think you and we, and our three children, started the summer season in the Midi! Alas, we lost our two sons, to our great sorrow — . . . How life changes!

Please accept all our fondest memories, and *all* our wishes for happiness, and long life, and just being happy — which you deserve.

The next year, a mutual acquaintance was traveling through Paris and stopped to give Picasso the Murphys' regards. "Tell Sara and Gerald that I am well," Picasso said, "but that I'm a millionaire and I'm all alone."

In September 1960 *Life* magazine published a two-part article by Ernest Hemingway, "The Dangerous Summer," his chronicle of the bullfighting duel between the matadors Antonio Ordóñez and Luis Miguel Dominguín — the latter the uncrowned king of Spanish bullfighters, the former the young prince vying to take the elder's place. Gerald thought the piece "stunning." It brought back with unexpected force his memories of his own dangerous summer with Ernest, in Pamplona in 1926. Hemingway had not been well recently: the injuries he had sustained in the two African plane crashes, along with the effects of too much alcohol and hard living, had resulted in headaches, kidney trouble, high blood pressure, mood swings, and depression. In addition he had begun to suffer from paranoid delusions that he was on the brink of financial ruin or that unidentified agents were out to kill him. Arriving in New York from Spain that autumn he went into seclusion at the apartment Mary Hemingway had taken there; he saw no one — certainly not the Murphys — and refused even to go out. By the end of November, when a return to his beloved ranch in Ketchum, Idaho, had done no good, he was hospitalized for a complete workup — and, finally, a course of electroshock therapy — at the Mayo Clinic in Rochester, Minnesota, where Gerald Murphy had brought Fred so many years ago.

Inevitably the news got into the papers, although they merely repeated the official story, that Hemingway was being treated for high blood pressure. Sara, with her infallible instinct for the bogus, and her laserlike attentiveness to those she loved, sensed something was really wrong.

Dear Ernest, —

We read — too often, in the papers — about your being in the Mayo Clinic, — mentioning various ailments, and please write me a card, saying it *isn't* so, — or at least that you are all recovered — It isn't in character for you to be ill — I want to picture you — as always — as a burly bearded young man — with a gun or on a boat — Just a line, please — I always remember old times with the *greatest* pleasure — and that you were helpful to me at a time when I certainly *needed* it.

Ten days after she wrote this, Ernest Hemingway crept downstairs at dawn to the gunroom in Ketchum, took his old double-barreled shotgun, and blew himself into oblivion.

When she heard the news, Sara was devastated. It wasn't just the loss, so terrible and final, of someone she loved. It was his failure to keep faith with her creed that "If you just won't admit a thing it doesn't exist (as much)," that even "rebelling, dragging one's feet & fighting every inch of the way, one must admit one can't *control* it — one has to *take* it." His action was a rebuke to her, a refutation of all she had lived by. "Sara is repairing slowly," said Gerald to Calvin Tomkins, "but it's been a wretched business. Ernest's death affected her deeply. . . . He always warned us he would terminate any such situation. Possibly one has the right. I don't know. But what happens to 'grace under pressure?'" Grace under pressure — that elusive quality that Ernest had described in him on the slopes at Schruns and in the ring at Pamplona — was what Hemingway had most admired about him, and most despised. In the end, somehow, it marked the sad difference between them.

In July 1962 *The New Yorker* published Calvin Tomkins's profile of the two of them, entitled "Living Well Is the Best Revenge." Although the piece eloquently evoked the life they had made in Paris and Antibes in the twenties, and portrayed them with affection and sensitivity, neither Gerald nor Sara felt entirely easy about it. Sara disliked the feeling of being transformed into a kind of secondary celebrity, someone famous for knowing famous people. And Gerald objected to the title. For one thing, the "living well" part of it sounded frivolous, as if he were a Lucius Beebe–like *bon vivant*; for another, he claimed, he had never wanted to have revenge on anyone, for anything. He had in fact mentioned the phrase to Tomkins himself, claiming it was a Spanish proverb, which may have been a typical Murphy improvisation to cover a lapse of memory. For although it sounds like one of Patrick Murphy's *bon mots* for a Mark Cross ad, the saying comes from a miscellany compiled by that wisest and most tender of the English metaphysical poets, George Herbert — a miscellany whose first entry reads: "Man Proposeth, God disposeth."

Earlier that year a film version of *Tender Is the Night* had appeared, starring Jason Robards as Dick Diver, Jennifer Jones as Nicole, and Joan Fontaine as Nicole's sister, Baby Warren. The reviews of the film (most of them negative) revived Sara's feelings of outrage about the book — "so *shallow*," she had complained to Calvin Tomkins — and she refused to go see it. So Gerald went alone, to the little movie theater in Nyack. He was the only person in the audience, an experience which, he told Tomkins, "was oddly appropriate somehow to the unreality of the film." For two hours he sat alone in the dark, watching scenes he had lived being reenacted, sometimes clumsily, by people who bore not the slightest resemblance to the people who had lived them. Increasingly, he must have felt, he and Sara were like ghosts at the feast.

That autumn they had received news that Esther Murphy had died in Paris. She and Gerald had been on cordial if not intimate terms: intimacy, in their family, had always been something to be avoided at all costs, and matters were complicated by Esther's personal life. There were the two unhappy marriages — Gerald had paid for her divorce, in France, from Chester Arthur, an expensive and complicated proposition — and the relationships with Natalie Barney, Muriel Draper, Mercedes de Acosta, and Sybille Bedford. For Gerald, who had carefully hidden, even from himself, any ghost of sexual ambiguity, her behavior was a rebuke. Then there was her rather manic, unfulfilled brilliance, so uncomfortably similar to, and yet vastly different from, his own unfulfilled painting career: the book, written out in longhand, on Madame de Maintenon, which she never even attempted to have published, although she knew more than anyone in the world about Louis XIV's famous mistress; the other book, unwritten so far as anyone knew, on her friend Edith Wharton. There were her embarrassing personal habits, about which she remained cheerfully unembarrassed — wetting the bed at night (Sara always made up the guest room with rubber sheets for her), relieving herself, in fact, wherever she happened to be, because it was too much trouble to stop talking long enough to find the bathroom.

She had been in straitened financial circumstances for some time, despite the income from a trust left by her mother and various loans and gifts from Gerald; and she frequently had to ask him for money. "I am sorry to be just another middle aged failure," she had told him, pitifully, in one such request. Lamenting that "our relationship has ever been plagued by the question of money," Gerald nonetheless always tried to help, though he insisted that money paid to Esther should come out of *his* funds, not Sara's. Her death — alone, far from her family — filled him with regret. As he told Dawn Powell: "It was my irreparable loss not to have been able for reasons of difference in age, location, interests, friends . . . to share more in her life. As a proud older brother — proud of her — I urged her too much to write. She was no doubt not meant to, — but to share brilliantly with others the workings of her mind. I think she took satisfaction in this. I hope so."

When her ashes were shipped home from France for burial, Gerald paid her the best tribute he could think of, which was to design her memorial stone himself, and to have her laid to rest in the East Hampton churchyard next to Baoth and Patrick.

In that bleak winter when Patrick died, Scott Fitzgerald had tried to comfort Sara and Gerald with his vision of "another generation growing up around Honoria and an eventual peace somewhere, an occasional port of call as we all sail deathward." With mortality in the air again, the Murphys found enormous satisfaction in their grandchildren, John, Sherman, and Laura Sara, who had been born in 1954, as well as in the grandchildren of friends like the MacLeishes and Myerses. Sara's relationship with them was serene and comforting, Gerald's more stimulating: he made up games and virgin varieties of the house cocktail; and he opened their eyes and ears to new things. It was Gerald who, in the early autumn of 1963, called his grandchildren into the living room to show them a record album called "Meet the Beatles" — "grandchildren," he said, "pay attention. These young men are going to be very, very important." It was Gerald who read them books by Edward Gorey, Gerald who taught them to swim beyond the treacherous East Hampton breakers, Gerald who told his granddaughter — as she watched him shaving in the morning — never to brush her teeth with her eyes open because it was vain.

Sometimes the games he concocted for them had an edge: on summer nights in East Hampton, Gerald would take the young ones for rides in his black 1955 Pontiac with the searchlight on the roof, telling them ghost stories while they shrieked with laughter and protested that he couldn't scare *them*; then he would let them out by the side of the road and drive off. The children, who were dressed in their nightclothes, would laugh, then pretend to be bored, then begin to wonder where he was — and just as they were on the point of actual terror he would reappear as if by magic and they would all pile into the car again, claiming they *knew* he'd been fooling them.

Usually the entertainments were more benign; if there were no treasure expeditions to deserted beaches, like the one Gerald and Sara had organized so long ago in Antibes, there were picnics on the beach at East Hampton, which Gerald would rake "like a Japanese garden," says a grandson, or Easter egg hunts at Sneden's Landing. "Dow was in charge," remembers William MacLeish of one such party, "and he did everything" — he even made a garland of flowers, like the ones Honoria had worn as a child, for Laura Donnelly to wear in her hair. At the end of the party, when the young

MacLeishes were taking their leave, he saluted them by going down on one knee, like a medieval courtier, "his arm out — like that — with that wonderful Mick face." Says MacLeish now: "and I thought, Ah, Jesus, Murphy, I love you. God, what a man."

That Easter party was one of the last the Murphys gave at Cheer Hall; in the spring of 1963 they had decided to sell it. Gerald, who had stayed on as president of Mark Cross after the 1948 sale to the Drake America Corporation, had felt increasingly uncomfortable running somebody else's business, and in 1955 he had decided to retire. So he lost his $35,000 a year salary, and the burden of carrying the mortgage on Cheer Hall was, under the circumstances, considerable. Sara found the house gloomy in the summer, too many shade trees, not enough sun, and they had both felt it had been "a little too much for the past year — slippery road, remoteness, little or no help, etc." She added, in a letter to John and Betty Dos Passos, "We have always believed it good to leave a place before it leaves you."

In this case they left it with a farewell fireworks display: two parties for Gerald's seventy-fifth birthday; in June, a farewell dinner for the Dos Passoses, their little daughter, Lucy, and the Lowndses; and a lunch party for Edmund Wilson, long a friend of Esther's, intermittently a friend of Gerald's and Sara's, and Scott Fitzgerald's mentor and informal literary executor. Dawn Powell, a particular favorite of Wilson's, was invited as well, to provide "bufferage," and someone — Powell? Elena Wilson? — made a caricature drawing to celebrate the occasion. Entitled "Great White Father and friend approach Sneden's Landing," it depicts a square-faced, strong-jawed, scowling bald man (Wilson) and a little henlike woman with bangs and a feathered hat (Powell) crossing the Hudson in a rowboat with an American flag on its stern, like Washington crossing the Delaware in Gerald's least favorite picture.

The menu (inscribed, Wilson noticed, on little porcelain tablets put before each place) was a throwback to another era:

pâté et biscuits
poisson
selle d'agneau

pommes de terre Paillason
purée de petits pois
brioche avec fraises en sirop, crème Chantilly
fromage de Brie

In addition, there were "lots of *vins et liqueurs*," reported Sara proudly to Honoria. Unsure of whether they still had the ability to bring off such an occasion, they had hired a chef for the day to help with the cooking. Wilson was suitably impressed — "an incredible meal," was how he described it — but Gerald worried that they had perhaps gone a bit over the top. "We've never done it before," he reassured Powell anxiously: "and not knowing the W's really well we didn't want them to come all that distance for just-steak-and-a-baked-potato. . . . Tell them the whole thing was a 'HOMMAGES A M. ET MME. BONNIE VILSON.' All through it I kept thinking of the inordinate pleasure I'd had in all the years I was reading his books — all of them. And that's from the heart."

26

"Only half a person without you"

ALTHOUGH BOTH Gerald and Sara merrily claimed that leaving Cheer Hall made them feel "much more irresponsible than we did when we married in our late twenties," they felt some ambivalence as well. Gerald joked darkly that he and Sara might just drown themselves in the Hudson so that, like Tennyson's Lady of Shalott, their bodies could be borne downstream to New York on a funeral barge. At least that way they'd avoid clearing out the attics where, he said, "I feel sure I'll come across the skeletons of our two former selves."

Indeed there were skeletons aplenty: letters from Scott Fitzgerald and Ernest Hemingway and Katy Dos Passos; Gerald's painting of the objects in his father's library, *Bibliothèque*; table linens from Villa America; and cartons of photographs, which after 1929 Sara had not bothered to paste into albums. Exhuming them, and disposing of them — this piece of furniture to Honoria in McLean, Virginia, that box of photographs to East Hampton — seemed to bring a kind of conclusion. "Every once in a while," Gerald told Archie MacLeish, "we pull out a drawer and go through our memories of things we did together — we four. What an age of innocence it was, and how beautiful and free!"

Gerald and Sara planned to spend the summer before the move in East Hampton, where they were building a modest house — the first they had ever had constructed to their own specifications. La Petite Hutte stood just behind the dunes on the old Wiborg property, next to the pink stucco garage and chauffeur's quarters that the Murphys had been using after the sale of Swan Cove and Hook Pond in the 1950s. It was a low building that nestled protectively into its site, and its only extravagant feature was the spacious living room, with its cathedral ceiling, which overlooked the Atlantic; on the other side of the house the view, which could have been painted by Constable, extended over what had been the Wiborgs' fields to Hook Pond, and beyond to the treetops and steeple that marked East Hampton Village.

While they were still in East Hampton, Gerald had sobering news: his doctor, William Abel, discovered a cancerous tumor in his intestinal tract, which was removed by an operation in August. Gerald was more worried for Sara than anything else; but she and Honoria were both relieved when the operation seemed to be successful and he returned to East Hampton to recuperate. What they didn't know, but Gerald did, was that the surgery was merely "palliative." It had been undertaken simply to make him more comfortable, and it was only a matter of time before the cancer would recur, and with it, a lessened chance of survival.

He didn't tell Sara. Together they had heard hopeless news from doctors too many times for him to inflict more on her now. While he was in the hospital, Sara had written to him from East Hampton, as she had so often done in the days before their marriage when they were separated for a few days. It was a love letter, as those old ones had been, but distilled now to its essence:

> Dearest Gerald —
>
> Here I am "at home" — "without you," — and it is no longer a home, just a place to live — You *must know* that without you — *nothing* makes any sense — I am only half a person, — and you are the other half — it is *so*, however I may try — and always will be — *Please please* get well soon — and come back to me.
>
> With love — all I *have* —
> Sara

So he went home to East Hampton and spent the Indian summer days "sitting in the sun and gazing out over the Ocean to a featureless horizon" until he had "mended to the doctors' satisfaction," as he wrote Archie MacLeish. The phrase was an old one — he had noticed that same "featureless horizon" in Texas when he was stationed there in the First World War. Archie picked up on it at once.

Featureless horizon — yes. That is precisely what one sees from the unin-habited bare hills old men climb to, though only you would think of the just word. But the point is — or at least I think the point is — the horizon, not the featurelessness. When one expects to go on "forever" as one does in one's youth or even middle age, horizons are merely limits, not yet ends. It is when one first sees the horizon as an end that one first begins to *see*. And it is then that the featurelessness, which one would not have noticed, or would have taken for granted, before, becomes the feature. . . . So that this featureless sky is as far as it is possible to be from negation. It is affirmation. It says the world is possible to man because to man there are horizons, there are beginnings and ends, there are things known and things unknown.

Gerald's strength returned, and he and Sara finished clearing out Cheer Hall by November; then they went to Washington to spend the winter at the Fairfax Hotel, where they could help Honoria and William Donnelly settle in to their new house in McLean and visit with Ellen Barry, in Georgetown, and Scottie Fitzgerald, now married to a lawyer, Samuel Lanahan, and living near Honoria. Scottie (Sara reported to Dawn Powell) even gave a party for the Murphys, with "dinner and dancing, no less," that was written up in the gossip column of the *Washington Star* — the potent magic of Murphys and Fitzger-alds still had drawing power. To Sara, however — and to some of the gentle-men guests — the highlight of the party was a young woman wearing "one of the NEW Paris dresses, cut down to the waist *in front* — There *was* nothing there to hide, however — which makes it worse."

That spring of 1964 was a beautiful one, full of fair weather and promise — paradoxically so, Gerald thought, when all of a sudden he felt age (and death) creeping up on him "in the night or when one is off one's guard." Early in the year Washington's Corcoran Gallery of Art offered to mount a one-man show of his work, but although he had welcomed previous exhibitions in Dallas and San Francisco, Gerald seemed suddenly weary of the limelight, and turned the Corcoran down. "All of that is as if in a sealed chamber of the past and has somehow become unreal," he explained. "Je n'en peux plus. Trop tard." ("I can't do any more. Too late.")

In April, back in East Hampton, Sara learned that Hoytie had died in Paris, and the news upset her terribly. Not that she grieved for her sister — it was too late for that, too — but she realized that Hoytie "had been the only enemy she had ever had," said Gerald. The memory hurt still. But there was worse to come: in May, Sara and Gerald received the equivalent of a poison-pen letter sealed years ago in a bottle that had only just then washed up on the beach.

The "letter" was Ernest Hemingway's memoir of his early years in Paris, *A Moveable Feast*, which he had been working on in the late 1950s and had completed in 1960 shortly before his death. Although ostensibly a nostalgic reminiscence of "how Paris was in the old days when we were very poor and very happy," it was also the vehicle through which Hemingway, suffering through increasing depression, tried to rewrite the past and avoid self-recrimination for any of the wrong turnings his life had taken, to create for himself what one biographer has called "a life without consequences." How else can one explain his vicious treatment of people who had helped him when he most needed help, people like Gertrude Stein, Scott and Zelda Fitzgerald, Ford Madox Ford, John Dos Passos, and most spectacularly Gerald and Sara Murphy? Fitzgerald he was jealous of; Zelda he knew had distrusted him; and Dos Passos he had never forgiven for portraying him, thinly disguised, in his novel *Chosen Country*, as an "Indian-like boy with dirty fingernails" who runs off to join the Marines, a description Dos had clearly gleaned from Katy's memories of her childhood friend Ernie. He had already called Dos a "one-eyed Portuguese bastard" — a slur made worse by the fact that each word in it was true — and in 1957, when he was writing *A Moveable Feast*, he must have felt he still had a score to settle. But what score was he settling with Gerald and Sara?

Here is what he says about them:

The rich have a sort of pilot fish [Dos Passos] . . . who talks like this: ". . . I like them both. Yes, by God, Hem; I do like them. I see what you mean but I do like them truly and there's something damned fine about her . . . You'll like him (using his baby-talk nickname) when you know him. . . ."

Then you have the rich and nothing is ever as it was again. . . .

Hemingway blamed them for his own transgressions: it was the rich, he implied, who were responsible, by association, for his attraction to Pauline Pfeiffer ("another rich"), and who thereby corrupted his marriage to Hadley. And they did worse: "Under the charm of these rich I was as trusting and stupid as a bird dog. . . . I even read aloud a part of the novel I had rewritten, which is about as low as a writer can get . . . When they said, 'It's great, Ernest. Truly it's great. You cannot know the thing it has,' I wagged my tail in pleasure and plunged into the fiesta concept of life . . . instead of thinking, 'If these bastards like it what is wrong with it?'"

There was no way Gerald, or Sara, could have read these passages and not remembered Ernest reading *The Sun Also Rises* to them by the tile stove in Schruns, or heard the dim echo of their own voices, telling Ernest he had written a book so magnificent it was "hitched to the universe." Nor was there any way to avoid seeing *A Moveable Feast* stacked in bookstore windows and splashed across the front pages of book reviews. "I am — contre coeur [against my will] — in Ernest's book," wrote Gerald to Archie MacLeish in May. "What a strange kind of bitterness — or rather accusitoriness. . . . What shocking ethics! How well written, of course."

Sara's reaction went unmentioned. But it was during this spring that her memory began to fail: first for small things, like conversations she had just had, then for more significant ones, and possibly her forgetfulness shielded her from the effects of Ernest's posthumous vitriol. It was just as well that she never saw some of the passages that were deleted from the published text of the book: the one in which Hemingway referred to Gerald, not by name, of course, as someone who paints, but is not really a painter; or, worse, the one about "these rich" who "had backed me and encouraged me when I was doing wrong," which said that "They were bad luck to people but they were worse luck to themselves and they lived to have all their bad luck finally; and to the very worst end that all bad luck could go." Even posthumously and after the fact, it put Hoytie's curse to shame.

Shortly after *A Moveable Feast* appeared Gerald went into the hospital again; the cancer for which he had been operated on the previous summer had recurred, and this time there was no masking the consequences. Gerald was very firm with Dr. Abel: there were to be no heroic measures taken to prolong his life — it would end when his clock, his faulty *instrument de précision*, ran down. "I had so wanted to know and greet old age," he lamented to the MacLeishes; but instead he would try to cultivate Gerard Manley Hopkins's "'patience exquisite, which plumes to peace hereafter.'"

He spent the summer watching the sea or walking in the garden or sitting with Sara on the bench looking out over Hook Pond. When Dr. Abel called, as he did regularly, Gerald would proudly take him to see the roses, and then, still the perfect host, draw the doctor out about his work in Alsace or his travels in the tropics. Archie MacLeish had sent, at long last, a privately printed copy of the sermon he had given about Job to the Farmington Congregational Church; and during those summer months Gerald mulled over its contents. On the cover Archie had written:

> Dear Dow: I don't think I sent you this when I did it seven or eight years ago. Rereading it today I thought at once of you because you have said it all so much better. At bottom it is still a question of the love of life, isn't it? We will be down very soon
>
> love Archie

Gerald gracefully ignored the acknowledgment of his own gift to this old friend; instead he responded to the substance of the sermon itself. Recalling his own oppressive religious upbringing, and the "nightmare of bigotry" that the Catholic Church had made of "Sara's and my 'Mixed Marriage,'" he said that Archie's statement of faith "was like drinking from a pure source. I only wish it were not so late. I bless you for sending it. I heard every note of your clarion-call."

MacLeish had one last payback to make, however. Nearly twenty years previously, when he recited "The Windhover" aloud to Archie on that spring morning, Gerald had been trying to give him a renewed sense of himself as an artist; now Archie tried to do the same thing for him. The Museum of Modern Art had shown some interest in Gerald's painting, and MacLeish proposed to give them his picture *Wasp and Pear*, which he had exchanged years ago for *Watch*. Normally, such proposals take months, if not years, to be processed and accepted, but MacLeish wanted his friend to die "thinking of himself as a painter," and he persuaded the Modern's director, Alfred Barr, to make the acquisition official immediately. When Honoria told him the news Gerald was so weak that all he could do was smile, and say, "How wonderful."

On October 4 Sara wrote to Calvin Tomkins:

Dear Tad, —

I must write you — in all sadness, — Gerald is *very* ill, & the doctors have warned us that any day may be the last. . . . He simply sleeps waking only once in a while. . . . It is terrible to see him — once so strong — waste away. Honoria is with me most of the time — & we are doing our best — (whatever that is). . . .

Affectionately,
Sara

For almost two weeks more he drifted in and out of consciousness. On October 17, sensing the end was near, Honoria and William Donnelly asked if they could bring a Catholic priest, a former army chaplain, to give him last rites. They couldn't have known, and Gerald must have realized they couldn't have known, how bitterly he had expressed himself on the subject to Archie only the month before. "Get me the Army man," he said now; by then it hardly mattered, except to Honoria. Seeing her griefstricken face, and Sara's, hovering behind the priest, he smiled, muttered, "Smelling salts for the ladies," and slipped away forever.

"DEAREST SARA DEAREST SARA," went Dorothy Parker's telegram. It said everything. At Gerald's funeral, an elegantly brief service at the little Episcopal church on the green, "Sara was marvelous," reported Dawn Powell to John Dos Passos: "controlled & I believe relieved that Gerald did not have to go through any more of the unchic indignities and embarrassments of pain & dying." The funeral service was preceded by a gathering of friends at home and followed by "a small perfect Murphy party" with the bartender from the Maidstone Club mixing drinks and "four lovely local waitresses serving delicacies to about 20 or 25," including the MacLeishes, Powell, Fanny and Hank Brennan, Olga's son Stuyvesant Fish, Ellen Barry, and Calvin Tomkins, who was one of the pallbearers. (Among the absentees was Cole Porter, who had died two days before Gerald.) It was a perfect golden October afternoon, and as guests left for the long drive back up the island to New York or elsewhere, they stopped to kiss Sara good-bye. But instead of weeping, or pressing her hand, they said, "What a lovely party."

"It was," Dawn Powell said, "a lesson in courage disguised as *taste*."

After Gerald's death Sara carried on the way someone who has lost a limb carries on without it; she was not whole, but she functioned. Alone and increasingly frail, she took an apartment in New York at the Volney, a residential hotel on the Upper East Side where Dorothy Parker also lived, and the two of them kept an eye on each other. Parker's housekeeping had not improved over the years; she appeared to live on dust and drink, and Sara worried over her poor appetite. Dottie worried about Sara's "keepers," as she called the caregivers she relied on, and about her lapses of memory: "Don't go and see Sara," she told Lillian Hellman. "She won't know you."

Occasionally, though, Sara still showed her true steel. A year after Gerald's death she received a letter from an assistant to Mary Hemingway, telling of Mrs. Hemingway's intention to place Ernest's papers in the John F. Kennedy Library in Boston. "We know from the files," the letter said, "that Ernest corresponded with you and it would mean a great deal to have copies of those letters included in the Hemingway Collection." Sara, private as always, refused. "Dear Mrs. Hemingway," she wrote reprovingly, bypassing the nettlesome assistant: "Upon reflection, I do not think that Ernest would have liked a public exhibition of his letters to his friends. . . . [T]hey (the letters) are really personal & topical, & not necessarily interesting to the public view — I shall keep them for what they are: — amusing and affectionate letters from a good friend, who is gone."

Mary Hemingway couldn't accept defeat. She proposed to visit Sara personally at the Volney in the hopes of overriding her veto in person. But Sara, veteran of so many costume balls, had taken precautions: she sent her nurse-housekeeper, who normally dressed in street clothes, out to Bloomingdale's to get a nurse's uniform; she drew the blinds in her apartment, powdered her cheeks to produce a ghostly pallor, and lay down on a chaise longue. When Mary Hemingway arrived, she found an invalid, seemingly at death's door, whose "nurse" explained that Mrs. Murphy was resting, and mustn't be over-excited. Weakly, wordlessly, Sara waved away her visitor's entreaties. Mary Hemingway had no choice but to leave empty-handed, her breathing uneven and her face blotchy with fury.

Although Sara was more and more fragile and "stuck with rather unpleasant nurses . . . [who] *argue* every point until you are ready to drop," she still kept in touch with what remained of her and Gerald's extended "family." Ada and Archie MacLeish praised her "wonderful talking letters," and Dos Passos frequently called to see her when he was in New York. She read his 1966 memoir, *The Best Times*, with a mixture of delight and painful nostalgia. "It is such fun to read that I dread finishing it!!!" she wrote. "So I reward myself (when I've been a good girl, & often finished the Soup! —) I do wish I could *see you all.*" And she still went to East Hampton in the summers to sit by the sea she had always loved.

In 1974, partly at the urging of Archie MacLeish, the Museum of Modern Art mounted a retrospective exhibition of the work of Gerald Murphy. For the first time, all the extant canvases from Gerald's *anni mirabili* in France were reunited: the missing *Boatdeck, Portrait,* and *Engine Room/Pression* were represented by blown-up black-and-white photographs, and *Turbines* (MOMA called it *Pressure*), *Laboratoire,* and *Roulement à Billes,* for which no photos were available, were represented by plaques on the wall. The catalogue, by William Rubin, then curator of painting and sculpture at the museum and one of the world's foremost modern art historians, referred to Gerald as "a major American artist"; the *New York Times*'s John Russell, reviewing the exhibit, called it "a distinct contribution to the history of American painting"; and Hayden Herrera, writing in *Art in America,* said he was "an astonishingly original, witty and prophetic painter." The show earned for him what he had never had in his lifetime, not even when he had been "discovered" in Dallas in 1960 — crowds, admiring and influential reviews in both the scholarly and mainstream press, a real place at the table of American twentieth-century art.

Although Honoria stood in the receiving line at the exhibition opening, looking more and more like her mother, with the same slanting blue eyes and merry smile, Sara was not able to attend. That year she had become too frail and forgetful to be left on her own, and she had moved to Virginia to live with the Donnellys. By then her mind often wandered far afield, and she spent much of her time cutting out photographs from magazines and pasting them into scrapbooks. What the images meant to her, what she kept them for, no one knew. She had grown her hair long again, as it had been in her youth, and at night, preparing for bed, she would brush it out, to her granddaughter's delight, for minutes at a time, the way the beautiful Wiborg girls had done in the duchess of Rutland's boudoir at Belvoir.

When she caught pneumonia in the fall of 1975 it was clear that this would be the end. Like Baoth and Patrick and Gerald, she would go with her family around her. On October 9, Honoria was holding her mother's hand when Sara began to sing. "Here comes the bride," she quavered in her husky contralto — it was Wagner's wedding march from *Lohengrin*, which the musicians had played for her marriage to Gerald sixty years before. "She was going to Dowdow," Honoria said.

A week later her ashes were laid beside Gerald's — and Patrick's and Baoth's — in the South End Cemetery in East Hampton. It had been a long journey, from the New World to the Old and back again, from the nineteenth century to the twentieth — and neither of them would have undertaken it alone. Almost from the beginning their adventure had been a shared enterprise, a relationship that, as Gerald had hoped, let loose the imagination — for themselves and for those they loved. "Don't let's ever separate again," Sara had written to Gerald after they had been apart during World War I; now they wouldn't have to.

Author's Note and Acknowledgments

I met Gerald and Sara Murphy on a wintry afternoon when I was a little girl of (I think) eight or nine. My parents, who were friends of Honoria's, took me to tea at a maisonette that the Murphys had rented for a month or so in the East Fifties or Sixties. As childhood memories often are, this one is oddly disembodied: I remember books and firelight, tea in fragile little cups and cucumber sandwiches on a flowered plate, but I cannot summon up the house itself. I can hear the Murphys' voices, see their faces, but I have no recollection of what they were wearing or, curiously, how old they seemed to me.

I had brought my set of Chinese checkers with me as a hedge against the boredom of adult conversation, fully expecting to spend the afternoon playing a kind of invented solitaire by myself in a corner. But Gerald asked if he might join me and we sat by the window and played with great seriousness, the colored marbles making a satisfying *thunk* as we skipped them across the board. I don't remember who won. I was given extra sugar lumps with my tea, and Sara plied me with questions about my school (which she and Honoria had both attended), my activities, my friends, my opinion on interesting things to do in the city. I was made to feel as if I were the most fascinating person in the world.

When we left, Gerald gave me a keepsake: a little crocheted Moroccan cap, the sort Muslim boys wear on their shaved heads and which he himself wore as a protection against sunburn. I have it still, wrapped in tissue paper in my bureau drawer; sewn on the inside is a blue and white nametape that says "Gerald Murphy." *Tender Is the Night*'s Rosemary Hoyt, leaving the Divers' Villa Diana with the yellow evening bag that Nicole Diver has pressed on her because "I think things ought to belong to the people that like them," could not have felt more special than I with my crocheted cap on that winter afternoon.

Years later, when I came to read the novel that Scott Fitzgerald had dedicated "to Gerald and Sara — many fêtes," I was to remember that feeling, and to wonder whether it accounted for the way their names cropped up, again and again, in so many tales of the era in which they'd lived. What I discovered was inevitably more complex than that, and the truth was often hard to discern under the layers of embroidery, error, and contradiction that settle onto legends like the Murphys. At the heart of all the complexity, however, lay the gift that Gerald and Sara Murphy indisputably gave to each other and to all their friends, a sense of specialness and delight in a century when those qualities have come to seem rare. I hope that its spirit is somewhere perceptible in these pages.

I could not have written this book without the generosity, kindness, and support of Honoria Murphy Donnelly. She gave me unconditional access to all her family's papers, photographs, tapes, and films, furnished lists of contacts' names and addresses, entrusted me with information and anecdotes, allowed me to question her endlessly and repetitively in person and on the telephone, and, most notably, made me welcome in true Murphy fashion on my numerous visits to her house in East Hampton. Although she has not always agreed with my interpretations, she has always supported my efforts. There is no way that I can adequately thank her, but I would like to tell her, in Scott Fitzgerald's and Cole Porter's phrase, "how *great* you are."

I'm also ineffably indebted to Frances Myers Brennan for her unstinting help, wonderful memory, and wise counsel. By making available to me her father's engagement diaries, as well as her parents' letters (now on deposit at Yale University), she enabled me to date certain events with a precision any biographer would envy. And her tact and perceptiveness, her encyclopedic knowledge of the world in which the Murphys lived, and her awareness of when it was time to ask *me* questions, rather than the other way around, were invaluable.

Many others contributed recollections to my portrait of the Murphys. Gerald and Sara Murphy's grandchildren, John, Sherman, and Laura Donnelly, shared both memories and feelings with me, and put up good-naturedly with my intrusions into their family. The late Ellen Barry spoke with me at length, and her son, Philip Barry, Jr., his wife, Patricia, and their daughter Miranda were helpful as well. Calvin Tomkins, whose legendary *Living Well Is the Best Revenge* was both an inspiration and a formidable challenge to me, was generous with his memories of both Murphys as well as his sympathetic understanding; in addition, he gave me permission to use his own interview tapes, notes, and correspondence. I am also grateful to William Astor Chanler, Edward T. Chase, Roderick Coupe, James Douglas, Diane Fish, Frederic Franklin, Martha Gellhorn, Charles Getchell, Mimi MacLeish Grimm, Richard Hare, John Hemingway, the late Lincoln Kirstein, Jacques Livet, the late Yvonne Roussel Luff, William MacLeish, Mrs. John McCarthy, Mrs. Paul Mellon, David Pickman, Stewart Preston, Frances Ring, the late Vittorio Rieti, and Marian Seldes.

Much of my research was inevitably archival in nature: most of the individual actors in my story were gone, but fortunately they had left behind a rich record of letters, diaries, and other papers, and many people helped me to mine it. My warmest thanks for this go to Wayne Furman, overseer of the Berg Collection at the New York Public Library; the librarians of the Periodical Department of the Bibliothèque Nationale, the Bibliothèque de l'Opéra, and the Bibliothèque d'Art et Archéologie, Université de Paris; Dr. Howard Gotlieb, director of special collections at the Mugar Library, Boston University; Judy Malone of the Cincinnati Historical Society; Jean Ashton and Bernard Crystal of the Columbia University Rare Book and Manuscript Library, and Tim Page, donor of the Dawn Powell papers; Dorothy Kosinski, curator of the Douglas Cooper Collection; Madeline Nichols, curator of the Dance Collection, New York Public Library, and her staff, particularly Monica Moseley; Erik Naslund, director of the Dansmuseet in Stockholm; Ornella Volta, curator of the Fondation Erik Satie; Susan Sinclair of the Isabella Stewart Gardner Museum; George Barringer and the staff of the Special Collections department at the Lauinger Library, Georgetown University; Margaret Howland, curator of the Archibald MacLeish collection at Greenfield Community College; Laura Snowden, registrar of the Graduate School of Design, Harvard

University; Leslie Morris, curator of the Houghton Library, Harvard University, and his associate Mark Kille; Teresa Odean of the Hotchkiss School; Megan Desnoyers, former curator of the Ernest Hemingway Collection at the John Fitzgerald Kennedy Presidential Library, and its present curator, Steven Plotkin; the staff of the Manuscript Division of the Library of Congress; James LaForce of LaForce and Stevens and Andrea Mathewson and Stephanie Sarka of Mark Cross; Gérard Regnier, director, and Sylvie Fresnault, Anne Baldassari, and Yvon de Monbison of the Picasso Archives, Musée Picasso; William Joyce, associate university librarian, and Margaret M. Sherry, reference librarian and archivist, Rare Books and Special Collections, Princeton University; Ned Comstock and Steve Hansen of the Cinema-Television Library of the University of Southern California; Dr. Thomas Staley, Kathy Henderson, and Rich Oram of the Harry Ransom Humanities Research Center of the University of Texas; Edna Hajnal of the Thomas Fisher Rare Book Library at the University of Toronto; Greg Johnson of the Special Collections department at the Alderman Library of the University of Virginia; John Maeske, registrar of Yale College; Judith Schiff and Bill Massa of the Sterling Memorial Library, Yale University; and Patricia Willis, curator of the Yale Collection of American Literature at the Beinecke Rare Book and Manuscript Library of Yale University, and her colleagues Ellen Cordes and Ken Crilly.

Many scholars, writers, and critics contributed information or insight to my understanding of the times and figures I was writing about, and any list of them is bound to contain omissions. Nonetheless I wish to mention in particular Linda Patterson Miller, whose anthology of the letters among the Murphys and their circle was one of the inspirations for this book and a continuing resource for it, as well as Nancy Van Norman Baer, Matthew Bruccoli, Jackson Bryer, Pierre Cabanne, Mary Dearborn, Scott Donaldson, Ann Douglas, Elizabeth Garrity Ellis, Kristen Erickson, the late Robert Fizdale, Judi Freeman, Joe Haldeman, Brigitte Hedel-Samson, Diane Johnson, Bernice Kert, Robert Kimball, Eleanor Lanahan, Carolyn Lanchner, Nelly Maillard, William McBrien, Marion Meade, the late James Mellow, Nancy Milford, Bernard Minoret, Robert Murdock, Ronald Pisano, George Plimpton, Michael Reynolds, John Richardson, William Rubin, Elizabeth Hutton Turner, Linda Wagner-Martin, and Robert Westbrook.

I'm also grateful to all those who pointed me in the direction of illuminating material or useful sources, or helped in other material ways, including Compte Henri de Beaumont and Gaia de Beaumont; Mrs. Nathaniel Benchley; Lucy Dos Passos Coggin; Fereshteh Daftari of the Department of Painting and Sculpture, Museum of Modern Art; James R. Gaines; David Goddard; Sandra Aerey, the assessor for Harrietstown, New York; Edna Finn, the town historian; and Margaret Haig, the town clerk; the Honorable Jan H. Plumadore; Joan Schenkor; Guy-Patrice and Michel Dauberville; James Lord; Melissa de Medeiros of the Knoedler Gallery, John Reed, and Helen Miranda Wilson.

A network of friends sustained me, emotionally, artistically, and materially, at various points during the writing of this book. A list of all of them would fill its pages, but special mention must go to Paul Alexander, Gwendolyn Chabrier, Carol Easton, Terry Fox and Susan Lerner, Dan Greenberg, Lindy Hess, John and Chris Jerome, Louise Levathes, Charles Lockwood, Michael Lloyd, Honor Moore, Suzanne O'Malley, Leonora Prowell, Constance Sayre, Stacy Schiff, Michele Slung, William Stadiem, and Parmelee Welles Tolkan.

Special thanks are due to my agent, Kristine Dahl, who made an enormous leap of faith when she took me on as a client; to Dorothea Herrey and Kim Kanner of International Creative Management; to Laura Morris of the Abner Stein Agency; to the deft, perceptive, and ever understanding Jayne Yaffe; to Anne Chalmers for her inspired design; as well as Heidi Pitlor, Liz Vitale, Becky Saikia-Wilson — all of Houghton Mifflin; and to Houghton Mifflin's editorial director, Janet Silver, who somehow combines in one person the patience of Penelope, the wisdom of Athena, and the tact of P. G. Wodehouse's Jeeves.

Finally, I could not have undertaken or continued this project without the inspiration, love, and support of my family. My father, John Vaill, has given me advice and encouragement, and an invaluable sense of the context of my story. My husband, Tom Stewart, and our children, Pamela and Patrick, have gracefully put up with temper tantrums, crises of confidence, late meals, wrinkled laundry, long-winded anecdotes about people they've never heard of, and general dysfunction; more important, they have provided a center for my cosmos. My mother, the late Patricia Schepps Vaill, to whom this book is dedicated, is really its "onlie begetter": it was she who told me stories of her childhood in Paris and Cannes in the twenties, taught me French, and introduced me to the novels of Fitzgerald and Hemingway, the poetry of Archibald MacLeish, the music of Cole Porter. Because of her, the world Gerald and Sara Murphy created and lived in was always a reality to me, not something intangible and fantastic. For a gift like this, mere gratitude seems paltry.

Notes

Abbreviations for frequently cited sources

ESB	Ellen Barry
PB	Philip Barry
RB	Robert Benchley
BU	Mugar Library, Boston University
FMB	Frances Myers Brennan/Frances Myers Brennan archives
CUL	Rare Book and Manuscript Library, Columbia University
DC/NYPL	Dance Collection/New York Public Library, Lincoln Center
HMD	Honoria Murphy Donnelly/Honoria Murphy Donnelly archives
JDP	John Dos Passos
KDP	Katy Dos Passos
FSF	F. Scott Fitzgerald
AJ	Alan Jarvis
FL	Fernand Léger
GUL	Lauinger Library, Georgetown University
HU	Houghton Library, Harvard University
EH	Ernest Hemingway
PH	Pauline Hemingway
JFK	Ernest Hemingway collection, John F. Kennedy Presidential Library
LOC	Archibald MacLeish papers, Library of Congress
LW	*Living Well Is the Best Revenge* (Calvin Tomkins)
AMacL	Archibald MacLeish
GCM	Gerald Clery Murphy
PFM	Patrick Francis Murphy

SWM	Sara Wiborg Murphy
ALM	Alice Lee Myers
REM	Richard Myers
DP	Dorothy Parker
DaP	Dawn Powell
DOS	Donald Ogden Stewart
TITN	*Tender Is the Night* (F. Scott Fitzgerald)
CT	Calvin Tomkins
UTo	University of Toronto Rare Book and Manuscript Library
ASW	Adeline Sherman Wiborg
FBW	Frank Wiborg

Prologue: *Antibes, May 28, 1926*

1 "hard and lovely . . . a remarkable experience": F. Scott Fitzgerald, *TITN*, pp. 6–7, 18–19, 27.

"I used you again and again": FSF to SWM, 15 Aug. 1935, HMD.

"I hated the book": SWM to CT, 26 Nov. 1961, HMD.

2 "I know . . . any beauty": GCM to FSF, 31 Dec. 1935, PUL.

May 28, 1926: For the precise date of these events, and for other chronological details in this chapter, I'm indebted to Michael Reynolds, specifically to his *Hemingway: The American Homecoming*, p. 38.

But Gerald saw . . . of the sand: GCM/CT taped interview, HMD.

In fact . . . not speaking to him: FSF to Ludlow Fowler, undated, summer 1926, PUL; Donaldson, *Archibald MacLeish*, p. 159.

3 who . . . opium habit: Carr, *Dos Passos*, p. 203.

who swathes . . . germs: Donnelly, *S&G*, p. 32; HMD/Noel Murphy interview, HMD. Sara also made the children wear white gloves for traveling.

4 Edouard Baudoin . . . French Miami: Blume, *Côte d'Azur*, p. 90.

Fresh caviar . . . development: GCM/CT interview, HMD.

"Viking madonna": *TITN*, p. 33.

"stage manag[ing] . . . should tell": David Pickman interview.

"you drank" . . . that summer: ZSF to FSF, late summer/early fall 1930, PUL.

5 He finds a small throw rug . . . fun: GCM/CT interviews, HMD.

Early in the novel . . . "Christmas tree": *TITN*, p.34.

6 "the golden couple": Marian Seldes to author, 25 Jun. 1996 (postmark).

"No one has ever . . . ask me how": AMacL, "The Art of Poetry," interview in *The Paris Review*, vol. 14, no. 58, p. 70.

1. *"My father, of course, had wanted* boys"

7 Her father, Frank Bestow Wiborg: Information on FBW's origins comes from interviews with HMD; from *S&G*, p. 123; from Charles Theodore Greve, *Centennial History of Cincinnati and Representative Citizens*, vol. II; and from FBW's obituary in the *Cincinnati Enquirer*, 12 May, 1930.

8 the beautiful Misia Natanson: Gold and Fizdale, *Misia*, p. 41.
Major Hoyt Sherman: Greve, *Centennial History of Cincinnati and Representative Citizens*; *S&G*.
"After an awful struggle": FBW diary, 1883, HMD.
"My father, of course": SWM, untitled, unpublished memoir, HMD.
The new house . . . "and remain unseen": Details from *Cincinnati Enquirer*, 14 Feb. 1965 ("Historic Mansion Yields To Wreckers") and 9 Dec. 1906.

9 They attended Miss Ely's . . . "pale and shaken": SWM, untitled, unpublished memoir, HMD.
At Miss Ely's . . . in the pasture: Dachshunds and wolfhounds mentioned in *Cincinnati Enquirer*, 14 Feb. 1965; other details from SWM diary for 1896.
At other times . . . *King Arthur:* 1896 SWM diary, HMD.
"I think drawing . . . Thursdays!!!": 9 Jan. 1896 diary, HMD.

10 "It's raining on *me!*": HMD interview.
exacting but fair: Greve, *Centennial History of Cincinnati and Representative Citizens*, p. 819.
"kissed us all around": SWM to "Aunt Helen," 23 Jul. 1897, HMD.
At the palace . . . tried to help him: SWM, unpublished memoir: "Our Visit to the Kaiser," 21 Feb. 1898, HMD.

12 Perhaps, as her granddaughter: HMD interview.
only two years previously . . . Boxer Rebellion: Lord, *The Good Years*, p. 37.
the rather advanced . . . household accounting: Edmondson, *Profiles in Leadership*, pp. 9–10.

13 "*so* harmful": SWM to GCM, 10 Feb. 1918, HMD.
trip started out badly: Details from SWM travel diary (1904), HMD.

15 In 1895 Frank Wiborg . . . exponential increase in value: Description of house, HMD interview and Pease & Elliman real estate advertisement

[1940]. Other details, 1902, 1916, and 1930 surveyors' maps of East Hampton, courtesy of David Goddard.

16 sound of the surf: HMD interview.
"based on a community . . . New York society": *S&G*, p. 122.
"the women all had tiny waists": Mrs. Paul Mellon interview.

17 "a wise old Aunt": SWM to GCM, [Sept. 1908], HMD.

2. *"Gerald's besetting sin is inattention"*

18 graduated in 1875 . . . fashionable shopping venue: All information about PFM and Mark Cross comes from GCM's unpublished memoirs, written in response to Douglas MacAgy's questions and collected as the Murphy/MacAgy papers in the Archives of American Art, Smithsonian Institution.
GCM birth date: Registry Department of the City of Boston; ARM's alteration: HMD interview and *S&G*, p. 11.
"a stagnant community . . . educated mispronunciation" : GCM to SSW, 7 Jun. 1915, HMD.

19 He rented premises . . . Clarence Mackay: GCM, Murphy/MacAgy papers.
But Anna Murphy refused . . . packed and followed: *S&G*, p. 124.
"close relationships": GCM to Esther Murphy, 1957, HMD.
He seemed to think . . . standing guard: GCM's recollection, MacAgy/Murphy papers.
"some other gray-haired . . . Sweet Adeline": Wilson, *The Twenties*, p. 192. Whether this was meant as a melodic tribute to Mrs. Wiborg is an unanswered question.

20 He also possessed . . . arms of a chair: GCM/CT interview notes; Hester Pickman/HMD interview, HMD.
At Mark Cross . . . United States: GCM, *To Be Continued . . .: The Mark Cross Story* (company history of the Mark Cross Company), Mark Cross archives.
"A woman with a Cross bag . . . woman she likes least": PFM, advertising copy in Mark Cross Company files.
"Give a woman . . . harvest of regrets": Excerpts from PFM's speeches, collected as "Wit and Humor of New York's Famous After-Dinner Speaker," commemorative pamphlet (unpublished), HMD.

"Impromptu speeches": "Mr. Patrick F. Murphy Talks on Speechmaking," *Paris Herald*, undated, HMD.
He evolved . . . laughter and applause: GCM, Murphy/MacAgy papers.
"didn't believe in being sick": HMD interview.
He disdained overcoats . . . year round: GCM to JDP, 12 Sept. 1963, UVA.

21 one winter afternoon . . . finished their walk: *LW*, p.13.
"devoted, possessive, ambitious": GCM to Esther Murphy, 1957, HMD.
When he took Fred . . . "her glove": Noel Murphy/HMD interview, HMD.

Gerald had been attending . . . Dorothy Parker: Meade, *Dorothy Parker*, pp. 14–15; Sister Rita King, Order of the Sisters of Charity, interview.

22 took him to the woodshed: *LW*, p. 13.
Gerald now began to spell: 1907 *Mischianza* (Hotchkiss yearbook).
join the adults in the library . . . "interest in painting": GCM, MacAgy/Murphy papers.
"rebelled and chose": GCM to AMacL, 4 Sept. 1964, LOC.
"I will not put up . . . bilious temperament": All quotations are from letters from ARM to Huber Buehler, Hotchkiss School archives.

24 "a defect over which . . . incapable of a full one": GCM to AMacL, 22 Jan. 1931, LOC.
On Friday evening . . . down to coincidence: Program from *Mrs. Clymer's Regrets*, HMD.

25 squire about with some frequency: HMD interviews, Richard Preston interview.
Yale Glee Club's concert: *Cincinnati Enquirer* [Dec. 1905].
he told her how much: SWM to GCM, Sept. 1908, HMD.

26 "helped a lot . . . Here I am!!! — H": Postcard from Sara, Mary Hoyt, and Olga Wiborg to GCM, Feb. 1907, HMD.
"the likeness of popularity and success": GCM to AMacL, 22 Jan. 1931, LOC.
"social light": 1907 *Mischianza* (Hotchkiss yearbook).

3. "New clothes, new friends, and lots of parties"

27 "*what* a job . . . lots of parties": SWM untitled, unpublished memoir, HMD.
On December 30, 1905 . . . some green liquid: Cincinnati *Enquirer*.

27 "dressed to the teeth": SWM untitled, unpublished memoir, HMD.

After a ritual unmasking . . . to her guests: Cincinnati *Enquirer*, 31 Dec. 1905.

28 "the 1st real grief . . . weeping for 2 days": SWM untitled, unpublished memoir, HMD.

"very feminine": ESB interview.

"they told her not to wear": HMD interview.

29 "Palatial domicile . . . Little H. & Sara W.": SWM to GCM, 18 May 1907, HMD.

So it was a momentous . . . foreign secretary: "Court Circular," *The Times* (London), 7 Jun. 1907.

Frank even thought . . . reelection in 1910: *Cincinnati Enquirer*, 5 and 7 Dec. 1909.

30 Olga in her turn: "Young American Women Presented at Court of St. James's," *New York Tribune*, Jun. 1909. The *Tribune* was betraying its ignorance: the Court of St. James's is where ambassadors present their credentials, while ladies are presented to the king or queen at the royal residence, traditionally Buckingham Palace.

"Miss Sara's chic . . . delicate fairness": "Is She A Lord's Most Beautiful?" *New York World*, May 1911.

A favorite showstopper . . . suggestively: *LW*, p. 10.

Their act was so polished : "Shock for Misses Wiborg," *New York Tribune*, 1 Jul. 1913.

"Our girls are so thoughtless": FBW diaries, 1913, HMD.

Sara's behavior . . . digestive upsets: Details from SWM diary, 1910–1915, HMD.

31 "This is a word . . . miss out again": SWM to GCM, Sept. 1908, HMD.

Andover was a notion . . . instead of Yale: This is the version of events presented in *S&G*, p. 126.

32 The 407 members . . . Connecticut: *Yale Daily News*, 16 Oct. 1909.

On his first evening . . . *sauve qui peut*: Details come from Yale University, *History of the Class of 1912*, pp. 8–9.

"a general tacit Philistinism": *LW*, p. 14.

crossing the campus in riding clothes: GCM to CT, undated, HMD.

finished up his freshman year . . . failure: Yale College — Scholarship Record, Gerald C. Murphy, Class of 1912, courtesy of the Registrar's Office, Yale University.

33 "go free of care": ARM to GCM, [Jul. 1909], HMD.

"mak[ing] Fred look after": Ibid., 20 Jun. 1909, HMD.

"They always appeared": Edwin M. Woolley to CT, 26 Dec. 1961, HMD.

Patrick and Anna took . . . European specialist: ARM to GCM, 1 Aug. 1909, HMD.

"the belle of the ship . . . persecutor": Ibid., [Jun. 1909], HMD.

"Tess is a wonder . . . 'genius'": PFM to GCM, 26 Jul. 1909, HMD.

34 "Your environment": Ibid., 21 May 1909, HMD.

"the aesthetic side": Yale College, *History of the Class of* 1912.

reputation for wit . . . go more smoothly: Class rankings, Yale College, *History of the Class of* 1912.

Robert Gardner . . . make it correct: Robert Gardner told Sara this story in a letter after her engagement to Gerald in 1915; the undated note was enclosed in a letter from SWM to GCM, 18 Oct. 1915, HMD.

in late November . . . "to his studies": Report from the Office of the Dean, Yale College, HMD.

35 "Come, brace up . . . office for me?": PFM to GCM, 20 Nov. 1909, HMD.

"I can still see" . . . brought down the house: GCM, quoted in *LW*, pp. 15–16.

36 Glee Club appeared at the Waldorf-Astoria: *Yale Daily News*, 5 Feb. 1911.

Wiborg girls didn't come . . . in the evenings: SWM diary, 1910–1915: 21 Feb., 22 Jun., 26–28 Jun., 28 Jul., 1–3 Aug., 23 Aug., and 31 Aug., 1911, HMD.

Gerald was one of the eight organizers: Yale College, *History of the Class of* 1912, p. 27.

"Galahad the Pure": Robert Gardner to SWM, enclosed in SWM to GCM, 18 Oct. 1915, HMD.

37 She shared . . . amusement: SWM to GCM, 26 Oct. 1909, HMD.

"I have no idea": *LW*, p. 11.

4. *"Thinking how nice you are"*

38 "The saddest people": SWM to GCM, 16 Mar. 1918, HMD.

"Spent day in bed . . . depressed": SWM diary 1910–1915: 8 Aug. 1915, HMD.

taking classes . . . afternoons and evenings: Ibid.: 17, 18, 25, and 30 Jan. 1910.

"Went to H. Mann's" . . . louche manner: Ibid.: 3 Feb.1911.

39 "never even to glance": Mrs. Paul Mellon interview.

little Esther Murphy . . . luncheon table: SWM to GCM, [1915], HMD.

de rigueur . . . Whitneys': Ibid.: 8 and 10 Feb. 1910, HMD.

tableaux at the Clarence Mackays': *Vogue*, 15 Nov. 1914.

39 Strauss's *Elektra* . . . second time: SWM diary 1910–1915: Feb.–Mar. 1910, HMD.

"*awful* pains": Ibid.: 13 Jun. 1910.

"much depressed . . . fearfully depressed": Ibid.: 13, 17, 19 Feb. 1910.

family trip . . . empty and sad: Ibid.: 2 and 3 May 1910.

Sara Sherman . . . groom in sight for her: Ibid.: 18 Jul. 1910.

40 "people just fell in love": Mrs. Paul Mellon interview.

she didn't accompany . . . recorded in her diary: SWM diary 1910–1915: April 1910, HMD.

41 "She had a sense": ESB interview; see also *S&G*, p. 168.

Halley's comet . . . directly afterward: SWM diary 1910–1915: 26 May 1910, 11 Sept. 1912, 17 Nov. 1910, HMD.

"Will you ever forget": Yale College, *History of the Class of 1912*, p. 30.

The next day . . . "rheumatism in knees": Ibid., p. 31, *S&G*, p. 128; and SWM diary 1910–1915: 17 Jan. 1911, HMD.

42 "in bed" . . . for Adeline: SWM diary 1910–1915: 22 and 28 Jan. 1911, HMD.

"unspeakable": SWM to GCM, 18 Jun. 1911, HMD.

"in society as a lady": Stella Campbell, quoted in Peters, *Mrs. Pat*, p. 226.

43 "Sara, darling": *LW*, p. 11.

"We sang afterwards": SWM diary 1910–1915: 12 Mar. 1911, HMD.

duchess was a notable . . . drop earrings: Cooper, *The Rainbow Comes and Goes*, p. 44.

"a rather self-conscious": Havighurst, *Twentieth Century Britain*, p. 34.

"I love Sara . . . goes her own way": *LW*, p. 11.

"I think I shall": SWM to GCM, 18 Jun. 1911, HMD.

"dressed for tea" . . . Sara craved: Cooper, *The Rainbow Comes and Goes*, pp. 63–64; SWM diary 1910–1915: 26 Mar. 1911, HMD.

44 April 5 . . . Belvoir in March: SWM diary 1910–1915: 5 Apr. and 31 Mar. 1911, HMD.

secured a letter . . . Steichen had also studied: Ibid.: 14 and 18 Apr. 1911.

live nude model: Morton, *Americans in Paris*, pp. 68–69.

"one of the most fearful": SWM 1919–1915 diary: 14 May 1911, HMD.

"nice day but bored": Ibid.: 15 Jun. 1911.

Albert Hall was transformed . . . blue silk: "The Shakespeare Ball: Brilliant Scenes at Albert Hall," *Morning Leader* (London), 21 Jun. 1911.

45 nearly four thousand . . . midnight: "Shakespeare Ball: Visit by the King and Queen," unattributed, 19 Jun. 1911, clipping, FBW papers, HMD.

customary twenty-one-gun . . . morning's proceedings: SWM diary 1910–1915: 22 Jun. 1911, HMD.

"We have been having . . . enjoyed myself more": SWM to GCM, 18 Jun. 1911, HMD.

"Would you mind . . . 'out of it'": Ibid.

46 Elizabethan Club . . . Stuart writers: *Yale Daily News*, 31 Oct., 21 and 27 Nov., 8 Dec. 1911, and 10 Jan. 1912.

"cussing and drinking lemonade": Yale College, *History of the Class of 1912*, p.27.

February . . . Most Brilliant: Ibid.

"I am not disappointed . . . value it so lightly": PFM to GCM, 18 Aug. 1911, HMD.

"I cannot accept . . . at the dock": Ibid., Mar. 1911.

47 "I'm proud of you": Ibid., Feb. 1911.

"Only in my senior year": GCM to CT, undated, HMD.

"distortion of myself": GCM to AMacL, 22 Jan. 1931, LOC.

Gerald, for his part, spent . . . planned European trip: SWM diary 1910–1915: 3 Jan., Feb., 18 Apr., 1912, HMD.

"*Gerard's birthday*": Ibid.: 15 May 1912.

East Hampton summer . . . broke out: Ibid.: 28 May, 1 Jul., 14 Aug., 9 Oct. 1912.

48 "terrific crowds" . . . love a Scene: Ibid.: 19, 20, and 22 Jun. 1912.

returned to East Hampton . . . September 17: Ibid.: 30 Jun., 2 and 6 Jul., 17 Sept. 1912.

fun to camp . . . from the beach: SWM to GCM, 8 Feb. 1918, HMD. Sara couldn't remember the year (she says it was "years ago, *long* before we were engaged); the chronology of the Wiborgs' comings and goings, and the development of Sara's and Gerald's relationship, makes summer 1912 the likeliest time.

5. "*I must ask you endless questions*"

50 During the previous winter . . . 25th Street: SWM diary 1910–1915: Dec. 1911, HMD. Sara's December entries refer only to "Mr. Chase's" studio, but Ronald Pisano, author of William Merritt Chase's *catalogue raisonné*, confirms that Chase's studio at this time was located at 333 Fourth Avenue.

evening of *tableaux vivants* . . . Mrs. J. Pierpont Morgan: "Beautiful Women

Pose in Tableaux Vivants," *New York Herald*, 29 Jan. 1913; program from the tableaux, HMD.

50 quarreling with her family . . . one occasion: SWM diary 1910–1915: 30 Sept., 9 Oct., 11 Oct., and 17 Nov. 1912, HMD.

51 Esther worried so . . . take care of her: Esther Murphy to GCM, 18 Nov. 1916, HMD.

"I shall see your saddened . . . pretty Sal": SWM to GCM, 9 Mar. and 16 Mar. 1913, HMD.

Having dispatched Frank . . . Poiret: SWM diary 1910–1915: 20 Mar., 26 Mar., and 9–23 Apr. 1913, HMD.

"*Dreadful* day . . . not going back": Ibid., 23 Mar. 1913.

"preliminary scrimmage" . . . red, green, and yellow brocade: *Cincinnati Enquirer*, 24 Jul. 1913.

52 much more impressed . . . *Le Sacre du printemps*: SWM diary 1910–1915: 22 and 23 Jul. 1913, HMD.

Smartly dressed . . . "shut up": Buckle, *Diaghilev*, pp. 299–301.

"continuous thudding": Beaumont, *Bookseller at the Ballet*, pp. 137–38.

"musically and choreographically": Garafola, *Diaghilev's Ballets Russes*, p. 64.

"It must be wonderful . . . in detail": GCM to SWM, 29 Jul. 1913, HMD.

53 "I only wish": ARM to GCM, 13 Aug. 1913, HMD.

Esther, who was now . . . "is it so?": GCM to SWM, 28 Jul. 1913, HMD.

54 Frank was in a foul . . . "no end of bustle": FBW diary 1913: 5 Sept. 1913, HMD.

To make matters worse . . . penny more: "Wiborg Case Settled," *New York Press*, 24 Oct. 1913.

Curiously . . . Stanchfield: FBW diary 1913: 12 Sept. 1913, HMD.

"MRS. F. WIBORG . . . FINED AS SMUGGLER": United Press dispatch, 27 Sept. 1913; *New York Journal*, 23 Oct. 1913; *New York Evening Mail*, 23 Oct. 1913; *New York Press*, 24 Oct. 1913.

55 "Most horrible day . . . [G]erard and us": SWM diary 1910–1915: 29 Sept. 1913, HMD.

On October 23 . . . letting her go: Details from newspaper stories previously cited.

It was proposed . . . "*years* of business": SWM to GCM, 12 Jan. 1914, HMD.

"I sleep in trains": Ibid., 27 Dec. 1913, HMD.

Christmas at Belvoir . . . "dead with it": Ibid.

56 "Arriving at Port Said . . . subtle mixed in": Ibid., 12 Jan. 1914, HMD.

display of pukka-sahib festivity . . . retired early: FBW diary 1914: 12 Feb. 1914, HMD.

so many waltzes . . . "Miss Ragtime?": Dance card labeled "Viceregal Lodge, Delhi. Feb. 12, 1914," HMD.

following evening . . . "coon song snatches": Program labeled "Imperial Delhi Gymkhana Club, Indian Cavalry Polo Week, 1914," HMD; "Theatricals at the Gymkhana Club," clipping, Saturday, 14 Feb. 1914, source unknown, HMD.

"they looked beautifully . . . poor selection": FBW diary 1914: 13 Feb. 1914, HMD.

"hot unkempt and tawdry": Ibid., 7 Jan. 1914.

But Gerald . . . that autumn: GCM to SWM, [7 Sept. 1913], HMD.

"the most marvelous": SWM to GCM, 18 Jan. 1914, HMD.

57 "'transported me beyond delight'": GCM to SWM, 9 Apr. 1914, HMD.

"Lately I have been made . . . of the pavement": Ibid.

"Gerald Murphy showed up": FBW diary 1914: 27 Mar. 1914, HMD.

"[H]e was playing . . . no one at all": GCM to SWM, 9 Apr. 1914, HMD.

58 two of them went . . . "G": Ibid., 10 Jun. 1914, HMD.

6. "A *relationship that* so lets loose *the imagination!*"

59 "Damp day . . . Halifax": SWM diary 1910–1915: 5 Aug. 1914, HMD.

For his part, Gerald . . . New York: GCM to SWM, 9 Sept. and 9 Nov. 1914, HMD.

60 "cold-cuts and mustard" . . . Keats: Ibid., undated, 1915.

"How differently I feel . . . enjoys them": SWM to GCM, 2 Jun. 1915, HMD.

They decided to shun . . . "holes stick up?": GCM to SWM, undated, 1914, HMD.

"*Aristocrats!! bah!!*": Ibid., undated card.

To Sara, and only . . . position afforded him: Ibid., 12 Jan. and 29 Jun. 1915.

"My heart is full . . . beauty you feel": Ibid., 19 May 1915.

"we've both lived": Ibid., 26 Feb. 1915.

"*What* a gloomy thing . . . don't you think?": SWM to GCM, 19 May 1915, HMD.

61 "You asked the other . . . I thought of you!": GCM to SWM, 18 Feb. 1915, HMD.

61 "It is generally remarked": Ibid., 14 Oct. 1914.
"Can you see me": Ibid., 12 Jan. 1915.
"Who is there . . . Am I clear?": Ibid., 15 Jan. 1915.
"Are we peculiar": Ibid., 26 Jan. 1915.
"Sal mine": Ibid., 4 Feb. 1915 (postmarked 7:30 P.M.).
"My Sal": Ibid., 9 Feb. 1915.

62 "I never dreamed . . . We *are* each other": SWM to GCM, [1915], HMD.
This letter is dated in *S&G* as Aug. 1914, but it's out of keeping with the tone
of Sara's correspondence at that point. The year 1915 is much more likely.
"I am beginning to believe": GCM to SWM, 11 Feb. 1915, HMD. Sara's letter
itself is lost, but quoted in Gerald's to her.
"I put [the seal] . . . remove it": Ibid.
stone wall . . . picnicked: Honoria Donnelly believes this bottle was buried
and unearthed in Sara's East Hampton garden. But in a letter of Feb. 12
Gerald refers to "our little corner by the wall" at St. Andrew's, where he was
when he wrote the buried missive. And in another letter from St. Andrew's
dated May 24, 1915, he speaks of being able to see, from his window, "our
little corner by the wall where we lunched on that day when we sort of
realized we were engaged."
he buried . . . "tears of this night": GCM, 11 Feb. 1915, HMD. The little
bottle, with the rolled-up note still inside it, secured with the (now faded)
green ribbon, is in the file.
"ᶻas much": GCM to SWM, 13 Feb. 1915, HMD.
"Were you here . . . meager words!": Ibid.

63 "'loaded and fragrant'": Ibid., 10 Feb. 1915.
"Can't you see . . . finish it": Ibid., 10 Mar. 1915.
"I am disappointed . . . their ignorance?": Ibid., 24 Feb. 1915.
But Sara was apprehensive . . . at least once: Ibid.
"last night left me . . . all day": Ibid., 2 Mar. 1915.
"I tell you frankly . . . much longer": Ibid., 3 Mar. 1915.
"ply my suit . . . is at stake": Ibid., 5 Mar. 1915.

64 "I'm marrying Gerald": HMD interview.
Adeline wept . . . inestimable loss: Although there is no actual record of
Adeline Wiborg's reaction to *this* news, a letter from Sara to Gerald, 7 Jun.
1915, describes such a response to Olga's engagement, and says she "behaved
much the same as before."

"life and the living": GCM to SWM, 25 Aug. 1915, HMD.

refused to receive: Ibid., 8 Mar. 1915.

"an autopsy": Ibid., 10 Mar. 1915.

"Sara Wiborg . . . I don't like it": FBW diary 1914: 11 Nov. 1914, HMD.

"very fond of": GCM to SWM, 8 Mar. 1915, HMD.

"great disappointment . . . to be married": Ibid., 26 Aug. 1915.

65 "I can't see that age . . . Affectionately, Sara": Sara Sherman Mitchell to SWM, 8 Mar. 1915, HMD.

Adeline Wiborg hoped . . . engagement officially: S&G, p. 142.

"You have no adequate idea": Frederic T. Murphy to SWM, [Mar. 1915], HMD.

"I've never seen you" . . . quiz Gerald mercilessly: GCM to SWM, 22 May 1915, HMD.

66 "*Everyone* is agog": Ibid., 30 Mar, 1915.

"nooks in the library": Ibid., 3 May 1915.

"on public fire-escapes, etc.": Ibid., [1915].

"I think the tension . . . for you in return": Ibid., 22 Apr. 1915.

"I come wailing": SWM to GCM, 15 Jun. 1915, HMD.

she blushed uncontrollably: Ibid., 2 Jun. 1915.

"Thank Eliz. . . . leaving the room, too!": GCM to SWM, 4 Jun. 1915, HMD.

"I *miss* you so": SWM to GCM, 4 Jun. 1915, HMD.

67 "stalking up and down . . . sort of *left*": Ibid., 7 Jun. 1915.

"*What* do I know . . . seemed long to *me*": Ibid.

"What an agonizing . . . in the least": Ibid., [Jun. 1915].

"I wonder if I shall ever . . . accounts for a lot": GCM to SWM, 21 Jun. 1915, HMD.

But once among them . . . "Stone Henge": Ibid., 25 Jun. 1915.

68 "the men I admire most . . . smudged years of mine": Ibid., 29 Jun. 1915.

Frank agreed: Ibid., 28 Jul. 1915. This letter maintains that Sara should contribute only as much to the couple's income as Gerald did, a contention that Frank Wiborg clearly ignored, because another letter (GCM to SWM, 8 Aug. 1915, HMD) speaks of their plans to "run #50 on $18, a year."

Patrick Murphy: This information is extrapolated from letters from GCM to SWM, 13 Jul., 8 Aug., and 4 Oct. 1915.

"in a different place": GCM to SWM, 26 Feb. 1915, HMD.

68 Venetian glass . . . pink lusterware: Ibid., [undated, 1915], 3 May, 27 Jul., and 24 Aug., 1915.

"Such wantable things . . . among trash": SWM to GCM, 30 Sept. 1915, HMD.

"Better men than I": GCM to SWM, 29 Jun. 1915, HMD.

69 "I hope your father": SWM to GCM, [July 1915], HMD.

"court martial . . . can *confuse* them": GCM to SWM, 20 Aug. 1915, HMD.

"I think I am right . . .with your work": SWM to GCM, 15 Sept. 1915, HMD.

In late July . . . in Europe: GCM to SWM, 29 Jul. 1915, HMD.

"Her tenderness . . . their avoidance — !!": Ibid., 7 Aug. 1915.

70 "mange-cures" . . . full evening dress: Ibid., 8 Aug. 1915.

"long, hard journey . . . *never* seen it fail": SWM to GCM, 3 Aug. 1915, HMD.

he now reneged . . . price of $25,: GCM to SWM, 3 Aug. 1915, HMD.

71 "The youngest newsboy": SWM to GCM, 29 Oct. 1915, HMD.

A friend living in Panama . . . for the jungle: Ibid., 20 Sept. 1915.

"*Won't* it seem . . . Home to 11th Street!": Ibid., 19 Oct. 1915.

"I am *delighted* . . . pulverize them yet!": Ibid., 15 Nov. 1915.

72 "Here are some blossoms": GCM to SWM, [30 Dec. 1915], HMD.

That afternoon . . . man and wife: "Miss Wiborg Weds Gerald C. Murphy," *New York Times*, 31 Dec. 1915.

"Think of a relationship . . . thank heaven!": GCM to SWM, 4 Feb. 1915, HMD.

7. *"Don't let's* ever *separate again"*

73 "communicated affection": GCM to SWM, 18 Apr. 1936, HMD.

At the end of the block . . . brick walk behind: White and Willensky, *AIA Guide to New York City (Revised Edition)*, p. 75.

74 Around the corner . . . artists and illustrators: Kouwenhovem, *The Columbia Historical Portrait of New York*, p. 373.

Number 50 . . . rather than wealthy: Lockwood, *Bricks and Brownstone*, p. 85. Other details about the house's and street's appearance come from personal observation.

four stories high . . . Mollie, the maid: GCM to SWM, 14 Aug. 1915, HMD.

single sitting room . . . rooms had fireplaces: Floor plan of 50 West 11th Street, in SWM to GCM, Aug. 1915, HMD.

brick facade freshly . . . hung in the hall: GCM to SSW, 8 Aug. 1915, HMD.

wide-plank floors . . . Dunes: SWM to GCM, 15 Nov. 1915, HMD.

Gerald and Sara filled . . . opalescent glass jugs: Ibid., 10 Feb. 1918, HMD.

75 "a black and white": GCM to SWM, 27 Jul. 1915, HMD.

"It's very old": Ibid., 5 Apr. 1915.

"how much and how dearly I love you": SWM to GCM, 17 Mar. 1916, HMD.

76 "2 blue vases . . . out into the street": GCM to SWM, 15 Aug. 1916, HMD.

"this A.M. . . . bottom of your mattress": SWM to GCM, 23 Aug. 1916, HMD.

"the real rock" . . . in the autumn: GCM to SWM, 12 Aug. 1916, HMD.

"The work you are doing . . . infection": ASW to SWM, 18 Oct. 1916, HMD.

"I'm so glad . . . Do it for me": GCM to SWM, 12 Nov. 1916, HMD.

77 Adeline Wiborg's tersely: *New York Times*, 4 Jan. 1917.

"Your little hands": SWM scrapbook, HMD.

"Honoria Adeline": SWM diary 1917–18: 19 Dec. 1917, HMD.

Gerald always claimed . . . either family: *LW*, p. 19.

she carried the name . . . in 1832: *S&G*, p. 124.

Among the papers . . . Honoria Adeline Murphy: These papers are undated; the loose sheet is on paper (and in handwriting) consistent with the years 1916-17; the pigskin notebook also contains addresses for Murphy friends and suppliers of the late 1920s and early 1930s, HMD.

78 "my friend, Gerald Murphy": Ida Tarbell to W. S. Gifford, 9 Aug. 1917, HMD.

he was discouraged . . . commissioned: GCM to SWM, 10 Nov. 1917, HMD.

On November 22 . . . as a private: GCM, World War I service cards, New York State Archives, Albany, New York.

Sara was confined . . . difficult delivery: GCM to SWM, 2 Feb. 1918, HMD.

small Christmas tree . . . little tree: SWM diary 1917–18, HMD.

"royal and overpowering": Ibid., 16 Dec. 1917.

"courting mirror" . . . the baby nurse: Ibid., 30 Dec. 1917.

Frank Wiborg bought . . . son-in-law: GCM to SWM, 7 Jan. 1918, HMD.

"the greatest anguish of our lives": Ibid., 1 Jan. 1918.

79 bitterly cold . . . "candle-light and flowers": Ibid., 2 Jan. 1918.

Rows of dark khaki . . . four layers of blankets: Ibid., 15 Jan. 1918.

Sara, distressed . . . bran muffins: SWM to GCM, [winter 1918], HMD.

80 squares of washed cheesecloth: Ibid., 31 Jan. 1918.

80 "that I must get a lot . . . anything with ourselves": GCM to SWM, 18 Jan. and 2 Feb. 1918, HMD.

The train trip . . . fine adventure: Ibid., 25 Jan. 1918.

"It has made me" . . . Honoria had kissed: SWM to GCM, 24 Jan. 1918, HMD.

"*brilliant* dark gray" . . . mother's face: Ibid., 22 Jan. 1918, HMD.

She was keeping up . . . along the Marne: Ibid.

81 "What a triumph . . . shouldn't we?": Ibid., 2 Feb. 1918, HMD.

her old friend Rue Carpenter . . . New York: Ibid., 27 Jan. 1918.

Monty Woolley . . . military service: Ibid., 22 Jan. 1918.

He was charmed . . . surprise: Ibid., 2 Feb. 1918.

"the *most fearful*": Ibid., 15 Feb. 1918.

"miserable" . . . any attention: Ibid., 3 Feb, 1918.

"exactly as though": Ibid., 9 Feb. 1918.

"surrounded by the beautiful": Ibid., 10 Feb. 1918.

82 "our little farm": GCM to SWM, 15 Jan. 1918, HMD.

"our beautiful house": Ibid., 14 Mar. 1918.

Empire chest . . . eccentric list: Ibid. (postcards), 3 Jan., 14 Jan., and 17 Jan. 1918.

Now Sara was . . . between the windows: SWM to GCM, 7 Feb. 1918, HMD.

"our house . . . half of myself": Ibid., 9 Feb. 1918.

"I was thinking . . . very soon": Ibid., 30 Jan. 1918.

"in rusty black": Ibid., 8 Feb. 1918, HMD.

Gerald's own temper . . . arranged for himself: Ibid., 19 Feb. 1918.

83 they could share meals . . . night together: Ibid., 20 Mar. 1918.

Sara was desolate . . . entourage home: Ibid., 4 Mar. 1918.

"You see . . . where you are": Ibid., 20 Mar. 1918.

woke at 3:30 . . . until 6:00: GCM to SWM, 17 Feb. 1918, HMD.

By the end of March . . . New York: Item no. 33, Special Orders no. 73, War Department, 28 Mar. 1918.

"casual" . . . blow to his pride: GCM to SWM, 27 Aug. 1918, HMD.

"while the British . . . given a dance": Ibid., 25 Sept. 1918.

84 approached a former Yale . . . Henry T. Allen in France: Ibid., 23 Sept. 1918.

"everything I properly can": J. M. Tumulty to PFM, 14 Sept. 1918, HMD.

"What fun we had" . . . in the train afterward: SWM to GCM, 1 Sept. 1918, HMD.

Gerald found her unfinished . . . saved the holder: GCM to SWM, [Aug./Sept. 1918], HMD.

By the end of September . . . health or the baby's: Ibid., [Sept. 1918], 23 Sept. and 25 Sept. 1918.

Soon there was more . . . Long Island: P. C. Harris to J. M. Tumulty, 24 Sept. 1918; PFM to GCM, 25 Sept. 1918; HMD.

"You ought to be proud": J. M. Tumulty to PFM, 8 Oct. 1918, HMD.

"Jerry my Berry . . . Your wife, Sal": SWM to GCM, [Nov. 1918], HMD.

85 "completely knocked out": GCM to SWM, 11 Dec. 1918, HMD.

8. *"The idea is thrilling to me"*

86 Sara was already planning . . . baby arrived: SWM to GCM, 7 Feb. 1918, HMD.

When Honoria was separated . . . mark on it: SWM scrapbooks, HMD.

"get a grip on our future": GCM to SWM, 9 Jun. 1919, HMD.

In 1915 . . . his own version: *LW*, p. 134.

87 as he did Fred . . . Cross in England: Noel Murphy/HMD interview, HMD.

"I had to say . . . what came out": *LW*, p. 20.

Mexican market . . . street fair: GCM to SWM, 19 Jan. 1919, HMD.

"enormously fat Percherons . . . down the back": Ibid., 29 Jan. 1919.

That winter . . . Liberal Arts: GCM's application to the Harvard University School of Landscape Architecture lists "freehand drawing" at the School of Design and Liberal Arts under the heading "Special Preparation"; letters between GCM and SWM in 1919 supply Miss Weir's name.

"I do think . . . *amazing*": SWM to GCM, 8 Jun. 1919, HMD.

"My parents" . . . shoulder to shoulder: HMD interview.

"When we wake up": GCM to SWM, 9 Jun. 1919, HMD.

he swallowed it . . . son's decision: SWM to GCM, [May 1919], HMD.

88 "male Murphy . . . son himself": SWM scrapbook, and Ibid., 2 Jun. 1919.

"Dubbedy" . . . done of Honoria: SWM scrapbooks, HMD.

He was immediately enthralled . . . New York society: GCM to SWM, 9 Jun., 10 Jun., 15 Jun., and 18 Jun. 1919, HMD.

"one *manor*" . . . that very evening: Ibid., 9 Jul. 1919.

89 in addition to her passion . . . coaching: Catalogue of the manuscript and rare book collections of Amy Lowell, Amy Lowell papers, HU.

89 After dinner . . . "cordial and human": GCM to SWM, 9 Jul. and 11 Jul. 1919, HMD.

90 "to anticipate the need . . . evidence of it up here": Ibid., 11 Jul. 1919.
"Who can we get . . . Columbia Trust Co.?": SWM to GCM, 12 Jul. 1919, HMD.
"Nothing, I think": Ibid., 15 Sept. 1919.
"exasperated . . . still in me": Ibid.
"running the legs off his guests": Ibid., 14 Jul. 1919.
Hoytie and Olga . . . "nothing but *things*": Ibid., 16 Jul. 1919.

91 "I believe in you . . . forbade you to?!": GCM to SWM, 21 Jul. 1919, HMD.
And when her train . . . "glad that she wasn't": SWM to GCM, 24 Jul. 1919, HMD.

92 "We *need* a new . . . outlook it gives one?": Ibid., 15 Sept. 1919.
he had done unusually . . . courses in landscaping: GCM transcripts, Harvard Graduate School of Design.
Her scrapbooks tell . . . *properly*: SWM scrapbooks, HMD.
John Singer Sargent . . . Boston Museum of Fine Arts: GCM, Murphy/MacAgy papers, p.3.

93 "He isn't the real thing": AMacL, *Reflections*, p. 42.
"I would like . . . well-laundered": *S&G*, p. 9.
"the next-best Raphael I ever saw": Crosby, *Shadows of the Sun*, 27 Jul. 1926.
Gerald had been collecting . . . late nineteenth century: AMacL, *Reflections*, p. 93
Boston Public Library: In *Living Well Is the Best Revenge*, Calvin Tomkins reports that the source was old magazines; in a letter of May 29, 1964, to Douglas MacAgy, GCM insists he got the material from "original manuscripts" of "the drummer boy Higginson" in the Music Room of the Boston Public Library — an assertion also made by Honoria Donnelly in *Sara & Gerald*. There are, however, no such manuscripts in the Boston Public Library (and Higginson was no drummer boy, but the commander of a unit).
Mrs. Gardner he mingled . . . "Motherless Child": HMD interview; also *S&G*, p. 39.
The next day . . . bread-and-butter present: Isabella Stewart Gardner, guest book for May 12, 1921; copy of *Afro-American Folk Songs: A Study*, by Henry Edward Krehbiel, with card from Mr. and Mrs. Gerald Murphy, signed and inscribed by GCM; collection of the Isabella Stewart Gardner Museum.

94 "Make a poet black": Cullen, "Yet Do I Marvel," *Color*, p. 3.

Fats Waller: FMB interview.

"dissuaded by reactionaries": GCM to FMB, 11 Nov. 1949.

"A little of Roerich's virus": GCM, MacAgy/Murphy papers.

95 In Connecticut . . . wisps in her scrapbook: SWM scrapbooks, HMD.

"veering away from . . . Unsatisfactory": GCM, MacAgy/Murphy papers.

Gerald's work . . . course assignments: GCM transcripts, Harvard Graduate School of Design.

"Cambridge in the early 1900s . . . ceased to be civilized": Cowley, *A Second Flowering*, pp. 90–91.

essays by Harold Stearns: Harold Stearns, *America and the Young Intellectual*; discussed in Hoffman, *The 20s*, p. 27.

96 Waldo Frank: GCM, MacAgy/Murphy papers.

"Whole departments": Waldo Frank, *Our America*, quoted in Hoffman, *The 20s*, p. 31.

"a government that could pass": *LW*, p. 21.

He and Sara . . . "old sandstone houses: GCM to Nancy Milford, quoted in Milford, *Zelda*, p. 105.

"feeling like aliens . . . steamer tickets": Cowley, *Exile's Return*, p. 6.

In Europe . . . $7, a year: *LW*, p. 21.

he hadn't completed . . . his degree: GCM transcripts, Harvard Graduate School of Design.

97 "Foreign Residents": *S&G*, p. 8.

June 11, 1921 . . . *SS Cedric*: SWM scrapbooks, HMD.

9. *"An entirely new orbit"*

98 The summer of 1921 . . . parched and brown: Hester Pickman/HMD interview, Jul. 1981, HMD.

"didn't seem to fill the bill": SWM/CT interview, HMD.

September 3 . . . Étoile: SWM scrapbooks, HMD.

But then they discovered . . . material for a book: Hester Pickman/HMD interview, HMD.

"overdressed": Ibid.

So Gerald and Sara . . . rue Greuze: SWM scrapbooks, HMD.

99 "The thing I used . . . slaughtered": AMacL, *Reflections*, p. 23.

100 this first *manifestation* . . . delighted dadaists: Daix, *Picasso*, p. 172; and Wiser, *The Crazy Years*, pp. 40–41.

100 walls were covered . . . wee hours: Wiser, *The Crazy Years*, p. 134.

program note . . . popular lexicon: Cronin, *Paris*, p. 63.

Now he celebrated . . . drop curtain by Picasso: The first two of these were revivals of productions that premiered at the Alhambra Theatre, London, in 1919; *Le Chant du Rossignol* had opened at the Opéra in February, so, strictly speaking, only *Pulcinella* was new.

101 "The ground floor": Hugo, *Le Regard de la mémoire*, p. 158 (my translation).

conceived a hopeless crush . . . José María Sert: Gold and Fizdale, *Misia*, p. 233.

102 *l'emmerdeuse:* Ibid.

"subjugation and domination": GCM, quoted in *S&G*, p. 11.

"she knew everybody": Noel Murphy/HMD interview, HMD.

A tall, long-faced . . . blue eyes: de Faucigny-Lucinge, *Un gentilhomme cosmopolite*, p. 105.

By the time . . . ill from anxiety: Ibid., p. 106.

"In India": Gold and Fizdale, *Misia*, p. 239.

103 "there was a stir": Hugo, *Le Regard de la mémoire*, p. 206 (my translation).

"a world somewhere . . . men as women": de Faucigny-Lucinge, *Un gentilhomme cosmopolite*, pp. 105 and 108 (my translation).

forthcoming sale . . . Picasso: Daix, *Picasso*, pp. 173, 176, and 178.

"There was . . . new orbit": GCM, Murphy/MacAgy papers.

He couldn't remember . . . that autumn day: Although Gerald told Calvin Tomkins that he saw all these artists in Paul Rosenberg's gallery, that would have been impossible; Matisse was represented by Bernheim Jeune and Gris by Kahnweiler (as William Rubin points out in note 3, p. 44, *The Paintings of Gerald Murphy*), and their paintings would not have been hanging in Rosenberg's window.

104 "I was astounded . . . like to do": GCM/CT interview, HMD. Quoted, with alterations, in *LW*, p. 25.

"a crazy Russian . . . and irresponsible childishness": SWM to GCM, 16 Mar. 1918, HMD.

"charming, extraordinarily attractive": Hester Pickman/HMD interview, HMD.

"She started us . . . non-representational": GCM/CT interview, HMD.

They would subdivide . . . stronger ones less so: Rubin, *The Paintings of Gerald Murphy*, p. 9..

105 "No apple on a dish": SWM/CT interview, HMD.

The kind of art . . . simply pleased him: "Real objects which I admired had become for me abstractions, or objects in a world of abstractions," wrote Gerald to Douglas MacAgy. "My hope was to somehow digest them along with purely abstract forms and *re*-present them."

He and Sara and Hester . . . six months: MacAgy/Murphy papers.

"was still Mademoiselle": Hester Pickman/HMD interview, HMD.

"a huge, blond" . . . all his work for him: Stravinsky and Craft, *Conversations with Igor Stravinsky*, p. 111.

"how he rushed up": GCM, MacAgy/Murphy papers.

"a sad business": Charnot, *Gontcharova*, p. 77 (my translation). Gerald and Sara couldn't agree about why the scenery needed repainting: Gerald said later that a fire had destroyed all the company's sets, but Sara maintained (SWM/CT interview) that "it was just used up, worn out." The fire makes a better story, but there's no record of this event; wear and tear makes more sense.

Would Mademoiselle . . . scenery shop?: GCM and SWM/CT interview, HMD.

"serious and trying work": GCM, MacAgy/Murphy papers.

Diaghilev's atelier . . . proper perspective: GCM/CT interview, CT notes, HMD.

106 "hovered, — but pleasantly": GCM, MacAgy/Murphy papers.

peering through . . . offer corrections: GCM and SWM/CT interview, HMD; also MacAgy/Murphy papers.

"A dark, powerful": GCM, MacAgy/Murphy papers.

"very attractive": Hester Pickman/HMD interview, HMD.

"What are you all": Ibid. *S&G*, p. 15, using the same source, says the location was the Opéra, but Pickman clearly places the conversation at the atelier.

"a sort of *movement* . . . discussed it with you": GCM/CT interview, HMD.

Sometimes the new recruits . . . fondly afterward: SWM/CT interview, HMD.

107 Gerald's quarters . . . other supplies: Description of the studio's interior is from Ernest Hemingway, Item 648A, p. 14, JFK. The description of the exterior of the building, and the surrounding neighborhood, is based on personal observation.

108 broad-brimmed black . . . Toulouse-Lautrec poster: Reminiscence of William Lord, Yale class of 1922, quoted in *S&G*, p. 10.

"I seemed to see . . . giant scale": GCM, MacAgy/Murphy papers.

108 "iron, glass, concrete": Louis Lozowick, "Tatlin's Monument to the Third International," *Broom*, III, Oct. 1922, pp. 232–34.

He called one of them . . . engine block: Although William Rubin's catalogue for Murphy's MOMA show in 1974 has become the accepted chronology of his works, I differ from it on a few significant points. One concerns the identification of Murphy's first two paintings, listed in the catalogue of the Salon des Artistes Indépendents (34e Exposition) as *Turbines* and *Pression*. Without any visual record to guide him, Rubin posited, not illogically, that *Turbines* is the painting now known as *Engine Room* and that *Pression* (or *Pressure*) is lost. However, the arts journal *Shadowland* published an article on the 1922 Salon des Indépendents illustrated by a photograph of *Turbines* on which I have based my description; I therefore assume that the picture we know as *Engine Room* is the original *Pression*.

He worked on . . . oils on the canvas: GCM. MacAgy/Murphy papers.

109 He had never . . . until that moment: GCM to Rudi Blesh, quoted in Blesh, *Modern Art USA*, p. 95.

They settled in . . . digging in the sand: SWM scrapbooks, HMD.

"always had a great flair . . . crystalline water": GCM/CT interview, HMD.

10. *"A prince and a princess"*

110 "Think for a moment": Allan Ross Macdougall, "Independence and Otherwise in Paris," *Shadowland*, Jun. 1923.

111 "cubistic studies of machinery": Ibid.

"very personal . . . decorative effect": "American Art in Salon," *New York Herald* (Paris), 9 Feb 1923.

This four-day bazaar . . . American artist had arrived: "Foire de Nuit à Bullier," *Comoedia*, 22 Feb. 1923, p. 2; and "Le Bal des Artistes Russes," *Comoedia*, 25 Feb. 1923, p. 2.

112 Seldes considered . . . sublime: Kammen, *The Lively Arts*, p. 96.

returned from the Côte d'Azur . . . Versailles: SWM scrapbooks, HMD.

Sara delighted in prowling . . . antiques shops: SWM to FMB, 15 Jan. 1952, FMB.

But it was small . . . rats on the stairs: GCM/CT interview; HMD. In addition, GCM mentions the remodeling in the MacAgy/Murphy papers.

It wouldn't do . . . residence at Versailles: Although Honoria Donnelly maintains in her book that the family didn't acquire the quai des Grands-

Augustins apartment until the fall of 1925, other evidence contradicts this date. The catalogues for the Salon des Indépendents for 1923, 1924, and 1925 give Gerald Murphy's address as 23 quai des Grands-Augustins; and ESB, JDP, DOS, and Gerald Murphy himself placed the Murphys on the quai in 1923.

And they could justify . . . in February: SWM tax return for 1923, HMD.

The Kamerny actors . . . set was wide: Hugo, *Le Regard de la mémoire*, p. 224.

113 *The Man Who Was Thursday* . . . "out of the country": This account of the Kamerny Theater, and of the Murphys' dinner party, is drawn from GCM, MacAgy/Murphy papers.

114 "Once upon a time . . . be their friends": DOS, *By a Stroke of Luck!* p. 117.

"Sara was obviously . . . brisk and preoccupied": JDP, *The Best Times*, p. 145.

"an apostle": GCM, MacAgy/Murphy papers.

115 "tugs clustered": GCM art notebook, HMD.

"The banks of the Seine": JDP, *The Best Times*, p. 146.

"had never had . . . three little towheads": Ibid., p. 147.

Donald Ogden Stewart . . . visitors mistook it for: ESB interview.

116 Gerald said . . . pale green celery: Marcel Espiau, "Chez M. Gérard Murphy, peintre 'bien américain,'" *L'Éclair*, 18 Feb. 1924, p. 1.

black or white opalescent vases: These vases are still in Honoria Donnelly's possession.

spare cubicle . . . paintings afterward: GCM, MacAgy/Murphy papers. The rose — or, more accurately, roses on a single stem — appear in *La rose et le compas, Roses et compas, Le Buste, Nature morte aux livres*, and other paintings of 1925.

117 "The Murphys were . . . United States": Quoted in LW, p. 8.

"this year's gift": Louis Laloy, *Comoedia* (front page), Monday, 4 Jun. 1923.

"an aesthetic revelation": Paul Roche, "Les Ballets russes à Paris," *Le Gaulois* (front page), 1 Jun. 1923.

The music . . . xylophone: Stravinsky, *Chroniques de ma vie*, pp. 41–43.

traditional gender divisions . . . as it was musically: See Garafola, *Diaghilev's Ballets Russes*, pp. 125–29.

Natalia Goncharova . . . tight schedule: Nathalie Gontcharova [*sic*], "The Creation of 'Les Noces,'" *Ballet and Opera*, Sept. 1949; and Bronislava Nijinska, "The Creation of 'Les Noces'" (translated and introduced by Jean M. Serafetinedes and Irina Nijinska, *Dance*, Dec. 1974).

He also seized . . . finished their task: JDP, *The Best Times*, p. 148.

118 considered squalor: See Cowley, A *Second Flowering*, pp. 91–98.

although Dos Passos . . . embarrassed: *S&G*, p. 13.

"everyone directly connected . . . worthy of the event": GCM, quoted in *LW*, p. 31

Winnie de Polignac's . . . Louis XIV: Description of the princess's house comes from Jacques Brindejont-Offenbach, "Chez La Princesse Edmond de Polignac: "Une Répétition des 'Noces' de Stravinsky," Tuesday, 12 Jun. 1923; the source of this clipping, in the press book for Les Noces in the Fonds Kochno, Musée de l'Opera, is unknown.

"The Cirque Médrano" . . . Germaine Taillefer: Sources for the description of the barge party are GCM's interviews with CT, HMD; the MacAgy/Murphy papers; *LW*, pp. 31–33.

119 "preferred pianist of *les Six*": Survage, "Larionov, homme actif/Gontcharova, femme douce et discrète," in Tatiana Loguine (ed.), *Gontcharova et Larionov, cinquante ans à Saint-Germain-des-près*, p. 134 (my translation).

"*Depuis le jour* . . . my life": Gerald thought Seldes had inscribed the menu, but Seldes was a Jew and unlikely to have had a first communion.

11. "There *is American elegance*"

121 "On the pleasant . . . north in April": *TITN*, p. 3.

July 3, 1923: SWM scrapbooks, HMD.

Sella rationalized . . . south for the sun: Blume, *Côte d'Azur*, p. 75.

122 Antibes was a sleepy . . . unpaved: HMD interviews, personal observation, and *LW*, p. 96.

Before he left Paris . . . in February: Rubin, *The Paintings of Gerald Murphy*, p. 20, suggests that this painting, *Boatdeck*, was designed as an opening curtain for the ballet *Within the Quota*, but a simple consideration of the painting's dimensions suggests otherwise. A painting eighteen feet high and twelve feet wide, while massive, would not begin to fill the proscenium space of the Théâtre des Champs-Élysées, where the Ballets Suédois played, and would have had the wrong proportions besides. Drop curtains are generally wider than they are tall.

Possibly inspired . . . fall of 1921: Ibid., p. 22.

Gerald had taken more . . . *Aquitania*: Marcel Espiau, "*Chez M. Gérard Murphy, peintre 'bien américain*,'" *L'Eclair*, 18 Feb. 1924.

By 1923 . . . Bonnard, and Léger: For a fuller discussion of the place of the Ballets Suédois in the Parisian avant-garde, see Bengt Häger, *Ballets Suédois,* and Lynn Garafola, "Rivals for the New: The Ballets Suédois and the Ballets Russes," in Nancy Van Norman Baer, ed., *Paris Modern: The Swedish Ballet, 1920–1925,* pp. 66–83.

123 She had even asked Igor . . . had declined: LW, p. 39.

One day . . . meet her grandson: GCM, MacAgy/Murphy papers; and Daix, *Picasso,* p. 182.

124 wanted to come back: Ibid.

"didn't speak a *word*" . . . Spanish: SWM/CT interview, HMD.

"entirely prosaic" . . . small talk: *LW,* p. 35.

"*Chère Madame Picasso* . . . American canoe": SWM to Olga Picasso, undated letter on Hôtel du Cap stationery, Musée Picasso (my translation).

when the de Beaumonts . . . Garoupe beach: ESB interview.

The de Beaumonts planned . . . Friday noon: Undated invitation, Étienne and Édith de Beaumont to Pablo Picasso, Musée Picasso.

125 They all clowned . . . grinning hugely: Photographs in SWM scrapbooks, HMD.

Picasso and Sara . . . end of his life: Rubin, "Reflections on Picasso and Portraiture," *Picasso and Portraiture,* p. 55.

Picasso alone . . . shadowy and indistinct: Photographs in SWM scrapbooks, HMD.

Olga's tension . . . delight in her children: William Rubin interview.

"She is never coy": GCM/CT interview.

One day she was . . . "*festin*": GCM to CT, 4 Sept. 1960, HMD.

126 "sense of the grotesque . . . *un chien*": LW, p. 36.

Opéra in Paris . . . "American elegance!": GCM to CT, 25 Apr. 1962, HMD.

They rarely talked . . . El Greco's model: GCM, MacAgy/Murphy papers.

During those golden July . . . rope of pearls: These conclusions are the result of personal observations, made from examination of the Musée Picasso's microfilms of Picasso's 1923 sketchbook, now in the possession of Marina Picasso, and of conversations with William Rubin.

Some of these pictures . . . as a given: ESB interview; GCM/CT interview; Daix, *Picasso,* pp. 182–83. See also Cabanne, *Le Siècle de Picasso,* pp. 637ff.

"Picasso was in love . . . sexual adventure": William Rubin interview.

"I would have thought . . . hard for her to resist": John Richardson interview.

127 "The Man of Taste" . . . feast with her tempter: Philip Barry, "The Man of Taste," unproduced manuscript, GUL.

128 "chers Picassos . . . Sara": SWM to Pablo and Olga Picasso, undated (but internal evidence places it in Jul.–Aug. 1923), Musée Picasso.
They posed like tourists . . . but at Sara: Photograph in SWM scrapbooks, HMD.
Sara felt . . . different reasons: ESB interview.
And Cole and Linda . . . for pleasure: James Douglas and Roderick Coupe interview.
After two weeks . . . work with Cole: HMD interview.
The two of them . . . went on swimming: S&G, p. 22.

129 As someone who . . . not his type: James Douglas and Roderick Coupe interview.
X-ray examinations . . . alter the painting: William Rubin, "The Pipes of Pan: Picasso's Aborted Love Song to Sara Murphy," ArtNews, May 1994.
It's difficult . . . two people: HMD interview.
"Will you come" . . . in the margin: SWM to Pablo and Olga Picasso, undated, Musée Picasso (my translation).

130 But after seeing the rehearsals . . . to the audience: LW, p. 41.
"nothing but a translation": "American Ballet in Paris Tonight," New York Herald (Paris), 25 Oct. 1923.
"It's easier to write": Ibid.
Within the Quota . . . action on stage: Within the Quota scenario described by La Revue de France and quoted in Häger, Ballets Suédois, p. 44. The original scenario has apparently been lost, and this is the only source.
Parade . . . inside the circus tent: An interesting discussion of Parade in this context appears in Siegel, Bohemian Paris, pp. 360–65.

131 costumes . . . specifications: Although Gerald is listed as the costume designer for Within the Quota on the ballet's program, a personal comparison of the costume sketches with Sara's scrapbooks inevitably suggests that the renderings of the women's costumes, at least are her work and not Gerald's — a view that is supported by Honoria Donnelly. In addition, in an interview with Calvin Tomkins, Gerald referred to the Sweetheart costume as Sara's work.
"the most powerful symbol": GCM to CT, 3 Jan. 1962, HMD.
"a study of American women": GCM quoted in "American Ballet in Paris Tonight," New York Herald (Paris), 25 Oct. 1923.

132 "DANCER RENEWS": *New York Herald (Paris)*, 13 Oct. 1923, p. 1.

"the Jazz Baby": *Within the Quota* scenario described by *La Revue de France* and quoted in Häger, *Ballets Suédois*, p. 44.

"fashionable and artistic . . . laughter and applause": "American Ballet Pleases Gathering at Paris Theatre," *New York Herald (Paris)*, 26 Oct. 1923.

Reviews . . . "American theme": Gilbert Seldes, "Within the Quota," *Paris-Journal*, 1923. See also Fokine, et al., *Les Ballets Suédois dans l'art contemporain*.

133 But it was not performed . . . *L'Homme et son désir*: Gail Levin, "The Ballets Suédois and American Culture," *Paris Modern*, pp. 123–24.

This tactic . . . discarded after one performance: DOS, *By a Stroke of Luck!* pp. 122–23.

only "modernist" . . . rest having been dropped: Gail Levin, "The Ballets Suédois and American Culture," *Paris Modern*, p. 124.

Stuart Davis's 1924 painting . . . enormous newspaper: See Sims, *Stuart Davis*, p. 174. The art historian Elizabeth Garrity Ellis points out that the Suédois toured extensively in Davis's home state of Pennsylvania, and he would very likely have seen the production either there or in New York.

nine years later . . . come to life: Bergreen, *As Thousands Cheer*, p. 313.

"Paris is bound to": "American Ballet in Paris Tonight," *New York Herald (Paris)*, 25 Oct. 1923.

134 "Twenty-three Liners": *New York Herald (Paris)*, 19 May 1923.

The *Herald* . . . "any fun left": "News of Americans Day by Day," *New York Herald (Paris)*, 7 Apr. 1923.

"practically nothing a year": Le Vot, *F. Scott Fitzgerald*, p. 172.

12. *"Very serious over trivialities and rather wise about art and life"*

135 On February 7 . . . *Boatdeck*: "American's Eighteen-Foot Picture Nearly Splits Independent Artists," *New York Herald (Paris)*, 8 Feb. 1924, p. 1.

"struck by the look": GCM, MacAgy/Murphy papers.

An emergency meeting . . . withdrew their resignations: "American's Eighteen-Foot Picture Nearly Splits Independent Artists," *New York Herald (Paris)*, 8 Feb. 1924, p. 1.

"It could scarcely": "Curious Art Seen at Indépendents," *New York Herald (Paris)*, 9 Feb. 1924, p. 2.

136 "If they think . . . Grand Palais": "American's Eighteen-Foot Picture Nearly Splits Independent Artists," *New York Herald (Paris)*, 8 Feb. 1924, pp. 1–2.

137 "truly sorry" . . . freight terminal: Marcel Espiau, "Chez M. Gérard Murphy, peintre 'bien américain,'" *L'Éclair*, 18 Feb. 1924, p. 1 (my translation).

In the spring . . . hubcaps or headlamps: Photograph is in HMD's collection; the attribution to Man Ray is by Turner, in "Paris: Capital of America," *Americans in Paris*, p. 26. Additional details from AMacL, *Riders on the Earth*, p. 124.

"To be done . . . rated as somebody": Sylvia Beach, *Shakespeare and Company*, quoted in Turner, *Americans in Paris*, p. 19.

"Mr. and Mrs. [Gerald] Murphy . . . when she danced": Harry Crosby to Henrietta Crosby, 20 Dec. 1924, quoted in Wolff, *Black Sun*, p. 155.

one of his parties . . . like a butler: Wolff, *Black Sun*, p. 147.

138 "we always thought . . . with many people": GCM to CT, 24 Aug. 1960, HMD.

"chic (which was unpardonable)" . . . living room: Ibid.

"the most beautiful": FSF comment to Dorothy Parker, quoted in Milford, *Zelda*, p. 67.

Christmas dinner in 1923 . . . Princeton: Edmund Wilson to John Peale Bishop, 15 Jan. 1924, in Wilson, *Letters on Literature and Politics*, pp. 117–18.

139 "We four communicate . . . affection for Scott": GCM to FSF and Zelda Fitzgerald, 19 Sept. 1925, PUL.

"My father is a moron": FSF to Maxwell Perkins, 20 Feb. 1926, *The Letters of F. Scott Fitzgerald*, p. 199.

they, like Dos Passos . . . "Da-da": S&G, p. 7; Miller, *Letters from the Lost Generation*, p. xxvi; JDP, *The Best Times*, p. 170.

140 "full of money": FSF, *The Great Gatsby*, p. 120.

dresses from Poiret . . . Palais Royale: GCM to CT, 4 Sept. 1960, HMD; ESB interview.

"It was a colossal frost . . . impatient whispers": FSF, "How to Live on $36, a Year," *Afternoon of an Author*, p. 118.

"When I like men . . . leave him out": FSF, *The Notebooks of F. Scott Fitzgerald*, p. 146.

Three stories high . . . across the river: Personal observation.

The Gounod family . . . jumped at it: GCM/CT interview, HMD; Noel Murphy to ARM, 6 Feb. 1924, HMD.

141 fifteen minutes . . . back and forth: Ada MacLeish to Maurice Firuski, 28
Feb. 1924, Berg Collection, New York Public Library.

art notebook . . . didn't seem sure: GCM art notebook, HMD. William
Rubin, in *The Paintings of Gerald Murphy* (p. 15), seems to believe this
passage was a proposal for a ballet, but unlike the other ballet scenario in the
book it describes only a static set piece, not a continuum of imagery and
action.

welcome both grandfathers: Photograph in SWM's scrapbooks, HMD.

142 "the trouble with his father": Noel Murphy to ARM, 6 Feb. 1924, HMD.

"quite off": Ibid.

long-limbed . . . linen pillowcase: HMD interview.

"all agree . . . made myself plain": Noel Murphy to ARM, 6 Feb. 1924,
HMD.

On May 23 . . . never entirely clear: Frederic Murphy's obituaries in *Morn-*
ing Telegraph (London), 25 May 1924, and *Yale Alumni News*, undated; both
HMD.

143 "Picture . . . big match box": GCM art notebook, HMD.

"mechanically, in profile": GCM, quoted in Hayden Herrera, "Gerald Murphy, An Amurikin in Paris," *Art in America*, Sept.–Oct. 1974.

"re-present . . . interior of a watch": GCM, MacAgy/Murphy papers.

144 By his own admission . . . piano at home: Ibid.

1924 rayograph . . . clock's works: Man Ray, *Untitled*, 1924, collection of
Arnold Crane, New York, in Turner, *Americans in Paris*, p. 84.

"never had anything valuable": GCM to SWM, 16 Jun. 1915, HMD.

As one critic . . . time is king: Hayden Herrera, "Gerald Murphy: An
Amurikin in Paris," *Art in America*, Sept.–Oct. 1974.

145 *instrument de précision*: GCM to AMacL, 22 Jan. 1930, LOC; GCM to AJ, 13
Jun. 1946, UT.

nightly dinner guest . . . "prettiest girls": DOS, *By a Stroke of Luck!* pp. 130–
31.

Stewart finally . . . Ada MacLeish: Ibid., p. 130.

"was just instinctively": AMacL, *Reflections*, p. 42.

146 "We went . . . later for Noces": AMacL to John Peale Bishop, 30 Jul. 1924,
Letters of Archibald MacLeish, p. 150.

"I must say . . . but Scott": SWM/Nancy Milford interview, quoted in Milford, *Zelda*, p. 110.

146 "I don't know how": GCM/Nancy Milford interview, quoted in Milford, *Zelda*, p. 110.

"He was bronze . . . she didn't care": Zelda Fitzgerald, *Save Me the Waltz*, p. 89.

"It did upset . . . his own fault?": GCM/Nancy Milford interview, quoted in Milford, *Zelda*, p. 110.

147 "locked in my villa . . . [Jozan]": Milford, *Zelda*, p. 174.

Gilbert Seldes brought . . . side of the road: Ibid., p. 111.

"unflinching gaze": GCM, quoted in *LW*, p. 102.

"But Say-ra": *LW*, p. 42.

Outside stood Scott . . . "did it on purpose": Ibid.

When she found out . . . never mentioned again: GCM/Nancy Milford interview, Milford, *Zelda*, p. 111.

That summer . . . hazed over with smoke: Details from Gertrude Benchley to Nancy Milford, Milford, *Zelda*, p. 107.

148 The owner . . . "people I don't know?": Blume, *Côte d'Azur*, p. 77.

Noel Murphy . . . six-cylinder Renault: Noel Murphy/HMD interview, HMD.

The nearsighted Stewart . . . bull come at him: GCM/CT interview, HMD; DOS, *By a Stroke of Luck!* pp. 132–33.

But Gerald and Sara . . . advertised on the cover: DOS, *By a Stroke of Luck!* p. 134.

Johnny Lucinge . . . Riviera in the summer: Bernard Minoret interview.

"we saw what was happening": GCM/CT interview, HMD.

On the slope . . . near the house: Description of shrubs from personal observation; *S&G*, p. 19; and Previews Incorporated real estate sell sheet, May 1949, no. 42833.

149 "I think . . . *own* way": GCM to SWM, [1915], HMD.

"*artiste peintre*": Deed is on file at Hôtel de Ville, Antibes.

13. "Our real home"

150 "the Gerald Murphys": Ada MacLeish to Maurice Firuski, 28 Sept. 1924, Berg Collection, New York Public Library.

"had all his life": AMacL, "The Intimate Poems of L. T. Carnavel," LOC.

151 "Gerald was a remarkable . . . very knowledgeable": AMacL, *Reflections*, p. 42.

He and Sara had sung . . . "any other way": *LW*, p. 29.

Marcelle Meyer . . . baby to be admired: SWM scrapbooks, HMD.

"les Murphy . . . *very important*": Eric Satie to Vincente Huidobro, 28 Jun. 1924, Fondation Erik Satie.

Gerald was a friend . . . quite so close: AMacL, *Reflections*, p. 45.

"stirred by poetry": AMacL to Betty Choate, 12 Feb. 1925, in Donaldson, *Archibald MacLeish*, p. 148.

"A poem should": AMacL, "Ars poetica," *New and Collected Poems, 1917–1976*, pp. 106–107.

152 "in French terms": AMacL, *Reflections*, p. 43.

"very easy . . . see them": AMacL/Drabeck and Ellis interview transcript, Archibald MacLeish Collection, Greenfield Community College.

"very solid . . . in the spring": Ada MacLeish to Maurice Firuski, 5 Jan. 1926, Berg Collection, New York Public Library.

"Stripes of mustard . . . *sur le chameau*": All quotes from AMacL, 1926, *Notes & Drafts for The Hamlet of A. MacLeish*, LOC (my translations).

The preceding spring . . . return to New York: Donaldson, *Archibald MacLeish*, pp. 136–38. William MacLeish, in an interview with the author, said that his father denied having such an affair — at least to him.

153 perhaps not so coincidentally . . . made notes: GCM art notebook, HMD.

"lace, globe, black stems": Ibid.

"Sara never lodged": Unpublished, crossed-out draft of "Portrait of Mme. G—— M——," in Notebook 1924–25, MacLeish Papers, LOC.

"Her room": AMacL, "Sketch for a Portrait of Mme. G—— M——," *New and Collected Poems, 1917–1976*, pp. 107–109.

154 "1000 parties": FSF, *Ledger*, p. 179.

"weren't really party people" . . . kept coming back: GCM/CT interview, HMD.

"sentimentally disturbed": GCM to CT, [1961], HMD.

"in love . . . kiss between friends?": GCM/CT and SWM/CT interview tapes, HMD.

155 "Sara, look at me": CT notes, HMD.

Once, in a taxi . . . banknotes into his mouth: *LW*, p. 101.

who used to wash coins: Noel Murphy/HMD interview, HMD; also *S&G*, p. 32.

uninterested in food . . . prewar years: GCM/CT interview notes, HMD.

"Scott used to . . . not your roommate": ESB interview.

155 literary advice: *LW*, p. 105.

he made Gerald repeat . . . so unlike Gerald: GCM/CT interview notes, HMD.

"Are you what they . . . wanted to, always": GCM to CT, [1960], HMD.

156 "I hear a pulsing motor . . . dates you!": *LW*, p. 106.

"I've been watching . . . buckles and straps": GCM/CT interview, HMD.

"about myself . . . ever invented": FSF to H. L. Mencken, 4 May 1925, *The Letters of F. Scott Fitzgerald*, p. 491.

157 matters had been sticky . . . brother-in-law: HMD interview.

"noted for her Enthusiasm . . . Concentration": Barnes, *Ladies Almanack*, p. 32.

"an idiot savant": James Douglas interview.

"on her back in bed" . . . to get relief: Esther Murphy to Muriel Draper, [Aug. 1926], Muriel Draper papers, Beinecke Library.

attachment to Janet Flanner . . . his own sexuality: FMB interview.

158 "our real home": *S&G*, p. 15.

Its limestone walls . . . another balcony: Layout described in HMD and FMB interviews; also in an advertisement for the Villa America by Previews Incorporated, listing no. 42833), May 1949.

In the main reception . . . completed the look: Descriptions based on photographs and interviews with HMD, FMB, ESB, and Yvonne Roussel Luff.

Sara enlivened . . . found a new home: Linens and furniture listed in Villa America household inventory, HMD.

159 Throughout the house . . . green lace: HMD interview.

Gerald had found . . . silver radiator paint: ESB interview.

In July they purchased . . . farmhouse: Deed on file at Hôtel de Ville, Antibes.

giving each: Yvonne Roussel Luff interview.

Sara wrote . . . plant sweet corn: SWM to "Mr. Steinmetz," undated [1929], HMD.

She and Gerald . . . variety of nut trees: Previews Incorporated advertisement, HMD.

they acquired two cows . . . chauffeur, Albert: HMD interview.

160 Sara had tried to learn . . . gave up trying: *S&G*, p. 32.

Vladimir Orloff . . . Englishman called Kipling: HMD interview.

"do the things we want": GCM to SWM, quoted in *LW*, pp. 18–19.

In the mornings . . . what needed to be done: Schedule from interviews with HMD and Yvonne Roussel Luff.

161 Sometimes the mornings . . . cut Gerald's hair: *S&G*, p. 30.

"Think . . . tender weight, gone!": *LW*, p. 94.

There the children . . . toe touches: Exercise sheet in SWM's handwriting in "Valuable Data" file, HMD.

"recondite *hors d'oeuvres*": JDP, *The Best Times*, p. 150.

probably the delicious . . . Honoria still remembers: *S&G*, p. 31.

They ate at the big . . . fresh parsley: Menus from HMD interviews, JDP, *The Best Times*, p. 150; and AMacL, *Reflections*, p. 46.

162 Once when the Picassos . . . different from girls: HMD interview.

"*Chere mecie picaso*" . . . *Guernica:* HMD to Pablo Picasso, 26 Sept. 1925, Musée Picasso.

Late in the afternoon . . . highest point: S&G, p. 31.

Cannes . . . railroad tracks: GCM to ESB, 18 Jun. 1950, GUL.

"holocausts": *LW*, p. 41

"just the juice": HMD interview.

"invented by me" . . . mint in each glass: GCM to Alexander Woollcott, 15 Feb. 1939, HU.

163 These Gerald mixed . . . preparing Mass: *S&G*, p. 31.

served them ritually . . . drink before dinner: Hester Pickman/HMD interview, HMD.

Honoria practiced . . . Jimmy Durante's band: *S&G*, p. 31.

"there was no one": FSF to John Peale Bishop, [Sept. 1925], *The Letters of F. Scott Fitzgerald*, pp. 358–59.

Donald Ogden Stewart . . . Plage de la Garoupe: DOS, *By a Stroke of Luck!* pp. 144–45.

"Most of them": SWM to CT, 1 Jul. 1969, HMD.

164 Manuel Ortiz de Zarate . . . *interesting:* SWM to Pablo Picasso, undated, Musée Picasso.

That night . . . *happy* she was to be there: FSF to Marya Mannes, [Oct. 1925], *The Letters of F. Scott Fitzgerald*, pp. 488–89.

In thanks . . . "never been so moved": GCM/CT interview, HMD.

The parties weren't always . . . complete success: HMD interview.

"Life gets a little denser": GCM to EH, 18 Jun. 1927, JFK.

164 "it is the horror": AMacL to John Peale Bishop, 8 Aug. 1925, *Letters of Archibald MacLeish*, p. 169.

165 So in June . . . "STUPIDITY": Interview with Jacques Livet, friend of Vladimir Orloff; telegram quoted in Jacques Livet to the author, 7 Jul. 1994 (my translation).
"always became a native": David Pickman/HMD interview.
In July . . . Don Stewart: ESB interview.

166 "at first astonishing . . . Cézanne's apples": Florent Fels, "Le Salon des Indépendants," *L'Art vivant*, vol. 1, no. 6, 20 Mar. 1925, p. 27.
Archibald MacLeish . . . for himself: It's not clear when MacLeish acquired this painting, but it must have been around this time: a letter to John Peale Bishop dated 3 Feb. 1926 mentions MacLeish's "Juan Gris & Gerald Murphy bedecked atelier." (AMacL, *Letters of Archibald MacLeish*, p. 176.)
"L'Art d'aujourd'hui . . . certainly not European": Rubin, *The Paintings of Gerald Murphy*, p. 30.
"Gerald Murphy . . . in Paris": *LW*, p. 26.
The writer . . . getting to know them: Reynolds, *Hemingway: The Paris Years*, p. 325.
when he struck up . . . impressed: GCM to CT, 4 Sept. 1960.

14. *"The kind of man to whom men, women, children, and dogs were attracted"*

167 "the kind of man": Hadley Hemingway to Nancy Milford, quoted in Milford, *Zelda*, p. 117.
"promises to remove him": Wilson, *Paris on Parade*, p. 248.

168 Hemingway often wrote . . . drink or a coffee: EH, *A Moveable Feast*, pp. 91–92.
"a writer's job": EH, quoted in Mellow, *Hemingway*, p. 187.
"alpha male": William MacLeish interview.
"he was such an enveloping": GCM/CT interview notes, HMD.
"Sara loved very male": FMB interview.
"nobody is as male": *S&G*, p. 21.

169 "a nice, plain girl . . . carry the burden": GCM and SWM/CT interview (taped), HMD.
"swell": EH to FSF, 24 Dec. 1925, EH, *Ernest Hemingway: Selected Letters*, p. 182.

"Picture: — Finish": GCM art notebook, HMD.

"that big green": EH, "My Old Man," *The Short Stories of Ernest Hemingway*, p. 193.

"with rich food": EH to Bill Smith, 2 Jan 1926, private collection; Reynolds, *Ernest Hemingway: The American Homecoming*, p. 9.

fly to the Silvretta . . . ski down: EH to Grace Hemingway, 14 Dec. 1925, JFK.

toyed with the idea . . . January: GCM to FSF, 19 Sept. 1925, PUL.

And for Ernest . . . friends and family: Reynolds, *Ernest Hemingway: The American Homecoming*, p. 9.

170 returned to him, unread . . . Oak Park: EH to Dr. C. E. Hemingway, 20 Mar. 1925, *Ernest Hemingway: Selected Letters*, p. 153.

"You see . . . working toward something": Ibid.

"Those God-damn . . . promise to yourself": GCM to EH, in *S&G*, p. 21.

171 proceeded to read . . . single evening: EH to FSF, 15 Dec. 1925, *Ernest Hemingway: Selected Letters*, p. 176.

Sara dozed off . . . applauded its author: *LW*, p. 27.

"I have known . . . 10th printing": EH to FSF, 31 Dec. 1925, *Ernest Hemingway: Selected Letters*, p. 183.

"I'm loose": Ibid.

promising . . . developments: EH notebook, quoted in Reynolds, *Hemingway: The Paris Years*, p. 350.

left a manuscript copy: GCM to Hadley Hemingway, 3 Mar. 1926, JFK; Miller, *Letters from the Lost Generation*, p. 15.

"Gosh, what news . . . water afresh": Ibid.

172 "felt like skunks": Ibid.

"spent two days . . . absolutely elated": GCM/CT interview notes, HMD.

evening, all five . . . Gerald and Sara as well?: Details from Reynolds, *Hemingway: The American Homecoming*, pp. 11–12.

173 "nucleus": GCM art notebook, HMD.

"the last unalloyed": JDP, *The Best Times*, p. 158.

That spring Gerald . . . withdrawn or damaged: Catalogue, *Société des Artistes Indépendants, 37e Exposition* (held at Palais de Bois, Porte Maillot, 20 Mar. to 2 May 1926). The catalogue lists two pictures by Gerald Murphy: no. 2635 *bis*, *Laboratoire* and no. 2635 *ter*, *Nature Morte*. The *bis* and *ter* numerations indicate that they were the second and third entries; the first entry, not listed, must have been withdrawn after its number was assigned.

"group of chemical retorts": GCM art notebook, HMD.

173 "a table with real objects": Ibid. All these notes precede a dated entry from Oct. 1926; any note on pages after that could not refer to paintings executed, or exhibited, before then.

174 "'painting' forms . . . human relations": GCM art notebook, HMD.
"Is there dramatic . . . human beings": GCM to Philip Barry, [1925–26], GUL.

175 "Hadley seemed so tired . . . Don't worry — you": GCM to EH, 22 May 1926, JFK; Miller, *Letters from the Lost Generation*, pp. 16–17.
What they didn't tell . . . other expenses: Hadley Hemingway to EH, 24 May 1926, JFK; Reynolds, *Hemingway: The American Homecoming*, p. 35.
Gerald Cohn: *The Sun Also Rises* manuscript 194-I-13, JFK. See also Mellow, *Hemingway*, p. 304.
"By the time we left . . . great fun": Hadley Hemingway to Nancy Milford, quoted in Milford, *Zelda*, p. 119.

176 "I made one of those mistakes": FSF to Zelda Fitzgerald, [summer] 1930, PUL; *Correspondence of F. Scott Fitzgerald*, p. 239.
Why did they rave . . . about his own: GCM/CT interview notes, HMD.
"I suppose you have": *LW*, p. 106, and CT interview.
promising composer ruined . . . "Seth with you": *TITN*, pencil ms. 2, the Melarky version, PUL. See also Bruccoli, ed., *F. Scott Fitzgerald Manuscripts*, vol. IVa: *Tender Is the Night: The Melarky and Kelly Versions*, Part 1.
"It's hardly likely": SWM to FSF, [summer 1926], PUL.
"cooled relation" . . . Sara too: *TITN*, p. 75; CT transcriptions of GCM interviews, HMD.

177 "So was Ernest": ESB interview.
When Archie MacLeish . . . liner's bridge: Donaldson, *Archibald MacLeish*, p. 157.
Indian war dance on the pier: AMacL, *Reflections*, p. 41.
They organized morning . . . smiling to herself: All photographs, SWM scrapbooks, HMD.

178 Strange music . . . giants and dwarfs: GCM/CT taped interview, HMD.
The Hemingway party . . . chairs at their feet: Ibid.
"these men, living": GCM to Hadley Hemingway and EH, [14 Jul. 1926], JFK.
"you two children": Ibid.

"dow dow": Reynolds, *Hemingway: The American Homecoming*, p. 49.

Before they went to Spain . . . relinquish the habit: GCM to CT, 7 Nov. 1963, HMD.

"Papa": GCM to Hadley Hemingway and EH, [14 Jul. 1926], JFK.

179   "I didn't want . . . think it's fine": GCM/CT interview, HMD.

"to look or feel . . . do it well, Papa": GCM to Hadley Hemingway and EH, [14 Jul. 1926], JFK.

"He was watching me": GCM/CT interview, HMD.

"everybody yelled 'Olé'": GCM and SWM/CT taped interview, HMD.

"a little silk dress . . . all my diamonds": SWM/CT taped interview, HMD.

paid for by Gerald: Baker, *Ernest Hemingway*, p. 172.

"I stamped out . . . He didn't notice": SWM/CT taped interview, HMD.

180   "no one has anything": SWM to Hadley Hemingway and EH, [14 Jul. 1926], JFK.

"kept unearthing": GCM to Hadley Hemingway and EH, [14 Jul. 1926], JFK.

guitar for Baoth . . . Sara herself: SWM to Hadley Hemingway and EH, [14 Jul. 1926], JFK.

fireworks display . . . cheering crowd: GCM/CT taped interview, HMD.

Monty Woolley . . . Bulldog banter: HMD interview.

They also became fascinated . . . "crinkly-toes!": HMD and CT interviews.

181   "Gaytrûd": GCM to SWM and HMD, 4–9 Sept. 1937, HMD.

The Murphys greeted . . . Sara's drum: SWM to Hadley Hemingway and EH, [14 Jul. 1926], JFK.

"Brides, I find . . . seem to have??": SWM to Pablo Picasso, undated, Musée Picasso.

"She was dancing . . . unladylike": GCM quoted in Milford, *Zelda*, p. 120.

182   "I was sure . . . over and over again": Ibid., pp. 117–18.

Why did they seem . . . "anything about people": GCM/CT interview, HMD.

"Dear Scott . . . *Theories about friends*": SWM to FSF, [summer 1926], PUL. This letter is often assumed to follow the champagne-and-caviar party at the casino but cannot have been written then, as it refers to the MacLeishes (plural), and Archie MacLeish didn't arrive in Antibes from Persia until June 16.

183   an apology: Inferred from an undated letter of acknowledgment from SWM to FSF in which she writes, "Thanks for your note. Don't you think of it again — I haven't," PUL.

183 following two young . . . dancing with one of them: Milford, *Zelda*, p. 120.

The Murphys were going . . . "knocked him cold": GCM/CT interview notes, HMD. MacLeish, according to his biographer Scott Donaldson, denied punching Fitzgerald but claimed Scott had thrown a punch at *him* — to no effect. But MacLeish often liked to remember himself as more pacific than he always was.

184 "We saw the Murphys . . . much any more": FSF to EH, [fall 1926], *The Letters of F. Scott Fitzgerald*, p. 297.

Murphys had lent . . . remainder of the autumn: SMW to Zelda Fitzgerald, 28 Jun. 1927, PUL; "you were *too lovely* about running our entire place while we were away" is Sara's characteristic comment.

"depressed and . . . baffled": FSF to EH, [fall 1926], *The Letters of F. Scott Fitzgerald*, p. 297.

"Dear Hadern . . . hitched up to the universe": GCM to Hadley Hemingway and EH, [14 Jul. 1926], JFK.

"When life gets bumpy . . . talk about it after": GCM to EH, 6 Sept. 1926?, JFK.

Ernest had guessed . . . finances as a result: EH to Hadley Hemingway, 19 Nov. 1926, JFK.

"Hadley and you": GCM to EH, 6 Sept. 1926?, JFK.

He didn't tell them . . . returned to America: Because the Murphys knew and were fond of Pauline, it would have been natural for Ernest to refer to her and her plans in at least one of the letters he wrote them that autumn; but there is no mention of her in their correspondence until the following spring, just before she and Ernest married.

185 "Love Pirates . . . for my work": EH to Clarence Hemingway, 14 Sept. 1927, in *Ernest Hemingway: Selected Letters*, pp. 258–59.

"We said to each other . . . don't ever budge": GCM and SWM to EH, [fall 1926], JFK.

15. *"How can a wise man have two countries?"*

186 "Everyone in America": GCM to EH, 13 Feb. 1927, JFK.

"Therefore shall a man": Gen. 2: 23–24, in GCM "Notebooks" file, HMD. The quotation is undated but it is written on stationery from the Savoy Plaza Hotel, where Gerald and Sara stayed during New York visits in 1926 and 1929.

"*grang pere . . . tent n'etait pas la*": HMD diary, 1 Jan 1927, HMD.

"three nigger hives . . . adorable": PH to EH, 5 Oct. 1927, JFK.

Don Stewart . . . "false goatsbeard": DOS, *By a Stroke of Luck!* p. 157.

187 "Picture . . . windows": GCM art notebook, HMD.

"Capital, ionic": Ibid.

recoiled . . . cooing: FMB interview.

newly acquired cowboy . . . raids on the kitchen: HMD diary, 1 Feb., 3 Feb., 1928, HMD.

188 "the theatres . . . Executions": SWM to Zelda Fitzgerald, 28 Jun. [1927], PUL.

"a new opera": GCM to EH, 19 Mar. [1927], JFK.

concert at the Conservatoire . . . Scarlatti: Poster for Ada MacLeish concert in Myers papers, FMB.

"We wanted our children": AMacL, *Reflections*, p. 66.

Frenchified upbringing: DP to RB, 7 Nov. 1929, BU.

189 "They really couldn't": AMacL to EH, 19 Jun. [1927], *Letters of Archibald MacLeish*, p. 202.

"these damn school girl . . . his affection": AMacL to EH and PH, 13 Aug. [1927]; Ibid., p. 206.

encouraged him . . . year to paint: GCM to EH, 6 Sept. [1926], JFK.

more and more carrying . . . household alone: Yvonne Roussel Luff/HMD interview, HMD.

occasionally complained: William MacLeish interview.

"You're right . . . for a while": GCM to EH, 18 Jun. 1927, JFK.

"ballet of *métiers*" . . . cranes and warehouses: GCM art notebook, HMD.

filmed in a large, light . . . 69 rue Froidevaux: This idea was first proposed to me by Nelly Maillard, *documentaliste* of the Musée National Fernand Léger in Biot.

190 "my testicles give me": AMacL to EH, [Jun. 1926], JFK; AMacL, *Letters of Archibald MacLeish*, p. 178.

"He walks with Ernest": AMacL, *Collected Poems*, p. 146.

"all Fairies": EH to GCM and SWM, [late autumn 1926], HMD.

"was extremely sensitive": GCM/CT interview, HMD.

"You are quite sure" . . . lied to him: EH, "A Simple Enquiry," *The Short Stories of Ernest Hemingway*, pp. 327–30.

Hemingway began a novel . . . lousy writers: Item 529 B Ch 20, p. 1, JFK.

191 "a 4cv Terrot . . . without losing a spangle": GCM to EH, 18 Jun. 1927, JFK.

191 sometimes ride tandem . . . whizzing by: *S&G*, p. 29; HMD interview.
choosing dresses . . . Ellen Barry: ESB interview.
That spring . . . complained about it later to Gerald: SWM to PH, 17 Jun.
1927, PUL; GCM to EH, 18 Jun. 1927, JFK.
"What a remarkable . . . *La Mère Dante*": GCM to CT, 24 Aug. 1960, HMD.
spoke French like a butcher: AMacL, *Reflections*, p. 67.
"Gerald would get over . . . Gerald ditto": AMacL to EH, 13 Aug. [1927],
Letters of Archibald MacLeish, p. 206.

192 "People have now started . . . give us time": SWM to Zelda Fitzgerald, 28
Jun. [1927], PUL.
Harpo Marx . . . trip to Pamplona: GCM to EH, 15 Jun. 1927, JFK.
At a Paris concert . . . cut Picasso dead: AMacL interview, "The Art of
Poetry," *The Paris Review*, vol. 14, no. 58, p. 69.
"*Hélas, alors*": GCM to Pablo Picasso (postcard), 19 Sept. 1927, Musée
Picasso.
"I'm working . . . work quietly": GCM to EH, 18 Jun. 1927, JFK.

193 "such as the Greeks": *LW*, p. 144.
"blk. fond": GCM art notebook, HMD.
Its inspiration . . . bar tray: GCM, MacAgy/Murphy papers, HMD.

194 objects . . . personal iconography: See also Rubin, *The Paintings of Gerald
Murphy*, p. 37.
"faultily faultless": GCM to EH, 18 Jun. 1927, HMD.
They had been cruising . . . drop anchor in time: JDP, *The Best Times*,
pp. 150–51.
"hot boat": GCM to EH, 18 Jun. 1927, JFK.
"the child of my old age": Donaldson, *Archibald MacLeish*, p. 176.

195 "I don't mind a fairy" . . . same between them: GCM/CT interview; HMD.
Gerald Murphy's memory of this incident placed it shortly after their first
meeting; but he distinctly remembered Hemingway wearing a bandage
around his head at the time, something that happened after an accident with
a bathroom skylight in the spring of 1928.
"They were on their way . . . glad to be going": Zelda Fitzgerald, *Save Me the
Waltz*, p. 98.
"We are very fond . . . important thing: GCM to FSF, 15 May 1928, PUL.
"We are friends . . . so far away": FSF to EH, [Jul. 1928], JFK; *Correspondence
of F. Scott Fitzgerald*, p. 220.

The Murphys had recently . . . Scott and Zelda: Morton, *Americans in Paris*, p. 279.

"it looks like the setting": Zelda Fitzgerald to Mr. E. E. Addison, 29 May 1928; in Milford, *Zelda*, p. 140. Milford quotes it as "Madame Tausand's," which is clearly a mistranscription.

196 "There are limits . . . something awful would happen": Ibid., p. 141.

"I hope you die . . . next to her": Ibid., p. 142.

"The view was not . . . what she looked like": Ibid., pp. 141–42.

One morning, soon after . . . flea markets: HMD interview.

197 "It was such a . . . didn't ever happen": GCM to JDP, [19 Jan. 1929], UVA.

198 "I've never been exposed" . . . second place: Ibid., 5 Aug. 1928.

In the summer of 1928 . . . *Metropolis*: King Vidor interview in Schickel, *The Men Who Made the Movies*, p. 147.

consciously adopted the "shadowy effects": King Vidor interview by Dowd and Shepard, *King Vidor*, p. 48.

"a lot . . . the viewer": Schickel, *The Men Who Made the Movies*, p. 143.

199 "a classic country": King Vidor interview, quoted in Miller, *Letters from the Lost Generation*, p. 8.

"in my home town . . . singing songs": King Vidor interview by Dowd and Shepard, *King Vidor*, p. 102.

Scott Fitzgerald . . . Gerald Murphy: GCM to FSF, 15 May 1928, PUL.

Vidor came . . . Gerald's pictures: HMD interview.

"I thought that the type": King Vidor interview, quoted in Miller, *Letters from the Lost Generation*, p. 8.

Gerald had been impressed . . . *The Crowd*: GCM to FSF, 15 May 1928, PUL.

"My latest things . . . liberation": GCM to JDP, 5 Aug. 1928, UVA.

"An eye . . . foot in picture": GCM art notebook, HMD.

200 All were presented . . . experimenting: Léger had been to stay at the *bastide* for three weeks that summer, and he and Gerald had long talks about their work and the direction of painting. In Léger's view, surrealism was "the end of something and not the beginning, but with all the revolutions in art . . . it has dragged some real values onto the stage." GCM, MacAgy/Murphy papers; HMD.

"conglomerate standard": GCM, MacAgy/Murphy papers.

"Dear G . . . old call us": AMacL to GCM, 1 Sept. 1928, HMD.

16. "A *dismantled house where people have once been gay*"

202 Sara's bottle bag . . . evade customs: Yvonne Roussel Luff interview.
"I'm afraid we traveled": HMD interview.
Their rooms at the Savoy . . . assured one another: S&G, p. 123.

203 Don Stewart . . . *Holiday*: DOS, *By a Stroke of Luck!* p. 166.
most Indians had . . . no uncertain terms: HMD interview.
1737 Angelo Drive . . . Dicky, for Honoria: HMD and Patrick Murphy to Yvonne Roussel, undated; Yvonne Roussel Luff.
Marion Davies . . . Charlie Chaplin: S&G, p. 40.
"Patrick . . . Indians": Baoth Wiborg (Murphy) to Yvonne Roussel, undated; Yvonne Roussel Luff; description of the cowboy outfits from a photograph in SWM's albums, HMD.
"My God . . . Cupid Chips!": GCM to JDP, [19 Jan. 1929], UVA.

204 "It saves . . . Mary Pickford": Ibid.
Dorothy Parker . . . office door: Meade, *Dorothy Parker*, p. 198.
"a $150, . . . heart out of you": GCM to JDP, [19 Jan. 1929], UVA.
In Chicago . . . in that city: Vidor, *King Vidor*, pp. 99–100.

205 "SINCERELY HOPE . . . BEST REGARDS": Telegram from Irving Thalberg to King Vidor, 27 Oct. 1928, *Hallelujah!* production files, King Vidor collection, University of Southern California.
In the earliest stages . . . not been resolved: Vidor, *King Vidor*, p. 100.
The first script . . . verses of the song: Aug. 1928 script for *Hallelujah!*, King Vidor collection, University of Southern California.
The opening . . . "make it permanent": Ibid., 25 Sept. 1928.

206 "[I]n two weeks . . . Minstrels": GCM to JDP, 19 Jan. 1928, UVA.
When Thalberg heard . . . picture in droves: Daily memoranda, *Hallelujah!* studio files, King Vidor collection, University of Southern California.
To lighten things up . . . uplifting finale: Miscellaneous scripts, *Hallelujah!* and final credit sheet, *Hallelujah!* studio file; ibid.
"LIONEL BARRYMORE . . . Zowie": GCM to JDP, [19 Jan. 1929], UVA.
It was still . . . ranch house: Diane Fish interview.
Murphy children adored . . . picnicking: S&G, p. 42.

207 "It seems the most . . . trouble later": SWM to FBW, [Mar. 1929], HMD.
Rather than "letting everything" . . . addition to his own: Ibid.
Murphys on shipboard . . . somthing to happen: Photograph, SWM scrapbooks, HMD.

208 "Ireland is doomed": GCM to JDP, quoted in *S&G*, p. 29.

"Ernie" in the first draft: Item 618, JFK.

"I can blow him": EH, "Fathers and Sons," *The Short Stories of Ernest Hemingway*, p. 496.

"My Dear Boy . . . (french spelling)": GCM to EH, 16 Oct. 1927, JFK.

"Every other day": EH to JDP, [Dec. 1928], JFK.

209 "I know how the death": AMacL to EH, 14 Dec. 1928, JFK. According to notes in the Hemingway collection, the letter was not opened until 5 May 1978, after Hemingway's death.

Gerald asked Ernest . . . Marseille and Majorca: GCM to EH, [spring 1929], JFK..

proofs of his new novel . . . *Honoria's* crew: EH to AMacL, 18 Jul. 1929, *Ernest Hemingway: Selected Letters*, p. 300.

On his insistence . . . handsome dowry: Thomas, *John Strachey*, p. 71.

Strachey was already . . . day by herself: Ibid., p. 78.

210 "I hate figs": DP to Helen Droste, Sept. 1929, quoted in Meade, *Dorothy Parker*, p. 202.

smoking solitary cigarettes . . . gamine countenance: Yvonne Roussel Luff interview.

Baoth went so far . . . patois: DP to Alexander Woollcott, in Meade, *Dorothy Parker*, pp. 201–204.

"the Murphys have given their": FSF to EH, 9 Sept. 1929, *The Letters of F. Scott Fitzgerald*, pp. 305–306.

Gerald, at least . . . Antibes that summer: ZF to FSF, [late summer/early fall 1930], PUL.

Zelda became terrified . . . drowning victim: GCM interview with Nancy Milford, *Zelda*, p. 155.

"It's been gay here . . . five years": FSF to EH, 23 Aug. 1929, *The Letters of F. Scott Fitzgerald*, p. 305.

211 "absolutely blotto": Meade, *Dorothy Parker*, p. 204.

Another day, driving in Nice . . . fifteen days' imprisonment: The information about Robert Benchley and Gerald Murphy's run-in with the French authorities comes from a 13 Nov. 1919 letter from Charles D. Morgan, Gerald's Paris lawyer, to Benchley, asking for an affidavit. Morgan's version contradicts that given by Honoria Murphy Donnelly in *Sara and Gerald*, where she claims the car was impounded when left unattended, and says that Gerald, "realizing that he was in the wrong . . . quickly apologized" (*S&G*, p. 32).

211 "Green fruit softening": GCM to JDP, [19 Jan. 1929], UVA.

Wasp and Pear: There is some dispute about the date of this painting. Murphy, of course, rarely dated his own paintings and had difficulty remembering their chronology when attempting to reconstruct it in later life. Douglas MacAgy, in his catalogue for *American Genius in Review*, assigned it to 1927; but William Rubin, in his Museum of Modern Art retrospective *The Paintings of Gerald Murphy*, dated it 1929. Elizabeth Hutton Turner reverted to the 1927 date for her Phillips Gallery exhibit, *Americans in Paris*. It seems to me impossible, however, for someone who painted as slowly and painstakingly as Murphy did to have executed four canvases in the 1927–28 period that also included *Doves, Cocktail,* and *Portrait.* And it seems equally unlikely in the face of documentary evidence that he painted *no* pictures after 1927 — yet he described *Wasp and Pear* to Douglas MacAgy as "illustrating the direction in which my work was going when I was obliged to stop painting." He painted nothing while he was in America from Oct. 1928 until Mar. 1929 — so it seems likely that 1929 is indeed the only date that can be assigned to *Wasp and Pear.* The "green fruit" imagery, which dates from his Jan. 1929 letter to Dos Passos, only underscores this logic.

"hornet (colossal)" . . . seen from below: GCM art notebook, HMD.

212 "bed of crimson" . . . dark secret love": Blake, *Songs of Innocence and Experience,* unpaged facsimile edition.

"it was his duty": DP to RB, [7 Nov. 1929], BU.

213 "a wire from Gerald": EH to FSF, 4 Sept. 1929, *Ernest Hemingway: Selected Letters,* p. 304.

"at an altitude . . . fruits, etc.": GCM to Mary Hoyt Wiborg, 7 Sept. 1929, HMD.

"He's taking the injections . . . two years": GCM to EH, 12 Oct. 1929, JFK.

"bronchials showed speckly": SWM to PH, [12 Oct. 1929], JFK.

214 "My mother wants me . . . you to America": Baoth Wiborg (Murphy) to EH and PH, [Nov. 1929], quoted in *S&G,* p. 93.

worst decision . . . also the kindest: Meade, *Dorothy Parker,* p. 206.

"Sometime you must . . . coat or the muffler": Quotations are from DP to RB, [7 Nov. 1929], BU.

215 Ernestine took care . . . children's lessons: Yvonne Roussel Luff interview.

"isolated himself . . . 'poor Gerald'": Quotations are all from DP to RB, [7 Nov. 1929], BU.

17. "The invented *part, for me, is what has meaning*"

217 "laughing our heads off": JDP, *The Best Times*, p. 203.

Sara roasted . . . Christmas carols: HMD interview.

"big arty rout" . . . it was the Murphys: AMacL to EH, [10 Feb. 1930], *Letters of Archibald MacLeish*, p. 232.

"an *impossible* sort of cheque": Bankers Trust Company check dated 18 Dec. 1929, and made out to SWM, BU.

"*Don't* be mad . . . eternal snows": SWM to RB, [1 Jan. 1929], BU.

218 He would sit for hours . . . Miss Roussel or Gerald: Yvonne Roussel Luff interview.

February . . . visit to Antibes: HMD to Yvonne Roussel, [spring 1930], Yvonne R. Luff.

"DEUX CENTS FRANCS . . . MURPHYS" GCM cablegram to RB, 7 Feb. 1930; BU.

"Were you talking . . . right there with them!": GCM to Nancy Milford, in *Zelda*, p. 157.

219 Meanwhile the Murphys . . . Montana to Vermala: HMD to Yvonne Roussel, [spring 1930], Yvonne R. Luff.

"melancholly skenery": HMD interview.

"there is no more": HMD to Yvonne Roussel, [spring 1930], Yvonne R. Luff.

"Harry's Bar" . . . piano and sing: DOS, *By a Stroke of Luck!* p. 187.

220 "My father holds": HMD to YR, [spring 1930], Yvonne R. Luff.

Sara had tried . . . he refused it: SWM telegram to RB, [spring 1931], BU.

Because of the potency . . . hair of the dog: Meade, *Dorothy Parker*, pp. 211-12.

"I have a great surprise": HMD to YR, [spring 1930], Yvonne R. Luff.

221 "I don't suppose": SWM to FSF, 3 Apr. [1936], PUL; see also Meade, *Dorothy Parker*, p. 213.

"even though Patrick": DOS, *By a Stroke of Luck!* p. 187.

Gerald rented current . . . Saturday nights: HMD to Yvonne Roussel, [spring 1930], Yvonne R. Luff.

In addition to the Murphys' . . . rabbit: PFM II to GCM, [Sept. 1930], HMD.

parrot named Cocotte . . . shoulder everywhere: DP to RB, [7 Nov. 1929], BU.

"and two enormous turtles": HMD to Yvonne Roussel, [spring 1930], Yvonne R. Luff.

222 "that morbid, turned-in thing": DP to RB, 7 Nov. 1929, BU.

One day he became enraged . . . slipper: Yvonne Roussel Luff interview.

There was another row . . . avoid everyone else: GCM to AMacL, 22 Jan. 1931, LOC.

"Gerald is here . . . breathe in it": AMacL to FSF, 15 Sept. [1930], *Letters of Archibald MacLeish*, p. 236.

"After all these years": GCM to AMacL, 22 Jan. 1929, LOC.

224 "I hope . . . without offending you": Ibid.

"a long hike": *S&G*, p. 56.

225 "he'd had a kind": Hester Pickman/HMD interview, HMD.

"because I never believed": Lillian Hellman/HMD interview, HMD.

"authenticity . . . prospects": "Les Expositions/Exposition Murphy" (article signed "E.T."), *L'Intransigeant*, 29 Jan. 1929, p. 5.

226 "specialized in Anglo-Saxons": GCM/CT interview, HMD.

"for me only the invented": GCM/CT interview notes, HMD.

"He talked thoughtfully . . . undiscovered gold": GCM to SWM, undated letter, quoted by GCM in a letter to CT, 12 Apr. 1962, HMD.

"very painful": GCM to FSF, 9 Jun. 1937, PUL.

227 "were the only other Americans . . . contralto": *Tender Is the Night* pencil ms. 2, "The Melarkey Case," PUL.

"Gerald's Irishness": FSF, *The Notebooks of F. Scott Fitzgerald*, p. 149.

"Seth is quite amusing . . . who was with him": *Tender Is the Night* pencil ms. 2, "The Melarkey Case," PUL.

228 "I don't kiss people . . . hard woman": Ibid. The line "I'm a hard woman" appears in Nicole's dialogue in the published version of *Tender Is the Night*: "'I'm a mean, hard woman,' she explained to Rosemary" (p. 21).

"You thought I was": Callaghan, *That Summer in Paris*, p. 207. Callaghan and the bisexual Robert McAlmon had each recently been challenged to write stories about two homosexuals for *This Quarter* — Callaghan's entry, entitled "Now That Apr.'s Here," dealt with a gay man leaving his lover for a woman — and this commission may have made Fitzgerald oversensitive.

229 "The novel should": Fitzgerald papers, PUL.

18. *"The geodetic points of our lost topography"*

230 "The orderliness": GCM to AMacL, 22 Jan. 1931, LOC.

Gerald and Sara decided . . . sell Villa America: Ibid.

231 They had given Léger . . . another collector: The panels, entitled *Queues de comets sur fond noir*, were painted *"pour la Villa de Gérald Murphy à Antibes"* in 1930, and are listed as number 750 in Georges Bauquier's *catalogue raisonné* of Léger's work.

"In spite of thunder" . . . Mediterranean coast: GCM to AMacL, 22 Jan. 1931, LOC.

He soon seemed improved . . . Baoth to Venice: HMD diary 1931, HMD.

232 The cook, Frau July . . . rolling countryside: Ibid.

struck by the regulated . . . "dominates everything": Léger, *Lettres à Simone*, p. 18.

"Absolutely terrified . . . at the idea": Milford, *Zelda*, pp. 188–89 and 190.

"great . . . that you all": GCM to FSF, [summer 1931], PUL.

"Scotty + the little Murphys": FSF to ALM, [ca. summer 1931], Myers papers.

233 Shortly after the Fitzgeralds' . . . Miss Stewart: HMD diary 1931, HMD.

"She was terribly . . . just typical": *S&G*, p. 60.

"My God": GCM to AMacL, 22 Jan. 1931, LOC.

they took Honoria . . . for the first time: HMD diary 1931, HMD.

They also brought Fernand Léger . . . "delighted him": GCM, Mac-Agy/Murphy papers; Léger, *Lettres à Simone*, p. 29.

234 Countess Lieven . . . daughter Fanny: HMD diary 1931, HMD.

"gorgeous . . . Madame Bovary dress": ESB interview.

"She used Helena Rubinstein" . . . fur piece: HMD interview.

In the end . . . ruinously expensive: GCM to AMacL, 4 Feb. 1932, LOC.

235 Neither of his surviving . . . Senator Robert F. Wagner: "Many Pay Tribute to P. F. Murphy," unattributed, undated newspaper clipping, GCM papers, HMD.

"my father left a company": GCM, quoted in *S&G*, p. 45.

"take care of Esther": HMD interview.

"He cannot be . . . kill us for their sport": GCM, undated notes on *Europa* stationery; HMD. GCM also quotes many of the same lines in his 8 Jan. 1932 letter to AMacL.

236 "a paradise": GCM to AMacL, 4 Feb. 1932, LOC.

Sara made a ceremony . . . for a month: HMD diary 1932–35: Mar. and Apr. 1932, HMD.

"A thing of great": GCM to AMacL, 4 Feb. 1932, LOC.

The galley had . . . water to fill it: AMacL to EH, 31 May 1933, JFK.

236 "poor little Pook . . . sickness!": GCM to AMacL, 8 Jan. 1932, LOC.

237 visits from the Barrys . . . *Concurrence:* REM diary: 29 Mar. 1932; ALM to REM, [May 1932]; Myers papers.

"he kisses me": Jeanne Léger's postscript to FL's letter to SWM, 18 Jun. 1932, HMD.

"Put away my house": HMD diary 1932–35: 5 Jul. 1932, HMD.

"the era": *S&G*, p. 51.

"Some day we'll all": GCM to AMacL, 4 Feb 1932, LOC.

"lost [her] shirt": Mary Hoyt Wiborg to SWM, 6 Dec. 1929, HMD.

had invested heavily . . . deed to it: *S&G*, p. 69.

238 Now, however, she owed . . . an additional $1,: All details and quotations from SWM handwritten affidavit, 10 Aug. 1942, prepared for presentation in *Wiborg v. Murphy*, HMD.

239 John and Katy . . . frequent guest on weekends: HMD diary 1932–35, HMD.

"adore[d] it . . . arranging their lives": GCM to AMacL, 8 Sept. 1932, LOC.

240 "performed well for Ernest": *S&G*, pp. 67–68.

"lovely trails . . . moon cocktails": SWM to EH and PH, 29 Jul. [1936], JFK.

It was the custom . . . three hours: Carlos Baker, notes from interview with Olive Nordquist, Carlos Baker/Hemingway papers, PUL.

"good for her": HMD interview.

"tasteless, without variety . . . no longer respects": GCM to AMacL, 8 Sept. 1932, LOC.

241 Sara and Gerald dropped him . . . train from New York: SWM travel and residence affidavit; notes for *Wiborg v. Murphy*, HMD.

Baoth and Patrick and Honoria . . . horse-drawn sleigh: Murphy home movies, HMD.

Ada and Sara cooked . . . liqueurs: GCM to AMacL, 8 Sept. 1932, LOC.

"restor[ed] a few": AMacL to John Peale Bishop, [ca. Apr. 1933], *Letters of Archibald MacLeish*, p. 256.

"nasty mean operation. . . agonies": REM to ALM, 9 Feb. and 20 Feb. 1933, FMB.

242 "rather rickety": GCM to JDP, 9 Mar. 1933, UVA.

He and Sara wrote . . . more if need be: REM to ALM, [Feb. 1933], FMB.

"a chip of a little legacy": GCM to JDP, 9 Mar. 1933, UVA.

he and Gerald were thinking . . . one of them: Ibid. There is no further record of any attempts to produce these works, so it must be assumed their discussions came to nothing.

Archie MacLeish had been approached . . . basis of his score: AMacL, *Reflections*, p. 93.

243 "white Russian crook": Donaldson, *Archibald MacLeish*, p. 236.

Sara Murphy, Hoytie Wiborg . . . Esther Murphy Strachey: AMacL correspondence with Alice de la Mar, Mrs. Harrison Williams, and Sol Hurok, *Union Pacific* file, Ballets Russes archives, DC/NYPL.

In March . . . Virgil Thomson: REM diary: 12 Mar. 1934, FMB.

distinguished himself . . . immediately afterward: GCM to CT, 4 Sept. 1960, HMD.

"What carried that ballet . . . Gerald's music": AMacL, *Reflections*, p. 94.

Nor were Sara . . . first night's proceeds: Correspondence in *Union Pacific* file, Ballets Russes archives, DC/NYPL.

"Archie has hurt . . . can change that": ALM to RLM, Jun. 1934, FMB.

"He's a pretty lonely . . . knows it now": AMacL to H. Phelps Putnam, [Jun. 1934], *Letters of Archibald MacLeish*, pp. 266–68.

244 The weather in Key West was bad: EH to GCM, 27 Apr. 1934, HMD.

fishing with the Dosses . . . stared down at them: PH to SWM, 17 May 1934, HMD.

"It was lovely . . . I think": EH to GCM, 27 Apr. 1934, HMD.

"Dearest Sara . . . sea-sick": EH to SWM, 27 Apr. 1934, HMD.

more than twenty-five . . . without indignation: See "Prologue," pp. 1–2.

245 "Scotts book, I'm sorry": EH to GCM, 27 Apr. 1934, HMD.

"I liked it . . . if it were true": EH to FSF, 28 May 1934, *Ernest Hemingway: Selected Letters*, p. 407.

dark, swashbuckling man . . . "adventurers in the movies": Many years later Gerald told Calvin Tomkins that Tommy Barban was based on Mario (Tunti) Braggiotti, a pianist who, with his partner Jacques Frey, had a popular concert career in the 1930s and 1940s. Fitzgerald himself said that Barban had elements of Tommy Hitchcock, the society polo player — but, as Ernest pointed out, the characters in *Tender Is the Night* are composites.

246 "Dear Scott": SWM to FSF, [spring 1934], PUL.

She had been getting . . . her own correspondence: Milford, *Zelda*, pp. 284–86.

"Jazz Age Priestess . . . audience for background": Ibid., pp. 291–92.

247 Sara paid $200 . . . Cary Ross took in: Cary Ross to FSF, 4 May 1934, *Correspondence of F. Scott Fitzgerald*, pp. 359–60.

"Those monstrous . . . morbid": Milford, *Zelda*, p. 290.

247 "I am going . . . their garden has conveyed": Zelda Fitzgerald to FSF, Milford, *Zelda*, p. 290.

Mediterranean Midi . . . lifetime ago: Mediterranean Midi is pictured on p. 75 of *Zelda, An Illustrated Life: The Private World of Zelda Fitzgerald*, edited by Eleanor Lanahan; the caption says it "probably dates from the 1940s"; but the caption also says it is "suggestive of Capri where Zelda in 1925 is reported to have taken her earliest painting lesson." Neither assignment is definitive; equally persuasive are the visual references in the painting to the Murphys' garden and linden tree, and (of course) the title.

248 "I had the pleasure . . . expensive rugs": John O'Hara to EH, [spring 1934], *Selected Letters of John O'Hara*; see also Meade, *Dorothy Parker*, p. 234.

"THIS IS TO REPORT": DP to GCM and SWM, 8 Jun. 1934, HMD.

249 "YOU WILL NOT HAVE": Mary Hoyt Wiborg to SWM, 8 Jun. 1934, HMD.

19. "We try to be like what you want us to be"

250 flag Gerald designed . . . Picasso so admired: GCM, MacAgy/Murphy papers.

"260 kilometres . . . (or so blue)": SWM and GCM to PH and EH; 21 Jun. 1934, JFK.

251 bringing prints of *Ballet mécanique* . . . to screen: Léger, *Lettres à Simone*, p. 114.

"*A Sara à Gerald*": FL, *Weatherbird* sketchbook, HMD.

"small checks": FL to GCM, Mar. 1934, HMD.

Gerald . . . take home as presents: *S&G*, p. 83.

One evening . . . "if you stand tall": FMB interview.

252 "Children . . . *rechute*": *S&G*, p. 83.

Honoria came to visit . . . practically transparent: HMD interview.

"Isn't it *horrid?* . . . some more words": SWM to EH and PH, 18 Sept. 1934, JFK.

"the doctors have told": Esther Murphey Strachey to Muriel Draper, 17 Apr. 1935, Muriel Draper papers, Beinecke Library.

"either a Grants Gazelle . . . each others backs": EH to GCM and SWM, 30 Sept. 1934, HMD.

253 "I thought as I carried": AMacL to PFM II, 26 Oct. 1934, HMD.

254 "I didn't know one thing": GCM, quoted in *S&G*, p. 78.

He hired Tomi Parzinger . . . "Leather": FMB interview.

"spend[ing] all his time": JDP to EH, [23 Jul. 1935], *The Fourteenth Chronicle*, p. 479.

"'Trade . . . harmful but efficient": GCM to FSF, 31 Dec. 1935, PUL.

He told a friend . . . sleepwalking: *LW*, p. 125; CT interview.

255 "to the value . . . God awful expenses": EH to GCM and SWM, 16 Nov. [1934], HMD.

"YOUR RECORDS SHIPPED": GCM and SWM to EH, 21 Nov. 1934, JFK.

"turned into various things": JDP to GCM, 11 Jan. [1935], HMD; Miller, *Letters from the Lost Generation*, p. 106.

Murphys proposed to rent . . . Mark Cross permitted: KDP to SWM, 12 Jan. 1935, UVA.

"Welcome Home, Baoth": *S&G*, p. 86.

256 "Dos and Ernest": KDP to SWM, [Feb. 1935], UVA; Miller, *Letters from the Lost Generation*, p. 112.

"a tendency to be": Ibid., [2 Dec. 1934].

he still looked . . . records Gerald had sent: EH to GCM and SWM, 14 Dec. [1934], HMD; and home movie shot by Hemingway during that winter and sent to Patrick Murphy, HMD.

And the Hemingways' new house . . . palm trees all around: John Hemingway interview; EH home movie, HMD.

"John was very dishonest . . . dirty sheets and everything": Noel Murphy/HMD interview, HMD.

About the closest . . . Muriel Draper: There are four folders of correspondence between Esther and Muriel Draper in Draper's papers at Yale's Beinecke Library, some of it salaciously jokey, some of it warm and passionate.

257 "[A]pparently . . . know what they're doing": GCM to SWM, 15 Feb. 193[5], HMD. Gerald's letter is actually dated 1934 — an indication of how preoccupied he was.

"an actual relief . . . any such programmes": Ibid.

"The leaning tower of Baoth": *S&G*, p. 88.

"We *are* still behind": GCM to SWM, 18 Feb. 1935, HMD.

258 "ten days of hideous": Esther Murphy to Muriel Draper, 17 Apr. 1935, Muriel Draper papers, Beinecke Library.

Significantly Hoytie . . . believe was a curse: HMD, Noel Murphy/HMD, and William MacLeish interviews.

258 Archie could not stay . . . "she cried and cried": This account is drawn from interviews with HMD, William MacLeish, and Hester Pickman (the last by HMD); HMD's book, *S&G*; and letters from Esther Murphy Strachey to Muriel Draper (17 Apr. 1935), AMacL to JDP and KDP ([20 Mar. 1935] in *Letters of Archibald MacLeish*, p. 275); and the diaries of REM (entries for 14 and 17 Mar. 1935).

259 "Darlings . . . dear to us all": KDP to SWM and GCM, 18 Mar. 1935, UVA.
"You've been so brave . . . be brave": JDP to SWM and GCM, 18 Mar. 1935, HMD.
"It is not so bad . . . be brave about": EH to SWM and GCM, [19 Mar. 1935], HMD.
"courage & grace . . . mystery of pain": AMacL to GCM and SWM, [29 Mar. 1935], HMD.
"fancy . . . one like that": AMacL to JDP and KDP, [20 Mar. 1935], *Letters of Archibald MacLeish*, p. 275.
"BAOTHS ASHES STAND": GCM and SWM to KDP, JDP, EH, and PH, 21 Mar., 1935, UVA.
In the taxicab . . . cursing God: *S&G*, p. 91; HMD interviews.
"The news . . . Baoth and Patrick": William MacLeish interview.
Alexander Woollcott . . . "feeling better": *S&G*, p. 94.

260 "The difficulty will be . . . visor on backwards": EH to PFM II, 5 Apr. 1935, HMD.
Unlike many tuberculosis . . . disease and its treatment: Gallos, *Cure Cottages of Saranac Lake*, pp. 24–25.

261 local radio station . . . "rest hour": Ibid., p. 168.
classic Adirondack . . . enough to stand in: The description of the house, which burned down in 1967, came from interviews with Judge Jan Plumadore of Saranac Lake, whose family owned it in the 1960s. Other details are from personal observation.
"the Merchant Prince" . . . Saranac every other weekend: SWM to EH and PH, 11 Sept. 1935, JFK.
The Big Money . . . collapsed from the inside: JDP, *The Big Money*, p. 550.
"Sara very thin": JDP to EH, [23 Jul. 1935], *The Fourteenth Chronicle*, p. 479.

262 All his big canvases . . . "for all eternity": FL to GCM and SWM, 27 Jul. 1935, HMD (my translation). To Simone Herman, Léger confided that the only way he could afford this career move was to live with the Murphys "for six months to a year." (Léger, *Lettres à Simone*, p. 132, my translation.)

ten thousand viewers . . . twenty days: FL to GCM, undated, HMD.

Sara was able to get . . . *"Pour Sara et Gérald"*: *S&G*, p. 98; *LW*, p. 127.

Gerald was putting Léger up: Léger, *Lettres à Simone*, pp. 166–67.

"We're both at the complete": FL to GCM, undated [Saturday 16], HMD (my translation).

263 "the price isn't important": Ibid., undated, HMD (my translation).

"We don't buy pictures . . . all right": GCM to SWM, 5 Feb. 1936, HMD.

Thus the Murphys acquired . . . *grande feuille*: The Murphys seem to have owned at least three Légers — this one, which was painted in 1927; *Composition à un profil*; and *Accordion*, which was painted in 1924 and dedicated to Sara at that time with an inscription on the back reading *"à la bonne amitié."* *Nature morte* was sold in April 1989 by the dealer Guy Loudmer in Paris after having been in the possession of another owner; there is no definitive documentation that this *was* the painting taken in exchange for the gift of $1,, but the process of elimination suggests it. Gerald Murphy later said that he and Sara had given two other Légers to the Museum of Modern Art in 1931, but there is no record of these paintings in the Léger *catalogue raisonné*.

"thanks to you two . . . eternally grateful": FL to GCM, 23 Jan. 1936, HMD (my translation).

He weighed only fifty-nine pounds: SWM to FSF, 3 Apr. 1935, PUL.

"on the mend": SWM to EH and PH, 11 Sept. 1935, JFK.

"Dear Scott": GCM to FSF, 11 Aug. 1935, PUL.

264 "Dearest Sara": FSF to SWM, 15 Aug. 1935, HMD.

20. *"Life itself has stepped in now"*

266 "raw to the feelings . . . lot of good": SWM to FSF, 20 Aug. [1935], PUL.

"very unhappy": AMacL to EH, [14 Oct. 1936], JFK; *Letters of Archibald MacLeish*, pp. 284–85.

"My Dearest Scott": SWM to FSF, 20 Aug. 1935, PUL.

"My *Dearest* Hemingways": SWM to PH and EH, 11 Sept. 1935, JFK.

267 "My Dearest Pauline": SWM to PH, 18 Sept. [1935], JFK.

"My dearest Ernest": SWM to EH, 18 Sept. [1935], JFK.

268 "even though I knew . . . nobody coming": EH to JDP, 17 Dec. 1935; *Ernest Hemingway: Selected Letters*, pp. 425–26.

"a crush": James Mellow interview.

"maybe I am bad luck": EH to SWM, 12 Sept. 1935, HMD.

268 "It isn't true": SWM to EH, 18 Sept. [1935], JFK.

"Only place . . . sleep alone": EH to SWM, 8 Dec. [1935], HMD.

By the winter . . . relationship had cooled: Mellow, *Ernest Hemingway*, pp. 462–63.

"With very much love": EH to SWM, 8 Dec. [1935], HMD.

Gerald did his part. . . shape of a bell: "'Town Crier' Scoops the City!" advertisement in GCM/Alexander Woollcott file, HU.

269 "You show signs . . . strange gentlemen?": GCM to Alexander Woollcott, [summer 1939], HU.

"gift . . . valuable": GCM to AMacL, 8 Feb. 1943, LOC.

lofty barn . . . four different churches: Description of house and location from personal on-site observation.

Dick and Alice Lee . . . Lake Placid in February: REM diary: Feb. 1936.

Honoria remembers her mother . . . doesn't try to guess: HMD interview.

270 "Of all our friends": GCM to FSF, 31 Dec. 1935, PUL.

"Damn I wish . . . you were here, Sara": EH to SWM, 11 Feb. 1936, HMD.

"Poor Sara" . . . mutual friend: Ibid., [27 Feb. 1936].

271 "There is one . . . emotional pressure": GCM to SWM, 16 Apr. 1936, HMD.

"Dear Sal . . . nothing much": Ibid., 18 Apr. 1936.

272 "active love": *TITN*, p. 75.

"Thank God": Gill, *A New York Life*, p. 324.

"deficiency . . . rotten": GCM to SWM, 18 Apr. 1936, HMD.

After an inauspicious . . . bonito within two days: EH Notebooks 1936: 4–10 May, JFK.

"whining in public": EH to Maxwell Perkins, 7 Feb. 1936; *Ernest Hemingway: Selected Letters*, pp. 437–38.

"Do you *really* . . . all I know": SWM to FSF, 3 Apr. [1936], PUL.

273 One day . . . secluded cove: EH to SWM, 13 Jun. [1939], HMD.

And sometime during . . . their lives: SWM to EH, 20 May 1936, JFK.

"Some people . . . can't imagine it": John Hemingway interview.

"like a delicious": SWM to EH, 20 May 1936, JFK.

"beautiful . . . turned out to be me": PH to GCM, 17 Jul. [1935], HMD.

"About being snooty . . . yourself and Pauline": SWM to EH, 20 May [1936], JFK.

274 Now, in a story . . . "Kilimanjaro": EH to Maxwell Perkins, 9 Apr. 1936, *Ernest Hemingway: Selected Letters*, pp. 442–44. Hemingway's biographer

Michael Reynolds believes "Snows" was completed in April, but this letter to Perkins indicates it was still a work in progress at this point.

Although Hemingway had berated . . . kept in his files: Reynolds, *Hemingway: The 1930s*, p. 324.

275 it was Sara Murphy . . . sent it to her: HMD is unsure of who found the picture, but thinks it might have been Hemingway. As related by Carlos Baker in *Ernest Hemingway: A Life Story* (pp. 258–59 and 66n), Hemingway later said that "The Snows of Kilimanjaro" had been inspired by an unnamed rich woman who, after his return from his 1934 African safari, had offered to stake him to a return trip. He didn't take her up on the offer; "Snows," he implied, is the story of what might have happened if he had done so.

"Every woman's husband . . . Mrs. Parker's confidante": EH to AMacL, [undated], LOC. There is no date on this letter, nor has a postmarked envelope survived. Although Michael Reynolds, in *Hemingway: The 1930s*, confidently assigns it a July 23, 1933, date, this is by no means certain. References to Jane Mason's back injury indicate only that the letter was written during or after the summer of 1933. Although most of this letter concerns Jane Mason, there's no evidence that she was "Mrs. Parker's confidante" or that she or her husband knew "Mr. Benchley."

"terribly, terribly sorry": GCM to SWM, 26 Jun. 1936, HMD.

Camp Adeline . . . main living quarters: Patrick Murphy diary: 11 Jul. 1936, HMD.

filled with bright . . . plants and flowers: GCM to FSF, 30 Jul. 1936, PUL.

276 "like his old self": REM to ALM, 8 Aug. 1936, FMB.

One after-supper musicale . . . fandango: FMB interview.

"a black and chromium . . . junketing": GCM to Alexander Woollcott, 25 May 1936, HU.

Back at Camp Adeline . . . away in the Adirondacks: SWM to EH and PH, 29 Jul. [1936], JFK.

277 series of projects . . . engaged his imagination now: GCM art notebook, HMD.

278 "Honoria, I think you": HMD interview; *S&G*, p. 111.

"it is still a very doubtful": REM to ALM, 13 Aug. 1936, FMB.

"everyone remarks on": GCM to FSF, [ca. Aug. 1936], PUL.

"[s]he refuses to release": Ibid., 30 Jul. 1936.

"I want new clothes": SWM to EH and PH, 29 Jul. [1936], JFK.

278 The previous summer . . . change the fuse: Gallos, *Cure Cottages of Saranac Lake*, p. 125.

Murphys were paying . . . tuition and board: FMB interview.

279 "I spend three . . . doctors are uneasy": GCM to Bernardine Fritz-Szold, 12 Dec. 1936, Beinecke Library.

"Patrick is an adult . . . great deal": GCM to Alexander Woollcott, [ca. Nov. 1936], HU.

"Patrick is no more": Alexander Woollcott to GCM, 20 Nov. 1936, HU.

"pretty horrible . . . heartbreaking": JDP to EH, 9 Jan. [1936], *The Fourteenth Chronicle*, p. 504.

"Jan 1" . . . snow with Gerald : PFM II diary: 23 and 24 Jan. 1937, HMD.

Alice Lee ran interference . . . cajole him into eating: REM to ALM, 19 Jan. [1937], FMB.

Patrick had to have . . . wobbly scrawl: PFM II diary 1937, HMD.

Ernestine Leray . . . customs agents impounded it: REM to ALM, 5 Jan. 1937, FMB.

280 "noted and only american . . . not ready yet": PFM II diary: 16 Jan. 1937, HMD.

When Ernest emerged . . . "boy look so sick": S&G, p. 115. Honoria Donnelly says that Hemingway made this visit alone, and she places it in the fall of 1936. But Hemingway doesn't appear to have visited Saranac then — only in the autumn of 1935 and in January 1937.

"mother's milk": GCM to PH, 22 Jan. 1937, JFK.

"animal magnetism" . . . put-downs wearying: REM to ALM, 21 Jan. [1937], FMB.

"I feel as if we": GCM to Alexander Woollcott, 29 Jan. 1937, HU.

Honoria and Fanny Myers . . . now so acute: S&G, p. 118.

On the morning of January 30 . . . "be with you": Ibid., p. 119.

"Fate can't have . . . away from you now": FSF to GCM and SWM, 31 Jan. 1937, HMD.

21. "Not on the same course, nor for the same port"

281 "There is something . . . same port": GCM to CT, [1960], HMD.

Alice Lee Myers helped . . . heads to the Hemingways: ALM to EH [6 Feb. 1937], JFK.

Sara simply gave . . . Boys Club of New York: Title Search of Kirchner Camp, Franklin County Courthouse, Saranac Lake, New York.

"Dear Scott": GCM to FSF, 9 Jun. 1937, PUL.

282 "choir-boys' gowns": GCM to CT, 4 Sept. 1960, HMD.

"Gerald threw everything out": AMacL, "The Art of Poetry," *The Paris Review*, vol. 14, no. 58, p. 69.

"He was a painter . . . masochist to do that": William MacLeish interview.

"It tightens the main-spring": GCM to EH, 22 May 1927, JFK.

283 "grimly socio-politico-economic": GCM to SWM, 26 Jul. 1939, HMD.

"some labor issue . . . longer [an] ingenue": RB to GCM and SWM, 1 Jul. 1937, HMD.

"she never joked": Meade, *Dorothy Parker*, p. 222.

"clear, objective statement": AMacL, quoted in Donaldson, *Archibald MacLeish*, p. 264.

Virgil Thomson . . . *The Spanish Earth*: GCM to CT, 4 Sept. 1950, HMD.

Don Stewart . . . Hollywood Anti-Nazi League: DOS, *By a Stroke of Luck!* p. 231.

Archie and Ernest . . . Earl Browder on the platform: Donaldson, *Archibald MacLeish*, pp. 264–65.

284 "if there was a fascist . . . most intelligent audience": SWM to PH, 22 Jun. [1937], JFK.

"The future . . . mine shall be": Ibid.

"pitiful . . . dissatisf[ied] at everything": REM to ALM, 3 Aug. 1937, and ALM to REM, 2 Aug. 1937, FMB.

"We get up . . . bed at 10 P.M.": GCM to HMD, 13 Aug. 1937, HMD.

"I know that it doesn't . . . better time": GCM to SWM, [summer 1937], HMD.

285 "with fantastic hats": REM to ALM, 5 Aug. 1937, FMB.

"they now need . . . they'll like you": Lillian Hellman/HMD interview, HMD.

Hellman was on her own . . . other friends: Meade, *Dorothy Parker*, pp. 282–83; REM diary: summer 1937.

"private blonde": DaP to JDP, quoted in Mellow, *Ernest Hemingway*, p. 499.

Although Gellhorn was not . . . ever meeting the Murphys: Martha Gellhorn to the author, 20 May 1994. Honoria Donnelly, however, has a vivid if imprecise memory of Sara and Gellhorn having some kind of confrontation involving a locked gate. "Mother was standing outside and Martha Gellhorn wouldn't let her in," she says; but where or when this scene might have occurred she cannot remember.

285 "my great 37–38 epoch": EH to AMacL, 4 Apr. 1943, LOC.

"Never having been . . . comes to nothing": GCM to SWM, 4–9 Sept. 1937, HMD.

286 With it went a chatty note . . . "this autumn": SWM to EH, 20 Sept. 1937, JFK.

Sara went through all . . . birthday in November: REM diary: 1937, FMB.

But Gerald was careful . . . still too fragile: GCM to Alexander Woollcott, 16 Dec. 1938, HU.

"given up being . . . Hollywood": Stella Campbell to SWM, Jan. 1937, in S&G, p. 190.

she had not endeared . . . "tiny eyes?": Patricia Vaill interview.

287 Sara had hoped . . . flat in London: ALM to REM, 5 Aug. 1937, FMB.

Swan Cove . . . down to the water: Much of this description is from personal observation and from Murphy home movies, HMD.

"Arabian Nights house": KDP to SWM, 15 Jan. 1938, UVA.

"an oasis . . . both of them": GCM to Hale Walker and Harold Heller, [May 1938], HMD.

288 Patrick's death . . . "far afield": GCM to FSF, 29 Jan. and 1 Mar. 1938, PUL.

Sheilah Graham . . . drank cocoa: HMD interview.

"you were awfully damn kind": FSF to GCM, 11 Mar. 1938, PUL.

"Pears like nobody gits": KDP to SWM, 20 Mar. 1938, UVA.

Gerald arrived in June . . . "Bed early": SWM, 1938 *Weatherbird* trip log, HMD.

289 "very engaging . . . happiness already had": Zelda Fitzgerald to FSF, [Sept. 1938] and [autumn 1939], Milford, *Zelda*, p. 324.

"Look" . . . without speaking to each other: FMB interview.

Now, returning to Swan Cove . . . helplessly in the orchard: GCM to HMD, 14 Sept. 1938, and SWM, *Weatherbird* trip log, HMD; GCM to Alexander Woollcott, 28 Sept. 1938, HU.

290 "Hurricane — garden gone": SWM, 1938 *Weatherbird* trip log, HMD.

Sara had a quiet birthday . . . few hours at least: GCM to HMD, 5 Nov. 1938, and SWM to HMD, 16 Nov. 1938, HMD.

Tallulah quickly . . . "beautiful voice?": Lillian Hellman/HMD interview, HMD.

291 "ordering endless dishes": Lillian Hellman, quoted in "Hellman on the Time of the 'Foxes,'" undated newspaper clipping, HMD.

"I've got a favorite lady": REM, "To Sara," FMB.

Sara drove down . . . stayed three weeks: SWM trip log 1939, HMD.

"Dearest Sara . . . count on it": EH to SWM, 13 Jun. [1939], HMD.

292 "I had that orchestra . . . lovely Sara": Ibid., 27 Dec. [1939].

"I liked Gerald . . . I love Sara": EH to AMacL, 27 Aug. 1948, LOC

22. *"Enough to make the angels weep"*

293 "A list of the painters": Janet Flanner, *Paris Was Yesterday*, pp. 218–19.

"with *Manners* . . . even in my heyday": SWM to GCM, [Jun. 1939]. This letter was transcribed and enclosed in a letter from GCM to Alexander Woollcott, 22 Jun. 1939, HU; the original has been lost.

294 While the *Weatherbird* . . . Juan-les-Pins casino: SWM trip log 1939, HMD.

"The girls, I *hope* . . . lines of the Ritz": SWM to JDP and KDP, 18 Jul. [1939], UVA.

"disappointed": SWM trip log 1939: 22 Jul., 5 Aug., 6 Aug., 13 Aug., HMD.

3,300 people . . . "all milling": SWM to JDP and KDP, 17 Dec. 1938, UVA.

295 "rake the Avenue": GCM to Alexander Woollcott, [late 1930s], HU.

Alice Lee Myers . . . language of flowers: FMB interview.

There was a leather . . . name stuck: Rosmond, *Robert Benchley*, p. 141ff; HMD interview.

company still wasn't . . . Mark Cross were to survive: GCM to SWM, 2 Aug. 1939, HMD.

Murphys' investment adviser . . . robust $201,: Ibid., 7 Jul. 1939, HMD.

Cole Porter . . . unreachable and uninterested: Leonard Hanna telegram to Serge Denham, 11 Feb. 1939; *Ghost Town* files, Records of the Ballet Russe de Monte Carlo, DC/NYPL.

296 Irving Berlin . . . "completely out of my field": Serge Libidins telegram to Serge Denham, 21 Feb. 1939; *Ghost Town* files/Ballet Russe archive, DC/NYPL.

At the end of February . . . "Top Hat": Irving Berlin to Serge Denham, 6 Mar. 1939, *Ghost Town files*/Ballet Russe archive, DC/NYPL.

296 The person who . . . Gerald Murphy: Rodgers, *Musical Stages*, p. 194.
Rodgers, as it happened . . . understanding with Berlin: All documents are in *Ghost Town* files, Serge Denham Records of the Ballet Russe de Monte Carlo, DC/NYPL.

297 "he was a very, very good . . . sense of humor": Frederic Franklin interview.
"We all had crushes": HMD interview.
"O worst imprisonment": GCM to Alexander Woollcott, 20 Oct. 1939, HU.
"notes, records" . . . Raoul Pène DuBois: GCM to SD, 3 Apr. 1939, *Ghost Town* files, Records of the Ballet Russe de Monte Carlo, DC/NYPL.
popular nineteenth-century . . . even dances: GCM, "Ghost Town" scenario; *Ghost Town* files, Records of the Ballet Russe de Monte Carlo, DC/NYPL.
"it was so exciting . . . arts again": HMD interview.
"furious . . . 3 days and that is all": REM to ALM, 10 Jul. 1939, FMB.

298 recordings of *Ghost Town's* score . . . unavailable: Nicolas de Gunzbourg to GCM, 16 Jun. 1939, *Ghost Town* files, Records of the Ballet Russe de Monte Carlo, DC/NYPL.
The scene allows . . . top-heavy company roster: Besides Franklin and Platoff (or Platov, as he sometimes appears) the men included Serge Lifar, Michel Paniev, Roland Guérard, and Igor Youskevitch; the women, Alexandra Danilova, Alicia Markova, Tamara Toumanova, Nina Tarakaova, Mia Slavenska, Lubov Rostova, and Nathalie Leslie; "there are so many stars," wrote one company member, "that I cannot see how there will be enough ballets to go around" (Walker, *De Basil's Ballets Russes*, p. 82).
"The . . . story . . . much simpler form": Serge Denham to Léonide Massine, 5 Apr. 1939, *Ghost Town* files, Records of the Ballet Russe de Monte Carlo, DC/NYPL.
"complicate our work . . . on the increase": Serge Denham to Jacques Rubinstein, 11 May 1939, *Ghost Town* files, Records of the Ballet Russe de Monte Carlo, DC/NYPL.

299 Ballet Russe used Gerald's . . . popular ballet reference book: "Ghost Town," in Goode, ed., *The Book of Ballets*, pp. 114–18. The typewritten version of the scenario, which is identical, was produced on GCM's typewriter, samples of which appear elsewhere in the Ballet Russe files and in GCM's own personal files.
some tricky maneuvering . . . fourth speeding offense: GCM to Alexander Woollcott, [Jun. 1939], HU.

"Thanks for the film . . . Aff'y. Gerald": Ibid., 21 Apr. 1939.

300 felt the redirection of his attention: SWM trip log 1939: 13 Aug., HMD
"the English": GCM to SWM, 26 Jul. 1939, HMD.
"Very lovely . . . all fell asleep": SWM trip log 1939: 19 Aug., HMD
"Paris is on a wartime": REM to ALM, 31 Aug. 1939, FMB.
At Maxim's . . . "perfectly normally": HMD interview.
"gave us advice" . . . Sara declined: SWM trip log 1939: 3 Sept., HMD.

301 "For heaven's sake . . . come back": Noel Murphy to SWM, undated [1939], HMD.

301 soldiers' canteen: REM to GCM, 27 Aug. 1939, FMB.
dissuaded only when Honoria . . . without her mother: GCM to Alexander Woollcott, [postmarked] 11 Sept. 1939, HU.
"very angoissante day": SWM trip log 1939: 1 Sept., HMD.
The Guaranty Trust . . . carting it around: REM to ALM, 31 Aug. 1939, FMB.
Sara, Honoria, and the Myeres . . . Southampton and New York: SWM trip log 1939: 1–18 Sept., HMD.
There were nearly two thousand . . . "holding someone's thumb": GCM to JDP and KDP, 21 Sept. 1939, UVA.
"greedy sense of being included": GCM to Alexander Woollcott, 17 Oct., 1939, HU.

302 Gerald had attended only a few rehearsals: Frederic Franklin, in an interview, does not recall Gerald ever attending one; but in a letter written that autumn [and not dated] Gerald told Alexander Woollcott that "I have a ballet rehearsal Thursday."
Opening the program . . . luscious figure: Ballet Russe souvenir season's program, *Ghost Town* files/Records of Ballet Russe de Monte Carlo, DC/NYPL.
"Richard Rodgers, in collaboration": Serge Denham to Miss A. B. McNamara, [spring 1939], *Ghost Town* files, Records of Ballet Russe de Monte Carlo, DC/NYPL.
There was tumultuous applause . . . six curtain calls: Irving Kolodin, review in *New York Sun*, 13 Nov. 1939.
He and Platt . . . friendship into the 1940s: HMD interview.
"WAS TAKEN ILL": FSF to GCM, 21 Sept. 1939, HMD.
"What a strange . . . necessary to keep": All quotations from ibid., [21 Sept. 1939].
"Please don't keep": GCM to FSF, 29 Sept. 1939, HMD.
"I do not like": Ibid., 26 Aug. 1940, PUL.

303 "I don't think the world": SWM to FSF, 30 Aug. 1935, PUL.
"He was against . . . dusting mornings": GCM to Alexander Woollcott, 13 Jun. 1939, HU.

304 "We ate a very great deal . . . snored for about an hour": William MacLeish interview.
"The play depressed . . . fond I am of you": GCM to Alexander Woollcott, 17 Oct. 1939, HU.
"the last tie to the boys": GCM to JDP and KDP, 21 Feb. 1940, UVA.
"Will one's heart . . . talk to you": GCM to Alexander Woollcott, 24 Jun. 1940, HU.

305 Bumby, who was now . . . *Hellzapoppin:* John Hemingway interview.
"forlorn": GCM to FSF, 24 Apr. 1940, PUL.
"would like to be": PH to SWM, 1 Mar. 1940, HMD.
After stopping . . . covered the earth: SWM trip log 1940: 7 Apr., HMD.
"Yr old shipmate, Sara": SWM to EH, 29 Jul. 1940, JFK.
"I felt sort . . . same as always": EH to SWM, [Dec. 1940], HMD.

306 "the people he spoke": Frances Kroll Ring interview.
"Yr cheque gave me": GCM to FSF, 3 Oct. 1940, PUL.
"How cruelly the world": GCM to Alexander Woollcott, 26 Dec. 1940, HU.
"Those tragicly ecstatic . . . grievous to envisage": Zelda Fitzgerald to GCM and SWM, [Dec. 1940 or Jan. 1941], HMD.
"Poor Scott . . . more than anyone": EH to SWM, [Dec. 1940], HMD.

23. *"One's very Life seems at stake"*

307 "What sad days . . . all our time & $": GCM to AMacL, 20 Aug. 1940, LOC.
Sara was acting . . . war relief: GCM to Alexander Woollcott, 24 Jun. 1940, HU.
"One's very Life": GCM to AMacL, 20 Aug. 1940, LOC.
In the spring of 1940 . . . Cimetière Urbain at Pau: Margot Peters, *Mrs. Pat*, pp. 450–58.

308 "Everything goes so slowly! . . . something like that": FL to SWM, 5 Oct. 1940, HMD (my translation).
"a Frenchman" . . . tanks aren't sketches: FL to GCM and SWM, 18 Sept. 1940, HMD (my translation).
"They're whispering in Vichy": FL to SWM, 6 Oct. 1940, HMD.

From Marseille . . . that very day: FL to GCM and SWM, 17 Sept. 1940; GCM to Thos. Cook and Son, 17 Sept. 1940, 17 Sept. 1940 banking draft, Thos. Cook and Son; HMD.

309 "You have always . . . every part of my life": FL to SWM, 6 Oct. 1940, HMD.

He went to work against inaction . . . "classic to ourselves": GCM to AMacL, [Oct. 1941], LOC

311 Léger . . . picture in the house: Daisy and Jane Pickman/HMD interview, FMB interview.

"more than simply": Gill, *A New York Life*, p. 317.

Watch . . . Alexandria house: Lillian Hellman/HMD interview, HMD.

"the inside cabin": HMD interview.

"They started . . . tell us what you did": Grand jury notes, GCM notebook, HMD.

312 teaching a course . . . Dawn Powell was enrolled: DaP diary: 18 Feb. 1940.

Gerald made up . . . study of Bach: GCM New School notebooks, HMD.

American literature . . . Alfred Kazin: GCM's "Miscellaneous and Marginalia" file, HMD.

She was having dinner . . . It was Hopkins: Hellman, *An Unfinished Woman*, pp. 216–17.

313 "Poetry doesn't become": David Pickman interview.

"yards and yards" . . . killed in a shipwreck: David Pickman/HMD interview, HMD.

"Thou mastering me": Hopkins, "The Wreck of the Deutschland," *Poems of Gerard Manley Hopkins*, p. 55.

"refused to meet": GCM to AMacL, 22 Jan. 1931, LOC.

In 1940 Fanny Myers . . . delighted to welcome him: FMB interview.

314 Jarvis was . . . beneath the curl: Ibid.

Despite Sara's assertion . . . "cure" himself: For this information, and for further insights on Jarvis, I am indebted to the work of the late Norman Hay, who died before he completed his Jarvis biography.

He kept this turmoil . . . son-in-law: HMD and FMB interviews.

"Dow used to advise me": William MacLeish interview.

put him together . . . publishers: Norman Hay biographical note on Alan Jarvis, private collection.

wrote him a letter . . . Archie MacLeish: copy of a letter from GCM to AMacL, 4 Oct. 1941, UTo.

314 "a fierce and joyous": Norman Hay biographical note, 6 Jan. 1983, private collection.

"A. amatus" . . . since he was fifteen: Ibid.

315 "defects" . . . heart: GCM to AMacL, 22 Jan. 1930, LOC.

In later life Alan Jarvis . . . physical: Norman Hay biographical note, 25 Sept. 1987, private collection.

"She was rather edgy": FMB interview.

Sara went away . . . go with their steaks: SWM trip log 1941: spring, HMD.

316 "Gerald agreed" . . . America had also entered the war: Norman Hay biographical note, 6 Jan. 1983, private collection.

accepted a cache of Jarvis's . . . "zinc-lined": GCM to AJ, [Dec. 1941], Norman Hay collection, UTo.

Alan Campbell . . . "queer as a goat": Meade, *Dorothy Parker*, pp. 307 and 311.

317 "flatly stated . . . would be a sin": Lillian Hellman/HMD interview.

"We all talked about": JDP to AMacL, 4 Jan. 1942, LOC.

318 "What you write . . . write about it": EH to AMacL, 30 Jun. [1943], LOC.

"the aid of a court": The language in the decision on *Wiborg v. Murphy*, recorded in the Supreme Court of the State of New York in Riverhead, New York, in the spring of 1944, is quoted in *S&G*, p. 215.

defending herself . . . considerable anguish: *S&G*, p. 217.

Unable to find . . . oversee the job: GCM to Alexander Woollcott, 23 Jul. 1941, HU.

"I have contributed . . . do not like or admire": SWM affidavit, HMD.

"1) dinner Tuesday . . . New School": GCM to Alexander Woollcott, 23 Jan. 1942, HU.

319 "(just because they're not in your set)": Ibid., 24 Jan. 1942.

"His gift": GCM to AMacL, 8 Feb. 1943, LOC.

"what kind of service . . . took out of us": Ibid.

"that monument to the inessential": Ibid.

written hardly a line . . . war began: William MacLeish interview.

"charmingly civilized": Felix Frankfurter, note in margin of GCM to AMacL, 14 Apr. 1943, LOC.

"first Stravinsky performance": AMacL to GCM, telegram 23 Oct. 1944; LOC.

simply at-home evenings . . . Ada sang: SWM trip diary 1943: May, HMD.

"Archie is being pulled . . . farther away": GCM to Alexander Woollcott, 24 Jun. 1940, HU; [Miller, *Letters from a Lost Generation*, p. 251].

320 "like a stone bruise": AMacL, quoted in Donaldson, *Archibald MacLeish*, p. 383.

Gerald exerted himself . . . "great times with Dow": William MacLeish interview.

24. "Isn't it strange how life goes on?"

321 "People should never": Quoted in DaP to SWM, 22 Sept. 1947, HMD.

"the revisitation . . . Love . . . Gerald": GCM to AJ, 21 May 1946, UTo.

"grave but harmonious . . . I feel it": Ibid., 13 Jun. 1946.

322 "the Polyglot Rim . . . obliged to work": Wood Memorial Day Nursery fundraising brochure, manuscript draft with SWM's notes, HMD.

Every morning . . . three and six months: SWM black notebooks from Wood Memorial Day Nursery, HMD.

323 One day Honoria . . . room in tears: S&G, p. 212.

Sara even brought two . . . opposed the adoption: Ibid.

Gerald had likened . . . view of the water: GCM to KDP, 26 Jan. 1942, UVA.

"the constant aeroplane": JDP to GCM and SWM, 21 Feb. 1945, UVA.

"Mimi looked like": Donaldson, *Archibald MacLeish*, p. 389.

"the pearls went crunch . . . damned thing off": Mimi MacLeish Grimm interview.

324 "It's just like me": Donaldson, *Archibald MacLeish*, p. 396.

"went with an infantry . . . break for me": EH to SWM, 5 May 1945, HMD.

"As you know . . . 1942 to 1945": EH to Charles Poore, 23 Jan. 1953; *Ernest Hemingway: Selected Letters*, p. 800.

325 "I enclose . . . never hurt anybody": SWM to DaP, 9 Mar. 1964, CUL.

"I don't really . . . Love, G.": GCM to DaP, 25 Apr. 1942, CUL.

Powell wrote the ending . . . Swan Cove: DaP, *The Diaries of Dawn Powell*, 24 Jul. 1944, p. 233.

The Wicked Pavilion . . . *The Creevey Papers*: Ibid., 16 and 31 Jan. 1950, pp. 288, 289; DaP to John Hall Wheelock, 18 Sept. 1950, CUL.

"This conquering of the deep": DaP, *The Diaries of Dawn Powell*, 6 Sept. 1947, p. 262.

Talking to Gerald . . . pointing at him: Ibid., 11 Oct. 1947, p. 265.

326 "Sal dear . . . when he wakes": GCM to SWM, 13 Sept. 1947, HMD.

"deflected to Katy": DaP, *The Diaries of Dawn Powell*, 11 Oct. 1947, p. 265.

"Where can he put . . . I guess": GCM to SWM, 13 Sept. 1947, HMD.

helped make arrangements . . . funeral in Truro: Esther Andrews to DaP, undated, CUL.

urged Dawn . . . New York: DaP to SWM, 22 Sept. 1947, HMD.

327 "[Y]ou and I . . . do not know": AMacL to GCM, [autumn 1948], HMD.

"I cant yet find": JDP to SWM, 7 Nov. 1948, HMD.

For his birthday . . . "birthday before": Ibid., 15 Jan. 1949, HMD; GCM to SWM, 16 Jan. 1949, HMD.

it was owned . . . house was for sale: Marion Lowndes, quoted in John Dalmas, "Living Well Was His Best Revenge," *Westchester/Rockland Journal-News*, 12 May 1974.

328 "highly marginal": Jacques Livet, "La Baraka de Vladimir" (unpublished memoir); courtesy of the author (my translation).

Vladimir had managed . . . Gerald in 1945: FMB interview.

"dark seal brown": GCM to SWM, 22 Feb. 1949, HMD.

They added a small wing . . . stone for the addition: CT interview.

sometimes Black Velvets . . . hollowed-out coconut: GCM, miscellaneous clipping file; Daisy Pickman/HMD interview; HMD.

"looking up into the branches": CT interview.

Sara would light . . . little paper bags: Ibid.

329 squares of whole-grain . . . horseradish: FMB interview.

pheasant with bread sauce . . . poached in broth: DaP diaries: 11 Jan. 1958 and 1 Mar. 1959, CUL.

"wondrous black hushed sleep": Ibid., 19 Jul. 1956.

"curiously beautiful . . . private cemetery: Ibid., 12 Nov. 1949.

stories of patroons . . . Hudson River steamboats: GCM, miscellaneous notes file, HMD.

costume was a surprise even to Sara: Marion Lowndes, quoted in John Dalmas, "Living Well Was His Best Revenge," *Westchester/Rockland Journal-News*, 12 May 1974.

"still reeling . . . George and Martha": DaP to GCM and SWM, 28 Feb. 1950, HMD.

330 "the increasing growth": Harold L. Ickes to GCM, 15 May 1946, HMD.

"any number of times": Lillian Hellman/HMD interview, HMD.

Hellman had invited . . . "make her throw up?": Ibid.

Dashiell Hammett . . . $10,: Johnson, *Dashiell Hammett*, pp. 238–45. In the end the judge refused bail and Hammett went to prison.

331 "made up to save": Lillian Hellman/HMD interview, HMD.

"Gerald Murphy was always": *S&G*, p. 210.

"formidable and far . . . luncheon there every day": GCM to SWM, 26 Jul. 1939, HMD.

"To be anti-Communist": *S&G*, p. 211.

332 "a pernicious nonsense . . . agu'd fear!": *Coriolanus*, act I, scenes i and iv; GCM, loose notes, HMD. As was often the case, GCM cobbled the quotation together from hearing or memory, conflating two separate speech fragments into one.

"By and large . . . anywhere today": GCM to ESB, 14 Nov. 1952, GUL.

"always smelled of wet tweed": HMD interview.

"provocative and sympathetic": GCM to CT, undated, HMD.

333 Linda was also . . . adjoining suites: HMD interview.

"Very stunning . . . freshness for me": GCM to SWM, 16 Jan. 1949, HMD.

"never set foot": Mimi MacLeish Grimm interview.

"they realized it was what": *S&G*, p. 222.

334 "spoiled the Côte d'Azur": GCM to SWM, 23 Apr. [May?] 1950, HMD.

"Immediately one is caught . . . secret garden": Ibid., 30 Jun. 1959.

"Patrick at his little garden": GCM to ESB, 12 Jun. 1950, GUL.

"Isn't it strange . . . Honoria has her child": GCM to HMD, 21 Jun. 1951, HMD.

335 "How different . . . come into it": GCM to SWM, 11 Jun. 1953, HMD.

25. *"Back there where they were"*

336 Either Gerald had tracked sand . . . powerful club denizens: DaP to Edmund Wilson, 19 Mar. 1959, CUL.

"the question of belief . . . lovely things?": AMacL, *The Book of Job*, sermon at the First Church of Christ, Congregational, Farmington, Connecticut, 8 May 1955, privately printed, limited edition, Archibald MacLeish collection, Greenfield Community College.

337 "had never been 'rich'": AMacL, "The Art of Poetry" interview, *The Paris Review*, vol. 14, no. 58, p. 69.

337 "Then said his wife": GCM, notes on SS *Majestic* stationery, miscellaneous papers, HMD.

"an almost total invention": AMacL, Stuart Drabeck interview transcript (section A, p. 13), Archibald MacLeish collection, Greenfield Community College.

338 "Pretty . . . published": AMacL, *J.B.*, manuscript draft, 1958, LOC.

"There is no such . . . never called Sarah": AMacL, Stuart Drabeck interview transcript (section A, p. 13), Archibald MacLeish collection, Greenfield Community College.

"the confrontation": AMacL, *Riders on the Earth*, p. 125.

"the fable": Brooks Atkinson, "From 'Job' to 'J.B.,'" *New York Times*, 4 May 1958.

"brilliant . . . works of the century": Reviews quoted in Donaldson, *Archibald MacLeish*, p. 457.

didn't see the play . . . March 18: DaP diary 1959: 18 Mar., CUL.

"If Hamlet was your Omelette . . . big cookie": DaP to Edmund Wilson, 19 Mar. 1959, CUL.

339 "Gerald was going . . . very bad patch there": William MacLeish interview.

"You can never know": HMD interview.

"Blow on the coal of the heart": AMacL, *J.B.*, p. 153.

340 "sat between Gerald and Sara . . . where they were": AMacL to EH, [30 Sept. 1958], *Letters of Archibald MacLeish*, pp. 411–12.

"that nuisance . . . you and Ada": GCM to AMacL, 11 Jun. 1956, LOC.

341 "I always loved . . . kid about": EH to DaP, 31 Jan. 1944, CUL.

"Poor Sara and Gerald . . . but I did": EH to AMacL, 15 Oct. 1958, *Ernest Hemingway: Selected Letters*, p. 885.

"heard of his death": AMacL to GCM, 2 Feb. [1954], HMD.

Dawn Powell . . . Rudolph Valentino: DaP diary 1955: 21 Jan., CUL.

"I don't consider . . . figs at people": DaP, *The Diaries of Dawn Powell*, 7 Jan. 1950, p. 287.

"they were a great source": CT interview.

"I'd never met an older woman . . . second-rate practitioner": Ibid.

342 "he didn't seem the type": John Hemingway interview.

"thought I knew . . . never talked about it": Jane Pickman/HMD interview, HMD.

There were . . . put in the attic: *LW*, p. 132; CT interview; William Donnelly/HMD interview, HMD.

343 "A series of semi-abstract . . . in their wit": Blesh, *Modern Art USA*, pp. 93–96.

"I've been discovered . . . does one wear?": HMD and John Donnelly interviews.

"ironic distance": CT interview.

He was even unable . . . self-assurance: Blesh, *Modern Art USA* (p. 95), and MacAgy (in the catalogue for "American Genius in Review No. I," p. 56) both list Bernheim Jeune as the gallery where Murphy had his one-man show, although MacAgy — on the strength of a "correction" from Murphy — has the date as 1936. Calvin Tomkins, in the last chapter of *Living Well Is the Best Revenge*, uses MacAgy's date. William Rubin, in his catalogue for Murphy's 1974 retrospective at the Museum of Modern Art, could find no references to *any* Murphy show in Paris, and was inclined to suspect he had fabricated it. He hadn't, of course, he had just misremembered it.

344 "There's nothing more to be done": GCM to CT, [1963], HMD.

"O to be young . . . painting at 60!": Ibid., [undated].

"but returned to painting": GCM to Rudi Blesh, undated, quoted in Blesh, *Modern Art USA*, p. 96.

345 "he had to keep . . . the way you wanted": Sherman Donnelly interview.

"One remembers . . . you deserve": SWM to Pablo Picasso, 14 Mar. 1961, Musée Picasso (my translation).

"Tell Sara . . . I'm all alone": *LW*, p. 126.

346 "Dear Ernest": SWM to EH, 24 May 1960, JFK.

"If you just won't admit . . . *take* it": SWM to FSF, 3 Apr. [1936], PUL.

"Sara is repairing . . . 'grace under pressure?'": GCM to CT, 10 Jul. 1961, HMD.

347 Sara disliked . . . for anything: HMD interview.

Spanish proverb: Ibid., p. 126.

"Man Proposeth": No. 524, "Outlandish Proverbs, compiled by Mr. G. H.," in Sir John Mennes and James Smith, *Facetiae. Musarum Deliciae: or The Muses Recreation*.

"was oddly appropriate": *LW*, p. 128.

348 Gerald had paid for . . . complicated proposition: GCM to E. R. Cawdron, 12 Mar. 1951, HMD. It was important to have the case handled by a French lawyer because Esther was a French resident; the cost for this was 28, francs.

"I am sorry": Esther Murphy to GCM, 9 Sept. 1950, HMD.

348 "our relationship" . . . not Sara's: GCM to Esther Murphy, undated, HMD.
"It was my irreparable": GCM to DP, 17 Dec. 1962, CUL.

349 "another generation growing": FSF to GCM and SWM, 31 Jan. 1937, HMD.
It was Gerald . . . "very important": Sherman Donnelly interview.
Edward Gorey . . . it was vain: John Donnelly and Laura Donnelly Taylor interviews.
Sometimes the games . . . he'd been fooling them: Laura Donnelly Taylor interview.
"like a Japanese garden": Sherman Donnelly interview.
"Dow was in charge . . . what a man": William MacLeish interview; additional details, HMD interview.

350 "a little too much . . . it leaves you": SWM to JDP and Elizabeth Dos Passos, S&G, p. 231.
Edmund Wilson . . . "bufferage": DaP to JDP, 19 Mar. 1963, CUL.
"Great White Father" . . . least favorite picture: Undated, unsigned drawing in Edmund Wilson file, Dawn Powell papers, CUL.
inscribed . . . "fromage de Brie": Edmund Wilson to JDP, 2 May 1963, in Wilson, *Letters on Literature and Politics*, pp. 638–39.

351 "lots of *vins et liqueurs*": S&G, p. 230.
"an incredible meal": Edmund Wilson to JDP, 2 May 1963, in Wilson, *Letters on Literature and Politics*, pp. 638–39.
"We've never done . . . from the heart": GCM to DaP, 5 Apr. 1963, CUL.

26. *"Only half a person without you"*

352 "much more irresponsible" . . . funeral barge: GCM to DaP, 5 Apr. 1963, CUL.
"I feel sure I'll come": GCM to AMacL, 15 Sept. 1963, LOC.
"Every once in a while . . . beautiful and free!": Ibid., 30 May 1964.

353 What they didn't know . . . chance of survival: William Abel interview.
"Dearest Gerald": SWM to GCM, 7 Aug. 1963, HMD.
"sitting in the sun . . . doctors' satisfaction": GCM to AMacL, 15 Sept. 1963, LOC.

354 "Featureless horizon . . . things unknown": AMacL to GCM, 19 Sept. 1963, HMD.
"dinner and dancing . . . makes it worse": SWM to DaP, 9 Mar. 1964, CUL.

"in the night": GCM to AMacL, 30 May 1964, LOC.

"All of that . . . Trop tard": GCM to CT, [Apr. 1964], HMD.

355 "had been the only": *S&G*, p. 238.

"how Paris was": EH, *A Moveable Feast*, p. 211.

"a life without consequences": Mellow, *Hemingway: A Life Without Consequences.*

"The rich have . . . wrong with it?": EH, *A Moveable Feast*, pp. 207–209.

356 "I am — contre coeur . . . of course": GCM to AMacL, 30 May 1964, LOC.

paints, but is not really a painter: Item 841, JFK.

"these rich . . . bad luck could go": Baker, *Ernest Hemingway: A Life Story*, p. 593n.

Gerald was very firm . . . ran down: William Abel interview.

357 "I had so wanted . . . peace hereafter": GCM to Ada MacLeish and AMacL, 18 Jul. 1964, LOC.

When Dr. Abel . . . travels in the tropics: William Abel interview.

"Dear Dow": AMacL inscription to GCM, HMD.

Recalling . . . "clarion-call": GCM to AMacL, 4 Sept. 1964, LOC.

"thinking of himself": AMacL, "The Art of Poetry" interview, *The Paris Review*, vol. 14, no. 58, p. 70.

358 "How wonderful": HMD interview.

"Dear Tad": SWM to CT, 4 Oct. [1964], HMD.

On October 17 . . . slipped away forever: HMD interview.

"DEAREST SARA . . . disguised as *taste*": DP to SWM, quoted in Miller, *Letters from the Lost Generation*, p. 275; DaP to JDP, 26 Oct. 1964, CUL. Other details from interviews with CT, FMB, Patricia Vaill, and others.

359 "Don't go . . . know you": Lillian Hellman/HMD interview, HMD.

"We know . . . Hemingway Collection": Valerie Danby-Smith to SWM, 15 Dec. 1965, HMD.

"Dear Mrs. Hemingway . . . who is gone": SWM to Mary Hemingway, handwritten copy, [14 Jan. 1966], HMD.

But Sara, veteran . . . blotchy with fury: FMB interview.

360 "stuck with rather unpleasant": SWM to FMB, 12 Nov. [late 1960s], FMB.

"wonderful talking letters": AMacL to SWM 3 Dec. [1964], HMD.

"It is such fun . . . *see you all*": SWM to JDP, [1966], UVA.

missing *Boatdeck* . . . plaques on the wall: In fact, as discussed earlier, the titles of *Turbines* and *Pression* were confused, with the former being applied as an alternative title to the painting *Engine Room*. I have tried to adhere to what I believe to be the original titles in describing and discussing all works.

360 "a major American artist": *S&G*, p. 3.

"a distinct contribution": John Russell, "Surviving Murphy Art Is at the Modern," *New York Times*, 11 Apr. 1974.

"an astonishingly original": Hayden Herrera, "Gerald Murphy, An Amurikin in Paris," *Art in America*, Sept./Oct. 1974.

361 she spent much . . . Belvoir: Laura Donnelly Taylor interview.

On October 9 . . . "going to Dowdow": HMD interview.

Selected Bibliography

A book like this one has many sources, some indirect, some cumulative; the following list names those (including works mentioned in the endnotes) of which I have made the most direct use. Page numbers in the notes are to the editions I used, although they are not in every case the original ones.

Adams, Franklin P. *The Diary of Our Own Samuel Pepys, 1926–1934.* New York: Simon and Schuster, 1935.

Baedeker's New York 1899 (facsimile edition of most of the New York and Northeast excursions taken from *Baedeker's United States, Second Edition, 1899.* Leipzig: Karl Baedeker; New York: Charles Scribner's Sons). New York: Hippocrene Books; and London: David and Charles, 1985.

Baer, Nancy Van Norman, ed. *Paris Modern: The Swedish Ballet 1920–1925.* San Francisco: Fine Arts Museums of San Francisco, 1995.

Baker, Carlos. *Ernest Hemingway: A Life Story.* New York: Charles Scribner's Sons, 1969.

Barnes, Djuna. *Ladies Almanack: showing their Signs and their tides; their Moons and their Changes; the Seasons as it is with them; their Eclipses and Equinoxes; as well as a full Record of diurnal and nocturnal Distempers.* New York: Harper and Row, 1972.

Bauquier, Georges, with Nelly Maillard. *Fernand Léger: Catalogue raisonné* (5 vols.: 1903–1919, 1920–1924, 1925–1928, 1929–1931, 1932–1937). Paris: Adrian Maeght, 1991–1996.

Beaumont, Cyril. *Bookseller at the Ballet: Memoirs 1891 to 1929, Incorporating the Diaghilev Ballet in London.* London: C. W. Beaumont, 1975.

Benchley, Robert. *The Best of Robert Benchley.* New York: Wings Books, 1995.

Bergreen, Laurence. *As Thousands Cheer: The Life of Irving Berlin*. New York: Viking, 1989.

Bernier, Olivier. *Fireworks at Dusk: Paris in the Thirties*. New York: Little, Brown, 1993.

Blake, William. *Songs of Innocence and Experience,* unpaged facsimile edition. New York: Orion Press, 1967.

Blesh, Rudi. *Modern Art USA: Men, Rebellion, Conquest, 1900–1956*. New York: Alfred A. Knopf, 1956.

Blume, Mary. *Côte d'Azur: Inventing the French Riviera*. New York: Thames and Hudson, 1992.

Buckle, Richard. *Diaghilev*. New York: Atheneum, 1979.

Cabanne, Pierre. *Le Siècle de Picasso (2): L'époque des métamorphoses (1912– 1937)*. Paris: Gallimard, 1992.

Callaghan, Morley. *That Summer in Paris*. New York: Penguin Books, 1963.

Carr, Virginia Spencer. *Dos Passos: A Life*. Garden City, N.Y.: Doubleday, 1984.

Charnot, Mary. *Gontcharova*. Paris: La Bibliothèque des Arts, 1972.

Chernow, Ron. *The House of Morgan*. New York: Atlantic Monthly Press, 1990.

Cooper, Lady Diana. *The Rainbow Comes and Goes*. Boston: Houghton Mifflin, 1958.

Cowley, Malcolm. *Exile's Return*. New York: Viking Press, 1969.

———. *A Second Flowering: Works and Days of the Lost Generation*. New York: Viking Press, 1973.

Cronin, Vincent. *Paris: City of Light 1919–1939*. London: HarperCollins, 1994.

Crosby, Harry. *Shadows of the Sun: The Diaries of Harry Crosby*. Santa Barbara, Calif.: Black Sparrow Press, 1977.

Cullen, Countee. *Color*. New York and London: Harper and Brothers, 1925.

Daix, Pierre. *Picasso: Life and Art* (Olivia Emmet, trans.). New York: HarperCollins/Icon, 1994.

Dau's New York Blue Book: Containing the Names and Addresses of Thirty Thousand Prominent Residents Arranged Alphabetically. New York: Dau, 1914.

Delavoy, Robert L. *Léger*. Cleveland, Ohio: World Publishing Company, 1962.

Donaldson, Scott. *Archibald MacLeish: An American Life*. Boston: Houghton Mifflin, 1992.

Donnelly, Honoria Murphy, with Richard N. Billings. *Sara & Gerald: Villa America and After*. New York: Times Books, 1982.

Dos Passos, John. *The Best Times*. New York: New American Library, 1966.

———. *The Big Money*. New York: Signet Books, 1969.

————. *The Fourteenth Chronicle: Letters and Diaries of John Dos Passos* (Townsend Ludington, ed.). Boston: Gambit, 1973.

————. *Manhattan Transfer*. Boston: Houghton Mifflin, 1925.

Douglas, Ann. *Terrible Honesty: Mongrel Manhattan in the 1920s*. New York: Farrar, Straus & Giroux, 1995.

Edmondson, Mary. *Profiles in Leadership: A History of the Spence School*. West Kennebunk, Me.: Phoenix Publishing, 1991.

Faucigny-Lucinge, Jean Louis de. *Un gentilhomme cosmopolite*. Paris: Perrin, 1990.

Fitzgerald, F. Scott. *Afternoon of an Author*. Princeton, N.J.: Princeton University Press, 1957.

————. *Correspondence of F. Scott Fitzgerald* (Matthew J. Bruccoli and Margaret M. Duggan, eds., with the assistance of Susan Walker). New York: Random House, 1980.

————. *The Crack-Up*. New York: New Directions, 1956.

————. *The Great Gatsby*. New York: Charles Scribner's Sons, 1925.

————. *Ledger*. Washington, D.C.: NCR/Microcard Editions (A Bruccoli/Clark Book), 1972.

————. *The Letters of F. Scott Fitzgerald* (Andrew Turnbull, ed.). New York: Charles Scribner's Sons, 1963.

————. *The Notebooks of F. Scott Fitzgerald* (Matthew J. Bruccoli, ed.). New York: Harcourt Brace Jovanovich, 1978.

————. *Tender Is the Night*. New York: Charles Scribner's Sons, 1934.

————. *Tender Is the Night: The Melarky and Kelly Versions, Part 1*, vol. IVa (Matthew J. Bruccoli, ed.). New York and London: Garland Publishing, 1990.

Fitzgerald, Zelda. *Save Me the Waltz*. Carbondale, Ill.: Southern Illinois University Press, 1967.

Flanner, Janet. *Paris Was Yesterday: 1925–1939*. New York: Viking Press, 1972.

Fokine, Michel, et al. *Les Ballets Suédois dans l'art contemporain*. Paris: Editions du Trianon, 1991.

Ford, Hugh. *Published in Paris: American and British Writers, Printers, and Publishers in Paris, 1920–1939*. New York: Macmillan, 1975.

Gaines, James R. *Wit's End: Days and Nights of the Algonquin Round Table*. New York: Harcourt Brace Jovanovich, 1977.

Gallos, Philip L. *Cure Cottages of Saranac Lake: Architecture and History of a Pioneer Health Resort*. Saranac Lake, N.Y.: Historic Saranac Lake, 1985.

Garafola, Lynn. *Diaghilev's Ballets Russes*. New York: Oxford University Press, 1989.

Gill, Brendan. *A New York Life: Of Friends and Others*. New York: Poseidon Press, 1990.

Gold, Arthur, and Robert Fizdale. *Misia*. New York: Alfred A. Knopf, 1980.

Goode, Gerald, ed. *The Book of Ballets: Classic and Modern*. Garden City, N.Y.: Doubleday, 1939.

Greve, Charles Theodore. *Centennial History of Cincinnati and Representative Citizens*, vol. II. Chicago: Biographical Publishing, 1904.

Häger, Bengt. *Ballets Suédois*. New York: Harry N. Abrams, 1990.

Havighurst. *Twentieth Century Britain*. New York: Harper and Row, 1962.

Hellman, Lillian. *An Unfinished Woman*. Boston: Little, Brown, 1969.

Hemingway, Ernest. *Ernest Hemingway: Selected Letters* (Carlos Baker, ed.). New York: Charles Scribner's Sons, 1981.

———. *A Moveable Feast*. New York: Collier Books, 1987.

———. *The Short Stories of Ernest Hemingway*. New York: Charles Scribner's Sons, 1953.

———. *The Sun Also Rises*. New York: Charles Scribner's Sons, 1926.

———. *The Torrents of Spring*. New York: Charles Scribner's Sons, 1972.

History of the Class of 1912, Yale University. New Haven: Yale University Press, 1912.

Hoffman, Frederick J. *The 20's: American Writing in the Postwar Decade*. New York: Free Press, 1966.

Hopkins, Gerard Manley. *Poems of Gerard Manley Hopkins*. London: Oxford University Press, 1965.

Huddleston, Sisley. *Paris Salons, Cafés, Studios: Being Social and Artistic Memories*. Philadelphia: J. B. Lippincott, 1928.

Hugo, Jean. *Le Regard de la mémoire*. Paris: Actes Sud, 1983.

Johnson, Diane. *Dashiell Hammett: A Life*. New York: Random House, 1983.

Kammen, Michael. *The Lively Arts: Gilbert Seldes and the Transformation of Cultural Criticism in the United States*. New York: Oxford University Press, 1996.

Kert, Bernice. *The Hemingway Women*. New York: W. W. Norton, 1983.

Klüver, Billy, and Julie Martin. *Kiki's Paris*. New York: Harry N. Abrams, 1989.

Kouwenhoven, John A. *The Columbia Historical Portrait of New York*. Garden City, N.Y.: Doubleday, 1953.

Lanahan, Eleanor. *Zelda, an Illustrated Life: The Private World of Zelda Fitzgerald*. New York: Harry N. Abrams, 1996.

Lancaster, Clay, Robert A. M. Stern, and Robert Hefner. *East Hampton's Heritage: An Illustrated Architectural Record*. New York: W. W. Norton, 1982.

Léger, Fernand. *Lettres à Simone*. Zurich: Skira/Musée National d'Art Moderne/Centre Georges Pompidou, 1987.

Le Vot, André. *F. Scott Fitzgerald: A Biography*. Garden City, N.Y.: Doubleday, 1983.

Lifar, Serge. *Serge Diaghilev: His Life, His Work, His Legend: An Intimate Biography*. New York: G. P. Putnam's Sons, 1940.

Lockwood, Charles. *Bricks and Brownstone: The New York Row House, 1783–1929: An Architectural and Social History*. New York: McGraw-Hill, 1972.

Lord, Walter. *The Good Years*. New York: Harper and Brothers, 1960.

MacLeish, Archibald. *The Collected Poems of Archibald MacLeish*. Boston: Houghton Mifflin, 1962.

———. *J.B.: A Play in Verse*. Boston: Houghton Mifflin, 1957.

———. *Letters of Archibald MacLeish, 1907–1982* (R. H. Winnick, ed.). Boston: Houghton Mifflin, 1983.

———. *New and Collected Poems, 1917–1976*. Boston: Houghton Mifflin, 1976.

———. *Reflections* (Bernard A. Drabeck and Helen E. Ellis, eds.). Amherst, Mass.: University of Massachusetts Press, 1986.

———. *Riders on the Earth: Essays and Recollections*. Boston: Houghton Mifflin, 1978.

Maine, Barry, ed. *Dos Passos: The Critical Heritage*. London: Routledge, 1988.

Meade, Marion. *Dorothy Parker: What Fresh Hell Is This?* New York: Villard, 1988.

Mellow, James R. *Charmed Circle: Gertrude Stein & Company*. New York: Praeger Publishers, 1972.

———. *Hemingway: A Life Without Consequences*. Boston: Houghton Mifflin, 1992.

———. *Invented Lives: F. Scott & Zelda Fitzgerald*. Boston: Houghton Mifflin, 1984.

Milford, Nancy. *Zelda*. New York: Harper and Row, 1970.

Miller, Linda Patterson, ed. *Letters from the Lost Generation: Gerald and Sara Murphy and Friends*. New Brunswick, N.J.: Rutgers University Press, 1991.

Morton, Brian N. *Americans in Paris: An Anecdotal Street Guide.* Ann Arbor, Mich.: Olivia and Hill Press, 1984.

O'Hara, John. *Selected Letters of John O'Hara* (Matthew J. Bruccoli, ed.). New York: Random House, 1978.

Peters, Margot. *Mrs. Pat: The Life of Mrs. Patrick Campbell.* New York: Alfred A. Knopf, 1984.

Powell, Dawn. *The Diaries of Dawn Powell: 1931–1965* (Tim Page, ed.). South Royalton, Vt.: Steerforth Press, 1995.

———. *The Wicked Pavilion.* South Royalton, Vt.: Steerforth Press, 1996.

Reynolds, Michael. *Hemingway: The American Homecoming.* Cambridge, Mass.: Blackwell Publishers, 1992.

———. *Hemingway: The 1930s.* New York: W. W. Norton, 1997.

———. *Hemingway: The Paris Years.* Cambridge, Mass.: Basil Blackwell, 1989.

Rodgers, Richard. *Musical Stages: An Autobiography.* New York: Random House, 1975.

Rosmond, Babette. *Robert Benchley: His Life and Good Times.* Garden City, N.Y.: Doubleday, 1970.

Rubin, William. *The Paintings of Gerald Murphy.* New York: Museum of Modern Art, 1974.

———. *Picasso and Portraiture: Representation and Transformation.* New York: Museum of Modern Art, 1996.

Schickel, Richard. *The Men Who Made the Movies.* New York: Atheneum Publishers, 1975.

Seldes, Gilbert. *The 7 Lively Arts.* New York: Harper and Brothers, 1924.

Siegel, Jerrold. *Bohemian Paris: Culture, Politics, and the Boundaries of Bourgeois Life, 1830–1930.* New York: Elisabeth Sifton Books/Penguin Books, 1970.

Sims, Lowery Stokes. *Stuart Davis: American Painter.* New York: Metropolitan Museum of Art, 1991.

Société des Artistes Indépendents, 34e Exposition (1923), 35e Exposition (1924), 36e Exposition (1925), and 37e Exposition (1926). Paris: Société des Artistes Indépendents, 1923, 1924, 1925, and 1926.

———. *La Conquête de la liberté artistique* (catalogue of the 100th exhibition). Paris: 1989.

Steegmuller, Francis. *Cocteau: A Biography.* Boston: Little, Brown, 1970.

Stewart, Donald Ogden. *By a Stroke of Luck! An Autobiography.* New York: Paddington Press/Two Continents, 1975.

Stravinsky, Igor. *Chroniques de ma vie,* vols. I and II. Paris: Denoël et Steele, 1935.

———, and Robert Craft. *Conversations with Igor Stravinsky.* Garden City, N.Y.: Doubleday, 1959.

———. *Expositions and Developments.* Garden City, N.Y.: Doubleday, 1962.

Survage, Léopold. "Larionov, homme actif/Gontcharova, femme douce et discrète," *Gontcharova et Larionov, cinquante ans à Saint-Germain-des-près* (Tatiana Loguine, ed.). Paris: Klincksieck, 1971.

Thomas, Hugh. *John Strachey.* New York: Harper and Row, 1973.

Tomkins, Calvin. *Living Well Is the Best Revenge.* New York: Viking Press, 1971.

Turner, Elizabeth Hutton, ed. *Americans in Paris (1921–1931): Man Ray, Gerald Murphy, Stuart Davis, Alexander Calder.* Washington, D.C.: Counterpoint, 1996.

Vidor, King. *King Vidor,* interviewed by Nancy Dowd and David Shepard, Directors Guild of America Oral History Series. Metuchen, N.J., and London: Scarecrow Press, 1988.

Wagner, Linda M. *Dos Passos: Artist as American.* Austin: University of Texas Press, 1979.

Walker, Kathrine Sorley. *De Basil's Ballets Russes.* New York: Atheneum Publishers, 1982.

White, Norval, and Eliot Willensky. *AIA Guide to New York City (revised ed.).* New York: Collier Books, 1978.

Wilson, Edmund. *Letters on Literature and Politics: 1912–1972* (Elena Wilson, ed.). New York: Farrar, Straus & Giroux, 1977.

———. *The Twenties.* (Leon Edel, ed.). New York: Farrar, Straus & Giroux, 1975.

Wilson, Robert Forrest. *Paris on Parade.* Indianapolis: Bobbs Merrill, 1925.

Wiser, William. *The Crazy Years.* New York: Thames and Hudson, 1990.

Wolff, Geoffrey. *Black Sun: The Brief Transit and Violent Eclipse of Harry Crosby.* New York: Random House, 1976.

Index

Excerpts from letters from Dorothy Parker to Robert Benchley, November 7, 1929, and to Gerald and Sara Murphy, June 8, 1934: The author wishes to thank the National Association for the Advancement of Colored People for authorizing the use of Dorothy Parker's work.

Excerpts from letters of Fernand Léger to Gerald and Sara Murphy: © 1998 Artists Rights Society (ARS), NY/ADAGP, Paris.

Letters and notebooks in the Musée Picasso, courtesy of the Archives Picasso, Paris, and Conte Henri de Beaumont.

Letter from Erik Satie to Vincent Huidobro, Fundación Vincente Huidobro, Santiago de Chile.

Telegram and *Hallelujah!* screenplay excerpts in the King Vidor papers, Doheny Library, University of Southern California, King Vidor Collection, USC Cinema-Television Library.

Unpublished manuscript of "The Man of Taste," Philip Barry Papers, Georgetown University Library.

ILLUSTRATION CREDITS

With the following exceptions, all photographs in this book are from the collection of Honoria Murphy Donnelly and are its property. Used by permission.

Portrait of Sara Murphy, by Pablo Picasso. Private collection, Switzerland; © 1996 Estate of Pablo Picasso/Artists Rights Society (ARS), N.Y. Photograph © 1996 The Museum of Modern Art, NY.

Femme au collier encoudée, by Pablo Picasso. Property of the Musée Picasso. Used by permission.

Photographs of Archibald and Ada MacLeish, Gerald Murphy in Chinese robes, and Gerald Murphy and Alexander Woollcott, Steele Camp, and Honoria Murphy and John Shelton are all by Richard Myers. Used by permission of Frances Myers Brennan.

Photograph of F. Scott Fitzgerald. Used by permission of Corbis-Bettmann.

Photograph of Gerald and Sara Murphy, Ernest and Hadley Hemingway, and John Dos Passos. Property of the Ernest Hemingway Collection, John F. Kennedy Library. Used by permission.

Patrick Murphy by Fernand Léger. Collection of Honoria Murphy Donnelly. Used by permission of Artists Rights Society (ARS), N.Y.

Photograph of Marc Platt, and of Frederic Franklin and Mia Slavenska in *Ghost Town,* are used by courtesy of the Dance Collection, New York Public Library, Astor, Lenox and Tilden Foundations.

Photograph of Dawn Powell used by permission of Tim Page and Columbia University, Rare Book and Manuscript Library.

Watch by Gerald Murphy, courtesy of the Dallas Museum of Art, Foundation for the Arts Collection, gift of the artist.

Cocktail by Gerald Murphy, courtesy of the Whitney Museum of American Art, New York. Purchase, with funds from Evelyn and Leonard A. Lauder, Thomas H. Lee and the Modern Painting and Sculpture Committee.

Wasp and Pear by Gerald Murphy (1927). Oil on canvas, 36¾ × 38⅝" (93.3 × 97.9 cm). The Museum of Modern Art, New York. Gift of Archibald MacLeish. Photograph © 1998 The Museum of Modern Art, New York.